MORMON MISSIONARIES
AMONG THE CATAWBA INDIANS

1881 to 1938

By Judy Canty Martin

&

Shirley Hamblin

Mormon's (The Church of Jesus Christ of Latter-Day Saints)

Backintyme

History of the U.S. Color Line

Published by Backintyme Publishing
Crofton, Kentucky, U.S.A.

Copyright @ 2018 by Backintyme Publishing
ALL RIGHTS RESERVED
1341 Grapevine Rd.
Crofton, KY. 42217
Website: www.backintyme.biz
Email: backintyme@mehrapublishing.com
Printed United States of America
February 2019

ISBN-978-0-939479-57-3

Cover Art by

T-riffic Design
Pam Goyens Tatum

ACKNOWLEDGEMENTS

My thanks to those who contributed to my projects.

Edrie Linn Cleaver who gave me her grandfather's missionary journals. She then scanned and sent his mission photos. Most only had elder so and so. We had to try to find who they were and find homes for them. By homes I mean on family search and to the families. I would have liked to send the photos to family. The amount of information she sent made a whole new chapter. While Elder Bingham had only fleeting contact with the Catawba, his photos and other papers contributed an account of Elder Clarks death in South Carolina and other bits and pieces of missionary work. Not only did we obtain new information, but I acquired a good friend in Edrie. Ronette and Rick Mecham entered information on Willard Eugene Bingham's profile on family search. When I put a photo on his sheet, hoping to contact a family member I saw their names. I contacted them and they sent his missionary journal. He died on his mission but his journal was another side of his mission.

Jan Gerber had already transcribed Elder Alexander Redd's journal. I obtained that on line and since Elder Redd was close to the Watts family in Cedar City, I chased the whole journal. I wanted to share with that family for another friend Monty Woodbury of Cedar City, Utah who was a source of photos and inspiration for all my books. She and Thora Wright who started this journey with me years ago. When I finished the first 3 books, I sent them to her. She had been going blind and we lost contact. I sent them anyway and several weeks later I got a check for them and Thora had passed away. Her daughter assured me she had them read to her before she passed which is what these projects are for. To know her relatives as much as I knew at that time.

PREFACE

The Catawba , also knowIswa are a federally recognized tribe of Native Americans , known as the Catawba Indian Nation. They live in the Southeastern United States, on the Catawba River at the border of North Carolina, near the city of Rock Hill, South Carolina. They were once considered one of the most powerful Southeastern Siouan -speaking tribes in the Carolina Piedmont, as well as one of the most powerful tribes in the South as a whole.

The legend is that they may have been the folks that greeted Columbus and were once a very populous tribe which was decimated by small pox and alcohol use. By the 1880's it was supposed that there were only 60 to 80 left in and around York county, South Carolina and Cherokee, North Carolina.

This was the condition of the nation until the Mormon missionaries found them. They joined the church nearly in mass, 2/3 of the tribe, however the number was around 60.

FORWARD

I have so much enjoyed my working with my friend and fellow genealogist Judy Canty Martin. Judy has worked in the genealogy field for over 40 years and has spent many an hour hunting up records, documents and pictures to trace her ancestors. One of her favorite research projects has ben her fathers people, the Catawba Indian Tribe. She has worked diligently for years researching and diging out information on the tribe and her ancestors in that tribe. This book moves away a little from the ancestrial side to the religious beliefs of her tribal ancestors. When the whiteman contacted them about relition and how they responded to it. Then on to the Missionaries of the Church of Jesus Christ of Latter Day Saints, and who they were and how they taught and worked with the Catawba. Inspiring them and teaching them to except the teachings of their church.

I have so enjoyed working with and learning from Judy over the years and all the knowledge and researching stratigies we have shared through out the years.

Shirley Hamblin

Table Of Contents

Religion of the Catawba Indians............................1

Southern States Missionaries serving between 1901-1920

Southern States Missionaries who served between 1921-1935

South Carolina people who helped the LDS Missionaries that served in that area.

Religion of the Catawba Indians

Catholic: In 1526 Lucas De Allyon was the first Spaniard in Carolina with Priests. Although the Spanish were welcomed and given gifts and other fineries, the Indians were repaid by being killed and robbed by these Men of God.

1537: Hernando De Soto, was the first Spanish explorer at <u>Catawba</u> with Priests.[1] De Soto followed the fine old tradition of enslaving and robbing the natives, then took hostages to use as guides and moved on.

1566: November, Captain Juan Pardo came from Fort San Felipe, now Port Royal, to explore and conquer from that point, to Mexico. He was also to make friends with the Indians and convert them to the Catholic Gospel. Pardo had 125 men, supplies and ammunition. He marched for 10 days northwesterly, or about 50 leagues, coming to the convergence of the Canos or Cofitachequi River, which would be about. the Congaree River, and the Wateree River and would be near Columbia; South Carolina. The people of Cofitacheque were cordial, just as

Presbyterian: In 1759 Reverend William Richardson had preached to the Cherokee, without much success, under the Society for the Propagation of the Gospel, and settled in the Waxhaws. He passed through Catawba in 1759 and was told by his Savona guide that the "old Indian make no Sabbath and young Indian make no Sabbath."[2] November 8, Richardson tried to speak to King Hagler using One Waters as an interpreter. On the 11th, Richardson finally met with King Hagler. He continued to preach to the lesser Catawba towns, including the Cheraw about schools and the need for education He tried to preach to King Hagler, and Hagler "would not listen to preaching" because Hagler believed that there was no afterlife.

1755: The first Christian minister who left a written account of his attempts was the Reverend Hugh McAden, a Presbyterian minister from Pennsylvania. He came primarily to serve the Scotch - Irish people who had settled near the Catawba Nation.

He and his party passed near a Catawba hunting camp below Charlotte, North Carolina without incidence. However, when they stopped to eat, the "Catawba" surrounded them, searched their baggage, screaming and shouting and scaring their horses. His party moved away as soon as possible; however, the party was soon accosted by another group of Indians. Their party finally escaped but McAden was driven out of the Catawba nation without any Catawba converts.[3]

1802: Reverend W. C. Davis started a missionary effort, but it was not successful.

1897: The Presbyterians built a school, and employed a teacher Mrs. Dunlap, and began efforts to convert the Catawba. She had some success with the school, in spite of a lot of fighting over who owned the house she was given, she was well thought of by most of the Catawba.

Baptists: During the Revolution, Reverend John Rooker settled near the Catawba towns. When he left stated that he had . left them worse than he had found them. Perhaps one example of this is that

---

[1] Roger Trimnal Genealogy and Research.
[2] Brown page 249.
[3] North Carolina Colonial Records Vol. V, page 1207.

Molly RedHead a Catawba women had a child she called John Rooker Redhead, John Rooker being his father.[4]

1804: The Rev. Robert Mush-Marsh. a Pamunkey Indian of Virginia, who had married a Catawba, Betsy Scott-Quash, preached in conjunction with Rev. Rooker. Robert and Betsy were progenitors of many of present day Catawba. 7 [5]Although her husband was a Baptist Preacher, Robert's wife never embraced the religion.

1840: After the Nation's Ford Treaty was signed, I l men and 22 women were allied with the Baptist Church at Echota Mission, North Carolina. which amounted to nearly the entire tribe. The list included Chief William Morrison and his family, the Stevens, Red Head, George, Joe, Canty, and David Harris families, and most of the rest of the Catawba on the 1847 census, residing among the Cherokee. 6[6]

Methodists: In 1780 Rev. Michael Budge erected a church, but nothing more was heard.

1791: Rev. Thomas Coors church and school failed, however a Catawba named Tarn Cook fought in the Revolutionary War, and is listed on Drennen's Paybill of 1780, so it is possible that he, like Reverend Rooker left a child.

1870: Dr. Maurice Moore said that he was told by a fellow minister to Catawba, although they understood English and had been preached to by all denominations, up until that time, "not one of the Indians ever professed conversion or became consecrated with a Christian Church."[7]

Church of Jesus Christ of Latter Day Saints: In 1838-39, Elder E. M. Murray was sent to South Carolina. The first Elder, L. M. Davis baptized 10 in Union County, SC.[8]

1841: 11 were baptized into the LDS Church in Charleston, SC.

1881: November, Elder John Easton of Beaver, Utah and Elder Willard Burton[9] were sent to organize the Kings Mt. Branch. James Henry Moyle pleaded for re-opening of South Carolina, and had a vision of a SC town with a branch.

1882: March, 3, at the home of William Nelson Gordon, in Rack Hill, South Carolina, Elder Willard Burton's dream became a reality.

1882: August, Anti Mormon indignation is aroused and directed by a Rev. White. Elders Henry Miller and C. E. Robison left south easterly to Rock Hill and Lancaster, but were treated coldly, and returned to Catawba.[10]

June 3, 1882: Elder Robison became sick with chills and fever in the home of Evan and Lucy Quash-Mursh Wats.[11] He died in the presence of Elder Joseph Willey on September 26, 1882. "The first Elders who came in this locality were Elders Henry Miller and Charles Robison; They visited the Catawba Nation for the first time in May 1883.

They began holding meetings here during the summer of that year.

---

[4] Roger Trimnal research.
[5] Ibid
[6] List of Echotä Mission, in collection of Judy Cantu Martin.
[7] Maurice, Augustus Moore, Reminiscences of York, page 4.
[8] Ci- Lee; Jerry, Masters Thesis, Brigham Young University, December 1 976, page 24.
[9] Elder Burton had a vision about a South Carolina town that had a branch organized in it.
[10] Trimnal Research.
[11] Lucy is the granddaughter of the Reverend Robert Mush-Marsh, and a Catawba.

After holding one meeting Eider Robison took sick and Elder Miller held one meeting alone. Elder Robison, after lingering for some time died at Kings Mountain (South Carolina) in the later part of September, 1883. Elder Joseph Willey then joined Elder Miller and they held meetings here about every other Sunday up till December 1883, when Elder Miller took the chills and fever, and Elder J. J. Humphreys took his place.

Elders Humphreys and Willey held meetings every other Sunday up till about the 1st of May, then Elder R. S. Humphreys became the companion of Elder Willey. They held meetings here every other Sunday until the 1st of September, when owing to threats of mobs the Elders had to hide in the woods for about a week. There were not more meetings held here till February 1885. Elders Joseph Willey and W. S. Cragun held six meetings in one month.   The 6th of April, 1885 and in May 1885, Elders Cragun and F. A. Fraughton came and held two meetings. They were mobbed on the night of May 25, 1885 by twenty-three men about 10 o'clock in the evening. Running to Mr. A. Tims[12] house, Elder Cragun made his escape to the woods. About fifteen or twenty shots were fired at him, but one of three or four shots from a shot gun hit him on the chin inflicting a slight wound."[13]

In the book entitled The Life and Ministry of John Morgan.

comes the following:

"The brethren report that in South Carolina, a mob of 23 men, in daylight and not under the influence of liquor, ordered the Elders out of the State. in another - district a party of men raided the house of one of the Saints where Elders W. G. Cragun and F. A. Fraughton were staying. Elder Cragun made good his escape out of the back door, but was fired on by the mob. Fortunately none of the shots took effect, except d slight mark on the chin. Elder Fraughton was captured and whipped, but not seriously."[14]

Charles Hudson, a researcher of the Catawba in South Carolina, and not a member of the Church stated:

They tried to make them promise not to come back, but they would not promise.[15]

Hudson also noted that the whites around the Catawba did not want the Catawba to become "Christians" because so many Catawba women babies were fathered by the whites of the area. The best example of Hudson's theory being true is found in Joseph Willey's Journal:

"June 8, nothing of any importance since last date. Visited around among the Saints. Elders W. G. Cragun and F. A. Fraughton arrived from the Indian Nation, York Co. They had sad news. on May 18th, they received the following notice" -- We the undersigned citizens of the state and county aforesaid have been informed that you the Mormon Elders are preaching and practicing your polygamis doctrine in Catawba Nation, York County and we respectfully request you to leave the state and county aforsaid and on your refusal to comply with this request we will not be responsible for the consequences." There was about 70 names signed to the article, the ones who brought it to them were; Maj. Botch, Mr. Crook Sr., Take Crook, Robert Cornwell, Frank Collins,[16] 10 John

---

[12] John Alexander (Alec) Tims, son of Rachel Quash-Mursh and John Alexander Tims.
[13] Catawba Branch Records.
[14] The Life and Minstry of John Morgan, Historical Research and Publication, 1965, page 413-417, 448.
[15] Hudson, Charles, The Catawba, Georgia Press, Athens, 1970 pages 78-79.
[16] Bear in mind that Frank Collins fathered the children of the Catawba woman Harriet Harris, ta the white men were anxious ta keep the Catawba from bei nq Christianized for selfish reasons.

Allen. Pirce Giles. This notice was fixed up to run Elder Cragun and I out of the Nation, but we left on the 10th. The Elders paid know attention, but continued preaching."

Frank Collins was reportedly the father of Harriet Harris's children, and only one of the whites who fathered Catawba children.

The house in which Eider Cragan found shelter was that of James Goodwin and Elizabeth Missouri White Patterson.

Sister Elizabeth Patterson tended the wound, and the family hid the Elder until the next day when he was re-united with Elder Fraughton.[17]

"l don't know how long they stayed. The mob went to where the Elders were staying and the Elders ran into the woods to prevent another whipping."[18]

1883, October, Elders Willey and Miller preached to the Catawba. After the October 26th meeting the first Catawba "in this dispensation ta accept the truth" applied for baptism, that man was James Goodwin Patterson.[19]

On November 4 four more atawba applied for baptism.

1883. November 11, Those Catawba who were baptized were James Goodwin Patterson, Mrs. Lucy Wats James Henry Wats (mother and son), Mrs. Mary Jane Wats, Taylor George.[20]

February 24, 1884, Canty, son of Eliza Scott Canty and Thomas Whitesides was baptized by Elder Willey. Pinkney H. Head, was baptized on March 16, 1884 also by Elder Willey.[21]

May 18, 1884, Mrs. Mary Jane Wat, daughter of Eliza Scott Canty and Thomas Whitesides, took very sick, and was administered to by Elder Willey and his companion. Her brother and sister,[22] who were not of the faith, sent for 3 doctors, who promptly told them she would be dead in 24 hours. The Elders administered to her and then left. When they came back she was on the mend, and within 2 days was well.[23]

By June 1, 1884, the branch has 31 members, 25 of whom are Catawba. Elder James Goodwin Patterson was called to serve as first Branch President of the Branch that was called the Rack Hill Branch.[24]

The following message from the mob' came from the Missionary Journal of Joseph Willey:

"August 23, 1884 Notice, Messrs Willey, Humphreys, Humphrey. We the peaceable citizens of this surrounding country have been pained to learn that you three men professing to be Mormon missionaries have taken up your quarters with an ignorant class of our   people and are denominating doctrines among them calculated to disorganize human society and adverse to the peace and well being of our people and country. To the laws and dignity of the State, now therefore

---

[17] Patterson Genealogy.

[18] Joseph Willey Diary.

[19] Joseph Willey Diary

[20] James Goodwin Patterson, son of Martha Patterson and Laban Chappell; Lucy Wats, daughter of Robert Marsh and Betsy Quash Scott; Mrs. jane Wats, daughter of Thomas Whitesides and Eliza Scott Canty, wife of James Henry Wats; James Henry Watts, son of Evan and Lucy Quash- Mursh Wats; Taylor George, son of Anthony (Zacharia Taylor) George and Rebecca Mursh.

[21] Joseph Willey Journal.

[22] The sister is Fannie Whitesides Harris, daughter of Thomas Whitesides and Eliza Scott Canty, the brother is in realith a half brother, George Washington Canty, who was baptized March 8, 1885. The twin brother of Fannie was John Alonzo Canty, who was just baptized just prior to this incident.

[23] Joseph Willey Diary.

[24] Ibid

these presents are to civily and peaceably request and command you to vacate the State and to return no more among us and you are hereby allowed five days to obey this order to peaceably absent yourselves from the State without hurt or molestation but if you are found within the limits of the State after the expiration of that time you may charge consequences to disobedience to this order. We are going to be rid of you." Capt. of the mob, Wm. Kithcart, Wm. Carethers, Charles Harrison, Paul Harrison, Alexander Millens, Clarence Cotter. The names of the rest of the mob we did not get. This notice had been received while we was gone and the 5 days was up."

On November 30, 1884, the branch was disbanded because of persecution. The Catawba went   to Spartanburg, South Carolina, it.js unknown if the few whites who were also converted including the Gordon Family, went also. The Catawba were back at the Nation early in February, 1885.

July 31, 1885, The mobs were so bad, the Elders, Bingham and Cragun, hide in the woods, and were piloted through the swamps for 30 miles, by James Patterson, James Wats,[25] so they arrived in the Nation without it being known.

On August 2, 1885, John AlonzoCanty was ordained the first Branch President of the Catawba Nation Branch, Rock Hill, South Carolina.[26] 26 He later moved to Colorado with his family and the families of 4 other Catawba, namely, Head, Patterson, Harris and Tims.

John Alonzo Canty

In his journal entitled "My Mission to the Cherokee of North Carolina,

Pinkney Henry Head, the son of Sarah Ann Evans-Canty and Robert Head, writes:

"October 31, 1885, me and Brother Alonzo Canty received a letter from Elder W. E. Bingharn stating that our names had been suggested that we was worthy young men to take a mission among the Cherokee Lamintes in North Carolina, Swain County and Jackson County. He told us that we could gether our crops before we started but we was willing to go at any time. We was glad to think that we was worthy to go and teach others the Gospel."

They left for their mission on December 1, 1885.

The persecution was still a problem, although the violence had ceased.

February 19, 1885; Rock Hill Herald "A Raleigh dispatch says three Mormon elders are preaching in Rutherford County, N.C. near the South Carolina line. They have with them twenty-three converts from Rock Hill, SC. They are holding meetings and are preparing to build a church." There is considerable excitement in the community."

The elders were even threatened with prosecution.

We do not think it is true that the Mormons have any converts with them from this section. They may be accompanied by a few of the Catawba Indians and if so, they are welcome to them".

These are the words Pinkney wrote in his journal about leaving South Carolina.

"February 28, 1887 Left Spartanburg, SC at am, bound for Zion."

Between 1885-1890, 5 families of Catawba moved west with Elder John Morgan to Manassa, Colorado and then to Sanford, Colorado and beyond. The Catawba had dwindled down to about 60 men, women and children, the 26 who moved were the families of James and Elizabeth White

---

[25] James Goodwin Patterson and James Harvey Wats-Watts, James Harvey being the husband of Mary Jane Watts, and a brother in law to John Alonzo Canty.

[26] . Catawba Branch Records and letter from Jeffery 0. Johnson, Historical Department of LDS Church, dated November 3, 1981.

Patterson and unmarried daughters, Bell, Lula, Dora, Emma, Maud, Abbie and son Joseph; married daughter another husband, Henrietta Patterson and Canty; another married daughter Martha Jane Patterson and her husband and daughter Pinkney and Sarah Head; Pinkney's mother and his step father, Sarah Evans-Canty Head Tims and husband John Alexander Tims; Alec's first wife and his son, Martha Cottsky-Scott Tims and son Harvey; another daughter of Alec and Martha Tims and her husband Hillery and Rachel Tims Harris and son Josiah. Later Evan and Lucy Quash-Wats and family moved to Harmony, Utah and Lillie Susan Harris Ballard went to Oklahoma. Lillie Susan and her family did not come to the west because of the Mormon Church however, all the rest did.

1896, After their arrival in Manassa, Colorado, James Goodwin Patterson was ordained as Branch President of the Los Cerritos Branch, San Luis Stake, Colorado. Los Cerritos is closer to the San Juan Mountains and north of Manassa, along the San Antonio River. It was disbanded in 1900.[27] The family then moved to Sanford, Colorado, where they remained until their deaths.

1928: The 2nd LDS Chapel building is built at Catawba, South Carolina, with Charles Casslis as Mission President, he was followed by Elder LeGrand Richards.[28] I

The Church then has its influence felt on Catawba Indians in as far away Brazjl.

1913: Sister Lucy Head Marcelino and her husband and one son, left the United States for Brazil. On the trip, all her books, including her precious Book of Mormon were lost.

1937: The Church first sent missionaries to Londrina, Brazil.

1950: The Rock Hill Branch of the Church, refounded by Woodrow Trimnal, Connie Lee and Mercelle Cabaniss.[29]

October 6, 1956: Guilherme Albert Marcelino was baptized in Londrina, Brazil. Guilherme is the son of Lucy Head Marcelino, he is the grandson of Pinkney and Martha Jane Patterson; and the great-grandson of James Goodwin and Elizabeth Missouri White Patterson.

1956: Lucy Head Marcelino and her stepdaughter Emma Marcelino are called as the first Relief Society Presidency in Londrina, Brazil. Lucy is the daughter of Pinkney and Martha Jane Patterson Head, married to Manuel Marcelino, the father of Emma. Lucy is the step-mother of Emma.

In the months and years following his baptism in 1956 Guilherme or Bill's first calling in the Church was as a teacher for the Genealogy Class in Sunday School. At that time, he did not even know what Genealogy was. He soon learned, along with the others in his class and then he has done a great deal of genealogy, primarily on his father's side, the Marcelino's were Portuguese. Guilherme then served as Branch President for several gears, much as his great-grandfather James Goodwin Patterson.[30]

1961: Elder Donald Guy Croasmun, eldest living son of John and May Garcia Croasmun. of Pueblo, Colorado died in Sao Paulo. Brazil, while serving a mission there. Elder Croasmun is the grandson of Abbie Patterson Garcia, and the great-grandson of James G. and Elizabeth M. White Patterson. Elder Croasmun also was a cousin of the family of Lucy Head Marcelino who lived in Sao Paulo. They were connected both in family and in being Catawba, and never knowing the others.

---

[27] Jersen, page 448.
[28] Trimnal Research
[29] Blumer, page 355.
[30] Foster, Mark, page 6/8.

1962: In Sanford, Colorado, San Luis Stake, William Franklin (Buck) Canty, son of John Alonzo and Georgia Henrietta Patterson Canty was called as the first Lamanite Patriarch.[31]
William is the grandson of James Goodwin Patterson. William is shown here with his youngest brother in the headdress that was presented to him at BYU where he was a frequent speaker at Brigham Young University's Indian Week. He also toured with the Lamanite Generation in 1978.

1970's: Guilherme Marcelino is interviewed for the calling of the regions first Patriarch of the Londrina, Brazil region. His health prevented him from accepting the calling. However this would have made him the second Patriarch within the family of James Goodwin Patterson.

1985: In a special Lamanite session of the Mesa, Arizona temple, the temple ordinances were completed for the identified Catawba tribe, fulfilling a promise made by William F. Canty to his niece Judy Canty Martin, that he would send her a COD letter after he died with genealogical answers on it. The work was done on his birthday, April 26, 1985, (which was not a special request by Judy) just three years after his death.[32]

1987: Raymond Harris, a grandson of Hillery and Rachel Tims Harris, Western Catawba, was called as Patriarch, 'Of the Kirtland, New Mexica Stake. making this the second Patriarch out of the 5 families of Western Catawba.[33]

1991 November, The LDS Church Historical Department noted that the Catawba Ward is the oldest Lamanite unit of continual existence in the Church.[34]

---

[31] Canty Genealogy.
[32] Ibid
[33] Raymond Harris genealogy.
[34] Trimnal Research.

LDS Catawba Missionaries
Among the Catawba Indian People

The Church of Jesus Christ of Latter Day Saints

(Mormons)

Elder John Alonzo Canty - m 1885

PHOTO 1 -- JOHN ALONZO CANTY

Catawba Indian John Alonzo Canty, born 9 November 1859, Catawba Reservation, York, County, South Carolina and died 1 February 1938 - (age at Death 79) in Sanford, Conejos County, Colorado. He was the son of a white man, named Thomas Patrick Whitesides who was the Indian Agent and a Catawba woman Eliza Scott.

"Sunday February 24, Sunday school was held at Bro. Evan Wats. This was the first Sunday school the Lamanites had ever attended. They seemed to take a lively interest. After Sunday school a young man by the name of John Lonzo Canty was baptized. John Alonzo Canty was also called as the first Branch president of the Catawba Branch, after it had been disbanded and moved to Spartanburg, South Carolina. It had originally been the Rock Hill Branch, led by James Goodwin Patterson.

Pinkney Head writes in his Journal of his Mission to the Cherokee: "October 31, 1885, me and Brother Alonzo Canty received a letter from Elder W E. Bingham stating that our names had been suggested that we were worthy young men to take a mission among the Cherokee Laminates in Swain county and Jackson county. He told us that we could gather our crops before we started but we was willing to go at any time. we was glad to think that we was worthy to go and teach others the Gospel. so, I left my home."

From Jerry D Lee's Master thesis:

Elders Bingham and Cragun under the protection of the Catawba organized the Catawba Nation Branch on August 2, 1885. There were about 50 present and an excellent spirit. bro. Alonzo Canty was called as president of the branch and unanimously sustained by vote of the saints and was ordained a priest by elders Bingham and Cragun. A Sunday school was organized on the same day apparently the members who organized the branch attended Sunday school as fifty were present at Sunday school when six members were appointed teachers and classes were formed.

December 1885 the Catawba nation branch had a new president appointed to take the place of Alonzo Canty who was called on a mission to the Cherokee Indian nation in North Carolina.

It appeared to be a tactical move on the part of the Mormons to send an Indian missionary among Indians although this procedure later was to be adopted by the church in the southwest. In this early case it apparently created no positive results other than enabling Elder Canty to speak to the Cherokees bear his testimony and leave copies of the book of Mormon. Canty's mission did not last very long for he was again presiding at the Catawba nation branch on June 13, 1886."

PHOTO 2 -- JOHN ALONZO CANTY

Elder Pinkney Head   -   M 1885

PHOTO 3 -- PINKNEY HEAD

Catawba Indian Pinkney Henry Head was born 26 October 1862, Catawba Reservation, York, South Carolina and he died 25 May 1951, Farmington, San Juan, New Mexico.
Father: Robert Henry Head (1841–1864)   Mother: Sarah Ann Evans-Canty

Baptized into the Church of Jesus Christ of Latter Day Saints - 6 Mar 1884

Called on an LDS mission - 31 Oct 1885

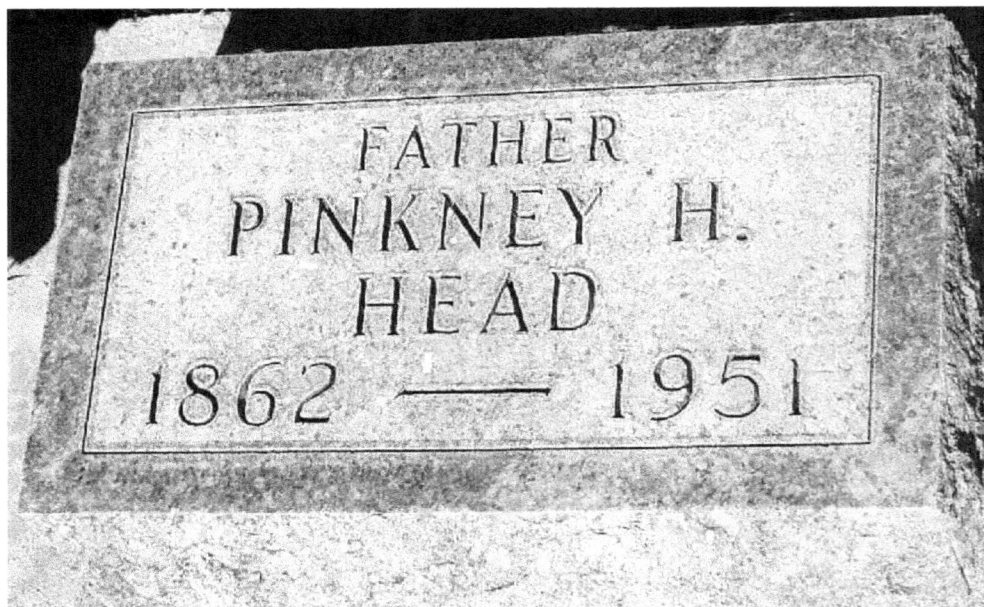

PHOTO 4   HEADSTONE FOR PINKNEY H HEAD

Journal of Pinkney Head,

(Journal of my Missionary travels to the Cherokee)

---my book. After while I raised my head and looked up the street and saw Bro. Patterson.[35] I lift my head down again and he would come up on the steps and look and then come a few more steps and look until] he found me out. Then he said hello and come and shook hands then walk back up the street.

Next with Bro. Taylor George[36] and had quite a lively time and staid in the city till late in the evening and started to J.C. Russells place which was 12 miles west. The evening was very cold. We reached Bro. Russells place about 9 o'clock in the night where I met with my aunt and 4 cousins of that family and 4 cousins of another family. I met with Elders Joseph Willey who had been laboring in our part for some time and Elders W. E. Bingham and Cragun. They had a fine time that night singing the songs of Zion. I concluded that I would stay at Bro. Pattersons and write for the company that was going in February and about the same time had found out that they were no company going from SC. I staid in the country and worked until April 1. I heard they was some Saints going to Colorado, so I thought I would go then and the 3rd day of April I quit work to fix up to go. I left and walked 10 miles that evening.

Come to Martinsville P.O. SC and there I got a letter from home stating that my mother[37] was sick, bad off, no life expected for her. She said that she wanted me to come home and, see her one more time so went on to Bro. Russells got there about sundown. Staid there till 12 o'clock that night getting ready to go home. One of my cousins went with me down to Mr. Blacks,[38] which was about 10 miles. We got there just at daylight, went to Grandmothers [39] house and had breakfast and then went with my Uncle J. H. Watts [40] to Gaffney Station which was 10 miles and There waited for the train which came at 4 PM. I got on and rode 66 miles and come to Charlotte, NC about dark. I check my bundle and started a foot on home, 35 miles that night, is they was in town until Next day late I travel all night on the railroad until! about one hour before day. I went out in the woods a little ways and made me a little fire. I awoke next morning about daylight and started on to the Catawba Nation which was 10 miles. I call at some five houses along the railroad for something to eat. At last I got a little to eat and then I

---

[35] James Goodwin Patterson, son of Laban Chappell and Martha Patterson.
[36] Taylor George, son of Zacharia Anthony Taylor George.
[37] Sarah Ann Evans-Canty Head, daughter of Peggy Canty and Chancy Evans, widow of Robert Henry Head.
[38] John S Black a white friend of the Catawba.
[39] Lucy Quash-Marsh Watts.
[40] James Henry Watts, son of Evans and Lucy Quash-Marsh Watts.

went and with haste to get home. I got in about 1/2 half (mile) home. I met up with one of my old friends. tie told me my mother was a little better. I then began to feel better. I went on home and saw my mother very low and there I met with Elders Joseph Willey and W. E. Cragun again.

April 5. 1884, on Sunday morning or about noon the Elders had meeting appointments at Bro. George's[41] house which was about 1 1/2 miles from our place. I thought I would go to this meeting with them, so I went and seen all of the Catawba Saints and them that was not Saints also. I heard the Elders preach and that was the last time I heard Elder Willey preach, for he and Elder Cragun left the county that same week. Elder Willey was released to return le in July following so I did not see him anymore. The same year I taught school in the Catawba Nation, South Carolina for months four $30.00. & had in 3 acres of cotton that year but did not do much good it made me 21 dollars and on the 16 day of May Elders Cragan and F.A. Fraughton came back to stop with us all the summer season they had been there one week and one day they was about 12 men came where we was teaching school and the Elders was there with me in the house. One of the men came to the door and called for Elder Cragan. [Tim and Elders Fraughton went out to talk to them. They gave the Elders a pertisehen (petition) that had about 33 names signed to it telling them that they had to leave the County. They told them that they were citizens of the United States and thought they had as good to stay in the country is any other citizens. They gave the Elders 6 days to leave the place, but the Elders did not pay any attention to it much. They staid on and on the 25 nights of May they was 32 men came on the Elders at our house about 10 oclock. Came running up to the house all well arm. Elder Cragan had just taken off his shoes to retire to bed when he heard the noise someone said run and Elder Cragan made his escape out of the north door and run for the woods which was about 30 yards and while on his way to the woods they was about 25 or 30 shots fired at him, one shot just grazes him on the chin and Elder Fraughton had no chance to get out and the mobs came in about 8 of them and caught Fraughton and led him away and gave him 50 lashes with hickory switches and turned him loose charging him to leave the country. The next day he came back to our house, then we all looked for Elder Cragun for about 2 hours before we found him. Both staid in the woods the rest of the night and next morning came to the house and got breakfast. Appointed meeting that day at Wm. Georges house.

They was one couple married and baptize that day about 10 o'clock instant namely James Harris

---

[41] William-Billy George, son of Nelson and Sarah Ayers George.

and Fanny Whitesides[42] in the same stream I was baptized. After baptism we all went to the house. The Elders council led the Saints a little. Elder Cragun remarks was this, "be good to everybody, pray for them that despitefully use you and lift up your head and rejoice for being persecuted for so good a cause," and after they had talked to us, they left for Spartanburg County, South Carolina. Brother John Sanders[43] accompanied them 10 miles leading them mostly through the woods. Then the Elders did not walk openly there much anymore after that time. John Allen[44] was the leader of the mob.

The Elders slipped back in on the last day of July. Elder W. E. Bingham and Elders Cragun, James Patterson and James Watts accompanying them from Spartanburg County. And the first day of August they organized Sunday school Brother Alonzo Canty[45] was ordained a Priest to preside over the Sunday school.

In September me and Brother Alonzo (John Alonzo) Canty started on horses to go to Spartanburg County, which was about 80 miles. We got to Brother Patterson's house on the 13th day of the month, at about 8 o'clock on Sunday morning. We found Marth Jane Paterson[46] my (future) wife sick bad off of the Eresiples (I have no idea what he means) Staid there until the 23 day and started back home and on the 27th of the month I was-taking sick with the chills and fever and boils, so I was useless for some time. I had two spells of sickness during the year 1885.

My first prayer in public was on the 25th day of May 1885.

Some of the Lamanites was the starters of getting up the mobs to run off the Elders from our mists. Brother Joseph Willey and Bro. Humphrey traveled sometime in the southern part of South Carolina trying to open up new fields but failed to do so on account mobs and had to return back to York County. They came to our house about 10 o'clock in the night. The mobs was ragin at the same time there also so they was compelled to hide up a little season. They staid in the stable loft at our house and were often unsettled by our neighbors, after while the Elders was there but they did not nowhere the Elders was. They thought they had left the country. One morning Brother George Canty[47] came to our house and was surprised to see Elders there and to hear them say they had been there all the time.

---

[42] James Jr, son of James and Sarah Jane Ayers Harris, Fannie, twin to John Alonzo Canty, daughter of Thomas Whitesides and Eliza Scott Canty.

[43] John Idle Sanders, son of Lucinda Harris.

[44] John Allen fathered a Catawba child.

[45] John Alonzo Canty, son of Thomas Whitesides and Eliza Scott Canty.

[46] Martha Jane Patterson, daughter of James and Elizabeth White Patterson.

[47] George Washington Canty, son of Franklin and Eliza Scott Canty, half brother of John Alonzo, Fannie and Mary Jane.

October 31,1885, me and Brother Alonzo Canty received a letter from Elder W. E. Bingham stating that our names had been suggested that we was worthy young men to take a mission among the Cherokee Laminates in North Carolina, Swain County and Jackson County. He told us that we could gather our crops before we started but we was willing to go at any time. We was glad to think that we was worthy to go and teach others the Gospel.

So, I left my home at Catawba Nation, Carolina on the first day of December 1885 to go to the Cherokee Nation. Brother John Sanders and B. P. Harris[48] accompanied us 12 miles. We all stopped and staid all night at Lucindas[49] house 6 miles above Rock Hill. Next morning started for Kings Mountain. We walked hard all day in the rain and mud but failed to reach the place. We stopped all night with Mr. and Mrs. Brown, 3 miles above Yorkville. Had a good supper, good bed and paid 50 cents. Started soon next morning travel all day and come to a man's place. Staid overnight. The next morning the man we staid with went to the man of the place and told him that we was at his house. Then the man began to curse and spring about saying that we had to leave his place, or he would make us go. Saying the Mormons was bad enough, but the Indians was worse. So, we left soon and walked about 5 miles and met up with Elder W. E. Bingham and went with him to Brother James Smith house at Whittier.

We staid there a while and started fore Hampton Robisons about 2 miles and went a little ways in the woods all three of us and was set apart for to take a mission among the Indians in Swain County,[50] South Carolina. We traveled all day and came to Bro. Robersons house about dark and staid all night and had a good time together and left next morning about 10 o'clock and traveled 15 miles. Came to brother Evans Watts house there I met my Grandmother and 3 uncles and some of my cousins. Had a good time with them all night and the rest of the day until! 3 o'clock and then started for Bro. Pattersons house about sundown. There we met up with Bro. F. A. Fraughton and Elder Anderson. While stopping with Bro. Patterson, I went hunting on the 9th of December and killed two rabbits and I started to the post office for mail. Got about half way and met Bro. Patterson with a letter for me from home stating that all was well which gave me great satisfaction. I then went back to the house with Bro. Patterson.

On the 11th day of December I thought it wisdom to send my money to Chattanooga, Tennessee to Elder John Morgan. So, I wrote a letter and went down to Paris P.O., Spartanburg County, SC and

---

[48] Benjamin Perry Harris.
[49] Lucinda Harris.
[50] Cherokee

requested 65 dollars to Mr. Morgan. Came out of the office and there I met Rachel Tims[51] that was from our place, left home after I did. I went up in the cotton field where brother Patterson's family and he was picking cotton and stayed until night.

The 12th of December 1885 they was a few of us went to meeting at Mr. Black's place, names Pinkney Head and Alonzo Canty were accompanying Miss Martha and Henrietta Patterson[52] all the way which was 10 miles and heard Elder F. A. Fraughton and W. E. Anderson preach a great sermon. On the 13th there was a lot of sleet, so we could not travel so we stayed at Brother Watts house until the 14th day. Started for Brother Patterson's place in company with Martha Patterson and Henrietta Patterson. Reached there at 12 o'clock and met with 4 Elders. We all stayed all night, and a fine time, leaving together on the 15th, we bid all the folks good bye. Then started far the Cherokee Nation. We walked hard all day and until 8 o'clock in the night and stayed all night with a man by the name of Wilkie. Had a good supper and breakfast. Then went on and walked 7 miles. Overtook a wagon and got to ride 7 miles with an old man by the name of Hills. He gave us a good dinner of beef and bread and apples. After we left him, we went to Broad River again and had no way to cross. We had to wade the stream which was very cold (because of the) weather. Walked till 8 o'clock in the night and got in a house at an old widow woman with one grown son and daughter. We had a fine supper and good warm bed all night. Her name was Mary Harris.[53] She did not charge us anything for stopping. We left them our names and tract and started on. We walked 15 miles from 1/2 past 9 o'clock till sunset. We called at a man's house by the name of Henderson to stay all night. He came out and asked our business. We told him we was ministers of the Gospel traveling without purse or script. He said, "Well how do you get along?" I told him when we tell our business then we get a stopping place. He said, " you two are too young to preach." I told him we read that the Lord takes the weak things of the world to confound the mighty. Then he said that was so and asked us in the house. While at supper the man said the folks was mighty bad there. The preachers would not preach without a heap of money. I told him we did not charge anything far preaching for I did not think that was right to charge for preaching. Next morning, we had a good breakfast and then bid them good-by. We walked 14 miles without anything to eat. Next morning, they was a man came and asked us to hold meeting at his house that night. We told him we would and night came we went down and there got a Cherokee to interpret for us. We held meeting one hour and 20 minutes, good attention was paid to what was said. Then we went back to our good old friend house, Will Tarber and stayed there 4 days with him Then

---

[51] Rachel is the daughter of John Alexander and Martha Ann Cottsky-Scott Tims.
[52] Both daughters of James and Elizabeth White Patterson.
[53] Mary George Harris, first wife of Epp Harris, daughter of Patsy George.

went across the river to James WalkingSticks house and there stayed with him 3 days. On the 8th of January 1886 there fell a big snow on the 9th we walked 8 miles and came to Jessie Reeds house. Stayed overnight with him. He claims to be a leading man in the Babts. Church leader. But did not hold any pray before going to bed. In all our travels we did not staid with anyone that would have his prays before going to bed. On the 1st day of the month we went to hear a Quacker (Quaker) minister preach to the Cherokees. The same hour when we had a Bro Preaching to them and while this man was opening the meeting with prays, he said 0 Lord help us to love those that love us and help us and help us to hate them that use us. I thought he was not fit to teach anybody how to live then we had a little talk with him concerning New Revelations and he said there was no need of New Revelations. So, after meeting we went about two miles and staged over night with a man by the name of Dawson George.

The next day went and stayed all-day and over night with a Methodist preacher and had a long talk with him that night. We then went to Bird Town which was 9 miles and held meeting at Mr. John Peckerwoods[54] house and went home with Bill Peckerwood and stayed overnight with him. The next day his wife washed some clothes for us and dun them up in good shape for us, not charging us anything for it. We stayed with him a few days. He told us we could stay with him long as we wanted and make that our home.

On the 15th we went to James WalkingSticks house and stayed overnight with them, had a good time. On the next day walked about 8 miles to the post office through the snow but did not get any mail. We went back to Bird Town and while there we went to James Kagg (Kegg)[55] house. He was one of the tribe of Catawbas. I had a long chat with him and returned to Will Peckerwoods house.

We had a meeting appointed at Will Peckerwoods house on the 17th day of January. So, the crowd came together that night, early candle light. Just before meeting began they was two young men come in one was named Martan the other was Show. Martan asked me was I the preacher. I told him I was. He asked me that church did belong. I said the Church of Jesus Christ of Latter Day Saint. I asked him did he ever hear any of our Doctrines. Yes, he said, we had it here long time. I told him there was no Mormons then. The two men set and whispered and said "lets us go then the men will leave" and the other said, "Lets stay little while longer " and soon after we commenced our meeting, then there was about 3 men more came in the house and set down. I asked the Lord to help me at that time and I proved to them that the Gospel had been took off the earth and that the time had come it was restored

---

[54] Yes, this is really a Cherokee name.

[55] James Kegg was actually a Pamunkey Indian who had married a Catawba woman, thus making him a Catawba.

back again and proved to them that we was teaching it. I spoke better that night then I ever did. I thought I felt the Spirit of God with in me more at that time. I spoke about one hour. After meeting they was one of the men said, it seems like your Doctrine was true. Then he said "I thought you would be frightened when we came in. You would have thought we was mobs." I told him if they was mobs, it would not be any news to me for I had seen (them before). He said he wanted to know something about the Mormons, and have they got that name. I told him that Mormon was one of the olden Prophets and if we was going to go by a Prophet we could go by Jaramiah or Joshua and it would be just as good. Then I quoted some scriptures to him and he said, "I do not profess to argue on anything and your Doctrine sounds true. I would like to hear you again some time and will come if I know when you hold meeting. I said to him, "You will know I suppose when we hold meeting." He said again, I did not come for any harm only came for curiosity." I told him it was a wonder to all that hear it and that I was glad he came just for that purpose so I could get to bare my testimony to him. I told him we was called Mormons but (if) everybody would believe in their own Bibles, then they would all be Mormons. We wound up the chat. The man of the house told us if anybody done anything to us he would skin them and I do believe he would too.

A day later we started to the post office to get mail, while on our way we met a man that we had been talking to about our Doctrine. He became interested in the same, we had a long talk with him. On the 22nd of December they was a man come and told us there was a mob crowd made up for us and they had mode threats that they would have us caught before long. Saying they would get a load of hickory switches for us, so we thought they was no good to be done there then. We calculated to leave on the 23rd but it came a lot of rain so we did not get off but on the 24th we started anyway and walked 12 miles and found the roads so bad we could not go. We went back and stayed two weeks longer. Sent home for a little money and we were on our way westwards we cross a fence and found some walnuts there. We made our dinner on them. We thought then we would sell our watches and go back on the train. I tried with all of my might to sell my watch, but failed to do so. I don't think the folks had any money for I seen that a lot of the Cherokees going barefooted and it being in the months of December and January 1886, the ground was covered with snow. The people there had gave us one week to leave, but we did not go thinking it best to stay and meet Elder W. E. Bingham, the President of the S.C. Conference. At last we left the Cherokees on the 7th of February 1886. We walked hard all day through the mountains and got a lunch a man's house by the name of Garitt and went on. We walked 22 miles through snow that day and was wearied down. We stayed overnight with a man by the name of Shehand. Got an early start next morning and walked 13 miles. Came to Piggon River and got on the cars. We went to Ashville City, NC and stayed overnight with a man by the name of More. Started next morning soon for Hendersonville, which was 20 miles. Walked hard all day and came to the town just dark. Went to the hotel stayed all night which cost us one dollar. Got on the cars again next morning at day light and came to Spartanburg City at 12 o'clock. There was a man of our faith living in that city which we knew well, so we went and took dinner with him. I wrote a letter to my mother while I was stopping and then left on the 2 o'clock train, PM. Got off at Cowpens Station, SC. Walked about 12 miles that night and came to Brother Watts house and stayed overnight with him. Then we stayed around there for some time among the saints and our relatives. On the 15th day of February 1886, Elders W. E. Bingham and W. G. Cragun bid us farewell as he was released to go home.

On the 17th day, I was married to Martha Jane Patterson by Elder Heber Wright. Alonzo Canty my companion was married to Henrietta Patterson at the same time in Spartanburg, South Carolina at John Black's place. We left that place on the 18th walked 3 days and most of the time till late in the night. On the 19th it was terrible cold night. We got home on the 21st day of the month at Catawba Nation, South Carolina.

The whole amount of money I used while on my trip to the Cherokee Lamanites was $44.55 during the months. This is the end of my travels to the Cherokees.

On the 13th me and A. Tims[56] was to settle. 1 being anxious for him to raise means to go to Colorado when I told him I would take $30 out of the crops, so he gave me 30 dollars. On the 14th, it being the Sabbath, Sunday school and meeting was held at the schoolhouse in Catawba Nation. Some good instruction was given, some bore a faithful testimony. In the evening there was a singing appointment at Brother John Sanders house which we all attended. Had an enjoyable time together.

February 26, 1887 Left Spartanburg, SC at am, bound for Zion.

March 5, 1887, I then arrived to the San Luis Stake of Zion with a company of 140 Saints in which my mother and wife and one child, step farther and father in law, and two of his small children.[57] All making 6 souls. We then stopped with Brother Nelson Gordon two days and got a house, moved in. I stayed in that town which was called Manassa, until the last of August and then removed to Sanford, 6 miles north. That was a town just started up 4 miles east of the D. & R. G. W. Railroad up on a bench about 12 feet higher than the rest of the valley. I like the place well when I first saw it, so I took me up a town lot on the west side of town. Being scares of means to build any I made me a dug out on my lot. My wife helps me all she could. We soon got it finished in October 1887 and moved in. I still keep at work all the time thinking that I would do better before long.

---

[56] John Alexander Tims, son of Rachel Quash-Marsh and John Alexander Tims Sr. should be 19
[57] Sarah Head Tims, Alexander Tims, Martha Patterson Head, Jaames Patterson, 2 children

In the summer of 1886 1 bought seven thousand bricks from Bishop S.C. Berthelson. I then worked for a time and went to hauling the bricks. My wife helped me haul them and we built us a house that fall and winter. It was 14 by 20 with 6 windows and 3 doors one chimney. During this long time living in the ground our baby had some bad spells of sickness. I think on account of it being so damp, but we was proud when the day came for us to leave our dug out and move into our new house. April 26, 1889, the wind blowed very hard (at) night, but we felt to thank the Lord for his goodness unto us. During the summer of 1889, I labored all the time at the house trying to do the best I could carrying the United States mail.

Three times a week Bishop S. C. Berthelsen bring the contractor. I also worked a few acres of land that I rented. Continued carrying the mail until October 14th, then the mail service was increased to 6 days in the week. I then bought another house. I went through some very hard storms.

October 11th, on October first me and my wife started to go to Logan Temple which our tickets cost us fifty dollars from La Jara Colorado to Salt Lake City, Utah. We left La Jara on the first day of October at half past 4 PM. and got to Salt Lake City on the 3rd day. We met some people we was acquainted with before we left the state of SC. Also, one of the Elders we got acquainted with in SC. We stopped with them and on Saturday went to Conference. Saw more Elders we knew in the south. On Sunday we attended Conference at 2 o'clock, I met Brother Joseph Willey which I had not seen for 4 years. He was proud to see us. So, me and my wife went up on the cars 10 miles to Bountiful on the 6th where Brother Wiley met us with a wagon. He drove us to his brother Jed's house. We had supper and after supper the folks sing songs, pretty songs, and then we went to his mother's house and stayed all night.

Next morning soon, he carried me around and showed me the country. Also went to two of his brothers houses. Saw them all and came back, had breakfast and went to the railroad and went to Salt Lake City. This was on the 7th and on Tuesday, me and my wife started to Logan Temple leaving Salt Lake City at 7 o'clock. Arrived at Logan City about 3 o'clock the same day. We went to Brother Washington B. Rogers house and stayed with him all the time we stopped in Logan. While stopping there, they was a lot of snow and rain fell which made a very disagreeable time for us. We stayed in Logan City 7 days and then we went back down to Salt Lake City, stopping with Brother John Gordon for a few days. On the 19th we started for home, we was on the road until the 21st day. We reached home and found all of the folks well and feeling pretty well. This ends our journey which cost us seventy-five dollars.

I had to go to the Court House and buy my license before I could be married in the Temple. October 4 arrived to La Jara Station which was a few miles west of Sanford where we live. I was expecting a team to meet me there but by some misunderstanding it failed to come. So, me and my wife walked with our bundels and two little children, Sarah J. E. and Rosey. We reached home just a little before sundown and found everything moving along well. We then enjoy ourselves, to think we had been able to go to the Temple of the Lord and receive our Endowments and was united together in marriage by W.W. Wenell, one of the Servants of the Lord for Time and all Eternity. Also had our two little girls sealed to us, Sarah Jane Elizabeth and Rosey Lee.

I then worked for Brother H. Corey and earned 20.00. I paid two dollars of it on the church we was going to build there in Sanford. Sot the rest in wheat, 8 hundred pounds. I worked for Brother James Read and earned 10.00 which got grain, paid some debts that I owed at the Sanford COOP Store, had near about six hundred pounds left which made me 14 hundred pounds which I sent to the mill and made me my winters bread. Work then closed out, so did nothing then only haul wood on shares.

On the 25th day of February I had a payment due on my lot which was ten dollars and 35 cents. Paid that off all right and felt glad to think that the Lord had blessed me so far as he had.

I was at that time thinking of going on to New Mexico some 90 miles to look for a better climate as Colorado was a cold place where I was living. In the month of June, I started down with Brother R. F. Humphrey and Brother A. S. Fuller with two wagons and 13 head or cattle. Part of the country was dry so we had to haul water. Was five days on the road and reached a little settlement of Saints called 7797797, but since then name was changed to-

Here ends the copies of the journal of my Great Uncle Pinkney Henry Head, in my possession.

From the journal of Pinkney Head, we read of the friendship that Elder Willey especially had built with the Catawba he converted.

Elder Samuel Taylor Blue

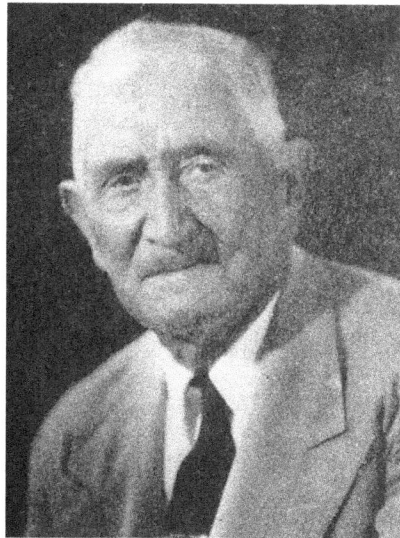

PHOTO 5 -- SAMUEL TAYLOR BLUE

Samuel Taylor Blue – born 15 August 1872, Catawba Indian Reservation, York, South Carolina and died 16 April 1959, Rock Hill, York, South Carolina.
Father – Samuel Blue Mother – Margaret Marsh-Ayers-George

Baptized – 7 May 1897 – by J A Gordon
Served a Mission - 1916-1917

No. 22 {Cancellation} Name in Full Samuel Taylor Blue
Father's Name
Member (Yes, No) Samuel Blue
Mother's Maiden Name
Member (Yes, No) Margaret
Born at York Co., S. C. Day 15 Month Aug. Year 1873
Received from
Blessed by
Mission to
Baptized by J. A. Gordon 7 May 1897
Married {Temple / Civil} to Louisa Canty
Confirmed by J. W. Parker Not Given
Priesthood when received
Ordained by
Removed to
Ordained by
Excommunicated for
Ordained by
Died of
Ordained by
Canceled for

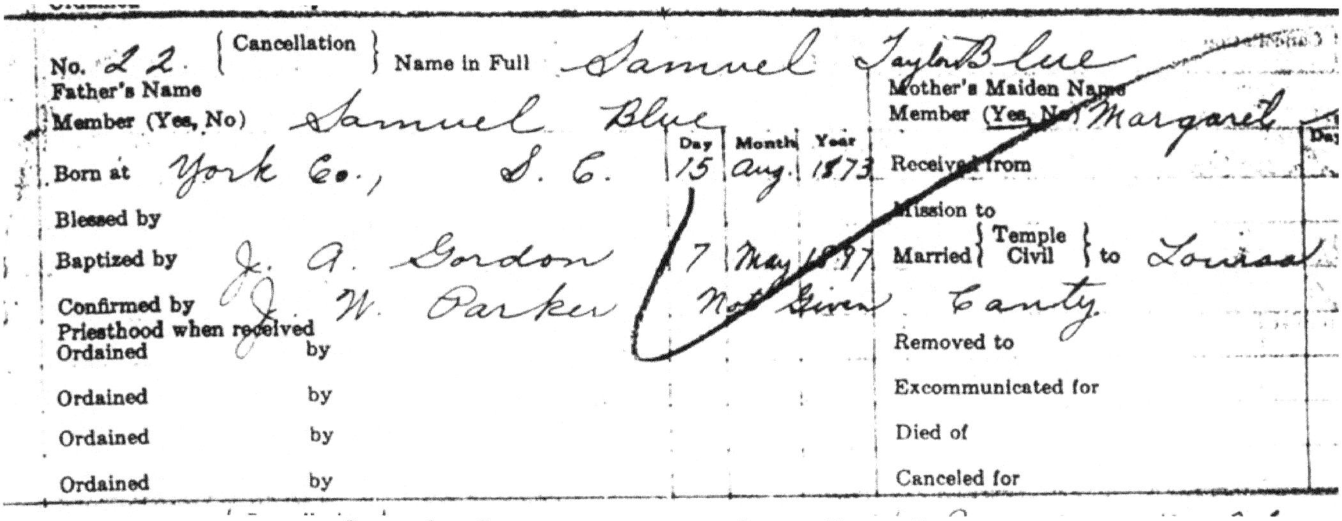

PHOTO 6 -- BAPTISMAL RECORD FOR SAMUEL TAYLOR BLUE

Elder Sam Blue assisted by John Brown and Alonzo Canty. Elder Robert Harris presided over the branch. The Indians served another mission to their Lamanite brothers in 1916-17. Elders Sam T. Blue and Ben P. Harris taught the gospel to a tribe of Pembroke Indians in North Carolina:
Elder Samuel T. Blue, one of the Lamanite brethren, and president of the Catawba Indian Nation

branch, in a letter to President Callis says:

Chief Sam Blue born in 1873 stated they brought a book which is known as the book of Mormon this book was the direct history of our forefathers which we had no other history before this book came along. Herbert Blue son of chief Sam Blue recounted his earliest recollection passed down to him concerning the motivation behind accepting Mormonism. "The missionaries read the book of Mormon --- the history of the American Indian and the Indians believed the story they told them. The relationship between the Catawbas and Mormonism which resulted in the establishment of the LDS church in South Carolina grew increasingly stronger until Mormonism became the dominant factor in Catawba society.

The Church and the Catawbas continued to grow and prosper during the next few years with little outside interference. In 1911 the chapel was found to be too small and was enlarged by twelve feet, the tribe now possessed a schoolhouse, a chapel, and a well. With the help of Sister Barrus, the Relief Society was organized on March 7, 1910, with sisters Mary C. Barrus, Mary J, Watts, and Eliza Blue as the presidency, and Sister Lucy George as secretary. The Sunday School was operating very smoothly with upwards of sixty pupils and an efficient teaching core under the able direction of Elder Sam Blue assisted by John Brown and Alonzo Canty. Elder Robert Harris presided over the branch.

The Indians served another mission to their Lamanite brothers in 1916-17. Elders Sam T. Blue and Ben P. Harris taught the gospel to a tribe of Pembroke Indians in North Carolina:

Elder Samuel T. Blue, one of the Lamanite brethren, and president of the Catawba Indian Nation branch, in a letter to President Callis says:

"on Friday, the 9th, Brother Ben P. Harris and I went to Pembroke to visit the Indians in that place. We had a nice time there. We had several Gospel conversations and we left all of our literature with them, also a Book of Mormon. They seem to think a great deal of us."

Elder Benjamin Perry Harris

PHOTO 7 -- BENJAMIN PERRY HARRIS

Benjamin Perry Harris --born February 1871, Catawba Indian Reservation, Rock Hill South Carolina and died 15 December 1930, Rock Hill, York, South Carolina. The son of John "Mush" and Nancy Harris Harris, the seventh child.

"The Church and the Catawbas continued to grow and prosper during the next few years with
little outside interference. In 1911 the chapel was found to be too small and was enlarged by
twelve feet, the tribe now possessed a schoolhouse, a chapel, and a well. With the help of
Sister Barrus, the Relief Society was organized on March 7, 1910, with sisters Mary C.
Barrus, Mary J, Watts, and Eliza Blue as the presidency, and Sister Lucy George as secretary.
c the Sunday School was operating very smoothly with upwards of sixty pupils and an
efficient teaching core under the able direction of Elder Sam Blue, assisted by John Brown
and Alonzo Canty. Elder Robert Harris presided over the branch. The Indians served another
mission to their Lamanite brothers in 1916-17. Elders Sam T. Blue and Ben P. Harris taught
the gospel to a tribe of Pembroke Indians in North Carolina:

Elder Samuel T. Blue, one of the Lamanite brethren, and president of the Catawba Indian Nation branch, in a letter to President Callis says:

"on Friday, the 9th, Brother Ben P. Harris and I went to Pembroke to visit the Indians in that place. We had a nice time there. We had several Gospel conversations and we left all of our literature with them, also a Book of Mormon. They seem to think a great deal of us.'[58]

Elder Chester Gilbert Harris -- SSM 1935

PHOTO 8 -- ELDER CHESTER GILBERT HARRIS

Catawba Indian Elder Chester Gilbert Harris born 15 Aug 1909 in Catawba, York, South Carolina and died December 1970, Columbia, Richland, South Carolina.
Son of David Adam and Margaret Della George Harris.

Called as Missionary in 1935 served in the "Nation" 1935 along with Brigham D Madsen.

Chester Gilbert Harris is mentioned by Brigham D Madsen in his book Against the Grain, the following are Madsen's observations about Chester.
"In addition to one month with the in- active missionary, I spent another month with James Simmons, a former football player, from Brigham Young University; two months with Clint Adair, a cowboy and rancher from Luna, New Mexico; and four months with Chester G Harris, a full-blooded

---

[58] Pembroke was the name of the town in Robeson County, North Carolina. The Indians were Lumbee.

Catawba Indian from Greenville, South Carolina. At other times I would work with a newly arrived elder for a week or two while waiting for a good place to assign him. I very much enjoyed my labors was Simmons, Adair, and Harris.

Chester G Harris and about 300 of the remnants of the once mighty Catawba nation formed the branch of the LDS church at Greenville under the leadership of Harris's uncle, Chief Blue, who according to Harris and other members of the tribe, was gradually becoming "white and delight some "as prophesied in the book of Mormon. Harris believed this promise with all his heart and proved to be a very effective missionary and speaker for the Mormon cause. He had practically no money or means of getting any; because I felt that I could keep him going financially and also because of my interest in his people, I selected him as a companion for about four months.

In September 1935 he and I undertook to proselyte without purse or scrip in Robeson County, the home of a few thousand Lumbee Indians. These people, a mixture of whites and Indians, claimed descent from Sir Walter Raleigh's lost colony of Roanoke Island and had formally been known as Croatans. Harris was roly-poly, only 5 foot four in contrast to my six-foot four, he was an ever smiling, fun-loving, and hard-working missionary. During our work together, I usually gave a short introduction explaining the purposes of our church with a brief description of the Book of Mormon. Then Harris would take over for about 50 minutes giving an impassioned recital of the wrongs perpetrated by white people in the US government on the American Indians, the broken promises and the forgotten and treaties. During his sermons, he would be transformed his eyes would flash and his audience would see a real Indian orator fighting for his people. We nearly always had turn away crowds because many North Carolinians had never seen a real live American Indian. One preacher listened to our sermon to an Indian audience, then congratulated us on the truthfulness of our message.

The only time I traveled extensively without purse or scrip in North Carolina was when Harris and I were companions. Perhaps my most important contribution to the church in eastern North Carolina was building two chapels. I convinced Pres. Kirkham that he would see in new Chapel in short order if the mission would help with the financing. He agreed, and on November 6, 1935 I delivered a set of ready-made church plans to a brother Barnhill, the only Mormon carpenter in the town he had agreed to work for minimum wage to help construct the building. He, Harris and I began on November 19 and had it ready to meet in exactly 2 months later. When Barnhill didn't show up to work, Harris and I would work alone. Once when Harris became so ill he had to go to the hospital, I worked by myself for two days. On January 19 we held our first meeting in the new building. I proudly wrote "we had about 50 out. Harris and I preached up a storm. Apostle Melvin J Ballard dedicated the Chapel on

June 1. This ends the remembrances of Madsen about Chester Harris.

PHOTO 9 -- BRIGHAM STANDING 6' 5" AND CHESTER STANDING 5' 5"

From the book <u>Against the Grain</u> written by Brigham D Madsen in 2004

'Quote the only time I traveled extensively without purse or scrip in North Carolina was when Harris and I were companions. One evening in Pembroke, Robeson County, we had difficulty getting lodging for the night. The fifth place we asked to stay, they said they were going to the show and so couldn't keep us, so I said well we'd be glad to go to the show with you. So, we did. Such gall astonishes me in my Pocatello days I was even timid about answering the telephone. The next evening, we found a place to stay with Willie Prevatt on the condition that we attend a revival with him. We went. There were only about five whites and about 300 Indians. The evangelist could not get the congregation stirred up and finally announced that all those who had not repented and had not been saved would be killed, because

"God's going to kill you for not repenting." Once in September 1935 we walked 9 miles asking at every farmhouse for lodging and finally found a place at 9:30 PM. As I wrote I never heard so many excuses in all my life.

Working with Arthur Clinton Adair was just as enjoyable, but for different reasons. His ranching background had given him a quiet strength, a mirthful sense of humor, and an understanding of other two-legged creatures. He was somewhat diffident about speaking in public or pushing himself to the front at social affairs but was very effective as a missionary one to one. We spent the two months from mid-March to mid-May of 1936 tracting and holding meetings in the small town of Kinston and had a week together without purse or scrip in Robeson County. An excerpt from my March 1936 diary brings back fond memories of Clint Adair.

"Adair decided to preach on Word of Wisdom (at the Albertson Chapel) which he had never attempted before. He said that some scientists allowed a leech to suck the blood from a person who was a habitual tobacco user. The leech was not long in dying after gorging itself on this contaminated blood. Then this man of science allowed a leech to fill itself on the blood of a person who didn't use tobacco and it thrived. Adair said that he could prove it from his own experience for he had spent the night at a member's home in the hills of North Carolina, and the next morning he was covered with bed- bug bites and he could see stuffed bed- bugs crawling away. He said that the people up there use tobacco and liquor and therefore bed-bugs couldn't live off them, but when they got near these two Elders they knew that the famine was over."

Adair and I did our job and enjoyed each other's company. In September 1935 while we were traveling for a few days without purse or scrip, Adair and I went methodically from door to door for two hours in Parkton (population 450), starting with the minister, asking for a night's lodging. We finally found hospitality in the fourth to the last house; but later I recorded, "Got a place to stay at first house we asked which is unusual" It was with a certain amount of relief that I recorded returning to the home of a good Saint Furnie Harper in Deep Run: first square meal I've had for a month.

When one elderly woman asked me for baptism I agreed to perform the ceremony but becoming slightly ill asked if Adair could officiate. She refused. If I wouldn't baptize her she wouldn't join the church I acquiesced, though with some personal misgivings about the strength of her convictions.

Adair played the guitar and had a good tenor voice, in Kingston we got in the habit of taking his guitar to our cottage meetings then singing for the congregation afterwards. We were soon at attracting such large crowds that our sermons became shorter and our performances stretched out to as much as two hours. Adair's favorite music was cowboy songs, so we soon branched out from hymns, and I developed a real fondness for Western music as well including Adair's signature tune When It's Night Time in Nevada. We made a lot of friends for our church. Who knows perhaps this pleasant approach was as effective in improving the reputation of the Mormons and leading some to investigate as my public sparring with ministers in Tennessee.

Money was always tight in contrast to the present, there was no great emphasis on placing or selling copies of the book of Mormon, but at least once such a sale was a godsend. Harris and I sold one to the barber in the small town of Pembroke: we have had $.20 apiece for about two weeks now-no more, no less so it ($.50) came in handy. On another occasion Adar and I got down to $.13 between us but were saved when he received a money order for $40. My diary records frequent disapproval of the prices charged in 1936. $12 a month for room in Kinston and $.10 for a large hamburger with all the trimmings. When Adair's trousers needed mending in April 1936, he had to stay in our room all day while the tailor worked.

Holding open and street meetings was much more difficult in North Carolina than in Tennessee where they had been part of the Bible Belt culture. A carnival was set up just across the street from our meeting place as we started to sing our opening him the carnival Calliope started up at full volume. Our meeting came to an abrupt end and I silently paid my compliments to a very devious official. In Kinston, Adair and I were unable to get permission to hold street meetings, and the city officials just laughed when we asked to hold a preaching service in the courthouse. At Parkton in Roberson County when Adair and I attended a Baptist Sunday school, the minister asked Adair to give the opening prayer and had me teach the adult class. One day Adair and I caught a ride with the man to whom, as we rolled along, we explained Mormonism and that our church did not believe in paid ministry. Only as we were getting out of the car did he politely mention that he was a Methodist minister.

PHOTO 10 -- ELDER CLINTON ADAIR AND CHESTER HARRIS - 1935

Missionaries who served in the Southern States Mission
(founded in 1876)

and worked with and among the Catawba Indian People
in the Carolina's

Southern State Missionaries from 1880 - 1900

President John Hamilton Morgan – SSM 1881-1888

PHOTO 11 -- PRESIDENT JOHN HAMILTON MORGAN

Birth date, place - 8 August 1842, Greensburg, Decatur, Indiana, United States
Death date - 14 August 1894
Baptism date - 23 November 1867 - Baptism by - Robert L. Campbell
Father's name - Gerrard Morgan -- Mother's name - Eliza Ann Hamilton

Southern States -- October 1875–December 1877 - Age Called: 33
Set Apart: 11 October 1875
Called: 8 October 1875
Departed From Home: 28 October 1875
Arrived At Home: 7 December 1877
Mission type: Proselytizing
Marital Status: Married
Priesthood office: Seventy
Called From: Salt Lake City, Salt Lake, Utah, United States
Set apart by: Joseph Young

Southern States - January 1878–January 1888 - Age Called: 35
Served as Mission President
Set Apart: 25 January 1878 - Set Apart: 29 January 1881 - Set Apart: 29 March 1882
Released: 4 January 1888
Arrived At Home: 5 April 1879
Arrived At Home: 7 December 1881
Mission type: Proselytizing
Marital Status: Plurally Married
Priesthood office: Seventy - Quorum: 8th
Called From: Salt Lake City, Utah Territory, United States
Set apart by: Orson Pratt, George Q. Cannon

> Notes: There is some confusion about his actual dates of service due to multiple entries in the missionary registers. He returned home numerous times, but was still referred to as the president in the mission records during his absence. The confusion is compounded since he was set apart and entered into the missionary registers multiple times as he would return to the mission.
>
> Orson Pratt is listed as setting him apart in January 1878, but George Q. Cannon is listed for the January 1881 and March 1882 entries.

United States - January 1890–Unknown - Age Called: 47
United States
Set Apart: 4 January 1890
Mission type: Proselytizing
Marital Status: Married
Priesthood office: Seventy
Called From: Salt Lake City, Salt Lake, Utah, United States

Missionary Department missionary registers, 1860-1959, Vol. 1, p. 29, line 1247.
Missionary Department missionary registers, 1860-1959, Vol. 2, p. 32, line 1247.
Missionary Department missionary registers, 1860-1959, Vol. 1, p. 40, line 1726.
Missionary Department missionary registers, 1860-1959, Vol. 2, p. 44, line 1726.
Missionary Department missionary registers, 1860-1959, Vol. 1, p. 53, line 2287.
Missionary Department missionary registers, 1860-1959, Vol. 2, p. 58, line 2287.
Missionary Department missionary registers, 1860-1959, Vol. 1, p. 63, line 2697.
Missionary Department missionary registers, 1860-1959, Vol. 2, p. 68, line 2697.
Missionary Department missionary registers, 1860-1959, Vol. 1, p. 104, line 4.
Missionary Department missionary registers, 1860-1959, Vol. 2, p. 111, line 4.

John Morgan journals, 1875-1892, Church History Library.

Account of his missionary activities in the Southern States.

Southern States Mission history, 1832-1964, Church History Library.
See the index in volume 1 for entries on his service.

John Morgan scrapbooks and correspondence, 1863-1881, Church History Library.
Contains newspaper clippings from various papers concerning the Southern States Mission

Andrew Jenson, "Morgan, John," Latter-day Saint Biographical Encyclopedia, vol. 1 (Salt Lake City: Andrew Jenson History Company, 1901), 204-05.

John Morgan journals, 1875-1892, Church History Library.

Account of his missionary activities in the Southern States.
Southern States Mission history, 1832-1964, Church History Library.
See the index in volume 1 for entries on his service.

John Morgan scrapbooks and correspondence, 1863-1881, Church History Library.
Contains newspaper clippings from various papers concerning the Southern States Mission
Andrew Jenson, "Morgan, John," Latter-day Saint Biographical Encyclopedia, vol. 1 (Salt Lake City: Andrew Jenson History Company, 1901), 204-05.

"President John Morgan wrote that it would be well, if possible for the Elders to come in here and organize a branch. He desired the Elders to use their own judgement about coming. Accordingly on July 31, 1885, Elders W. E. Bingham and W. G. Cragun walked about 30 miles part of the distance through the woods and after night, they staid all night at Mr. Bailey Barkers'. Next day, Brothers James Patterson[59] and James Watts[60] piloted them through the woods for about 15 miles, so they arrived in the nation without it being known in the country round about. They spent part of a day and two nights in the woods while they remained in the Nation. "

---

[59]James Goodwin Patterson,
[60]James Harvey Watts.

Elder Joseph Willey   -   SSM 1883-1885

PHOTO 12 -- JOSEPH WILLEY   (PICTURE FROM FAMILYSEARCH.ORG AND SANDRA M STOUT)

Birth date, place - 17 May 1859 - East Bountiful, Davis, Utah
Baptism date - 20 June 1867 -- Baptism by -- W W Willey
Died - 10 Oct 1943 - Ogden, Weber County, Utah,
Father s name - Jeremiah Willey -- Mother's name - Nancy Call

Southern States -- 9 April 1883 – 6 July 1885 -- Age Called: 23
 Southern States
Set Apart: 9 April 1883   -   Released Date: 13 July 1885
       Arrived At Home: 13 July 1885
Mission type: Proselytizing
Marital Status: Single
Served with companion: Henry Miller, John M Easton, Angus McKay, John James Humpherys,
Richard Miles Humphrey and Wiley Gidoni Cragun
Priesthood office: Elder   -   Priesthood: Elder
Called From: E Bountiful, Davis, Utah, United States   -   Set apart by: Jacob Gates

First Presidency missionary calls and recommendations 1877-1918, CR 1 168, Church History Library.
On March 14, 1883, Joseph Willey accepts his mission call.
First Presidency missionary calls and recommendations 1877-1918, CR 1 168, Church History Library.
March 14, 1883, bishop's endorsement
Missionary Department missionary registers, 1860-1959, Vol. 1, p. 64, line 2765.
Missionary Department missionary registers, 1860-1959, Vol. 2, p. 70, line 2765.

Southern States Mission history, 1832-1964: LR 8557 2, Church History Library.

    Mission index

Southern States Mission history, 1832-1964: LR 8557 2, Church History Library.

    April 11, 1883 departure for mission

Southern States Mission history, 1832-1964: LR 8557 2, Church History Library.

    May 10, 1884 summary of service in North Carolina and among the Catawba Indians

Southern States Mission history, 1832-1964: LR 8557 2, Church History Library.

    July 6, 1885 release

Southern States Mission history, 1832-1964: LR 8557 2, Church History Library.

    July 31, 1885 review of service

Missionary journals: journal or diary's of two LDS missionaries to the Catawba Indians (Joseph Willey and Catawba Pinkney Head) transcribed and footnoted by Judy Canty Martin: M256.08 M6785 1995, Church History Library.

Joseph Willey was born 17 May 1859 in Bountiful, Utah. He married Amy Maud Thurgood and died 10 Oct 1943 in Ogden, Utah, buried in the Kaysville Cemetery.

Elder Willey kept a wonderful and detailed journal. I have a copy in my possession, it is well over 100 pages. With this journal, I have been able to do genealogy for the Catawba Indians. Without this journal, I could not have completed any of the books I have authored about them. He is responsible for baptizing my daddy's family, great grandpa James Patterson, who is the "first Catawba Lamanite" mentioned in the summary, He blessed many of his children, one of whom Emma died young, as well as baptizing my great grandmother Elizabeth Patterson and my grandfather John Alonzo Canty and his twin sister Fannie. This was the first time I ever found Fannie listed in any records. The list is too long to use here.

"On the 18th they received the following notice, from an undisclosed friend "we the undersigned citizens of the state and county aforesaid have been informed that you Mormon elders are preaching and practicing your polygamist ways in the Catawba nation, York County South Carolina and we respectfully request that you leave the state and county aforesaid and, on your refusal, to comply with this request we will not be responsible for the consequences of your actions." There were about 70 names attached to it, the ones who brought it were Maj. Boarch, Mr. Crook, Take Crook,, Robert Cromwell, Frank Collins, John Allen and Pierce Giles. (Boarch, Collins and Allen all had children with Catawba women.)

Again, they received another notice.

On August 23, 1884 "Notice, Messrs Willey, Humphreys, Humphrey, We the peaceable citizens of this surround country have been pained to learn that you three men profession to be Mormon missionaries have taken up your quarters with an ignorant class of our people and are denonating doctrines among them calculated to disorganize human society and adverse to the peace and wellbeing of our people and country, to the laws and dignity of the State. Now therefore these presents are to civilly and peaceable request and command you to vacate the State and to return no more among us and you are hereby allowed five days to obey this order to peaceable absent yourselves from the State without hurt or molestation, but if you are found within the limits of the State, after the expiration of that time you may charge consequences to disobedience to this order. We are going to be rid of you."

Capt. of the mob, Wm Kithcart, Wm Carethers, Charles Harrison, Paul Harrison, Alexander Millens, Clarence Cotter. The names of the rest of the mob we did not get."

These threats and the violence did not hamper the conversion of the people, especially the Catawba Indians. In fact, after one of the petitions was delivered, they baptized John Gandy, who was a Catawba.

"This completes my labors as a missionary: signed Joseph Wiley. Items of interest on my mission: August 1883, visited the Cherokee Indians. September 26, 1883, I stood over elder C.E. Robison when he breathed his last breath. September 28, we put his corpse on the train home, got bit by a dog had one meeting broken up by two Baptist ministers. Had one gun pointed at me. Laid out 15 nights. Went 30 hours without food. Walked 3,600 miles. Held 113 meetings. Organized one Sunday school, ordained one priest. (John Alonzo Canty) Baptized 34 and assisted in baptizing 59. Baptize the first Catawba Lamanite that ever give obedience to the gospel in this dispensation.[61]

Baptized one preacher (Richie Hartness) blessed 10 children. Received two notices to leave the state. Traveled with seven elders as traveling companions. February 28, 1885 I was appointed President of the South Carolina conference. Traveled in 16 counties and North Carolina: York, Chester, Fairfield, Richland, Kershaw, Lancaster, Spartanburg South Carolina in North Carolina Greenville, Henderson, Transylvania, Jackson, Swaim, Union, Polk, Cleveland."

---

[61] James Goodwin Patterson.

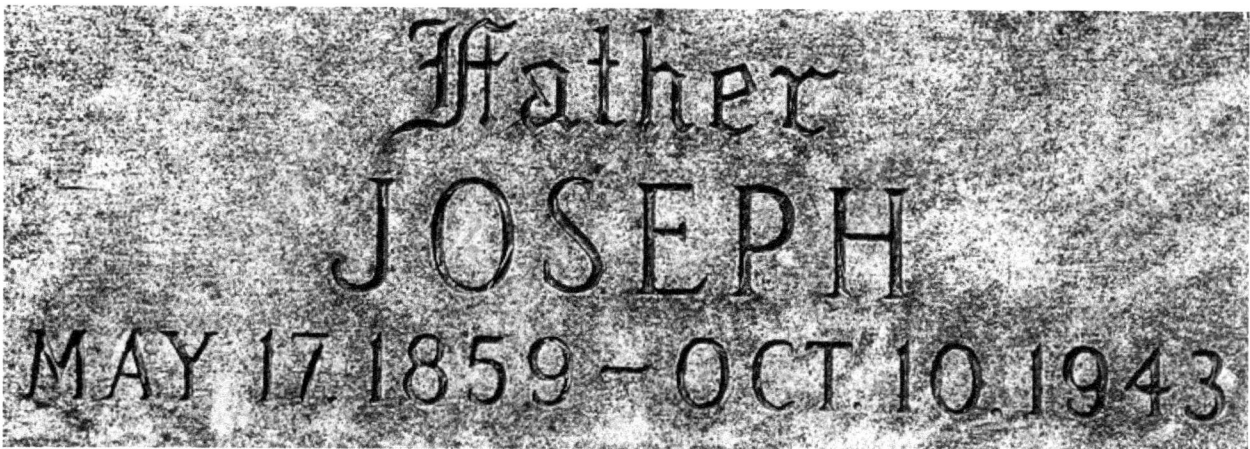

PHOTO 13 -- HEADSTONE OF JOSEPH WILLEY   1859-1943

East Bountiful   March the 14 1883

Brother John Taylor
Dear sir I received your letter
and in as much as I have been
called to preach the Gospel
I am ready to go and do the
best I can from your brother
in the Gospel
              Joseph Willey

PHOTO 14 -- JOSEPH WILLEY'S LETTER ACCEPTING HIS MISSIONARY CALLING (MARCH 1883)

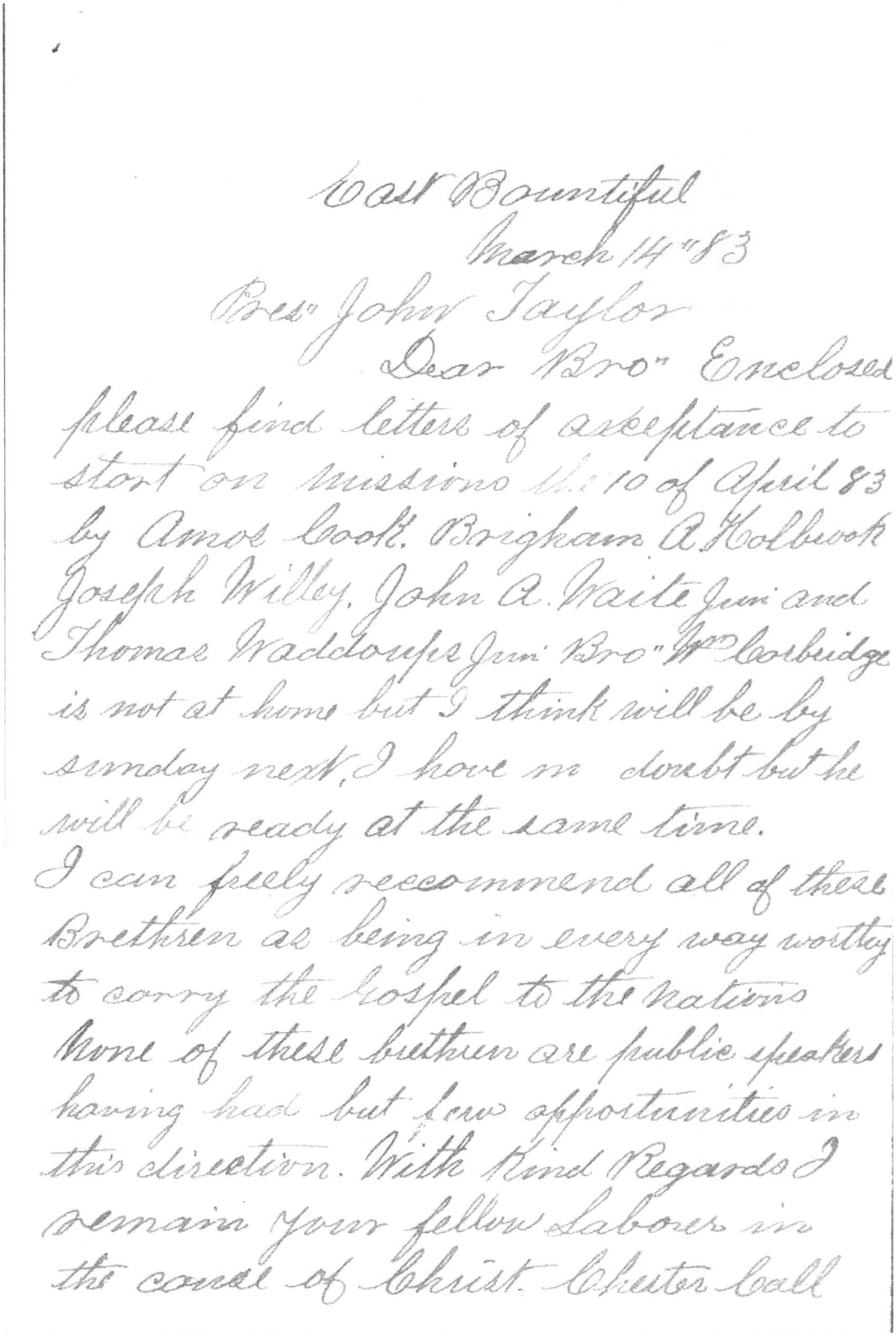

East Bountiful
March 14" 83

Pres. John Taylor
          Dear Bro. Enclosed
please find letters of aceptance to
start on missions the 10 of April 83
by Amos Cook. Brigham A. Holbrook
Joseph Willey. John A. Waite Jun. and
Thomas Waddoups Jun. Bro. Wm Corbridge
is not at home but I think will be by
sunday next, I have no doubt but he
will be ready at the same time.
I can freely reccommend all of these
Brethren as being in every way worthy
to carry the Gospel to the nations
None of these brethren are public speakers
having had but low opportunities in
this direction. With Kind Regards I
remain your fellow Laborer in
the canal of Christ. Chester Call

PHOTO 15   LETTER TO PRES. JOHN TAYLOR ABOUT JOSEPH WILLEY (MARCHJ 1883)

JOSEPH WILLEY'S MISSIONARY JOURNAL

March 1883, I was called to go to the Southern Sates to preach the gospel 15th March 1883 by President John Taylor. I went through the Indowment (Endowment) house the 29 of March 1883. I was set apart in April to go on my mission. I started on my mission on April the 10th 1883. Held a meeting on the cars that night I stand gard (guard) that night on the cars. Met B. H. Roberts at Salida (Colorado) 1 Opm Color.[62] changed cars to Kansas City. Arrived at Chattanooga April 16, 8 PM. Left Chattanooga in the AM for Whittaker, South Car.[63] Arrived at Whittaker 1pm. Staid in the station that night. Got up at 7, walked 7 miles and found the Elders at Brother Gordon. We was treated very kindly. The next day 14 miles south to the Elders apt. (appointment) Walked 10 miles April 22, held our first meeting at Brother Gordons house about one day we was there

23rd went a fishing and walked 8 miles to Brother David Wells.

25th walked 20 miles.

27th walked 5 miles.

28th walked? -miles.

29th rested.

30th walked 17 miles. 31st walked 7 miles to -_____ Smiths. There was a few came in to us.[64] They told us to much we was hungry but to call for they wished to hear us and to hold meeting in the house. (this is so faint, it is a guess on most of the sentence.) Thare I got a letter from my mother. The first letter I received after I had left my home.

May 1883:

May 2rd 1883 walked 5 miles to Mr. Rippys. Was treated very kindly & walked to brother Hampton Robinsons who had his house burned by Miss (a woman's name?) while the saints was in meeting. I gave them--- .

3rd walked 8 miles to brother ---.

4th walked 4 miles to Mr.----

5th walked 7 miles to Brother Gordons. May 6th held meeting at Brother Gordons. May 6th walked 8 miles to R. Willeys house. His wife was a blind woman. She was educated to a blind school. She has a Bible with raised letters and she understands the Bible well.

10th walked 5 miles.

---

[62] Willey's Abbreviation of Colorado.
[63] Willeys abbreviation for Carolina
[64] I am unsure of what this says the writing is so faded This is the best I can do

11th walked Smiles.

May 12, I Baptized Sylvana B Gordon the first person I ever baptized. Elder McKay confirmed SB Gordon.

13th walked 14 miles.

May the 10th started with Br. John W. Easton to open a new field of labor. Walked 11 miles.

May 5th Br Easton baptized one Mrs. Jane Idet. I confirmed her after baptism. We held meeting in the Grove. I spoke for my first time outdoors I stud (stood) up about 3 minutes. We had very (good?) time. We walked 11 miles.

May 22nd walked 8 miles.

23rd walked 15 miles.

24th walked miles held meeting. Thar was about one hundred there.

June 3rd held meeting In Spartanburg, Co South Car. Thar was a full house.

The 6th, walked 7 miles June to hold meeting, full house. Some were there drunk with liquor. They were very noisy and very insulting.

11th walked 6 miles.

12th walked 3 miles;

16th walked 5 miles.

17th walked 7 miles held meeting about 10 there very good on ----. The first question that was asked me was how I new (knew) that Joseph Smith was a prophet of God. They wished me to explain to them how I new it. I told them the Spirit of God bore witness with my spirit and told me so.

June 19 walked 6 miles

21st walked 9 miles staid to one Mr. Craferds.[65] We was treated very kindly. The 22nd went to one Mr. Paynes. He sent his son to git (get) a man to come and play on the banjo. He made music for us till 11 o'clock at night. 23rd went to see Mr. Corns. He said he did not believe in our doctrines but said we was welcome to come and we should fair as he fared

June the 24 we held meeting. We had more to our meeting than the house would hold and very good order. Staid to Mr. Russells that night. 25th started to one Mr. Childers. He took my address and said he wished to keep up correspondence with me when I went home. 26th staid to 28th with one Mr. Latters who was a member of the Dunkers Church. He said we had tore him up so he could not sleep.

June 20th. Started for our conference the distance of 10 miles. Walked 10 miles and staid at one Mr. Burnetts who lived in Pope Co., NC. He had laid in bed for 22 years with a bad back. He treated

---

[65] Crawford.

us very kindly and wished us to come again.

The 29th walked 17 miles. Ask to stay at night at 3 different houses but was refused. About 7 we got to stay to one Mr. Thompsons he charged us 18 cents for night.

30th walked 8 miles to one Mr. Goens who treated us very kindly. His wife said she was ready from baptism but she would wait and see if her husband was willing.

July the 1St walked Smiles to Bro. Robersons, Haveland Co. There we met Elders McKay and Davidson, then we went up to Bro. Gordons where we met the saints The next day we went to the station met Pres. B. H. Roberts. He was well. We went and staid to one Mr. Rippeys. The next day we went back to attend conference. There we met all the Elders in South Car.

We held conference the13, 14 and 15 of July. We had a very good time. The saints spread the table each day under the harbor[66] with plenty of good food. We held Preasthood (Priesthood) meeting in the woods ever morning. There we got some very good counsel from Pres. B. H. Roberts. The first day the Elders was called on to give a report of there (their) labors then Pres. B. H. Roberts spoke on the literal gathering (gathering) of Israel. He spoke each day the conference went of very smoothly.

After conference we was sent to our various fields of labors. Elders Angus McKay & myself was sent to Spartanburg Co, SC when we got back the people treated us very cool. They had got the history of the Mountain Meadow massacre which made them very much opposed to us as a people. We held two meetings there. Thar was only one family interested so we left him a Voice of Warning and left the place

We did not know where we was going but we was determined to effect a opening if possible. We traveled through Poke Co. We never held meetings in the country but talked to a good deal by the fireside. Then we travel to a Henderson meeting. Nothing of important transpired in that county. We past on through Transylvania & Jackson County in to Swain Co. Thar we come to what is name as the Cherokee Nation of Indians called the Cherokee Indians. We went and inquired for the chief & found him and we told him we was Latter Day Saints, name in the world as Mormons. He said thar was some of our people there. We was much surprised to hear that thar was Mormons there. He referred us to one Mr. Parsis. We went to see him and told him we was Mormon Elders. He said they called him a Mormon but he said we was the first Mormons he ever saw. We found out that he was a free--- or a Freemason. We went back and told the Chief we did not claim any of such doctrine. I told him we would like to have a interview with him. We told him we had a history of their

---

[66] Elder Willey must mean an arbor.

forefathers called the Book of Mormon. I left it with him.

He apportioned a time for us to come and see him and we left him and tried to get a stopping place for a few weeks. We tried several places but failed. We went out in the woods and asked God to open the way for us. We traveled about 4 miles and found a stopping place. We went back in a few days and had a talk with the chief. He said was much interested in the Book of Mormon and he said he would like to hear us preach, thar was a counsil among them and some officials thar from Washington and he was so busy he could not attend. But he apportioned a meeting among the Indians for us but the whites told them we was false prophets and thar (there) was not many out to our meeting, not many Indians.

The next Sunday thar was a large revival or Protracted[67] meeting nigroes & whites. We went and the preacher took for his text beware of false Prophets. He told the people that false prophets was among them right then. He give us a tongue-lashing. We prayed in our hearts that he mint (might) be confounded and he was for two men a few rows began to fight. The people all left the preacher standing alone. Then two women commenced to fight and the meeting was broke up. Thar (there) we see the hand of God manifested in our behalf.

We went to see the chief again; the chief's name I forgot to mention his name is Nymrod Jorret Smith.[68] He told us to come the following Sunday and he would have all the Indians preachers thar which was very incurging to us. So when Sunday came we went expecting to meet them. But when we got thar the Chief was sick a bed it seamed as if the Devil was to work hedging up our way so we returned back to our boarding place. With (out) any meetings we went to in a few days and told the chief we was going to leave he said he wanted us to leave the Book of Mormon with him. The Voice of Warning he said he would read them and ask God to inlighten his mind that he mint no wether they was true or not. He said he was going to Washington soon and he wished a letter of interduction to our delagate John T. Cane. He said he wished to corespond with us. Our expenses was so tight we was oblige to return to headquarters, so the following Tuesday we started. We averaged 20 miles a day. One night was obliged to travel all night. We arrived to headquarters in good health. To our surprise, we found our President J. M. Easton had received his release to return home on the following Tuesday. and heard that one of the Elders, Bro. Robison was sick. The President appointed me to go with a new elder who had just come out to go see Bro. Robison and fetch him to headquarters (where)

---

[67] In the missionary diary of Nathaniel Alvin Decker, I found the same name. Evidently, this was a denomination in the South, because his mission was to Florida and Georgia, around 1899.

[68] Nimrod Jerrett Smith, one of two of the most outstanding chiefs in the Eastern Cherokee Nation, source, Milling, Chapman, Red Carolinians, Chapel Hill, University of N.C. Press, 1940 page 372.

the saints could take care of him. Elder Easton, Elder /?? and myself started Friday the 21st Got to Mr. Watses[69] 8 AM. We walked 35 miles. We found Brother Robison very sick. He was very glad to see us. We anointed him with oil and administered to him. Pres Easton and myself set up with him till twelve o'clock. He was in much pain-slept one hour. The next day we took him to Rock Hill to Br Smiths. Got a light wagon and took him to the depot at three fifteen we took the train. It created quite an excitement at the station Elder Miller and myself got off at Fort Mills 8 miles from Rock Hill. Staid to Sister Bunches.[70]

The next morning started to headquarters walked 2 miles found Br. Robison very low. He was in great pain all day. He said he wanted to go home. He asked us if would get a team and wagon and take him to the depot. Elder Easton went to the station and telegraphed to President B. H. Roberts to know what t doe about taking him home. He waited but could not get any answer to his dispatch.

he was in great pain all-day and gradually sinking. He had the hickups and was still pleading for us to take him home. Brother Miller and Mckay set up with him the first part of the night. We anointed and administered to him and prayed for him by day and by night but his time had come. At twelve o'clock Brother Davidson and myself got up. He had took a change for the worse to all appearance. They pain had left him, he was dieing. Bro. Davidson went over to Bro. Moses Gordons to wake up the elders. He died at ten minutes to two on the 26th. He died without a struggle.

Elder Easton sent a telegram to Pres. B. H. Roberts of his death, also for a coffin and burial clothing. His coffin came on the three am train. We took him to the depot on 28 September.

We had quite a lift to get him on the cars. Thar (there) was a good many to the depot but they would not help us life him on the cars.[71] He started fifteen minutes to five PM.

I started to travel with Bro. Henry Miller. We went to Buffalow, staid to Mr. Rippeys, was treated very kindly. Visited among the Saints one week. One of the preachers of the Baptist Church said it was more honorable to be called a murderer than to be called a Mormon. He said he felt sorry for them that had joined the Mormon Church.

I was appointed to labor with Elder Henry Miller and to fill the place of Bro. Robison. Elder Miller and I started for the Indian Nation. We walked 29 miles that day. Staid to Sister Bunches. The next day we went over to Mr. Wats.[72] This was where Bro. Robison staid while he was sick. They received us very kindly. They wished us to hold meeting in their house that night. The neighbors all come in

---

[69] The home of Evan and Lucy Quash-Marsh Watts.
[70] Delphi Quash-Mush-Marsh Bunch, daughter of John and Betsy Scott-Quash Mush, wife of Howard Bunch.
[71] Native Americans have an aversion to dead bodies
[72] Evans and Lucy Marsh Watts

and we had a good meeting. Thare was 25 persons to meeting, all Indians. Next day Bro. James Smith sent for us. He had his lips poisoned. He had four doctors, they said they could do nothing for him. We anointed and administered to him. The next day he was well and to work.

Next day we come back to Mr. Pattersons.1° (there) was a good many of the Indians come in that night and we had a good time. They helped us to sing a good many Hymns. We appointed a meeting for the following Sunday. We held meeting in an empty house. The house was packed to the utmost capacity and the Spirit of God was in our midst. I think we made an impression on the Indians. They said they wished to meet that night and learn more of our Hymns. We sang till ten o'clock at night.

The next day (there) was two wagonloads of Indians went to Rock Hill. I went with them to Rock Hill to Bro. Smiths. (there) we had a long talk with his brothers. We explained the principles of marriage to him. He said he liked the plan of being married for time and all eternity. We sang a few hymns and went to bed. Next day his brother quit his work and talked with us all day. He said he was convinced we had the truth and said he expected to be baptized. Also Bro. Smith's wife applied for baptism. She appointed the time and place. She said she would be ready October 28th, then we went to Mr. Pattersons, helped him pick cotton on half day.

Went to go get our mail. We had five miles to go for mail and had the Catawba river to cross. Went down to the Nation. Two-wagon load of Indians went down with us. Held meetings, (there) was about fifty Indians out to hear us speak. They wished us to come back the next Sunday. We appointed a meeting two weeks from then in the same house. Went back to Mr. Pattersons staid the night.

Next day went down to Bro. Smiths set up till eleven o'clock. I will not give the particulars as we was visiting among the Indians. We went over the river every week for our mail. It cost us 20 cents a trip boat fair.

Sunday October 28, 1883. Baptized Hannah Smith. Elder Miller baptized her, I confirmed her in meeting. We had a large congregation and a good meeting. (there) was two ministers (there). They had a good many questions to ask us after meeting. They said we had to much scripture for them to attempt to oppose us. After meeting we went up to Mr. Wats and sang hymns till nine o'clock. After singing. they said they wished us to hold prayers. We done so after prayers, one of the leading Indians. Bro. Patterson [73] applied for baptism. He said he wished to be baptized on the 11th of November. The Indians called us their preachers and the white people called us the Indian preachers.

---

[73] James Goodwin Patterson.

October 30, 1883 went down to Rock Hill and got a little of oil and anointed and administered to Mrs. Smith. She had a swelling on her neck. It had been growing for 16 years.

We went to the post office. (there) was three ministers (there) that had met (there) to have a talk with us- they did not know how to broch (broach) the subject. One of them steps up to us and said you are the followers of Jo Smith. You follow Jo Smith. We follow Jesus Christ and the Bible. The people came rushing from all sides to hear the argument. They wanted to see if we could prove that Joseph Smith was a prophet. We told them we could and give them a track (tract) called <u>The Modern Prophet.</u> They said they was not prepared to talk on scripture. They said they would be to our meeting the following Sunday. They told us we could prepare for an argument. We told them we would be pleased to meet them with the Bible. They throwed out a good many insults and slurs at us. When Sunday came (there) was none of them come out to talk with us.

Bro. Miller got a letter from Bro. Robisons wife. She felt very sorry that she could not be with her husband in his last moments. We also got a letter from Bro. McKay. He stated he was released to go to Scotland and said he would be over to see us before he went. He also said (there) was two more Elders come from Utah, their names was Wiley Cragan (and) Bro. Bingham.

We then went down to the Nation. While we was eating breakfast Pres. McKay came. I felt like he had lifted a burden from my shoulders as I did not know what subject I could speak from. Nov. 4th, 1883, after meeting they said they wished us to give it out that we would hold meeting to the Nation that night. There was some of them walked ten miles to meeting in the Nation. Had a good meeting. After the meeting, five of them applied for baptism. They said they would baptized the next Sunday. Mr. Wats was sick a bed. He wished us to administer to him. We did and the next day he was able to go to work. He said it was a great testamony to him and he demanded baptism. Then we went to Mr. Pattersons, staid all day. That night the neighbors come in and we had a good time singing hymns. Mr. Patterson wished us to hold meeting at his house the next night. We did so. The next day Pres. McKay went back to headquarters. We went to Yorkville and took our pictures ---- ----We tried some three places to stay all night but was refused. The fourth place they took us in. The man of the house was reading a Book, the title of the book was Life Among the Mormons and the life of Joseph Smith. They said they give five dollars for the book. It was the worst book I ever read. It said Joseph Smith was a murderer and after supper, the battle began. It got hot and hotter. They said every word in the book was true. We told them Joseph Smith was the best man that ever lived excepting Jesus Christ. We was the first Mormons they ever had seen. We said the first principles before them. They was surprised to hear that the so-called Mormons had so much scripture for to back them. Next morning we bore our testimony to them and paid our fair, which was 1.00 and went to Mr. Pattersons. Thare we married five couples, which had been living together but was not married. One couple had lived 30 years. We married them. We had considerable spirit. We eat corn bread and buttermilk for the wedding supper.

Sunday Nov_ I baptized five Indians. After meeting, we confirmed them. Thare was about fifty to the baptism. After meeting, we sang a few hymns. The next day my companion Elder Miller was appointed President over the branch, as he was the oldest Elder in the field. It was very cold and stormy We went over the river and got our mail. Went to Bro. Pattersons, staid two days and nights with him. His wife[74] applied for baptism. We forwarded to the Desert News for books to organize a Sunday School among the Indians.

Sunday Nov 15, 1883 held meeting to the Indian Nation. There was a good many come out to meeting had a chill in meeting. It was the first chill I ever had. My companion had the chills also. He had lost his appetite.

Nov 20, we walked 12 miles. It rained on us all day. The next day my companion was quite sick. I anointed and administered to him. He got better. I ate a harty dinner.

Nov 21, one of Mr. ----daughters died. She had opposed us and was very angry because her father took us in. She left home and died away from home. Her parents took it very hard, I felt very bad.

Nov 22, 1883 Elder Miller was quite weak. We went that night to Bro. --- and had a good time. (there) was 15 or 20 there. We sang hymns; I talked on the principles of the gospel. 23rd we went over the river to Fort Mill and got our mail. We was very late when we got back to Bro. Pattersons.

On the 24th had a long talk with Mr. Barker on the principles of the Gospel.

The 25th it was very stormy, so stormy that the people could not come out to meeting, so we had no meeting. This was the first Sunday we had missed since we had been among the Lamanites.

On the 26th we went over to Mr. E. Wats, found the folks all well to Br. Wats.

Nov. 27 1883. I anointed with oil and administered to Elder Miller also anointed and administered to Sister Lucy Wats.[75] They was both well the next morning.

Went down to William Wats, staid all day. Then went back to Mr. E. Wats and staid that night and the next night. We went to Brother J. Pattersons. I read the <u>Voice of Warning</u> all day. Next day Elder

---

[74] Elizabeth Missouri White, daughter of George and Margareth-Peggy Quash-Marsh White.
[75] Lucy Quash-Marsh, daughter of John and Betsy Scott-Quash Mush-Marsh, wife of Evan or Evans Watt.

Miller and myself received a letter from Bro. Johnson, state of Georgia. He stated the Saints was all well in Georgia and everything quiet. We read the letter to the folks. Elder Miller set up till eleven o'clock and talked with Bro. Patterson and Brother Taylor George and Mr. P Hanis[76] on the Book of Mormon.

Sunday December 2, 1883, I baptized four persons, Evans Wats, Wm. Wats, Nancy Wats & Betsy Patterson.[77] After baptism, we confirmed them in meeting. We had a very good meeting and kept very good order. Visited around among them talking and explained the Gospel to them next day and every night by the fireside. My companion Elder Miller was having chills every third day and every night. He had it gone to bed when his chills come on him.

Sunday, we held meeting at Bro. Evans Wats. There was not many out on account of the weather being so cold. We held a very good meeting.

December 13, 1883, we went to rock Hill. Elder Miller took the cars for Whittaker or Kings Mountain and left me to labor alone until another Elder come.

Dec 16, 1883 held meeting to the Indian Nation alone. There was a good turn out if I ever felt the Spirit of God; I felt it there while speaking. I spoke three quarters of an hour. This was the first meeting I ever held alone, you can imagine my feeling. I walked back to Bro. Wats visited around among the Saints read the Book of Mormon.

Dec. 21, 1883 President Miller sent me a companion; his name was H. Humphreys.

He arrived here on the 21st. The next day we went over to Sister Bunches, staid that night. The next day we started back. We had a letter to mail so we went through Fort Mill. It being the day before Christmas we found many under the influence of liquor. When the drinking men seen us they began to cry out, there was eight or ten followed us through the town cursing and swaring at us and making many threats. We expected every minnitm (minuet) they would take holt of us but we escapt unhurt.

Christmas Dec 25, 1883 We was to brother Pattersons. Thar was twenty-five Indians thare. Thar was twelve of them going a shooting. They wished me to go with them. 1 did so. We had a good time altho it was quite stormy all day. This was the first Christmas I ever spent away from home. We was reading and talking with the people every night through hollowday (holiday) and we was not well. We had a very bad cold. We held meeting. Dec. 30 (there) was quite a number out. One white man by the name of Barker. I explained the coming forth of the Book of Mormon. He said it was plain to him.

January 1884. We spent New Year's Bro. Pattersons. We had a very good time. We set up until ten

---

[76] Benjamin Perry Harris, son of James and Sarah Jane Ayers Harris.
[77] Evans Wats, husband of Lucy Quash-Marsh Watts, William David Watts, their son, Nancy Christine Wats Patterson Watts, wife of William David and Betsy-Elizabeth White Patterson.

o'clock at night, talked on the principles of the Gospel. January the 5th we started to the Nation to fill an appointment. It snowed all day on us. This was the first snow I had seen in the south. It was very cold and windy. It snowed five Inches. Thar was some people making good use of the snow, slay riding. We got fast and traveled about twenty miles that day through the snow. Sunday.

Jan. 6th 1884. Held meeting at Mr. William Georges.[78] The weather was so cold there was only about twelve out to our meeting. They kept good order and we had a good time together. We staid there three days reading the book of Mormon and explained to them. Also we read several sermons from the Deseret News. The weather is very cold. One of the Indians told us the river was froze over so we walked to Bro. Watses, a distance of 9 miles. While thar we received a letter from Elder Miller stating he was quite sick.

Sunday January 13, 1884 we held meeting at Bro. Evan Watses. Sunday February 17, 1964, We held a testamony meeting at brother Nelson Gordons. Many of the Saints bore thear testamony. We had a good meeting and a good spirit prevailed.

February 20, Two of the Lamanites came with a carriage to Kings Mountain to take us back as they were very anxious for us to organize a Sunday School. We arrived back to our old field of labor among the Lamanites to Brother Pattersons at 5pm. They were all well. Some 20 of them came to Brother Pattersons, we had a singing, and we were pleased to meet again. They said it seemed like we had been gone 2 months.

Sunday February 24, 1884 Sunday School was held at bro. Evans Wats. This was the first Sunday school the Lamanites had ever attended. They seemed to take a lively interest. After Sunday School a young man by the name of John Lonzo Canty[79] was baptized. After baptism, we held meeting. Thar was a good turn out and all seamed to be interested. We appointed a meeting to the Nation for the next Sunday.

Feb 26, one of the Lamanites Jane Wats[80] was very sick with a cramp in her stomache. She wished me to administer to her which I did and she got well immediately which was a great testamony to her and to me.

February 29th, 1884. My companion led two young women down in the waters of baptism; viz.

---

[78] William (Billy) George, son of Nelson and Sarah Ayers George, married 1St. to Betsy Mush, 2nd to Margaret McLonah or McClure.

[79] John Alonzo Canty-Whitesides, son of Thomas Whitesides and Eliza Scott Canty.

[80] Older sister of John Alonzo and Fannie, daughter of Thomas Whitesides and Eliza Scott Canty, wife of James Harvey Watts.

(namely) Marthy and Heneretta Patterson[81] confirmed them at Bro. Evans Wats and we blessed two of brother Pattersons children, Eldora and Emma Patterson. I being the mouth on Emma. This was the first child I ever blessed.

March 1, Walked ten miles to the Indian Nation then held meeting at Mr. Georges. Thar was not many out but a good spirit prevailed. March 3, walked ten miles to Bro. James Wats.[82] It was a very cold day, windy cold and then we had a good nights rest.

March 6, 1884 I baptized two Lamanites, Margaret Jane George[83] and Miss Alice Ayers.[84] 7th, My companion J. J. Humphreys baptized Jefferson Davis Ayers.[85]

Sunday, 9th, held Sunday School at Bro. Wats. Thar we blessed two (more) of Bro. Pattersons children, namely Abby & Maude Mary Patterson, I being mouth on Abby. After Sunday school I had the privilege of baptizing five, we confirmed them in meeting. We had a good meeting and a good spirit prevailed. We visited around among the Saints reading the paper and teaching them the first principles of the Gospel.

March 15, 1884 We walked to the Indian Nation a distant of ten miles to fill an appointment. Staid all night to one Mr. Georges.

Sunday March 18, Held meeting at Mr. Georges. Thar was a good many out to our meeting. We had a splendid meeting. After meeting, Mr. George, Pinkney Head and Robert Harris[86] were baptized and confirmed. There was a woman by the name of Whiteside[87] said she understood her Bible and she wished to have a talk with me. They gathered around to hear the argument. I find her so close she became excited and unreasonable and her relatives took her away. They were disgusted with her.

March 1884. We blessed one of Bro. Georges children namely John N. P. George.[88] We were invited to call on several of the Lamanites and had a good time. All seemed to be much interested. 8th, walked 10 miles to Bro. Watses, found the Saints all feeling well. Nuthing of any importance transpired until the following Sunday,

March 23. We had a good Sunday school. After Sunday school I baptized five namely Peter Harris,

---

[81] Martha Jane and Georgia Henrietta Patterson, daughters of James and Elizabeth Patterson.

[82] James Harvey Watts, son of Evan and Lucy Quash-Marsh Watts, husband of Mary Jane Whitesides Watts.

[83] Margaret McClure daughter of Robert McClure and Lucy Marsh.

[84] Margaret-Peggy Jane McClure or McLonah, daughter of Frank and Lucy Quash Marsh, and Alice, daughter of Jefferson and Emily Cobb Ayers.

[85] Alice and Jefferson are children of Jefferson and Emily Cobb Ayers.

[86] William-Billy George, husband of Margaret Jane-Peggy Jane Wats George, Pinkney Head, son of Robert Henry and Sarah Ann Evans-Canty Head and Robert Lee Harris, son of James and Sarah Jane Ayers Harris.

[87] Fannie, twin sister of John Alonzo Canty, daughter of Thomas Whitesides and Eliza Scott Canty, wife of James Harris jr.

[88] John Nelson Pierce George.

Margaret Harris, Nancy George, Minna George, and Ellen Bunch.[89] We confirmed them in meeting. We had a splendid meeting and all were well paid for coming.

March 30, 1884. Walked to the Indian Nation found the folks all well. 31st, we held meeting at Bro. Georges. There was not many out to our meeting on account of false reports which was circulated about us, although those who were out listened attentively. After meeting, we had several invitations to dinner. We staid there till Tuesday as my companion was not well. The next day we went back to Bro. Watses. We visited around among the Saints teaching them by the fireside. On Thursday night we met together with some 25 and had a good time togeather singing hymns and talking with the people on the first principles of the Gospel.

Sunday April 8, 1884 walked 28 miles to Kings Mountain, found the folks all well. Next day went to Whittaker to Bro. Weavers. His neighbors had made many threats. We were insulted on the streets many times but was not harmed. Sunday April 13 1884 held testamony meeting at Nelson Gordons. Many of the Saints bore a faithful testamony a good spirit prevailed.

Thursday April 17th met Elder R. M. Humphrey at Whittaker. He was direct from Utah. Staid to Bro. Weavers that night. Next day walked back to Kings Mountain. Sunday 20th, held meeting at Bro. Nelson Gordons thar was some 35 persons present. Several of them had never heard Later Day Saint speak before. All seemed to be much interested and wished to investigate. All said they were well paid for coming to meeting.

April 26, 1884 walked eleven miles to Bro. Prear Aydelotte. Sunday April 27th held meeting at Bro. Aydelottes. Some twelve being present. After I blest Bro. Aydelottes child named Mary Susan. 28th walked 14 miles, staid to Bro. John Gordons.

Elder R. M. Humphrey was appointed as my traveling companion. Next day we walked 30 miles to Bro. James Pattersons. We found the Saints all enjoying good health. They were pleased to see us as they were anxious for to hear preaching, as we had just been gone three weeks.

May 1 held a short meeting at Bro. James Pattersons, a good spirit prevailed.

Saturday, May 3, 1884 walked ten miles, staid all night with Bro. Georges. Sunday held meeting to Bro.Wm. Georges some 15 being present. Held meeting one hour and a half. All seemed to enjoy the meeting. After meeting, we met a learned Doctor by the name of Maul. I talked with him one hour. He denyed his own Bible and talked very unreasonable. Next day we walked ten miles ate strawberry pie and stayed all night with Bro. James Wats. Visited around among the Saints, preaching by the fireside.

---

[89] Peter, son of David and Little Nancy George Harris, husband of Margaret Harris. She was the daughter of Jim and Nancy Quash-Marsh Sanders; Minna is Minnie George, daughter of Taylor and Emily Cobb Ayers George; Ellen Bunch is either Delphi Quash-Marsh Bunch, or a previously unidentified child of Delphi and Howard Bunch.

Read to the Saints the sermons in the Deseret News and writing letters.

Sunday May 11, 1884 held Sunday School at Bro. Evans Wats. After Sunday School, I baptized Emily George, who had been investigating the word one-year.[90] After baptism, we held meeting at the same place. The house was well filled and we had a rich portion of the good spirit in our speaking. After meeting the Saints brought the bands in the door yard and sang hymns and had an enjoyable time together. Saturday

May 17th was my birthday and walked ten miles to the Indian Nation, took dinner with Mr. Tims.[91] After dinner took a boat ride on the Catawba River had fish and honey for my birthday supper.

Sunday May 18, 1884 held meeting at Bro. Wm. Georges. The house was filled to the utmost capacity. Good attention was given and a good spirit prevailed. We spoke on the signs that was to follow the true believers.

March 16, 17,18, 19, after meeting one sister Mary Jane Wats[92] who had come ten miles to meeting took very sick. We administered to her according to her request. She grew weaker and weaker. We set up with her that night. She grew even weaker the next night; some thirty Lamanites set up with her. We prayed for her, day and night. Thar was something wrong inwardly. Her bro. and sister[93] who was not of our faith sent for three doctors who was very bitterly opposed to us and our teachings. Two of the doctors gave her up and said thar was no hope of her recovery and said, "Them Mormon Elders says they can heal the sick" and said she would he a corpse in twenty-four hours. We administered to her and started 10 miles to get some clean clothes. We had not been there long when they sent us word she was still no better. We started back at 5pm and walked until midnight to get back, taking a small Indian boy 14 years old to pilot the way. When we arrived, we found her on the mend. The house was filled with her friends and relatives. We again administered to her and in two days she was around the house

May 25th held meeting at Bro. Wm. Georges. A good spirit prevailed. On the 26th walked 12 miles to Bro. James Pattersons. The 28th Pres J. J. Humphreys arrived. He had come down to visit us in organizing a Branch of the Church.

June 1, 1884 held meeting at or near Bro. William Watses[94] in a house had had fixed for that purpose. Elders Humphreys, myself and M. Humphrey being present we appointed another meeting at the 4th, at the same place and requested all the Saints to be present as we was going to organize a Branch of

---

[90] Emily Cobb Ayers George, daughter of John D. Cobb and Lucy Quash-Marsh, wife of Taylor George.
[91] John Alexander-Alec Tims, son of John Alexander Tims and Rachel Quash-Marsh.
[92] Mary Jane Whitesides Watts
[93] Fannie Whitesides Harris and George Washington Canty.
[94] William David Watts, son of Evan and Lucy Quash-Marsh Watts.

the Church. We organized a Branch of the Church of Jesus Christ of Later Day Saints and set Bro. James Patterson apart to preside over the Branch. It was called the Rock Hill Branch. The Saints numbered 31 in all, 25 of the number was Lamanites.

Saturday June 3, 1884 walked 10 miles staid all night at Bro. Wm. Georges. Sunday 5th, held meeting at the same place. Our congregation was small, a good spirit prevailed and good attention was given by all present. The next day we walked back to Bro. Wats. From there we went and paid Mr. Barker a visit. Staid all day talked on the first principles of the Gospel.

Sunday June 15,1884 held meeting at Bro. Evans Wats. We partook of the Sacrament for the first time among the Catawba, we had an enjoyable time and the good spirit attended us in our meeting. Elders J. J. Humphrey, R. M. Humphrey and myself address the Saints and a good spirit prevailed although it was very cold and snowed on the same date. Such weather was never known. In the evening Elder R. M. Humphrey and myself went to hear a man preach. 21st walked ten miles to one Mr. Tims.[95] Got thar (there) at 9pm eat supper outdoors under the trees. Staid all night, next morning we walked one mile.

It being Sunday June 22, 1884 held meeting at bra. Wm. Georges. Thar being some 35 present. Many of the Saints come 10 miles to meeting. A good spirit prevailed. After meeting I had a long talk with 2 men. They seemed to be very reasonable. We then walked 10 miles to Bro. Harrises[96] whar we found him very sick. We administered to him and he had a good night's rest.

June 24th, we started to try and affect an opening where the Gospel had never been preached by an Elder. We walked some 4 miles came to a bridge 475 yards wide and 55 feet high. We walked over on the cross ties. We met a negro who ask us our business. We told him we was ministers of the Gospel of Christ. We explained the principles to him. When we got ready to leave he offered us some money to help us on our way. We traveled on some two miles inquired the road of a gentleman who ask us in and gave us a good dinner. Told us it we, ever came that way to call on him. We thanked the Lord for the friends he had raised up for us and went on in the rain until we came to one Mr. Kimbles (where) we was obliged to stop on account of high water. We staid all night with him got a good breakfast without charge.

June 25th very rainy walked all day without dinner. Met the Justice of the Peace and told him our business. He abused us shamefully with his tongue. We ask him if he would come out and hear us preach. He said yes if he could get in some dark corner whare he could not be seen.

---

[95] John Alexander Tims
[96] Peter Farris.

We traveled on but could get no place to hold meeting. After walking 25 miles, we stayed all night with one Mr. Winchester. We explained the principles of the Gospel to him. We got a good supper and bed and breakfast.

26th walked all day without any dinner. Went that night and staid all night with a preacher. He told us he knew more about Mormonism than either of us. He ask us who was the founder of the Mormon Church. I told him Jesus Christ. He invited us in the sitten (sitting) room and informed us he was a well-read man and had preached the Gospel 15 years. I prayed in my heart that he might not confound me, as I was the one that had to do all the talking, as this was the first trip my companion had ever made among his enemies. We brought our Bible and started. We talked until eleven o'clock and we agreed that it would be continued till next morning. We had a good bed and breakfast and talked untill 11 AM. We proved by the scriptures that he had no authority to preach also that he was a preaching a man-made Gospel. We bare a faithfull testimony to him. He shook hands with us and wished us God speed. We went on our way rejoicing. Walked all day could not get any place to hold meetings on account of so many false reports about the Mormons through the papers. Staid all night with one Mr. Kimble. He was much opposed to us and would not reason with us. Next day we returned and round that Bro. Peter Harris was dead and his wife[97] and children and the Saints was very low-spirited.

Sunday, June 30, 1884 held Meeting. A testimony meeting at Bro. Wm. Watts. Many of the Lamanites bore a faithful testimony to the truthfulness of the gospel I think if thar ever was a good meeting it was one. After meeting we and 40 of us met to together and enjoyed ourselves singing Hymns. We staid among the Lamanites visiting the sick., encouraging them to live their religion. Teaching them to keep the word of wisdom.

Nothing of any interest transpired until Jun 19. When we started to visit one Mr. Kimble. On arrival at his place, we found he had moved. We was shamefully abused by one Mrs. Merit.

July 17, 1884 after walking 20 miles through the hot sun we staid with one Mr. Dunkens who treated us very kindly. Gave us a good supper. After supper he called his family to gather to hear us explain the principals of the Gospel. He gave us a good bed to lay our worn out bodies on and a good breakfast without charge and invited us to call again.

July 18th, we then went to the Indian Nation whar (where) we staid over. Sunday, July 19, went to visit one Mr. Harris,[98] who kept the Ferry on the Catawba River. We held meeting in his house that night. Very few were present and on the 20th went back to the Nation.

---

[97] Margaret Elizabeth Harris Harris
[98] James Harris, son of James and Sarah Jane Ayers Harris Sr.

July 2C, 1884 set up until 1 AM accorden to request with sick Lamanite. Some 15 were setting up. I asked the privilege of talking a few moments, it was granted. I stood at the sick persons bed and addressed them a short time.

21st, walked 10 miles to Bro. Watses. July 25th called on to go to the funeral. We stayed that night at Bro. Wm. Georges. Next morning we was sent for to preach the funeral sermon. We arrived at the house at 11 PM when found a big assembly. More than the house would hold They said I was the one they wished to do the speaking. We called the large congregation to order. I called on them to sing. My companion Elder R. M. Humphrey offered prayer. They sang another hymn. I arose stood some 3 minutes without uttering a word when the man--¬spirit left me. The Lord blessed one with a rich portion of his spirit. I addressed them about one hour. They payed strick attention. After services they followed the corpse to the place of burial 2 by 2 after the body was laid away we all fell on our knees and offered up prayer. My companion being mouth. We then returned to Bro. James Pattersons.

July 2ᴄth, 1884, we held meeting at Bro. Wm. Wats. A good Spirit prevailed. After meeting, we all went over to Bro. Georges and had singing. Bro. Wm. George had concluded to quit using tobacco and gave us his tobacco to get it out of his site.

25th read my Bible most.

29th Went and I took dinner with Bro. Thomas Harris. Administered to his wife. 30th went and visited 3 of the Watses.

31st got a letter from Elder Henry Miller. Went over to Bro. Pattersons. Administered to Bro. James Patterson who soon recovered.

Augus˞ 1, 1884 very rainy weather. 2nd gathering watermellons and I administered to Bro. Evans Wats who had been to the post office and come home quite sick with a chill. Sunday 3rd, had Sunday School. After Sunday School we had testimony meeting of the Saints bore a faithful testimony. After meeting at 4 PM we had singing and had an enjoyable time together. After singing we went and staid all night with Bro. James Wats.

Augus˞ 4 1884, very fogy and dusty weather. Went to the melon patch and got melon. While we were laying on the ground eating melon, I was taken with a chill. My teeth began to chatter I went to the house went to bed and covered up with quilts. This was the first time I was ever cold in the month of Augus˞. After it was over, I had a high fever and rose quite early and felt well after my chill. Spent most of the day in reading and spent the day in visiting and administering to the sick.

Augus˞ 7 1884, weather fine, spent the day in reading and visiting the Saints that were sick. 5th nothing of any importance transpired. 9th washed our bodies and changed our clothes took them in the name of the Lord. Sunday, we held meeting only 15 persons were present. A good spirit prevailed.

After meeting we went and staid all night at Mr. Tims. Monday.

August 11, Spent the forenoon talking on the principles of the Gospel. After dinner, we went to Mr. James Harrises who lives some 5 miles from the Nation and keeps the ferry on the Catawba river. We set up until 11 pm and read and talked with them on the Gospel.

12th walked back to Mr. Tims. 13th went fishing with Mr. Tims in the Catawba river in the four noon. In the evening, we went to Bro. Georges and set up quite late and talked on family duties.

14th we in company with Bro. Patterson and wife and several of the ---. Started for Point Look Out or Br B---. On the road we met a man with a gun who thawed it on us and cursed and swore, but we passed on unharmed. On our return to Bro. Patterson we found Elder J. J. Humphreys.

15th wrote home. 16th, had a long talk with a Mr. Steel and Mr. Barker. Bore our testimony to them then washed and put on our clean clothing.

17th held Sunday School and meeting a good spirit prevailed. 17th visited the Saints. 19th, one sister Martha Patterson[99] was taken very sick. Elder Humphrey had gone to visit one Mr. Bailey so I administered to her alone. She was healed almost instantly and in 30 minutes she was able to be up and around.

August 20, 1884, we received a paper confirming the fact that 2 of our Elders had been murdered in Tennessee for preaching the Gospel of Christ.

22nd, last night I dreamed I made a fence around a flock of sheep. After I had got them fenced in, I dreamed that there was 2 large bulls came and broke the fence down and let all the sheep out. After we got our breakfast, we started to try and open a new field of labor. We was to be gone one week and then returned---.

Walked 10 miles to-visit with- Mr. Tims. Walked 5 miles to Mr. Harrises, staid all night got a good supper & breakfast & went on our way rejoicing.

23rd continued to travel east stopped within 3 mi of Lancaster City in Lancaster Co. I had a 2 hours talk with a Mr. Wilson but got no dinner walked on in a eastern direction come to the house of Mr. Sims ask if we could stay all night but was refused on account of some visitors he had. One of his sons told us we could get to stay at the next house & went & showed us the road. We was taken in that night by a Mr. R. Burton.

August 24, Mr. Burton after hearing the message we were on explained, gave us a good breakfast. It being Sunday morning he put his horse on his buggy and took us some 6 miles on our road. On parting, he wished us Gods speed. We passed on without any dinner until we came to a small village

---

[99] Daughter of James and Elizabeth Patterson

called Waxehaw. There we inquired for a minister. The people directed us to one Rev. Phail. We ask him to keep us all night but was refused. We told him we had a message to deliver to the people. We passed on and staid with one Mr. John C. Blackburn. We talked until 1 pm with him and a schoolteacher the latter was very prejudiced. Monday

August 25th, Mr. Blackburn said he would get us a house to preach in he being one of the directors of a large schoolhouse. He got that and stopped his work and informed the people there would be a meeting at 5pm. At time appointed we was on hand we found on our arrival at the school house some one hundred were there to hear the Mormons. We both felt well and had a good meeting. My comp. (companion) spoke first on the first principles and then spoke on apostacy and restoration. We told them we had to return to Rock Hill in a few days. They wished us to hold meeting the next evening in the same place, so we appointed a meeting for the next evening at the same hour at the same place. Tuesday.

August 26, 1884, spent the day reading our Bibles and eating watermelons at Mr. Blackburns. We talked with several of the leading men of the place, the name of the place we are in is called Charlesburough. When we arrived at the time and place appointed we found the large schoolhouse well filled with people. On calling the congregation to order we ask if there was anyone that would please sing a hymn. One said he would so we invited singing. When my companion opened by prayer as I arose to speak three school teachers and two Baptists preachers took there seats by us. Took out there books and pencils and took chapter and verses they felt from our help. I spoke on authority and the organization of the Church of Christ. The Lord blessed me with- His Holy Spirit in my speaking. My companion Elder Humphrey then spoke a short time when he got through, I arose. I told them if there was any questions to be ask we would be pleased to answer after the close of the meeting. One of the preachers arose and said he something to tell the people. We ask to please wait until we closed our meeting. He would not so I told him to speak, with humble spirit, he started and you may judge whether he had the Spirit of God. He told the people we were mugers, adulterers, false prophets. After he set down, another Baptist preacher arose and abused in the same manner as the other. They never brought any scriptures against us. They excited the people so that our meeting was broken up without any chance to reply to their abuse. They left the house and the congregation followed. After our meeting was broke up a man came to us and told us to leave the place. He said he was a friend to us but said it was not safe for us to come any father in the daytime but to come in the night. That night he had received a notice from eight men who came with it which reads as follows: "August 23, 1884 Notice, Messrs Willey, Humphreys, Humphrey, We the peaceable citizens of this surrounding country have been pained to learn that you three men professing to be Mormon missionaries have taken up your quarters with an ignorant class of our people and are denominating doctrines among them calculated to disorganize human society and adverse to the peace and well being of our people and country to the laws and dignity of the State. Now

therefore, these presents are to civilly and peaceably request and command you to vacate the State and to return no more among us and you are hereby allowed five days to obey this order to peaceably absent yourselves from the State without hurt or molestation but if you are found within the limits of the State after the expiration of that time you may charge consequences to disobedience to this order. We are going to be rid of you."

Capt. of the mob, Wm. Kithcart, Wm. Carethers, Charles Harrison, Paul Harrison, Alexander Millens, Clarence Cotter. The names of the rest of the mob we did not get. This notice had been received while we was gone and the 5 days was up. President Humphreys was afraid we would run in their hands unknowingly. We learned he was staying in the woods nights. We got a good supper and started at 11PM to where he was but there came a hard rain and raised the creek so we could not reach him. We was obliged to retrace our steps so we went back to the Indian to Bro. Wm. Georges. When we reached his place, it was 2 AM Next morning, President Humphreys sent us word and for us to keep out of site until father orders from him.

August 29, 1884, went in the woods where was fed by Bro. Wm. George.

That day one of the Saints come from Rock Hill, brought my companion a letter from home and some papers. We spent our time in reading. Did not rest much that night. We arose next morning the 30th, commended ourselves to the Lord as commonly before eating our breakfast. Bro. Georges brought us a good breakfast. After breakfast we went to a small stream in the woods and washed our bodies and put on our clean clothes which Bro. James Patterson had brought to us 10 miles.

September 1, 1884, we left our hiding place in the woods at Bro. Georges and moved to Mr. Tims and stayed in the loft of his stable. Mr. Tims brought us food 3 times a day. We wrote a letter to President Humphreys to know what to do as we did not think it safe to be seen by our enemies.

Sept 2nd, we were both well had a good night's rest, received a letter from Elder Lamoni Call from VA. 3rd read our Bibles and kept out of site. I was not feeling well in body, but well in spirits.

September 4,1884, layed in the loft read, prayed and fasted. We had concluded to go up to Bro. Pattersons so that night at 11 pm we started. We arrived Bro. Pattersons at 3 AM. There we found Bro., James Smith who President Humphreys had got to come down to see what had become of us. We got our breakfast before daylight and took 2 quilts and went to the woods for safety. That day several spies came around inquiring for us. Had a good nights rest.

Layed in the woods until 10 AM when Elders Bingham and Cragun came from Spartenburg Co., SC.

As they satisfied there would be conference. President Humphrey's had wrote and told them there would be no conference but there letter had never reached them. They was somewhat disappointed we all got dinner and left at 4pm and started for Kings Mountain a distance of 30 miles to see Elder Humphreys and the Saints. We traveled most all night, arrived at Bro. Gordons at 3 AM. We found President Humphreys had been keeping out of site. We all went in the woods and held council meeting and had a good time together. This was the first time we had ever all been together.

September 8, 1884. Elders Bingham & Cragun went back to there labors in Spartenburg County. Elder Humphreys stayed around Kings Mountain and visited the Saints. Nothing of any importance transpired until! Wednesday the 17th. Elder J. J. Humphrey baptized Catherine Gordon. 18th we walked 28 miles to Bro. James Patterson we found the Saints feeling well. Things seemed to be quiet here at the Rock Hill Branch. It was instructions from headquarters to hold no public meetings so we visited quietly among the Saints until further orders.

September 26, 1884 staid all night at Bro. James Pattersons. Neither of us could sleep. We both felt very gloomy and uneasy. We felt as though there was something wrong. The 30th, we went down to the Nation, found the Saints and friends all well and feeling well. We staid and visited the Saints arid friends until! October 6. Went on the riverbanks gathering fruit called musquedines every day. Left the night of the 6th at 8pm to go to Bro. Pattersons as we did not consider it safe to go in the day time. We got some 4 miles on the road.

Oct 6th 1884, when we heard a crowd of drunken men cursing and swaring so we layed down on the grass and slep until they left. We arrived at Bro. Pattersons at 1 AM found all well, nothing of interest transpired. On the 9th we received a letter from Pres. J. J. Humphreys instructing us to leave our present field of labor and go beyond the circle of bitterness where an Elder was never seen or heard and warn and preach to all that come under the sound of our voice. This being Thursday we concluded to stay until Monday the 13th, so we appointed a meeting at our usual place.

October 12,1884, Sunday, had a good Sunday School. After Sunday School my companion led David and Butlar Harris[100] into the waters of baptism. After baptism we had a good meeting. This was the first meeting we had held for two months. After meeting we attended to confirmation, I also blessed Howard Harris. Monday, October 13th, weather fine. Started Southwest to open a new field of labor. Walked 18 miles, slept in a stable, but we had plenty of food which the Saints put up for us.

Tuesday Oct 14, we arose at 7 AM walked 2 miles. Eat our breakfast and walked 20 miles come to a small village called Battenrust. Staid all night with Mr. A. D. Dorbby who was a lawer (Lawyer). He

---

[100] Taylor Butler and his brother James David Harris are children of Peter and Margaret Sanders Harris.

said he did not want to talk on religion. He said he was matured and could not be changed. He said he always calculated to stick to the Church that was the most popular. We left him a discourse delivered by Pres. George G. Cannon.

15th We walked 15 miles staid all night at one Mr. J. N. Dickersons, was treated well. Set up until! 1 pm talked on the Gospel to him and his large family.

October 16, 1884 went in Fairfield Co. Posted a letter at Crosbyville.

Walked 10 miles called at two places to stay overnight but was refused. Finally one Mr. J. F. Sytes took us in. We set up until 10 PM and talked over the scriptures. He was on the road to infidelity he said. He had never met a man that believed the Bible. We could do but little good with him as he would not stick to any one point

Friday October 17 1884 Weather fine. Walked 4 miles. We met 5 men in the road. We talked some time with them. The gentleman of the house Mr. Matthew Pettergrue ask us to the house. We laid the first principles of the Gospel before the. Set up very late and talked on the scripture, bore our testimony to them in the morning when we left them.

October 18, Saturday, Called at Mr. Murphy. My companion learned that he was a distant relative of his. He got the names of many of his dead relatives. Mr. Murphy seemed to be very indifferent about our message. We got a good dinner, went on our way rejoycing. We walked until dark. We called at one Mr. Yarbers for nights lodgen. He took us in but on finding out who we were said he could not keep us. We tried to reason but all in vane. We had a long argument bore our testimony to him and passed on. We was turned out three times but about 5 PM we got entertainment at one Mr. Curries who treates us very kindly. Set up very late, got a good supper and bed and breakfast. Staid until 9 am, tried to get an appointment to preach, could not.

Sunday, Oct 19th, Staid in the woods the most of the day and read our Bibles. Walked 2 miles called at a Mr. McMulken who took us in. He had company, we had an elegant supper. He called on me to return thanks after supper. He ask me to dismiss the table. I responded all though it was something new to me to dismiss a table after supper. Explained the Gospel to him. We had prayers and retired at a late hour. At breakfast the gentleman left us before we got half through eating. The company had then gone home. Monday October 20th walked 20 miles into Richland Co. Took dinner at Mr. Fridays, staid all night at Mr. Wm. Smiths who was an old batchlar. Tuesday Oct. 21 Weather fine. Arrived in the City of Columbia at 12 o'clock. We learned that the population of Columbia City was 11 thousand. We went through the main street of the city and visited some of the prominent buildings. Among the number was the Asylum. We went all through the building. There was 750 inmates among the number of insane was several young women who played on the orgen. (Organ) We staid some 5 hours in the city and passed through. Went 5 miles out of town and staid all night with a Mr. Green. He was an old batchler and had a black wench to cook. Treated us well, give us a good breakfast. Wednesday

Oct. 22, Traveled SW. 15 miles, saw great destruction caused from the cyclone. Trees blown up by the roots 2 ft through. Large trees twisted off some had dug holes in the earth to escape the cyclones. Their hearts failed them. Called to stay all night at a Mr. Buchaster who was a class leader of the Baptist Church. He would not take us in but treated us with contempt. We slept in the cotton at Mr. G. S. Rawlisons.

Oct. Thursday 23rd walked 10 miles. Had a talk with a man who did not believe the Bible. Staid all night with a Mr. Mclechlin. Set up late talked on the Gospel. Friday,

Oct.24th, 1884, in Kershaw Co., Fine weather. Walked 20 miles over a very sandy road. There was hundreds of colored people on the road, only 3 or 4 whites on the road. Staid all night at Mr. W. T Hammond, who was a negro driver. On the road was many turpentine farms.

Saturday, Oct 25, Heavy frost last night. Started at 10 am, walked 6 miles through the sand. Called to get a drink of water and the Ladie of the house ask us to come in the house and take a seat in the piazza. We told her our business, she got us some dinner and said she wished us to go and see her son John Robin. She said he would be pleased to entertain us over night so we went. When we reached his place we found he was not at home, but there was a Baptist preacher there who was calculating to preach near there. he next day when he found out we were ministers he sent a boy off to get help. Soon the man of the house came and brought several with him. After supper Mr. Harten and the minister ask where the thief that hung with Jesus went to. I readily answered his questions which seemed to astonish him as it was never answered before to his satisfaction. We divided the time and talked some three hours on the first principles of the Gospel. He became excited and said he would retire for the night. The gentleman of the house tried to get him to stay all night, but he would not. I ask him where he got the authority to preach. He said he took his authority from the Bible, Mark, chapter 8, where Jesus commanded his Disciples to go and preach. I then asked him if he believed the Father, Son and Holy Ghost to be one or three separate persons. He said the "Bible could not be understood, good night!"

Sunday Oct.26, Weather fine. We was calculating to go and hear Mr. Harten preach but a gentleman came to us and said it would not be safe for us to go to meeting. He said he was a friend to us and knew that the people would not reason with us but would use violence and mob us. So, we passed on. We met Mr. Harten and a minister of the Methodist church in the road early that morning but they seemed to be very distant. Walked several miles through the sand. Was turned off several times, staid with a gentleman, but could not learn his name.

Monday, Oct. 27, Chester Co. Weather fine. Walked 20 miles without any dinner. Called at an old gentlemans to get entertainment but was refused. Called at a Mr. Onleys who concluded to keep us over nights but on inquiring who we were said he would not keep a Mormon overnight. He said if he should his neighbors would look down on him. He said he had heard a great deal about Mormonism and he believed them to be a corrupt lot. We could not reason with him. We bore our testimonies to him and past on. We was turned out several times but was taken in at 8pm by Mr. Goden who treated us kindly without charge.

Tuesday Oct 28th, Weather cloudy and cool. Started at 9 AM walked 30 miles without letting ourselves be known as we was getting back near Rock Hill where excitement ran high, when we left we arrived at Mr. Tims at 11 pm foot sore & tired as we had been walking 15 miles & never got the chance to hold no public meetings. Found the Saints & Friends all well. Oct 28 went & visited Bro. Wm George & staid to Bro Georges & rested up.

November 3, Weather cloudy. President J. J. Humphryes who was at Kings Mountain Branch had sent us word that he was honorably released or transferred to go to England and wished us to come at once. In 2 hours we was on the road. Arrived at Bro. John Gordons at 9pm, walked a distance of 28 miles. Tuesday 4th, walked 4 miles, to Bro. M. M Gordon. There we met Elders J. J. Humphreys, W. J. Cragun, W. E. Bingham and rejoiced to be together. Wednesday Nov. 5 my traveling companion R. M. Humphrey was now assigned to go to Spartenburg County with Elder W. F. Bingham as traveling companion. We went to the depot to see Pres. J. J Humphreys off but his money did not come, so him and I went to Bro. Aydelottes, the next day he borrowed the money of him. Friday Nov 7 at 3 AM, I give him the farewell shake, his instructions was for me to take charge of the Rock Hill Branch until further orders.

Friday staid all night at Bro. Aydelottes. The 8th walked 11 miles to W. N. Gordons.

Sunday Nov 9 held meeting at W. N. Gordons. Elders present were Bro. Cragun and myself a good spirit prevailed. Monday

Nov. 10th, walked 28 miles to Rock Hill Branch, where I was to labor and travel alone until! further instructions from Chattenooga. On my return I learned that Bro. Taylor George and Thomas Harris both Lamanites, had been drinking.

Nov 11, 12, 13, nothing of any importance transpired. I visited around among the Saints. Nov 16 held meeting at Bro. Evans Watts. The house was filled to the utmost capacity. My tongue was loosened and I spoke in great power. After meeting, Mr. Wiley applied for baptism. He had been our most bitter enemy. I told him to bring forth furst (1st) meet (meat) for repentance and he could be baptized.

Nov 16, 1884, 1 spent most of the day talking with one Mr. Simkin.

Nov 18, 19, 20, 21 and 22, visited around among the Saints, teaching them to keep the Word of Wisdom. Also visited one Mr. Baily Barker.

Nov 23 held meeting at Bro. Evans Wats, a good spirit prevailed. Many had come ten miles to meeting. Many of the Lamanites bore a faithful testimony to the truth of .the Gospel. I read the papers to the Saints.

Nov 25, 26, 27, 28, nothing of any importance transpired.

Nov. 29th had a long talk with Mr. Simkins and Mr. Mathews. Mr. Mathews said he was a Bible lover. I had a long talk on apostacy from the primitive church. Mr. Mathews got very angry that evening. I called a meeting a requested all the Saints to come together. I called on Br. George and Harris to make a public confession for getting intoxicated and ask the Saints forgiveness. They made a humble confession and the Saints freely forgave them. I spoke some time on the duty of the Saints. Bro. Russell had come to move the Saints.

November 30, 1884, Sunday, I preached my farewell sermon at the Rock Hill Branch. A good spirit prevailed. Bro. James Russell had now come to move the Saints to his place to tend his farm in Spartenburg Co. The Lamanites that went with him numbered 22. This broke up the Rock Hill Branch of the Church. The Saints wished be to go with them as several of them was sick with the chills and fever. I did so. The distance they had to move was 65 miles over a very rough road. They had two wagons to and took to cows.

December 1, 1884. We started for Spartanburg Co. Traveled 9 miles camped in the woods. Had a large fire, cooked supper, had prayers and all laid down on the ground.

Dec. 2, weather very cold and cloudy. We started on our journey as soon as it was light. It was so cold that most of the children was obliged to walk to keep warm. We reached Bro. Moses Gordons at 6 PM a distance of 20 miles. Camped in an old house that is the Lamanites did. I slept with Elder W. S. Cragun who was laboring thar.

Dec. 3, The weather was fine. We camped in the woods that night. Everything was all right. We ask the Lord night and morning to temper the elements.

Dec. 4, 1 1884, We had a good nights rest. The night of the 3rd, I went with Bro. Russell to see one Mr. Blacks who was a strong believer in the Gospel, to see if he wished to rent his large plantation td some of the Rock Hill Saints. We got enough land for 6 of the Saints and wrote for them to make calculations to move in 2 weeks. On the 4th we reached Bro. Russells at 2pm without an accident and we all gave the Lord the praise for taking us safe through. It never rained or snowed on the road. After we got moved in the houses the rain come down in torrents and continued to rain all night. 5th and 6th visited the Saints and read the papers.

Dec, Sunday, the 7th 1 held a meeting at Bro. James Russells. Thar was quite a number of the neighbors come. After meeting I baptized Edward Harris[101] in the Pacolet River. December 8, Elders W. E. Bingham and R .M. Humphrey who had been trying to open a new field of arrived at Bro. Russells (where) I met them.

Dec. 9, we was invited to visit Mr. Croford. I formed acquaintance with when I first come on my mission. Mr. Croford was a Baptist --. He said he was a Later Day Saint in principle. We talked--

Dec 10,11,12 & 13, I visited among my old friend s who was kind to me but was not willing to give obedience to the truth. Sunday, the 14th we had a meeting appointed but the weather was so bad there was no meeting. Tuesday the 16th Started back to Rock Hill Branch in company with Bro. James Patterson & Bro. Davis Ayers,[102] we camped in the woods that night.

Dec 18th, arrived at Bro. Nelson Gordons. Dec. 18, arrived at Rock Hill, found the Saints well Dec 19. wrote home to my folks. Dec 20, visited one Mr. Barker. Dec 21st very rainy weather Dec 22, weather very cold. Dec 23rd, I walked 28 miles to Bro. Nelson Gordons (where) (where) I found Elder W. S. Cragun as traveling companion.

Dec 24, we visited bro. John Gordon. One Mr. Richy Hartness a Baptist preacher came to Bro. Gordons. He invited us to come and see him. Christmas Dec., 25, 1884, Spent the day with Rev. Hartness talking on the Gospel. Slept that night on a feather bed which was once offered to feather the Elders with some months before.

Dec.26. We returned to Bro. John Gordons. Mr. Hartness come with us to hear us talk. Dec 27, we walked two miles to Bro. N. Gordons. Sunday, the 28th held testimony meeting at Bro Nelson Gordons. A bad spirit prevailed. After meeting went home with Bro. James Smith. Dec.29, paid Bro. James Smith a visit.

Dec 30, had our picture taken. Dec .31, took dinner with Mr. James Rippy.

January 1, 1885, spent our new years with bro. P. Aydolette and his wife was gone and we got our own dinner. Jan 2, went to Whitaker and mailed some letters, staid all night with Bro. J. Smith. Jan 3, staid all night with Bro. Givans, very rainy. Jan 4, Sunday held meeting at bro. Nelson Gordons a good spirit prevailed. Rev. Hartness was there he invited us home. We could not go. Jan 5, weather very rainy spent the day in reading. Jan. 6, I had the priviledge of leading Rev. Hartness in the waters of baptism. Jan 7, walked 6 miles to Bro. James Smiths. Staid all night. Jan 8, walked to Whittaker staid

---

[101] Eldest son of Peter and Margaret Sanders Harris.
[102] Jefferson Davis Ayers.

all night to Bro. Smiths. Jan 9, I walked 13 miles. Staid all night at Bro. Robinsons. Jan 10th walked 15 miles staid all night at Mr. John Blacks. Several of the Catawba Lamanites from Rock Hill had rented M Blacks place. We staid with them the 11th.

Jan 12th, walked 10 miles to Bro. James Russells where we met Elders W. E. Bingham and R.M. Humphrey. Jan 13, spent the day in reading the papers.

Jan 14, held council meeting in the woods. Jan 15 made an appointment for a meeting and wrote a letter home. Jan 16, visited the Saints. Jan 17th, went to meeting and heard a Baptist preacher preach. He took his text from Rom.(Romans) 5, verse 6. After meeting he gave it out that we would preach the next day at Bro. James Pattersons. Sunday, 18th, Held meeting at Bro. James Pattersons. There was 34 present, a good spirit prevailed. Jan 19 Elders Bingham and Cragun took a trip to North Carolina.

Jan 20, we went to the post office. Jan 21, Elder Humphrey and I went to Spartanburg and had our pictures taken. Went that night and called on one Mr. S. W. Aydairs. He treated us well. We set up until 1 pm and talked on the principles of the Gospel. He wished us to call again. Jan 22, weather clear and cold. We went to Spartanburg City, and staid hours then went back to Mr. Aydairs, and staid all night, talked till 11 pm.

He seemed to be much interested. We left him a Voice of Warning.

Jan 23, the snow was falling very fast. We walked 11 miles through the snow. It snowed all day. We arrived at Mr. Pools at 5 AM (where) we had a meeting appointed. He had a large family and a large house with 17 rooms.

Jan 24, weather very had, snow two inches deep. Sunday, Jan 25, held meeting in one of the large rooms. The congregation was small. I spoke about one hour a good spirit prevailed. Jan 26, walked 17 miles arrived to brother James Russells 5pm, found the Elders and Saints well. Jan 27, wrote a letter and read my Bible. Jan 28 wrote up my journal. Jan 29th got my watch fixed, went to the post office. Jan 30th left -¬12 o'clock, walked 10 miles to fill an appointment at Mr. Blacks. Found the Saints all well. Jan 31, visited and encouraged the Saints.

Sunday, Feb 1, weather cloudy. Held meeting at brother Watses. There was some 35 present. We went and staid all night at Mr. Williams. Feb 2, I went a shooting rabbits with two of the Lamanite Brothers. Feb 3, walked 15 miles to Brother Robisons, setup till 1 pm. Feb 4, walked 9 miles to brother Aydoletts. Feb 5, walked 10 miles staid all night at Bro. Givans. Feb 6 weather fine. Feb 7, weather fine walked 3 miles. Sunday, held meeting at Bro. James Smiths. Thirty persons were present a good spirit prevailed. Feb 9, very rainy. Went and staid all night with Bro. Weaver. Feb 10, walked 16 miles to Bro. Wm. Gordons. I had a very ---back Feb 11, very cold, , walked 2 miles to Bro. John

Gordons. Feb 12, snowed two inches in the night, snowing heavy this morning. Feb 13, staid that day and night with brother Hartness. Feb 14, the snow was 4 or 5 inches deep. We started to Bro. Givans but the path was narrow through the thick woods and we got lost. We wandered around through the wood but finally came to brother Smiths at a late hour where we got a good supper, sang a few hymns and retired to rest. Sunday, Feb 15, had meeting appointed but the weather was so bad there was no meeting. One man came there under the influence of liquor. His name was Lay. He tried to open my shirt to examine my underclothing. I threw him off and he left. Feb 16, we walked 7 miles to Brother John Gordons and staid all night. Feb 17, staid and took dinner with Bro. Hartness then walked 4 miles to Mr. John R. Harrises. Set up very late and talked on every subjects.

Feb 16, there was some two men come to a wood chopping. They were all drinking liquor so we left there and went and stayd all night with one Mr. Bowlen who seemed to be much interested in the Gospel. Feb 19, Left Mr. Bowlens at 8 AM and took dinner with Bro. John Gordons, staid all night with Bro. Hartness. Talked on the Gospel until 2 AM. There was one Mrs. Lanier present.

Feb 20, walked 25 miles. While we was setting in the woods by a fire eating a lunch which Mrs. Hartness had put up, our umbrellas caught on fire. Elder Craguns was burned up and there was a large hole burnt in mine. Staid that night with Bro. Thom Harris.

Feb 21 arrived at the Catawba nation, staid that night at Mr. Tims. They was all glad to see us.

Feb 22, Sunday, held meeting at Bro. Wm. Georges. A large congregation was present a good spirit prevailed. Those that was present was Lamanites.

Feb 23, visited the Saints, found them all firm in the truth. Staid all night at Mr. James Harrises. Set up until 12 o'clock and talked on the Gospel. They wished us to hold another meeting. We was calculating to go on and open a new field of labor. I felt as though there was some honest in hart in that country as I dreamed I was standing on the banks of a large stream of water and Elder Cragun was in the water baptizing. We made another appointment to hold meeting at Bro. Georges.

Feb 24, weather very stormy but warm. Spent the day in reading. The hour of meeting come but the weather was so bad there was no one come. We appointed a meeting at the same place to be held the next night at 6pm

Feb 25, cloudy and warm. Held meeting. Elder Cragun done the speaking. Feb 26, held meeting at Mrs. Harrises, some 30 was present. I done the speaking. Feb 27, weather pleasant. The house was well filled. Elder Cragun done the speaking. Feb 28, I was appointed to preside over the South Carolina Conference. We held meeting at Mr. Tims. The house was packed to its utmost capacity. I done the speaking. People paid good attention and considerable interest was manifested. Sunday March 1, geld meeting at Bro. Wm. Georges. Several strangers was present.

March 2, held meeting at 7pm at Mr. John Sanders.[103] March 3, held meeting at Mrs. Sarah Harrises.[104] March 4, held meeting at Mrs. Mary Harrises.[105] The meetings were well attended by the Lamanites. March 5, weather cloudy. Walked 7 miles to see one Mr. L. M. Din---. Several of his neighbors came in to spend the evening and hear us talk. We set up quite late and explained the Gospel. We was well treated

March 9, had a good nights rest, got & good breakfast and went back to the Catawba Nation. Had singing at Bro. Georges, a good many Lamanites were present. March 7, spent the day in reading our Bibles. We ware most wore out for the want of sleep. We were invited to stay all night at Mr. John Sanders, which invitation we accepted. Sunday March 8, weather fine, my companion Elder Cragun married Mr. John Sanders and Miss Martha Harris.[106] They had been living together several years and had three children. It was rulable among the Lamanites to take up without marriage. Mr. John Sanders and Mr. George Canty[107] was baptized. On the next nite after baptism we held meeting and confirmed them in meeting. We had singing that night at James Harrises.[108] March 9, spent the day in reading. March 10, visited around among our friends and met at 7pm at Mr. Tims and had a good time singing hymns.

 March 11, went a fishing but caught none. Some 25 met at James Harris and sang hymns.

March 12, we read our Bibles and went a boat riding on Catawba river. March 13 we all met at Mrs. Sarah Harrises and sang hymns. We had a enjoyable time and most of the Lamanites in the Nation were present.

March 14, 1885, 20 of the Lamanites wished us to take a boat ride, so we took several hymn books and rode the boats out in the center of the Catawba River and song hymns. March 15, we had a good meeting at Bro. Wm. Georges and met at Mrs. Sarah Harrises at 7pm to sing hymns. After we got through singing we blessed two of Brother Sanders children.

March 16, weather very pleasant and warm. March 17, very cloudy read most of the day. There was 5 inches of snow fell that night. This was the most snow that all night at brother Wm. Georges. March 19, I baptized four young women, two married and two single namely Mrs. Betsy Canty and Martha

---

[103] Son of John Sanders SR and Lucinda Harris.

[104] Sarah Jane Ayers Harris, daughter of Edmund and Rebecca Quash-Marsh Ayers, widow of James Harris sr.

[105] Mary George Harris, daughter of Patsey George, first wife of Epp Harris.

[106] John son of Lucinda, earlier, Martha, daughter of James and Sarah Jane Ayers Harris.

[107] George Washington Canty, son of Franklin and Eliza Scott Canty, half brother of John Alonzo, Fannie and Mary Jane Canty or Whitesides.

[108] James Harris, JR, son of James SR and Sarah Jane Ayers Harris, husband of Fannie Whitesides.

Sanders and Miss Rachel Tims and Betsy Crofford.[109] While on the banks of the river we appointed a meeting at Mrs. Ann Tims,[110] where we confirmed the sisters. While I was speaking Bro. Ritchy Hartness came in. He lived 30 miles from there. After we got through speaking we called on him to bear his testimony. He bore a powerful testimony and said he had left home on account of persecution.

March 20, received a letter from home. Met at 7pm at Mrs. Sarah Harrises and sang hymns.

March 21, Elder Cragun baptized Mrs. Sarah Harris, David Harris, Franklin Canty.[111] There was upwards of 25 Lamanites on the banks of the river. Held singing at 7pm at Bro. John Sanders, a good spirit was manifested. March 22, held meeting at Bro. Wm. Georges. We confirmed those that had been baptized. We had a splendid meeting. March 23, wrote a letter to Pres. Morgan.

March 23, had a long talk with MISS -- who was Baptist. Staid at Bro. Wm. Georges.

March 25, spent the most of the day with Mr. James Harris. March 26, I accidently through Mr. Brown out of the boat- I was some what excited but I handed him my ?? pole and he got in the boat safe. March 27, staid with Bro. Sanders. March 25, went and visited one Mr. Oceola Whiteside who was a mullattar.[112] He was the first man I had ever visited that had negro blood in him. He was well oft, highly respected by the whites and blacks. He seemed to be much interested in the Gospel and wished us to call again.

We only took dinner with him. March 29, held meeting at Bro. Wm. Georges. Our congregation was quite small.

March 30, Mrs. Sarah Head,[113] was taken very sick. She send for us to come and administer to her. We did so, she was a very sick woman. She seemed to rest better after she had had been administered to

March 31, went a fishing with Mr. Harris. He caught a fish 22 inches long and weighed 5 pounds.

April 1, 1885. Wrote several letters home. April 2nd, we went and helped to turn over a large flatt (boat) 38 ft long and put it in the Catawba River

April 3, very rainy. Went in bathing, staid at Mrs. Ann Tims. Sunday April 5, had a long talk with Dr. White who was said to be the best-informed man in York Co. He said he did not believe in persecuting

---

[109] Betsy Canty, daughter of William and Margaret-Peggy Jane McLonah or McClure Watts George, wife of George Washington Canty; Martha Sanders, wife of John Sanders earlier; Rachel Tims, daughter of John Alexander-Alec and Martha Ann Cottsky or Kilishy Scott.

[110] Daughter of William Cotttsky or Kilsky and Betsy Mush Scott, first wife of John Alexander Tims jr.

[111] Sarah Jane, daughter of Edmund and Rebecca Ayers, widow of James Harris SR; David Harris is actually James David Harris, son of Peter and Margaret Sanders Harris; Franklin is the son of George Washington and Betsy Mush Canty.

[112] Mulatto, half black. The Whitesides family was white, Thomas Whitesides the Indian Agent, fathered Catawba babies as well as white children. Evidently either he or one of his relatives had a black woman also, not an uncommon act in the South in those days.

[113] Sarah Ann Evans-Canty Head, daughter of Peggy Canty and Chancy Evans, who was white, she was the widow of Robert Henry Head, Civil War soldier.

any religious detonations. We fond (loaned) him a book called Mormon Doctrine We held meeting at Bro. Wm. Georges on the same date. April 6, wrote several letters talked several hours with Mr. James Harris on the principles of the Gospel.

April 7, went fishing. April 8, read the paper and had singing at Mr. Tims. April 8 wrote out a pertition and got signers enough to start a school. We hired a teacher for them. School was to start the 13th of the same month. We staid all night at Mr. Tiros. April 10, two years this morning since I left my lovely mountain home.

Today we was going to bid the Lamanite Brothers and sisters goodby. We went and seen the most of them. Many of them wept like children when we gave the parting hand. We walked 10 miles and staid all night with one Mr. Barker who gave us a good supper and breakfast.

April 11, walked 28 miles arrived at Bro. Hartness at 5 PM, found the family all well. April 11, excitement seemed to run high. Bro. Hartness had received several threats if he did not give up Mormonism. One Mrs. Lather and Mrs. Hartness wished to be baptized before they laid down that night so bro. Hartness lead us to a place where they could be buried in water. At 11 PM Elder Cragun lead them in the waters of baptism we confirmed them the same night and all retired to rest for the night.

April 12 Sunday, we blessed 2 of Bro. Hartnesses and one of Sister Laniers children. We walked 4 miles to King Mountain where we found the Saints had met in a meeting capacity an a large mountain where they could worship God without being molested by mobs. We preached to the Saints and imprest upon them the necessity of observing the Word of Wisdom. After meeting I baptized Misses Mary and Frances Hartness. We confirmed them on the banks of the stream. We walked 3 miles.

April 13, Bro. Givans, Elder Cragun baptized Miss Stacy Ann Dover confirmed her the same night. Staid all night at Bro. Givans. April 13 walked 7 miles to get our mail, returned staid at Bro Givans.

April 14, brother Nelson Gordon took the cars for Colorado, the gathering place for the Saints. I gave him a letter to give to the Bishop of Manassa, Colorado, stating the kindness he had shown to the Elders etc. April 15, weather fine, read the news and staid at Bro. A. J. Smiths. April 16, fixed up the Branch record. April 17, went to see Sister Wiley who was very sick, staid at Bro. Givans. April 18, started for Spartanburg, Co., walked 12 miles to Bro. H. Robisons, found them feeling well.

April 19, staid all day and night at the same place. April 20, walked 15 miles to Bro. Watses, found the Saints feeling well. April 21, read and counciled the Saints and encouraged them to live their religion.

April 22, walked 10 miles to Bro. James Pattersons, found the Saints feeling well in the Gospel. April 23, I received a letter from home with $75.00 in it.

April 24, wrote a letter to Chattanooga and one home.

April 15, weather fine, went and heard a Dunkard preach. His name was Rev, Frans--- we setup until 12 o clock at night and talked.

Sunday, 25th, we held meeting at Bro. James Pattersons. A good spirit Prevailed. One Mr. Black came 10 miles to see us. April 27, one of the Saints had got in difficulty and we wished us to come at once and settle the trouble.

April 27, took a walk around the farm of Mr. Black. April 28, weather fine, walked 10 miles to Bro. James Russells, and found on our return that Bros. Bingham and Humphrey had returned. Also Elders F. A. Fraughton and Heber Wright had arrived from Utah. They informed us that Pres. Morgan was so busy he could not get time to write. April 29, all had our pictures taken. April 30, went and found a secluded spot of ground and set it apart for prayers.

May 1, 1885, I wired $55.00 to Chattanooga and walked 25 miles to Spartanburg City, and got one new suit of cloths. May 10 walked 10 miles all six of us Elders. May 13, we held two meetings on Mr. Black's place at Bro. Watses. Good attention was payd in both meetings. We all six spoke and a good spirit prevailed. May 4, we administered to Br Wm. Wats who was very sick with the chills. He was heald all most instantly. May 5, we parted with Elders W. S. Cragun and F. A. Fraughton who started for the Catawba Nation, York Co. to labor in my old field among the Lamanites. Elders Bingham and Humphrey, Wright and myself walked 10 miles to Bro. Russells. May 6, read a true account of the Mountain Meadow Massacre. May 7, Elders Humphrey, Wright started to Mr. Pools to try and make a appointment. May 8, weather fine statened up my journal. May 9, walked 17 miles to Mr. Pools.

May 10, we held two meetings. I occupied the most of the afternoon meeting speaking on apostasy from the Primitive Church. A considerable interest was manifested. May 11, walked 17 miles, visited Clifton factory, arrived at Bro. Pattersons at 7 PM. May 12, all went to the post office 12 miles. May 13, Elders R. .M. Humphrey, Wright started to ---NC to try and open a new field of labor. May 14, Elder Bingham and I started to labor to together. We walked 17 miles, staid with M. V. Gowans who was very much interested in the Gospel. May 15, we had a long talk with the magistrate who was very much opposed to Mormonism. He told us we were imposters and tramps. He was drinking whiskey. Sunday May 16, staid at the same place. Sunday May 17, my birthday. We held meeting at Mr. James Tuckers. We had a splendid meeting. May 18, weather fine, visited several families who seemed to be much interested in the Gospel. Staid that night Father Lawrence who was in his 90th year. He wished us to call again. May 19, walked 4 miles to see one Mr. Hammot. His mind had been poisoned against us and he would not keep us over night. We returned to Mr. Gowans at an late hour, they got out of bed and got us a good supper and we retired for the night.

May 20, I read the Voice of Warning to Mrs. Gowans. Went and staid all night with one Jackson

Stone. May 21, staid at Mr. A. T. Turners. His wife said she was convinced of the truth or the Gospel and she said she calculated to be baptized. May 22, went and staid at Mrs. Stones. We was treated well. May 23, staid at Father Lawrences who seemed to mainfest considerable interest in trying to understand the Gospel. May 24, held meeting at James Tuckers, about 40 persons was present, all payd good attention.

May 25, walked 17 miles, arrived at Brother James Pattersons at 3pm and found the Saints all feeling well. May 26, wrote a letter to my Brother W. W. Willey

May 27, Elders Humphrey and Wright returned from there new field in Polk Co. They was met by a mob of 25 men who ordered them to leave Polk and Spartanburg Counties. It was all the leader could do to keep some of the men from whipping the Elders. The Elders left Polk Co the same night. May 28 read my Bible.

May 29, Elders Bingham and Humphrey started to Mr. Pools to hold meeting. May 30, Elder Wright and I went to the post office. We went a fishing a caught I fish each. May 31, held meeting at Bro. Pattersons and my companion lead 4 in the waters of baptism. This was the first baptizing he had ever done.

June 1, staid at Bro. Georges. June 2, mailed some books to the Catawba Nation so they could start a Sunday School. June 8, nuthing of any importance since last date. Visited around among the Saints. Elders W. G. Cragun and F. A. Fraughton arrived from the received the Indian Nation, York Co., they had sad news. On my 18th they received the following notice-¬"We the undersigned citizens of the state and county aforesaid have been informed that you the Mormon Elders are preaching and practicing your polygamis doctrine in Catawba Nation, York County and we respectfully request you to leave the state and county aforsaid and on your refusal to comply with this request we will not be responsible for the consequence." There was about 70 names signed to the article, the ones who brought It to them were; Maj. Botch, Mr. Crook sr., Take Crook, Robert Cornwell, Frank Collins, John Allen, Pirce Giles.[114] This notice was fixed up to run Elder Cragun and out of the Nation, but we left on the 10th. The Elders paid know attention, but continued preaching. June 6, On May 25 Elder Cragun and Fraughton was visiting one of our Lamanite friends, Mr. Alexander Tims and Elder Cragun had his shoes off ready to go to bed for the night. When a mob of about 20 men rushed in them. Mr. Tims said to the Elders, Run. Elder Cragun ran out the back door. Some 10 or 12 shots was fired at him. He fell but rose again and got in the woods. He received a slight wound on the chin.

---

[114] It is probably more than a coincidence that Maj Botch is Boartch, Frank Collins and John Allen had fathered Catawba women's babies.

Several fine shot hit him on the right side of the chin. The wound was not serious. Elder Fraughton concealed himself under the bed but was brought out at the point of several pistols. They took him about one mile out of the Nation and the men whipped him, giving him 10 lashes each, 40 lashes in all. He returned to the house and they spent a the night in the woods. Sunday, June 7, we held meeting at Bro. James Pattersons. All six of us Elders was present and we all spoke, good spirit prevailed. After meeting I baptized Mr. John Gandy in Pacolet River.[115] We confirmed him on the banks of the river.

June 6, we walked 2 miles. We spend the day councilling together and reading our Bibles. June 9, very rainy, walked 2 miles. Elders Humphrey and Wright started for Kings Mountain.

June 10 weather cloudy, walked to the post office. June 11, helped Bro. James Patterson hoe cotton. June 12, walked 17 miles up Pacolet River to our new field of labor, staid at Mr. T. A. Tuners. June 13, visited several of our friends. We was refused the houses we had been holding meeting in. Staid with Joseph Lawrence. Sunday June 14, held meeting at Mr. M. V. Gowans, our congreagation numbered 8 persons, all felt well. June15, walked 4 miles staid at Father Lawrences. When we got up in the morning we found the following notice had been slipped in the door while we was asleep in the night. "Mr. Joseph Willey and Bingham, We ask you to leave this place and stay away, never come back here know more. We ask you polittely to never show yourselves no more. We will give you next week to leave this place." June 16, walked 18 miles to Bro. James Pattersons. We found the Saints all well, many threats was being made against the Saints.

 June 17, 18 7 18th wrote letters, straitened up my journal, hoed cotton, went to the post office, visited around among the Saints etc. June 20 we was looking for Pres. John Morgan. Elder W. E. Bingham went to the city of Spartanburg where he expected to meet Pres. Morgan but for some cause he did not come. We were all much disappointed as all of the Elders was together and several of the Saints had come 30 miles to preaching. We met at Bro. James Russells and sang hymns until a late hour and had a good time together.

Sunday June 21, we held two meetings at Bro. James Pattersons. One at 10 AM and one at 2 PM. The time was occupied by Elder Bingham, Humphrey and Fraughton. At the meeting held at 10AM and the meeting held at 2 PM Elders Cragun, Wright and myself all the Elders spoke with great power. We had a time of rejoicing. There was about 40 persons and they all felt well paid for there coming to meeting. We also held councils meeting in the woods. June 22, helped Bro. James Patterson hoe cotton. June 23rd, did the same as yesterday. June 24, weather very cloudy and sang hymns. The 25,

---

[115] John Gandy, a Catawba, son of Lucy Quash-Marsh and a white man named Thomas Gandy.

26 & 27, visited around among the Saints. Sunday, June 28, held Sunday School and meeting at Brother James Pattersons. I dreamed that night I was honorably released to return home. I told the brethren my release wuld come in the next letter from Pres. Morgan.

July 1, I received a letter from Pres Morgan stating I was honorably released to return home. He also instructed me to select on of the Elders to preside over the SC Conferenece.

July 2nd Elder Heber Wright and I walked 10 miles to bid the Saints farewell. Staid all night bore my testimony to a number of strangers. July 4, walked 10 miles to brother James Pattersons, found several of the Saints sick.

Sunday July 5, held meeting on brother James Russells place. Elders present, R. M. Humprhey, F. A. Fraughton and Heber Wright. I occupied the time and preached my farewell sermon. I felt well and spoke an hour and twenty-five minutes. The house was well filled with people. Several had come 10 miles to meeting

July 6, packed up my things and got ready to start for home. July 7, I bid farewell to the Saints who wept like children. Bro. James Russell and James Patterson took me to Spartanburg City a distance of twelve miles. Elders R. M. Humphrey and Heber Wright went to the city to see me take the train. We put up that night at the hotel.

July 8, I took the train at 6 AM. On arriving at Chattanooga, Pres. John Morgan informed me that I would travel alone. This was a disappointment to me as I anticipated having company home. I arrived home July 13, at 6 PM. July 15, 1 went to Pres. Taylors office and reported my labors. This completed my labors as a missionary.

Signed Joseph Willey

Items of Interest while on my mission. August 1883, 1 visited the Cherokee Indians. September 26, 1883, I stood over Elder C. E. Robisons when he breathed his last. September 28th we put the coprse on the train home (got bit by a dog.) had one meeting broken up by two Baptist preachers. Had one gun pointed at me. Laid out fifteen nights. Went thirty hours without food. Walked 3,600 miles. Held one hundred and thirteen meetings. Organized one Sunday School, ordained one Priest.[116] Baptized 34, baptized and assisted in baptizing 59. Baptized the first Catawba Lamanite that ever give obedience to the Gospel in this dispensation.[117]

Baptized one preacher, blessed 10 children. Received 2 notices to leave the state. Traveled with 7 Elders as traveling companions. February the 28th, 1885, 1 was appointed President of the South

---

[116] John Alonzo Canty.
[117] James Goodwin Patterson.

Carolina Conference. Traveled in 16 counties in South and North Carolina; York, Chested Fairfield, Richland, Kershaw, Lancaster, Spartanburg, SC. In North Carolina, Greenville, Henderson, Transylvania, Jackson, Swain, Macklanburg, Union, Polk, Cleavland Counties.

Marriage Ceremony; "You each of your own free will and choice, choose each other to be companions through life and you do solumenly covenant before God and these witnesses that you will not lawyfully cohabit with any other? Do You? Salute the Bride. I pronounce you man and wife until death doth you part. And I do it by virtue and authority of the Holy Priesthood invested in me in the name of Jesus Christ, Amen.

Children blessed on my mission: Emma Patterson, Feb.29, 1884; Abby Patterson, March 9, 1884; Delvina George, April 6, 1884; Mary Susan Aydelotte, April 27, 1884; Moroni James Joseph George, Sept 6, 1885; William Thomas Sanders, March 15, 1885; Luiza H, J. Canty, March 19,1885; William David Hartness, April 12, 1885; Mary Lanier, April 12, 1885; Walter Russell, July 5, 1885.

Baptisms while on my mission in the Southern States. John Gandy, June 7, 1885; David Harris, Oct.12, 1884; George Canty, March 8, 1885; John Sanders, March 8 , 1885; Betsy Canty, March 19, 1885; Martha Sanders, March 19, 1885; Betsy Crofford, March 19, 1885; Rachel Tiros, March 19, 1885; Sarah Harris, March 21, 1885; David Harris, March 21, 1885;

Franklin Canty, March 21, 1885; Mary L. Lather April 11, 1885; Mary E. Hartness, April 11, 1885; Mary F. Hartness jr. April 12, 1885; Frances L. Hartness, April 12, 1885; Stacy A. Dover, April 12, 1885; Lora Russell, May 31, 1885; Minnie M.. Russell , Mar 31, 1885; Mary George, May 31, 1885; Theodore Russell, May 31, 1885; Sylvanna B. Gordon, May 12, 1883; Mrs. Jane Idlet, May 30, 1883; Mrs. Lucy Wats, May 11, 1883; James Henry L

Wats, Nov 11, 1883; Mrs. Mary Jane Wats, Nov 11; 1883; James Patterson, Nov 11, 1883; Taylor George, Nov 11, 1883; Mrs. Hannah Smith, Oct. 1883;

Elizabeth M.. Patterson, Oct. 1883; Nancy Wats, Dec 5, 1883; William David Wats, Oct 1883,; Evans Wats, 1883; John Jones Smith, John Alonzo Canty, Feb 26, 1884; Margaret Jane George, March 6, 1884; Miss A 1 ice Ayers, March 15, 1884; Jefferson Davis Ayers, March 15, 1884----March 9, 1884; Nancy George, March 9, 1664; Lizzie Paterson, March 9, 1884; Lula Patterson March 9, 1884; Lena Wats, March 9. 1884; Pinkney H. Head, March 16, 1884; William George, March 16, 1064; Robert Harris, March 16, 1884; Peter Harris, March 29, 1884; Margaret Harris, March 23, 1884; Nancy J. George, March 23, 1884; Minna George, March 23, 1884; Lena Wats, March 23, 1884;--- George, April 6, 1884; Elizabeth Wats, April 6, 1884; Emily George, May 11, 1884; Mitchel Ann Gordon, Sep 10, 1884; Butler Harris, Edward Harris, Ritchey Hartness.

Elder Henry Miller - SSM 1882-1884

PHOTO 16 -- ELDER HENRY MILLER

Birth date, place: 4 June 1845, Nauvoo, Hancock, Illinois
Death date: 22 January 1923
Baptism by - Thos Crooks
Father's name - John Miller -- Mother's name - Jeannett Crook

Southern States - June 1882–February 1884 - Age Called: 37

Southern States -- Set Apart: 12 June 1882 -- End Date: 20 February 1884
Priesthood office: Seventy - Quorum: 44th
Priesthood: 44th Seventies
Called From: American Fork, Utah, Utah, United States
Set apart by: Jos F Smith
Stories and Documents

Missionary Department missionary registers, 1860-1959, Vol. 1, p. 60, line 2564.
Missionary Department missionary registers, 1860-1959, Vol. 2, p. 65, line 2564.
First Presidency missionary calls and recommendations 1877-1918, CR 1 168, Church History Library..

From Troy Miller:

Here is what his biography said: "He filled a mission to the Southern States in 1882, laboring in the State of Carolina. On account of contacting the chills and fever, he was honorably released to return home after one year and nine months of faithful service."

From Mormon Enclave:

"In 1883, Mormon Elders Henry Miller and Charles E Robison met with a number of other missionaries at King's Mountain, North Carolina. It was there that the pair discerned an opportunity in York County, South Carolina to work among the Catawba tribe. They first visited the Catawba Reservation in May and held a meting at the home of a Catawba woman, Mrs. Nancy Harris Brady, where they sang the Mormon hymn, "We Thank Thee O God For a Prophet" and expounded on their Beliefs.

Journal History, May 28, 1883, Bro. D Osborn.

In January, five Latter-day Saints in the mission died of illness.

Young Women's lessons:

On June 3, 1883, Elders Henry Miller and C. E. Robinson walked out of the South Carolina forest and first greeted the Indians of the Catawba tribe. Eventually, almost the whole tribe accepted the restored gospel. The Church was less successful with the Catawba's white neighbors, however, and mobs rose up repeatedly to try to extinguish the work. The Catawbas defended the missionaries against these attacks, and the reservation became a safe refuge from which the gospel message could go forth. This small offshoot of Israel grew into an unshakable outpost of Zion.

PIONEER DROPS DEAD.

AMERICAN FORK, Jan. 24.—Henry Miller, an old resident of this place, was found by his wife Monday morning sitting dead on a sack of potatoes in the basement of his home. Apoplexy was certified as the cause of death.

Mr. Miller started out in the morning as usual to milk his cows. For this purpose he went to the basement to get some potatoes, and had apparently been sitting on a sack cutting the potatoes when the fatal attack seized him.

Mr. Miller was born in Garden Grove, Ill., June 6, 1845. He came to Utah with a pioneer company in 1851, settling in American Fork, and had been engaged in farming in this vicinity since that time.

He is survived by his wife, Caroline, and the following children: Henry Miller, Jr., Genevieve Miller Andreason, of this city, and Katie Miller Faulken of Salt Lake City.

Elder Charles Edward Robison   -   SSM 1882

PHOTO 17 -- CHARLES EDWARD ROBISON

Charles E Robinson born 2 December 1845, Nauvoo, Hancock, Illinois
Died 26 September 1883, York County, South Carolina (while on his mission)
Father - Lewis Robison   --   Mother - Clarissa M Duzett

Southern States - April 1883–September 1883 -   Age Called: 37

Southern States
Set Apart: 9 April 1883
End Date: 26 September 1883
Died In The Field: 26 September 1883
Mission type: Proselytizing
Marital Status: Married
Priesthood office: High Priest
Called From: Montpelier, Bear Lake, Idaho Territory, United States
Set apart by: Lorenzo Snow
Notes: President of the South Carolina Conference.

Missionary Department missionary registers, 1860-1959, Vol. 1, p. 60, line 2564.
Missionary Department missionary registers, 1860-1959, Vol. 2, p. 65, line 2564.
First Presidency missionary calls and recommendations 1877-1918, CR 1 168, Church History Library

Charles Edward Robison

"The sad intelligence was received of the death of Elder Charles E. Robison, which occurred at 1:15 o'clock on the morning of the 26th. Elder Robinson's home was in Montpelier, Bear Lake county, Idaho. He died near Whitaker, York county ,S.C." From the History of the Southern States Mission.

Since the death of Elder Robinson and J M Easton's help with the body are so interconnected, they are put together here.

August 1882, anti-Mormon sentiments are aroused and Reverend White directs actions. Elders Henry Miller and C. E. Robison left southeasterly to Rock Hill and to Lancaster County, but they were treated coldly by the white population and returned to Catawba.[20]

June 3, 1882, Elder Robison became sick with chills and fever in the home of Evan and Lucy Quash-Mush[21] Watts. Evan was a white man, married to a Pamunkey-Catawba woman, Lucy Quash-Mush; they had two boys together. Lucy had several grown children, including Pinkney Head's father Robert Head. Elder Robisonn died there in the presence of Elder Joseph Willey on September 25, 1882.[22]

THE MEMORY OF ELDER ROBISON.

We returned to headquarters, where we learned that Elder C. E. Robison was very sick. Elder J. M. Easton, J. J. Humpherys and myself went and assisted his companion, Elder H. Miller, to bring him to headquarters as he had been laboring among the Catawba Indians. He was beloved by all that knew him and sowed seed in his last days that since his demise has taken root. He departed this life at 10 minutes to 2 p. m., Sept. 26th, 1883.

PHOTO 18 -- NEWSPAPER CLIPPING OF   C. E. ROBISON'S DEATH

706   LATTER-DAY SAINT   BIOGRAPHICAL ENCYCLOPEDIA

ROBISON, Charles Edward, an Elder who died in the missionary field, was born Dec. 2, 1845, in Nauvoo, Hancock county, Ill., the son of Lewis Robison and Clarissa M. Durette. In the spring of 1883 he was called on a mission to the Southern States and left Salt Lake City for his field of labor April 10, 1883, having been set apart the day before by Apostle Lorenzo Snow. He labored diligently and faithfully until September, 1893, when he was taken ill with an attack of chills and fever, combined with yellow jaundice. He gradually grew worse until the 26th of the month, when he passed away near Whitaker, York county, South Carolina. He was a High Priest (Bishop of Montpelier, Bear Lake county, Idaho), and at the time of his death was president of the South Carolina conference.

SOUTHERN STATES MISSION

1883

Wednesday, September 26.   Elder Charles E. Robinson of Montpelier, Idaho, died near Whitaker, York County, South Carolina. He passed away at 1:15 A.M. on this date, having been sick for several days with chills and fever. He was also afflicted with yellow jaundice.

He had just been appointed president of the South Carolina conference, succeeding Elder Easton who was released to return home. Elder Robinson's companion, Elder Miller, and Elders Easton and Humphreys were with Elder Robinson and did all they could for him. Elder Easton will accompany the body to Utah.
                    (So. Star 1:145,153. Des. News, Oct. 3.)

PHOTO 19 -- ARTICLE FROM THE SOUTHERN STATES MISSION SITE ON DEATH OF C E ROBISON

South Carolina

DEATH OF BISHOP ROBISON.

By courtesy of Elder John Morgan, we are enabled to publish the following from a letter addressed to him by Elder B. H. Roberts, written at Chattanooga, and dated Sept. 20th.

It is our unpleasant duty to inform you of the death of Elder Charles E. Robison, of Montpelier, Bear Lake County, Idaho. He died near Whitaker, York Co., S. C., at 1.15 this morning.

The first information we had of his illness was in a letter from Elder Davidson, bearing date 21st of Sept., and received here on the 23d. The information was to the effect that Elder Robison was low with the chills and fever, and also had the yellow jaundice. His companion, Elder Miller, had sent for Brother Easton to come and assist him with Brother Robison, as he was worn out with watching. Elders Easton, Miller and Humphries went down to where he was.

Our next information was received to-day, and that was that he had died as above stated. A telegram was sent by Elder Easton on the 24th inst., stating the condition of Brother Robison, but it was not received until the message was that announced his death.

We immediately telegraphed Prest. Taylor of the sad occurrence. We also telegraphed President Wm. Budge, at Paris, Bear Lake County, Idaho, and asked him to inform the family, as the place where they reside has no telegraph office.

We have instructed Elder Easton to use all diligence to preserve the body, and given directions in relation to dressing it. We have expressed him a metallic coffin, and he will bring the body to Chattanooga and from here will accompany it on through to Utah.

Brother Robison was a High Priest, and started on his mission with the company that left Salt Lake on the 10th of April last. He was faithful and energetic in the discharge of his duties as Traveling Elder in this mission, and had just been appointed President of the South Carolina Conference, succeeding Elder Easton, who had been honorably released to return home.

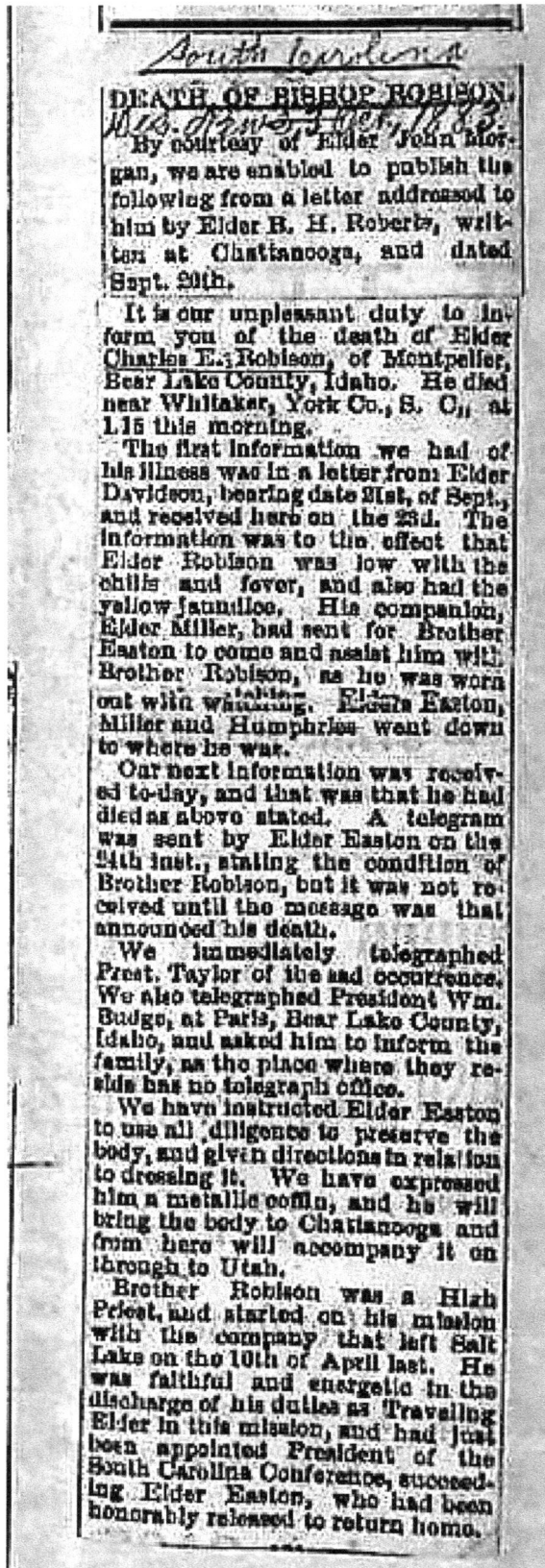

PHOTO 20 NEWSPAPER ARTICLE OF C E ROBISON'S DEATH

Elder Brigham Henry Roberts - SSM 1880-1884

PHOTO 21   BRIGHAM HENRY ROBERTS

Birth date, place - 13 March 1857, Warrington, Lancashire, England
Death date -- 27 September 1933
Baptism date - March 1867   --   Baptism by -- Seth Dustin
Father's name -- Benjamin Roberts   --   Mother's name - Ann Everington

Southern States - April 1880–May 1882 - Age Called: 23
United States
Set Apart: 9 April 1880 -- End Date: 24 May 1882
Mission type: Proselytizing
Marital Status: Married
Priesthood office: Seventy -- Quorum: 19th
Called From: Warrington, Lancashire, England, United States
Set apart by: C C Rich
Notes: Alternate residence: Centerville, Davis, Utah, United States

Southern States -- March 1883–1884 - Age Called: 26
Set Apart: 29 March 1883 -- End Date: 1884
Mission type: Proselytizing
Marital Status: Married
Priesthood office: Seventy - Quorum: 19th
Called From: Centerville, Davis, Utah, United States
Set apart by: John Taylor

Notes: He was appointed assistant mission president 29 March 1883.

Missionary Department missionary registers, 1860-1959, vol. 1, p. 49, line 2083
Missionary Department missionary registers, 1860-1959, vol. 2, p. 53, line 2083
Missionary Department missionary registers, 1860-1959, vol. 1, p. 64, line 2740
Missionary Department missionary registers, 1860-1959, vol. 2, p. 69, line 2083.
Missionary Department missionary registers, 1860-1959, vol. 1, p. 104, line 3
Missionary Department missionary registers, 1860-1959, vol. 2, p. 111, line 3
Missionary Department missionary registers, 1860-1959, vol. 5, p. 68, line 233
First Presidency missionary calls and recommendations, 1877-1918, Church History Library.

Letter dated 30 March 1880 accepting a mission call to the United States.
First Presidency missionary calls and recommendations, 1877-1918, Church History Library.
Letter dated 18 February 1883 recommending him for missionary service.
First Presidency missionary calls and recommendations, 1877-1918, Church History Library.
Letter dated 18 February 1883 accepting a mission call to the Southern States Mission.
Southern States Mission history, 1832-1964, Church History Library.
See the index in volume 1 for entries on his service.
Eastern States Mission history, 1830-1977, Church History Library.
See the index in volume 1 for entries on his service.
Andrew Jenson, "Roberts, Brigham Henry," Latter-day Saint Biographical Encyclopedia, vol. 1 (Salt Lake City: Andrew Jenson History Company, 1901), 205-06.

PHOTO 22 -- PRESIDENT ROBERTS IN DISGUISE --- PORTRAIT OF BRIGHAM H. ROBERTS TAKEN IN NASHVILLE, TENNESSEE, CIRCA 1884. HE WORE THIS DISGUISE TO RETRIEVE THE BODIES OF MISSIONARIES WILLIAM S. BERRY AND JOHN H. GIBBS WHO WERE KILLED BY A MOB IN LEWIS COUNTY, TENNESSEE. CHL PH 1300.

Elder W C (Willard Cushing) Burton -- SSM 1881-1882

PHOTO 23   W C (WILLARD CUSHING) BURTON

Birth date, place - 1 December 1856, Salt Lake City, Utah, United States
Death date - 12 June 1949
Baptism date - 7 February 1866 -- Baptism by - R T Burton
Father's name - R T Burton --- Mother's name - Susan E McBride
Family Search logo

Southern States - January 1881–December 1882 - Age Called: 24
Southern States
Set Apart: 21 January 1881 -- End Date: 25 December 1882
Priesthood office: Seventy - Quorum: 32nd -- Priesthood: 32nd 70s
Called From: Salt Lake City, Salt Lake, Utah, United States
Set apart by: J H Smith

Missionary Department missionary registers, 1860-1959, Vol. 1, p. 53, line 2281.
Missionary Department missionary registers, 1860-1959, Vol. 2, p. 58, line 2281.

BURTON, Willard Cushing a home missionary in the Salt Lake Stake a member of the 2nd Quorum of Seventies and of the Fifteenth Ward Salt Lake City is a son of Bishop Robert T Burton and Susan E McBride and was born in Salt Lake City Utah Dec 1 1856 was baptized Nov 7 1866 by his father and ordained to the Priesthood about nine years later Jan 6 1881 he married Mary Jane Gardner and 18 days later Jan 24th started on a mission to the Southern States agreeable to a call from the authorities of the Church He was appointed to labor in the State of South Carolina where he baptized Edward M Green and wife Jan 27 1882 He and his missionary companion Elder E Easton of Beaver were the first Elders to introduce the fullness of the Gospel in that State and after laboring successfully for several months they had the satisfaction of organizing a branch of the Church known as the Kings Mountain Branch York County appointing EM Green to preside over the same after first having ordained him to the office of an Elder When the South Carolina Conference subsequently was organized Elder Burton was appointed to preside over the same continuing to act in that position until he was released to return home in December 1882 Also at home Elder Burton has ever been an active member of the Church and has filled various positions of honor and responsibility.

PHOTO 24 HEADSTONE FOR WILLARD CUSHING BURTON 1856-1949

Elder Angus McKay - SSM 1882-

PHOTO 25 -- ANGUS MCKAY

Birth date, place - 3 June 1838, Farr, Sutherland, Scotland
Death date - 13 January 1926
Baptism date - 19 August 1860   --   Baptism by - William McKay
Father's name - William McKay - Mother's name - Grace Gunn

Southern States - December 1882–Unknown   --   Age Called: 44
Southern States
Set Apart: 15 December 1882
Priesthood office: Seventy -- Quorum: 75th - Priesthood: 75th Seventies
Called From: Huntsville, Weber, Utah, United States
Set apart by: W Woodruff

The third mission call came in 1882 for him to go to the Southern States. The fourth call came while he was still in the Southern States to go to the Scottish mission without coming home, family or loved ones.

Angus McKay
Missionary Department missionary registers, 1860-1959, Vol. 1, p. 70, line 2995.
Missionary Department missionary registers, 1860-1959, Vol. 2, p. 76, line 2995.
First Presidency missionary calls and recommendations 1877-1918, CR 1 168, Church History Library.
Southern States Mission manuscript history and historical reports, 1832-1978: LR 8557 2, Church History Library.
        Southern States Mission index
Southern States Mission manuscript history and historical reports, 1832-1978: LR 8557 2, Church History Library.
        November 13, 1883 departure for Scotland

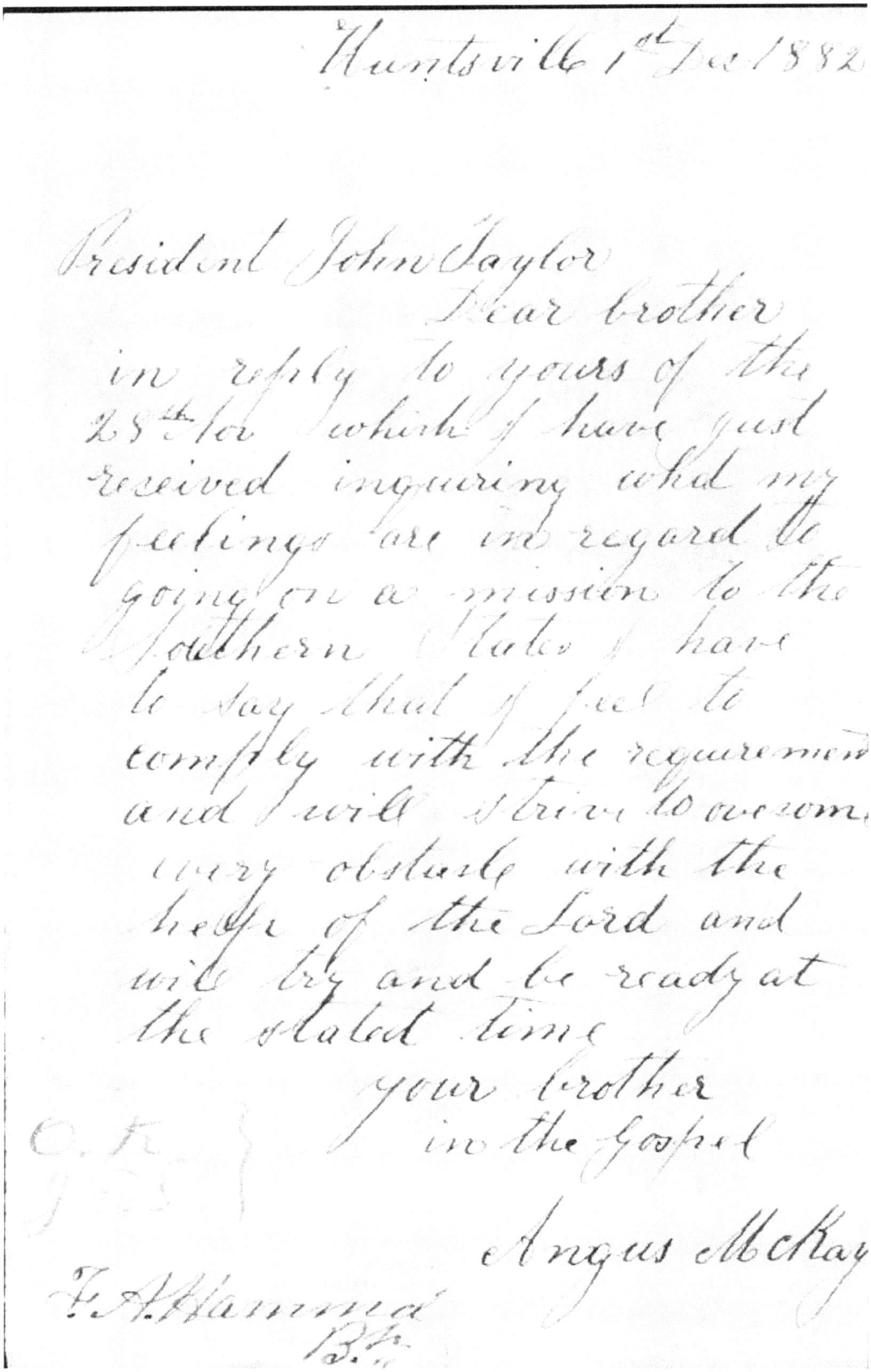

Huntsville 1st Dec 1882

President John Taylor

Dear brother

in reply to yours of the 25th Nov which I have just received inquiring what my feelings are in regard to going on a mission to the Southern States I have to say that I feel to comply with the requirements and will strive to overcome every obstacle with the help of the Lord and will try and be ready at the stated time

your brother
in the Gospel

Angus McKay

O.K.

F A Hammond
B.P.

PHOTO 26 -- ANGUS MCKAY'S LETTER TO THE FRIST PRESIDENT OF THE LDS CHURCH EXCEPTING HIS MISSION CALL

Elder John Miller Easton -- SSM 1881-1883

We have found no picture of him so far.

PHOTO 27 HEADSTONE FOR JOHN MILLER EASTON 1850-1905

John Miller Easton was born 16 Dec 1850 in Grovie, St. Louis, Missouri. He married Elizabeth Hearst or Hurst and had a small family. He died 10 Jan 1905 in Greenville, Beaver, Utah.

Baptism date - 9 June 1861 -- Baptism by - Lester J Herrick
Father's name - John Easton -- Mother's name - Margaret Fife

Southern States -- October 1881–October 1883 -- Age Called: 30

Southern States
Set Apart: 24 October 1881 -- End Date: 6 October 1883
Served with companion: Joseph Willey
Priesthood office: High Priest
Called From: Greenville, Beaver, Utah, United States
Set apart by: W Woodruff

Missionary Department missionary registers, 1860-1959, Vol. 1, p. 57, line 2456.
First Presidency missionary calls and recommendations 1877-1918, CR 1 168, Church History Library.

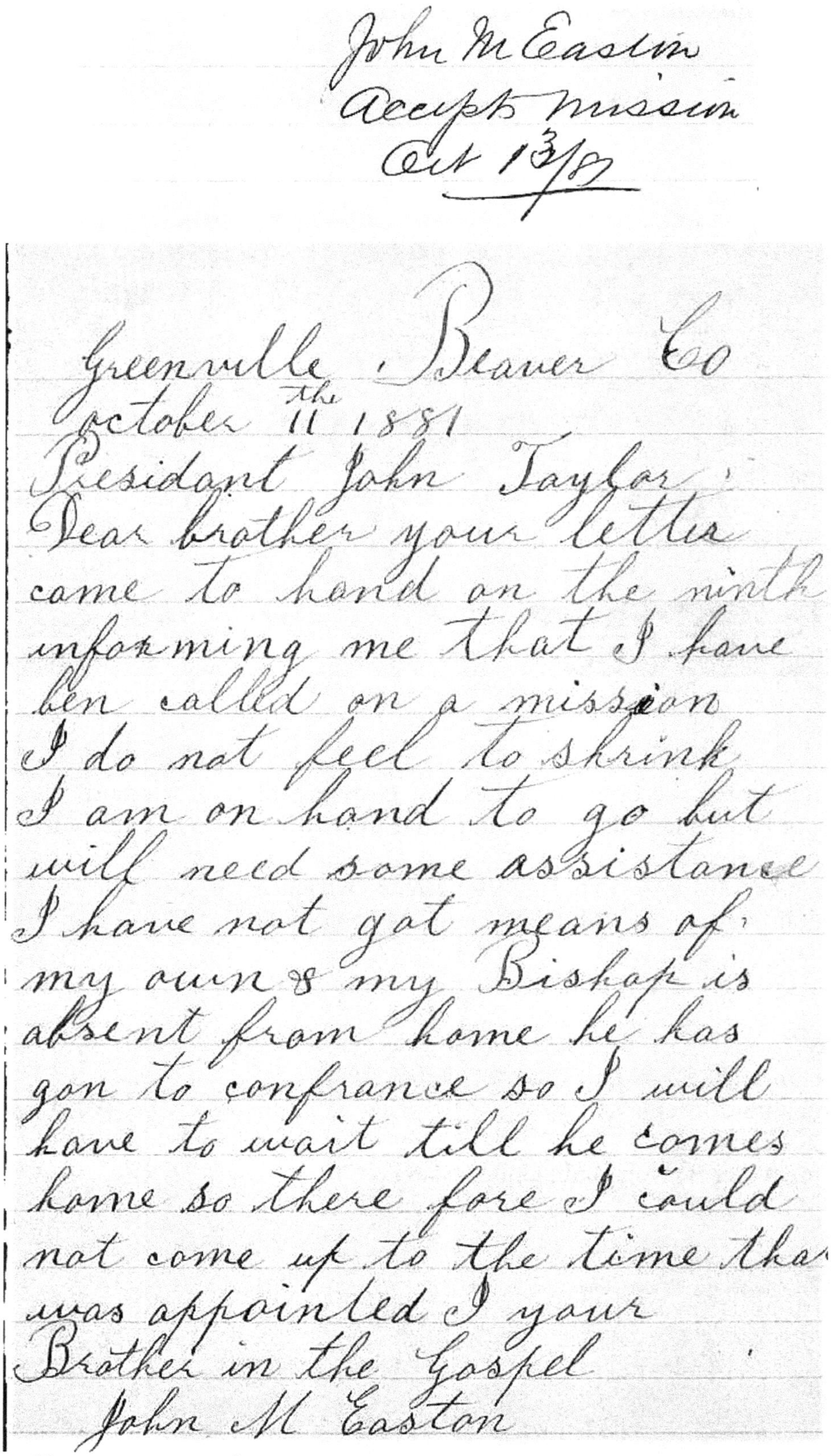

John M Easton
Accepts mission
Oct 13/81

Greenville, Beaver Co
October 11th 1881
Presidant John Taylor
Dear brother your letter
came to hand on the ninth
informing me that I have
ben called on a mission
I do not feel to shrink
I am on hand to go but
will need some assistanse
I have not got means of
my own & my Bishop is
absent from home he has
gon to confrance so I will
have to wait till he comes
home so there fore I could
not come up to the time that
was appointed I your
Brother in the Gospel
John M Easton

PHOTO 28 -- JOHN M EASTON'S LETTER OF MISSION ACCEPTANCE TO FIRST PRESIDENT JOHN TAYLOR

1883

Southern States Mission.

Monday, Sept. 10. Elder John M. Easton (of Greenville, *Beaver Co., Utah*), was released from his missionary labors in the South Carolina conference to return to his home. The "Deseret Evening News" of Oct. 9, 1883, noted his return as follows:

From the Southern States.—Elder John M. Easton, who left here on a mission to the Southern States, October 25th, 1881, arrived back on the evening of the 6th inst. He accompanied the body of Elder Charles E. Robinson, who died in York County, South Carolina, on the 26th of last September, from Whittaker station in that State to Montpelier, Idaho, where the family of the deceased reside. He reached there on the evening of the 3rd inst., and after delivering his charge into proper hands came down to the city in time to attend the closing part of Conference. While on his mission he labored in North and South Carolina, part of the time with Elder W. C. Burton, with whom he went soon after his arrival there, to open up a new field of labor in Burk County, South Carolina. He also labored in York and Cleveland Counties. During his mission 43 were added to the Church in that field, 19 of whom he baptized himself and assisted in initiating 18 others. He enjoyed his labors and had good health, with the exception of about ten months in 1882, when he suffered considerably with chills and fever.

(Des. News 32: 601)

PHOTO 29 -- ELDER JOHN M EASTON'S RELEASE FROM HIS MISSION CALL

91

Southern States Mission.

1883

Sunday, July 15. On this and the two preceding days a conference of the South Carolina conference was held on the premises
of W. N. Gordon, King's Mountain, York county, South Carolina,
the following account of which was published in the "Deseret
Evening News" of July 27, 1883:   (Des. News 32: 450)

(See Journal History of July 15, 1883)

Conference convened on Friday, 10 a.m. Missionaries present, B. H.
Roberts of the Presidency of the Southern States Mission. President of the
conference, John M. Easton and Elders Henry Miller, Angus McKay, John M. Davidson, Charles E. Robison, Joseph Willey. After the usual opening exercises,
Prest. Easton spoke of the object of our Conference, made a report of his labors
in the field and dwelt for some time on the order of the Kingdom of God.

Elder Robison reported his labors among the Catawba Indians expressed his
desire to do his duty and trust in the Lord, and testified to the truth of the
Gospel. Elder Miller related some of his experience in introducing the Gospel
among strangers, and felt to be humble that he might have the Spirit of the
Lord to be with him, to assist him in his labors.

At 2 p.m. Elder Davidson spoke of the good feeling among the Saints where he
labored, and exhorted them to faithfulness; referred to the ordinances of the
Gospel and our duty to obey them.

Elder Willey testified to the truth of the Gospel and desired to put his
trust in the Lord, so that he might be successful in delivering the gospel message
to those that are seeking after truth.

President B. H. Roberts read Jere. 31st chapter and 10th verse. Spoke of
the dispersion of Israel and referred to many passages to prove that Israel will
be gathered in the last days.

Saturday speakers were Elder Angus McKay, John M. Easton, and Pres. Roberts.
On Sunday Elder Davidson, Elder Miller, and President Roberts were the speakers.

Priesthood meetings were held every morning during the conference.
(Southern Star 1.145.)

Excerpts from Joseph Willey Journals

The next Sunday thar was a large revival or Protracted[6] meeting nigroes & whites. We went and the preacher took for his text beware of false Prophets. He told the people that false prophets was among them right then. He give us a tongue-lashing. We prayed in our hearts that he mint (might) be confounded and he was for two men a few rows began to fight. The people all left the preacher standing alone. Then two women commenced to fight and the meeting was broke up. Thar (there) we see the hand of God manifested in our behalf. We went to see the chief again; the chief's name I forgot to mention his name is Nymrod Jorret Smith.[7] He told us to come the following Sunday and he would have all the Indians preachers thar which was very incurging to us. So when Sunday came we went expecting to meet them. But when we got thar the Chief was sick a bed it seamed as if the Devil was to work hedging up our way so we returned back to our boarding place. With (out) any meetings we went to in a few days and told the chief we was going to leave he said he wanted us to leave the Book of Mormon with him. The Voice of Warning he said he would read them and ask God to inlighten his mind that he mint no wether they was true or not. He said he was going to Washington soon and he wished a letter of interduction to our delagate John T. Cane. He said he wished to corespond with us. Our expenses was so tight we was oblige to return to headquarters, so the following Tuesday we started. We averaged 20 miles a day. One night was obliged to travel all night. We arrived to head quarters in good health. To our suprise, we found our President J. M. Easton had received his release to return home on the following Tuesday. and heard that one of the Elders, Bro. Robison was sick. The President appointed me to go with a new elder who had just come out to go see Bro. Robison and fetch him to headquarters (where) the saints could

---

[6] In the missionary diary of Nathaniel Alvin Decker, I found the same name. Evidently, this was a denomination in the South, because his mission was to Florida and Georgia, around 1899.

[7] Nimrod Jerrett Smith, one of two of the most outstanding chiefs in the Eastern Cherokee Nation, source, Milling, Chapman, Red Carolinians, Chapel Hill, University of N.C. Press, 1940 page 372.

take care of him.   Elder Easton, Elder /??   and myself started Friday the 21st   Got to Mr.

Watses [8] 8 AM.   We walked 35 miles.   We found Brother Robison very sick.   He was very

glad to see us.   We anointed him with oil and administered to him.   Pres Easton and myself set

up with him till twelve o'clock.   He was in much pain-slept one hour.   The next day we took

him to Rock Hill to Br Smiths.   Got a light wagon and took him to the depot at three fifteen we

took the train.   It created quite an excitement at the station Elder Miller and myself got off at

Fort Mills 8 miles from Rock Hill.   Staid to Sister Bunches. [9]

The next morning started to head quarters walked 2S miles found Br. Robison very low.   He

was in great pain all day.   He said he wanted to go home.   He asked us if would get a team and

waggon and take him to the depot.   Elder Easton went to the station and telegraphed to President

B. H. Roberts to know what t doe about taking him home.   He waited but could not git any

answer to his dispatch.

25th, he was in great pain all-day and gradualy sinking.   He had the hickups and was still

pleading for us to take him home.   Brother Miller and Mckay set up with him the first part of the

night.   We annointed and administered to him and prayed for him by day and by night but his

time had come.   At twelve o'clock Brother Davidson and myself got up.   He had took a change

for the worse to all apperence.   They pain had left him, he was dieing.   Bro. Davidson went over

to Bro. Moses Gordons to wake up the elders.   He died at ten minutes to two on the 26th.   He died

without a struggle.

Elder Easton sent a telegram to Pres. B. H. Roberts of his death, also for a coffin and burial

clothing.   His coffin came on the three am train.   We took him to the depot on 28 September.

---

[8] The home of Evan and Lucy Quash-Marsh Watts.
[9] Delphi Quash-Mush-Marsh Bunch, daughter of John and Betsy Scott-Quash Mush, wife of Howard Bunch.

Elder Lamoni Call - SSM 1883-1885

PHOTO 30   LAMONI CALL

Birth date, place - 25 January 1865, East Bountiful, Davis, Utah
Death date - 26 October 1933
Baptism date - 4 June 1876   --   Baptism by - W W Willey
Father's name - Anson Vasco Call   --   Mother's name - Charlotte Holbrook

Southern States - April 1883–November 1885 - Age Called: 18
Southern States
Set Apart: 9 April 1883 - End Date: 23 November 1885
Priesthood office: Elder
Called From: East Bountiful, Davis, Utah, United States
Set apart by: E Snow

Missionary Department missionary registers, 1860-1959, Vol. 2, p. 70, line 2756.
Missionary Department missionary registers, 1860-1959, Vol. 1, p. 65, line 2766.
First Presidency missionary calls and recommendations 1877-1918, CR 1 168, Church History Library.

Bountiful,
Apr. 2 1883
Pres. Jos. F. Smith,
Dear Bro.
Your letter
of appointment came
duly to hand. I am
thankful to be counted
worthy to be an ambas-
sador of the Truth.
Your Respectfully
Lamoni Bell,

LAMONI CALL

Lamoni Call, 68, co-founder of the Davis County Clipper, merchant watchmaker and builder of the Bountiful opera house, died at his residence 844 South, Second East. Salt Lake City yesterday morning, of cancer of the stomach. He had been ailing for several months but worked about as hard as usual up to about ten days or two weeks before he died. For a number of years he had lived at 409 First avenue and had moved into his new home six weeks ago. He bought this place last spring and worked on it all summer remodeling and improving the same. He had done his own mason work, plumbing, electrical work, painting etc. in all of which lines he was proficient. He was very industrious and studious all his life. He never loafed nor stood on the street corner; he was always learning to do something. He started doing carpenter work when he was a boy and whenever anything was needed in that line he could do it. He also had a considerable knowledge of pharmacy.

While he had worked at these various occupations during his life he was mostly engaged in printing in his latter years.

He had some military training and served as captain of the Militia.

It was not his privilege to attend a university but he had as good a common school education as the average boy of his day. He, however, did not quit studying when he quit school but went on like Abraham Lincoln until he was quite a philosopher and writer being the author of a number of books. He was very much interested in religion and his writings mostly along that line. Being a printer, he could get out small books at very little cost except his own labor.

He was so well informed that he could converse with almost any one.

Mr. Call was born Jan. 25, 1865, in Bountiful, the son of the Vasco and Charlotte Holbrook Call. His father died on the plains while going back after emigrants as they used to do in those days. Lamoni was but a small boy then and his mother died too, so his uncle and aunt, Lamoni and Kate Holbrook, reared him. His uncle was the first mayor of Bountiful.

In 1882, he married Annie L. Barlow and immediately left on a mission to the southern states where he labored two years.

On his return he engaged in the store business and a few years later started printing.

His first wife died in 1918. Sept. 16, 1929, he married Carrie Gardner Buys.

Surviving are his widow; the following sons and daughters: Mrs Annie C. Carr, Bountiful; Mrs. Leonie L. Miller of Farmington; Mrs. Delila D. Causey and Mrs. Ardith Kreis of Lynwood, Cal.; L. B. and Emerson Call of California and La Mar W. Call of Salt Lake. Three sisters, Vinnie Nelson of Bountiful; Mary Muir of Logan and Hannah Hatch of Rigby and Anson V. and Joseph Call of Afton. Wyo. together with 16 grandchildren survive.

Funeral services will be held in the Bountiful tabernacle, Sunday, at 12:30 p. m. with burial in the Bountiful cemetery.

Friends may call at the home of his daughter, Mrs. Willard G. Carr (Putnam place 5th So. and Main) Saturday evening and Sunday morning.

Elder Wiley Gidoni Cragun   -   SSM 1883-1886

PHOTO 31   ELDER WILEY GIDONI CRAGUN

Birth date, place - 6 October 1860, North Ogden, Weber, Utah Territory
Death date - 14 January 1922
Baptism date - 1868   --   Baptism by - Thos Brown
Father's name - Simeon Cragun   --   Mother's name - Susan Mower

Southern States - October 1883–February 1886 - Age Called: 23

Southern States
Set Apart: 8 October 1883   -   End Date: 22 February 1886
Priesthood office: Seventy
Called From: Pleasant View, Weber, Utah, United States
Set apart by: Geo Teasdale

Missionary Department missionary registers, 1860-1959, Vol. 1, p. 68, line 2895.
Missionary Department missionary registers, 1860-1959, Vol. 2, p. 73, line 2895.
First Presidency missionary calls and recommendations 1877-1918: CR 1 168, Church History Library

Wiley Gidoni Cragun was born 6 Oct 1860 in Pleasant View, Utah. He married Joanna Dyan Seaman on 21 December 1894 and died on 14 Jan 1922 in Ogden Utah. He graduated from Normal school of Deseret in 1880, and then returned to graduate from the school of mathematics two years later. He was a school teacher, and during vacation was engaged in shipping Utah products for 11 years. In 1886, he and his brother Wilson E. Cragun established the fruit and produce firm of Cragun Brothers, and soon after shipped the first car-load of peaches that left the state of Utah. He was a director of the Utah State Fair for 14 years.

> Bro. Geo. Reynolds.
>
> Pleasant View, April 7. 04
>
> Salt Lake City, Utah.
>
> Dear Bro:
>
> I take great pleasure in recommending Bro. Wiley G. Cragun to do Missionary work. He is a capable good faithful worker as as such I fell he will ever be working for the advancement of the cause of Truth,
>
> C. A. Hickenlooper Bp/th

PHOTO 32   HEADSTONE FOR WILEY G CRAGUN   1860-1922

Returned Missionaries Report their Labors.

Of the eleven missionaries who returned from the Southern States on Monday evening we have had calls from quite a number, who, agreeably with the usual custom, have reported their labors while abroad upon this their first mission. In the case of most of them it was their first absence from the Territory, too, having been born and reared in Utah. As a whole they were a fine looking and intelligent lot of young men and worthy representatives of the Church of which they are me members and the doctrines they were sent forth to expound

Elder Wiley G Cragun,

Whose home is in Pleasant View, Weber Co., left here Oct. 16, 1883, and had South Carolina assigned him as a field of labor, where he remained during nearly the whole of his absence, only going into North Carolina a few times. Preminent among his interesting experience stands the mobbing to which he was subjected, while he and Elder Fraughton were together among the Catawba Indians, he having been there sometime and awakened considerable interest in the gospel besides baptizing quite a number; they were waited upon by the deputation of seven men with a paper signed by 70 names, warning them to leave the State. The bearers of this document claimed to be friendly, but said they would not be responsible for the consequences if the warning was not heeded. They charged the Elders with preaching and practicing polygamy among the Indians. This was not only denied by the Indians themselves; but it was shown that these seven men were of the kind who usually heap reproaches upon the "Mormons," for they themselves had been living in adultery with Indian women. A few days subsequently – on the night of the 25th of May, 1885 -- the house at which they were staying was suddenly surrounded by a mob and their host, on discovering the situation, yelled to the Elders to run. Elder Cragun, who had taken off his shoes to retire to bed, ran for the woods, and on the way a volley was fired at him. A bullet grazed his forehead, merely cutting through the skin, and knocking him down, and as he arose part of a load of shot struck him on the jaw and came out underneath his chin. None of the other shots touched him, although their effects were afterwards visible upon the trees and shrubbery all about where he was. He succeeded in hiding in the timber and remaining there until Elder Fraughton, who was taken by the mob into the woods and given forty lashes with green hickory withes, returned and found him. They remained there the rest of the night, too, for the family were afraid to have them return to the house. They baptized two persons the next morning, and continued so to do afterwards, though there subsequent visits to the place were made more secretly. The man who led the mob in that instance was an old KuKlax leader, and the others – 25 in all – were much of the same class. The wound Brother Cragun received in his chin has troubled him more or less ever since, not having been properly treated when it was first received.

While in Greenville County he and his companion held a meeting one night in a private house where they were strangers, and without making known to what Church they belonged. The audience was delighted and a wealthy man immediately invited them to hold forth the next evening at his house.

They did so, but by this time they had become known. However, many were still anxious to hear more and petitioned for the use of the church for them to preach in. Permission was granted, but before evening arrived a Baptist preacher by the name of Bowers, a noted moonshiner, had collected a mob and threatened if they preached it should be at their peril, and so they had to seek lodgings in the woods that night.

Brother Cragun related a number of other interesting incidents connected with his labors, illustrating the friendship and kindness of which he was the recipient, as well as persecution received, but we have not space to record them.

One case of healing, among a number related, however, we will mention. A lady – a member of the Church – had one side of her body paralyzed and was also afflicted with a very painful swelling under her arm. The Elders administered to her in the evening and the next morning she arose wholly restored to health.

From the Missionary Journal of Joseph Willey, part of the account is given.

"They stayed on and on the 25th night of May there was 32 men came on the elders at the house of Mr. Alexander Tims, at about 10 o'clock. Came running up to the house well armed. Elder Cragun had taken off his shoes to retire to bed when he heard the noise. Someone said run and Elder Cragun made his escape out of the north door and run for the woods which was of about 30 yards and while on his way to the woods there was about 25 or 30 shots fired at him one shot just grazed him on the chin and Elder Fraughton had no chance to get out and the mobs came in and took and led him away and gave him 50 lashes with hickory switches and turned him loose charging him to leave the country. The next day he came back to our house then we all looked for Elder Cragun for about two hours before we found him, both stayed in the woods overnight and next morning came to the house and got breakfast. Then the elders did not walk openly for some time."

From the Southern Star 1883-1884

On the 25th of this month Elders Wiley Cragun and F.A. Fraughton were stopping all night near the borders of the Catawba Indian reservation. At night an armed mob came to the house and demanded all the brethren to come out. Elder Cragun made his escape by the back door amid a shower of bullets, one of which struck him on the forehead, another in his face, neither inflicting a serious wound.

Elder Fraughton did not escape so well. He was caught by the mobocrats and given forty severe lashes. Among those prominent in the mob were John Allen, Fayette Crooks and Robert Cornwall."

1885—Apostle Franklin D. Richards returned from a trip to the east, during which he visited Pueblo, Independence, Richmond and Carthage, Mo., Nauvoo, Ill., and other places known in Mormon history. Peter Nebeker died at Willard, Box Elder county, Utah. Elders Wiley G. Cragun and Franklin A. Fraughton were mobbed in South Carolina; Fraughton received a whipping, and Cragun was shot in the chin.

1886—Thomas Porcher and John W.

PHOTO 33   ARTICLE ON ELDER WILEY G CRAGUN

Elder Richard Miles Humphrey --   SSM 1884-1885

PHOTO 34   RICHARD MILES HUMPHREYS

Birth date, place - 22 October 1848, Chattooga, Georgia, United States
Death date - 17 August 1925
Baptism date - 3 May 1868 --   Baptism by - J E Murphy
Father's name - John Humphrey -   Mother's name - Agnes Elmina Murphy

Southern States - April 1884–December 1885 -- Age Called: 35
Southern States
Set Apart: 7 April 1884 - Arrived At Home: 16 December 1885
Mission type: Proselytizing
Marital Status: Plurally Married
Priesthood office: Seventy
Called From: Salina, Sevier, Utah, United States
Set apart by: B Young

Missionary Department missionary registers, 1860-1959, Vol. 1, p. 70, line 2995.
Missionary Department missionary registers, 1860-1959, Vol. 2, p. 76, line 2995.
First Presidency missionary calls and recommendations 1877-1918, CR 1 168, Church History Library.

Richard Miles Humphreys was born 22 Oct 1848 in Rome, Georgia. He married Nancy Pruella Murphy and he died 17 Aug 1925 in Layton, Utah and is buried Salina, Sevier, Utah cemetery.

Taken from the mission Journal of Elder Joseph Willey.

RM was involved when Elder Charles E Robison died, and his subsequent removal from SC to Idaho. He helped administer to him and sat with him. He was also included in the violence in the Mission. The following is a petition they received:

On August 23, 1884 " Notice, Messrs Willey, Humphreys, Humphrey, We the peaceable citizens of this surround country have been pained to learn that you three men profession to be Mormon missionaries have taken up your quarters with an ignorant class of our people and are denonating doctrins among them calculated to disorganize human society and adverse to the peace and wellbeing of our people and country, to the laws and dignity of the State. Now therefore these presents are to civily and peaceable request and command you to vacate the State and to return no more among us and you are hereby allowed five days to obey this order to peaceable absent yourselves from the State without hurt or molestation, but if you are found within the limits of the State, after the expiration of that time you may charge consequences to disobedience to this order. We are going to be rid of you." Capt. of the mob, Wm Kithcart, Wm Carethers, Charles Harrison, Paul Harrison, Alexander Millens, Clarence Cotter. The names of the rest of the mob we did not get."

Elder John James Humpherys -- SSM 1883-1884

PHOTO 35   JOHN JAMES HUMPHERYS

Birth date, place - 31 October 1836, Mansfield, Nottinghamshire, England
Death date - 28 January 1921
Baptism date - 2 January 1852 -- Baptism by - Thomas Humpherys
Father's name - Thomas Humpherys -- Mother's name - Mary Sudbury

Southern States - September 1883–October 1884 -- Age Called: 46
South Carolina Conference
Set Apart: 3 September 1883 - Arrived In Field: 26 September 1883
Departed From Field: 30 October 1884
Mission type: Proselytizing
Marital Status: Plurally Married
Priesthood office: Seventy -- Quorum: 15th
Called From: Paris, Bear Lake, Idaho, United States
Set apart by: Heber J Grant

Notes: Transferred to the British mission October 30, 1884.

British - November 1884–August 1885 -- Age Called: 48
Manchester and Nottingham Conferences
Arrived In Field: 25 November 1884
Released: 3 August 1885
Departed From Field: 29 August 1885

Mission type: Proselytizing
Marital Status: Plurally Married
Priesthood office: Seventy   --   Quorum: 15th
Called From: Southern States Mission
Set apart by: Heber J Grant

Missionary Department missionary registers, 1860-1959, Vol. 1, p. 67, line 2883.
Missionary Department missionary registers, 1860-1959, Vol. 2, p. 73, line 2883.
Missionary reports, 1831-1900: MS 6104, Church History Library.
First Presidency missionary calls and recommendations, 1877-1918, Church History Library.
Southern States Mission history 1832-1964: LR 8557 2, Church History Library.

Elder Willard Eugene Bingham   --   SSM 1883-1886

PHOTO 36   WILLARD EUGENE BINGHAM

Birth date, place - 3 October 1856, Ogden, Weber, Utah Territory
Death date - 13 December 1918
Baptism date - April 1868 -- Baptism by - Jos Mulener
Father's name - Willard Bingham -- Mother's name - Amanda M Snow

Southern States -- October 1883–February 1886 -- Age Called: 27
Catawba reservation in York County, South Carolina
Set Apart: 15 October 1883 - End Date: 22 February 1886
Priesthood office: Seventy
Called From: Weber, Utah, United States -- Set apart by: H J Grant

> Missionary Department missionary registers, 1860-1959, Vol. 1, p. 69, line 2940.
> Missionary Department missionary registers, 1860-1959, Vol. 2, p. 74, line 230
> Southern States Mission history, 1832-1964: LR 8557 2, Church History Library.
> Southern States Mission history, 1832-1964: LR 8557 2, Church History Library.
> February 18, 1886 release and summary of service

May 31 1885
Elder W E Bingham was called to succeed Joseph Willey as President of the Southern Conference on July 6 1885 when Willey was released honorably to return to his home in Bountiful, Utah. Bingham and Cragun, under the protection of the Catawbas, they organized the Catawba Nation Branch on August 2, 1885.

WM. E. BINGHAM DIES AT HOSPITAL

Willard E. Bingham, 62 years of age, one of the old and respected residents of the county, died at 1

o'clock this morning at the Dee hospital of stomach trouble, after an illness of three months.

Mr. Bingham was born in Ogden October 3, 1856, the son of Willard and Amanda Bingham. He was a member of the high priest's quorum of the North Weber stake and served 16 years under Bishop Rackman of Wilson Lane; was a superintendent of the Sunday school and a leader in the Y. M. M. I. A. and a ward teacher of ability.

In 1880 he served his church on a mission to the <u>Southern States</u> and his death terminates a married life of forty years. He is survived by his widow and the following children:

Mrs. Mary E. Holmes, Eugene Bingham, Mrs. Edward Anderson, Adelbert W. Chas. J., Wm. S., and the Misses Duella, Luella, and John H., and Joseph H. Bingham, in addition to 18 grandchildren, four brothers, and ten sisters.

The remains are being cared for at the Larkin establishment and funeral announcement will be made later.

<u>The Ogden standard December 13, 1918</u>

<u>Early Days in Ogden   20 years ago</u>

Wilard E. Bingham, 62, died at the Dee hospital December 11. He was born in Ogden in 1856 and had resided in the city practically all his life.

Ogden Standard Examiner December 19, 1938

Returned Missionaries Report their Labors.

Of the eleven missionaries who returned from the Southern States on monday evening we have had calls from quite a number, who, agreeably with the usual custom, have reported their labors while abroad upon this their first mission. In the case of most of them it was their first absence from the Territory, too, having been born and reared in Utah. As a whole they were a fine looking and intelligent lot of young men and worthy representatives of the Church of which they are me members and the doctrines they were sent forth to expound

Elder Willard E Bingham

A resident of Willson Ward, Weber County, started upon his mission October 16, 1883, and during his absence labored almost exclusively in South Carolina, occasionally going over the border into North Carolina. When he went into this region it contained only one small branch of the Church, but since then two others have been established in York and Spartensburg counties, and during the present winter a new field has also been opened up in Oconee county, so that seven Elders now find employment in South Carolina in extending a knowledge of the Gospel among those who are strangers to it and encouraging those who have accepted of it. He labored considerably among the Catawba Indians, a small colony of whom have almost universally embraced the Gospel, and are making encouraging progress in conforming to its requirements as well as in the acquirement of general knowledge. There are now two good Sunday schools established among them by the Elders and well attended, and there branch organization is in good working order. Two of the young men of this tribe who had been ordained to the office of Priests were lately sent among the tribe of Cherokees living in the same State, and who number some 3,000, to introduce the Gospel among them, but were unable to accomplish much owing to the opposition of the sectanian Preachers among them.

Elder Bingham found many true friend in the south who would lay down their lives if necessary in the defense of the Elders, had great joy in his labors, saw the power of God made manifest upon many occasions in this on behalf as well as in the healing of the sick to whom the Elders administered, and returns home feeling thankful for the experience he has gained.

PHOTO 37   HEADSTONE FOR WILLARD BINGHAM 1830-1913

Elder Amos Cook -- SSM 1883-1885

PHOTO 38   AMOS COOK

Birth date, place - 3 February 1854, Salt Lake City, Utah
Death date - 13 December 1938
Baptism date - 3 May 1862 -- Baptism by - Seth Dustin
Father's name - Mark Cook   Mother's name - Ann Evans

Southern States - April 1883–February 1885 - Age Called: 29
Southern States
Set Apart: 9 April 1883 - End Date: 24 February 1885
Mission type: Proselytizing   -   Priesthood office: Elder
Called From: East Bountiful, Davis, Utah, United States
Set apart by: J Gates

Missionary Department missionary registers, 1860-1959, Vol. 1, p. 66, line 2831.
Missionary Department missionary registers, 1860-1959, Vol. 2, p. 72, line 2831.
First Presidency missionary calls and recommendations 1877-1918, CR 1 168, Church History Library.
First Presidency missionary calls and recommendations 1877-1918, CR 1 168, Church History Library.
Missionary Department missionary registers, 1860-1959, Vol. 5, p. 195, line 1192.
Southern States Mission history, 1832-1964: LR 8557 2, Church History Library.   Southern States Mission index

Life Story of Amos Cook

My father, Amos Cook, was born in Salt Lake City, Utah, on February 3, 1854. His parents were Mark Cook and Ann Evans Cook.

The Church was very dear to Amos and he was a willing worker all his life. He served two missions, one to the Southern States in 1883-1885. He left his family and loved ones behind and labored for the Church for two years. While on this mission he had Malaria fever many times. Also one of his children, Louisa, age thirteen months, died. His wife was home with five children. His father took care of his farm for him. In this way he was kept on his mission and his little family was cared for at home.   The Church was very dear to Amos and he was a willing worker all his life. He served two missions, one to the Southern States in 1883-1885. He left his family and loved ones behind and labored for the Church for two years. While on this mission he had Malaria fever many times. Also one of his children, Louisa, age thirteen months, died. His wife was home with five children. His father took care of his farm for him. In this way he was kept on his mission and his little family was cared for at home.

PHOTO 39   HEADSTONE FOR AMOS COOK 1854-1938

The Southern States Mission—Faithfulness of Young Elders—Opposition to the Truth—Gradual Spread of the Gospel—Changes in Religious and Political Sentiment—Hard Times in the South—Vice and Degradation—The Colorado Settlements

Elder Franklin Augustus Fraughton   -   SSM 1885-

PHOTO 40   FRANKLIN AUGUSTUS FRAUGHTON

Birth date, place - 31 January 1846, Westfield, Chautauqua, New York, United States
Death date - 4 May 1929
Baptism date - 15 March 1879   --   Baptism by - John Sessions
Father's name - George Fraughton   --   Mother's name - Henrietta Case
Family Search logo

Southern States - April 1885–Unknown - Age Called: 39
Southern States
Set Apart: 13 April 1885
Priesthood office: Seventy - Quorum: 20th
Priesthood: 20th Seventies
Called From: Heber City, Wasatch, Utah, United States
Set apart by: Heber J Grant

Northern States -- December 1907–November 1909 - Age Called: 61
Northern States
Set Apart: 10 December 1907
End Date: November 1909
Priesthood office: High Priest
Called From: Wellsburg, Wasatch, Utah, United States
Set apart by: Seymour B Young
Stories and Documents

Missionary Department missionary registers, 1860-1959, Vol. 1, p. 76, line 3241.
Missionary Department missionary registers, 1860-1959, Vol. 4, p. 27, line 874.
Missionary Department missionary registers, 1860-1959, Vol. 2, p. 82, line 3241.
First Presidency missionary calls and recommendations 1877-1918, CR 1 168, Church History Library.
Listed among other missionaries called on this letter.

Fraughton, Franklin Augustus, second Bishop of Wallsburg, Wasatch county, Utah, was born Jan. 31, 1846, at Westfield, Chautauqua county, N. Y., the son of George Fraughton and Heneretta Case. He emigrated with his parents to Utah in 1854, crossing the plains in an independent train. They settled in Provo, Utah County, where in the year 1855 Bro. Fraughton was baptized by John Sessions. The family remained in Provo until the spring of 1860, when they moved to what is now Heber City, Wasatch County, and in the year 1866 Bro. Fraughton went back to the Missouri river after the "Mormon" emigration as night herder in an ox-train. In the fall of 1866 and the summer of 1867 he acted as scout in what is known as the Black Hawk Indian war, and on August 12, 1867, he married Juliet Mott and made a home in Heber City. In 1870 he was ordained an Elder by Joseph Murdock and a few years later was ordained a Seventy and set apart as one of the presidents of the 20th quorum of Seventy. For a number of years he was in the Stake Superintendence of Y. M. M. I. A. He sawed the lumber that made the first house built in Park City; he also, in connection with three other men, purchased and operated the first steam saw mill which ever came into Wasatch county, and sawed hundreds of thousands of feet of lumber for the Ontario and other mines in the Park. In 1885 he was called on a mission to the Southern States and labored principally in the State of South Carolina. His first companion was Elder Wiley G. Cragun of North Ogden, Utah, and he first labored in York county. About the first experience he had there was an attack on himself and companion by a mob of about twenty-five armed men. Falling into their hands he was given forty stripes with oak sprouts. Elder Cragun made his escape to the woods under fire of about twenty-five shots. Bro. Fraughton was among the first Elders called to the South after the Cane Creek (Tennessee) massacre. He filled his mission and returned home in 1887 and was called and sent to Wallsburg to act as Bishop of Wallsburg Ward, being ordained a High Priest and Bishop by Franklin D. Richards. He acted as Bishop until May 1, 1903, when he was honorably released from that office. Together with Wm. P. Fullmer, Bro. Fraughton raised the first sugar beets under contract to the Sugar company at Lehi. They were also the first beets raised in Wasatch county. In 1907 he was called to take a mission to the Northern States and labored mostly in Indiana, returning in 1909. In 1912 (Jan. 28th) he was chosen as first counselor to Bishop Wm. P. Fullmer of the Wallsburg Ward, in which position he labored until April 2. 1916, when he was honorably released.

Elders Fraughton went out to talk to them. They gave the Elders a pertisehen (petition0 that had about 33 names sined to it telling them that they had to leave the County. They told them that they were citizens of the United States and thought they had as good   to stay in the country is any other citizens. They gave th Elders 6 days to leave the plase but the Elders did not pay any attention to it much. They staid on and on the 25 night of May they was 32 men came on the Elders at our house about 10 oclock. Came running up to the house all well arm. Elder Cragan had just taken off his shoes to retire to bed when he heard the noise some one said run and Elder Cragan made his eskape out of the north doore and run for the woods which was about 30 years and while on his way to the woods they was about 25 or 30 shots fired at him. one shot just graze him on the chin and Elder Fa. A. had no chance to get out and the mobs came in about 8 of them and caught Fraughton and led him away and gave him 50 lashes with hickory switches and turned him loose charging him to leave the country. The next day he came back to our house, then we all looked for Elder Cragun for about 2 hours before we found him. Both staid in the woods the rest of the night and next morning came to the house and got breakfast. Appointed meeting that day at Wm. Georges house.

They was one couple married and baptize that day about 10 o'clock instant namely James Harris and Fanny Whitesides [56] in the same stream I was baptized. After baptism we all went to the house. The Elders council led the Saints a little. Elder Cragun remarks was this, "be good to everybody, pray for them that despitefully use you and lift up your head and rejoice for being persecuted for so good a cause," and after they had talked to us, they left for Spartenburg County, South Carolina.

---

[55] William-Billy George, son of Nelson and Sarah Ayers George.
[56] James Jr, son of James and Sarah Jane Ayers Harris, Fannie, twin to John Alonzo Canty, daughter of Thomas Whitesides and Eliza Scott Canty.
[57] John Idle Sanders, son of Lucinda Harris.

OFFICE OF **A. Hatch & Co.,**

JOS. HATCH.
Purchasing Agent.

DEALERS IN

GENERAL MERCHANDISE,

AGRICULTURAL IMPLEMENTS,

AND

FURNITURE.

INDIAN TANNED
BUCKSKIN.
And all kinds of
Rocky Mountain Furs.

Best Brands of Flour
AND
Country Produce.

Heber City, Wasatch Co., Utah. March 2 1885

F. D. Richards

Dear Brother

according to your request
I submit the following
names for Missionaries

√ Franklin Fraughton
of Heber City

√ Edward J Clyde
of Heber City

√ William Gaybable
of Charleston

√ John Morton
of Midway

Isaac Watt
of Wallsburgh

The above are all young
& well Physically developed
and I think will make

Heber City, Wasatch Co., Utah. [Mar 24 1885]

Good faithful Elders—
none of them speak
only the English language
all of which
is Respectfully
Submitted by
Your Brother

Aram Hatch

In answer to yours of the 7ᵗʰ inst

Wallsburg, Utah, Aug 11ᵗʰ 1907

Dear Bro Reynolds

I will say that I think nothing would give me greater pleasure than to take a mission if I could see my way clear to do so. but I cannot. in the first place my Wife's Health is not good and it would be a Hardship for her to look after and direct our affairs here at Home, next my Education is very limited and my finance also is limited and I understd that the missionary fieald is not what it was 22 years ago when I went to the southern States, then we could travale without purse or scrip, and we labored amongst the poorer Classes and our education was not so assential as at the present amongst the more wealthy Classes.

I have no ready means sufficent to Keep my Family and suply me in the field with 10 or 15 dollars a month as I understand the Elders have to use at the present time and should I go to the northern States as your letter sugests I sorely stand in need of at least 2 year preparratory corse in the B.Y.U. and my means are lacking in this. I Have I beleave a fairly good understanding of the gospel, and also the ways of the world generly

but the polish and gift of delivery and so on is lacking
on account of education. I keep the Word of Wisdom so
far as tea coffee whisky and tobacco are conserned.
my health is fairly good, I am troubled a little with
my kidnies but not very mutch I dont consider for a man
of my age. I am 61 years old past last January
and I consider I am exceptionaly healthy and strong
for that age. I dont know as I could stand it to
labor as a travailing Elder I dont know, that would be
all right
if I could. ~~all right~~ if I could not perhaps I could do
something else. I speak no other language exept the
English and that only roughly as I before stated.
I beleave this answers all of your questions that it is
nessary to answer at this time and I beleave from the
statement I have made you can get a pretty good
understanding of my condition and circumstances and
when you have tharouly considered them all. and you
find that the Lord wants me to do this labor, I will make
any sacrefice and go to any extent that is nessary to go
and am ready at almost any time. your Bro, in the
Gospel   F. A. Fraughtain

F. A. Fraughton

Aug. 11, 1907.

RECEIVED
AUG
13
1907
PRESIDENT'S OFFICE

J. R.

Let him be
excused –
until he can
see his way
to go and
so reports.

PHOTO 41   HEADSTONE FOR F A FRAUGHTON 1845-1929

Elder William Nephi Anderson -- SSM 1885-1887

PHOTO 42 - ELDER WILLIAM NEPHI ANDERSON

Birth date, place -- 9 February 1859, Salt Lake City, Salt Lake, Utah Territory, United States
Death date -- 20 June 1922
Baptism date -- 7 May 1865
Baptism by - James Anderson
Father's name - James Anderson
Mother's name - Catherine M Cowley

Southern States -- October 1885–October 1887 -- Age Called: 26
Southern States
Set Apart: 12 October 1885 -- End Date: 18 October 1887
Priesthood office: Seventy - Quorum: 2nd -- Priesthood: 2nd Seventies
Called From: Salt Lake City, Salt Lake, Utah, United States
Set apart by: John W Taylor -- Date Set Apart: 12 Oct 1885

Missionary Department missionary registers, 1860-1959, Vol. 2, p. 85, line 3360.
Missionary Department missionary registers, 1860-1959, Vol. 1, p. 78, line 3360.
First Presidency missionary calls and recommendations 1877-1918: CR 1 168, Church History Library

Felt, Lambert & Young
Sept. 3. 1885.

Salt Lake City
Sept. 3rd 1885.

Pres't F. D. Richards
Dear Brother;

Bro. Lambert received a letter under date of Aug. 21st from Bro. Reynolds, in which we were requested to submit to you a number of names from the Young Men's Associations of this Stake; it was immediately forwarded to Bro. Felt but did not reach him until Aug. 31st — we now hasten to comply, and respectfully submit the names as per inclosed list.

Your Brethren in the Gospel

Joseph H. Felt.
Geo. C. Lambert
Royal B. Young

✗	Albert Brown	1st Ward	Francis B. Platt	13th Ward	
	Hans Sorenson	2nd "	Alonzo Young	" "	
✓	Theo. Angell	3rd "	Benj. R. Eldredge ✗	" " +	
✓	Wilford Smith	4th "	~~Fred W. Taylor~~ 14th		
✓	Arthur Sperry	4th "	~~~~ 15th		
✓ ✗	Wm. A. Cowan	5th "	David Emory	16th "	
✓	Wm. W. Anderson	6th "	Chas. R. Howe	17th "	
✓ ✗	Wm. J. Woodbury	7th "	Sam'l Sudbury	18th "	
✓	Albaroni H. Woolley	9th "	Horace G. Whitney	" " +	
✓ ✗	Royal A. Barney	8th "	Wm. Wood Jr.	19th "	
✓ Billy	✗ John H. Saunders	10th "	✗ Isaiah Burrows	21st "	
✓	Henry A. Tuckett	11th "	~~John Schofield~~	20th "	
✓	✗ Thomas A. Williams	12th "	Sam'l G. Spencer, Pleasant Green. ✗		

SOUTH CAROLINA

Interesting Report of Missionary Labors There - The Catawba Indians – The Preceptor a Benefit.

EZELL, Spartanburg County, South Carolina

May 2nd 1887.

Editor Deseret News:

I was appointed as President of the South Carolina Conference on the 20th of February last, and am doing all in my power to forward the work of God in this land, in connection with the rest of my brethren. There are now eight elders laboring in this state or Conference and we are expecting another to arrive soon. Two in Ocone County, two in Union County North Carolina, and four in Spartanburg County, covering an area of country of 200 miles east and west.

Interest in the different sections, as is usual at this season of year. Is decreasing although in Ocone County it is still comparatively good, and we are in hopes of reaping the reward of our labors during the past winter, in which I assisted by a bountiful harvest, as there seems to be some there who are honest in heart. The Elders in that county have baptized three lately and think that will break the ice for a number more.

Persecution is not prevalent at present but Satan's emissaries are still on hand to oppose the promulgation of the Gospel and we hear mutterings now and again in regard to what they will have to do to stop our making converts to the truth.

There are 140 members in the conference and most of them in good standing. We are using every endeavor to get them to gather to zion as soon as possible, realizing that the hour of God's judgments is near at hand. The Saints from this State generally emigrate to Colorado. There is another company going in June, but there are only three or four going from here that we know of.

A number of our Saints in South Carolina are Lamanites, known as the "Catawba Indians." Some of them are the best we have got, being full of faith and integrity and have taken hold with a zeal not commonly manifest with those who receive the truth nowadays.

The Catawbas are a small colony, situated on a reservation of thirty miles square, on the Catawba River, and were first visited by our Elders in 1883. They married and mixed with the white people, and the whites kept intruding upon them and cheating them out of their land, until now those these few who remain (about 100) have only a quarter section of land left. The majority of them have embraced the Gospel, but it is hard, under the influence of so called civilization, to get all of them to refrain from the evil habits which had such a hold upon them when the Gospel found them. When the Elders first went in among them, the neighboring whites had, in "The Nation," as they call it, a regular place of resort for lewd purposes. As soon as the principles of the Gospel were taught them, and they were made to sense their condition they ceased their evil practices and accepted the truth. This as a natural consequence, enraged some of the pious Christians, because they could not gratify their evil desires, and the spirit of mobbing was soon rife, and as the 'Mormons" were an unpopular sect, it was not difficult to get a crowd to drive them out. This state of affairs arising placed the Elders in jeopardy while prosecuting their labors and resulted in May 1884 in one of the Elders being shot at and the other given 40 lashes. Ever since that time there has been a standing threat toward the Elders: "If they are ever caught in there they will be similarly dealt with," and when ever we do visit them we have to slip about and be watchful.

We have a Sunday school organized in their midst and one of the Lamanite brethren to superintend it. We write to them quite often and do all we can in that direction to encourage them. We got a number of them to move away from their lands, up in this section, where we can be protected and visit them and teach them their duties. We learned lately that some of them who are yet in the nation are being overcome by the wicked ones around them, since we are, (while they remain there) deprived of teaching them.

All was peace throughout the conference at last accounts and Elders and Saints generally are enjoying a degree of good health. The weather is fine corn and wheat crops are beginning to adorn the cleared portions of land, which look like a sandy waste in winter time.

People are busy planting cotton and it will soon be flourishing when the sun shines hot. The woods are getting in full bloom, birds making the air ring with shrill notes in the day and whip-poor-will responds at night.

I have a good deal of walking to do in visiting around and looking after the welfare of those under my watchcare and sometimes it is tiresome, especially in hot weather. Still I rejoice, and as God has, so far, given me strength perform my duties according to His promises, by observing his laws. I will not complain.

The Preceptor has been a great benefit to the Elders in this section in getting them to present the principles of the the Gospel in order and simplicity. There is one prominent feature adopted by the Elders in their teachings that is contained in it and that is, "to avoid finishing and beginning several times in a discourse." This point always occurs to my mind when I am speaking and the effect of observing it is manifest. Also the plan of having an opposite to speak to is observed. The Preceptor has and is doing, in my judgment a great deal of good at home and abroad.

I remain your brother in the Gospel

W N Anderson.

Elder Joseph Thorup -- SSM 1885-

PHOTO 43 -- ELDER JOSEPH THORUP

Birth date, place - 8 December 1865, Copenhagen, Denmark
Death date - 21 April 1935
Baptism date - 1874 -- Baptism by - Thomas Johnson
Father's name - Herman A Thorup   Mother's name - Maria C Christensen

Joseph Thorup

 Southern States - September 1885–Unknown -- Age Called: 19
Southern States
Set Apart: 4 September 1885
Priesthood office: Seventy - Priesthood: Elder Ord Seventy
Called From: Salt Lake City, Salt Lake, Utah, United States
Set apart by: H J Grant

Missionary Department missionary registers, 1860-1959, Vol. 1, p. 77, line 3302.
Missionary Department missionary registers, 1860-1959, Vol. 2, p. 83, line 3302.
First Presidency missionary calls and recommendations 1877-1918, CR 1 168, Church History Library.

First Presidency missionary calls and recommendations 1877-1918, CR 1 168, Church History Library.
First Presidency missionary calls and recommendations 1877-1918: CR 1 168, Church History Library
Letter 3 Aug 1885 of a mission recommendation

Joseph Thorup
Utah, Missionary Department Missionary Registers, 1860-1937
Name: Joseph Thorup   --   Event Type: Mission
Event Date: 1885   -   Event Place: Southern States
Residence Place: Salt Lake City, Salt Lake, Utah, United States
Birth Date: 08 Dec 1865   Birthplace: Copenhagen, , Denmark
Baptism Date: 1874
Father's Name: Herman A Thorup   Mother's Name: Maria C Christensen
Page: 83   Volume: Missionary Register v. 2
By Whom Baptized: Thos Johnson
By Whom Set Apart: H J Grant
Date Set Apart: 04 Sep 1885

Jos. Thorup -   mentioned in the record of Thorup
Name: Jos. Thorup   -- Sex: Male
Wife: Romney
Daughter: Thorup
Other information in the record of Thorup from Utah Births and Christenings
Name: Thorup
Gender   Female
Birth Date: 01 Oct 1899
Birthplace: Salt Lake City, Salt Lake, Utah
Race: White
Father's Name: Jos. Thorup Mother's Name: Romney

Salt Lake City Aug 22/85

President
John Taylor

Dear Brother I feel thankful that I am considered worthy by you to be called as a missionary and if permited to go I will do all that I possibly can to fulfill my appointment as a missionary. I have no objections whatever in going on a mission. As I will have to go to the Temple for my blessings I therefor will not be able to start till about the middle of

September. if this will meet your approbation I will be very much pleased I would be very much pleased to get an answer whither the middle of September will answer the purpose or not

Your Brother in the Gospel

Joseph Thorup

Joseph Thorup Senior
Bishop
First Ward

Logan. City. Aug 28th 85

President. F.D. Richards
Dear Brother
According to appointment
I arrived here yesterday
and enquired at the
Temple for my reccomend
which I learned had not
arrived I was therefor
advised by Prest Merill
to send a telegram to you
which I did. but the
answer came an hour to
late so you see how I
am fixed up here. Brother
W.W Allen came up at
the same time as I did
also Bro J H Gleason
raither of these Bretheren
received their reccomend
in time so you see we are

all in the same fix.
We would be very much
pleased to heare from you
What we are to do. whether
to stay till next wednesday
(September 2nd) or come
home right away. We
would be pleased to get
an answere by return
mail.

 Your Brethern in the Gospel

   Joseph Thorup
   W. H. Allen
   J. H. Gleason

Joseph Warburton
Aug 3, 1885

Salt Lake City
Aug 3rd 1885
F. D. Richards
Dear Brother.

Brother Joseph Thorup.
the bearer of this note,
is a worthy young man.
an Elder in the Church,
and about Twenty Years
of Age, his parents desires
if agreeable, that he Should
go on a mission. and
he feels it a duty, and
a blessing for him to go.
if it could be So arranged
and he could have an
answer, I would like
for him to get his Endow-
ments, that he could do
forthwith.)

Some work in the Temple
with his parents for the
dead, before going on
mission, he will answer
you any question you
may ask.

please send me an
answer and oblige
          Your Brother in the
                    Gospel.

          Joseph Warburton
                    Bishop
                              First Ward.

Salt Lake City
Aug 5th 1885 -

This is to Certify that
Brother Joseph Thorup, is
a member of the Church
of Jesus Christ of Latter
Day Saints, in the First
Ward, of the Salt Lake Stake
in good Standing, and as
Such I recommend him
to take a mission, or any
other blessing you may
feel to confer upon him.
　　　Your Brother in the
　　　Gospel of Christ.
　　　Joseph Warburton
　　　Bishop
　　　　First Ward.

P.S.
Brother Thorup is an
Elder &c.

A History of Joseph Thorup, born Dec. 8, 1865
Compiled by Wilma T. Svedin
June 26, 1979

Joseph Thorup was born Dec. 8, 1865 in Copenhagen, Denmark (Skt. Johannes parish). He was the youngest in a family of 8 children, but two sisters had died in infancy. His parents, Herman August and Marie Christine Christensen Thorup, had joined the Church of Jesus Christ of Latterday Saints in 1853 and had known considerable persecution because of it. When Joseph was born, no name is recorded on the vital statistics, though the Parish was the record-keeping part of the government. His birth certificate is shown below.

So, though there was a parting with friends and a breaking with their native land, it was with somewhat of a relief from the persecution and an anticipation of better things in Zion that the family left Denmark and sailed for U.S.A. May 8, 1868. After a 14-month stay in Chicago because of bad connections and lack of communication, the family came west to Utah. By this time, the railroad had been established and they came by train. Had they come the year before, they would have been Pioneers.

In America there were hardships too. The Salt Lake Valley had not been settled many years, so there was much pioneering going on. There was plenty of work, and unless the work was done, there was nothing on which to survive. So there was the family garden. Joseph's mother was a good gardener, and took pride in what she raised and could sell. But the family couldn't eat from the garden until prices were low and selling was unprofitable. There was hay to be cut from the roadsides and brought home to cure for the winter. Joseph being the youngest was a part of all this activity.

Nor was life easy for immigrants. Little prejudices caused undue persecution of its own kind, and the youngsters were reluctant to admit their nationality. Joseph was one who felt it would be easier to say he was English, born in Chicago, than to admit he was from Denmark. He even practised speaking with an English accent. Since he was only three years old when he came to America, he had overcome any Danish accent.

Joseph attended school at the Hamilton School on 8th So. & 8th East, where most of the Thorups went. It was not far from the family home on 9th East & 7th So.. He attended Church at the First Ward meeting house. Then he received a call to fill a mission in the Southern States, and was set apart for that mission Sept. 4, 1885. Upon reaching the mission field, he was assigned to the South Carolina conference.

Though the Latterday Saints had been driven from their homes in 1847 and forced to go to the barren Salt Lake Valley, persecution had not been purged from their lives. Those who would agitate, condemn, or spread falsehoods followed the Saints here. Publication of unfavorable articles in the press of this country concerning the Latterday Saints and the constant repetition of falsehoods by enemies of the Church here in Salt Lake City caused much bitterness throughout the country. The missionaries of the Church were sorely abused, especially in the Southern States, where many of them were stripped of their clothes, tied to trees and brutally beaten by mobs until the blood ran from their wounded bodies. And when they were released they were ordered from that part of the country on pain of death if they remained. On July 21, 1878, a mob had seized Elder Joseph Standing and his companion, Rudgar Clawson in the state of Georgia, taking them to the woods for an apparent thrashing. Elder Standing made a show of resisting and was shot. They then turned to Elder Clawson and said, "Shoot him". Elder Clawson folded his arms and said, "Shoot".
- - - - - - -
Below, a copy of the birth record (Male births) of Joseph Thorup, listing his father as a cabinet maker.

Date	Child	Parents	and address

1865

December 8

311

*Thorup Herman August
und Ev
Marie Christens*

Ft 74

(Joseph Thorup (b. 1865) history, page 2)

This unnerved the mob and they put their guns away. Elder Clawson pleaded for permission to get help, and this was granted. But while he was gone, about 20 bullets were fired into the body of Elder Standing at close range.

It was only 7 years after this incident that Joseph Thorup began his mission in this area. He was not without trials and ridicule either for he had rotten eggs thrown at him. Reports from him and his companions can best tell of the circumstances under which he served. From the Deseret News, Oct. 17, 1885, we read, "Oct. 4, 1885 - On this day and the preceding day, meetings were held at Paris, Spartanburg Co., So. Carolina. The five Elders, Cragun, Fraughton, Heber Wright, Wm. H. Gardner, and Joseph Thorup now laboring in this state, and W. E. Bingham, met at this point Oct. 3 to welcome the president of the mission (John Morgan) and be instructed by him in relation to our duties as the servants of God. During his stay of two days we held three meetings, and the appreciation of the visit can best be understood by those who have experienced similar meetings.

The majority of this branch is made up of Catawba Lamanites, and it is gratifying to hear them bear their testimonies to the truth of the gospel and sing the songs of Zion, thus establishing the fact that the time for the redemption has come.

Proselyting here, to use a southern phrase, is "just sorta", but the mobocrat spirit has abated "right smart", and full of encouragement occasioned by our President's visit we feel confident that some of the seed now being scattered will fall upon good soil.
Heber Wright
Sec. pro tem"

In Sept. 1886 Elder Wm. N. Anderson wrote from Thickety Mountain, No. Carolina, that prejudice in the farming communities was not so rife, but in the cities it was so bad that the Elders were unable to teach them. The only times they visited the cities was to get their mail or to purchase something they needed.

"It is a noticeable feature that whenever some good is being done, the adversaries of the truth are enraged and they use every device to hinder the progress. The spirit of mobbing has been prevalent in this area the past few weeks, but owing to the many friends the Elders have, and the mobbers not being too strong, it has all passed off in threats.

The power of God, of late, has also been manifest in the shape of a terrific earthquake, which has caused the enemies of God's people to shake in their shoes and abandon, for the present at least, their nefarious designs.

It took place on the night of August 31st at 9:45 P.M. I was 3 miles from where I am at present, at the house of Mr. H. Bright, with Elder Joseph Thorup. It was the first one I had ever experienced. It was so severe that it made the frame building we were in reel to and fro, and was accompanied by a heavy rumbling sound. When it got to is height in shaking, we went to the doors to see what was the matter, and not till then did we realize what it was. We stepped out onto the ground to see how it felt. It sent a shock through us like that of an electric battery, as nearly as I can describe it. There were 3 shocks within 15 minutes. The first and most severe lasted about 4 minutes.

A great many people were panic stricken. A number of them left their houses and took to the woods. Others ran out and commenced praying. Some got their suns supposing it was somebody trying to upset the house. One man got so excited he fired a shot through his own door.

One man out where Elders Wright and Fraughton are staying exclaimed, "The time has come". His wife, who has been convinced of the truth for some time exclaimed, "I have known my duty and have put it off, and now it's too late".

The Deseret News printed a letter written by Joseph Thorup Mar. 10, 1887. Under the date of Feb. 27, 1887, Elder Joseph Thorup and his companion, laboring in Wolf Pond, North Carolina wrote of a discussion with a minister from "The True Church of Christ" on this date. "Upwards of 250 people assembled at the appointed time for the discussion. My companion took the stand at 10:30, setting forth our first principles, occupying one hour. Our opponent took the stand at 11:30, occupying one hour, but instead of refuting the first principles of our religion, he commenced an onslaught on our people. At seven minutes to one our opponent again took the stand. This time he was going to prove our doctrine false and us imposters. In his effort to quote scriptures he got badly confused, finding nothing in the Bible to condemn us, and he again began his harangues. At 7 minutes to two, I took the stand and opened fire, occupying one hour. I experienced no difficulty in proving him the imposter and his doctrine false and spurious. I also refuted his slander of our people amid the laughter of the congregation. When my hour had expired, he jumped to his feet and again commenced his harangue, but the people, much to his mortification, paid no attention to him, but crowded around us to get tracts treating our faith. We distributed upwards of 50 tracts among the people, and had we been better supplied we could have distributed thrice that amount. Giving God the glory, we went on our way rejoicing. Remarks of "Well, he was trimmed to the quick" were made on every side."
--Elder Joseph Thorup

April 5, 1887, working with Parley P. Bingham in North Carolina, they wrote: "Success in North Carolina. An interest has been awakened and many are following the admonition of the Savior--"Search the scriptures". Three persons were baptized recently. Two of them

(Joseph Thorup (b. 1865) history, page 3)

had been members of the Baptist Church 40 years. The spirit of opposition however is active and the Elders have to meet a great deal of falsehood and many alarming reports. But these things only strengthen the faith of the missionaries and cause them to press forward in the good work."   --Elder Joseph Thorup

In a letter dated June 12, 1887, Elder Joseph Thorup who is laboring in South Carolina conference, states he was taken down with typhoid fever at a town called Paary. He was a companion of Elder Wm. N. Anderson and nursed him before Elder Anderson came home.
(Des. News June 21, 1887)

It was about time for "Uncle Joe to be released from his mission to go home. His companion, Elder Wilcox, went to a neighboring county to arrange for his trip home. While he was gone the following took place:
"July 3, 1887, Elder Joseph Thorup and some of his friends were walking past a school-house where a meeting was being held in Oconee Co., So. Carolina. They stopped and listened a short time to the preacher, a man named Wright, who was bitterly abusing the "Mormons" and urging the people to drive them out. When Wright got through he came over to Elder Thorup and, shaking hands with him, said, "I am through now. You can speak to the people if you want to". At this time some of those assembled called on Bro. Thorup to talk to them, but the larger portion of the crowd howled derisively at him. One man drew a knife and started toward him, cursing and threatening. Miles Moss, one of the company interfered and ordered the would-be murderer to stand back. After a few hot words the crowd dispersed.
(Des. News 36:421)

Monday, July 4, 1887, Elder Joseph Thorup was arrested and thrown into prison at Walhalla, So. Carolina. The following was recorded in the Deseret News July 16, 1887:
"The next day was the 4th of July and Brother Thorup who was quite ill stopped at the house of one of the saints a short distance from the before mentioned schoolhouse. Toward evening he was lying on some sheepskins on the porch of the cabin when a man who was nearby remarked to him, 'Thorup, you are gone this time". Just then the deputy sheriff of the County stepped up and looking down at him said, "I've got an arrest for you", at the same time drawing a pistol and pointing it at him. Elder Thorup took up his hat and arose when the deputy said, "Come out here. There's 14 men waiting to see you. You're the presiding Elder about here, and we want you. We don't want any of your d--n doctrine".
Brother Thorup went to the place indicated, where the sheriff named Brazil served a warrant on him, charging him with assault and battery, and riot. Five of the men (all non-Mormons) who had taken Elder Thorup's part at the schoolhouse, were also arrested on the same charges. These were Miles Moss, James Woods, Thomas and Leland Honeycutt, and Beman Stansson. The complaint had been made by the preacher Wright who claimed that the assault had been made on him, though none of the accused had spoken to him except Elder Thorup, who had simply said, "How do you do", when Wright shook hands with him.
The five prisoners were required to travel all night to Walhalla to the prison. Elder Thorup was closely guarded all the way, but the others were not so carefully watched. Arriving at the prison, Moss and the two Honeycutts were released on bail. Woods and Stansson were unable to find sureties for $500. Some of Elder Thorup's friends offered bail for him, but no sum would be taken, bail being peremptorily refused. He was thrown into prison, and notwithstanding his enfeebled condition he was placed in a dirty cell, the only bedding being a rotten quilt, while bugs, worms, and other vermin crawled about the floor and walls which seemed literally alive with them.
There Elder Thorup was compelled to remain from early on Wednesday, July 6 until evening of Friday July 8. On that evening he was taken before the Justice of the Peace, Gaines by name. On the way the sheriff told Bro. Thorup there was nothing in the charge against him, as it had been trumped up by Wright for the purpose of driving the "Mormons" out,"for", said the sheriff, "they mean to hurt you and you better go. If any other Elders come in here they'll meet with violence".
About 200 of the mob tried to get at Bro. Thorup, but the sheriff prevented them. When they reached the courtroom it was found that Moss and the two Honeycutts had signed an agreement pledging their honor that Elder Thorup would leave. After reading this, Justice Gaines said to Brother Thorup, "We can't have Mormonism in our midst. We won't have this man Thorup about here. These men have pledged their honor that you will get out, and if you don't you will have to go back to jail". Brother Thorup replied that he had a right as an American citizen to stay there. He had broken no law, and no one had the right to inter-fere with him. He further stated that it did not make much difference, as he was preparing to go home anyhow, but would not guarantee that other Elders would stay away.
Without further proceedings, Brother Thorup and the others who had been arrested were liberated, no attempt being made to bring them to trial. Elder Thorup started for home on the following Monday, July 11, 1887.
--(Deseret News 36:421)

July 16, 1887 - "Elder Joseph Thorup arrived home at 2:45 this morning from the Southern States mission. He had left this city Sept. 11, 1885 and was assigned to labor in South Carolina conference. His first companion was Wiley G. Cragun. In November 1885, they ex-perienced mobbings at the hands of a mob, but were not injured bodily. At a town called

(Joseph Thorup (b. 1865) history, page 4)

Belton they were arrested by a vigilance committee, and after a mock trial were ordered
to leave the county on pain of death. Three weeks later they were warned of the approach
of a mob and escaped violence.

Elder Thorup labored in several counties in North and South Carolina, having varied
success. In June he was appointed to labor in Ocenee Co., South Carolina, and accompanied
William N. Anderson part of the way on the latter's journey home on June 13th. On that
day, Elder Thorup felt ill, and the next day was quite sick, being attacked with typhoid
fever. He managed to continue to his new field where he received attention from the Saints.

Though suffering considerably and having at times a high fever, he was enabled to move
about a little and was confined to bed only a portion of the time. About July 1st, he was
released to return home, and on the 2nd a committee of "regulators" waited on him and his
companion, Elder Wilcox of Garfield Co., and notified them to leave that part of the state.
The mob said that the ministers of the neighborhood had decided that the "Mormons" must go.
No attention was paid to the warning, and Elder Wilcox went over to the neighboring county
to make arrangements for Elder Thorup's return home."

--(Deseret News, July 16, 1887)

Regardless of his problems and disappointments in later years (as he did not remain
active in the Church), the fact remains that he did perform a great mission. He endured
much, with courage and dignity, and he was one of those stalwart leaders who blazed the way
for the teaching of the gospel of Jesus Christ in that area, making it possible for those
who were seeking the truth to hear it and have this blessing in their lives. We are proud
of his contribution to this great latterday work.

On March 28, 1895, he married Clara Romney. To them were born 5 children--Winnifred,
Joseph, Chauncey, Lucille, and Melvin. They lived at 735 So. 9th East, just south of his
parents' home, when the children were small.

Joseph's brother John had worked for Z.C.M.I. in the Grocery Dept. but had quit for
some other position. Then Z.C.M.I. came and asked John if he would return. John said he
couldn't because of his new commitment, but that he had a brother Joseph who could perhaps
help them. So Joseph was contacted and hired to be manager of the Grocery Dept. It was
here that I met him and had several visits with him as a child when going through the store
with my parents. He was always jovial and pleasant and treated us with much courtesy and
kindness. Others who knew him said he was kind to them and they enjoyed visiting him.

Later, Joseph quit Z.C.M.I. and moved to California. There he became a broker in the
wholesale grocery business. Sunfreeze Icecream had come into being about this time, and
this was one of the products he dealt with. It is also interesting to note that his niece,
Rae Thorup, was working in the office at Sunfreeze here in Salt Lake and she was the one
who received his checks in payment for that product.

Joseph was always good with children. May Clark recalls when she was a small child
living next door to him. It was her birthday and Joe was working out in his garden, so she
said, "Uncle Joe, it's my birthday". "Oh, it's your birthday, is it?" and he went on working. So she said it again, and he responded somewhat similarly. But when she repeated it
the 3rd time, he smiled, reached down in his pocket, and gave her a nickle.

Later, May was a 'baby sitter' for them, though the children weren't many years younger
than she. But she said she was reassured by the fact that her own mother was close enough
if help was needed.

Every year Joseph had fireworks for the 4th and 24th of July to delight the children.
Eva Bosworth recalls what a highlight it was for them because few could afford such things
in those days. Most of the homes on the block were those of the Thorup families, and all
would congregate on their front porches to see the display.

Joseph's children attended school at the Hamilton school as their father had done.
But for some reason, they attended Bryant Jr. High later. His daughter Lucille always
walked home from school with Marnee and Edna Thorup, and quite often walked to school as
well. So they were close friends, as well as cousins.

Joseph was very tender toward those who were persecuted for polygamy, and felt their
punishments were too harsh. He even tried to pursuade them to abandon their commitments in
order to free themselves of this constant threat on their well-being. It would not be easy
to stand by and see a brother so persistently persecuted by those who neither understood
the circumstances nor offered any assistance in the well-being of those involved. The in-
justice of it was most chafing. He had sympathy for the children who had to work hard and
long to make up for the hardships inflicted upon them by these enemies.

Joseph died Apr. 21, 1935 in California, and is buried beside his parents here in
Salt Lake City,

Elder Heber Jedediah Wright -- SSM 1885-

PHOTO 44 -- ELDER HEBER JEDEDAIH WRIGHT

Birth date, place - 19 January 1858, Brigham City, Box Elder, Utah
Death date -- 31 August 1914
Baptism date -- 1866
Father's name - Jonathan Calkin Wright   --   Mother's name -- Lois Susannah Moran

Southern States - April 1885–Unknown   Age Called: 27

Southern States
Set Apart: 7 April 1885
Served with companion: Wiley Gidoni, Cragun, Franklin Augustus Fraughton
Priesthood office: Seventy   --   Priesthood: Elder Ordained Seventy
Called From: Willard, Box Elder, United States
Set apart by: Jno W Taylor

Missionary Department missionary registers, 1860-1959, Vol. 1, p. 75, line 3213.
Missionary Department missionary registers, 1860-1959, Vol. 2, p. 81, line 3213.
First Presidency missionary calls and recommendations 1877-1918, CR 1 168, Church History Library.
First Presidency missionary calls and recommendations 1877-1918, CR 1 168, Church History Library.

Heber Wright
Willard
Mch. 22=(2) 85.

Willard City March 26/85

Mr. Geo Reynolds.
Salt Lake City.
Dear Brother:

Your letter
of enquiry was received by my
folks some time ago, but I
was away from home and did
not get it in due time.

In answer to it I can
say that I will be ready to
start on my mission at
the appointed time.

Will I have to visit Salt
Lake City to be set apart?

I understand our approaching
Conference is to be held in
Logan please instruct me
as to this matter and

Oblige Your Brother

P.S.
Direct to Willard
instead of Brigham

Heber Wright

Office of Boothe, Wilson & Co.,

DEALERS IN

DRUGS, DRY GOODS, GROCERIES, HATS, CAPS,

BOOTS, SHOES, GLOVES, NOTIONS, ETC.

ALSO, SHIPPERS OF GRAIN, BUTTER, EGGS, POULTRY, ETC.

Main Street,

Brigham City, Utah, Sep 1st 1884

(BOX ELDER COUNTY.)

Pres. John Taylor
Salt Lake City

Dear Brother: On account of being absent from home your letter was not received until Friday.

In regard to the call that has been made of me I can say that without sacrificing considerably I cannot leave my family comfortably at present; however my anxiety to assist in the great latter day work is great and if under the existing circumstances my labor is required in the field I will be ready at the appointed time

Please let me know your conclusion at as early a date as convenient that I may govern myself accordingly

Your Brother in the Gospel

Heler Wright

P.S. Direct to Willard instead of Brigham.

I believe this to be a true statement of Bro. Wrights feelings and circumstances.

George Facer Bp

135

Elder William Heber Gardner -- SSM 1885-1887

PHOTO 45 -- ELDER WILLIAM HEBER GARDNER

Birth date, place -- 7 February 1857, Payson, Utah, Utah Territory, United States
Death date -- 31 July 1927
Baptism by - Smith
Father's name - Walter Elias Gardner   Mother's name -- Martha Ann Tuttle

Southern States -- September 1885–June 1887   - Age Called: 28

Southern States
Set Apart: 5 September 1885   -   Arrived At Home: 18 June 1887
Mission type: Proselytizing
Marital Status: Married
Priesthood office: Seventy -- Quorum: 19th
Called From: Salem, Utah, United States
Set apart by: Andrew Carrington

> Missionary Department missionary registers, 1860-1959, Vol. 1, p. 77, line 3303.
> Missionary Department missionary registers, 1860-1959, Vol. 2, p. 83, line 3303.
> First Presidency missionary calls and recommendations 1877-1918, CR 1 168, Church History Library.
> On Setember 1, 1885, W H Gardner accepts his mission call.
> First Presidency missionary calls and recommendations 1877-1918: CR 1 168, Church History Library
> On September 10, 1885, his bishops states that Wm H Garder will leave with the next company.
> First Presidency missionary calls and recommendations 1877-1918: CR 1 168, Church History Library.
> On September 15, 1885, William H Garder makes a request.

Sept 5, 1885: Set apart as a missionary to the Southern States. Experienced much danger but was never harmed while serving. Returned home in June 1887, a bit earlier than intended due to his wife's poor health

Salem City Sept 1 1885

President John Taylor

Dear Brother
Yours of aug 31
come to hand
You wanted to know
my feeling in regards
to the call that was
made of me I feel
willing to respond
and do all
the good I can
in helping to spread
the truth with the
help of the lord

Your Brother
in the Gospel
W. H. Gardner

Wm H Gardner
Sept 1, 1880

Accepts Mission
Call

Chattanooga, Ten
September 15. 18 85

Prest. F. D. Richards
Dear Brother
I arrived here to day
And learned that it
was necessary for me
to have a letter of
appointment, which I have
not received. I would
be pleased if you would
have the kindness to forward
me one at your earliest
convenience
Your Brother in the Gospel
William H. Gardner

P. S
Please send the letter
to the office at Chatta
nooga. as I don't know
where I am going

Wm H. Gardner
Sept 15 1885
sent on the 22nd

Elder William Alexander Redd   -   SSM 1887-1889

PHOTO 46   WILLIAM ALEXANDER REDD

Birth date, place -   19 September 1861, Spanish Fork, Utah, Utah Territory
Death date - 6 January 1911
Father's name - Lemuel H Redd --   Mother's name - Keziah Jane Butler

Southern States - February 1887–March 1889 - Age Called: 25

Southern States
Set Apart: 14 February 1887 - End Date: 10 March 1889
Priesthood office: Seventy - Quorum: 9th - Priesthood: 9th Seventies

Called From: New Harmony, Washington, Utah Territory, United States
Set apart by: H J Grant

Missionary Department missionary registers, 1860-1959, Vol. 1, p. 85, line 15.
Missionary Department missionary registers, 1860-1959, Vol. 2, p. 92, line 15.
First Presidency missionary calls and recommendations 1877-1918, CR 1 168, Church History Library.

"At the priesthood meeting, he explained that he had been given instructions to open up the territory, long since unworked, where Brothers Berry and Gibbs had been killed by a mob. Higbee needed a companion to accompany him on this mission. After his explanation, he asked for a volunteer. Some shook their heads, but a new man, William A. Redd, was the first one to raise his hand and volunteer to go. He didn't take Father. Probably he wanted a more experienced man than this beginner, but it tells that Father was willing to meet all calls that came."

From Chattanooga he went to Atlanta, Georgia, and on to Cowpens, South Carolina. There they hired a vehicle to take them to Thickety Mountain, Spartanburg County, N.C., his first field of labor.

Here is where the Watts family lived, for he mentions them repeatedly.

Maybe it was like the place they directed me to when I was in that area. They said I could see the store from the station. I could see merely the corner of something, which proved to be a two-roomed house where the family lived in the back and a few shelves with mighty little to sell on them in the front room. The rest was country filled with forest. I can see that when I consider this place.

Around here were a few friendly people who took the Elders in and listened to them. From here they went in different directions on short trips to find people to talk gospel to. During his first months there he mentions meetings and Sunday schools frequently.

These are some of his entries:

1887 - Feb. 27th- Sunday held two meetings - considerable interest - went down to Cowpens at night to see Bros. Wright and Fraughten off for home - got back to J. Black's at daylight - slept till noon and heard John Black bear testimony of the blessings of the Lord manifested to him by feeding the servants of the Lord - in a public gathering when Elders Wright and Fraughten were leaving.

April 2nd - Saturday clear - after B went over to Bro. Surratt's and dinner held meeting - Elders Anderson, Ferrin and I talked - was about 28 present - good attention.

April 3rd - Sunday - clear fine weather - fast day - held S.S. and meeting - diner with sisters Jas. Patterson2 - stayed all night with John Black.

April 29th - Friday - took dinner with Sister Watts - helped Wm. Watts plant3 cotton and took supper with him - stayed all night with Webb Smith.

May 2nd - Monday - after B turned potato masher (How many of you remember Mother's old wooden potato masher? This is it. Stayed overnight with Harrison Bright. (It's too bad Father didn't know that one of his genealogical lines was Bright. He met several of them - C. Bright, Theodore Bright, William Bright, Hosea Bright and there was a place called Bright Town). (All these trips about were on foot.)

May 20th - Friday - go to John S. Black's - received a letter from Alonzo Redd --(I stayed with his son when I was down there.) took diner with Alonzo Canty4 - green peas - stay all night with Harrison Bright.

June 8th - Wednesday - go to Bro. Robinson's - eat mulberries - go to broad river fishing - had a powerful time - all catch 9 fish, 2 eels - eat strawberries - go home get supper and go to bed - tired out - Sister Robinson wash our clothes after night.

August 2nd - Tuesday - raining - go out in council with the rest of the Elders, and Elders Blackwood and Redd appointed to go on a trip up around Island Ford, N.C., to see if we could find anyone who wanted the gospel.

August 5th - Arose and took breakfast and continued our journey promiscuously through the woods until we felt hungry - stopped at one Mr. Rogers and applied for dinner but was given to understand at once we couldn't eat with him- our next application was at Mr. Miller Kenney's - he gave us dinner - then we traveled on - applied to Mr. James McKenney's to stay all night - we was refused - we then stopped at Mr. Joseph McKenney's who took us in overnight, gave us supper and breakfast - think our fare was begrudged us. (Rutherford Co., N.C.) (returned)

August 10th - Wednesday - arose - took B - go to Bro. Surratt's - bid the folks goodbye - take our grip sack and start on our designated trip in search of the honest in heart in a southerly direction - traveled about 8 miles and called on one Mr. Samuel Littlejohn for dinner who took us in and treated us very kindly - had a gospel chat of about two hours - left him an Articles of Faith and No. 1 tract - traveled on - call on Mr. Burgess (B preacher) for lodging - he kindly refused us - we then called on Mr. Mark Fowler who sent us to Mr. R.C. Littlejohn who, on account of sickness, took us back to the above vFowler to stay overnight and come after us in the morning for breakfast (a gentleman)

Union Co., S.C. (walked 15 miles this day)

August 11th - after breakfast - then on our way slowly, it being very warm - arrive at Mr. Wm. Paris's on Mr. Huse's place about 12 o'clock - take dinner - have a chat with him in regard to the principles of the gospel - he being interested goes and gets a school house for us to preach in and circulates the news - several come to interview us who expressed a desire to hear us preach - in the evening we hold a meeting - about 40 present – good attention and good spirit manifest - after meeting they gathered around to get some tracts and ask questions - received two invitations - appointed another meeting -

stay with Mr. Paris. (walked 8 miles that day)

4 John Alonzo Canty, with Rhett, also

August 13th - Saturday - warm - reading - Mr. J. F. Blackwood came in - talk awhile and invite us home to diner (accepted) - some friends come in - talked about two hours – go to Mr. Jackson Gregory's - hold meeting - had about 50 present - good spirit manifest - after meeting - talk - explaining scripture and singing until about 12:30 o'clock - retire - wore out.

August 14th - Sunday - arose - took breakfast - go up to Sunday school with Mr. Gregory - on arriving at the place was informed it was going to raise a disturbance so we turned off - had a long talk with a Mr. Whitlock (who had invited us to come and see him) and others who on account of his near and dear neighbors talking to him he refused to take us in so went back to Mr. Wm. Paris's for dinner - spent the afternoon in reading and talking to people that come in - go to Mr. Mace Garner's and hold meeting – about 20 present - quiet prevailed - retired about 10 o'clock.

August 15th - Monday - arose - took breakfast - start back for Spartenburg Co. – go through without dinner - arrive at Bro. Sarratt's about 4 o'clock - supper with Bro. Watts - slept with Bro. Sarratt. (walked 23 miles that day)

August 31st - Wednesday - go to Bro. Surratt's - read - take dinner - Elder Wilcox and I go out and have prayer - then we start on a trip to Cleveland Co., N.C.

Sept. 4th - Sunday - breakfast and went on - came to Mr. Wm. Long's in Gaston, N.C. He was not at home so went on after dinner to Bro. Gwin's - had a gospel chat till 12 o? clock with some strangers - put in the night there. (walked 18 miles that day)

Sept. 13th - all the Elders meet - tend to our prayers - then Houston and I take our equipment and start in a southerly direction - take D with Mr. Creek Lee Linder - call at Mr. Sam Littlejohn's - on account of sickness we move on - called on Squire Bonner – he refused to take us in - then we called on Mr. Smith who said we could stay, then repented and sent us adrift - called on Mr. Lipscum who fired us right now (wrathy) says, I have no use for you - you hadn't ought to be allowed in this country - you had ought to be run out - the first thing you know you won't know nothing - we bade him goodbye and traveled on - we next stopped at Mr. Gochers who took us in and treated us like gentlemen - gave them the gospel until bedtime - had prayer with them and retired. (walked 10 miles today)

September 19th - after B started up the road and met Mr. John Rippy who invited us to take the day with him - invitation accepted - witness the beginning of cotton for the first time - after D pick cotton awhile - write to my wife - take supper - hold meeting – about 40 present - good order - received no new invitations - got to bed at a reasonable hour.

September 23rd - then to Mr. Bill Rodes who took us in treated us kindly - his wife was a Red - her

Father's name was Thomas and Grandfather's name John Cross, Ancre, Spartenburg Co., S.C. (walked 10 miles)

September 24th - when B was over we travelled on and crossed into Laurens Co. – take D with Mr. John Wilbanks of the Methodist faith - spent the afternoon in the woods, reading - stay all night with Mr. G. C. Byrd a very clever gentleman - his daughter gave music on piano and sang - which reminded me very much of home - - (the little old organ we had in New Harmony belonged to Grandpa) had a good night's rest.

September 28th - (after sleeping well in an old gin house) - arose from our slumbers and traveled up the road - take breakfast with a Mr. Young - go to Clinton - call on Mr. Yerby a hotel keeper, for to stay the day but was refused - stopped in a store about an hour – the news went out that Mormon preachers were in town - all seemed anxious to see us - some came in and talked to us, some came to the door and daresn't venture their lives farther, others peeked in at the windows - from there we traveled toward Laurens – took D with Mr. Simpson but he didn't want any gospel - then traveled on slowly - was taken in at night on first application by Mr. John Godfrey and treated like gentlemen. Very wet and sloppy traveling, 11 miles.

October 2nd - Sunday - grease up our shoes and trudge along - call at Mr Sam Tumblin who kept us the day and night - very clever people the lady never used tea, coffee or tobacco nor never did.

October 3rd - arose - had B by daylight and went about 2 miles, Washed and changed clothes and washed our dirty ones first of such work have had to do. After our clothes dried we continued our travels called at the house of a Mr. Wood and applied for refreshments and a night's lodging which was granted us - we gave them the gospel by the fireside and sang a few hymns - then retired.

October 5th - Wednesday - another beautiful morning dawned and after B we found ourselves toddling along the big road - stopped by the wayside to read - a young Baptist preacher came along and invited us to preach in a school house in his neighborhood – we accepted the invitation - we ate dinner with the family of Mr. John Owens, a sanctified man - in the evening about 30 came out to hear - had a very good time - no questions asked after meeting - we ate supper and stay all night with Mr. Boland.

October 8th - arose this morning feeling much refreshed - after B we continued our travels calling at the residence of Mr. Barksdale - while sitting in the plaza resting I picked up the Goldville paper and saw a short account of our proceeding by the correspondent - myself and companion having passed through there on the 26th of September. It was as follows - "One day last week a couple of tramps passed through our neighborhood begging their way, saying they were preachers of the gospel, disciples of the meek and lowly Jesus, which we would advise to be arrested and sent to the nearest chain gang." After dinner we travelled on - called on Mr. B. Owens to stay with but was refused. A gentleman standing by says, "I will take you up to the next station on the hand car, there is a big meeting going on up there and ministers scarce and they would be glad to have you to help them out, but when the word `Mormon' came up, "that let's me out", says he. We traveled on - called and stayed all night with Mr. Dave Barton. (walked 12 miles today)

October 11th - after B we start on our way - met J. A. Dacus who invited us to stop for dinner - we did so and preached him the gospel and after dinner we traveled on reflecting on the good times we had anticipated in opening up a field in Laurens, but they were all blighted and we had found ourselves in the big road hitting the grit in getting away - called on Mr. Waddle to stay all night but didn't make the riffle - we then called on Mr. A. W. Parker. When he read our certificate and I commenced to tell him about it, he said See here, do you men want supper?? says I, "Yes, and we want to stay all night with you too." He took us in and we gave him the gospel straight out. He seemed when we left to be quite badly torn to pieces. (8 miles today)

October 15th - cold and windy - continued our march toward Spartenburg - we had supper with him and went to Mr. D. J. Farr and stayed all night. (17 miles)

October 18th - after B we continue - stop at Mr. T. Allen's to inquire the way - he invited us to stop for D which we did - had Possom - and toward evening we found ourselves at Bro. Pool's where we stayed all night.

October 27th - another rainy day dawned and after B. Wilcox and Redd go down and take D with Mr. Andrew Smith after which we all went to Bright Town and spent the night with Mr. Morgan Paris.

THERE IS A BREAK HERE UNTIL

February 25th when he is moving to another field of labor. A note book is missing. If anyone has it get some stuff out of it for this paper.

1888 - begins here:

Feb. 28th - had a early B go to Cowpens - I take the train to Spartenburg - go to the Merchant Hotel - stay until after dinner - then boarded the train for Augusta, Ga., where I arrived at 9:20 p.m. - stayed all night at the Central Hotel. (ride on the R. R. about 160 miles.)

March 3rd - Saturday - Go to Mr. Green's - get some tracts - take dinner with Mr. E. V. Lowe - from there we go to Mr. Nathaniel Walker's - wash all over - hold meeting at night - a goodly number present and a good spirit manifest. We stay all night with Mr. Walker.

March 8th - another beautiful day - after leaving Mr. Creggs we went to Mr. Lawrence Eubanks - no one at home - go to Mr. William Lowe - no one at home - take dinner with Mr. Evert V. Lowe - go to P. Heath's but on account of sickness we went to Mr. Plunket Tools and stayed all night.

March 9th - we go and stay all night with Mr. Ransom Lowe.

March 18th - Sunday - another beautiful day dawned - go without dinner -arrive at Mr. Walker's about l: 30 - meet Jeff Red - hold meeting in the open air - give out what tracts we have - go stay all night with Mr. Edward Key.

March 19th - after B go lay down in the woods - write letters to J. F. Pace and my wife - go take dinner with Mr. Wiley Lowe - supper and stay all night with Mr. Kenney Key.

March 22nd - Cold north wind - very disagreeable - write to Aunt Louisa and the children - read to the folks - take D with Mr. Cregg - go over and stay all night with Mr. Wyley Lowe.

March 24th - Saturday - after B go to the branch and take a bath and change clothes - take dinner with Bryant. Leave our valises - go from there to Mr. Jeff Redd's and stay all night. (walk 15 miles today)

March 25th - stay with Mr. Jeff Redd until after D then go over to Mr. Calhoun Redd's - hold meeting - talk until evening - go to Mr. Jeff Redd's - take supper - sing the songs of Zion - talk on the gospel until bedtime - then we retire.

March 26th - arose feeling fine - remain with Mr. Jeff Redd until after dinner, reading and explaining the gospel - rain - go down to Mr. Calhoun Redd's - take supper – then hold meeting - have a good time - retire at a reasonable hour - rain most of the night.

March 27th - after B start back to Lowe Town through the rain - take D with Mr. Bryant - go to the P.O., receive letter from Father - stay the balance of the day with Mr. Bryant and the night - rain most of the night.

April 3rd - spend the day watching the road for the new Elder - about 4 o'clock Bro. Henry Fairbanks of Payson arrived (He is the father of Miles and Viola F. Lamar who used to live in Raymond) All glad to see one another - go stay all night with Mr. John Cregg.

April 7th - after B continue our journey to Mr. Jeff Redd's where we take dinner – spend the balance of the day - supper and stay all night.

April 8th - spend the day with Mr. Redd - after D hold meeting - have a good time - supper and stay all night with Mr. Jeff Redd.

April 12th - Mr. Boyd and family being sick, Bro. Fairbanks and I conclude to help him plough and ongoing to the field my mule plowing took a fright and ran away - after we caught her we put in the day and stay all night with Mr. Joseph Boyd.

April 22nd - fast day - go to the other side of the runs to Calhoun Redd's - take dinner - hold meeting in the evening - have a good time - not many present but a good spirit manifested - supper and stay all night with Calhoun Redd.

April 23rd - spend the forenoon reading - take dinner with Mr. Cally Redd - go fishing but failed to catch any - replant corn for Mr. Jeff Redd - supper - sing the songs of Zion and go to bed about 10:30 o'clock at Mr. J. Redd's.

April 24th - replant corn for a while - plough a little for Cally Redd - dinner - supper - stay all night with Jeff Redd.

May 4th - go to the office - rec. letter from my wife with picture of self and children - also rec. letter from pap and coat from Bro. Humphrey the Boss - stay all night with Mr. J. Cregg.

May 8th - go to the office - get the paper - spent the afternoon reading - stay all night with Mr. Wyley Lowe.

May 17th - Thursday - after B we go to Bro. Andersons - meet the other Elders - get our equipment - bid the folks goodbye and start for our own field in S.C. - weather very warm - arrive at Mr. Nat Walker's about 5:30 o'clock where we stay all night.

May 28th - after a good night's rest and the morning refreshments we start on our way to Graniteville. After a walk of about 9 hours through the hot sun we arrived there and was very kindly received by Mr. Berry Washum's family where we stayed all night - talked some on the gospel and retired at a reasonable hour quite tired.

June 6th - Remain at Mr. Walker's until after dinner - write to Bro. Humphreys - then go to Mr. Benjamin Boyd's. He not being at home we went to Mr. Wily Lowe's and stay all night.

June 9th - After B go to the office - rec. letters from my wife, Sister Caroline, Elder Ferrin - learn of the death of my bro. John W. Redd - ate dinner - wash - and change clothes - stay all night.

June 19th - After taking the morning's refreshments go to the branch and take a bath - then go to the office - rec. letter from my wife, also a registered letter from Bro. Humphreys with one from my wife stating in it that she had sent me $25.00 - go down to the runs stay with Mr. Jeff Redd.

June 20th - Stay all day and night with Mr. Jeff Redd.

June 21st - Stay with Cally Redd all day and night.

July 3rd - Go to the office, rec. letters from my wife, Pres. Spry & Bro. A. R. Smith, pres. of the Georgia Conference. Go to Mr. Jeff Redd's and stay the night.

July 20th - Stay with Mr. Jeff Redd until after B and start back- go to the office - rec. letters from my wife and Bro. Humphreys stating we were permitted to go to Augusta for the 24th July celebration - D and stay all night with Mr. John Craig.

July 24th - Nine of the Georgia Elders had assembled with the saints to celebrate the day. Called to order at 10 o'clock by William A. Redd who was appointed master of ceremonies. The program was as follows - Music by band, singing by the choir, "Oh Ye Mountains High". Prayer by chaplain David F. Fawns. Singing "Up Awake Ye Defenders of Zion". Pioneer speech by pres. A. R. Smith - Choir sang, "Come, Come Ye Saints". Music by the band - speech by John M. Browning - Song by Jadediah Balentine "Latter Day Kingdom", recitation by David Bennion - closing hymn by the choir "Oh Say Have You Seen etc.". Benediction by the chaplain. The barbecue was then made ready and a glorious feast for all present. Thinking the time had not been sufficiently taken up so a meeting was held. Called to order at 3 o'clock by pres. A. R. Smith - after the usual exercises - singing and prayer, William A. Redd was called to address the congregation and followed by pres. Smith. Thus the day closed which was passed without a single word of disrespect or a strong phrase of any name or nature as I heard, something I never witnessed before in my life - I stayed all night at Bro. McLittle's, slept with Bro. Smith. (This celebration was held at Grovetown, Columbia Co., Ga.)

July 25th - The Elders all came in and after talking and singing a while we retire to the woods - hold meeting (the eleven Elders). The Spirit of God was present in rich abundance and a time of rejoicing was had by all. All being called to express his feelings, desires and determinations - to speak of the goodness of the Lord as he was so led. After we had all spoken pres. Smith delivered a very interesting and instructive sermon, exhorting all to faithfulness in performing our duties, especially in qualifying ourselves for future usefulness. The comfort, joy and satisfaction that was experienced is beyond description - Bro. Smith and I slept together at Bro. McLittle's.

August 7th - arriving at Jeff Redd's about 4 o'clock where we suppered and stayed all night.

August 8th - Stay all day with Mr. Redd - get Mrs. Redd to wash my coat and vest – read from Daniel 2nd chapter and explain to Mrs. Redd who was a warm investigator. Mr. Darlin Heath came home with Mr. Redd and we preached the gospel.

August 17th - Board the train for Spartanburg at which point we change cars for Cowpens. (He is going back to his first field of labor after six months away.) `R.R. ride 130 miles - walk to Bro. Sarratt's and stay all night - meet Bro. Jones on his way to the office. (That was Lehi Jones from Cedar City.)

Sept. 3rd - After B we go to Bro. James Watts5 spend the rest of the day after D finish writing to my Father - Bro. Humphrey (conf. pres.) feeling bad concluded to send me to Ocones to visit the Elders and saints in his stead.

Sept.5th - Get up at 5 - wash and fix for starting. Elder Fairbanks go with me to Cowpens where I take the train for Central (70 miles) where I met Elders Wilcox and Barker with a team to take me to where they were laboring 20 miles distant - arrive at Bro. Miles Mosses at about 5 o'clock where we stay all night. Continued rain all day and night.

Sept. 6th - And still it rains - feeling quite poorly - cause bad cold and a very bad headache - ate dinner with Bro. Miles Mosses - start down to Bro. Nathaniel Wilson's where we stay all night, but on the way on account of the branches being up from rain Bro. Wilcox had to strip twice and carry us across.

Sept. 9th - Sunday - raining - fast and pray - we hold S.S. and meeting - after exercises in S.S. Bro. Redd talk to them a short time - meeting was called to order by Bro. Wilcox - after singing and prayer Bro. W. talked awhile on the Kingdom of God and also our duties - Elder Redd then read from Matt. 10:34-38 and occupy about 3/4 of an hour dwelling mostly on the word of wisdom, occasionally quoting from the scriptures to substantiate my assertions - take dinner with Bro. Wilson - we go stay all night with Bro. Samuel Stuart.

Sept. 10th - After B go down to see the river - it was very high from recent rains – take dinner with Silas K. Wilson - go to Bro. Taylor Wilson's supper - hold a testimony meeting - 13 of the saints bore their testimony to the truth - then Bros. Wilcox, Baker and Redd speak a few minutes each and bear testimony. Have an excellent time - not one refused to get up when asked - stay all night with Brother S.K. Wilson.

Sept. 12th - Read awhile - go out in the woods hold a meeting ourselves - talk to one another - have a very good time giving our experiences and a short account of our labors and talking over the ways we should walk and talk among the people - go and take dinner with Sister Harriet Wilson - go from there to Bro. Mosses - supper and held meeting - Bro. Redd did the preaching - read from 1 Pet. 3, 15 about 40 present – good spirit prevail - stay with Bro. Moss.

James Harvey Watts and Mary Jane Whitesides his wife. James was the son of William and Lucy Watts

Sept. 13th - read and talk awhile - then we go to Bro. T. Wilson's - Bro. B. stay there and Wilcox and I go to S K. Wilson's - take dinner - wade little river - go to Mr. Gubly Rains hold meeting - Redd do the preaching - read from Matt. 7:21 from which I take the first principles of the gospel - occupy about 55 minutes - good spirit prevails - stay all night.

Sept. 20th - After B start for Seneca where I arrive quarter to twelve - board the train for Cowpens - leave train and walk to Bro. Bolen and stay all night. (Ride 80 miles on the train.)

Oct. 20th - Saturday - Bro. Spry arrive safe and sound - conference opened - Elders present - Pres. Wm. Spry, pres. of southern states mission - Hyrum T. Humphreys, pres. of South Carolina conf., traveling Elders, Barker, Jones, Wilcox, Jensen, Clark, Burgess, Fairbanks, Johnsen and Redd. 10 o'clock a.m. meeting called to order by Pres. Humphreys who made a few remarks - Bro. Jones followed, then Pres. Spry addressed us - adjourned until 2 p.m. then Barker, Johnsen, Redd and Fairbanks, D with Bro. Sarratt, supper and stay all night with Bro. Evan Watts. (The father of Billy of New Harmony fame.)

Oct. 21st - Sunday - meeting called to order by pres. Humphreys. Burgess, Jensen and Spry addressed the congregation - dinner with Bro. Evan Watts - meeting called to order by pres. H. Elders Clark and Spry did the preaching - which closed our conference. In the meantime we held 5 council meetings in the woods, where we received much valuable instruction - Bro. Humphreys was released to go home with the Nov. company and Bro. Redd to succeed him as presiding Elder (Pres) over the South Carolina conference - we make proposal to Pres. Spry to stay with us another day, which he willingly consented to do. I go with Bros. Fairbanks and Barker and stay all night with Bro. Bolin. (This Pres. Spry was later governor of Utah.)

Oct. 25th - write to Miss Emily Redd of Wilmington, N.C. - rain all day. (Lura says "When I was in Wilmington in 1918 I stayed with this Emily Redd and read the letter that Father wrote to her. I've wished ever since that I had copied it. He was preaching `gathering' to her which has been discontinued for many years.")

Oct. 28th - Sunday - go to Bro. Sarratt's meet the rest of the Elders. Hold S.S. and meeting. A general good time and lots of the Spirit of the Lord was enjoyed. Sister Robinson being sick sent for some of the Elders. Bro. Clark and I go down and administer to her. She was instantly healed by the power of God. Sing the songs of Zion.

Nov. 9th - Bro. and Sister Roop were going down toward Cowpens to visit some of their relatives - left Bro. Fairbanks and I with the house as we were going to the office when the mail came (with the understanding that we would lock the door when we left. They left the breakfast dishes dirty on the table, the beds unmade, the ovens and lids scattered around the fire as they had been used while cooking, the bread tray uncovered and exposed to mice, cats and flies, the churn with the fresh churned milk in it uncovered also, the floor un swept - in fact as it is generally termed by housekeepers - it was left upside down. We go to the office - rec. letters from wife, Elders Burgess, Wilcox, Barker and Jones. Write a note to Pres. Spry. Also write to Elders Wilcox and Burgess - stay all night with Bro. Sarratt.

Nov. 18th - Sunday - go to Bro. Sarratts - hold S.S. and meeting - not many present – a good spirit manifest - D, S and stay all night with Bro. Evan Watts.

"I don't have any more of his mission journal. I remember him saying that when he was released he didn't have the money to come home. Then the church didn't pay their way home as they do now. He went to Mr. Black who has been mentioned many times. Mr. Black was not a member, but a very good friend. He was a Justice of the Peace or some such thing and stood out on the courthouse steps and gave quite a speech.

He said he was going to lend this man $50.00. He had been out here paying his own way for them and their welfare. He wouldn't lend anything to a sectarian minister, but he was going to lend it to this man, Mr. William A. Redd from Utah, because he would pay it back. He was an honest man and could be trusted.

Too, this is not nearly all of the journal I have. As you will note, I have put in only the entries of a few days in each month that I have. He has an entry for every day."

by Jan Garbett

Elder Amasa Lyman Clark - SSM 1887-

PHOTO 47   AMASA LYMAN CLARK

Birth date, place - 6 June 1865, Farmington, Davis, Utah Territory
Death date - 25 May 1968
Baptism date - 12 October 1873   --   Baptism by - Oliver Robinson
Father's name - Ezra T Clark - Mother's name - Mary Stevenson

Southern States - November 1887–Unknown - Age Called: 22

Southern States
Set Apart: 12 November 1887
Priesthood office: Seventy - Quorum: 56th - Priesthood: 56th Seventies
Called From: Farmington, Davis, Utah, United States
Set apart by: A H Cannon

Central States -

Southwestern States - December 1925–May 1926 - Age Called: 60

Central States
Set Apart: 15 December 1925 - End Date: 27 May 1926
Departed From Home: 16 December 1925
Priesthood office: High Priest
Called From: Farmington, Davis, Utah, United States
Set apart by: Stephen L Richards

> Missionary Department missionary registers, 1860-1959, Vol. 5, p. 160, line 1234.
> Missionary Department missionary registers, 1860-1959, Vol. 1, p. 90, line 254.
> Missionary Department missionary registers, 1860-1959, Vol. 2, p. 98, line 254.
> First Presidency missionary calls and recommendations 1877-1918, CR 1 168, Church History Library.
> Site Map

Amasa Lyman Clark was born 6 Jun 1865 in Farmington, Utah. He married Alice Sneed, the other marriage was after his mission. He mentions Alice often in his journal. Amasa died 25 May 1968 in Salt Lake City, Utah and is buried in the Farmington Cemetery.

From his journal:

Nov. 22, 1887

"I received a letter of inquiry from the first Seven Presidents of Seventies dated Sept. 20, 1887, desiring to know my condition and feelings in regard to preforming a mission if my service should be needed within the next three years. In answer I said I was willing to do what was required at my hands.

On the 3rd of Nov. 1887 I received a letter from President (Wilford) Woodruff stating that my name had been accepted as a missionary to the Southern States & that I was expected to start on the 15th of the same month. Before starting I moved (d) Alice my wife down to my fathers and according to arrangements started from Salt Lake City on the 17th of November via of the Denver & Rio Grande Railway. "

The Missionary Journal Of Amasa Lyman Clark

November 1887

Journal of Amasa L. Clark

Nov. 22, 1887   I received a letter of inquiry from the first Seven Presidents of Seventies dated Sept. 20, 1887, desiring to know my condition and feelings in regard to performing a mission if my service should be needed within the next three years. In answer I said I was willing to do what was required at my hands.

On the 3rd of Nov. 1887 I received a letter from President (Wilford) Woodruff stating that my name had been accepted as a missionary to the Southern States & that I was expected to start on the 15th of the same month. Before starting I moved Alice my wife down to my fathers and according to arrangements started from Salt Lake City on the 17th of November via of the Denver & Rio Grande Railway.

Leaving Salt Lake (11-10 a.m.) I traveled south through an open country for about 15 mi. then descended into the river bottom of the Jordon where the train makes several nice curves. After abt 5 or 6 miles travel in the river bottom we came out on a level plain in Utah State, arrived at Provo at 1-10 p.m. here I met Bros. Moroni Dunford and Robert Skelton. Travel southeast through Springville and Spanish Fork and then up the Spanish Fork Canyon saw several charcoal kilns and a sand stone quarry and some slate colored rocky cliffs. The grade was so heavy another engine joined us until we reached Soldier's Summit (7465 ft. above sea level) we then passed through Pleasant Valley which is not settled very much. Continuing down grade we pass through Price Canyon.

It was quite difficult to construct a road through this canyon as it runs on the edge of rocky cliffs which shoot perpendicularly into the air for hundreds of feet. In the eve. We came to Castle Gate. The huge pillars of rock composing it are offshoots of the cliffs behind. One peak is 400 ft. high the other five (hundred). Travel over a desert company and arrive at Green River after dark. Had a talk with Wm Elliot of Rochester, Minn., an unbeliever in the Bible.

Nov. 18 (Friday) Wake up early in the morning and find myself traveling through up the Gunnison Canyon. through this canyon runs the Gunnison River which flows into the Colorado. This canyon affords very beautiful scenery. The road has been constructed in the side of solid cliffs which hand over the cars and shoot into the air for hundreds of feet. Leaving the canyon we follow up the river through a small valley about a mile wide. In this valley are hundreds of acres of meadow land. Saw great amount of hay and some nice beef cattle. Arrive at Gunnison for breakfast. Here another enjine joins us. Continue to the southeast from Gunnison up a very small canyon the grade being very heavy. At this time we begin ascending the Rocky Mountains. (This would have to have been the now Monarch Pass, down into Salida, over Marshall Pass coming out near Poncha Pass, south of Poncha Springs, Colorado.) The grade becomes heavier averaging about 270 feet to the mile. We gradually ascend the mts. winding around the hills forming very short curves. Near the summit the train runs around six miles of road in accomplishing three quarters of a mile. Reach the summit abt. Noon (10,952 ft. above the sea). In descending the mountain the train runs around similar curves forming curves a great deal like a letter S. On arriving at the bottom Moroni Dunford pulled a tooth for me. From the foot of the mountain, we run through a very narrow valley out into a plain country between two ranges of mts. In this valley are several small villages among which is Poucho (Poncha Springs). Here we cross the Arkansas River & follow it down through Grand Canyon. This canyon is about 30 mi. long and is very narrow. (The canyon is the one at the bottom of Royal Gorge.)

At one place it is so narrow that one end of a bridge is held up by two iron beams which extend above the track from one side of the canyon to the other. The other end is fastened to the cliff. Along through these canyons are found several (cake) kilns. The fire in thee kilns burns from top to bottom. After leaving this canyon we follow the Arkansas River southeast opening out into the great planes. Leaving the beautiful rocky mts. In the west. We soon arrive at Cannon City Col. Which is the same altitude as Salt Lake City also growing the same products. Here is situated the state prison of Colorado. This is a great mining district---coal. Forty miles farther brings us to Pueblo. Was much surprised to see the streets running off in different directions. Arrived here at 4-25 p.m. Change cars for Kansas City. Leave via. Atchison Topeka & Santa Fe at 6.50 wide. Travel through planes all night crossing the line between Col. and Kansas about 12-30 a.m. Wake up in the morning and still on the planes. The soil seems to be a light cast containing alkali and other minerals. Many towns & villages are built along the railroad. Corn is the principal product.

In the eastern part of Kansas the land seems to be better & several coal mines are also found here. Arrive at Kansas City at 5-10. While here I visited the Cable line also went out and saw the Missouri River by moonlight. The population is about 200,000. Streets run in different directions. Leave here at 9-20; via., of Fort Scott, Gulf R. R. Rode in a chair-car. We are at this point coming into the forests of white oak and other trees. Travel all night.

-20- (Sunday) The cotton plant soon begins to appear but is not cultivated as extensively as corn and lumber. Travel south-east through Missouri & the north-eastern part of Arkansas. Receive telegram that the trussell works are burned. Have to run around another road which is a great deal farther causing us to be late to connect with the other train at Memphis. Cross the Mississippi about 10 (p.m.) on a ferryboat-Charles Marion. Was taken in & shown the barge engine, electric engine, driving-wheel etc. Arrived at Peabody House, Memphis about 11-50 p.m. This city contains 60,000 inhabitants. Stay all night and start for Chattanooga at 10 a.m. via of the Memphis & Charleston. Along the road are seen cotton fields. A great many trees are cut from the forest. About one half the population seem to be Negroes. Droves of pigs are seen instead of herds of cattle.

This part of the country consists of rolling hills which are covered with trees. The people are generally very indolent. Children receive a very poor education having to work in the cotton from the last of April to late in the fall, sometimes until Christmas.

Travel from Memphis through the south-western part of Tenn., the north-eastern part of Miss., the northern part of Alabama, the north-western corner of Georgia, then back into Tenn. arriving at Chattanooga 10 p.m. and go to the Kennedy House.

(Nov. 22) (Thursday) In the morning take Dummy Line & go to Missouri Ridge. On this hill some hard fighting was done during the war between the north and the south. Obtained some wild raspberry leaves, also a small cedar bough from the tree where Gen. Bragg had his headquarters. In the afternoon went and visited the ice factory where water is distilled and frozen in vats by the use of compressed air.

Nov. 23 (Wednesday) Bro. Morgan left for the west the 22nd with a company of Emigrants. Bro. Spry (Bro. Morgan's assistant) and Heber Rich, who was assisting Bro. Spry, came to the Hotel and gave us some instructions regarding our responsibility as missionaries and the manner in which we should Conduct ourselves. Bro. Robt Skelton was appointed to labor in Clay Co., Tennessee. Bro. O. P. Jensen & myself were sent to Ezell, Spartanburg Co., S.C. Bro. Skelton started the next morning Nov. 24 abt. 5 o'clock. We were to start at 9.10 but on account of having to meet Bro. Spry we did not go until 1- p.m. Arrived in Atlanta at 6:50 p.m. , after traveling about 150 miles through a rolling country covered with pine, hickory, oak, and other trees. Could not make connection at Atlanta and stayed all night there. The people of Atlanta were divided in opinion about the liquor question & it was to be decided by ballot. Those opposed to the sale of liquor, The Prohibation Club, about 25,000 in number, were parading the streets, most of them having torches & preceded by a brass band. Stopped at hotel near the depot and started for Cowpens St. at 7:40 a.m.

Friday Nov. 25 Arrived at Cowpens St. or Hampton at 4:10 p.m. after traveling all day through a very rolling country covered with forest. The country is very thinly settled except for a settlements scattered along the railroad. At Hampton we met Bros. Humphery & Stookey who were just going to start south-west into a new field of labor. We also met Mr. Jno. Black who is a rough man but he is very friendly to the Elders; they having stayed to his house at times for four years. Twenty-five Elders have stayed at his house.

Walked home with Mr. Black about 7 ½ miles north-east of the Station. Here we found the S. C. conference of the Church presided over by Moroni D. Ferrin.

November Here I joined Bro. Wm. A. Redd in laboring with the members of the Church and holding Sunday School and Meeting at Tickety Mt. Every Sunday. Bro. Jensen labored with Elisha Peck, of Lehi three miles east of here in a Branch of the Church. Stayed all night with Mr. Jno. Black (7 ½ miles.

Saturday 26 1887. Ate dinner with Jno. Black. After dinner, met with Elder Ferrin who had been visiting the Saints south-west of here. The people are very thinly settled there being about three or four houses to the square mile. Stayed all night with Sydney Berry.[118]

Sunday 27. Attended Sunday School and meeting held on porch of Alonzo Canty's.[119] Spoke at each meeting. Stayed all night with Jno. Black, Esq.

Monday 28, Nov. Wrote to my wife, W. W. Clark, & to Wm. Spry, Chattanooga, informing him of our safe arrival. Met Elder Elisha Peck from Brighton Branch. He was acquainted with Ezra J. Clark in England. Stayed all night with James Watts.

Tuesday 29. Went to Ezell P.O. three miles distance. On returning visited Cowpen's Monument where the last battle of the Revolutionary War was fought. The monument is built upon a square rock. It was made of rock in an octagon shape upon which is placed a large white stone of the same shape. Height about seven feet. From the top extends a rod into the air about eight feet long

December 1887

Thursday Dec. 1. Met Elder Ferrin. Ate dinner with Alonzo Canty. Went with Elder Ferrin stayed all night with Davis Ayers. 2 miles.

Friday 2nd Dec. Ate dinner with Alonzo Canty.[120] Stayed all night with Sydney Berry.

Saturday 3rd Went to the post office stopped on the way back and ate dinner with Sister Lanier. Met with Bro. Jensen and Peck from Brighton. Stayed all nigh(t) with Bro. Jas. Watts. (7 ½ miles)

Sunday 4th Dec. Fast day. Sunday School and meeting at James Watts'.[121] Spoke at each meeting. Took dinner with Bro. Taylor George's.[122] Stayed all night with Bro. James Watts.

Monday 5- Took dinner with Alonzo Canty. Stayed all night with Davis Ayers.[123]

Tuesday 6 Went to Post Office came back to cotton picking at Davis Ayers had dinner and supper with him. Stayed all night with Jno. Black. 7 ½ miles.

Wednesday 7 Engaged in settling difficulty between Bro. Sydney Berry and family about working part of Mr. John Black's Farm. Took dinner with Sydney Berry & stayed all night with Alonzo Canty.

---

[118]Sydney was a white man.
[119]John Alonzo Canty- born 1859.
[120]Catawba John Alozno Canty Whitesides
[121]James Harvey Watts, son of William David and Nancy Christine Wats Watts, husband of Mary Jane Whitesides, sister of John Alonzo Canty.
[122]Taylor George, son of Zacharia and Emily Cobb George.
[123]Jefferson Davis Ayers, son o f Jefferson and Emily Cobb Ayers.

Thursday 8   Went to the post office coming back, took dinner with John Williams. Rec'd a...come from my wife. Stayed all night with John Black Esq. after holding a Testamony meeting at Bro. James Watts. 7 ½ mi.

Friday 9 Dec.   During the forenoon I attended a council meeting in the woods, by a fire, while it was raining. Moroni Ferrin, Wm A Redd and myself were present. Were engaged in settling a difficulty between Sydney Berry and family. His wife has (had) children from four other men before marrying Bro. Berry and according to the Law of S. C. he has no right to control them but we wish to have the children bound to them so he can control them, which he is not willing to have done.[124]

Ate dinner with Alonzo Canty. After dinner we met with Bro. Berry in a vacant cabin of John Blacks and held council until about four p.m. when we went and visited with Sister Berry and tried to persuade her to bind the children to him which she was not willing to do. West from there about 9-30 p.m. and stayed all night with Alonzo Canty.

Saturday 10 Dec.   Wrote a letter to Alice and went to the post office while Elders Ferrin and Redd went to visit Sister Berry. Stopped at Sister Linder's on my way back and had a nice dinner with her. On coming to headquarters met Bros. & Jensen, had a bath and Bro. Ferrin wished me to go with Elder Peck to a branch three miles east where a Sunday School and meeting are held every Sunday, average attendance about thirty. Arrived at Bro. Surratt's (headquarters) at 6-30 p.m. 10 ½ miles.

Sunday 11   Met with the saints and children about 10-30 a.m. After the reading exercises I spoke for about 15 mts. Between S. S. and meeting there was fifteen intermission. Meeting commenced at 12 o'clock. During meeting I was an instrument in speaking to the people for about thirty minutes upon the first principles of the Gospel, the Apostasy, & the Restorations of the Gospel. Bore testimony that the Gospel was restored in these last days. After dinner went from Bro. Surratt's and visited Sister Price and took supper with her-spent the evening there and returned to Bro. Surratt's where we stayed all night.

Monday 12-1887   Spent the forenoon in picking cotton for Mrs. Surratt. After dinner cut some wood-wrote in my journal and walked two miles and a half south. Stayed all night with Bros. Thos. Blackwood & family all have been baptized except the mother. Spent the evening in talking with the family about the Gospel. 2 ½ mi.

Tuesday Dec. 13, 1887   Left Bro. Blackwood's about 9 o'clock after chopping some wood, walked about one mile stayed all night with (Bro.) James Bowlin and family. Had a good time in talking

---

[124]Harriet Berry a white woman had a child by a man named Dye, not a Catawba, the result was Gertrude Dye who later 'married' James Harvey Watts; Harriet then 'married' Nephi Lehi Sydney and had an infant that might have died; Harriet then married Jefferson Davis Ayers and had several children.

about the Gospel. Sister Bowlin told of the ill-treatment she received from her folk. Her father went away from home when she went to visit him. Her folks with not have anything to do with her. Ate dinner there and stayed all night. Was treated very kindly. Enjoyed a nice dish for dinner and breakfast called stickies. Made by rolling out dough which spread with butter and brown-sugar then it is all rolled together making layers of dough, & butter & sugar. The roll is then cut into pieces about two inches long which are put into the baking oven-a little milk poured over them and then baked. 1 mi.

Wednesday 14   Left Bro. Bowlin's about 9 o'clock went about two miles-north-west to Mr. Henry Henderson's via of Bro. Blackwood's. His family have all been baptized. Here a young lady aged 15 was sick with a dizzy head blood having rushed to her head.

Her father also had a very bad cold. We administered to them and then went about ¾ of a mile to Bro. Blackwood's and got some herbs to make some herb tea for them. When we returned the girl was better-made some tea and gave them & he felt better. We then chopped up a pile of wood. After dinner we read the Book of Mormon to them until 4 p.m. and then walked three miles to Bro. Surratt's (headquarters). Ate supper with Sister Watts, and Stayed all night with Bro. Surratt. 5 miles.

Thursday 15   After breakfast spent some time in writing in my journal. Two years ago this moment I was going after My Alice to start to Logan. Left Bro. Surratt's at 10 a.m. & went two miles south two miles and took dinner at Thos. Blackwood's. Talked with Mrs. Linder upon the Principles of our religion. Ate some very nice popped-corn.

The "Knights of Labor" are holding meetings here and quite a number are joining them. There is a general feeling among the people that they are about to create trouble with the Nation. Left Bro. Blackwood's at 4 p.m. for Bro. Surratt's. On the road we met Elders Ferrin and Redd who accompanied us to Bro. Surratt's. Elder Peck and I went & spent the evening and stayed all night with Sister Cleveland Bright. Her husband has been excommunicated. 2 mi.

Friday 16-Dec.   My Wedding Day---Beautiful day. Met with Elders Ferrin & Redd & held a Council Meeting upon some difficulties to be settled in the Church. Ate dinner with Bro. Surratt. Wrote to my wife and Dr. Hetzler. Spent the evening with the wife of Hosea Bright-he has been excommunicated. Stayed all night with Bro. Surratt.

Saturday 17. Dec.   Ate breakfast with Bro. Surratt. Went up to Alonzo Canty's (headquarters). Had bath & changed clothes.

December

Ate dinner with Alonzo Canty. Held Council Meeting on the case of Mrs. Sydney Berry also James Watts for drunkenness. Has to make acknowledgement before the Church. Left for Bro. Surratt's with

Elders Peck & Jensen. Stayed all night for Bro. Surratt. 6 mi.

Sunday 18th, 1887.   No Sunday School was held on account of the children having the mumps. Meeting commenced at 11 a.m. at which each of us spoke. Testamony meeting at 6 p.m. was held at Bro. Evan Watts.[125] Several of Saints bore their testimony. Spent night Harrison Bright.

Monday 19   Helped Mrs. Surratt pick the last of her cotton while Bro. Peck carried a grist to the mill 21/2 miles away. Ate dinner with Bro. Surratt.

Spent the evening and stayed all night with Mr. Harrison Bright and family. Read to them from "The Martyrs" and explained the principles of the Gospel to them. Went to bed 11:40.

Tuesday, 20. Dec.   Has been raining during the night and all the morning. Ate dinner with Bro. Surratt. Wrote to Alice, Wm. Elliot (of) Rochester, Minn.2 And to Jos. S. Clark. Spent the evening with Hosea Bright and stayed all night with Bro. Surratt.

Wednesday 21,   Went with Elder Peck two miles to the Shoe-makers. Came back and had dinner with Bro. Surratt. Met with Elders Ferrin & Redd who had brought me a letter from Alice. Held Council Meeting over the difficulties existing in the Conference. Partook of the Sacrament and each of us spoke and desired to improve the condition of the Conference. After meeting left with Elder Ferrin went 2 miles south and spent the eve. & stayed all night with Bro. Thos. Blackwood. 2 miles.

(22) Thursday   Went to Mr. Henry Henderson at 8:30. Read the B of M to them; stayed until about 3 p.m. left to see Bro. Lee Linder-was away from home. We then went down towards Cowpens & stayed all night with Mr. Mat. Henderson. 4 miles.

Friday 23   Went and saw a Mr. Smith on some of Elder Ferrin's business, then went and had dinner with Mr. Jorden Blackwood's wife had been baptized.   Stayed all night. Had conversation with a woman who had not heard the Gospel. 3 mi.

Saturday 24   Started for headquarters Alonzo Canty's distance 5 miles. Has been raining all night. Ate dinner with Bro. Alonzo Canty. Started with Elder Peck & told the people there would be no meeting tomorrow on account of so much drunkenness going on it the being the custom of the country. Stayed all night with Bro. James Bowling.

Sunday 25 Christmas   Left for Bro. Surratt's 3 miles, had Christmas dinner with Bro. Surratt. Spent the day in singing hymns and talking. Ate supper with Bro. Surratt. Stayed all night with Bro. Evan Watts. 6 1/2 mi.

---

[125]Evans Watts was a white man who married into the tribe. He married Lucy Marsh who had children by several men, both Catawba and white, and the two had two more children, James Harvey and William David Watts. Evan and Lucy and William David and wife Nancy Christine moved to New Harmony, Utah, where they remained until their deaths.

December

Monday 26 Dec.   Wrote to Wife and Parents. Ate dinner with Bro. Surratt, also stayed all night with him. 3 mi.

Tuesday 27. Dec.   Went to the P.O. coming back ate dinner with Sister Lanier. Left headquarters with Elder OP Jensen stayed all night with Theodore Bright. 12 miles

Wednesday 28, Dec.   Went to Bro. Surratt's wrote to my Companion. Held Council Meeting in the afternoon and partook of the Sacrament. Elder Ferrin and I after meeting, started on a three weeks trip to Kings Mt. 25 miles east to look after the Saints there. Walked 8 miles in the evening stayed all night with Hampton Robinson who has been excommunicated for drunkenness . His wife is strong in the faith. Friends have abandoned her; her half-sister burned her house & continse (contents) down but cannot give her religion up. 8 ½ (miles)

Thursday 29. December   Stayed all day and night with Sister Robinson. Chopped a large pile of wood for her mother who has been opposed to LDS. She seemed pleased with my cutting the wood & felt better towards us. Made two pies for us for Christhmas presents.

Friday, Dec. 30.   Had a very nice chicken & dumplings for breakfast. Started on our journey at 1 p.m. went east 14 miles to Bro. Moses Gordon's on Buffalo Creek where we stayed all night & the next day and night. Read a pamplet entitled Mormon Exposed" The other side of Mr. Barclay, A Member of the British Parliament. 15 mi.

November | December   1888

New Years 1888. Sunday.

After breakfast we went one mile south in the rain & spent the day and night with Bro. Jno. Gordon on Mr. Humphrey's plantation. 1 mi.

Monday January 2   Administered to one of the children and left at 1 p.m. went to Bro. Wm Weavers three miles south east of Grover on Mr. Patterson's Plantation. [126] Stayed all night. 7 mi.

(Tuesday 3.)   Went and took dinner with Saister Dorer (Soer?) 11/2 mile(s) south. Her husband is opposed to our Faith. After dinner went 11/2 mi south and spent some time with Bro. Wiley. Sister Wiley is blind. She knows how to read with raised letters. Has the Testament in two volumes each being about the size of a large center-table Bible. She is very well versed in the Scriptures. Left in the evening and went back and stayed all night with Wm. Weaver. 5 mi.

Wednesday 4 Jan.   Wrote a letter to a to Alice. Went three miles and spent several hours with Mr.

---

[126]James Goodwin Patterson, born 1849 married Elizabeth Missouri White and had a large family. James was the son of Laban Chappell a white man and a Catawba woman named Martha Patterson. He never used his father's surname.

L.G. Wilson who has been investigating-lives one half mile n-e (northeast) from Grover. Went Back to Bro. Moses Gordon's 41/2 mi and stayed all night. 7-1/2 (miles)

Thursday 5, 1888.   Went 1 ½ mi. east. Took dinner with Bro. Jno. Gordon who has moved on Mr. Thos. Camps place. After dinner went to Shelby and found Bro. Jno. Gowins working in a small plaining mill; went from here 2 miles s-e (southeast) to his home got lost & went an extra mile. 12 ½ mi.

Friday Jan. 6   Stayed all day and night here. In the afternoon went to Shelby, N.C. Got some Olive O(il). 4 mi.

Saturday 7. 1888.   Had a bath in the creek and wore some other under ware while Sister Goins washed & dried ours. Went back to Bro. Jno. Gordon's 6 mi. where we stayed all night. Administered to Bro. Gordon's child. 6 mi

Sunday 8. Jan.   Held two meetings spoke at each. In the evening administered to Bro. Jno. Gordon's child. Stayed all night here. Had conversation with Mr. Camp who thought I was a young looking preacher. Seemed interested & accepted a tract with pleasure.

Monday Jan. 9   Went and spent the day with Bro. Moses Gordons wrote to Father-in-Law and Alice. Stayed all night with Mr. Jno. Patterson[127] treated kindly his wife would be baptized if he would permit. 3 mi.

-Tuesday 10-Jan.-   Went 8 miles s. (south) ate dinner with Bro. Wm. Weaver. Bro. Ferrin (re)baptized Sister Weaver for Adultery and I reconfirmed her. E. Ferrin went down to York Co. alone and in disguise to visit some of the Saints. I did not on account of raising suspicion as two generally travel alone. I accompanied him one mile and visited Kings Mt. Monument and then came back and stayed.

January

All night with Bro. Wiley. The King's Mt. Monument is twent(y)-five feet high built of granite; the same as in SLC. (Salt Lake City) Temple. Cost $2800.00. It is situated on a hill, one of the spurs of King Mt. Ridge. Build in honor of a successful Revolutionary Battle in which Gen. Furgerson at the head of English, who were camped on top of the hill, was defeated by the Americans who surrounded the hill. Here the tide of war turned in favor of America. Battled Oct. 7, 1780. Obtained a good view from the monument standing on its platform five or six feet from the ground. 10 mi

Wednesday Jan. 11, 1888   Went seven miles north-ate dinner with Bro. Wm. Weaver. Stayed all night with Mr. Lum Turner who wanted to see the Elders. He was much interested was treated kindly. I was

---

[127]James Patterson not Jno.

to ask him about wanting to see the E's if I saw him while going by; so as no one could be seen the dog come at me in such a fury that the man came out and invited me in. 7 mi.

Thursday 12 Took dinner with Bro. M. Gordon. 11/2 mi. After dinner went to Bro. Jno. Gordon's 11/2 miles east. Spent the evening & stayed all night with Mr. Thos. Camp who wanted to see the Elders. Stayed up talking until 12 p.m. His wife never talked with an LDS before thought men in Utah had 7 wives and to examined my Bible thinking it a "Mormon" Bible. 3 (miles)

January Friday 13. Ate dinner with Bro. Jno. Gordon and then went 6 mi. n (north) to Bro. Jno. Goins near Shelby N.C. Stayed all night. 6 mi.

Saturday 14 Jan. Had a bath in the creek some sleet was on the ground. Wrote to my wife. Left for Bro. Jno. Gordons at 4 p.m. here met Elder Ferrin who had returned from York Country. 6 mi

Sunday 15 Had meeting at 11 a.m. & ate dinner with Bro. Jno. Gordon. Stayed all night with Bro. Moses Gordon. 2 mi.

Monday 16 Jan. Had a fall in the old mill wheel feel and cut my head on a rock but soon got well. After dinner we went 5 mi.

Jan.   s-e (southeast). To Bro. Saml. Gordon's 2 mi north of Balck's Station near Whitacer Mt. His wife is non-Mormon. Held meeting with the family and I spoke about 30 minutes by the assistance of the Holy Spirit. Stormy weather. Stayed all night. 5 mi.

Tuesday Jan. 17 In the afternoon we held meeting with family of Ruphus McDade who invited us. One mile from Bro. Gordons.

Wednesday 18 Left Bro. Gordon's in the morning went 9 miles to Sister Robinson's. In the morning Sister (Robinson) mended my pants and coat. 9 mi.

Friday 19. Went to Bro. Surratts 10 miles via of Gaffneys here I had 7 letters, 4 from my Wife one from M.E. Clark (Mary Elizabeth) & Ezra, Wm Elliott & J.L.H. Stayed all night Bro. Evan Watts. 10 (miles)

January Friday-20 Wrote to C.W. Richards & Wife. Dinner with Bro. E. Watts also stayed all night with family of Bro. Wm Watts[128] with E. Jensen.

Saturday, 21 Went to P.O. by Alonzo Canty's where I found one letter from Wife and got 3 from office 2 from Alice and one from W. W. C. (Wilford Woodruff Clark). Had dinner with Bro. Canty.

---

[128]Evans and Lucy Marsh Watts and their son William David Watts and his wife Nancy Christine and their son.

Stayed all night at Morgan Paris (friend) with E. Redd. 13 (miles)

Sunday 22. No Sunday School on account of bad weather. Held meeting with Bro. Evan Watts. Stayed all night with Harrison Bright (friend).

Monday Jan. 23 Held Council Meeting---Elders Ferrin , Redd, Peck , Jensen & Clark. Partook sacrament. Each spoke.

January Wrote to Alice. Stayed all night with Bro. Evan Watts.

Tuesday 24 Wrote to Chas. R. Clark-dinner with Bro. E. Watts. Went two miles s.e. (southeast). Stayed all night with Bro. James Bolin on Mr. Harrison('s) Planatation. Administered to Bro. Bolin's little boy E. Peck & myself. 2 ½ (miles)

Wednesday 25. Spent the day in reading and talking about the Gospel. Stayed all night.

Thursday 26. Came up to Bro. Surratt here met Bro. Ferrin who has come from Mr. Blacks---had one letter from Alice. Had dinner with Bro. Evan Watts, also stayed all night. 2 ½ (miles)

Friday, January 27 Wrote to Alice and Dr. J. L. Hetzler. Went two miles north with Elder.

January

Peck to the Shoemakers. The weather is warm here while at home they are having a hard winter & cold weather 15" below zero at Farmington. About noon (Elders Ferrin, Peck & myself) commenced work on a rock chimney to Bro. Surratt's house where we have meetings so we can have a fire during meeting. Ate dinner and stayed all night with Bro. Surratt. 4 (miles)

Saturday Jan. 28 Worked all day on the chimney mixing mud etc. Ate dinner and stayed all night with Bro. Surratt.

Sunday Jan. 29. Held Sunday school and meeting at Bro. Surratts with large attendance. I spoke in Sunday S. Elders Ferrin & Peck in meeting. After dinner I went home with Bro. (Bolin) where I had dinner and stayed all night. Administered to Sister Lanier who is staying with or near Bro. Bolin.

Monday Jan. 30 Came with Bro. Bolin to Bro. X and continued work on the chimney. On our way we shock some locusts down from the tree and I enjoyed them very much. In the evening I left via. Mr. Black's for the P.O. Stayed all night with Bro. Davis Ayrs (Ayers) (On Mr. Black's plantation). 3 mi.

Tuesday-Jan. 30 (31 3 mi. Left for P.O. early in morning sat porch of P.O. & wrote a letter to Parents. Then walked 5 miles to Bro. Surratts for dinner. After dinner Elder Peck & I went three miles to mill with grist on our backs. On the way the string of my sack broke & let part of my corn on the ground & we had a picnic gathering & cleaning up the corn. Elder Ferrin & I went a short distance and spent the evening with Market Bridges, an old friend to the Elders, on account of his having company, we went and stayed all night with Bro. Surratt. 16 mi.

February 1 1888 Wednesday-   Completed the work on the chimney. Ate dinner at Bro. Surratt's. Stayed all night with Bro. Evan Watts.

Thursday Feb. 2   Half soled my boots & helped Bro. Surratt put a hearth in his fireplace. Ate dinner and stayed all night with Bro. Surratt.

Friday. Feb. 3   In the morning wrote a letter to my wife at Bro. E. Watts and went to P.O. 6 mi; received letter from Alice; went back to Bro. James Watt's[129] (on Mr. Black's place) & took dinner. Here met Elders Ferrin and Peck who had stayed all night with Bro. Lee Linder. Stayed all night with Bro. Davis Ayers (on Black's). 9 mi.

Saturday 4.   Went to Bro. J. Watt's in morning met Elders Ferrin & Peck, and soon after Elders Redd and Jensen came from a journey down the country south of Cowpens. According to request of E. Ferrin (Pres) Elder Redd and I were to go and visit King's Mt. Branch in Cleveland Co. NC. and on our way hold meeting at Hampton Robson's the next day. So I went to Bro. Bolin's

February   Changed clothes (4 miles) while Elder Redd went to Bro. Surratts and met us at Bro. Bolin's. We took dinner and started at 3-40 arriving at H. Robinson abt. 5-40 where we stayed all night. 11 mi.

Sunday 5   11 mi.   Held meeting at 11-40 a.m. six members present. After dinner I carried Mrs. Phillips (Sister Robson's) mother a bucket of water who lives nearby. She is an old lady. When she came to meeting she brought a bucket, so I carried it full of water back for her. She treated me very well. I ate dinner with her and stayed some time. This is the first time an Elder ate with her. At one time she threatened to throw hot water on the Elders for passing her door. Stayed all night with Sister Robson.

-Monday 6-   In the morning Sister Robson mended my pants and at 9-30 a.m. went across Broad R. (river) 9 miles and took dinner and stayed all night with Bro. Saml. Gordon. His wife and family have become friendly and are investigating. 9 mi.

Tuesday 7.   Left in morning and went 6 mi and spent the day, and stayed all night with Bro. Wm Weaver. Administered (his) to child which was having warm fits and it seemed better. 6 mi.

-Wednesday 8.-   Went to Bro. Wiley's near Kings Mt and on the way went a mile out of the way & visited the monument situated on the hill where the tide of battle in the Revolution turned in favor of America. 5 miles-7.

February   Took dinner with Bro. & Sister Wyley and after noon went two miles and stayed all night with Mr. & Mrs. L. Wilson ½ miles from Grover. In evening E. Redd & I explained the principles of

---

[129] At this time James Havey Watts was married to Mary Jane Whitesides, sister to John Alonzo Canty.

the Gospel to them in connection with a Mrs. Starns who came to visit, there, soon after we arrived. She had heard a great many tales about the "Awful Mormons" and when she found that we were Elders she wished she had not come. She afterwards found (we) were perfectly harmless, and accepted a tract and invited us to call and visit her.

Thursday 9. In the morning went to Brother Moses Gordon's 4 ½ mi spent the day and stayed all night with them. 4 ½ mi

Friday 10- Went one mile to See Mr. & Mrs. Patterson [130]and to Bro Jno Gordon's & took dinner with him. After dinner we went on to Bro. & Sister Jno. Goins+ 9 mi. Stayed all night. 9 mi.

Saturday-11 After dinner-Elder Redd & I administered to Dortha-the daughter and then went 6 mi and stayed all night with Bro. Jno Gordon where we hold meetings. 6- (miles)

Sunday 12. Held meeting at 10 a.m. Ate dinner with Bro. Gorden. Spent evening and stayed all night with Mr. & Mrs. Patterson-2 mi.

Monday 13 Took dinner with Bro. Moses M. Gordon. Stayed all night with Mrs. Turner.---3 mi.

Tuesday 14. In morning went and spent day with Bro. Saml Gordon. Held meeting with the family at night. Mrs. Gordon's sister (Bobbi) and her father were also present. We both spoke for ½ an hr. each. 5 miles

Wednesday 15 Left in the morning. As we were going along the track I sat upon a piece of timber and wrote a note to Alice & in closed (Introduced) it in Mary Elizabeth's letter; went across Broad River & called at Sister Robson's. She was away from home, so Elder Redd displayed his ability in getting dinner. We then went, by way of Gaffney to Bro. James Bolin & stayed all night. 18 miles.

Thursday 16. Went to Bro. Surratts in morn and met the Elders. Two new Elders, Lehi Jones Cedar City, Iron Co. Utah & G.E. Burgess, Pine Valley, Washington Co. Utah. Elder Redd & I ate dinner with Mr. & Sister Bright. After dinner all of us went & administered to Mrs. H. Bright who was very sick. Seemed better and at night sent for Elders again. Elder Burgess & I, as the other Elders were away, went & administered to her again. Stayed all night with Bro. Surratt. 3 miles.

Friday 17. Wrote letter to wife and posted my Journal. Took dinner with Bro. Evan Watts. Elder Jones and I stayed all night with Mr. Morgan Paris near Bro. Surratt's.

February Saturday 18, Elder Ferrin & Redd went to P.O. Jones & I went to Bro. Jas. Watts near Black's had a bath etc.: here met Elder Jensen & Peck who had been down the country a few miles holding meeting & also back to Bro. Surratt's. We all were called to go and administer to Mrs. Harrison Bright who would be baptized if her husband would consent. We administered to her and she

---

[130]James Goodwin and Elizabeth Missouri White Patterson.

seemed some better. The next day Mr. Bright went for a doctor, but she refused to take his medicine. She was afterwards administered to & got better very soon. Mr. Bright said, while she as sick, he would consent to her baptism. Then went to singing school. E. Peck & I stayed all night at Mr. (H) Bright. 7 miles. Elder Ferrin & Binham are released.

Sunday Feb. 19   Held S. S. & meeting Elders present - Ferrin, Redd, Peck, Jensen Clark and Jones & Burgess. After meeting Elder Burgess & I went home with Bro. James Bolin and spent the night. 2 ½ miles.

-Monday 20-   Went to Bro. Surratt's in morning. Wrote to Hyrum. Wilford & E. S. Cotton. On account of E. Ferrin & Bingham being released from their missions two new elders, Jones & Burgess were sent to the conference. Elder Alonzo J. Stookey & H.J. Humphrys traveling in new field. Elder S (Stookey) called to the office at Chattanooga to assist Pres Spry who presides over the mission as Bro Jno Morgan has been released. Elder H. follows E. Ferrin in presiding over conference. Spent night with Mr. C. Bright. 3 miles

Tuesday 21.   After breakfast went headquarters. All Elders present at Council Meeting-partook of the Sacrament & all spoke. E. Wm. A. Redd was app to go and take Elder Stookey's place and remain a short time with Elder Humphreys and another Elder will be sent from the office to join E. Redd. I was appointed to take Elder P. P. Bingham's place & join E. Johnson in Catawba Nation 70 miles east (100 by rail). Elders Ferrin, Redd & I made preparations to go to Spartansburg City and buy some clothing etc. etc. Went and spent night with Mr. And Sister Henderson 3 miles from Cowpens. On leaving Mr. Blacks was called back ¾ mile and pulled tooth for Mrs. Black. 9 miles.

Wednesday 22. 1888---   Rose at 2 a.m. Sister Blackwood got us an early breakfast & we went and took train about 5 a.m. Arrived at Spartanburg City after a ride of 10 miles before day. Bought summer clothes, shoes, penholders etc. Had a nice dinner in restaurant for 25 cents. In afternoon E. Redd & I returned to Cowpens and after walking 7 ½ miles & spent night with James Watts. At Spartanburg Elder Ferrin went the other way west to Oconee Co., to visit Saints, and as E. Redd would leave for new field before he returned, they bid each other good bye never more to meet in the Sunny South. 13 miles

Thursday 23   Ate breakfast with Sister Taylor George and accompanied E. Redd to Bro. Surratts' and made preparations to leave for Catawba Nation. Put tack in bottom of my shoes. Stayed all night with Bro. Surratt. 3 miles

Friday 24   Wrote letter in morning and at 11 a.m. bid Elders and Saints adieu, and went in a heavy rain to Gaffney's Station, stopped by the way, to Bro. James Bolin and ate dinner & got my clothing which Sister Bolin washed & then took train at Gaffneys at 4-30 p.m. arriving at (50mi) Charlotte in evening. Stayed all night at Snyder House. 7 miles.

Saturday 25   Spent some time in morning in drying my shoes which I got wet previous day. The train was to leave at 1 p.m. so I went and took a view of the City.   Contains 15,000 inhabitants one of the best locking cities I had seen in states. There are several nice houses, stores & churches. On one of the most elevated and central parts of the city stands an iron cistern, or tank about 20 feet in diameter & 130 in height. This is kept full of water to be used with engine in case of fire.

Train 1 hr. late. Left at 2 p.m. & arrived in R. H. [131] (25 mi) about 3 p.m. Left for Nation 10 miles; got off the road and walked two or three extra miles arriving in Nation at 8 p.m. Stayed all night with Bro. Alonzo Canty & James Harris[132] who are living together. Here I met & stayed all night with Elders P.P. Bingham of Wilson, Utah. 13 miles

Sunday 26   In morning met Elders Jos H Johnson of Johnson, Utah my intended companion. He is a young man aged 21 years old who came to mission one mo. before myself. Held S.S. & meeting in a log house with good attendance. Spoke at each place. Elder J and I went home and spent night with Bro. Wm T Ivey. Wrote letter to Wife. 3 miles

Monday 27.   Met Elder Bingham and we crossed the Catawba or Pedee R. in a batto or small boat and went three miles up the R & had dinner with his mother. Came back after dinner to Bro. Wm. Whitesides one mile from the ford and stayed all night and ate for supper some cat fish which were very nice. 7 ½ miles.

Tuesday 28.   Came back to Nation ate dinner with Mr. Louis Gordon, his wife belongs to Church. Supper with Bro. James Harris. Attended singing in the evening. Spent night with Mr. Ballard a friend was treated very kindly and slept for the first time under a feather bed. 4 miles

Wednesday 29   Wrote references in Bible took dinner with Mr. Ballard. E. Johnson

March 1888   And I spent the night with Sister Sarah Harris [133] & son. 1 mi

Thursday 1 March.   Went to R. L. Harris.[134] I spent the forenoon writing references in my Bible. After dinner E, Bingam cut my hair. Supper with (Bro) W T. Ivey after which we went and spent evening with Mr. Ballad, close by, when Elder J. & I stayed all night. 1 mi

Friday March 2   After breakfast we went to Bro. Ivey's, posted journal, wrote to Robt. Skelton. Ate dinner with Bro. Ivey also supper and went to testimony meeting.

Went to stay all night with Bro. R. L. Harris . Heard a false report that a mob of 16 men were in the

---

[131] Rock Hill, South Carolina
[132] James Harris, married to John Alonzo's twin sister Fannie.
[133] Sarah Jane Ayers Harris, widow of James Harris, daughter of Edmund and Rebecca Marsh Ayers.
[134] Robert Lee Harris born 1867, son of John "Mush" Harris and perhaps Jenny Ayers Harris.

Nation so as to be on the safe side E. B. & I went with bed & stayed in the woods. Elder J. stayed with W. T. Ivey.

Saturday Mar 3. 1888   Spent most of the day with R L Harris. After dinner went to Bro. Jas. Harris and had bath etc. During the day one or two strange men were seen in the Nation, we thought perhaps to see where (we) were going to stay all night; so we crossed river stayed all night with Bro. Wm W. Whitesides. 2 ½ miles.

Sunday Mar 4.   Crossed river again to S. S. & spoke in meeting. All day fast. Stayed all night with Bro. Geo. Canty.[135] 1 mi

Monday 5   We Elders and few Saints fixed up an old building to hold S. S. meeting in. Had been holding meeting in a private house. Ate dinner with Sister Sarah Harris. Ate supper with Bros Canty & Harris. Stayed all night with W T Ivey. Wrote to C. R. Savage and Wife. 2 miles.

Tuesday March 6-   In morning Bro. Ivey & I went to Rock Hill as Elder Ferrin was coming over from Spartanburg County to join E. Bingham and bid farewell to all, here. I got my shoes mended. Returned to Nation. Ate supper with Bros Harris & Canty---went to Singing at which E. Ferrin occupied part of the time in speaking to Saints. Stayed all night with Bro. R. L. Harris. 19 miles

Wednesday 7   Met E. Ferrin and Bingham in morning; crossed river and ate dinner with Bro. Wm H Whitesides. E. F & B went on to Union Co. to bid friends & saints adieu. Elder J & I stayed all night with Bro. Whitesides. During day went to river and saw baskets used in catching fish. 2 ½ (miles)

Thursday 8   Wrote to parents and J. L. Hetzler. Crossed river and ate dinner with Sister Tims[136]. Stayed all night with Bro. Wm George. [137]3 miles

Friday 9 1888.   After breakfast went to Sister Tims.   Elder J. wrote a letter for Sister H. Harris. Ate dinner I worte to C. R. C3. & wife. Testamony meeting. Spent eve. with Bro Ivey. 2mi

Elder J & I cleaned out the School House. Took dinner with Bros Harris & Canty. Spent night with R. L. Harris. 1 ½ mi

Sunday 11-   Held S. S. and meeting at usual time. E. Ferrin, Bingham, Johnson & Clark present. E. Ferrin spoke in S. S. Elders F. C. & B. in meeting. Elders F. & B. spoke their farewell sermon. We all took dinner with Bro. Wm George supper at Sarah Harris---spent eve together at R. L. Harris. E. J & I spent night with Bro. Jno. Sanders.[138] 2 miles

---

[135]George Washington Canty, half brother to John Alonzo Canty. George was the son of Franklin and Eliza Scott Canty. Eliza was the mother of the Whitesides children, John, Fannie and Mary Jane.

[136]Ann, daughter of Martha Ann Cottsky-Evans, first wife of Alexander Tims.

[137]William George, son of Nelson and Sarah Ayers George.

[138]John Idle Sanders, born 1862, son of Lucinda Harris and John Evins Sanders. Lucinda had 4 children, all by different men.

Monday 12. 1888- Met Elders Ferrin & Bingham in morning and they made preparations to leave. All ate dinner with Bro Geo Cantys where several of the Saints had gathered to bid them adieu. After their bidding good bye etc. Elder J. & I went with them to see them off. Went to Bro. Thos. Harris' 4 mi from Rock Hill as they did not have very many accommodations for so many of us. E. Ferrin & I went to a house by & asked if we could be accommodated there. The man of the house had gone to bed and received no, for answer, knowing who we were. We all four slept in one bed on floor and got along all right. 5 miles

Tuesday 13 The next morning we journeyed on with them stayed a short time in Rock Hill. E. Ferrin left his umbrella in P.O. & in a few moments went & found it had taken its departure.

March   Went on their way 3 miles past R. H. Here we held Council Meeting. Each spoke and rec'd instructions from E. Ferrin. We then gave them the parting hand. Returned to R. H. Had lunch, wrote to wife & after mail came in we returned to the Nation ate supper at Geo Canty's-went to singing and stayed all night with John Sanders. 19 miles-

Wednesday, 14 Helped Bro. Sanders in morning saw and split wood to build his chimney higher. Ate dinner at R. L. Harris. Spent night with Mr. Ballad. 1 ½ (miles)

Thursday, 15 Spent day and night with Wm T Ivey. Read testament. Talked to E. J. abt. Young Ladies.

Friday, 16- Went to Bro. Harris & Canty's in morning. Rec'd letters from Robt. Skelton an interesting one from Wife and Joseph S. Clark. Spent the whole day and night with Harris & Canty. Went to testimony meeting in evening. Pulled two teeth in afternoon. 1 ½ miles

Saturday, 17. Went & cut wood for schoolhouse-posted Journal at R. L. Harris where we took dinner. Spent the night with Bro. Geo. Canty.

Sunday 18- I was requested to take charge of the Sunday School also held meeting and spoke at each. Went home with R. L. Harris where we spent the night.

-March-

Monday 19-1888 Read in Testament. Ate dinner with Sister Wiley. Stayed all night with Mr. Ballard and was treated fine. 2 mi

Tuesday 20. Elder J. and I started to R. H. to P.O. Stopped about half way and took dinner with Bro. Thos. Harris[139] & wrote a letter to Robt. Skelton. Rec'd letter from wife desiring a new name, which I answered. Came back and spent the night with Bro. Harris. 14 mi.

Wednesday 21. Went to Nation in morning. Took dinner with Sister Ann Tims. After dinner we met

---

[139]This must be James Thomas Harris, son of David and Nancy George Harris, born 1833. He married Sarah Jane Ayers.

with the children and taught them their letters-how to read etc. after which I wrote a letter for Sister Rachel Harris.[140] Then cross Catawba River on way for Union Co to visit saints and friends there. Stayed all night with Bro Whitesides. 6 miles.

Thursday 22, 1888-   In morning started on our way for Union Co. After going two miles we came to 12 mi. creek which on account of such much rain was so high we could not cross with ought going up the creek two miles so we returned to Bro. Whitesides and spent remainder of the day and night. 4 mi

Friday 22…..(23)   After breakfast we started again on our journey. Went two miles extra & crossed bridge all right. Had successful journey. Before arriving at our destination we sat on a log near Walkerville P.O. and wrote a letter to our Better halves.

March

Arrived at Sally Jant & Rebecca Backer's at 3-30 p.m. These are two sisters who are widows and are and have been very true friends to the Elders. We had dinner & supper together. Here we spent the night. (17 miles)

-Saturday 24- Remained here until after dinner reading and chatting. Aunt Sally gave me $20.00 of the Confederate Money as a relic and a rose which had been pressed. Was treated very kind. After dinner we went and stayed (1 mile) with Bro. Bigham & family. 2 mi

Sunday 25 Spent the forenoon in singing and reading. After dinner two lady visitors came in and had a good look at Elders for the first time but nothing much to say.

In evening we went north a short distance and visited a good friend by the name of McMinice. In evening besides the family several young people came in to hear us sing as they liked to hear the Elders sing who had been here before. We sang to them a while and then I asked the man if it was intended that we should speak to them, who answered that he would leave that to us, so we held meeting at which each spoke. After which the man of the house and the young people sang. Spent night & was treated very kindly & asked to come again.

Monday March 26. 1888-   After breakfast we went and spent a short time with a young lady, according to request, (rec'd) the night previous by the name of Miss Ferguson.

Went and took dinner with John Bigham, Bro. Bigham's son-in-Law a friend where the Elders first stayed when they came in here. We then proceeded to go and visit other friends but as we could not get across the branch we returned and had supper and spent evening. Then went and stayed all night with Bro. & Sister Bigham. 2 mi.

---

[140]Rachel Jane Tims Harris, daughter of Alexander and Ann Tims, wife of Hillary Harris. She moved to Colorado where she died.

Tuesday 27   In morning we crossed branch went about 3 miles east called on a friend by name Mr. McNuley who is a very well read gentleman. He is and has been a good friend to the Elders. Had conversation upon different inventions and science, and for our religion. Poligamy seems to be stumbling block for both him and his wife. Spoke of the man who is trying to work a plan to make it rain on desserts & a scientist who predicts another Deluge in the 8th thousand year. While talking on matters of religion a visitor was in his house and when he heard me say we were anxious to get to preach he called Mr. McNuley out and told him to bring us down to his house in the evening. Sometime after supper we went down to the man's house and we held meeting & each spoke. I answered the question What for and why do we have Temples. After meeting we went back to Mr. McNuley and spent the night. 3 miles

-March-Wednesday-28   After breakfast we went to Mr. H. Baker's and took dinner after which we intended to start back for the Nation, but as it was raining so hard we stayed all night. The two sons played on the fiddle and Elder Johnson on the accordion-was treated very well. 1 mi.

Thursday 29.   After breakfast we intended to start off; went to bid Salley Johant & Reb. Baker goodbye as it was raining so very hard it was not hard to get us to stay over another day. Wrote a letter for them to Elder Alonzo J. Stookey, Chattanooga, Tennessee, and had conversation . Had a fine bed to sleep in which was enjoyed.

Friday-30-   E. Johnson & I left in company with Wm. T Ivey for Nation taking some biscuits in our pockets Posted a letter at Walkersville P.O. for Alice my wife. Came to Catawba River about 4 o'clock in afternoon. The three days of almost steady rain made the river rise away beyond its banks but we went and hollowed (hollered) and two young men came over and got us and we had a nice ride as we had to start across away above the ford in order to make our landing place.

Met with quite a large number of the saints on the edge of the high waters. We went to Bro. Canty's & Harris' and rec(')d letters from Mary Elizabeth & Father, W A Redd, E. Ferren and a card from Sister Smithy. Here rec'd word to the effect that I was Daddy Clark which was thankfully received. Mother and son were doing well. Took supper with and spent the night with Bros. Canty & Harris.

There were two persons from here expecting to start next Sunday with a company of emigrants but in the letter from Elder Ferrin I was informed that no arrangements had been made (except) for sending only Tersey Patterson[141] but if farther instructions should reach him from Pres. Spry he would send telegram, and requested me to be at R. H. 17 mi.

---

[141]Tarsa or Isabella Patterson, daughter of James and Elizabeth Missouri White Patterson

Saturday 31-   After breakfast I went to Rock Hill but no news came for Henryett Canty[142] to go to Zion. I wrote a letter to my wife-returned and stayed all night with Harris & Canty. 18 miles.

April 1888

Sunday April 1.   Went to S. S. in morning after which I went to James Harris and had dinner and went to R. H. to go as far as Charlotte (North Carolina) with Tersey Patterson to see her off all right. Started from Rock Hill abt. 5 p.m. arrived at Charlotte abt. 6 p.m. Put up at Snyder House and I went and looked around the town and about seven the sounds of more than half a dozen Church bells warning people of meeting. I attend the 2nd Presbyterian Church occupying seat in gallery directly opposite the minister.

April-

The singing (or music) was excellent. The choir sang twice, the minister offered prayer and read portion of a chapter from which he took text. Singing. For text he took II Cor. 5:11 & went on and showed how the terror of the Lord is manifested on ocean by storms or ship wrecks; on the earth by eruptions & quakings and referred to the sky as being the home of the terrible cyclones.

He told his audience they were not worshiping the right God hence, said in you are Idoliters. 11 mi.

Monday 2   Went and looked around the town for some time in the morning and bought collar tie, etc. After lunch I went and bought tickets and had quite a time changing money & it was not until a few minutes before the train started that I arranged everything. I returned to Rock Hill and rec'd word that Alice & babe were still doing still doing well. Arriving at Nation just in time to escape a heavy thunderstorm. Found Elder Johnson at Sister Mary Harris[143] where we spent the night. 10 mi.

Tuesday 3-   Pulled a tooth for Sister Jno Sanders in morning. Dinner at Sister Ann Tims. At 2 p.m. met with the children to teach them again. Spent night with Bro. Geo. Canty.

April Wednesday 4   Spent day & night with Bro. Wm T Ivey. Wrote to Parents and J. S. Clark & wife. 1 mi.

Thursday 5-   Went to Sister Ann Tims and spent forenoon & had dinner-wrote to W. A. Redd & Eddy & Wealthy. Went and spent the night with Bro Wm George. 2 mi

-Friday 6-   Read in D & C. Took dinner with Sister John Sanders and met with the children in the afternoon teaching them the rudiments of education. Elder Johnson went to P.O. to post 5 for me & 4 letters for himself. Rec'd letters from C. R. Savage and wife to which I answered. Crossed the river and stayed all night with Bro. Wm Whitesides (2 miles.)

---

[142]Henrietta Patterson Canty, daughter of James and Elizabeth Missouri White Patterson, wife of John Alonzo Canty.
[143]Mary George Harris, first wife of Epp Harris.

-Saturday 7, 1888- Came across river in the afternoon and Elder J. and I had a fine swim in the river. Spent night with Bro John Sanders.

-Sunday-8.-2 mi. Had a good S. S. and meeting. Spoke at meeting. Dinner at Jno. Sanders and spent night with R. L. Harris.

Monday 9. Spent most of the day with Sister Mary Ann Tims-wrote to T.B.C. Spent night with Bros. Harris and Canty.

Tuesday 10. Spent forenoon with Bros Harris & Canty. Dinner at Sister Sarah Harris' spent night with Mr. Benj. Ballard and was treated well. 1 mi.

April-Wednesday 11 Spent part of the forenoon explaining the Gospel to him. Had conversation after dinner. Spent night with Wm. T. Ivey.

Thursday 12 Read pamplet in forenoon. Dinner at Bro. Harris & Canty. Read Testament in afternoon and crossed river and stayed all night with Bro. Whiteside. 2 mi

Friday 13 Crossed river in the morning or rather afternoon, after waiting 3 hrs for the ferryman. Met with the children in the afternoon. Supper with Sister Jno. Sanders. Stayed all night in a house. 2 miles

Saturday 14 Ate breakfast at Bro. Geo Canty's. Wrote to wife went to P.O. and back after 11 .am. eating lunch at Bros. Harris' & Canty's. 18 miles.

Sunday 15- Met with well attended S. S. & meeting-spoke in latter. Ate dinner and spent night with John Sanders. Esq.

Monday 16 1888 Wrote a letter of three pages to Wm Elliott, Rochester, Minn. In answer to "Self Contradictions" etc. and one to Joseph Thorup for Alonzo Canty[144]. Spent night with Bros. Harris and Canty.

Tuesday 17. Spent part of the day and had dinner with sister Martha H. Tims. Met in afternoon with the children. Posted Journal and wrote to my companion.

April Wednesday 18 Elder J. went to P.O. Rec'd the News containing the Conference minutes. We spent the night with Sister Sarah Harris & Son.

Thursday 19. Had a good time reading the News. Called to see Sister Elizabeth Harris but she was not at home. Crossed the river in the evening and spent the night with Bro. Wm Whitesides. 2 mi.

Friday 20 Crossed river again in the morning went and spent the forenoon and took dinner with Sister Ann Tims. Elder J. wrote a letter for her and I wrote to Elder M. D. Ferrin. At 2 p.m. we met with the children and taught them. 2 mi Spent night with Bro. R. L. Harris

---

[144] This Alonzo Canty is Alonzo George Canty not John Alonzo Canty.

-Saturday 21-1888   Spent forenoon in reading etc. Took dinner and spent the night with Bros. Harris and Canty. Went to singing in the evening.

Sunday 22.   Had a good S.S. and meeting in the school-house. Spoke at each. Five were present who had never heard an Elder speak before; issued three tracts at their request. Took dinner and spent the night with Bro. John Sanders.

-Monday 23. 1888-   Spent the forenoon with Sister Jno. Sanders reading Testament, when we had dinner . Read newspaper and spent night with Mr. Benj. Ballard. Was treated fine. 1 mi.

April Tuesday 24. 1888-   Elder Johnson and I went into the field where Mr. Ballard & two sons were planting cotton. I took a mule and opened furrows, the seed being dropped by one following. E. Johnson followed with the other animal covering the seed over with a wooden implement.

After taking dinner we met with the children at 2 p.m. Spent the night with Bros. Wm. George. 2 miles.

Wednesday 25.   In the morning we started to go and visit some saints living 8 miles up and on the opposite side of the river, Bro. John Brown accompanying us. Crossed river at Mr. Braidy's ferry. On arriving we took dinner with Mr. Wyley his wife being a Mormon, and moved up there from the Nation. Went to a store, close by got some paper and wrote to wife. Spent night with Mr. Wyley. 8 miles

Thursday 26.   In forenoon wrote a letter for Sister Wyley. Dinner at her daughters Sister Sarah Gordon. On returning to Nation stopped at Belair P.O. and called and saw Mrs. Ivey a few minutes. Crossed at Nat. Ferry to get letters but none came. Crossed river again and spent the night with Bro. Wm Whitesides. 8 miles

Friday 27.   Crossed river in the morning & went from house to house via the trails trying to find the woman that brought the mail. Rec'd letters from Robt. Skelton and my Wife. The baby had been sick and she was not feeling very well. Took dinner with Sister Elizabeth Harris.[145] In evening two letter came for Elder J. one from E. Humpherys, and one from his wife unfolding the news that he was Father of a fine daughter. Folks all doing well.

Saturday 28.   Took dinner with Bro. Wm. George.   At 2 p.m. Gus Harris[146] and Johnny George being eight years old were baptized by Elder J and he confirmed one and I the other. Quite a large crowd of people were present.

Spent the night with Bros. Harris and Canty. 2 mi.

---

[145]Margaret Elizabeth Harris Harris, wife of Peter Harris, daughter of Epp and Matha Jane White Harris.
[146]Gus Howard Harris born 27 Jun 1879, son of Peter and Margaret Elizabeth Harris Harris.

Sunday 29.   Sunday School at 10 a.m. at which I spoke. Good attendance. Ate dinner with Bro. John Sanders. The meeting at 2 p.m. was well attended. Four or five were present and several colored men who could not get in the small house. We both spoke to the meeting.

Wrote a letter to Parents and one to Jas. Patterson for Alonzo Canty[147]. Spent the night with Bro. R. L. Harris.

Monday 30-   Wrote a letter to Pres. Humpherys. Went to P.O. and rec'd a letter from Wm. Redd Stating that an Elder. in some part of the Mission preached a sermon to a mob with a rope around his neck over a tree when the mob took off the rope and sneaked away leaving the E. preaching.

May-1888-   While at Rock Hill I wrote a letter to Wife.

Stayed all night with Bro. Thos. Harris three miles from R.H. 12 mi.

Tuesday 1st May   Had some nice sweet potatoes for breakfast and dinner which were a rarity. After dinner I went to the Nation and met with the children at 2 p.m. E. Johnson returned to R. H. to see if there was any mail but he received none. Spent the night with Bros. Harris & Canty. 7 miles.

Wednesday 2.   Posted Journal at R. L. Harris and read Testament. After dinner, spent the night with Sister Sarah Harris and son.[148]

Thursday 3.   Spent most of the forenoon at Sister Harris'. Took dinner with Mr. And Sister Gordon who were living nearby. Spent the night with Mr. Benj. Ballard with good treatment. 2 mi.

Friday 4.   Helped John Ballard (son) plant a melon patch. After dinner wrote a letter to Father and Mother-in-law. Forgot our meeting with the children at 2 p.m., thinking it was Thursday. We had that Miss. Smith (widow) living close by who has been opposed to us now desires to hear us preach. Spent the night with Bro. Geo. Canty. 1mi.

-Saturday 5-   We worked most of the day & finished Sister Sarah Harris' porch where we ate dinner. Spent the night with Bro. Jno. Sanders.

Sunday-6. 1888.   Held S.S. in Nation at 10 a.m. Meeting at 2 p.m. at which E. Johnson and self spoke. Took dinner with Bro. R. L. Harris. Spent night with Bro. James Harris.

Monday 7.   We started for Union Co. Had some difficulty in crossing the river, waiting for the batto which was in use down the river a short distance. Crossing the river we took dinner with Bro. Wm Whiteside and at 1-30 we continued our journey, and after 3 ½ hours of pleasant walking we arrived at Mr. McMinice. He was away from home but was to arrive soon. While sitting waiting on the porch, a large man came and took a seat nearby. After asking if we strangers I informed him who we were. He

---

[147]John Alonzo was the son in law of James Patterson.
[148]The son must be David Adam Harris, the youngest of Sarah's children.

said they had no use for Mormons in their country. I spoke of our misrepresentation. He then commenced on the chorus (polygamy), but it only took a little defense of that principle until he was gone. Had a pleasant time in remaining all night with Mc. 12 miles.

Tuesday 8, 1888. After breakfast we went down ½ mile and spent the day and night with Bro. Bigham.

Wednesday 9. We appointed meeting at Bro. Bigham's Saturday at 10 a.m. On our way over to Aunt Sally Ghent and Rebecca Baker's we called and notified a family of the meeting. We took dinner and stayed all night with them. 2 mi.

Thursday 10, 1888. In the forenoon I wrote a letter for Aunt Salley to A. J. Stookey & E Johnson wrote another for her. After dinner I wrote to wife and went and spent the night with Alexander Baker.

Friday 11. We called on Mr. McNuley in the forenoon remaining until after dinner and had a pleasant time. Left for Sister Bighams called by the way and bid aunt Sally and Rebecca good bye and to the P.O. posted our letters, arriving at Bro. Bighams in the evening where we spent the night. 6 miles.

Saturday 12. Commenced our meeting at 10:45 a.m. with three members besides the family. Aunt Salley Rebecca and Mr. Baker. We both spoke on the First Principles (etc). Took dinner with Mr. John Bigham. Started for the Nation at 1-30 p.m. When we started it was very hot, in about an hour it commenced raining very hard and we got a good soaking, wading branches etc. but we rejoiset on our journey. Arrived at Brother Whiteside 6 p.m. where we spent night. 14 mi.

Sunday 13. In morning we went down to the river to cross but the batto was gone. We therefore had to go up the river about a mile and cross at Mr. Braidy's Ferry. River was high & in crossing we went down some. We arrived at the School House sometime after S. S. was taken up.

May

Took dinner with Bro. Jno Sanders. Meeting at 2 p.m. I & E. Johnson spoke. There was a colored Baptist Minister present who was pleased with what he heard. He seemed to think that our belief was the same as his. While talking after meetings, the subject of the Thief on the cross came up. I asked him to explain I Peter 4: (6) 18, 19, 20. After pausing he said he had come for information. Preaching to the Spirits seemed a new thing to him, and he said he was quite unlearned only having been a preacher for fourteen years. Stayed all night with Alonzo Canty. Letter from E. B. & wife. 3 mi.

Monday 14. Helped Bro. Canty plant a melon patch. After dinner Elder J. & I took a bath in a creek near by.

Spent the night with R. L. Harris. Rec'd letter from F. D. Steed & wife.

Tuesday 15. Posted Journal in forenoon. Took dinner with Sister Ann Tims. Met with children at 2 p.m. Spent the night with Bro. Wm George. 1 mi

Wednesday 16.   Wrote a letter to my wife also to James Loynd.   Elder J. and self administered to Sister George. Took dinner with Sister Sarah Harris and spent the night with Bro. Geo. Canty.

Thursday 17   Took dinner with Sister Elizabeth.   Read a lecture given by Bro. J E Taylor on Priesthood. Rec (')d letters from John L. Hetzler, Dr. & Mrs. C.R. Clark.

Spent night with Bro. James Harris.

-May-Friday 18   Went to see how Bro. & Sister Wm George were getting along as they had been unwell & found them some better.

Ate dinner with Alonzo Canty. Met with the children at 2 p.m. Spent night with Mr. Benj Ballard and was treated well.

Saturday 19.   Read pamplet treating on the admission of Utah as a State. Dinner with Mr. Ballard. Ate supper with Bro. Jas. Harris. Singing School in the evening. Spent night with Robt. L. Harris Esq.

Sunday 20.   S. S. at 10 a.m. was well attended. Meeting was quite slimly attended on account of the rain. Spoke at each.

Dinner and spent night with Bro. John Sanders.

Monday 21.   Read Testament and posted Journal. Ate dinner at Sister Ann Tims. Spent night with Sister Sarah Harris & Son.

Tuesday 22.   Wrote to W. A. Redd. Took dinner at Sister S. Harris and spent the night with Bro. Alonzo Canty.

Wednesday -23-   Chopped wood for Uncle Billy George also took dinner. Took dinner with Robt Lee Harris. Rec'd letter from Wife.

Thursday 24   Dinner with Bro. Geo Canty. Bath in afternoon. Spent night with Bro. James Harris.

May 25 Friday-   Took dinner with Alonzo Canty. Met with children at 2 p.m. only one however was present. Wrote to J. L. Hetzler. Started for Rock Hill spent night-Bro. Thos Harris. 6 mi

Thursday

Spent the forenoon reading Congress pamplet on the Amission of Utah as State. After dinner we went into the Nation and stayed all night with James Harris Esq.

Saturday 26.   In morning wrote to Annie & Wife. Went on to Rock Hill. Bot me a hat, writing material, and medicine: Salts, siene (saline?) and a box of pills. On returning spent night with Bro. Thos. Harris 7 mi.

Sunday 27.   Walked to Nation in the morning and attended S. S. at 10 a.m. good attendance.

Dinner at Bro. John Sanders. Meeting at 2 p.m. medium attendance. After meeting went and spent night with Mr. Benj Ballard 7 mi.

Monday 28   Plowed cotton for Mr. B. and had quite a number of strawberries which we found in the woods. After dinner we replanted and hoed our melon patch. Went to the Nation in evening and spent night with Bro. Robt. Lee Harris. It was a very warm day and hot weather in commencing. 1 mi.

May Tuesday 29.   Spent some time mending pants. Ate dinner with Bro. James Harris and had the first mess of new Irish potatoes.

At 2 p.m. we went to the School House but no children came. Commenced work on a small arbor, or bowery to hold meeting in during the summer time. Spent the night with Bro. A. Canty. 1 mi 30.

Wednesday 30   Posted Journal in forenoon. Ate dinner with Sister Tims. Done some work on the bowery and spent night with Bro. Geo. Canty.

Thursday 31.   Ate dinner with Bro. Robt. L. Harris. Wrote to Companion; spent night Jno. Sanders. Had a feast of cherries for first time.

June

Friday 1. 1888-   Rained some in forenoon. We put top on the Bowery. Ate dinner at Bro. James Harris. Met with children at 2 p.m. after which we crossed river at Mr. Bradies Ferry to see Bro. Wm. Whiteside about getting some slabs from the saw-mill to make seats for the Bowery. Spent night with Bro. Whiteside. Had some cherries. 3 mi.

Saturday 2.   Crossed river again in morning and finding a tree of mulberries we had a feast for the first time. Got into some poison oak but washed in soda-water and it did not break out. Dinner at A. Canty's where I found a letter from Wife telling of her taking music lessons.

June. 3   Spent night with Bro. Canty and had some cherry pie for supper. Went to schoolhouse at 8 p.m. but as it was rainy the Saints did not come to Singing.

Sunday 3.   Sunday School at 10 a.m. moderate attendance. Spoke to Saints. Had dinner at Mr. Benj Ballards and meeting at 2 p.m. Elder J. and I spoke to about a dozen darkeys and several whites; issued six tracts. Spent night with Benj Ballard, Esq. 2 mi.

Monday 4.   Went and hoed cotton in the forenoon. Dinner = new potatoes and custard pie. Had some religious conversation with Mrs. Ballard and was treated fine. Had some mulberries. Worked on Bowery in the afternoon. Spent night with Sister Sarah Harrises Son. 1 mi.

Tuesday 5.   Hoed cotton in forenoon. Ate dinner with Sarah Harris. Posted Journal. Met with the children in the afternoon 4. o'clock. Had no school as children did not come. Spent night at Uncle Billy George's.

Wednesday 6   Went a short distance and picked an ate some dew-berries which are a good deal like blackberries also had some cherries. Hoed cotton for 2 ½ hrs. for A. Canty. Dinner at Bro. James

Harris & had the first mess of green peas. Wrote to Alice in the afternoon. Spent night with Bro. James Harris.

Thursday 7   Visited Bro. John Sanders in forenoon but was sick but, soon recovered. Took dinner with Sister Sarah Harris---new potatoes. Hoed cotton a short time for Bro. J. Sanders after which I started on my way to Rock Hill staying all night with Bro. Thos. Harris. 6 mi.

Friday 8.   Wrote to E.B.C. 6 and arrived in R. H. at 9 a.m. I had previously sold my light coat to Jas. Harris and I bought an alpaca coat & vest-cost. 2.90   Also bot small looking glass & presented it to Mrs. A. Canty[149] for her kindness to me in doing my washing etc. Arriving at the Nation in the evening I spent the night with Bro. Geo. Canty. 12 mi.

Saturday 9.   Hoed cotton for Bro. Geo. Canty for some time in forenoon where we also took dinner. Had bath in afternoon. Spent night with Bro. R. L. Harris.

-Sunday 10-   S.S. at 10 a.m. Spoke on history of Jos. Smith the Prophet. Dinner with Bro. R. L. Harris. Spoke in meeting of the First Principles. 2 mi.

Mr. Saml. Broom, a friend, was present; he told us one of his neighbors, Mr. Cullins desired to see us so we accompanied him there where we stayed all night and until eve the next day. Mr. C. was very sick & had been for about 2 weeks with the Flue.   He and his wife treated us very kindly. Had for supper fish and the first blackberry pie. He asked me who Mechesideic was; he had thought he was a spirit, but my answer seemed to satisfy his mind to the contrary. In talking about Negros, he said he thought they had no soul; he seemed to believe they were created and classed with the other animals. Thought they dwelt in the land of Knod as a kind of animal having no connection at all with the race of Adam.   Cain, he thought had a dark skin but he thought the darkey sprang from his marrying in the Land of Knod.

After eating a very nice dinner we spent a few moments with the wife of Mr. Broom and then via. Of Nation and spent night with Mr. Benj Ballard.

Tuesday (12)   Went to the field in the morning and had a time binding. Chopped some wood at the house. Had new potatoes and gravy for dinner. Hoed and replanted our melon-patch in the afternoon, also talked with Mrs. Smith widow, for some time . Spent the night with Bro. James Harris. 4 mi.

Wednesday 13.   Had slept during the previous night in J. Sanders house as Sister S. spent night with Sister Harris. Wrote letter to wife. Ate dinner with Sister Alonzo Canty and went up the river 8 miles and spent the night with Mr. Wiley crossing river at Mr. Braidies by the assistance of Bro. Ben

---

[149]Georgia Henrietta Patterson Canty, wife of John Alonzo Canty

Harris[150]. Was very much surprised to have Sister W. give us some ripe peaches as it was the first we had had and we did not know they were ripe. When Mr. Wiley came home from work, he brought us a few more ripe peaches. The next day we had a few more also a few ripe apples. 8 mi.

Thursday 14. 1888   Dinner with Mr. Wiley after which we visited an ancient burial ground which was in a hollow a short distance away. The creek had, when the water was high, washed the surface of the ground seemed to be of a sand loom while the top of the graves seemed to be more clay, hence the sand would wash away and leaves the graves. We could not tell how large the burying ground was as we could not distinguish them only where the creek had washed over which was only a small area. It is supposed the Catawba Nation was once quite a powerful one and they owned a large tract of land. They used to roam over the country as the wild Indians of the west, selling pottery and pipes which they made which trade is carried on at the present on a small scale.

They tell us that years ago they had kings to rule over them but since the whites settled in near them, they have been robbed of their lands and many of them killed, while others migrated and joined other tribes. The burying ground is supposed to have been one belonging to the Catawba Nation many years ago. Human bones have been found here and I also picked up part of a human jaw bone containing two teeth, but the bone was very badly decayed.

We were to spend the night with Mr. Louis Gordon[151] and while going home we picked up some blackberries & Sister G. made some pies for supper and breakfast. 2 mi

Friday 15   Left at 7 a.m. and arrived at Bro. Wm. Whiteside's at 10. In the afternoon we picked some more blackberries and Sister W. made some more pies for supper and breakfast.

Saturday 16   Crossed the river in the forenoon after waiting three hours for Mr. Braidy to come with them key to the batto. Took dinner with Bro. Alonzo Canty. Had no supper. Attended Singing in the evening (or night). Spent night with Sister Sarah Harris and son. 4 mi.

Sunday 17.   Sunday S. at 10 a.m. good attendance. Elder J. & I spoke. Spent noon with Bro. Sanders.

Meeting at 2 p.m. Had the Saints bear their testimony. I spoke on Authenticity of the Book of Mormon. Spent night with Bro. Jno. Sanders.

Monday 18   Posted Journal and spent some time talking with Sister Jane Sanders. Dinner---Sister Sarah Harris.

June

---

[150]Benjamin Perry Harris, son of John 'Mush' and Jenny Ayers Harris.
[151]Lewis was the son of Lucinda Harris and a white man named Stell Gordon. He married Sally Brown, daughter of Margaret Ayers George and Joe Cherry, a white man.

Spent the night with Bro. Geo. Canty.

Tuesday 19   Spent some time hoeing cotton for John Sanders. Dinner, Sister M. A. Tims. Wrote letter for her also to Pres. H. T. Humphreys reporting our labors. Stayed overnight at Bro. Alonzo Canty.

Wednesday 20   Hoed cotton part of forenoon for A. Canty. Spent some time at R. L. Harris. Dinner with Bro. James Harris. Hoed his melon patch in afternoon and helped him shock up grain. Spent the night with our old friend Benj. Ballard and was treated fine. (1mi)

Thursday 21.   Went into the field where Mr. B's son was cradling oats, and did some binding & was not outdone in a short race. Hoed our melons. Dinner---Mr. B's. All night R. L. Harris. 1 mi.

Friday 22.   Hoed some cotton for Bro. J. Sanders where we also had dinner. Spent night James Harris. Rainy afternoon.

Saturday 23.   Rec'd letter from Alice which one of the Saints handed me. While Elder J. was cutting my hair with Fanny Harris' [152] scissors, I laid them on a rock and with another one I tried to rivet them a little closer together and broke them. Afterwards paid 38 cents to replace the broken with another pair. With another pair I succeeded in getting my hair cut. Elder J. rec'd word that a registered package was at the office for him so he went to R. H. and received a new suit of clothes from his Bishop. I helped Bro. Jno. Sanders hoe cotton as he had been up the river and on the opposite side and floated some slabs down the river to the Nation landing which he paid 50 cents to have delivered upon the river banks above.

We carried these slabs from the river to Bro. James Harris where during the afternoon I with a little assistance made six benches for the Bowery. Dinner with Bro. Jno Sanders. Spent night with Bro. Geo. Canty. 1 mi.

Sunday 24.   Had bath in morning as I did not have time the night before. SS at 10 a.m. in the Bowery was not well attended. Had meeting at 2 p.m. with fair attendance. Elders J & C spoke. Dinner and spent the night with John Sanders

Monday 25.   Spent some time and had dinner with Sister Elizabeth Harris. Hoed cotton in the eve for Bro. Sanders. Spent night with Sister Sarah Harris & son.

Tuesday 26   Made more benches for Arbor. Dinner Bro. Wm George. Stayed all night with James Harris.

Wednesday 27.   Dinner Alonzo Canty. Lost my pocket-knife on my way to his house through a hole in my pocket. Started for Union Co. Crossed river at Mr. Brady's ferry and stayed during night with

---

[152] Fannie Whitesides Harris, wife of James Thomas Harris, twin to John Alonzo Canty.

William Whiteside. 3 miles.

Thursday 28. Arose at 3-20 a.m. rainy morning and did not start until 9 o'clock, arriving at Bro. Bigham's a little after dinner, where we spent the night. 12 mi.

Friday 29. Visited Mr. John Bigham where we took dinner. Went to visit Aunt Sally and Becky who were away on a visit; started the same day, but Mrs. Ghant, aunt Ricky's daughter who lives nearby received us with kindness and good treatment where we spent the night. Before leaving Bro. B's wrote a letter to Mother and Wife. 2 ½ miles.

Saturday 30 Saw Wm T. Ivey and conversed with about his duties and his conduct for it seems Bro. I. Although having been baptized the second time is loosing ground. Had gone to his original church. Went to-and returned from P.O. Took dinner with Mr. Ghant. Called on Mr. Baker in the evening. Soon after we called, two gents & 2 ladies called & after the evening was nearly spent Mr. Baker asked us to preach, so at 10:10 p.m. a small table was cleared for us to make use of. We both spoke and our meeting closed in about 1 ¼ hrs. After meeting several questions were asked & it was not until 1 o'clock that we found ourselves tying to close our eyes in happy dreams.

Sunday July 1. The next morning Elder J. was some unwell. He complained with his not knowing what was the matter, only that while young, he and other boys were playing; someone got behind him, stooped down, while another boy pushed E. Johnson over him, and liting on his back; for some time (after) his back troubled him very much, but since that time it has bothered him slightly not however as much as this morning. We were going about two miles and one-half to Bro. Bigham's. Along the road his back seemed to give completely away & he would have to stop. After going about ½ the journey his back was so bad he could not get along. I left him in the shade of a tree, went to Bro. B's procured team & wagon and took him to where we first started for. Sam & Bob Bigham were visiting their parents and Robt. Accompanied me after E. Johnson.

We were to have meeting at 2 p.m. none were present excepting the above named men. Elder J. not being able I took charge of the meeting alone, getting the folks to sing some hymns. 5 miles

Monday Tuesday Wednesday and Thursday we stayed with Bro. Bigham's. Helping plow, hoe, went to mill 1 ½ mi., one afternoon sheared seven sheep, the first I had ever attempted. 5 miles

Friday 6 Elder Johnson had quite a hard time of it for a few days but by this time was able to get around, so we started for Nation. Stopped at Mr. McMinis' and had a very nice dinner of applie pie, new milk and friend chicken. His themomiter registered 97 (degrees) in shade. Had some nice ripe apples.

Arrived at the Nation in eve & ate dinner with James Harris. Went two Geo. Canty' were I found one letter and one at A. Canty's where we spent night. 14 mi.

Saturday July 7. 1888-   Enjoyed bath in forenoon and dinner with Bro. Canty. Spent night with Bro. Robt. L. Harris.

Sunday 8.   S.S. at 10 in Arbor medium attendance John Sanders & A Clark speakers. Dinner, Jno Sanders.

At 2 p.m. Testimony meeting commenced Elder J. presiding. Several bore testimony after which the Elders spoke to a fair attendance. Our friend Mr. Ballard being present took us home with him where we spent the night and were treated finely. 1 mi.

Monday 9.   Sunday evening we sat up quite late explaining salvation for the dead to Mr. & Mrs. Ballard. Took dinner with Mrs. Smith who was living nearby. When we got through eating, she said "return thanks." This was something new for us as E. Johnson asked a blessing at the commencement and nudged me to return thanks which I attempted and got through in some shape. Spent night Uncle Billy Geo. 2 mi.

Tuesday 10   Wrote a letter to my wife and read a piece on the Priesthood by Jos. E. Taylor. Had dinner. Spent night with Bro. Geo. Canty.

Wednesday 11.   Left for R.H. in morning stayed at Thos. Harris wrote to E.B.C. Took dinner and pursued my journey rec'd one letter, from Alice. Had my 1st glass of soda water.   Bot pair scissors 38 cents at Racket Store for Fanny Harris. Returning we spent night with Thos. Harris. 12 mi

Thursday 12   Came to Nation, ate dinner Bro. James Harris also spent the night. Wrote to Ezra T Clark & Companion. 6mi

Friday 13.   Visited the iron bridge of the C. C. & A three miles below Nation. It will be a good bridge when completed, standing on three pillars and two buttments . Was not finished quite. Returning Mrs. Ballard had a nice dinner prepared for us. Spent night with Alonzo Canty. 7 miles.

Saturday 14   Cleaned a small clock. After dinner, enjoyed a nice bath in Catawba River. Singing at 8 p.m. Spent night with Sarah Harris and Son.

Sunday 15.   S.S. was held in the School House also meeting as it was rainy & cool. Elder Johnson spoke to a fairly attended school. Testimony meeting at 2 p.m. at which the Sacrament was administered. Several bore testimony after which the Elders spoke medium attendance. Took dinner with Sister Sarah Harris and spent the night with John Sanders.

Monday July 16.   We decided that I should go to Union County and assist Bro. Bigham in his work as, he is old and infirm, and Elder Johnson stay at the Nation. When we came to the river in the forenoon, the battoe was on the other side, so I stripped off swam the river came back with batto for Elder Johnson. We took dinner with Wm Whiteside after which I pursued my journey. Elder J. accompanying me as far as Twelve Mile Creek, a few miles distance. Arrived at Bro. Bigham in the evening---spent night. 13 mi

Tuesday 17   Went to hoeing corn & peas in the forenoon. The pasture that Bro. B. kept his cows in was very poor and Sister B. was in the habit of going some distance and cutting hay along the creek with a case knife for her cows, which job I looked after while there. While at the job I couldn't help contrasting such a manner of cutting to the way I was cutting it one year previous. Took dinner with Mr. John Bigham living nearby.

Wednesday 18   Went 1 ½ miles to mill, bot one bushel of corn, had it ground and "toated" the grist on by back the usual way. Plowed the remaining part of the forenoon and hoed cotton after.

Thursday 19. 1888.   Engaged in hoeing cotton in the forenoon and corn in the afternoon. During my stay with the old folks I had an interesting time as they are anxious to hear the Gospel principles explained.

-Friday 20-   During the night we had a nice rain and I went and called on "Aunt" Becky Baker. Aunt Sally had not returned from her visit. Aunt Rebecca was very interested in and was investigating the Gospel and I enjoyed myself with her, it being a treat to get to talk with a person thus interested. Had nice food and a good bed which I appreciated after being troubled with bed-bugs (chinches) at Bro. B. The first night at Bro. B's. was one not to be forgotten if desperately fighting bugs all night has anything to do with charging my memory withy such an affair. 3 mi.

Saturday 21   Wrote to Alice during the forenoon. Went via. Of P.O. to Bro. B's. After dinner wrote a letter for Sister Bigham and then started for the Nation where I arrived in the evening. Bro. Wm Whiteside helped me across the river in the batto and took it back again. Met Elder J at the river where I took a bath, took supper at James Harris and went to Singing in eve. Rec'd letters from W. W. C. stating he had rec'd letter of Inquiry also one from Alice. 18 miles.

Spent the night with R. L. Harris.

Sunday 22 1888.   Met with S.S. at 10 a.m. fair attendance. Elder C. spoke to the children. Spent noon with A Canty. Meeting at 2 p.m. was well attended. Elder Johnson and I spoke. Went and called on Mr. Ballard. Sat up until about eleven o'clock to see the eclipse of the moon which commenced at 10-28. 1 mi.

Monday 23.   Wrote a letter to E. A. Catterell posted my journal. Had a nice dinner and had some nice apples also. Spent the night with James Harris. Had a game of marbles in the evening with boys.

July Tuesday 24.   Posted the Nation Journal. Dinner Uncle Billy George, after which we went up the river 8 miles, talking some about home and about the Gospel, by the way; arrived at Mr. and Sister Wylies in the evening.

On our way we took a bath in the Catawba River. Spent the night at Mr. W's having some nice apples to eat in the evening. 8 miles.

Wednesday 25   We had heard that Mr. Solomon Harris, the owner of a large plantation, wished to talk with us on certain points. Prior to this we had sent him a Congress Record containing arguments of Richards & Caine in favor of Utah becoming a State. It treated on Celestial Marriage which he thought was all a humbug. He said woman was taken from man and she would return again in our future existence. While he said this, his wife stood by his side and seemed perfectly satisfied with the idea, believing as he seemed to, that the woman in this state could be happy. We told him no rib had been taken from him, or us. Also explained that we all had to stand before the Judgment seat etc. and that the "spirit must return to God who Gave" it. Ecc 12-7.

We told him he had a Spirit and a body also his wife, and that the blending of spirits would be something strange. Explained the Law of Moses of 7 brothers; also woman no without man. He had nothing more to say on the Marriage Question. He asked us in and we enjoyed a very nice dinner with him. Spent the night with Mr. Wyley. Had plenty of nice applies also some melons at Mr. Harris .

-Thursday 26 1888-   Commenced a letter to Companion. Called on Mr. Harris and again enjoyed ourselves sitting in the shade chatting with him. Helped him eat two melons in forenoon.   For dinner we had fried onions, tomatoes, apple-pie, and grape-pie etc…

We had understood that he had quite a number of religious subjects he wished to talk about but it seemed the youths hemmed him in too close and he preferred talking about something else. We talked about the different classes of people, their intelligence etc. After a while Mr. Wylie came and joined the conversation. He is the one who Mr. Harris told he wanted to talk with.

Mr. Wylie said, "he (Mr H) can prove there was two distinct creations," at this Mr H. tried to turn the subject in a different direction, but we didn't care to change. His proof was that "we read about God creating man in his own image a verse or two farther along it says he create man from the dust of the earth. ' One verse simply explaining another. I called for his Bible, when he stepped in the room and handed us each one.

The subject of preexistence was then sprung. I told him and explained from the Bible that man existed before he came here and that by creating Adam & Eve was the way the Lord appointed for us to come upon the earth & what was the need of two creations.

I turned to Job 47 Sons of God shouted for joy, etc. Mr. H seemed to thank that Sons of God means those who do his will. I referred to Heb. 12-9 We have had Fathers of our flesh, etc. alson Numv XVI 22. Ecc. 12-7-Jam 1 5 Titus 1-2.

He gave us saying "you've got me the there. That's new doctrine" etc. Went on to tell us how much more the Ministers of the Day cared for money rather than the soul.

Mr. H is an intelligent man and can plainly see that the Ministers speculate on the "Gospel." During our conversation he said he thought he could prove that the American Continent was inhabited before the flood. He referred to an ancient wall which was made visible by the water washing a gulley about 7 feet deep into the ground. In this gully, which he went with us to, can be seen a rude stone wall built by the ancient Nephites and buried during the period in which Christ was crucified.

We told Mr. H about the B of M[153]. and It's coming forth, but he didn't care much about listening about it, but he afterwards sent for a copy of the B of M. In the afternoon we went with him to the melon, took several to the house and we had another enjoyable feast.

Returning from visiting the ancient ruin we spent some time with Mr. Louis Gordon his wife being a member. At 8 p.m. we held meeting in the woods near an old school-house, having a few of the desks and benches for our accommodation. Our light was furnished by the bottom part of a lantern, the oil gave out leaving us in darkness to close our meeting. The attendance was small; three or four from the outside and a few members were present. Spent the night with Mr. Gordon. 2 mi.

Friday 27, 1888.   Started for the Nation 8.45 arriving at 12 o'clock. Took dinner with sister Sarah Harris. At Geo Canty's I received a letter from my Wife containing $5.00. Spent the night with A. Canty. 9 mi.

-Saturday July 28-   Went to Rock Hill taking dinner by the way with Thos. Harris. Rec'd letter from C.R.C. also one from companion containing proofs. Bot shoes (2) collar tie, etc. As it was late when we started for the Nation we concluded to spent the night with Thos. Harris. 13 mi

Sunday 29.   Arrived at the Nation about 9. met with S. S. at 10 a.m. good attendance. Speakers were E. Jos H Johnson and Wm Whiteside. Fasted all day. Went home with Geo Canty. There was a usual good attendance at the meeting at 2 p.m. Elder J. presiding. Speakers were Elders Johnson and Clark. Bros. Canty and Sanders. Spent the night with Bro. Sanders. 6 mi.

First wore my new shoes.

-Monday 31, (30) 1888-   Posted Nation Journal. Took dinner with Elizabeth Harris. Crossed the river and spent the night with Wm. Whiteside. 2 mi.

-Tuesday-1 Aug. (July 31) 1888.   After a few hours pleasant walk, we arrived at Bro. Bighams Union County, where we took dinner and spent the night. Hoed corn in the afternoon.

Wednesday Aug. 2 (1)   Until the afternoon we stayed with Bro. B. when we visited Aunt Bekey. Aunt Sally had not arrived from her visit. Here we had some very nice apples which she had been

---

[153]Book of Mormon

saving for us. Our conversation was about the Gospel as she was still investigating its principles. 3 mi.

Thursday 3. (2)   Stayed with her until evening, then we called upon Mr. Baker living a short distance away. Here we again had some nice apples; were treated fine

Friday 4 (3)   In the morning Elder J & I, also Mr. B. & son Robt. Pitched horse-shoes. Mr. B & I vs. Elder J & R. We left for Bro. B's going around via P.O. posting letter to C.R.C. and Wife. It was a cool reception, when we called on our Bro. Wm. T Ivey, who was working at J. J. McCaines. We heard he was taking up another Church which he had done before and for which he was excommunicated from our church; but repenting of his sins, he was again baptized. We called at the house, he to the door, and a heavy look came over his countenance as we took him by the hand calling him Bro. He went back into the house and we had to leave without having the privilege of seeing him more. 5 mi.

 Saturday Aug. 5 (4)   Elder J. and I went to mill for Sister Bigham, after which I plowed corn and peas until noon. After dinner we took bath and called upon Mr. McMinis ¾ (of a mile) where we spent the night having some talk about the Gospel.

1888- Sunday 5   Morning we went back to Bro. B's where we had meeting at 2 p.m. Four were present besides members & children. Elder C. presided. Spent the night with Bro. B.

-Monday 6.-   We went with John Bigham and sharpened our axes at Mr. McM and in the afternoon commences making a brush fence on three sides of about 5 acres for pasturage . The timber was so thick, that most of the fence could be made by felling the timber in the same way in a line. Ate dinner and spent the night with Bro. B's.

Tuesday 7   Continued our work on the pasture. Took dinner and spent the night with Bro. B Spent the eve with John Bigham.

Aug. Wednesday 8   Wrote part of Johns B.s genealogy in his Bible in morning. Bidding all good bye we left for the nation arrived at Bro. Whitesides and took dinner. During our journey I suffered some with the heat walking so fast. When we arrived at the river several of the Saints (male) went bathing in the river. Bro. Sanders came across after us in the batto.

Got a letter at Robert H's from Alice, also the News and Juveniles. S pent night with Alonzo Canty. 14 mi

Thursday 9.   Read the News and visited nearby all the people of the Nation with a petition to give Uncle Billy George extra help from the Government appropriation which was held back for Medical Purposes. The petition, not being made out correctly proved a failure. Dinner with A. Canty. Spent the night with R. L. Harris. 2 mi.

Friday 10.   Posted Journal at R. L. Harris' where we had lunch, the folks being away.

Had a talk with John Brown.[154] He had been drunk and swearing; we saw him about making the matter right before the Church. also saw Taylor George who had run away from the officers at Spartanburg while under arrest for stealing. By Pres. Humphery's request we saw him about going back and making the matter right.

Spent the night with Bro. Jno. Sanders.

August Saturday 11-   Ate dinner with M. A. Tims. Spent part of the afternoon with Sister Wylie. Took supper, after which we went to Singing School. Spent night with M. A. Tims, Hill Harris[155] being there.

Sunday 12.   S.S. at 10 a.m. Usual attendance. E. Johnson spoke. I read from the Juvenile Instructor. After SS. Called to see Sister Wylile (Wylie?) to have her come before the saints for profanity. Had an a talk with Bro. Thos. Harris.

2 p.m.   Meeting called to order by Elder C. Bro. Geo Canty & R.L. Harris, by request, made a few remarks. Elder C. spoke, faith repentance forgive one another etc. after which Elder J. occupied some time. Attendance was good.

Called on Mr. Ballard our old friend;--had nice peaches; also had the first mess of green corn. 1 mi.

Monday 13.   Visited our melon-patch, retired to the woods and ate two nice melons; carried two large ones to the house which we helped eat during the day. Had plenty of apples and peaches.

In the afternoon we called and saw Miss. Smith (age abt. 35) living nearby.

Before leaving Mrs. B gave us some apples in a sack to take with us. Spent the night with Geo. Canty. 2 mi.

Tuesday 14 Posted Journal at Bro. Geo. Canty's Dinner with Uncle Billy George. Spent night with Aunt Sarah Harris. 1 mi.

Wednesday 15. 1888   Had a morning walk and nearby some black berry bushes I found my knife which I had lost about 6 weeks before through a hole in my pocket while picking black berries. Wrote to Wm A Redd also to Wife. Chopped wood etc. After dinner did some writing & on my way to A Canty's called at Mr. Wylies and got two letters; on from Miss S and from Alice. All night---A. Canty's. 2m mi

Thursday 16.   Had bath in forenoon. Spent some time and took (dinner) with Elizabeth Harris. Spent night M.A. Tims.

---

[154]John Early Brown, son of John William and Sallie Rachel Brown.
[155]The first mention of Hillery Harris, who was the son of Nancy Harris and a white man named Kilpatrick. He married Rachel Jane Tims, daughter of MA Tims.

-Friday 17 Aug. -   Dinner with Sister Fanny Harris, James [156]being at Greensville as a witness. Had a talk (with) the Young men (3) of the Nation. Spent some time at Alonzo Cantys & spent the night with R L. Harris. 1 mi.

Saturday 18.   Spent most of the day at Alonzo Cantys. Before dinner went with David Harris to his melon patch helped eat two and brought one melon to the house.

Had game of marbles in the afternoon. After Singing School went home with A Canty. 2 mi.

Sunday 19.   S.S. at usual time and place. A.L.C. made some remarks and read from the Juvenile Instructor. Elder J. presided over a well attended meeting. He & I spoke upon the duties of the Saints. Called on Mr. Ballard after meeting; had some talk with Mr. and Mrs. B. 2 mi.

Monday 21 (20)   Sometime after breakfast James B. Elder J. & I went to melon patch & had all the melons we wished. By request we remained another night.

Tuesday 22, 1888 (21)   Did some reading in Testament. We again went to the melon patch and had some more bringing one to the house. Had for dinner the first mess of new sweet potatoes. As there is not much fruit in the Nation Mrs. B had us bring some away in a sack which we divided among the Saints   Had a bath at A. Cantys. Crossed the river in the evening and spent the night with Wm. Whiteside. Found Sister W. very sick with the measles . We stayed here until after dinner the next day. 3 mi.

Wednesday 23. (22)   Wrote to Alice. Had the good luck to meet Wm. Ivey and had talk with him. After dinner we went up to Mr. Solomon Harris' as we had understood he wanted to see us. When we arrived he and his son James were near the latter's house making baskets to pick cotton in. It was getting dusk and we were expecting an invitation from Mr. S. Harris to go and stay all night. Instead of this he walked off in a different direction from his house; we stood for a few moments laughing at our situation & gassing about where we would stay all night. We concluded to walk up the road with the intention of meeting the old gentleman & give him a fair chance to ask us. We had not gone far when we thought we heard his voice in the woods; we stopped to listen, and as we stood there, Mr. James Harris called us back, told us he would keep one of us while the (other) could stay all night with his hired man. We were glad enough to accept the invitation as the family living near by, with whom we intended to stay with, were away from home.

Elder J. decided I should stay with James H. young man (age abt. 26) having a wife and babe. He did not have much to say about Utah affairs. Bed time soon come, when, by request, I read a chapter (15th St. John) and took lead in prayer. Had a good bed in a room by myself-slept well as the night

---

[156]Fanny Whitsides Harris, James Harris was her husband.

was unusually cool. 8 mi.

Thursday 24 (23)   After Spending some time the next morning with them we went to the Nation in the afternoon; arriving in the afternoon. Took dinner and spent the night with Sarah Harris. Rec'd an interesting letter from Alice. 8 mi.

Friday 25. (24)   Posted Journal at Sarah Harris' and spent most of the day. Remained al night Jno. Sanders.

August Saturday 25.   Studied the subject of "Continuous revelation" and spoke upon the same the following Sunday. Elder Johnson & I had bath in the river. I dressed first and took a short ride in the Battoe. After my short ride was over I tied up the Battoe but while stepping on the bank by foot slipped and in the water I went up to my wallet. Just deep enough to save my watch from getting wet. Supper at James Harris. Changed clothes at A. Canty's and attended Singing at nigh(t). Spent night Hullery Harris[157] & Ann Tims. 2 mi.

Sunday 26   Usual attendance at S. S.; after exercises Elder J & I spoke.

Meeting at 2 p.m. at which Sacrament was administered but for some unknown reason few partook. Spoke also Elder Johnson. Spent night with Uncle Billy George.

Monday. 27.   Spent most of the day with Uncle Billy, did some writing. Went to their melon patch & had a good time eating melons brought and ate some at the house. Spent night Jas. Harris 2 mi.

Tuesday 28. 1888.   Remained until after dinner. Met with the children in the afternoon. All night A Canty.

Wednesday 29.   Wrote to Companion; remained until after dinner. On our way to Mr. Ballards we called to see, and administered to Sarah Harris. Spent night with Mr. B. 2 mi

Thursday. 30   Enjoyed melons and apples. Had chicken & dumplings for dinner. Spent the night Geo Canty. 1 mi.

Friday 31.   A few days before I had given Mr. Braidy some letter to post at R. H., he did not go so I went to see him in the morning early but as he was intending to go that day I left them. During the day we called upon Mr. B. had a talk. He is a wicked man living in adultery. Gave us a melon. We intended to cross river but waited for mail until it was too late. Rec'd letter from Wife also Mother & John from Georgetown. Spent night with John Sanders. 4 mi.

Saturday 1, 1888.   Started in the morning for Union Co. to meet an appointment the next day. Ate dinner with Wm. Whiteside. Crossing 12 mile creek on the log the water & was high and we had to wade keeping ourselves from falling off by a small pole with which we could reach the bottom.

---

[157]Hillery Harris

Arrived at Sister Bigham in the evening where we spent the night. 13 mi

Sunday 2.   Fast day. Held meeting at 3 p.m. about one dozen strangers were present. E Johnson spoke on the First Principles. I followed speaking on the Kingdom of God.

Monday 3   I went with John Bigham to Mr. Matisons abt. 2/3 mile after their gentleman ox (a two-old). While there I fixed, or set running the clock. Returning with the ox I took hold of the rope which was around his head when he started running as fast as he could. I held on for fear we would have a hard time catching him. It had been raining, the ground was slippery and I was afraid of falling if I should let loose. So I held on going at a faster rate than I had ever done before on foot. I left Mr. Bigham far behind who enjoyed a hearty laugh at the chase. Ate dinner with Bro. Bigham and called upon Aunt Sally in eve but found only Aunt Becky at home, Aunt S. was still on her visit.

Spent the night and was treated kindly. 4 mi

Tuesday. 4   Wrote to Mother and John in forenoon. After dinner, ate too much green melon which made me quite sick to my stomach & had some little trouble.

Called on, and spent the night with Mr. Baker

Wednesday 5.   We pitched horse-shoes in the morning with Mr. B. but he did the best work. Called on Mr. McNulley about 11-oclock. He was away from home, but intended to return in the evening. Mrs. Mc said she would have dinner for us. Before dinner we went 1 mi to post O. and posted letters. Returning had good dinner.

Elder Joseph Brockbank -- SSM 1887-

Photo 48 Joseph Brockbank

Birth date, place - 15 September 1859, Salt Lake City, Salt Lake, Utah Territory, United States
Death date - 4 March 1941
Baptism date - 8 September 1867 -- Baptism by - John Hopla
Father's name - Isaac Brockbank -- Mother's name - Sarah Brown

Sothern States -- November 1887 – Unknown -- Age Called: 28
Southern States - Set Apart: 14 November 1887
Mission type: Proselytizing
Marital Status: Married
Priesthood office: Seventy -- Quorum: 19th
Called From: Spanish Fork, Utah, Utah Territory, United States
Set apart by: H S Eldredge

Missionary Department missionary registers, 1860-1959, Vol. 1, p. 91, line 270.
Missionary Department missionary registers, 1860-1959, Vol. 2, p. 98, line 270.

On November 12, 1887, less than two years after his marriage, Joseph received a letter from President

Wilford Woodruff asking if he would go on a mission to the Southern States. He was to leave Salt

Lake City November 15, 1887 just three days later. He left his young wife and baby in Spanish Fork and reported in Salt Lake City on November 14.

He was set apart for his mission by President Woodruff, and then on the same day, President H. S. Eldredge of the First Seven Presidents of Seventies gave him a blessing. In part it reads: "We say unto you inasmuch as you seek continually for the spirit of God and yield obedience thereunto, you shall be blessed with wisdom, knowledge and understanding. Your mind shall be enlightened, your understanding enlarged, your tongue loosened and you shall be able to proclaim the principles of the everlasting gospel in its fullness with ability and in a way that will win many souls to a knowledge of the truth. And you shall be astonished in your heart at your labors. You shall be shielded and protected from all harm. Your life shall be precious in the sight of God and he will give his angels charge concerning you."

Joseph traveled much without purse or scrip. Through his teachings and his singing, many families opened their doors with greetings of welcome to him and the Mormon missionaries to follow. Upon returning home from his mission, Joseph bore testimony of the many blessings received during his mission and of his faith in the Church of Jesus Christ of Latter-day Saints and of the true Prophet, Joseph Smith.

Joseph was honorably released to return home November 19, 1889. The letter of release was written by William Spry, the Clerk to the Southern States Mission who later became the Governor of Utah. The letter in part reads: "We trust that in returning home you will not lay off the armor nor slacken the zeal which has characterized your labors while abroad as a Herald of Truth but that you will turn your attention in assisting to build up Zion and in establishing God's kingdom on the earth in the midst of the Saints." Joseph did continue his labors at home.

On August 17, 1902 he was chosen as second counselor to Benjamin Argyle. When the first counselor moved away in 1903, Joseph was called to be first counselor to Bishop Argyle. He served in this position until he was released on September 24, 1916.

Elder William Spry -- SSM 1885-1888

PHOTO 49   WILLIAM SPRY

Birth: 11 January 1864, Windsor, Windsor and Maidenhead Royal Borough, Berkshire, England
Death: 19 April,1929, Washington, District of Columbia, District Of Columbia, USA
Baptism date - July 1875   --   Baptism by - Mark Lindsey
Father's name - Philip Spry   Mother's name - Sarah Field Townsend

Politician. Two-term Governor of Utah. Born in England in 1864, he emigrated to the United States at the age of nine with his parents, who had converted to Mormonism shortly after his birth. In 1908, he was elected governor on the Republican ticket. He pushed for and received a large appropriation from the state legislature for the construction of the state capitol building. Spry also worked for food and drug legislation, promoted the development of the state's natural resources, and established committees on banking, industrial safety, and irrigation and water rights. He won re-election in 1912, achieving notoriety during his second term by refusing to intervene in the execution of labor organizer Joe Hill. In 1915 the Republican Party refused to nominate Spry for a third term because of his unpopular veto of a prohibition bill. (bio by: Thomas Fisher)

Burial: Salt Lake City Cemetery,   Salt Lake City, Salt Lake County, Utah, USA

Southern States --   October 1885–Unknown - Age Called: 21
Served as Mission President
Southern States

Set Apart: 12 October 1885 -- End Date: 4 January 1888
Priesthood office: Seventy -- Quorum: 24th -- Priesthood: 24th Seventies
Called From: Salt Lake City, Salt Lake, Utah, United States
Set apart by: Erastus Snow

Notes: He became president of the mission in 1888, replacing John Morgan.

Notes: Served as mission president from 1888 until 1891.

Start Date: 4 January 1888 -- Released: 13 August 1891

Notes: He briefly returned to Salt Lake City in 1890 to marry Mary Alice Wrathal.

Missionary Department missionary registers, 1860-1959, Vol. 1, p. 78, line 3359.
Missionary Department missionary registers, 1860-1959, Vol. 2, p. 85, line 3359.
First Presidency missionary calls and recommendations 1877-1918, Church History Library.
First Presidency missionary calls and recommendations 1877-1918, Church History Library.
Southern States Mission history, 1832-1964: LR 8557 2, Church History Library.
Andrew Jenson, "Spry, William." Latter-day Saint Biographical Encyclopedia, vol. 4 (Salt Lake City: Andrew Jenson Memorial
    Company, 1936): 381-82.
William L. Roper and Leonard J. Arrington, William Spry: Man of Firmness, Governor of Utah (Salt Lake City: Utah State Historical
    Society, 1971).

Elder Alonzo Jerome Stookey -- SSM 1887-

PHOTO 50   ALONZO JEROME STOOKEY

Birth date, place - 14 July 1861, Clover, Tooele, Utah Territory, United States
Death date - 26 September 1930
Baptism date - 1877   Baptism by - R W Green
Father's name - Enos Stookey   Mother's name - Jemima Elizabeth Child

Southern States -- March 1887–May 1889   -   Age Called: 25

Southern States - South Carolina Conference
Set Apart: 28 March 1887
Arrived At Home: 7 May 1889
Mission type: Proselytizing   -   Marital Status: Single
Served with companion: Hyrum Thomas Humpherys
Priesthood office: Elder
Called From: Clover, Tooele, Utah, United States
Set apart by: L Snow
Notes: Returned home due to the death of his father.

Missionary Department missionary registers, 1860-1959, Vol. 1, p. 86, line 47.
Missionary Department missionary registers, 1860-1959, Vol. 2, p. 93, line 47.
First Presidency missionary calls and recommendation 1877-1918: CR 1 168, Church History Library
Southern States Mission history, 1832-1964: LR 8557 2, Church History Library.
        Mission index
Southern States Mission history, 1832-1964: LR 8557 2, Church History Library.
        January 27, 1888 summary of service
Southern States Mission history, 1832-1964: LR 8557 2, Church History Library.   May 27, 1889 release

Alonzo Jerome Stookey was born in Clover, Tooele, Utah 14 Jul 1861 died 26 Sep 1930 in Salt Lake City, Utah. He married Fanny Ajax. He was called and served a mission in the Southern States Mission, and worked with the Catawba Indians there. He is mentioned many times as a companion and partnered up with Moroni Ferrin a good deal of the time, from his journal: " Elder Stookey was appointed secretary of the conference meetings. On Nov 11, 1887, "Elder Stookey baptized Fanny Black and Martha Blackwood. " From Ruben Gardner Miller's journal: " We reached Chatanooga at 11:00 AM and was met by Bro. Alonzo J. Stookey who -ushered us to the Hotel. Four or five of us went up to See Bro. Stookey who was feeling a little under the weather.

I purchased from him 150 tracts and Books. Took his keys and went to Post Office but as there was no mail for him didn't go back up."

Liberal educational opportunities were accorded Alonzo J. Stookey who was graduated from the University of Utah on the completion of a normal and mathematical course. Taking up the profession of teaching, he followed it for fourteen years and since that time has devoted his attention to stock raising and civil engineering. He was for fifteen years a United States deputy surveyor and has extended the government survey over portions of Tooele, Boxelder and Juab counties and has led a very active life, bringing him prominently before the public. During the fourteen years in which he was teaching he was continuously connected with the schools of Tooele county and was principal of the schools in the city of Tooele for four years, also principal at Grantsville for seven years and the first four years of his experience as a teacher were passed at Clover. He is now concentrating his efforts and attention upon ranching and cattle raising, and there is perhaps no one better able to judge of the value of stock in this section of the state than Mr. Stookey

His farm, which produces wheat, hay and other crops, is splendidly equipped with modern machinery.

Utah Since Statehood: Historical and Biographical. Volume III.

Elder Moroni Daniel Ferrin -- SSM 1886-1888

PHOTO 51   ELDER MORONI DANIEL FERRIN

Birth date, place - 6 July 1862, Oden, Weber, Utah
Death date - 5 June 1922
Baptism date - 4 August 1870 -- Baptism by - John Farrell
Father's name - Josiah M Ferrin -- Mother's name - Martha A Bronson

Southern States - January 1886–April 1888 - Age Called: 23

South Carolina Conference; Catawba Indian Nation, South Carolina
Set Apart: 24 January 1886
Arrived In Field: 31 January 1886
Released: 2 April 1888
Departed From Field: 3 April 1888
Arrived At Home: 12 April 1888
Mission type: Proselytizing
Marital Status: Married
Served with companion: Parley Pratt Bingham

Priesthood office: Seventy   --   Quorum: 75th Quorum Of Seventy
Called From: Eden, Weber, Utah, United States
Set apart by: A H Cannon

Notes: Served as President of South Carolina Conference

Missionary Department missionary registers, 1860-1959, Vol. 1, p. 80, line 4.
Missionary Department missionary registers, 1860-1959, Vol. 2, p. 86, line 4.
First Presidency missionary calls and recommendations 1877-1918, CR 1 168, Church History Library.
     28 September 1885 letter of recommendation
First Presidency missionary calls and recommendations 1877-1918, CR 1 168, Church History Library.
     Acceptance letter: 15 November 1885, Eden, Utah
Southern States Mission manuscript history and historical reports, 1832-1978: LR 8557 2, Church History Library.
     Mission index
Southern States Mission manuscript history and historical reports, 1832-1978: LR 8557 2, Church History Library.
     13 December 1886 report on work
Southern States Mission manuscript history and historical reports, 1832-1978: LR 8557 2, Church History Library.
     12 April 1888 return home
Moroni D. Ferrin journal 1887-1922, MS 7532, Church History Library.

He was born 6 Jul 1862, married twice, first to Rosella Bachman, second to Nancy Victoria Murphy. He was called to his mission in the Southern States Mission on 14 Nov 1885, and answered it on the 16th. He was set apart on January 26, 1886. His journal mentions the Catawba frequently, especially the Watts, Evan, James and William D and their families. He also ate and stayed with John Alonzo Canty, and speaks about Elizabeth Patterson and her baby and Bell leaving SC. He even mentions my great grandfather on my mother's side and gives the date his family left Georgia. He died in Utah on 5 Jun 1922 and is buried in Meadow View Cemetery, Eden, Weber, Utah.

Moroni Daniel
Ferrin   1887
in disguise to keep
from being recog-
nized by mob who
were attacking the
L. D. S. Missionaries
at that time.

Moroni D. Ferrin
Nov. 15, 1885

O cast Mission

Eden Nov., 15, 1885.
President Taylor
    Dear Brother
    I received your letter of
Nov., 10th inquiring my feelings
with regard to taking a Sothern
Mission.
    I feel my weakness, but by
the help of the Lord, I hope
that I may be enable to do
all that is required at my
hands for the advancement
of His cause here on the earth.
I have a testimony to bare
to the truth of the Gospel.
I know that God has again
spoken from the heavens and
that His Kingdom is set
upon the earth never more
to be thrown down nor given

to another people and I hope to be able to stand among the faithfull at the last day. For this reason I hold myself in readiness to comply with any request that is made of me by those who are placed over me in the Priesthood

Your Brother in the Gospl

Moroni D. Ferrin.

J M Ferrin Bishop

Elder Moroni Daniel Ferrin's Journal

Conference begins 1887 and meeting number 133

November 1-   I wrote a letter to Brother W. N. Givens, Elders Bingham, Johnson and I took dinner with E Watts. Elder Wilcox and I stayed overnight with Brother Taylor George. I wrote a letter to my wife. Elders Bingham, Redd, Wilcox, Humphreys, Johnson and I picked cotton for Brother H Surratt dinner with him. Elder Johnson and I Stayed overnight with Brother Lee Lindner. Walked 6 miles.

November 3-   we made some benches for conference. Elders Bingham, Wilcox and I took dinner with Sister Patterson. Elder Bingham and I stayed over night.

November 4-   Elder Redd, Wilcox, Humphrey and Johnson and I picked cotton in the forenoon for Alonzo Canty.   Elder Bingham, Wilcox, Johnson, and I took dinner was Sister Patterson.

John S Black furnished two teams and went with me to Cowpens Station after Pres. John Morgan and Brother John Wilson the former president of the southern states mission and the latter a local priest from Oconee County South Carolina. Received a letter from my wife. All of the South Carolina traveling Elders gathered at Mr. JS Blacks and spent the evening there with Pres. Morgan. Pres. Morgan and I stayed overnight with JS Black. Traveled by team16 miles.

We held Council meeting in the morning. Our conference meetings began at 10 o'clock at Brother Alonzo Canty's residence on J. S Black's plantation. Conference adjourned, baptism

1887 meeting number 134, 135, 136, and 137

November-it was a nice warm day and a fair congregation of people assembled. I was presiding and Elder Stookey was appointed secretary of the conference meetings. At 11:30 meeting adjourned. Elder Humphreys and I to dinner with Brother Jefferson Davis Ayers. At 2:00 PM meeting convened again at the same place in adjourned at 3:30 PM after which we held a council meeting until nearly dark. Elder William Cox and I took supper was Sister Patterson.

We held the testimony meeting in the evening and a good time was experienced. Pres. Morgan, while giving his testimony said that he had heard the voice of Angels. Elders Wilcox, Humphreys, Johnson and I stayed overnight with Mr. JS Black.

November 6- Sunday and fast day. We held Council meetings, meeting in the morning. Our conference meeting convened again at Alonzo Canty's at 10:00 AM and adjourned at 11:30. Elder Humphreys baptized Francis M Davis the widow all Mr. James Davis who died September 30, 1887. Pres. Morgan, Elders Wilcox, Stookey, Peck, Humphreys, Johnson and I all took dinner with JS Black Our meeting convened in at Alonzo Canty's at 2:00 PM and adjourned at 3:30 PM. In this meeting, Pres. Morgan confirmed Francis M Davis. Our conference meetings were now adjourned for the year. We held Council meeting again until nearly dark. Elder Morgan, Wilcox and I took supper with Brother Sidney M Berry. The Elders and a number of Saints and friends gathered in to Brother Berry s to have singing practice and Mr. J S Black requested us to go up to his house and hold meeting which we did. Pres. Morgan and Elder Peck occupying the time. Pres. Morgan and I stayed overnight with Brother Sidney M Berry.

November 7- we held Council meeting in the morning. Elders P. P. Bingham and J. H. Johnson were appointed to labor in Union County North Carolina. Elder Wilcox in Oconee County, SC. Elders Redd and Peck in Spartanburg County, South Carolina and Elder Stookey and Humphreys work to go into the southern part of the country and open up a new field of labor. Elder Redd baptized Mary Black, Mr. John S Blacks wife and Elder Bingham confirmed her. The confirmation took place after a short address by Pres. Morgan. Elders Morgan, Bingham and I took dinner with Brother AL Rupp, which Pres. Morgan boarded the train at Cowpen and Station and started back for Chattanooga Tennessee at the same time Elder Wilcox and Brother John Wilson boarded the train and went to

Oconee County South Carolina.

While Pres. Morgan was with us he gave us a great many valuable instructions and we felt to press forward with new vigor in our labors. While in one of our Council meetings Pres. Morgan told us that the Elders would find the honest in heart in the southern part of the kind County or words to that effect. Elder Bingham and I stayed overnight with S A Rupp.   Walked 10 miles.

November 8 -   Elders Bingham, Redd, Stookey, Humphreys and also Elder Johnson shucked and pulled corn for Sister Francis M Davis. Took dinner and supper with her. I stayed overnight with Alonzo Canty and received a letter from W. C. Burton. Walked 7 miles.

November 9-   I wrote a letter to my wife and to F A Fraughton and one to A Green Junior. I took dinner with Sister Patterson, went to Ezell Post Office and got a letter from Heber Wright and one from W N Anderson. The neighbors had a play at Brother Alonzo Canty's residence and Brother James Watts was intoxicated. I stayed overnight with Alonzo Canty walked 6 miles.

November 10th-   I wrote the letter to WC Burton, Elders Redd, Stookey and I took dinner with JS Black. Elders Humphreys, Peck, and I stayed overnight with JS Black.

November 11-   Elders Bingham, Humphreys Peck and I picked cotton for Sister Davis. We all took dinner with her also supper. Elder Peck and I stayed overnight with Mr. Jordan Blackwood. Walked 5 miles.

November 12-   the same Elders picked cotton for Sister Davis in the forenoon and took dinner with her. In the afternoon I went to Cowpen Station and wrote a letter to Pres. Morgan and one to JE Wilcox. I paid for collar buttons, five cents, for paper and postage $.10 for castor oil $.30. I took supper was Sister Patterson and stayed overnight with Brother Alonzo Canty. Walked 11 miles.

 Sunday--   Elder Stookey, Humphreys, Johnson and I held Sunday School and meeting at A. Canty's with a good attendance after which Elder Stookey baptized Fanny Black and Martha Blackwood. Elder Humphreys confirmed the former and I the latter. Elder Stookey, Humphreys, Johnson and I took dinner and supper combined with Sister Bolin and Lanier. Elder Humphrey and I stayed overnight with Mr Willis Martin.

14th-   Elder Peck and I went to Ezell Post Office. I posted a letter to Elder Wilcox. I received a letter from Elder Wilcox, one from John Wilson one from John Gould and one from Richie Hartness. Elder Peck and I took dinner with Sister Bolin and Lanier. I received from Rand. Westbrook two dollars for Brother Richie Hartness. Elders Stookey, Humphreys, Peck ,Johnson and I took supper with J S Willie and shucked corn for him at night. Elder Stookey, Humphreys and I stayed overnight with him walked 5 miles.

Elders Bingham, Redd and I to dinner with Sister Francis M Davis and then made freight boxes for her. Elders Bingham and I threshed out some peas for her took supper with her and stayed overnight with Jordan Blackwood. Walked 5 miles

November 16-- Elder Bingham and I to dinner with Sister F M Davis who sold her cow for $20 cash. I stayed overnight with Mr. Andrew Smith. Five miles

17th- Elders Stookey, Peck and I took dinner with Sister Patterson. I wrote a letter to WN Anderson, Elders Stookey, Humphryes, Redd, Peck, Johnson and I all took supper with J S Black and then helped him shucked corn after which the hands gathered in his house and spent the evening singing, playing and dancing.

18th- Elder Stookey and I took dinner with J S Black. I went to Sister Davises and met Elder Bingham who informed me that he had been assaulted at that place on the evening of the 16th instant and for self-defense was obliged to knock one of them down which he did in an excellent matter. He can got out of farther difficulty by being persuaded off from the spot by Sisters F M Davis and Ellen Price. Elders Bingham, Redd, Humphreys, Peck, Johnson and I all stayed overnight with Brother Alonzo Canty. We afterwords learn that there was a mob hunting for us on this night at Sister Davises. Walked 10 miles

19th- I borrowed a team from J S Black and Elder Bingham, Brother Sidney Berry and I went and got Sister. Davis her family and baggage and brought them to Brother A Canty's. We packed up part of Sister Davises things and also Sister Pattersons. Elders Humphreys, Peck, and I took supper with J S Black. Elders Bingham, Redd, Humphreys and I stayed overnight with him. Our enemies were here prowling around the house. Mr. Black got his gun and scared them away but no shooting was done as they stayed out of Mr. Blacks sight.

20th- Sunday we finished packing up the baggage for the Saints, held meeting and had a good time. The emegration Saints were taken to Cowpen Station with the team of JS Black and Alexander Bridges. Accompanied by a number of the Saints, friends and Elders. We hired a room in a hotel for the people to stay in overnight. Elders Bingham, Stookey, Redd, Humphreys, Johnson and I stayed with them. We had scarcely got settled we stayed up all night and sit by the fire in our room when the scoundrel (George Bishop a merchant at Cowpen Station) disturbed our peace by his demonic presents.

On learning that he had come therefore licentious purpose and had been insulting our Sisters we saw it was necessary to invite him from the room which we did, but he soon returned and continued. Returning making himself bolder and bolder until it became necessary to keep him out by force. But he made so much disturbance that we called upon the Constable of that place to take him and keep the peace.

The Constable replied by coming in and insulting one of our Sisters. The task of getting rid of them both was now before us, by the aid of our faithful friend J S Black, we finally succeeded in doing so without resorting to any great violence, although Mr. Blacks knife was waived through the air somewhat. Walked 8 miles

27th- I concluded to go with the company as far as Atlanta, Georgia as Clark's Jones for whom we were looking did not arrive to take charge of them. At 5:00 AM we boarded the train started for Atlanta, those in the company were Sister Patterson and baby, Lula Patterson, Nancy George, Francis M Davis, and her eight children, Willey and Wm M Givins and wife. We arrived in Atlanta at 4:20 PM the fare costing $6.55 here we met Elders SG Spencer, Lars P Madsen and John M Browning.

The Saints we met were Brothers T H Tydeman and family, G W Payne and family, and W A Ervins and family who were all on their way to Zion. We all stayed overnight at the Union House which costs 40 cents a bed with children free and no meals. Brother Givins was taken very sick and called upon Elders Spencer and I to administer to him. We did so and he recovered almost instantly.

22nd - return to Spartanburg learned that Newman H Barker had arrived from Utah and had joined Elder Wilcox in Oconee County, South Carolina.

At 7:30 AM Elder Spencer and the Saints boarded the ET and VA- GA. Train and started for Chattanooga Tennessee to meet the main body of immigrants.

Page 9

Elders Madsen, Browning and myself remained in the city. I wrote a letter to my wife. We took dinner at the Union House which costs $.25 apiece. I paid for popcorn five cents, for ticket back to Cowpens $6.55.

At 6:30 PM we boarded the Air Line train and left Atlanta. Elders Madsen and Bingham left me at Gainesville, Georgia and I proceeded on my way to Cowpens. Paid for coconuts $.10.

23rd - I arrived at Cowpens about 3:30 PM a distance of 202 miles from Atlanta, walked to Brother Alonzo Canty's where I arrived about daybreak. Elders Bingham and Humphreys and I took breakfast with Brother Canty, received a letter from Pres. Morgan. Elder Spencer and I stayed overnight with J S Black. Walked 8 miles

Received a letter from my wife, one from J C Ferrin and one from Wilmer Ferrin.

24th- Elders Bingham, Spencer and I took dinner with J S Black. Elders Bingham and Johnson started for Union County North Carolina to labor there. Elders Redd and me stayed overnight with John Williams.

25th- Elder Redd and I went to Ezell Post Office. I received a letter from Elder Wilcox stating that H

Barker from North Ogden, Weaver County, Utah had joined him.

Meet Elders Jensen & Clark 1887 Meeting No 141 SS No 53

I received a letter from A. Green Junior also a registered letter from Joseph Thorpe containing the balance of the money due me from him. I went nearly to Cowpens with Elder Stookey and Humphreys who started in a southwestern direction to open a new field of labor. We seperated and I stayed overnight with Jordan Blackwood walked 9 miles.

I took dinner with Mr. William Black then went to A, Canty's (rode part way with Swafford) where I met Elders Oley Peter Jensen of Ovid, Bear Lake County, Idaho and Amasa L Clark of Farmington, Davis County Utah who had just arrived from their home the day before. Elders Ole P Jensen and Peck and I administered to sister LUCY WATTS who was sick and stayed overnight with Henry Surratt walked 8 miles. Elders Peck, Jensen and I held SS and meeting at Brother Surratts. I wrote a letter to JE Wilcox and in NH Barker. We took dinner with E Watts. Elder Jensen and I stayed overnight with Smith Price.

28th-   I wrote a letter to John Morgan. One to J Gould, one to John Wilson and one to Heber Wright. Elders Peck, Jensen and I took dinner with H Surratt. Elder Jensen and all I stayed overnight with Morgan Paris.. Elder Jensen and I took dinner with Henry Surratt.   I wrote a letter to my wife, one to J C Ferrin, one to Wilmer Ferrin, one to Joseph Thorp and one to S C Mowson. Elders Redd, Jensen and I took supper with E Watts and stayed over night with H Surratt.

We took breakfast with E Watts and Elder Peck and I took dinner with Mr. Edward Linder. I stayed over night with A. Canty. Walked 7 miles.

I went to Ezell Post Office and took dinner with sister Bolin and Lanier. Elder Clark and I stayed overnight with JD Ayers. Walked 6 miles.

I wrote a letter to W , Elders Redd Clark and I took dinner with A Canty. Elder Redd and I stayed overnight with James Watts.

I took dinner with JS Black Elder J and I took supper with A. Canty. Elders Jensen, Clark and I went to Brother S Barry's to a cotton picking and a play.   I got a letter from my wife. Elder Jensen and I stayed overnight with Brother Barry.

Sunday and fast day -- Elder's Jensen, Clark and I held SS and meetings at A. Canty's and the spirit of the Lord was made manifest. Brother Taylor George made a public confession for getting drunk and asked the Saints to forgive him which was freely done. I took dinner with James Watts. Elder Clark, Easton and I took supper with Taylor George and stayed overnight with James Watts. Elder Jensen and I to dinner with JS Black and were engaged all day in searching out the truth or falsity of an accusation made against James Watts s for stealing cotton from Major Lender. The charge could not be sustained so Brother Watts remained at liberty. Walked 3 miles.

We took supper with Major Lender and stayed overnight with JS Blackwood.

I took dinner with A. Canty. I received a letter from my wife and stayed overnight with H Surratt.

Elders are Clark and I took dinner with Brother Sidney Barry. We administered to Sister Canty who was sick. I wrote a letter for Mr. Black. Elder Redd and I stayed overnight with him walked 3 miles.

I wrote a letter for Mr. Black and took dinner with him. Elder Redd and I took supper with Taylor George. In the evening we had a testimony meeting. A number of the Saints bore their testimony to the truth of the Gospel and a good time was experienced. I stayed overnight with A Canty.

Ninth – – I took breakfast with James Watts, Elder Redd and I took dinner with A. Canty and stayed overnight with him.

I wrote a letter to Elders Wilcox and Barker. Elder are and I took dinner with JS Wyllie. I received a letter from Elders Wilcox and the also one from John Wilson. Elder Redd and I took supper with Taylor George and administered to his little boy who was sick with the fever connected with the cold he had a good nites rest and in the morning appeared to be perfectly well. I stayed overnight with A. Canty.

On the eighth instant I administered to DC George who was sick with cold and fever and she's soon recovered.

11- – – Elders are Jensen and I held SS and meeting at A. Canty's was small attendance but a good spirit prevailing. I took dinner with Taylor George. Elder Jensen and I took supper was Sister Barry. We administered to T George's little daughter who was sick stayed overnight with Alonzo Canty.

I wrote a letter to my wife, Elders are J and I took dinner with Alonzo Canty. Elder and I stayed overnight with Brother JJ Bolin. Walked 5 miles.

Elder Jensen and I went to Ezell Post Office. I got a letter from Elders being him and Johnson. I paid $.10 for sugar. I took supper with Alonzo Canty. I wrote a letter to Elders Wilcox and Barker also one to John Wilson. I took supper with Alonzo Canty and Elders are Jensen and I stayed overnight with him walked 10 miles.

The 14th- – – I wrote a letter to Elders Bingham and Johnson. Elder Redd and I stayed overnight with Brother Lee Lender. We found him feeling very cold in regard to the Gospel but by talking to him we soon got him to feeling better. Walked 2 miles.

Elder Redd and I took dinner with Henry Henderson and stayed overnight with Mark Bridges. Walked 3 miles.

I wrote a letter to JD Bluth. Elders Redd, Peck and Clark and I took dinner with H Surratt. Elders Redd. Johnson and I took supper with Alonzo Canty. Elder Jensen and I stayed overnight with JS

Black. Walked 3 miles.

Elder Redd and I went to Ezell Post Office. Took dinner and also stayed overnight with JS Black. Walked 6 miles.

18—– Elder Redd and I held Sunday school and meeting at Alonzo Canty in this meeting Brother Roberson was excommunicated from the Church for drunkenness.

God dealt with this man in a manner that I consider is worthy of record. According to Brother Roberson's statement to me he was at this time about 40 years of age and had been habituated to drinking liquor from his youth and his appetite had come to that state that it was constantly craving for strong drink.

The Gospel came to him a few years previous to this date and he received it (I believe with full intent to over come evil even this habit of drinking) but his appetite was so strong for drink that it still overcame him. He therefore neglected to pray saying " I cannot pray while I am still doing wrong." Knowing that his appetite was so strong and be leaving that he had a heart which naturally desired to do right, we counseled him from time to time and board with his weakness until it seemed that patients had ceased to be a virtue, and that mercy would soon be robbing justice if it were continued. Many times has my heart been filled with sorrow to see him shed tears for talking about it and wishing he could overcome bad habit, but it seemed to be of no use he still had that long being and craving for whiskey, whiskey, whiskey.

One day one of the Elders went with me to see Brother Roberson and while talking to him we felt impressed to make him a promise which we did to this effect: that if he would attempt to his prayers, asked the Lord to assist him to overcome not have it and then extend the powers that God had given him to that and that the Lord would assist him to overcome it.

He concluded to accept our counsel secure the assistance of God and take a stand against liquor forever. As he in formed me, he began the task them all the appetite he ever have for strong drink was taken from him and he had no more desire for it then a man that had never tasted it. He continued in this condition for about five months, and no doubt would have continued forever had he been watchful, but it pretended friend persuaded him to take a taste of liquor as a token of friendship. This taste created again the old appetite for whiskey, whiskey, whiskey, and he was soon on another drunken spree. He had again fallen. His old appetite and craving had returned. God had assisted him but he had failed to appreciate it as he should and he was now like the Sow that was moist and had returned to her wallowing in mire. It finally became necessary to put the evil out of the Church by taking action against him which we did as stated above. He himself, although in sorrow for his weakness, acknowledged it to be in accordance to the laws of justice.

In this meeting James Watts made a public confession asked for forgiveness for drinking liquor. On coming out of meeting a note was found pinned to the middle of the road with the sticke. This note, besides containing the Vilest kind of language both in profanity and vulgarity was filled with accusations against us (the Elders) of all manner of wickedness coupled with threats of violence. I would here copy the note but the language therein contained is unfit for record. Before retiring to rest that night, the guilty party was proven to be our satisfaction to be one of our young sisters about 15 years of age (Marietta Berry). Two sisters in the Church testified to having seen her that morning on the spot where note was found and she denied having been there. The last she was proven in a lie as well as being guilty of the offense of placing this while note before the public. The contents of this note proved the consumption of her heart plainly and we had previously suspicion and that she was practicing evil.

Extra effort to search out evil

A few days previous to this date we D Elders had, we had come to the conclusion that there was evil practiced among the Saints secretly, that is they were keeping the truth from us as much as possible. We met together in counsel to decide upon the best means to find these things out that they might be eradicated from our midst. We decided to make it a special matter of prayer before the Lord that he would open these things to our view. We did so and the Lord answered our prayers. James Watts drunkenness and myriad of Barry's iniquity was soon brought to light Reddy noted, and the near future of this history will show other things.

Elder Redd and I took dinner and stayed overnight with J else block and J S Black. I wrote a letter to Pres. John Morgan. Elder Redd and I took dinner and stayed overnight with Alonzo Canty.

Elder Redd and I went to Ezell Post Office I received a letter from my wife and one from Elders Wilcox and Parker. Elder Redd and I took dinner with sister Lanier and stayed overnight with Alonzo Canty. Walked 6 miles.

Elder Peck and I took dinner with E Watts. . Elder Redd, Peck Jensen Clark and I held prayer circle on the spot that had been dedicated for that purpose, partook of the sacraments and held a council meeting each one are rising, expressing our feelings and giving instruction to each other as the Spirit gave us utterance. We had a time of rejoicing together. Elder Clark and I stayed overnight with JT Blackwood. Walked 5 miles.

Elder Clark and I took dinner with Henry Henderson in stayed overnight with Matthew Henderson. 5 miles

Elder Clark and I took dinner and stayed overnight with Jordan Blackwood I received a letter from Elder Stookey and Humphreys one from Mary A Bolin and one from Elder Stookey's mother. Paid for paper five cents. Elder Redd and I took dinner with James Watts. I stayed overnight with Alonzo Canty. Walked 5 miles. Christmas. No meeting. Elder Redd, Jensen, and I took dinner with Alonzo Canty. Elder Jensen and I stayed overnight with Sidney Barry.

I wrote two letters to Elders Wilcox and Barker and 1 to Elders Bingham and Johnson. I received a letter from Elders Wilcox and Barker also one from Elders Bingham and Johnson and one from Pres. Morgan. I sold a coat to Sid Barry for five dollars and got $2.50 paid down.

Elder Redd and I to dinner with JS Black. Elders Redd Jensen and I stayed overnight with Brother Alonzo Canty.

Healing the sick December 27, 1887:   by my own request I had no dinner. Elder Peck and I stayed overnight with JJ Bolin. Walked 4 miles.

28th- – – Elders Redd, Jensen and I took dinner with E Watts. Elder Clark and I started for North Carolina. We stayed one night with Hampton Roberson. Walked 11 miles.

I wrote a letter to Elder Stookey's mother. We stayed all day and night with H Roberson. We administered to sister Roberson who was sick with the mumps. We crossed into North Carolina and stayed overnight with M. M Gordon. Walked 14 miles.

The 3st- – – we stayed all day and night with Brother MM Gordon. Thus ended the year 1887.

January 1, 1888 Sunday we took dinner and stayed overnight with Brother John Gordon.

January 2 by our own request we took no dinner. We administered to John Gordon's baby that had been sick for about three months. Having no oil with which to anoint it we laid our hands upon it prayed to the Lord for it and rebuffed the disease in the name of the Lord. We then went to William Weavers and stayed overnight. About a week afterwords Brother Jordan told me that after we administered to his baby upon this occasion it recovered within a few minutes and had never since been afflicted in the same manner, although it had complained some otherwise.

I paid five cents for goobers and $.10 for candy. Walked 7 miles.

We took dinner with sister Rachel Dover and found the report to be true that (this part is blocked out) had been guilty of committing fornication. We called and stayed a few hours with Brother and sister Wiley. Sister Wyllie made me a present of a book entitled "leaves from my journal". These leaves being from Wilford Woodruff's journal. We returned to Brother William Weavers and stayed overnight. Walked 4 miles.

We took dinner with Lawson Wilson. I paid $.20 for paper and Sweet oil. We stayed overnight with in M M Gordon. Walked 7 miles we took dinner with John Gordon and stayed overnight with John Goins. Walked 10 miles

We went to Shelby city North Carolina I paid for Sweet oil $.25 for goobers $.10. We took dinner in stayed overnight with Brother John Goins. Walked 4 miles.

We took dinner with Brother John Goins. We administered to Brother John Gordon's baby that was sick. It was so bad the previous night that it's mother thought it would die. We stayed here overnight 5 miles.

Excommunicated acknowledgments of error January 8, 1888 Sunday

Brother Gordon's baby arose and was feeling considerable better. It engaged in its usual plays somewhat during the day.

We fasted and prayed. Held meetings in the forenoon at Brother John Gordon's. (Again it's blacked out, somebody) was excommunicated from the Church of Jesus Christ of latter-day Saints for fornication. Brother William Weaver made a public acknowledgment for drinking liquor and swearing and asked for forgiveness . (Blacked out again) made of public not acknowledgments and ask forgiveness for committing adultery, May 18 80 1887. The Saints agreed to forgive her on condition that she would be rebaptized. Brother John Gordon made a public acknowledgement and asked forgiveness for getting intoxicated. Sally Wiley, who had been disfellowshipped was restored to fellowship again.

Meeting was adjourned for about 40 minutes then another meeting was held in the same place. We spoke words of encouragement to the Saints and a good spirit prevailed. In connection with Brother blinds and family we took dinner with Brother John Gordon. We administered to Brother goings a the doubt was sick then he and family went home. As already observed we fasted and prayed this morning. Well on my way to a secret place of prayer I felt strongly impressed by the spirit to disguise myself leaving Elder Clark here in this neighborhood and goal Åland down into what we called the white nation where there were a few Saints living among those who were hostile to the cause of truth. The latter having driven those who held the priesthood from their minutes by mob force and had made threats of destruction against us, to be carried out if we should ever return.

This impression interfered with my arrangements a little as I had thought I would not go down there because of the danger, but return to Spartanburg. I thought the matter over for The Saints their needed counsel and encouragement. Should I go to give them that necessary instruction it was at this risk of my life. Even the Saints living there were threatened so heavily that they were in constant fear.

As such thoughts ran through my mind the spirit seemed to whisper that it was God's command and my duty to obey. The Lord was able to overrule all things at his pleasure, and even if I should be called upon to lay down my life for the cause of the truth walked was I better than others who had done the same? I therefore concluded to go use as much wisdom as the Lord would give me, and put my trust in him for the consequences.

We stayed overnight with John Gordon. We took dinner with Brother and my M Gordon. I wrote a letter to present John Morgan, one to the Elder in Spartanburg and one to my wife. We stayed overnight with Mr John Patterson. Walked 2 miles

We took dinner with Brother William Weaver. We then went to Kings Creek and I baptized married Jean Weaver for the remission of her sins. Elder Clark reconfirmed her. We visited the Kings mountain monument. I then gave Elder Clark the parting hand and started on my trip to the white nation. I borrowed pants from John Gordon, hat from Laura guard Gordon and a cold from William Weaver which constituted my disguise. This disguise would naturally indicate to the observer of the buyer was some farmer or tradesmen. I traveled along unmolested and as much unnoticed as a common citizen of the account County would be. So soon after dark I arrived at the house of Brother McAlpine world's in the white nation. I knocked at the door, Brother gross came and opened it fearing do should be in enemy in the house that would be pleased to inform the mob of my of arrival. I preferred not to go in until I could learn who was there, so I asked Brother gross to come out a moment. That he fearing that it was an enemy as he had been threatened by the mobs many times., Preferred not to come out so he invited me in. I then went in found that all of the inmates were friends and remained overnight with them, giving in such counsel and encouragement as was given to me like the spirit of the Lord for them.

Walked 18 miles

I took dinner and stayed overnight with Brother Robert a near who had also been threatened by mobs and was surprised at my appearing. About the first words that Brother the new said to me when he meant me was "young man, you had better be careful how you slip around here, or you will get a whipping" Some person told me I think it was Brother Lanier that if word should get out among our enemies that I were there, they would be after me inside of two hours. Brother Gross came town in the evening and stayed overnight with us. Walked 3 miles

I took dinner in stayed overnight with Brother Joseph Olin and found that his wife Tilda had joined Baptist Church walked 2 miles

I took dinner with Brother Calvin Gross. Having invited all the Saints in the white nation. White nation was given to the the of Hickory Grove York County South Carolina and given them such instruction and encouragement as was in my power, I considered that my mission to the white nation was completed so I started on my returned back to the Saints in North Carolina. I got on a strange road, but thinking it would come out all right I continued to travel until nearly dark and upon inquiry at a Negro house I learned that I was but a short distance (I think they said 2 miles) from Brother Gross house. This Negro told me as best he could how to find my way and I proceeded, but it was raining and the night was very dark and quite cold. I miss the way in the darkness but continued to travel thinking perhaps I was on the right road and would soon come to a familiar spot, but about 9 o'clock I found myself back again at the same old darkys house.

I saw that it was folly to make my further attempts to proceed until morning. The question arose in my mind what shall I do for a night's lodging I could call on the white inhabitants of the country for accommodations but I feared leastI should fall into the hands of my enemies, for I was still in the enemy's country. Could I return to Brother Gross? No, without was quiet and's impossible as it was to continue further on my journey.

To live without shelter overnight in such weather would not only be unpleasant but jepordizing might help. I did not like to stay with call collared people for it was considered a disgrace in that country, for white people to associate in such manner with the colored folk people.

I considered the matter over seriously and finally asked the colored man to allow me to sit by his fire overnight that he not knowing my situation, refuse saying there were plenty of white people in the neighborhood that I could stay with. I tried to prevail on him to let me stay but could not. He then told me of white man named Anderson Rippey living nearby. We had seen some people in North Carolina by the name of Rippey and although I was not acquainted with this man I felt that he could not be train me, at least, for he was a Rippey. I went to Mr. Rippey and applied for lodging and he received me with great kindness. And he and his wife, the latter especially, took great pleasure in listening to the Gospel as I explained it to them. I told them my situation and they seem to feel quite bad to think that it become necessary for a man to be disguised in order to preach the Gospel in their country. The solo was. Walked 13 miles

January 14, 1888:   I left Anderson Rippey's and received an invitation to call again and see them. I took dinner with Brother William Weaver. At Groves I spent $.15 for Cooper's and candy and $.15 for paper and envelopes. I met Elder Clark at Brother John Gordon's in Cleveland County North Carolina where we stayed overnight. Being a can out of danger I took off my disguise and we rejoiced and thanked the Lord that he had preserved me from harm while I was in the enemy country. Walked 18 miles

we held meeting at Brother John Gordon's will small attendance. Excommunicated from the Church Sister Bolin for apostasy. We administered to James Gordon who was sick and stayed overnight with Brother M M Court.

16th-   James Gordon rose from his bed feeling well. We took dinner with Brother M M Court, then reconnection connected with Brother John Gordon we went to Brother Samuel Gordons where we held meeting and stayed overnight. While it M M Gordon's I copied a prophecy that had been given by Abinadi Pratt predicting the overthrow of this nation but he soon afterwards confessed that he had been deceived by the devil. Walked 6 miles

We took dinner with Brother Samuel Gordon. Elder Clark and I went to Rufus McDades and held meeting they and returned to Brother Samuel Gordon's and stayed overnight.

Other John Gordon went with false to black Station. We'd been left him and went to Mr. Hampton wrote Robison's and stayed overnight. Walked 9 miles

After dinner we went to Gaffney city where I $1.50 for 2 white shirts, $.20 for a memorandum book, $.20 for pens and $.20 for notions. We then went to Brother Humphryes where we met Elders Peck and Jensen. I received a letter from my wife one from Sr. Davis one from Richie Hartness, one from Ammon Green Junior, one from John Gould, two from Elders Bingham and Johnson, one from Elder J V Blueth, three from Elder Stookey and Humphreys and two from Elders Wilcox and Barker, Elder Peck and I stayed overnight with Brother Surratt 9 miles.

The Brights apostasy

January 20th- by my own request I took no dinner. Received a letter from elders Stookey and Humphreys one from elder Wilcox and Barker and one from my father one from John Morgan. Wrote a letter to William M Anderson, one to Pres. John Morgan one to elders Wilcox and Barker and one to my father I met Elder Redd. He and I stayed overnight with brother James Watts.

I sent $18 to Chattanooga to pay for Sister Davises emigration paid $.12 to register of the letter. Paid $.12. Received a letter from John Sanders. We all took dinner with brother James Watts. Elder Jensen and I stayed overnight with Evan Watts. Walked 3 miles.

We had no Sunday school. Meeting was held at Evan Watts with a good spirit prevailing. Elders Redd, Peck, Jensen, Clark and I were present. I fasted that morning. I took dinner with brother H Surratt Elder Redd and I stayed overnight with brother T Bright. Found him feeling very cold in regard to the principles of the gospel and wanted his name taken off from the church books.

We held 2 Council meetings and administered the sacrament elders Redd and I took dinner with brother Evan Watts. I took supper with Taylor George and Elder Jensen

Elders Redd, Peck and I took dinner with brother Evan Watts. I took supper with Taylor George and Elder Jensen and I stayed overnight with brother James Watts. I wrote a letter to my wife, one to W N Gordon and one to M M Gordon. Walked 3 miles.

I stayed over night with Bro. James Watts. I wrote a letter to my wife, one to W N Gorden and one to M M Gorden. Walked 3 miles.

Elder J and I went to Ezell P.O. I received a leter from my wife, one from George E Ferrin, one from Wilmer Ferrin and one from Mrs. J E Stookey, the latter wanting to emigrate. Sister Mary A Bolin. I wrote a leter to Mary A Bolin, one to Mrs. Je. E Stookey and one to Calvin Groves. Elder J and I took diner with Bro. L A Rouppe. I piad for postage.05 cents, for led pencil, 05.cts. Elders Redd and Jensen started for John Pooleys. I stayed over night with Bro Taylor George, talked to him about swearing, which he had guilty of, but he seemed to have no spirit of repentance. He thought he could take the world for it after that. Wrote to Elders Bingham and Johnson, walked 6 miles

I went to Ezell P.O., had no dinner, paid for goobers, 10 cts., for ink.10 cts. For mending a shoe .10 cts, took supper with Mr Cole, spent the evening with W D Watts. Stayed over night with H. Sarratt. 8 miles

I took dinner with Bro H Surratt, wrote a letter to Richie Hartnes, one to John Sanders, one to J V Bluth and one to A Green jr. I stayed overnight with JJ Bolin. 2 miles

Elder Clark and I worked on a chimney for Bro Surrat. I took dinner with E Watts. I wrote a leter to John Gould, one to George Ferrin, and one to Wilmer Ferrin. Elder Peck and I stayed overnight with E Watts. Walked 2 miles.

Jan 28th- I went to Ezell P.O. Got a letter from Elders Stookey and Humphreys which informed me that they had been driven by a mob from Edgefield Co., SC. I had no diner. Elder Peck and I stayed over night with J T Blackwood. Walked 12 miles

29th- Sunday, Elders Peck, Clark and I held meeting and Sunday School at Bro. H Sarratts. Edward Harris made a public confession and asked forgiveness for drunkenness and swearing. Theodore Bright was excommunicated from the Church for apostacy. Elder Peck and I took dinner and stayed over night with Mr. Harris Bright. Walked 2 miles

30th- I took dinner with E Watts, wrote a lettter to Elders Stookey and Humphreys, Elder Peck and I stayed overnight with W D Wats.

I took diner with Bro. Sarratt and worked on his chimney. Received a letter from Elders Wilcox and Barker and one from Bro. Wm Spry. The latter brought the news that Prest. John Morgan had been honorably released from the Southern Mission and that Wm Spry was appointed to succeed as President of the Mission. Elder Clark and I took dinner with Park Bridges and stayed over night with H. Sarratt. Gave.05 cts to Mrs. Sarratt.

Feb 3- Bro Lee Linder told us to take his name off from the Church records. He would not listen to reason on the polygamy question but denounced it as an abomination in the sight of God

Elder Peck and I took dinner with Brother J D Ayers. I received a letter from J C Ferrin, one from Elders B and J, one from Johnie Brown and one from my wife.

I wrote a letter to my wife. Elder Peck and I stayed over night with Bro. Taylor George and talked with him about using profane lauguage which he had been guilty of. We wished him to repent of his sin and make acknowledgment before the Church that the matter might be set right; but he was very stuborne and determined not to do so. His offence was commited on Jan 22dn. I talked with him about in or about the 23rd. And gave him till this date to thoroughly consider the matter. He was still very stubborne and said we could cast him out of the Church if we pleased but he was determined not to make a public acknowledgement. Walked 1 mile

4th - Elders Redd and Jensen returned from Bro. Pooles. Elders Redd and I took dinner with Brother H. Sarratt. Elders Red and Clark started for the Kings 'Mountain Branch and took back the Branch Record. I wrote a letter to J C Ferrin. Elder Jensen and I stayed overnight with James Fowler. Walked 3 miles.

Sunday Elder Peck, Jensen and I held SS and testimony meeting at Bro Sarratts. Elder Jensen and I took dinner on with Evan Watts.

Bro. Lee Linder was excommunicated from the church for apostacy.

Feb. Wm Hosa and Theodor Bright (Two apostates) came before us and contended against the principles of the Gospel with all the power they possessed, but on being defeated in their arguments went their way. I stayed over night with Evan Watts.

I took dinner with Brother Sarratt. I stayed part of the day writing in my journal, wrote a letter to Elders B. & J. I stayed over night with Bro Henry Sarratt..

7th - Bro Sarratt and I took his team and went to Gaffney City and returned.

I paid for pants $3.50 for shoes $3.00 plaster (of) Parish, & for Branch Record for ??, $1.30.

Elder Jensen and I stayed over night with J.J Bolin and administered to Sister Lanier who was sick. Traveled by team 12 miles, walked 2 miles.

Elder Jensen and I took diner with Sister Lanier who was entirely healed of the sickness which had troubled her the night before. The above administration was proformed without oil, as we had none with us.

We sent Sister Mary Ann Bolin and made arrangements for her to go to Utah and I wrote a letter to Sister J. E. Stookey who had offered to forward the money for Sister Bolin's emigration

Elder Jensen and I stayed overnight with Bro. James Watts walked 4 miles

I wrote a letter to Heber Wright. I spent ???? of the day copying the Oconee Record. Received a letter from President Spry stating the company of Saints would leave

In the 3rd day of April night and also that he wanted Elder Stookey to come to the office.

I started in the morning but took diner with Bro Jas Watts. I wrote a letter to Elders W & R also one to Elders B & J. I Baptized Margaret Jane George.

PHOTO 52   HEADSTONE FOR MORONI DANIEL FERRIN 1862-1922

Elder Joseph Hills Johnson   --   SSM 1887-

PHOTO 53 ELDER JOSEPH HILLS JOHNSON

Birth date, place - 1 December 1866, Virgin City, Washington, Utah
Death date - 23 December 1908
Baptism date - 1 December 1874 -- Baptism by - J H Johnson
Father's name - Joel H Johnson -- Mother's name - Margaret Threlcald

Southern States - October 1887–Unknown - Age Called: 20
Southern States
Set Apart: 10 October 1887
Priesthood office: Elder
Called From: Johnson, Kane, Utah, United States
Set apart by: H J Grant
Stories and Documents

Missionary Department missionary registers, 1860-1959, Vol. 1, p. 89, line 206.
Missionary Department missionary registers, 1860-1959, Vol. 2, p. 96, line 206.
First Presidency missionary calls and recommendations 1877-1918, CR 1 168, Church History Library.
11/11/1906 In Provo in compliance with instructions to take a missionary course.

In March 1888 Elders Johnson and A L Clark met with the children of the Catawba Nation, to teach them their letters and how to read. A month later they met with them again and decided to keep teaching them as long as their mission lasted. Elders Parker and Gordon using indian labor erected a meeting house in 1897. The church was originally a twenty four by sixteen foot log building located about a mile the exception of 1897-98 the school was taught by Mormon Missionaries.

PHOTO 54   JOSEPH HILLS JOHNSON IS THE 3RD PERSON FROM THE LEFT STANDING IN BACK.

BACK OF PHOTO: TAKEN OCT 23, 1888 / IN GAFFNEY CITY / SPARTANBURG CR / S.C. / MARY / MISSIONARY GROUP TAKEN IN 1887

OR 8

RECEIVED
NOV
13

Provo Nov. 11, 1906

President J. F Smith
        S. L. City
        Dear Bro.
                I recieved your letter
advising me to take a
missionary course at the Brigha
Young University at and am
now at Provo in compliance
with your request
        I will start school Monday
Nov 12, 1906.
                Your bro. in the Gospel
                Joseph. H. Johnson

J. H. Johnson,
Johnson
June 29/97

Accepts Mission
Call

Johnson, Kane Co. Utah.
June 5. 1887.
First Elders.

I just received my notice as a
missionary. And I am willing to go
and do all I can. I have no means
to go with. I am not yet of age. And
I applied to the bishop of the Kanab
Ward to which I belong. He advised me to
write and state my circumstances.
I have no Father to assist me but I
will do the best I can to work for man.
Your bro. in the Gospel
Joseph. H. Johnson.

Elder John Elbert Wilcox -- SSM 1887-1889

PHOTO 55 -- JOHN ELBERT WILCOX

Birth date, place -- 28 August 1866, Paris, Bear Lake, Idaho Territory
Death date -- 17 October 1942
Baptism date -- 28 August 1874
Father's name - John Dingman Wilcox   Mother's name - Mary Theodocia Savage

Southern States - February 1887–March 1889 - Age Called: 20
Southern States
Set Apart: 15 February 1887
Arrived At Home: 5 March 1889
Marital Status: Married
Priesthood office: Seventy
Called From: Coyote, Garfield, Utah
Set apart by: John H Smith

Southern States   -April 1897–Unknown   - Age Called: 30
Southern States
Set Apart: 7 April 1897
Priesthood office: Seventy
Quorum: 88th   -   Priesthood: Seventy 88th Quor
Called From: Marion, Garfield, Utah, United States
Set apart by: Francis M Lyman

Southern States   -   December 1915–May 1916 -   Age Called: 49
Southern States
Set Apart: 7 December 1915
End Date: 4 May 1916
Departed From Home: 8 December 1915
Priesthood office: Seventy   -   Quorum: 166th
Priesthood: 166th Quo Seventy
Called From: Madison, Idaho, United States
Set apart by: Rulon S Wells

Missionary Department missionary registers, 1860-1959, Vol. 1, p. 85, line 23.
Missionary Department missionary registers, 1860-1959, Vol. 3, p. 44, line 203.
Missionary Department missionary registers, 1860-1959, Vol. 4, p. 196, line 578.
Missionary Department missionary registers, 1860-1959, Vol. 2, p. 92, line 23.
First Presidency missionary calls and recommendations 1877-1918, CR 1 168, Church History Library.
On January 16, 1887, from Coyote, John E. Wilcox accepted his mission call.
First Presidency missionary calls and recommendations 1877-1918, CR 1 168, Church History Library.
On October 21, 1886, the stake president recommends him and others for missions.
First Presidency missionary calls and recommendations 1877-1918, CR 1 168, Church History Library.
On January 13, 1897, John E. Wilcox accepted his mission call.
First Presidency missionary calls and recommendations 1877-1918: CR 1 168, Church History Library.
First Presidency missionary calls and recommendations 1877-1918, CR 1 168, Church History Library.
Stake president Recommendation

Southern States Missionaries 1897   -   Elders who arrived at Chattanooga 20 April 1897.

Row 1 (seated) L to R: Ether M Davey, SLC, UT; John Henry Wall, Santaquin, UT; Morris C Phelps, Mesa City, AZ; George E Hill, SLC, UT; Lewis J Bushman, Escalante, UT; Brigham B Mecham, St. George, UT.

Row 2 (seated) L to R: Joseph W Thompson, Henrieville, UT; Leonard R Lewis, Mesa City, AZ; John H Woodmansee, SLC, UT; William E Rydalch, Springville, UT; Elias S Kimball, Mission President, Logan, UT; St. Joseph W. Musser, SLC, UT; Thad W Naylor, SLC, UT; John E Wilcox, Marion, ID; Henry D. Smith, SLC, UT.

Row 3 (standing) L to R: Alonzo Shurtz, Escalante, UT; Cyrus B Halliday, Pleasant Grove, UT; Sanford Weeks, Pleasant Grove, UT.

Row 4 (standing) L to R: John A Winegar, Bountiful, UT; William J Shakespear, Tropic, UT; Asa H Chase, SLC, UT; Albert D Clark, Panquitch, UT; Louis J Myers, Riverton, UT; Joseph F Broadbent, Mesa City, AZ; George A MacDonald, Mesa City, AZ; Heber C Atkin, St. George, UT; Monroe Twitchell, Escalante, UT; John M Cloward, Salem, UT; Bryant H Jolley, Washington, UT; Lafayetter Dana, Mesa City, AZ.

Row 5 (standing) L to R: Newton Woodruff, Smithfield, UT; Lorenzo Jolley, Mt. Carmel, UT; Silas S. Topham, Paragonah, UT; Don C Babbitt, Mesa City, AZ; Collins R Hakes, Mesa City, AZ; John S Cram, Kanab, UT; Willard Gailey, Kaysville, UT; Eliis H Johnson, Mesa Maricopa, AZ; Adolphus R Whitehead, St. George, UT.

Elder Elisha Peck Sr. -- SSM 1887-

PHOTO 56   ELDER ELISHA PECK SR.

Birth date, place - 26 April 1850, Redlynch, Wiltshire, England
Death date - 23 March 1850
Baptism date - 1 May 1862 -- Baptism by - John Quinton
Father's name - Elisha Peck -- Mother's name - Phebe Turner

Southern States - October 1887–Unknown -- Age Called: 37

Southern States
Set Apart: 10 October 1887
Priesthood office: Seventy -- Quorum: 68th -- Priesthood: 68th Seventies
Called From: Lehi, Utah, Utah, United States
Set apart by: John H Smith

Missionary Department missionary registers, 1860-1959, Vol. 1, p. 89, line 202.
Missionary Department missionary registers, 1860-1959, Vol. 2, p. 96, line 202.
First Presidency missionary calls and recommendations 1877-1918, CR 1 168, Church History Library.
First Presidency missionary calls and recommendations 1877-1918, CR 1 168, Church History Library.

Born 26 Apr 1850 Redlynch, Wiltshire, England and died 23 Mar 1914 in Lehi, Utah, married Charlotte Russon.

In eighteen eighty seven, Elisha was called on his second mission. This time he went to the Southern States Mission, leaving his wife and six children and one was born while he was in the mission field.

Elisha Peck Sr.
History by W O Peck

Elisha Peck Sr., son of Elisha and Phebe Peck, was born April 26, 1850, in Redlynch Wilts., England. At the age of three his mother died and at eight his father died, leaving three orphans, Elizabeth, Mary Ann, and Elisha. He was baptized May 1, 1862, by John Quinton and confirmed by Wm. Bramhall of Springville. August 8, 1867, he went on a mission to his native country. He sailed for America on the boat "The Emerald Isle." It took eight weeks to cross and 33 died and were buried at sea. He arrived in Salt Lake City September 24, 1868. He married Charlotte Russon November 7, 1870. They were blessed with 11 children; Elisha Jr., Mary Amelia, Sarah Jane, Alice, Eliza Ann, Moroni, John H., Leonard W., Isaac R., Thomas J., and Charlotte Blanch, all born in Lehi. Elisha taught school in the winter and farmed on shares in the summer. He helped to build the People's Co-operative Store and then worked there for twenty years as a clerk. He was a faithful Latter-day Saint secretary for many of the quorums and church organizations; secretary of the Deacon's Quorum until his son Elisha was called by A.O. Peterson to take his place. He was secretary of the Sunday school for 30 years, and of the 127th Quorum of Seventy. He was loved by all who knew him and had a kind loving disposition"

Taken from familysearch.org Memories of Charlotte Russon Peck by W O Peck

"She wanted her folks to come to Zion but she told them she loved a young man in Lehi and she desired to become his wife. One of the Nebeker girls said "But father is wealthy and he hasn't anything." One of them commented, "It was not for riches you came here. I don't blame you Lottie, I would marry the one I loved if he did not have a shirt to his back." This young man in Lehi was Elisha Peck, another missionary whom she had met in England. He had filled a mission in his home land before immigrating to Utah. He came here before she did and when he saw her name on the immigration records, he walked from Lehi to Salt Lake City to find her. This started a courtship that lasted about a year. Love conquered and she and Elder Elisha Peck were married in the Endowment House the seventh of November, eighteen seventy. From the Nebeker's luxurious home she went to live in a little twelve by fourteen home in Lehi. The roof was thatched with straw and willows and the interior consisted of a dirt floor and furniture made from boxes. Even though she went the way her heart dictated, the Nebekers later loaned her parents the sum necessary for the rest of the family to come to Utah. The Russon family which consisted of eight children and the parents lived with Charlotte and Elisha in that small room for the first few months after they arrived. In eighteen eighty seven, Elisha was called on his second mission. This time he went to the Southern States Mission, leaving his wife and six children and one was born while he was in the mission field."

Lehi City Sept 17th/87

Prest W Woodruff
                    Dear Brother
Your notice of my being
selected as a Missionary
to the Southern States was
duly received, And my feelings
are in regard to the same
that I am willing to labour
in that part of the vineyard
or any other place the
servants of God sees fit to
appoint me to the best of
my ability with the help of
the Lord, Therefore I will
endeavour to be ready to
start with the rest of my
brethren from Salt Lake City

Oct 12th Hoping that I will
be able to do good & praying
for the welfare of Zion & Freemans
Your Brother, W. Peck

Lehi Sep 17/87

I can fully recommend
Bro Peck to fill the
position to which he
is called J R Carter
Bp

Lehi City Sept 30th/87

Pres W Woodruff

Dear Brother

I have been expecting more
instruction concerning the
departure of the missionaries
for the Southern States, from
Salt Lake City Oct 10th
I would feel pleased to know
how much it will cost for the
Railroad fare, also the time
when the Elders will be
called together for further
instructions. A communication
from you will be gladly
received, giving me the above
information. Your Brother
in the Gospel
E. Peck.

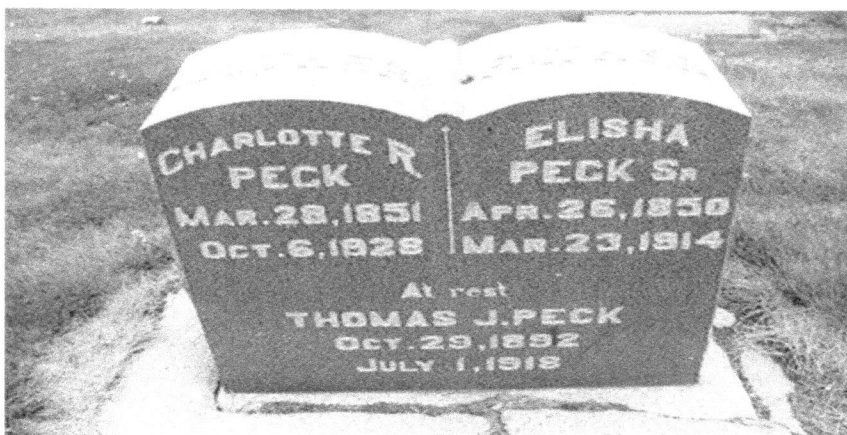

PHOTO 57   HEADSTONE FOR ELISHA PECK SR 1850-1914

Elder Reuben Gardner Miller   --   SSM 1888-1890

ELDER REUBEN G. MILLER.

PHOTO 58   REUBEN GARDNER MILLER

Birth date, place - 7 November 1861, Mill Creek, Salt Lake, Utah Territory
Death date - 8 June 1954
Baptism date - 4 August 1870   --   Baptism by - A J Rhynearson
Father's name - James Robison Miller   --   Mother's name - Mary Jane Gardner

Southern States -- November 1888–December 1890 - Age Called: 26

Southern States
Set Apart: 5 November 1888 -- End Date: 21 December 1890
Priesthood office: Seventy -- Quorum: 61st -- Priesthood: 61 Quo 70
Called From: Mill Creek, Salt Lake, Utah, United States
Set apart by: Heber J Grant

> Missionary Department missionary registers, 1860-1959, Vol. 1, p. 97, line 218.
> Missionary Department missionary registers, 1860-1959, Vol. 2, p. 104, line 218.
> First Presidency missionary calls and recommendations, 1877-1918, Church History Library.
> Mormon Missionary Diaries, Brigham Young University.
> Six journals spanning 1888 to 1890.

The dates in bold type have been added for clarity .
Green text indicates insertion in original diary.
Red text indicates deletion in original diary.
Southern States 1888-1889

Miller Reuben Gardner, 1861-

MSS 418 Vol. 1
[158] **1888-1890**
[159] **Mss 416**
Diary #1
Box 1 Ad2
[160] **Diary**
Diaries of, No 1 1888 to 1890 while in Southern States on a Church Mission
[161] **No 1   1888   MSS.   418**   [162]   [163]   [164]
[page [1]   [1]   [165]

Names of Elders who left with me!

John B. Reid, Salt lake City 16" Ward

William A Reeve, Duncan's Retreat * West Co.

John A. Spendlove, Virgin City " " " [166]

---

[158] There are black bindings visible over the bottom two corners. The front cover also appears to have markings with tape at the top and very faint writing.
[159] There is a white sticker in the top left corner with library markings as follows.
[160] The following word is very faint and difficult to read.
[161] There are black bindings visible over the top two corners and darker brown markings along the bottom where tape appears to be.
[162] The MSS number is circled.
[163] A large part of the bottom left corner and part of the bottom right corner are missing.
[164] The top two corners are torn
[165] The journalist places red check marks after several names on this page. They are denoted with an asterisks.
[166] All quotation marks on this page are on the bottom of the line.

James C. Orr, Clover, Toole Co.

Joseph R. Carlisle, Mill Roreck *

Henry Gardner, Spanish Fork *

Charles N. Hubboard Willard Box Elder Cr.

These boys took the other route and went at Kansas City [167]

Arthur Maxwell, Peor, Summit Co, *

Clark T. Brinkerhoff, Moab, Emery Co.

Williard Halliday, Pleasant Grove,

Isaac R. Vance, Alpine City Utah Co,

Carloss Rasmusen, Salina Sevene Co.

Haden W. Church Panginch, Garfield, Co *

Josiah F. Moretow, Salina Sevene Co.

Elias W. Crane " " "

Hyram S. Anderson " " " *

David Follick Dingie Bearlake * Co.

George Gates Salina Sevir Co.

November 06, 1888

Left - Home for Chattanooga Tennessee, on Mission Nov. 61888 in Company with Eight Elders by way of D&R.G.RR. Leaving home was one of the hardest trials which I had ever experienced to be separated from my Family, Relatives, and friends, gave me much grief and caused many a tear to flow. but after reaching the train and meeting the boys I was consoled as we could talk about what we would meet in a few days. The last friend who I met was Chas Taylor at Price and he bade me good bye will all his good wishes. It became dark on us about Lower Crossing of Price, Trains stopped twenty minutes for supper at -- Green River.

November 07, 1888   Wednesday Nov. 7 1888

We woke up very sleepy this morning as we hadn't been to bed last night. We had the priveledge of viewing a portion of the black canyon as it became day - light.- Trains stopped twenty minutes for breakfast at Gunnison He there started the Climb over Marshall Pass which was a fine sight all it terraced around in such a fine Climbing way We were much amused during last night at a Couple who were in the Pulman sleeper as they acted like they were caressing. We could see them through the car

---

[167] The text on this line is faded.

door. but to our surprise after we had gone to the foot of Marshall Sumit we saw the man a Corpse who was one of the Laughing stalk. We reached Pueblo in evening and laid over there two hours and a half. During which time we took a stroll around the lawn. He called at a Hotel for supper and had to order from Bill of Fare what we wanted. Four of us took Oister Stew and Joe Carlisle ordered a beef steak and then the waiter wanted to know what kind and Carlisle said a Beef Steak not mentioning the kind We were all a little green as to mode of Hotel ways. We boarded the Atchison and Topeka for Kansas City at 6:30 P.M. Reid and I were entertained by a lady who had been one of the Coro Boys. One who was out four years riding on the Range who for four years hadnt had a stich of womans Clothes on during that time. She now claims to be married and has a little Girl who is between three and four years of age Claims her husband's name is Dawley She I think is the Same one which. the Police Gazette made mention of a few years ago.

November 08, 1888   Thursday Nov. 8 1888

We were traveling on the Santefee Rout for Kansas City, Took breakfast Hutchison We crossed the old Hains this day but as it was Cloudy, misty and raining most of the time we were unable to See at a very great distance When we reached Kansas City one evening, about 6:30 P.M. we were much at a loss not knowing which way to go nor what to do but finally we caught on and then took. a portion of the town ins. We took a ride on the Cable Street Car to Post Office and all wrote a letter home and then returned to the Starting Point which was Depot Street. If I may give it that name. We then made for the Cars in which we were to ride to Memphis We there found the other Company of Elders and had a chat over our exploits and travels. We soon got stretched out in the Seits and were asleep.

November 09, 1888   Friday Nov. 9 1888

We breakfasted between Kansas City and Memphis We all tried to revive our spirits by singing Hymns and telling Anecdotes on the way but finally we are settled down Sober and quiet We crossed the Mississippi River on a steamer in evening about 5:30 where the stream was about a mile and half wide It was a picnic for us as it was the first steamer we or been on board. It was only a few minutes work to cross and was lauded and train run off to depot where we were switched around for an hour or two and then had to wait at the Charleston Depot till 10:45. We then took a stroll around Memphis where we saw some fine buildings and stores I purchased an Ivory Pocket Memoranda.

November 10, 1888   Saturday Nov. 10 1888

It became day light just before crossing the Tennessee River at a place called Decatuar. We had breakfast at a place called Stevenson about 39 miles from Chattanooga. We were all much interested in sight-searching as we new were nearing our destination and was running over a section of Country in which some of us might have to labor. We reached Chatanooga at 11:00 AM and was met by Bro.

Alonzo J. Stukey who -- ushered us to the Hotel Kennedy House, Chattanooga In afternoon and evening we all took a stroll taking in town. Went up on top of Cameron Hill which was a fine observatory to the City and surrounding Country. Reid and I went togater and after leaving the Cameron Hill went to the Beech where there was Saw Mills and foundries. We then made toward our room from there as darkness came on After supper we wrote a letter each and then were entertained by Bro. Stukey who gave us a little of his experience He called us togather and took our names and home residence & Adress, at 2: PM

November 11, 1888   Sunday Nov. 11 1888,

In morning after we had breakfasted we took a walk to National Cemetery where the remains of about 13000 souls were buried from the battle faught in the Rebellions. We could see from this cemetery where the three most Fated battles were faught. The battle of Mission Ridge " Chicanaugah " Lookout Mountain The Cemetery Contains 72 acres in the in closure In afternoon or toward--- evening went to Lookout Hill on the Dummy R.R. and there took the Inctire R.R. up on top. Saw Sunset Rock which is noted for being the place where the Signal was given to Grant when they had taken possession of the Mountain and driven the Confederates down to where the great battle had afterwards taken Place. We attended the Methodis Church in evening. the Text of the Pastor was the Glory of Paul or something to that effect.

November 12, 1888   Monday Nov. 12 1888.

Was at Kennedy House in Chattanooga Yet & was still taking in the town. Reid and I went down to the River and had a ride across and back on a steamer which was a treat to us We visited a saw mill and saw some quick Lumber making One log which Contained 250 feet or more was sawed in 3 ½ minutes. After leaving the saw was sent off on Rollers and cut up into lengths and certain widths The slabs edgings and Wunrie edge pieces were sent off to other departments and made into baths Pickets &C&C. The Mill is situated on the bank of Tenn., R. where all the Timber is driven down in Rafts. That is the logs are all pinned together and then floated down River. In after noon there was considerable excitement in the North West part of City by a fire breaking out, which got on a fair way before the firemen could get the waterworks to spray just right The Republic cause had a Torch Light prosession in the evening which was the noisiest crowd I ever heard & was principally Negros who formed the procession. Bro. Reid and I went to Theatre and while there heard of a fire being up near the Kenedy House but we knew that there as no use of us trying to go there as the crowd was so thick we could do no good. The play was the 12 temptations which was grand. The fire was East & across the Street from the Kennedy House where we were staying Four or five of us went up to See Bro. Stukey who was feeling a little under the weather I purchased from him 150 tracts and Books Took his keys and went to Post Office but as there was no mail for him didn't go back up.

November 13, 1888   Tuesday Nov. 13 1888

Went up to Bro. Stukey's Office but he had gone to Post Office and didn't get to see him. Reid was with me so we went back and I wrote a letter to Anna. Bro. Stuky came with cards. Reid went to see Iron works but as I was rather wearied concluded wouldn't go out. Bro. Spry came in on the 12:30 train from Alabama, and in afternoon went up to Kennedy House and gave us our appointment Some North Some South Some East and West. Four to Alabama Six in North Carolina Three to Georgia One East Tennessee Two to W. Verginia Self & Joe Carl Can't remember where the others were Sent. It seemed hard to part with them Joe and I were all of the Crowd who was left at the Hotel for the night. We went to the Depot with Six of them and bade them good bye. We were entertained till Midnight by Bro. Spry and Stukey in listing to their mission experiences. Three bodies were found in the ruins of the building which burned last Night Two men and a woman. A police man, was shot so that he died today and a man jumped from the 2nd story of the burning Hotel and strangled himself so he died today another dropped from the 3" Story and Spranied both Ancles so that he doubtless will be a Cripple for life. All this was caused through the Torchlight --- procession.

November 14, 1888

Wednesday Nov. 14 1888

Joe, R Carlisle and I wakened up at the Kenedy House and all the other boys gone. We barded the Cincinnata Southern for West Virginia at 7:55 A.M. Passed up through the Eastern part of Tenn, and through Kentucky to Lexington where we took the Chesepeake and Ohio to Huntington, at 10:55 P.M. Passing through Kentucky we saw some of the most beautiful Country one ever laid eyes upon and as nice Cattle were roaming over the fields as could be risen in any Country The Country is not quite so broken and hilly as other states which I passed through and of a much nicer Colored soil. Saw many droves of Hogs and Some Cotswool Sheep. Didn't notice many horses but what did see were good average ones.

November 15, 1888   Thursday Nov. 15 1888

We Joe and I landed at Huntington, W. Va at about 5:30 AM and went in to the Waiting room and Slept till about or a little after 7: then went to a Hotel and got our breakfast. We then went to a livery stable and Joe hired a Conveyance to take him to Wash Alkins about 30 miles distance from Lexington in Tooley, Wayne Co. It was a a hard task to bid good bye but we had it to do He started for his field of labor about 9 o'clock in a buggy and I took the train for Coalberg where I landed a little after 2: PM I then boarded the branch train raining to Coal mine where I was fortunate enough to meet a man by the name of Jas. Jarrell who pitated me to the House of Thos. Fosters, where I put up overnight. I think the Hand of Providence was placed over me as soon as I lighted from the Car as I met Jarrell and he proved to be going right to the place where I wanted to go. Had he not been there as a pilate for me there was nine Chances out of ten for me to have wandered off into the woods and not found my way. The Country is a mountainous or hilly Country. You can go up a gulch to its head where you come to a ridge separating three or four little Canyons or Hollows which if you follow will take you any place You want to go if you get on the right trail. I was received cordially at Mr. Fosters although he didn't belong to the Church. Mrs. Foster was a member and a very charitably old lady. This is a place where the elders meet for a kind of a home I was initiated into the ministry the first thing. At Supper Called on to ask blessing and to offer up prayer before going to bed. It was raining all day and when I retired

November 16, 1888   Friday Nov. 16 1888,

Got up at Thos Fosters in West Virginia, Boon Country it being the first night that I had ever Slept in this place or in West Virginia. I busyed myself till about noon in writing a letter to Anna and then Bro. Shepherd came an Elder from Richmond He had left his Companion at Bro. Hendrics he called the place. They were crossing one of the Streams and he sprained his ankel so that he was unable to travel. My Companion was unable to come and meet me on account of Streams being so swollen. Bro Shepherd entertained me and the day soon passed away In evening we went up on a hill and offered up Prayer. We sung a few Hymns in evening.

November 17, 1888   Saturday Nov. 17

We Bro. Shepherd and myself went from Uncle Tom Fosters to Coal mine in Cabbon Creek. a distance of about 2 miles with the intention of going to Coalberg on train but as the train wouldn't remain at Coalberd a sufficient length of time for us to attend our business and then ride back up we concluded it was useless to go down. We got dinner at Uncle Toms and then took over the hill and down into a hollow to a place known as ---- Velies where we remained but for a very few moments and then we went down the Creek Comonly known as Joes Creek where we met with friends and Saints. On our way passed the Grist Mill which is a building about 6X14 standing out in the Middle of the Stream on stilts. The dam was or formed a part of the foundation at the end and caused the Creek to look as though a beaver might have caused the water to back up. We stayed overnight at the House of a Saints by the Name of Alonzo Workman. where we passed a pleasant evening by fireside Chats and by singing Hymns.

November 18, 1888   Sunday Nov. 18

This was a remarkable day in many respects. Bro. Shepherd and I left Bro. Workmans on what is Known as Joes Creek, in Boon Co West Verginig, and went to Mr. Thos Fosters after which we went back on to Jos Creek to a place Knorowa Velies where we met ^some of the Saints and there Baptised James, Jarrell and Wife It was raw cold morning but we immersed them at any rate. We then Wended our way toward ColdBerg Station a distance of about 12 miles on foot. Took down the Cabbon Creek Rail Road. We couldn't do business satisfactory at this station and so we walked on down to Winefred Junction three miles. Our business was to find rates for the Company of Emigrant who were on their way for Colorado. They had started for the depot but as to what times they would arrive was uncertain for I think is uncertain for one to say when he will arrive at a place in West Verginia. James Jarrell and family got down at the Junction shortly after us and he and Wife each rode a horse which we Chartered to ride back up to Uncle Toms. Fosters but as we didn't meet the crew till about 11 o'clock up a Canyon known as Slaughters Canyon a distance of about 6 or 7 miles and the worst of all was the heavy rain which kept falling till after we were in shelter at the Station.

November 19, 1888   Monday Nov 19.

We Bro Powell and Timothy and I left Winefrede Junction on the Kanawah River and landed at uncle Tom Fosters where we remained overnight We had left the saints in Charge of Bro. Shepherd who was going as far as Huntington or Lexington with them It was Still raining and Continued mostly all day. We all had a Conveyance which was acceptable. I took any Valise out to a road and got a Bro. Andy Jarrell to Haul it over to his place a distance of about 12 miles. Bro Powell was feeling very poorly as he had a fever and Rash breaking out over him

November 20, 1888   Tuesday, Nov. 20

We Bro Powell, Timothy and I were at Uncle Tom Fosters all day till evening Reading talking and Singing and then Bro Timothy and I went down to a son in Laws of Fosters where we remained over night It was a never to be forgotten night for one as it was my first night out as a minister and we were cornered up on misteries such as being Baptized for the dead, How was it possible for Judas to be hanged and bursted at the Same time Bro. Timothy did the talking and singing and I listened Bro. Shepherd returned to Uncle Tom. Fosters from starting the emigration for Colorado.

November 21, 1888   Wednesday 21

We were at Mr. Caines Fosters Sons in Law. when we ate Breakfast. We Continued the talk on the baptism for the dead. Bro. Powell came about 9 o'clock A.M. and we sung a few hymns and then went to Uncle Toms Foster where we remained for a while and then we wended our way toward Bro Andy Jarrells on Coal River but when we got to the forks of White Oak, Bro Timothy and I went up White Oak to Bro Henry Foster and the other three Brothren went up to Bro Andies We met Bro. MCMaster at White Oak. We met Bro. Glines who was at Henry Fosters laid up with a sprained ancle or instep His foot was badly swollen

November 22, 1888   Thursday Nov 22

Bro.   Timothy and I left Bro. Henry Foster on White Oak and went over a mountain and up Coal River to Bro Andrew Jarrells. Where we met the Elders or four of them. We got dinner and there some of them engaged in a little recreation such as jumping. We then went with Bro. Andrew Jarrell to a Corn field and helped him pull corn. In evening we sung Hymns and recited. Bro. McMaster recited Barnards Del Carpio and --- --- ----- --- ---. Bro. Powell recited Bro Timothy sung Yes I will love you when you are Old.

November 23, 1888   Friday Nov. 23"

 Was at Bro Andy Jarrells till after 12 o'clock preparing to go into our several fields of Labor. We went to a secluded and dedicated spot and Held Prayer and received Council from the Bretheren. Bro. Timothy and I were assigned to a new field in Rawley Co and we started off in the highest glee. Bro Shepherd and Brockbank were sent into Fayette Co. We separated from where we crossed the river on a Gunnel about Â¾ miles below Jarrell Valley P.O. We called at a Bro John Jarrell Did remained there over night [168]

November 24, 1888   Saturday Nov. 24"

We Bro. Timothy and I ate breakfast a Bro. John Jarrells in Jarrells Valley where we had been over night and then got him to put us to the other side of River on a Gunnel after which we went up to a Mr. Petries who kept a stone where we remained a good Part of the day while Bro. Timothy repaired his shoes. Mr. Pettry was having a Husking Bee which is the Custom in in this this Country They all turn loose and Huck the Corn out and then eat a big dinner and supper.

We remained over night with Mr. Pettry and were very cooly treated. November 25, 1888 Sunday Nov. 25" We ate breakfast at Mr. Pettrys after which we went down to Jarrall Valley P.O. and then back up the Coal River where we crossed on a Gunnel to the other side and went up what in Known as the Little Marsh River at the mouth of which we called in to the House of Mr Jas. Jarralls and were lucky enough to strike on to a dinner after which we journeyed on up the River to a side draw or Canyon about a mile and half which we went up till we came to a Mr. Floid Williams at the head of Canyon where we remained overnight. Bro. Timothy gave them the First Principals of the Gospel. We sung a few Hymns. and I wrote a letter to Anna.

November 26, 1888   Monday Nov. 26"

We left Mr. Floid WIlliamsn on Mountain between the Little Marsh and Clear Fork and went to Lawson Post Office after which we went up the Clear Fork to Harpers Store a distance of about

---

[168] The last five words of the previous sentence are written in smaller text so it will fit on one line.

twelve miles where we took up another Canyon and went to where Bro Timothy had left his satchel and there journeyed on to a Mr David Colins over a Mountain about three miles where we remained over night.

November 27, 1888   Tuesday Nov. 27."

We left Mr. David Colins in the Pauit River Country and went up in timber off from the Side of Road and built a fire and sewed our pants where we remained a good portion of the day and then we went to Lewis Hemphreys and put up for the night but were very coolly received. We sung a few Hymns and Bro Timothy talked a little Gospel Mr. Humphrey became a little more socible and sat a pan of apples before us which we soon put out of sight

November 28, 1888   Wednesday Nov 28"

We left Mr. Lewis Hymphreys on Paint Creek and went to the Curts Ville P.O. and then across a mountain to a Mr. Cragers on Packs Branch where we ate dinner. We talked the people for a while and found they were almost Saints were very favorable and told us of some of their friends and relatives who were in Burks Gardens in Taswell Co. which they wished us to Call upon if we went there. We then journeyed on to a Mr. Geo. M. Powers where we were kindly received and remained overnight. Had lively Chat yet couldn't talk very much Scripture. They were favorable with the Mormons from the facts they had known them from childhood and that a Mormon preacher had married them About bed time two Gentlemen by the names of Woro Weece and Fontes Devecse Came in They had a talk about showing charity to Elders

November 29, 1888   Thursday Nov. 29"

Thanks Giving Day. We ate breakfast at Mr. G.M. Powers where we had remained over night and were much welcomed. We then went to the Mt. Hope P.O. about a mile from Mr. Powers.. We journeyed there on what is Known as the turn Pike to a Mr. Weese's where we got our dinner and then Bro. Timothy began to preach Gospel and got them much interested so much that we were   requested to remain overnight and so we did. We got them all interested and began to investigate. Showed them where we got our authority from to preach the gospel and a administer therein Miss Weese allowed one was soft to go to the table and not get enough to eat, this was said because I didn't take the last apple which was in the pan while talking around the fire hearth.

November 30, 1888   Friday Nov. 30"

We left Mr. Weeses on Look Creek and went to Rawleigh where I bought a pair of shoes and Bro Timothy a hat. We called at a place about three miles North of Raleigh Town and got our dinner We then got to talk with a Christian Baptist, We left a good spirit and were invited back We made three calls before finding a place to put up for the evening and there stopped at a man's House by

Name of Smith, We were not much welcomed although made very comfortable He and family kept one room and a boarder and us the other Stormed a little all day

December 01, 1888   Saturday Dec. 1" 1888

Ate Breakfast at Mr; Jack Smiths about a mile and a half west of Rawleigh Court House. and then wrote a few letters. We remained there till after we had dinner and then went to Raleigh C.H. where we mailed our letters. We then took a Road and went South to a place called Pincy where we were then directed to a new Church a distance of about a mile and half where we were   in hopes of holding meeting We called at three places before finding a place where we could stay overnight We caught on to a fine Place at Mr. J.S. Lewis in Daniels, Raleigh Co. We were treated very kindly yet there wasn't much stock taken in our Religion. We were assigned to a room ourselves shortly after Eight o'clock.

December 02, 1888   Sunday Dec. 2"

We were at Mr. J S Lewis till 11:30 and then we wended our way Eastward to the Feret School- House when we inquired and asked for the privilege to preach. We ate dinner at a Mr. Solesberrys who was Trustee of School House He granted us the use of House and Sent a boy around the Neighborhood to scatter news that we would hold meeting in evening. We held meeting according to appointment, but there were but few present. We were provided for by some people by Name of McDow. Baily. Bro. Timothy occupied the time of Meeting talked on first principles of Gospel.

December 03, 1888   Monday Dec. 3"

We left Mr. McDow, Baileys in a place called Dawels about 6 miles from Raleigh Court House, and went to Half way branch between Beaner Creek and Shady Spring and stayed overnight with Mr. Crockett Wadell a man 75 years old who was just turning grey, and a very peart man We had an argument with him on Repentance. He claimed one must receive a Testimony of God that he is a fit subject for heaven before he can be baptized He must see the working of this spirit in some way or other before He can confess his Sins. He wouldn't listen to what the bible said in relations to Repentance but requested us to say what the Spirit had done for us. He was all Baptis. We were very kindly treated and made welcome.

December 04, 1888   Tuesday, Dec. 4"

We left Mr. Crockett Wadells place about eleven miles from Raleigh Court House and went South West about three miles what was known as Chapple where we remained over night with a Mr. Clarkson P. Phillips who treated us very kindly. both before and after finding out that we were Mormons. When we asked him for permission to stay overnight he said. Yes Sir. I wouldn't turn such men as you away under any consideration. He was very clever until he found out that we were

Mormons and then he seemed to be paralyzed for a minute or two and then began to Recover. He was all but Converted when we retired for rest. He agreed with everything we said. and then said it was funny that a man should live till he became 55 years old before he could hear the truth once. Ate dinner with Mr. Smith.

December 05, 1888   Wednesday Dec. 5

Left Mr. Clarkson P. Phillips place in Shady Spring district and went westward tow. ard Trap Hill Country and passed over a Mountain's to Mr. C.E. Tolleys in a part of Country Known as Bacon, Town. Mr. Tolley lives one mile below the School House When we asked permission to stay overnight it was granted us yet in a very cool way. There being so much predguice existing among them In the evening chat we met up with many outrageous yarns which had been told about the Saints. Such as Jno. D. Lee and Mt. meadow massacre and other barbarous lies They were not in a fit state to receive the Gospel

December 06, 1888   Thursday Dec. 6"

Left Mr C.E. Tolleys in Bacon Town Country and went west to the Raleigh Road where we took a road to go in the Trap Hill Country. We went into the timber from the Roadside where we built a fire and informed our minds, Bro. Timothy read from the voice of warning. while I patched my pantaloons. We then wended our way to a store Known as the where we were refusd to remain overnight. We then went about a mile farther on the Maple Meadow Road to a Mr. Jacob Seslers who received us very kindly and was very sociable. He didn't profess to belong to any sect therefore he wasn't so much predguis to us as some people are He was anxious to know our belief and Bro Timothy gave him the First Principles of the Gospel straight. This Gentleman was in an Invalad from being hurt across the Small of the Back.

December 07, 1888   Friday Dec. 7"

We remained at Mr. Jacob Seslers till after dinner as he was much interested in what we were teaching. Bro Timothy gave him a little sketch of the obtaining of the Book of Mormon and of the Visitation of an Angel to Jos. Smith. We sung some Hymns which caused Mr. Sesler to weep We were invited to calla nd stay with them again if we ever passed through that Part of country We traveled on about 4 or 5 miles to a Mr. Isaac Snuffers on the Maple Meadow Road where we remained overnight Was coolly treated by Mrs Snuffer but more kindly by Mr. Snuffer. He was of the Dun Kard faith and didn't care much to hear the principles of our Gospel, We showed him the new translation of 1881 in his bible which he didn't know was there. He drifted off on the financial affairs of Utah and then we retired We removed Considerable prejudice from him before retiring

December 08, 1888   Saturday Dec 8

Left Mr. Isaac Snuffer near the Luster P. Office and went to the Office where we remained till after 1: P.M. writing letters. Wrote One to Bro, Alonzo J Stookey for Fifty Tracts No 1 and $5:00 One to JR.M and another to Anna. We were kindly invited into dinner by Mr. Luster the P.O. Master. We then continued our Journey westward toward Maple Meadow and remained over night with a Mr. Perry Oniel. We called at a place close to Mr Onils but were refused.

December 09, 1888   Sunday Dec 9

We wended our way from Mr. Perry Oniels place in Maple Meadows through Mud and rain to Mr. Clarkson Adkinsons in the Brackin Ridge Country a distance of about 9 mi. We went to Chas. Stausberrys place in the Trap Hill Country and got dinner When Bro. Timothy asked to dine with him he said Its pretty late isn't it. it being then 1:20 P.M. We were just turning on our heels to go and his heart was softened and said Come in and I guess can get dinner. We had a splendid dinner and were very kindly treated and invited to Come again if happen back that way.

December 10, 1888   Monday Dec. 10 Went from Clarkson Adkinsons over to a Mr. Farmers in the Bracken Ridge Country. Before going down to the House we sat on top of Hill reading till noon and then went down and got dinner after which we went into the Corn field with them and helped shuck Corn. We remained overnight with him

December 11, 1888   Tuesday Dec 11

He left Mr. Cris Farmers in Bracken Ridge country and went to Trap Hill Country. We built a fire in the Woods and read till in evening then went in search of a place where we could remain overnight and found Mr. Henry Snuffer who was justice of Piece. We were coolly treated but not out of respect. We had to sleep in the Same room as he and wife. As we Passed the Trap Hill Mill we were steared at and could hear them say to one another "There goes Some Mormons."

December 12, 1888   Wednesday Dec 12

Went from Mr. Henry Snuffers in the Trap Hill Country toward Raleigh C.H. and lodged with a Mr. J.W. Harper who was Sherriff of the County When we applied for lodgings we Consented but had he known who we were before don't believe he would allowed us to have shaded his door for when we told him who we were, He said, Well Gentlemen it won't do you any good to stay in this Country .but in as much as I promised you lodgings here will aim to treat you as Gentlemen and that will be all We thanked him for the promise at the same time laughed to ourselves to see the Change which came upon him He kept up a Conversation about temporal affairs until he became quite sociable and finally said Well you have head; face arms and hands just like other people and look like gentlemen. He became quite nice before retiring.

December 13, 1888   Thursday Dec. 13.

Was snowing when we got up we lit out in it shortly after breakfast. We were at Mr. J W. Harpers the Sherriff, and went back to a road leading to Prosperity where we secluded ourselves in the woods and made a fire where we staid till after three o'clock and then we hit the Road and went to Mr. Wm. Baileys and applied for lodgings and was refused We were asked what denomination we belonged to and after telling the lady seemed frightened and said no you can't stay. We don't believe in that Society because they had heard quite Smart about them, Called at Old Grandma Baileys and were kindly received.

December 14, 1888   Friday Dec. 14

We wrote a letter each before leaving Mrs. Baileys and then went to Prosperity P.O. to mail letters and then called at another Store after which we went into the woods and made a fire where we remained till after 4: PM. We then started for Raleigh Calling on the way for nights lodgings and were refused six times and finally had to Call at Hotel in Raleigh and were granted. We stopped in among a member of men in office and told we were Ministers of the Gospel without Purse or Scrip.

December 15, 1888   Saturday 15

We remained in Raleigh C.H. town till after the Mail Came from Mt. Hope. I received four letters, one from Jos Carlisle and three from Anna. Also a Paper. We had been at the Semmon House overnight where there were quite a number of roughs who used some foul language. They sprung the Poligamy questions which we Protected and Caused them to Change the Subject We went west of town and made a fire in Woods where we informed our minds   We then traveled on to a Mr. Cooks where we were kindly received and well Provided for. We had a quite a roundabout way of talking of the Gospel December 16, 1888 Sunday Dec. 16" We left Mr. Cooks about 2Â½ miles west of Raleigh CH on the Maple Meadow Road and went to the Court House to Meeting which was held at from 11:AM till 12 noon We were not much built up in the Faith from the Sermon from the fact it was Simply fiction taking the IX Chap. of Acts. From 23 Verse and that new revised addition changing the meaning of the Chapter. He dwelt on the alms deeds which Tabitha or Dorcas by in -- terpitation did. and then flattered the women by telling them what good works they do &C&C. We wended our way back west to the place in the woods where we had been yesterday and mad a fire and read some of our Church works and informed our mind a little. We then went farther west and applied for Lodgings and were refused by three and granted by the fourth but by the worst heresy we have met Since I left home. He was fairly in - salting as soon as he found out who we were. He said his Book didn't teach such stuff as Visions Revelations, Prophets &C-- Said he didn't blame the inhabitants of any Country for mobbing and driving our people if they believed any such stuff. He harped on Folks any for a time and we were mute and finally we were shown our bed and we retired leaving him quite Hostile.

December 17, 1888   Monday Dec. 17.

We left Mr. Evans shortly after breakfast and he said after we had bade him good bye; Now if you fellows are teaching what you professed to be last night You had better go right home tomorrow. for he didn't believe one word of it. We said all people didn't believe as he did. It was raining lively and we waded through the Mud to Mr. Jack Smiths where we first remained overnight in this Country and where we left Clothes + Boots.

We then went toward Raleigh and went into woods where we had been two days previous where we built a fire and Sat under our umbrellas for shelter while we wrote letters and read. I wrote to Anna and Bro Timothy read a Tract. We then journeyed towards Raleigh again and Called upon a Man living in a Large White House who had buried his wife but two day before and Consequently couldn't grant us Entertainment. We Called at Post Office and I received two letters and two Papers which had been forwarded from Lawson. We went East in a Part Called Little White Stick to Mr. Stewart Hurt

December 18, 1888   Tuesday Dec. 18

We left Mr. Stewart Hurts on the Prince Stalion Road about three miles from Raleigh C.H. and went to the Youth of Piney where we were directed to Carper Ville by going up a trail of 2¾ miles. We called upon a man for Lodgings and was directed to a Ministers where we went and was received and Cared for. The Minister was a Baptist and didn't Catch on to us till we asked a Blessing on the Food when he said what denomination do You Gentlemen Rep. His name was A J Carper December 19, 1888 Wednesday Dec. 19" We left Mr. A.J. Carpers in Grand View and went to Mr. and asked for dinner and remained there for a while and then went to the P.O. and Posted letters from which we went to a Mr. Lewis Worleys in Shady district. We were refused once before reaching this place. It snowed all day and was snowing when we retired.

December 20, 1888   Thursday Dec. 20

We went from Mr. Lewis Worleys in Shady Spring District and went to a Mr Abraham Bears in the Daniels District where we remained from before noon till time to hunt a place to remain overnight and got permission to stay where we were Mr. Bear asked a number of questions which we answered satisfactory for he soon quit. Asked our opinion on "Foot washing."

Baptism, Falling from grace and others I can't remember. We kindly treated by the whole family.

December 21, 1888   Friday Dec. 21

Went from Mr. Abram Bears to Raleigh C.H. for mail and returned to his sons in Daniels He was one of the most inquisitive persons we met on our trip around the Co. We had quite a time with him before would give us permission to remain overnight I got a letter from Anna and a register and Tracts from Bro. Sookey.

December 22, 1888   Saturday Dec. 22

Went from Mr. Wm Bears, the Miller to Mr. Solesberry. where we just made a call and to Mr. C Baileys when we remained till after 2: P.M. and then went to Mr. Joab. Meadors where we happened just at meal time. This was one of the many changes which we meet up with from time to time, an extreme to the opposite from what we had ever had before. The whole crowd, Six in number would take it in turn to talk about us among themselves and we were unable to tell one word that was being said. But we were positive they were talking about us from the way that would look and Laugh at us. As I said before their meal was all ready and as we stepped in they all sat holding their hands for a few minutes and then two stepped outside and held council which was to set the food on table and give us a show. It was Cornbread, Pork and Molasses. Also stewd turnips. This cooking was done on the hearth in an Old Duch Oven. After we had retired I overhead them talking about us and from the conversation they were very suspicious of us.

December 23, 1888   Sunday Dec. 23

We remained with the above mentioned people till after dinner and then wended our way toward Shady and posted a letter from where we went to a Mr. Joshua Lillys where we remained overnight. We were very kindly treated We called at his closest neighbors for lodgings and was refused on account of being Mormon.

December 24, 1888   Monday Dec. 24

Went up on Side Hill from Mr. Joshua Lilly s and Sat in spent the greatest part of the day reading and crossed over to Mr. Robt, Smiths where we were permitted to remain overnight.

December 25, 1888   Tuesday Dec. 25

Christmas Was in shady spring destrict about ten miles from Raleigh C.H. in the woods till nearly four o'clock from which we wended our way to a Mr. Clark Phillips where we had thought would be a good place to remain overnight but it proved he didn't want us to stay. Bro. Timothy showed them how to play the Banjoe before leaving. We then wended our way through the mud to a Mr. Jas. Meadors when we were received and kindly treated but we had been refused lodgings at three places before reaching this place the third one being the worst one. Said when asked if could get entertainment, Yes Sir You Can if you have money to pay for it and the lady then spoke up and said. Yes and you will have to pay before you stop too. I have heard of Ministers being in this Country before. Our Christmas dinner was eaten together with our supper which ^was a Cold lunch. but a very good one there geing quite a variety Fried Pork, Stewd apples, apple-- Butter, Molasses, Black Berries, also Dumplings that had been cooked with Chicken.   The weather was warm and delightful so warm we remained in a Cecluded spot in the woods reading a good portion of the day without a fire.

December 26, 1888   Wednesday 26

We left Mr. James Meadore in Shady Spring destrict and went toward Flat. Top. where we called on Mr. George Sweeney and were privileged to remain over night with him We had only been in his House but a few minutes when it Began to rain and Kept it up till after we retired. We couldn't enter into much of a talk about scripture.

We met a man by the name of Charles Ashworth who said he lived about two and a half miles from Flat Top Store. He said that the Mormons taught things that is hard to get around Said he had read lots about Mormons. We gave him a Tracts and also let him take a voice of Warning

December 27, 1888   Thursday Dec 27

It began storming when we got up and Continued all day We left Mr. Geo. Sweeneys and went to his father's where we remained till middle of Afternoon. And then went to Mr. Ashworths where we thought could have remained overnight but he was not at home So we kept traveling and went down to Mr. Tolleys in the Bacon Town Country. We were after dark getting there being turned from three doors after dark. The first two were Coopers and last Mr. Tolleys sons who gave us a lantern to gide our footsteps.

December 28, 1888   Friday Dec. 28.

Remained at Mr. Cled Tolleys till ten o'clock from where we wended our way to the Main Road till we came to the little church and then took a side Road and went off into the woods where we lodged with a Mr. Green Wood who was living in the old style cooking on hearths with Dutch Oven We couldn't talk much with him as he didn't see me to take any stick

December 29, 1888   Saturday 29 Dec.

Went from Mr. Green Words in Abner district and went to Mr. Jacob Seslers where we remained overnight We built a fire in the woods and remained there till nearly noon writing letter and reading thinking we would go to a meeting in the Abner School House but no one seemed to come We were received very kindly at Mr. Sesler,

December 30, 1888   Sunday Dec. 30

Went from Mr. Jacob Sesler toward Raleigh C.H. and lodged with a man by name of Jacob Bowers who was very kind and sociable to us. Before reaching there we sidled off in the woods where we passed off a good portion of the day reading scripture.

December 31, 1888   Monday Dec. 31 1888

Mobbed out of Raleigh. We went from Mr. Jacob Bowers to Raleigh where we received our mail and had done a part of our business when a man came into P.O. and said are you Gentlemen from Utah.

We are? Well we have a little bet over at the other store. Some say there are different denominations in Utah and Some say not. We would like you to come over and decide this case We went and to our surprise there was a Mob of regular Demons, who were ready to wipe us out. Mr. Prince came in and Said Are you Gentlemen from Salt Lake: We are not right from Salt Lake but from Utah. You are Mormons. Yes Sir. Well the Citizens of this place requested me to tell you to leave this Town. Why don't they want us here. Because we don't believe in the doctrine you teach. What do we teach Don't know but don't want you here but Poligamy is one of the things we don't uphold and that is something Old Brigham Young Claimed to have had a direct Rev. on We are not teaching Poligamy. No, but you practice it, Our Articles of Faith tell what we are willing to do and that we do. Don't Care for your articles of Faith. You Can teach one thing and Practice another. We obey the law What about the Mt Meadow Massacre? Well what about it. Did you Kill Garfield No Sir. Neither did we nor did we kill those people at the Mt. Meadow Well the leaders of your Church did: No indeed they did not. Well John D. Lee said they were at the head of it It matters not what he said that didn't make it so. He was executed for the deed and that through Mormon evidence. You people believe in Blood atonement. We do not. Brigham Young did No Sir: How Many tongues have you cut out of men. Not one Sir nor has that ever been the Case in our Country. We wished them good day and then went back into the Post Office where we tried to get some pants but Couldn't find any that would do so when we had finished trading we left but during the mean time we were requested by Note to leave the Town in ten minutes It read Thus. We will give^ you 10 minutes to leave this town and be sure never to come back again, in the event you do you will wear a coat of tar and feathers. Committee We were fully 20 minutes doing our trading and then mosied off very quiet as though we had not heard from them. We had gone but two or three Rods when one from the other side of the Street and back of us said Don't Shoot----if they are going. We never looked back to see what kind of preformances they were going through. We went to Mr. Jacob Medors about 8 miles where we remained overnight. It rained on us all the time from Raleigh.

January 01, 1889   Tuesday Jan. 1 1889

Happy New Year. Went from Mr. Joab Meadors to Mr Joshuas Lillys but before reaching there we called at Mr. Crockett Waddles and from there to Mr Wards on Beaver where we ate dinner and then to Mr David Meadors, a Mr. Lillys a Mr. Waddles another ---- Lillys a Smiths and there over the Hill to where we Remained

January 02, 1889   Wednesday Jan 2

Were requested by Mr. Joshua Lilly to never Call at his place again as his wife was so opposed to us, We went from there to Mr. Wm. Sweeneys Close to Flat Top where we remained overnight and then sung two or three Hymns and went to bed

January 03, 1889   Thursday Jan 3

Went from Mr. Wm Sweeneys after writing letters to Flat Top Store and then North East about 4 miles to a Mr. Franklyn Sanes where we were kindly received by both he and family. We had all the nice apples we could eat. Didn't talk about Religion much mostly about temporal affairs, We held prayers and went to bed.

January 04, 1889   Friday Jan 4

Went from Mr. Franklyn Lones to Jumping Branch a distance of about 9 miles and purchased us each a pair of Pants and then returned to a Mr John J. Vest about a mile from store where we remained overnight He didn't know we were Mormons even when we retired. We taught him the first principles of Gospel.

January 05, 1889   Saturday, Jan 5

Went from John J Vests to Jumping Branch where we posted letters and Bro Timothy exchanged his Pantaloons which he purchased yesterday. We then took out on the road toward Hunton till where it forked and then took the Right Hand the Second wine till we reached a Mr. Josephus Lilly place at the Fork of the Blue Store Roads and then we remained overnight. It rained furiously all day and was raining when we retired

January 06, 1889   Sunday Jan 6 1889

We went from Mr Josephus Lillys to a Joshephite Mormons down toward the Little Blue Stone in Summer Co. We were Kindly received by him as he though we were of the Same Faith. His name is John Houghman He is a Cripple and in very Humble Circumstances living in one old log Room with a Hundred Sky lites or holes where Cold and light shines in. We read the Book of Mormon to him till dark and then talked the remainder of the evening

January 07, 1889   Monday Jan 7 1889

Went back north from the Josephite Mormons to the Turn Pike and then went to Andrew Williams another of the Josephite Mormons where we got our dinner and remained overnight. We held a little meeting in the evening that there was only about 15 in all large and small I spoke a few words and then Bro Timothy occupied the time The whole family seemed to use tobacco or the Old Gentleman, Old Lady and Boys even to the Small one.

January 08, 1889   Tuesday Jan 8

Went down on New River from Mr. Andrew Williams the Josephite Mormon and followed up at to where Blue Stone empties in and there got under a Clift of Rocks and we read the Book of Mormon. I sewed Buttons on my Pantaloons. It was a very warm and mild day. We went about a mile up the

River and remained over night with a Geo. Frazier who was a Renter on a Mr. James Farms. Clouded up about dark and looked like raining when we retired

January 09, 1889   Wednesday Jan 9

Went up Blue Stone River to South Bluestone and there called at the House of a Mr. Lilly where we talked a short time and then continued our Journey up the River till we reached Matthew Hedrick where we remained overnight. The Gentleman wasn't any way religious so little could be done

January 10, 1889   Thursday. Jan. 10

Went up the Bluestone River from Mr. Matthew Hedricks to where Mountain Creek empties in and there Crossed it and went up on Mountains to Widow Manns where we remained overnight. All her children were affected or lacking few buttons. We were kindly treated.

January 11, 1889   Friday Jan. 11

Wrote two letters and there went to Mountain Creek Stores where we roamed around nearly all day getting Permission to preach in the Church the Coming Sunday which we got and then went South to Mr. Wand Meadows a blind Mans and remained over night

January 12, 1889   Saturday Jan. 12

Went from the Blind man Meadows along the Road west and Secluded ourselves most of the day and there went down on Mountain Creek where we remained with a Man named John Wood. The finest kind of weather prevailed all day.

January 13, 1889   Sunday Jan 13

We held meeting on Mountain Creek Mercer Co, W. Va. at the Church I occupied a few minutes and was overcome by timidity. Bro Timothy occupied the time in speaking on the First Principles of Gospel We had an attendance of about 65 or 70. and from what we heard afterward all seemed well pleased with what was said We were invited to dinner by the Deacon Jas. Lilly and thus invited to remain over night with him

January 14, 1889   Monday Jan 14

We went up right hand Fork of Mountain Creek to Mr. Roser's to have our shoes stiched a little and then left him Orson Pratts work to read Went to Mr. Robt Lillys 3 miles North of Flat Top about 9 miles from Mt. Creek and remained overnight Received letter and Pictures from Home,

January 15, 1889   Tuesday Jan. 15

We were at Mr. Robt. Lillys where we wrote letters and went then to Flat Top and mailed them. We then went south to Mr. Burtons where we remained overnight He was a Methodist and was one of these long faced ones. In the evening prayer he moaned and croaked which was odd to us for This was the first case of this kind. Bro T. bought a pair of shoes at F.T. Store.

January 16, 1889   Wednesday. 16

Went to F.T. Store from Mr. Burtons and mailed letters and set out in search for Trustees to the Church but were unsuccessful as Couldn't find any one that had it in Charge We then Concluded to go toward Fayette so Called at Mr. Jos Meadows but as he was so crowded with Lumber in House couldn't remain over night but went to their neighbors by name of Moye where we were Kindly treated. These people had been visited by Elders before and as nearly as I can learn one was Golden Kimball

January 17, 1889   Thursday. Jan. 17

Went from Wm. Moyes in Snik H.C. Country to Mr. Joab Meadors in Shady Spring We got under a cliff of Rocks in the sun and read during the middle part of day. We called at Shady Store and Bro. T. got sole leather for his shoes.

January 18, 1889   Friday Jan. 18

We took across the Country from Mr. Joab Meadors to Mr. Jacob. Seslers by crossing the Bearer Stream and Pinery a distance of about 12 miles. It was a beautifully warm day Mr Sesler acknowledged to us he wasnt any way religious yet he didn't want to deprive others from their Religious Views, We were kindly treated by him and his wife.

January 19, 1889   Saturday Jan. 19

We remained at Mr. Jacob Seslers till after dinner, and then wended our way back across the Country toward Mr. Joab Meador and remained over night at a Mr. Furrows about three miles from Clouds Store. It Clouded up in the evening and wind blew furiously almost the time we retired

January 20, 1889   Sunday Jan. 20

We left Mr. Furrows in a Snow Storm and went to Mr. John Wards on the Beaver Creek where we called in for a while and got our dinners and then went to Louis Meadors where we remained overnight It stormed all day and was severely cold:

January 21, 1889   Monday Jan. 21

We went to Mr. Joab Meadors where we remained all day and night. I wrote two letters and we Chatted with the family

They gave us the news Concerning the Mormon Elders all what was said in the whole Neighborhood.

January 22, 1889   Tuesday Jan. 22

We went from Mr. Joab Meadors in Daniels to Mr. Weise's in Fayette Co a distance of about 17 miles. We called at the Prosperity Stores and rested a while, Ate a few Ginger Snaps. It was beautifully warm all day We had snow to walk through which was hard on Bro Timothy as his shoes were slippery We were Kindly treated by the Weise Family as the had the appearance of Saints.

January 23, 1889   Wednesday Jan. 23.

We went to Mr. Wm. Weises and he repaired Bro Timothy shoes and we had a real sociable time talking on points of scripture and reading voice of Warning. We remained overnight there and had a real sociable time Miss Rhoda Weice Came over and She remained there overnight. We sung a few Hymns and then they sang. We had the finest Beans for dinner that I ever ate or equally as good. The Old Lady Weise came there in the evening and merely made a Call as she was on her way home from nursing a neighbor sick woman. She told us she had heard that we had converted Mr Andrew Jackson Carper of Carpers Ville, Raleigh Co. He is a minister of the Christian Baptist Church We. remained over night with him and left a tract. As yet we don't Know whether the report is true or not.

January 24, 1889   Thursday Jan 24

We went from Wm Weises to Mt. Hope P.O. and from there to Mr Powers where we received kind treatment and got our dinner. We met Mr. Barnes and Wife who had come from Kentuckey with their Child to bury it at Packs Branch near Mr. Crager. We then went to Mr Cragers where we remained overnight Those people were very kind and sociable and Saint like

January 25, 1889   Friday Jan. 25

Went from Mr. Jos. Cragers on Packs Branch Fayette Co to the Lawson P.O. in Raleigh Co on our way to Andrew Jarrolds on Coal River, a distance of about 27 miles. It had rained nearly all night so that the Roads were fearfully muddy.

January 26, 1889   Saturday Jan. 26

Went down the Coal river to Bro. Andrew Jarrolds from Lawson P.O a distance of about 9 miles Rained nearly all day. Met Bro. McMaster [169] and Brockbank there.

January 27, 1889   Sunday Jan 27 1889

Was at Bro. Andrew Jarrolds on Coal River Boon Co. in Company with three other Elders Bros. Timothy, Brockbank and MCMaster. This was quite a day of rest for us as it was a change from what we had been used to in the two months past. Had a Sunday School in evening which was very interesting as the family had their lesson well learned.

John Cardall   Salt Lake City,   2E. St. 5 5 7.

Wishes a sample Cotton and Tobacco plant.

---

[169] the bottom left corner of the page is missing

Elder William Charles Parker Winder   -   SSM 1891-1893

PHOTO 59   WILLIAM CHARLES PARKER WINDER

Birth date, place - 30 September 1858, Salt Lake City, Salt Lake, Utah
Death date - 19 June 1937
Father's name - John R Winder   --   Mother's name - Elizabeth Parker

Southern States   --   November 1891–October 1893   -   Age Called: 33

Southern States
Set Apart: 30 November 1891   --   End Date: 27 October 1893
Mission type: Proselytizing
Marital Status: Married
Priesthood: Seventy
Called From: Mill Creek, Salt Lake, Utah, United States
Set apart by: A H Cannon

Notes: Served as President of the North Carolina Conference
   Missionary Department missionary registers, 1860-1959, Vol. 1, p. 118, line 317.
   Southern States Mission history, 1832-1964: LR 8557 2, Church History Library.
    Mission index
   Southern States Mission history, 1832-1964: LR 8557 2, Church History Library.
    March 31, 1892 experience being driven out by a mob
   Southern States Mission history, 1832-1964: LR 8557 2, Church History Library.
    September 24, 1893 release
   Southern States Mission history, 1832-1964: LR 8557 2, Church History Library.
    October 27, 1893 summary of service and return home

Elder Joseph William Parker   --   SSM 1895-1897

PHOTO 60 JOSEPH WILLIAM PARKER

Birth date, place - 19 November 1864, Heber City, Wasatch, Utah
Death date - 3 September 1930
Baptism date - December 1854   --   Baptism by - Elder
Father's name - Joseph F Parker   --   Mother's name - Mary E Ross

Southern States - February 1895–July 1897   --   Age Called: 30

Southern States
Set Apart: 22 February 1895 - End Date: July 1897
Priesthood office: Seventy - Priesthood: Ord Seventy
Called From: Joseph, Sevier, Utah, United States
Set apart by: Edward Stevenson
Stories and Documents

Missionary Department missionary registers, 1860-1959, Vol. 3, p. 8, line 57.
Missionary reports, 1831-1900, MS 6104, Church History Library.
First Presidency missionary calls and recommendations 1877-1918, CR 1 168, Church History Library.

'in March 1888 Elders Johnson and A L Clark met with the children of the Catawba nation to teach them their letters and how to read A month later they met with them again and decided to keep teaching them as long as their mission lasted.   Elders Parker and Gordon using indian labor erected a meeting house in 1897 the church was originally a twenty four by sixteen foot log building located about a mile the exception of 1897-98 the school was taught by Mormon missionaries.'   (from Jerry D Lee thesis)

```
                          1907 Nov  6  Released   Nov 12
Parker, Joseph William    1895 Feb 22  Set apart  Mar 19 in S Car  Oct 26,27
                          1896 Apr  1, 11  Jun 6  Sep 10, 28 in S Car
                          1897 Jun 23  Released    Sep 26
Parker, Leo Hall          1948 Jul  3  Arr in Miss:to Ga Dist
                          1949 Jan 10  To orch  Apr 4 tr to S Fla  Dec 27 to orch
```

```
                    SOUTHERN STATES MISSION

        1897

            Wednesday, June 23.   Elder Arta McLain Seeley, East Mill Creek, Utah,

        arrived in South Alabama Conference, and will labor in Dallas County, Alabama.
                                (So. Alabama Conf. Record, p. 53.)
                                        (No. 6716.)


            In South Carolina Conference, a Sunday School was organized at Packsville,

        with R. T. McLeod as superintendent.  (So. Carolina Conf. Record, p. 90.)
                                        (No. 6820..)


            Elder Joseph W. Parker, Joseph City, Utah, and John S. Cram, Kanab,

        Utah, were released from the South Carolina Conference.  Elder Cram was re-

        leased because of illness.  (So. Carolina Conference Record, 6820, p. 70.)
```

Joseph & Co Jan 17. 1895
Presd Wilford Woodruff
      Salt Lake City
Dear Brother

          I have received
notice from you dated Jan 24. 1895
that my name has been accepted
as a Missionary to Southern
States. If the Lord will assist me
in obtaining means I will be on
hand, Feb. 23, 1895
      Your Brother in the Gospel,
            J. N. Parker.

George. Charlesworth. Bp.

July 5, 1897.

Returned Missionary,
J. W. Parker

Southern States Mission,
Church of Jesus Christ of Latter Day Saints.
Headquarters, P. O. Box 103, Chattanooga, Tenn.

South Carolina Conference.
Conference Address, Box 71, Ridgeway, S. C.

Joseph Sevier S. C, Utah July 5, 1897

Prest. Wilford Woodruff
Salt Lake City, Utah.

Dear Bro,

Having returned from a mission
to the Southern States without the
privilege of meeting with or visiting
any of the Apostles I thought I
would write you a few lines that
you might know of the safe arrival
of myself and Elder J. R.
Cram of Kanab. It was my
desire to report to you in person
but because of the illness of Elder
Cram I was instructed by Pres.
Elias S. Kimball & Prest S. N.
Oldham of the S. C. Conference
to see to his safe arrival at Bel
nap station on the Riogrand Western

Ry. six miles above here, where his folks would meet and take care of him. Before we reached here we learned that his folks were waiting for him at Defune, and as he had improved some in health on the journey he thought it unnecessary for me to go on with him to that place. I was set apart for a mission to the Southern States Feb. 2nd 1895. and started out on the following day. On arriving at Chattanooga Tenn. I was appointed to labor in the S. C. Conference, & In company with Elders Bond & Stephenson & Portie I went to Columbia where we met Prest Keate. We first labored with Elder — S. Bradley in Chester Co. Then with Elder J. F. Hyatt in York Co. After conference which was held in Williamsburg Co. in the month of October I was sent Prest H. P. Oldham to open up from

Southern States Mission,
Church of Jesus Christ of Latter Day Saints.
Headquarters, P. O. Box 103, Chattanooga, Tenn.

South Carolina Conference.
Conference Address, Box 71, Ridgeway, S. C.

S. C., ... 189

THE TEMPLE, SALT LAKE CITY.

well Co. I remained there untill Aug 1896.
My next field of labor was York Co
which place I continued untill my
release which was June 23. 1897.
Because of false reports the people of
York. Co are generally very much oppos
ed to Mormons and Mormonism untill
it was often that we could not get to talk
or hold meetings with the people as we
would have liked. But with all I think
a greate deal of prejudice has and will
continue to be alayed. Twenty or more
persons have been united to the church
since Elder Wyatt and I went to that
Co and I think there are several
others amongst the first friends that
the Lord raised up to us that will come
into the Church before very very much longer

255

~~the ... Shelbyburg (which ...~~ now cut off and formerly part of Cherokee (?) a Sunday School with about forty members.

My health was very good the most of the time. While traveling I was greately blessed and protected of the Lord and have received many testimonies that the work is of the Lord. These blessings and testimonies will be given to every elder that will do the best he can however weak he may be.

& I believe the S. C. Conference is in a thriving condition and will no doubt continue to prosper for I believe the elders do desire and are trying to carry out council. Well Dear President I feel that I have not lost anything by going on this mission and if there is any other labor the Lord desires me to preform with His blessings I hope to be able to preform it.

May the Lord help us to preform every duty and labor and keep us in the faith is the prayer of Your Bro.
J. W. Parker.

The receipt of this letter should be kindly ac- knowledged, and the letter should be filed at the H. D. ...

Elder John Gordon   SSM 1895-1898

PHOTO 61   ELDER JOHN GORDON

Birth date, place   2 September 1846, York, York, South Carolina, United States
Death date   20 March 1913 --   American Fork, Utah, Utah,
Baptism date   27 January 1882   Baptism by   Willard C Burton
Father's name Moses Moore Gordon   Mother's name Catherine Inmon

    John Alonzo and his family heard the message of the restored gospel taught by missionaries from the Church of Jesus Christ of Latter-day Saints early in 1882. He and his wife were baptized members of the Church on 27 January 1882 by Elder Willard C. Burton. Eventually other members of the family were baptized as well.

    Like other converts of the "unpopular religion," the Gordon family became the target of persecution for their acceptance of the Mormon faith. Because of increasing difficulties, the decision was finally made to leave the area and join the Saints in the Salt Lake Valley.

    In the spring of 1888, John and his family moved to Spartanburg, South Carolina, in preparation for their move to the West. While waiting for travel arrangements to be finalized, the family, with other LDS converts, lived temporarily in some empty houses in Spartanburg. The night before they were to board the train for Utah, the anti-Mormon mobs came to town. According to Katie, the family "was kneeling in prayer when the mob broke the door down, whipped the elders, and drove all the men and boys into the woods" where they remained hidden for three days. They were finally able to board the train and begin their journey westward.

John Alonzo Gordon

Southern States   **December 1895–September 1898**   **Age Called: 49**

Southern States
Set Apart: 6 December 1895
Arrived At Home: 26 September 1898
Mission type: Proselytizing   Priesthood office: Seventy
Called From: American Fork, Utah, Utah Territory, United States
Set apart by: J Golden Kimball

Missionary Department missionary registers, 1860-1959, Vol. 3, p. 19, line 519.
First Presidency missionary calls and recommendations 1877-1918, CR 1 168, Church History Library.

Southern States Missionaries
Serving between 1901-1920

Elder Charles Christian Martensson -- SSM 1908-1910

Scrapbook of Charles Christian MARTINSON

C. C. Martinson ~ Missionary picture

PHOTO 62   CHARLES CHRISTIAN MARTENSSON

Birth date, place - 5 February 1867 - Ysta, Malmo, Sweden
Death date - 4 July 1923
Baptism by - Qvist
Father's name - Mons Martinson   --   Mother's name - Bertha Nilson

Southern States - July 1908–December 1910 - Age Called: 41
North Carolina Conference
Set Apart: 7 July 1908   -   Released: 18 December 1910
Arrived In Field: 12 July 1908
Mission type: Proselytizing
Priesthood office: Elder
Called From: Salt Lake City, Salt Lake, Utah, United States
Set apart by: Seymour B Young

Elder Charles Barnes Jr.   --   SSM 1909-

The First Barnes Missionary

PHOTO 63 CHARLES BARNES JR.

PHOTO 64   INSCRIBED: "THE LONG AND SHORT OF MORMONISM" L TO R: CHARLES FREDRICK BARNES; JOSEPH EUGENE COBBLEY.

Birth date, place - 13 July 1886, Lehi, Utah, Utah, United States
Death date - 22 July 1935
Baptism date - 2 September 1894 -- Baptism by - William Sharp
Father's name - Charles Henry Barnes -- Mother's name - Amelia Christina Goss

Southern States - November 1909–Unknown - Age Called: 23

Southern States -- South Carolina Conference
Set Apart: 23 November 1909 -- Arrived In Field: 28 November 1909
Released: 26 March 1912

Mission type: Proselytizing
Marital Status: Single
Priesthood office: Elder
Called From: Parker, Fremont, Idaho, United States
Set apart by: Seymour Bicknell Young

Notes: Served as President of the South Carolina Conference

Missionary Department missionary registers, 1860-1959, Vol. 4, p. 74, line 889.
Southern States Mission history, 1832-1964: LR 8557 2, Church History Library.
        Mission index
Southern States Mission history, 1832-1964: LR 8557 2, Church History Library.
        November 2, 1910 appointed president of South Carolina Conference
Southern States Mission history, 1832-1964: LR 8557 2, Church History Library.
        March 26, 1912 release to return home

In the late 1840s, Charles Barnes Jr. was doing a fair amount of open-air preaching to the crowds at the statue of William the 3rd in Hull, Yorkshire, England. Seventy years later, his grandson, Charles Frederick, was the first Barnes officially called to serve a mission. In November of 1909, Charles rode the train south to Salt Lake City to complete his temple ordinances.

He then boarded another train for Chattanooga, Tennessee. When he arrived, he was greeted at the train station by President Charles A. Callis. President Callis was serving as a missionary in the Southern States Mission when he was called as its president in 1908 at the age of 42.

One former president, Benjamin Erastus Rich had been transferred to the Eastern States Mission but still provided publishing services for the missionaries in the Southern States. President Rich was frequently compiling new illustrated tracting pamphlets and lecture compendiums for the Elders.

 Radio was another medium used to spread the good news in the South. President Callis and his band of Gospel messengers also pioneered the member referral technique of missionary work. The local Church members best knew who else might be interested and socially able to accept the Gospel message. Elder Barnes frequently asked for member referrals, despite there being only about 2,000 members of the Church in both North and South Carolina at the time. Quickly the missionaries of the Southern States recognized the perils of working on member referrals. President Callis straightly limited the number of hours a missionary could spend interacting with members. "I am fully persuaded that every day tracting contributes largely to the spiritual depth of the missionaries. It strengthens testimony," Callis wrote. "Countless thousands of people have been converted by reading the tracts and by listening to the Elders expound the principles of the Gospel." And again, "I do not know of anything that will spoil an elder quicker than long visits with the Saints. He becomes spiritually lazy – he is not out on the battle line."

PHOTO 65 -- BEN ERASTUS RICH

PHOTO 66 -- ORLANDO

Elder Barnes spent 5 hours a day minimum tracting and contacting the lost sheep of the Carolinas and tracted every district in North Carolina three times or more. If one town was unfriendly, he walked to the next one. Years after his mission, Charles would be rejected from military conscription due to "bad ankles". Elder Barnes' first letters are filled with descriptions of the oddities of the Carolinas. "The people down here eat peanuts raw ... All of the women here use tobacco. Down here they think it is so funny that none of the girls or women home use it." "We are 6 miles from the Atlantic ocean and I can hear it. I should see it tomorrow." "The capitol building of S. C. has been shot all to pieces in the war, even the capitol building has marks of cannon balls and corners of it are shot off."

To Charles, a Mormon descended from European immigrants who waited out the American's Civil War during the '60s, this place was as different as another planet. Elder Barnes had only been in the field for a few weeks when he and his companion stumbled upon the Salvation Army. As the Salvation Army planned a Christmas party for a local Catholic orphanage – a rather remarkable convergence of three very different religions – Charles acted as Santa Claus to entertain the children. Luckily, he captured a photograph of the moment to send home.

On January 25th, Charles and his companion were let in by a 60-year-old man and the subject turned to religion. The greenie Elder Barnes preached for an hour straight. The next morning the man's sons and grandsons ran all over the town inviting neighbors to hear the Mormon preachers. During several days lodging with the man, Elder Barnes and Elder Bagley held 6 meetings with the townsfolk of Ash, North Carolina

After several weeks in Ash and Supply, North Carolina, the elders moved on to Clarendon, North Carolina, and there attended a Holiness Meeting at a small Methodist congregation. The Methodist preacher told the congregation that baptism wasn't necessarily a requirement from God and that every man held the "Priesthood of the Believers". So went the reasoning of a religion which "denies the power thereof". Elder Barnes and Elder Bagley approached the preacher. "After the meeting we went up to the preacher and asked if he could prove that baptism was not essential to salvation … He could not do it." Elder Barnes read from his New Testament, St. John 3:5: "Jesus answered, saying, Verily, verily I say unto you, except a man be born of water and the spirit, he cannot enter into the Kingdom of God." Acts 8: 38 & 39: "And he commanded the chariot to stand still: and they went down both into the water, both Philip and the eunuch; and he baptized him. And when they were come up out of the water, the Spirit of the Lord caught away Philip, that the eunuch saw him no more: and he went on his way rejoicing."

By this time a small crowd began to gather around the dueling preachers. The Elders recited Romans 6:3-6, Colossians 2:12 and 1st Epistle of Peter 3: 18 and 20. The crowd could plainly see that the Elders knew their cannon. The preacher was flustered – "we beat him so bad that he soon went off", Charles writes. "It certainly meant victory for us everybody could see he was beat and beat bad." Filled with new confidence, the Elders eventually found their way back north to Pireway and Ash. In Pireway, a local church invited the orators to preach to the congregation one Sunday. Charles' sermon was recorded by his companion: "Seek the Lord for wisdom and we promise that if you approach the throne of grace humbly that the Lord will manifest to you by His Spirit that the message we are delivering to you is of God." After the meeting, several new members were promptly baptized. The Elder's examples were beginning to impress the people of Pireway, who began to remark that "if any people on Earth live Christian lives, it is they.."

 Not all residents of Pireway were so friendly, especially not the local Methodist Deacon whose congregation was enjoying the doctrine of the Mormons. This deacon began to notice his wages were being garnished by low attendance whenever the Elders were around. Several times he accosted the young farm-boys, accusing them of heresy and polygamy. His sermons began to address polygamy directly and Charles' letters begin to record some of his battles with anti-Mormon propaganda. The Methodist Deacon eventually persuaded the superintendent of schools to eject the Elders from the local school house where they had been meeting. This didn't help the reputation of the Deacon, whose earnings kept dropping as the Elders winnowed his congregation. These vagrant, penniless, homeless farm-boys were spoiling the business of the sermonizer with a house, a chapel and nice clean suits. The Deacon fancied himself entitled to some help, and, like Jesus wandering through the cornfields on the Sabbath, he stole some corn. Unfortunately for the Deacon, the citizens of Pireway were not persuaded by his analogy to Jesus' disciples in St. Matthew 12, verse 1. He was arrested and convicted of theft. The Pireway locals felt so ashamed of their preacher that "the friends and members worked hard and moved a log house and fixed it up for us as soon as we got back, it has been a fine thing."

In March of 1910, 4 months into his mission, Charles held his 100th meeting with the newly sympathetic locals. Baptisms continued almost each weekend through May. While they wandered, the Elders kept record of their distances and expenses. In the month of April, as the season heated up and the hearts of many southerners cooled down, the Elders spent more nights sleeping with Uncle Sam and more days turned away. This meant even more walking. Elder Barnes walked 192 miles in the month of April 1910. On April 14th, Elder Barnes and his companion reported 4 more baptisms in Pireway as well as 6 meetings over 2 weeks that had over 100 persons in attendance. "I tell you, it means something when a large crowd of people gathers to be edified by a young person who has been working on the farm all the time." The next month they reported 5 more convert baptisms as well as 5 baby blessings.

In June 1910, Elder Barnes and Bagley left Pireway to Elders Hart and Black and made their way south. "We walked 8 miles along the beach when the water was out," Charles writes.

Charles was the first Barnes to see an ocean since his grandfather crossed it in 1853. From Myrtle Beach South Carolina, the Elders turned west toward Camden, South Carolina. The Elders then turned north until Yorkville (now York). In 1910, the center of the South Carolina Conference was a tiny town called Roddey, which no longer exists. The closest modern town is called Catawba, named after the Indian nation which dwelt there most of the season. Conference President Barrus had been called specifically to the Catawba Indian Nation by the Prophet in 1908. Upon arriving at Roddey (Catawba), Elder Barrus' wife, Mary Elizabeth Clark (granddaughter of Ezra T. Clark), met the chief elders of the tribe, one of whom remarked to her: "I saw you in a vision." [170] The Barrus' arrival marked the fulfillment of a long-standing prophecy in the tribe that a knowledge of their ancestors would be returned to them. Wholly 85% of the tribe converted, hundreds were baptized. [171] In 1910, there were as many Catawba Indians members of the Church as all other members in North and South Carolina. For this reason, the Conference was centered here. In mid-June, Charles and his companion, Elder Bagley reached York County and the Indian Nation. Their first assignment was in Yorkville where they met with considerable hostility. In a letter to his mother he confesses: "We have been assigned to labor in two counties that are pretty bitter enemies to the Mormons ... The last Elders that

---

[170]

[171] Not quite, there were only 60 or so Catawba left in 1880, nearly all the adults joined the church.

were in there were run out – that is, out of the county … Two of the Elders were arrested here last week but the foolish people could not prove anything against them worthy of a sentence so they were turned loose … The Lord said to his Apostles when he sent them out: 'Fear not therefore for there is nothing covered that shall not be revealed, and hid that shall not be known'." This is in stark contrast to the growing friendliness with which southern North Carolina had been receiving the Gospel of late.

Just as the two Elders were departing for the south, the members announced that they would be donating land and lumber for the construction of a meetinghouse! Their replacements, Elder Hart and Elder Black, began construction in June 1910 on the Bug Hill Mormon Chapel, a one-room, 60 square foot wooden church at the corner of Swamp Fox and Savannah Road. Leaving the white field of Pireway after so much hard work -- and just as it was paying off -- must have been a bit sad for the Elders, but they wasted no time laying foundations elsewhere. On the train running from Camden to Yorkville, Charles happened to sit next to a "well-to-do man" and struck up a conversation with him. Elder Barnes quickly turned the chit-chat to religion. The man "at first thought that it did not matter at all which denomination any one belonged to, just so one lived right," as many Protestants maintained at the time. Elder Barnes recited 1st Corinthians, verse 10: "Now I beseech you, brethren, by the name of our Lord Jesus Christ, that ye all speak the same thing, and that there be no divisions among you; but that ye be perfectly joined together in the same mind and in the same judgment." Still sensing skepticism, Charles continued with Galatians 1:9: "If any man preach any other gospel unto you than that ye have received, let him be accursed." The man was struck, "I've changed my mind," he said. "I know the people out there must be blessed from some source" (referring to the Mormons in the Rocky Mountains). Elder Barnes presented the stranger with a Book of Mormon and the man promised to "read after it".

In Roddey, Elder Barnes and Bagley lodged with the Barrus family. Elder Orlando Barrus, his wife and seven children lived in a crowded wooden house on the Indian Reservation. Charles and his companion frequented this household as the eastern headquarters of the mission, close to their newly assigned area of labor, Yorkville. The labor in Yorkville had progressed slowly for years, primarily among the poor of the city – "poor people, not much in society".

The reputation of the Church was already shaky when one of the few members was caught having incestuous relations with his own daughter. Immediately the word spread that the Mormons were preaching incest and adultery to the citizens of the city. Lying about Mormonism has always been an easy thing, even for half-witted eastern journalists in the early 20th century. Spurred by news of the recent scandal of the Mormon Prophet running a fabulously successful sugar business (can you believe such a scandal!?), a wave of anti-Mormonism spewed out over the American magazines and newspapers in 1910 and 1911.

Accusations of polygamy were resurrected yet again by Collier's, Pearson's, Cosmopolitan, McClure's and Everybody's magazines. The Church was compared to a viper with tentacles reaching for wealth and power. Joseph F. Smith was portrayed as an evil corporatist and greedy capitalist in light of the accusations against the Utah Idaho Sugar Company being run by many General Authorities of the Church. The editors labeled The Church of Jesus Christ a "loathsome institution" whose 'slimy grip" had served only the accumulation of political and economic power in a dozen western states to pad the pocketbooks of exploitative Church leaders.

This sudden (and short-lived) assault on the reputation of the Church for a year starting in the summer of 1910 is referred to as the "Magazine Crusade". The Magazine Crusade only complicated Elder Barnes' work with the people of Yorkville. His letters speak of "many enemies" with "prejudices" and "unutterable lies" that the Mormons "still practice polygamy" and are "a low down adulterous, ignorant class of people who lived like dogs and cats." "The people have heard things that would almost make the Lord startle Himself," Charles noted.

He was pleased if the townsfolk "treated them as humans anyways". After a full month of effort, the Elders held just one street meeting (consider that in Pireway they held 3 meetings a week). Elder Barnes and Bagley spent the 4th of July in strange company. Former and future chieftains joined them for the celebrations. David "Toad" Harris and Samuel Taylor Blue provided prayers and music for the group. While at other times, these two great men assisted the Elders greatly and would later become influential leaders in the community.

The Catawba Indians; who had seen their tribe almost completely eradicated by European-imported Small Pox, and the Mormons; who had been legally murdered for their religious beliefs by governments in the United States, gathered to celebrate Independence Day. The program (as noted in one of Charles' letters to his family) ran as follows: Song – America – by all; Prayer – by Bro/Chief (Samuel Taylor Blue) Blue; an Indian Song ; Columbia the Gem of the Ocean – by all; Oration – by C. F. Barnes; Toast – by Elder Graff; Music – on Graphone by chief; Song – "Mormon Elders" by Elder Bagley; Comments on "Declaration of Independence" by Pres. Barrus; Battle of Waterloo – an Instrumental – on organ by Mrs. Barrus; Story of "Spanish-American War" by Elder Call; Music – on Graphone – by Chief; Song – Star Spangled Banner – by all; Prayer – by Bro. Toad Harris (David Adam Harris) – an Indian.   In the afternoon, the Elders played ball with the Indians, the single men (mostly the Elders) against the married men (mostly the Indians). The single men lost.

PHOTO 67 LEFT SAM BLUE AND RIGHT BRO. TOAD HARRIS

After nearly 7 months severing together, Elder Barnes and Elder Bagley were separated in late July. Elder Barnes was reassigned by a visiting President Callis to labor with an older, mustachioed Elder whose name Charles curiously omits. Charles notes off-hand that the Elder was bed-ridden sick for the first week of their companionship and the pair had to stay home – "I guess he will be well enough so we can go tomorrow."

The two Elders were stationed in Salem, 50 miles west of York County. The semi-migratory Catawba Indians had constructed a chapel here a decade or so before. The members were many and friendly so Charles expected work to be light, though he found himself dragging his companion along. The older Elder shied from speaking with people and sermonizing – "my companion won't speak over five or ten minutes" – and Charles took the lead in their companionship.

Charles conducted the meeti   , as well as a conf   y. Before long, the members began to recognize Charles as an excellent missionary and mentioned so to his companion. Elder Barnes' senior companion was offended, declaring that if "they all say you are so great, then you outta do all the work". Elder Barnes obliged by holding 13 conferences for the members in two counties over the course of a week. The meetings were so well attended that the Indian Chapel couldn't hold them. Nearly 1,000 people attended the conferences and each meeting was conducted and presided over by Elder Barnes: "I guess if you heard me speak now, I don't suppose you would believe it. A number have said I was equal to President Callis and others have said they never did hear better speaking. But don't believe this. I know better myself. –

Letter from Salem, August 28th, 1910" Elder Barnes then proceeded to organize a second branch in the city of Salem. The first branch consisted almost entirely of Catawba Indians. On August 28th, he organized the first white Sunday School in the area and additional quorums came later. While Charles was hurrying to build the Church in Salem and nearby Seneca, his companion was not. "The man I am with now is a pretty poor elder," he writes home. "He is 36 years old, but he is not obedient to instructions. [He] don't try to preach nor do anything else … He thinks I ought to do everything … [He] is supposed to take the lead but he won't hardly do any thing only just run around from one friend or member to another. He is a good enough man, but has not got the spirit of his mission. He does not use wisdom in his actions and talk. He claims to be sick about half the time but when he gets around the girls and children he is as well as anybody. Hardly any of the Saints like him – he is quite familiar with some of the women – writes to as many of the girls as he feels like he wants to and never has been known to stay with his companion as he is instructed to do … President Callis sure gave him a courching when he was here and almost sent him home. I have never had the least bit of trouble with him because I just let him have his own way. I have finally persuaded him to ask for a release. He does more harm than good." President Callis had also been impressed with Elder Barnes when they preached together in Yorkville that summer. He also noticed the degree of patience and endurance with which Charles handled his loafing companion. In letters to President Barrus, President Callis discussed the "especially" effective Elder Barnes who continued to submit such "good reports" of investigators and baptisms. As President Barrus prepared to return home with his family, Presidents Callis decided to appoint the young Elder Barnes in his place as Conference President.

After his companion was finally released, Charles was appointed President of the South Carolina Conference, encompassing all of North and South Carolina. His new companion was one stalwart Elder Miles Greener from Hinckley, Utah, a sharp change from his former companion. Their first order of business was to relocate the headquarters of the South Carolina Conference to Columbia, the state capitol, instead of at the Indian Nation in Roddey. Charles located an apartment at 719 Main Street in Columbia where he and Elder Greener rented out a one-bedroom apartment that provided three meals a day. Most convenient was that the landlord did not charge rent if the men were absent for a day. This was most convenient for the traveling elders, who spent many days at a time traveling across the Carolinas and returned home so briefly that preparing their own food would have been troublesome. After rearranging the companion ships, Elder Barnes and Greener packed their bags back up and headed for North Carolina. President Barnes was now responsible for the Elders in the

Carolinas, which totaled about 40 missionaries, or 20 companion ships. Additionally, there were 2,000 white members scattered throughout North and South Carolina.

President Charles Albert Callis   --   SSM 1906-1908

PHOTO 68   CHARLES ALBERT CALLIS

Charles Albert Callis was born 4 May 1865 in Dublin, Ireland and died 21 January 1947
Baptism date - 12 September 1875 --   Baptism by - John Williamson
Father's name - John Callis   --   Mother's name - Charlotte Quilliam

Southern States   --   April 1906–March 1908   --   Age Called: 39

Set Apart: 25 April 1906 --   End Date: 11 March 1908
Mission type: Proselytizing   --   Marital Status: Married   --   Served with children
Priesthood office: High Priest
Called From: Coalville, Summit, Utah, United States
Set apart by: Anthon H Lund
Notes: He was originally called to the Eastern States Mission, but his assignment was changed in early 1906. He served with his wife, Grace Elizabeth Pack.

Southern States   April 1908–February 1934   --   Age Called: 41.

Served as Mission President

Set Apart: 14 April 1908 -- End Date: 3 February 1934

Mission type: Proselytizing

Marital Status: Married -- Served with children

Priesthood office: High Priest

Called From: Coalville, Summit, Utah, United States

Set apart by: John Henry Smith

Notes: He served with his wife, Grace Elizabeth Pack.

Missionary Department missionary registers, 1860-1959, Vol. 1, p. 128, line 68.

Missionary Department missionary registers, 1860-1959, Vol. 2, p. 137, line 68.

Missionary Department missionary registers, 1860-1959, Vol. 3, p. 235, line 293.

Missionary Department missionary registers, 1860-1959, Vol. 4, p. 33, line 172.

First Presidency missionary calls and recommendations, 1877-1918, Church History Library.
Letter dated 3 January 1893 accepting his call to serve a mission in Great Britain.

First Presidency missionary calls and recommendations, 1877-1918, Church History Library.
Letter dated 21 December 1905 stating that he is willing to serve another mission.

First Presidency missionary calls and recommendations, 1877-1918, Church History Library.
Letter dated 30 January 1906 stating his readiness to serve a mission to the Eastern States.

First Presidency missionary calls and recommendations, 1877-1918, Church History Library.
Letter dated 13 February 1906 accepting the call to serve in the Eastern States Mission.

First Presidency missionary calls and recommendations, 1877-1918, Church History Library.
Letter dated 27 March 1906 stating his willingness for his assignment to change from the Eastern States to the Southern States Mission.

Southern States Mission history, 1832-1964, Church History Library.
See the index in volume 1 for entries on his service.

Charles A. Callis collection, circa 1908-1938, Church History Library.

Materials collected by David Yarn relating to the service of Charles and Grace Callis in the Southern States Mission.

Andrew Jenson, "Callis, Charles A.," Latter-day Saint Biographical Encyclopedia, vol. 4 (Salt Lake City: Andrew Jenson Memorial Association, 1936), 380-81.

Kathleen Callis Larsen, A biography of Charles Albert Callis and Grace Elizabeth Pack Callis (N.p.: published by the author, 1974).
Account of the life of Charles and Grace Callis, particularly while serving in the Southern States Mission and his subsequent call to be an apostle. Copy available at the Church History Library.

Colorado Denver South Mission manuscript history and historical reports 1896-1977: LR 10111 2, Church History Library.

" Those of us who have served missions have seen the miracle in the lives of some we have taught as they have come to realize that they are sons and daughters of God. Many years ago an elder who served a mission in the British Isles said at the end of his labors, "I think my mission has been a failure. I have labored all my days as a missionary here and I have only baptized one dirty little Irish kid. That is all I baptized." Years later, after his return to his home in Montana, he had a visitor come to his home who asked, "Are you the elder who served a mission in the British Isles in 1873?" "Yes." Then the man went on, "And do you remember having said that you thought your mission was a failure because you had only baptized one dirty little Irish kid?" He said, "Yes." The visitor put out his hand and said, "I would like to shake hands with you. My name is Charles A. Callis, of the Council of the Twelve of The Church of Jesus Christ of Latter-day Saints. 1 am that dirty little Irish kid that you baptized on your mission." [172]

President Callis was serving as a missionary in the Southern States Mission when he was called as its president in 1908 at the age of 42.

PHOTO 69   CHARLES ALBERT CALLIS

When the call came to serve as president, Elder Callis was laboring in Columbia, South Carolina as president of the Conference there. His first order as president was to call his own replacement and send one Elder Orlando Barrus to South Carolina to run the conference. Upon arriving in Chattanooga, Elder Barnes was first assigned to Ash, North Carolina under Elder Barrus and his companion was one Elder George Alma Bagley from Koosharem, Utah. President Callis traveled with Elder Barnes to the Carolinas, where the President was dispatched to defend a missionary in court. One elder was being tried for inciting a mob, after said mob had incidentally burned his house to the ground. Fortunately, President Callis' skill as a lawyer later saw the poor accused Elder acquitted. [173] Missionary work in the South during the early 20th century was often quite dangerous. Just a few years before Charles' arrival, the missionary force had been drastically cut from more than 450 Elders to about 150. Charles' mission president, President Charles Callis, kept with him a box of pictures of

---

[172] The Teachings of Harold B. Lee," ed. Clyde J. Williams (1996), 602-3
[173]

Elders who had been murdered by angry mobs during their service in the South. Missionaries were whipped, tarred-and-feathered or, at the very least, chased from most towns. Besides being a heroic missionary to a biblical degree, President Callis was a very effective lawyer, which skill he was exercising on a weekly basis to rescue his Elders from imprisonment or worse.

From Elsie Inez Blue, daughter of Samuel Taylor and Louisa Canty Blue of the Catawba Nation, South Carolina, the following is found. " Well this was in Spartanburg, I believe it was. President Callis was our Mission President and my daddy (Chief Samuel Taylor Blue) loved him. He said that he (President Callis) was his Savior, because he saved his life one time. He said he thought that maybe if it was not for President Callis, he might have been a murderer, because I had a brother killed (this was before I was born).[174] He was accidentally shot by a bunch of men, Indian men that were hunting. When my daddy came home that night, my brother was dead.[175] My daddy said that the men that were hunting in that hunting group were there that night, out in the yard; and he said that he wanted to get his gun and shoot them too. But he said he went down in threw woods and he prayed about it, and he came back. He did this several times, but in the meantime, he sent a telegram to President Callis in Atlanta. He came and he talked to my daddy. He always called him his savior, because he saved his life, saved him from being a murderer."

---

[174] Harvey Blue
[175] Chief Blue says he came home and then his son died. The full account is in Marion G Romney's book

ELDERS OF THE SOUTHERN STATES MISSION.
Top Row from Left to Right:—Charles J. Housley, John H. Stevenson, Francis S. Lundell, Henry Child, Harvey Dalton, Wm. S. Hamblin. Bottom Row:—Samuel S. Whitehead, Conway Wilkes, John L. Gleave, Conference President, Ira Gardner, Mission President, Charles A. Callis, Thomas Wilson, Clarence H. Yates.

PHOTO 70   ELDERS OF THE MIDDLE TENNESSEE CONFERENCE OF THE SOUTHERN STATES MISSION (SEPTEMBER 1915)

Elder Orrin Orlando Barrus   --   SSM 1908-1910

PHOTO 71   ORRIN ORLANDO BARRUS

Birth date, place -- 29 May 1870, Grantsville, Tooele, Utah Territory, United States
Death date -- 6 October 1958
Baptism date - 29 May 1878   --   Baptism by - Benjamin Franlin Barrus
Father's name - Benjamin Franklin Barrus   --   Mother's name - Lovina Ann Steel

Southern States -- December 1908–November 1910 -- Age Called: 38

Catawba Indian Nation, South Carolina Conference
Set Apart: 8 December 1908 -- Arrived In Field: 14 December 1908
Released: 2 November 1910   --   Arrived At Home: December 1910
Mission type: Proselytizing
Marital Status: Married
Served with spouse: Mary Elizabeth Mamie Clark
Served with children
Priesthood office: Seventy
Called From: Fairview, Uinta, Wyoming, United States
Set apart by: Francis M Lyman

Notes: He served with his family among the Catawba Indian Nation, as well as serving as President of the South Carolina Conference.

Missionary Department missionary registers, 1860-1959, Vol. 1, p. 131, line 212.
Missionary Department missionary registers, 1860-1959, Vol. 2, p. 140, line 212.
Missionary Department missionary registers, 1860-1959, Vol. 4, p. 51, line 909.
Southern States Mission history, 1832-1964: LR 8557 2, Church History Library.

PHOTO 72   ORLANDO BARRUS FAMILY,   BACK- LEONE AGUSTA, ORLANDO CLARK, ZINA CLOENE,

PHOTO 73 -- BARRUS FAMILY ABOUT 1914 ---- LEONE AUGUSTA = 1897-1963: ORLANDO CLARK = 1902-1922: ZINA CLOENE = 1903-1986: ORRIN ORLANDO = 1870-1958: MARY ELIZABETH MAMIE CLARK BARRUS = 1873-1961: RUTH = 1911-1993: LERA = 1907-2003: MERLE = 1913-2007: THAYER CLARK BARROWES =1909-2004 (TWO CHILDREN HATTIE THELMA AND STERLING CLARK PASSED AWAY BEFORE THIS PICTURE WAS TAKEN)

Mary Clark Barrus   --   SSM 1908-1910

PHOTO 74   MARY CLARK BARRUS

Birth date, place - 13 March 1873, Farmington, Davis, Utah Territory, United States
Death date - 4 November 1961
Baptism date - 1 January 1882   --   Baptism by - Oliver L Robinson
Father's name - Timothy Baldwin Clark   --   Mother's name - Lucy Augusta Rice

Southern States -- December 1908–December 1910 - Age Called: 35

Catawba Indian Nation, South Carolina
Set Apart: 8 December 1908   --   Arrived In Field: 14 December 1908
Released: 2 November 1910   ---   Arrived At Home: December 1910
Mission type: Proselytizing
Marital Status: Married
Served with spouse: Orrin Orlando Barrus
Served with children
Called From: Fairview, Uinta, Wyoming, United States
Set apart by: Geoge Franklin Richards
Notes: Served as President of the Relief Society, Catawba Indian branch

> Missionary Department missionary registers, 1860-1959, Vol. 4, p. 51, line 911.
> Mary C. Barrus typescript journal, 1909 February-1910; 1950, MS 28251, Church History Library.
> Southern States Mission history, 1832-1964: LR 8557 2, Church History Library.

From the Journal kept by Sister Barrus

Our South Carolina Mission When we had been married about 12 years, we attended stake conference in Afton with our five children. President Joseph F. Smith and Apostle George F. Richards were in charge. Brother Richards asked me how I would like to go on a mission with my husband. I answered, "If there is anything I could do with these five children, my hand and my heart are ready." Brother Richards reported to President Smith, saying, "I have just called a woman with five children on a mission." President Smith reminded him he had been appointed to find a family to go to the Indian reservation in South Carolina. "I have found the family," said Brother Richards. Next day at noon, Sunday, we met with them to discuss the mission. Orlando wondered with quivering lips how I could ever justify taking a family into that hot malaria country. When we learned that the venture would be at our own expense entirely, we were left to think it over and then report our decision. September passed. We often discussed the mission but came to no definite conclusions. At the October conference in Salt Lake, Orlando's brothers, Emery and Albert, took pains to discuss the undertaking with both President Charles A. Callis and George F. Richards. After they returned, I remarked one day to Albert, the bishop of our ward, that I wondered why we didn't hear from Salt Lake about our mission. Albert said, "I know why. Emery and I told them you could not afford it, and that we couldn't help you." I said, "Did you tell them that?" Why In a rush I ran home and told Orlando of the conversation. He immediately wrote to Brother Richards telling him that we were ready to make any sacrifice necessary to fill the mission. A letter came right away giving us an official call to be in Salt Lake to go with a company of missionaries on December 9, 1908. Because I had been promised in two patriarchal blessings I would fill a mission, I did not doubt that I should accept an opportunity if one presented itself. When we had only been married a short time, Cyrus Tolman gave Orlando and me a blessing. These promises to him were unusual: "You will be called to fill another mission. A woman will say to you, 'I know you are a servant of the Lord, for I saw you in a vision, also your family and the house with glass windows you will build." My promise by the same patriarch was: "You will have the privilege of going with your husband if you desire it with all your heart." I had full confidence in the Lord's help. After a month's preparation we were ready to go. We were prepared in every way. We offered everything for sale but the house and land, including the furniture in our new house. I could not help shedding a few tears as I witnessed the organ and other articles I prized loaded into wagons and moved away, everything gone but the beds we were sleeping in. Before daylight of the morning we were to start I felt pretty serious, not knowing whether we would live in a tent or under trees, and I had a natural fear of Indians. I was shown a scene of the house we would live in and was comforted. I was not asleep. Three and a half year old Sterling was taken suddenly ill with every symptom of pneumonia. The night before we started neighbors tried to discourage us. They said, "You surely won't take that sick child out in this cold weather." I said, "We are going on the Lord's business, and he will care for me and heal our boy" and He did. Two large trunks packed full of clothing and the necessary articles needed and a roll of bedding were arranged in the wagon with hay for the horses. A bed for Sterling was made in the hay. His father carried him to it, too sick to hold up his little head. Before we left the house, Orlando dedicated us all to the care of Heavenly Father, and we did not trust Him in vain. When we camped the first night, Sterling sat up and ate supper, greatly improved. The next night he was lively as the other children–healed. While we were selling our possessions to raise money to carry out our venture, people seemed eager to pay more than we asked for everything. A sheep herder insisted on us taking $16 for four quilts we weren't taking with us. One good friend offered $4 for Leone's big doll. As she kissed it good-bye she told it, "I'm going on a mission." The nest egg that we arrived in Star Valley with in 1897 was 40 cents. It had surely multiplied. In 1908, from the sale of our accumulations, we realized $2,000. We still had our house and land, about 120 acres, all paid for. They would be waiting for us when we returned someday, we knew not when. Orlando stored his harnesses and wagon wheels in the front room. We might need them some day. The members of my associates on the stake board came over and spent a day helping with sewing children's clothes. The children of the stake presented me with a gold watch and chain. I wrote these verses while making preparations to go: Farewell, farewell, our beloved mountain home, Farewell, farewell, we leave you now to roam In southern climes where falls no winter snow. Our call has come, and cheerfully we go., To those we came in early wedded bliss Like birds we came afar to build our nest Where little birds might learn to fly and rest. Our handiwork Father in Heaven hath blessed.

There's one we miss, One we must leave behind Upon the hill she sleeps neath grassy mound. A vacancy we feel so hard to fill But now, we bow, oh Father, to thy will. Farewell, farewell, loved home and friends most dear, Remember us when you are bowed in prayer That we may be faithful, trustworthy and true, If God wills, may we return home to you. Oh, yes, I desired to go "with my husband with all of my heart. While coming down stairs with baby Lera in my arms, I missed a step and sprained my ankle at Uncle Amasa's house. A taunting voice whispered, "Now you can't go on your mission." I thought, "This will not hinder me." I was carried to the kitchen. I was prompted to use hot packs, then wrap my feet with a wide strip of cloth snugly from foot to shoe top. The right thing to do, I learned later. While in Salt Lake City that same day making purchases of clothing, my ankle turned again, a terrific pain. I remarked to a friend at my side, "If I were only where my husband could administer to me." A whisper from my guardian angel spoke, "Thy faith hath made thee whole." From that moment I forgot about the sprain, yet I used my foot as usual the next ten days caring for the family during the trip to our destination. The morning we left Salt Lake, I was wondering about the Indians we would meet. In a sort of dream I heard the Indians singing, Jesus, Lover of My Soul. I saw the group as we met them later in reality. During our visit to Grantsville, Sterling was entirely well. We had quite an experience changing trains on our way. Leone was now 11 years old, Zina, 5 ½, Clark 7 1/2, Sterling 3 and Lera was 1 ½. The children would go to sleep on benches without complaint. At Saint Louis we visited headquarters of the Church, and with a group of Elders and Miss Pack - we visited the site where the Jackson County Temple is to be erected. We rode on the elevated railway ascending flights of stairs to the station. "Adam and Eve walked over this part of the world, perhaps," I commented. Orlando brought me back to earth with, "I wonder if that tree over there is the one where Adam boosted Eve up to get him an apple." We were quite a novelty to some people. They asked us, "Are all those children yours?" Answer: "They certainly are our own." The conference president met us at Columbia, South Carolina. We spent one night there in a hotel over a furniture store. When we were informed plans had been made for us to live in one room of John Brown's house, I knew we would need furniture, beds, etc. Orlando suggested that I see what I could find in a second hand store nearby while he tended the children. As I hurried down the stairs, I prayed, "Oh, Lord, if there is anything in this city we need in the line of furniture, please guide me to it." That voice which has prompted me often, spoke again, "Go straight across the street." I did and met the clerk of a used furniture store who was anxious to clear out of the way the following items: a washer, nearly new for $1; 2 iron bed steads with springs for $5; an army cot bed, bugs and all for $2.50; a dresser with a good mirror for $1.50; wash stand, $.50; 5 chairs, including a rocking chair, for $1.25; and a sewing machine for $2. I stepped into another shop and bought an extension table for $2.50 and an organ for $20 and a good baby buggy for $1.50. I mentioned to the clerk that we wanted them shipped to the Catawba Indian Reservation. The clerk followed me to the hotel for more detail of the address and added, "I'll pay the freight and send the things at once." He volunteered to do that. All of this was accomplished in one hour. On the streets in Columbia we met more Negroes than white people. They seemed arrogant in their appearance. We were not out to see the sights, but we did see them. A few hours ride on the train brought us to the end of our journey through rural districts. We could see many humble shanty-like dwellings with groups of Negro children in the yard. Apparently, there is a more numerous increase among the Negroes than the white people. Chief Blue met us at the Rock Hill station, and after a ten-mile ride, we were welcomed by a gathering of the Indians in the home of John Brown. It was the same group I saw in a dream in Salt Lake before leaving home. Sister Brown, when introduced to Orlando, said, "I know you are a servant of the Lord for I saw you I in a vision, also your family and I saw you go over the way and build a house with glass windows." Most of their homes had wooden shutters for windows for windows. These were closed in storms. Some had coal-oil lamps for light and heat. Every Indian family owned a lantern to light their way along the trail at night. When we opened our trunk and put the lamp I had brought in use, it was a real novelty. The next morning, I asked Sister Brown which way was east. She answered, "I don't know. Ask Sally. I can't read and write." There were tall pine trees in every direction- a house on a hill here and there. Springs in the hollows furnished water supply. Such filth - rain washed refuge from the hills into the springs. No wonder there was malaria prevalent. President Callis came a day after we arrived. He slept with two of our children on a couch. At his suggestion, a meeting of the chief's was held to determine the possibility of building a house. All the men were anxious to contribute freely of their means and labor. One offered $1, another $3, several offered 50 cents each. The total contribution was $7.00. Everyone offered to help build. The men cut tall pine trees, hauled them to the saw mill, and in one month we were moved into the house. On Christmas day, while we were at John Browns, we heard confusing noises outside. Two Indians were having a combat. Mr. Wheelock, a Cherokee Indian,[176] had been drinking. John Brown was taking him home. Wheelock was quarrelsome and tried to choke John. Wheelock's ear and John's teeth became entangled. Wheelock lost his ear. The next day Orlando and John called on the Cherokee to make peace. John said, "I'm sorry about our quarrel last night." Wheelock said, "Oh, that's all right, John. If I ever get drunk again, I hope you'll chew my other ear off." Soon after we arrived, Lera had an upset from drinking bad milk. Orlando and Clark filled their pockets with tracts and set out to find a milk cow outside the reservation. They bought a

---

[176]Actually Archie Wheelock was an Onieda from Wisconsin who had married Edna, a Catawba girl.

cow and a calf for $20. With the calf in the lead, the cow swam across the river in pursuit. While they were on their way home in the river bed, they lost their way. Rain set in. Clark, only 7 ½ years old, said, "Pa, let's pray." They knelt in the mud and asked the Lord to help them find the right trail. At that very moment, we were sitting around the fireplace worrying about them. John Brown arose suddenly and said, " I'm going to find Elder Barrus." From his door he shouted, "Elder Barrus." Orlando was at that time more than a mile away, but he answered, "Down Here." They shouted back and forth neared each other voices until they met - all of the three wet through, but very thankful. The Indians had a one room school house. Orlando taught, and used the money the Government supplied for buying desks, books, maps, etc. I held school at home for our children. We held Sunday School, Primary and Relief Society, with the Indians for Assistants. They were efficient and bright - only lacking in development and opportunity. They seemed more like a Nephite than a Lamanite people. We held night school for parents who could not read and write. Singing practice was held one night a week. The Indians were good singers and learned easily. I sang each part with them. We had the only organ in the community, but we helped buy one for the Church house and I taught the girls to play the hymns. The Indians helped us dig the only well on the reservation. About two feet of good soil covered volcanic rock. We bought powder for blasting through it to very good water. We lived on the main road through the reservation, and whenever strangers called at the well for a cool drink, Orlando would empty the water buckets at once and fill his pockets with tracts to give to callers. A Catholic priest heard of our living there and knocked at our door, ate dinner with us, and I gave him a Book of Mormon. We learned that we were accepted by all of the Indians. There were about twenty-five Indians who are not members, but they came to Church. Some of the Indian parents had never been officially married. Chief Toad Harris invited us over one evening to his official wedding. I was a witness to the ceremony. He had about a dozen children. Indian custom, we learned, in marriage was merely common consent - nothing promiscuous, though. A few Indians married white wives, whom they were proud to claim. We held Relief Society in our large front room. While one was in session, a little 4-year-old girl slipped behind her mother and whispered, "Mummy, I ant some Teet." A sagging breast was tucked in under the mother's arm, and the child, standing behind the mother, nursed in sweet content. Our house was built close to a shanty we used for a summer kitchen. An old hen stole her nest under it and delighted our children one morning as she appeared, displaying her brood of a dozen little chicks. These, with a few others contributed, set us up in the chicken business. Elders who came to headquarters after Orlando was made president of the South Carolina Conference - were made to feel at home when they were at our table eating the chicken they had prepared for cooking, with an abundance of cream and Jersey milk, home-made bread and butter, cream gravy and black berry jam that we made. Black berries grew in abundance. Chiggers claimed the crop, but we learned how to defeat them by tying a cord string saturated with kerosene or turpentine around our wrists and ankles. Because of heavy rains, we planted our garden several times before it rewarded us with vegetables. We planted a bushel of Irish potatoes and harvested a peck. When we were planting peanuts, little Sterling said, "Why not plant candy, too, Pa?" Each peanut blossom must be covered with soil. They are gathered and roasted–no candy with them. Sweet potatoes were the main crop, also peas, beans and corn. We thought we could raise onions because the climate was warm, but the soil was not suitable; and the ones we planted ripened when they were the size of a baseball. When we asked for a few bushel of Irish potatoes at Rock Hill, the clerk said, "We've never sold a bushel at a time." Irish potatoes were a rarity. The Indians thought potato soup was a real treat. President Callis advised me to teach the Indian women to make yeast bread. Some of them brought us very fine samples of it. Nancy Harris was an expert bread maker. She was one who learned from me. One day Nancy Harris asked me for some oil to doctor her finger. She had crushed it and proud flesh formed in it. I told her to use something stronger than oil to kill infection. The next day she returned with the same request. I poured oil over it as she uttered a prayer. In a few days she showed me a well finger, healed by her faith, no trace of the infection. We bought olive oil by the quart. The Indians had faith and they brought bottles to be filled for all kinds of sickness. A Dr. Hill visited the reservation once a month and prescribed calomel for most everything. He delivered our baby son Thayer, September 1, 1908. Dr. Hill spoke of his only son. He said,"I wouldn't take $1,000 for him or give a plug of tobacco for another child. President Callis transferred Brother and Sister Huskinson to our home during my confinement. Brother Huskinson took charge as conference secretary while Orlando was away visiting branches of the Church during six months. Little Sterling was taken ill with lung trouble again. Brother and Sister Huskinson and Brother Blue joined with us in a special fast and while they were administering to him his fever left - healed instantly. His father was now able to fill an appointment in a distant part of the state. While Sterling was so sick, I made a promise to the Lord that if He would spare the little boy till our mission was finished, I would be willing to give him up. I was taken at my word; a few years later he was called to leave us. Brother Blue told us of the time he fell while hunting and broke his leg, the splinters of bone protruding through the flesh. Blood poison set in and doctors said the only way to save his life was to amputate the fractured limb. Brother Blue refused to have it done. He prayed for Elders to come. Two Elders were impressed to go to the reservation. The united faith and administration of the Elders and faith of the Blue family resulted in a complete recovery. Brother Blue walked to Church about a week later. I think he is almost perfect in his living up to the teachings of the gospel. Brother Blue raised cotton. When he sold a bale of cotton in rock

Hill, too much money was given him and when he found a mistake had been made, he returned to the cotton mill. The dealer was astonished. When he was asked what kind of a man he was, Brother Blue replied, "A Mormon and I was taught to be honest." Brother Blue took a load of wood to the city often. The Indians would send for provision in small amounts, 25 and 50 cents from a dozen or more families. The money jolted out of his pocket. He felt responsible and knelt in a humble prayer; with perfect faith he asked the Lord to guide him to that money. Walking a short distance back he found every penny of it carefully piled up in an orderly way, the small coins on top. He thought the angels must have come to his assistance. When we needed to borrow finishing materials for our house, we had to borrow $200 until we could get that much from home. We had to be identified at the bank. We were asked if we knew Chief Ben Blue. We were told that if Chief Blue would recommend us, that we could have any amount of money we wanted to borrow. Orlando administered to a lady with smallpox and was vaccinated. Soon after, he filled an appointment in a distant part of the state and returned late at night in a rain storm. The children and I were worried. When he came in the door, Sterling said, "Ma, I told you Pa wouldn't go dead." Orlando had to walk five miles from the station to the reservation. The family and I often met him on his return, and it was a happy occasion. I had the privilege of re-clothing Elders with dry apparel, mending and pressing suits when they called on us in a rain storm. Our extension table proved its worth when we entertained groups of Elders and Saints. Brother Huskinson and Orlando were born on the same day: 40 years old on May 29, 1910. Sister Huskinson and I celebrated for them with an extra chicken and lemon pie dinner. Two pairs of Elders happened along for advice from their conference president. We enjoyed the reunion and feasted together. We divided our bedding with them. They slept on the floor and had fun when bats entered the scene and claimed a place with them in bed. President Callis advised us to visit the Saints in Charleston, South Carolina. One of the Indian women stayed with Leone and the children. We took the baby, six months old, with us. Sister Dupont, a missionary mother, made us welcome. We rode on a big steamer to the Isle of Palms, 20 miles off the coast. A real thrill—on the Atlantic Ocean. We passed Fort Sumpter of Civil War historical fame. A fine outing. The main street of Charleston reminded us of the letter S, crooked, yes. Stores dilapidated. Numerous Negroes around. When we received word our mission was for 2 years, we made preparations for leaving. Chief Blue took a wagon loaded with his family and ours on a picnic to Charlotte, North Carolina. We visited a big circus there. Indians sat along with white people, Negroes by themselves. The day before we left the reservation, at our farewell party, we sang "God Be With You Till we Meet Again." At the end of the hymn, nearly everyone was in tears. Brother Blue said, "I worship the ground Brother and Sister Barrus walks on." While we were packing the next day, I handed dishes and things to the friends looking on. Several Elders were there for dinner. We were to leave at one o-clock. The trunks were closed, but Orlando opened one of them to receive the silver knives and forks. They rode home along with Leone's and Zina's leghorn hats. No hats left after this trip. "

Transcription of the Daily Journal of Mrs. Orlando Barrus

Daily Journal of Mrs. Orlando Barrus

Feb. 1st, 1909.   Roddey, S.C.   1908 to 1910

Thoughts written while on my mission to the Southern States with my husband.

We were set apart Dec 8" 1908 at Salt Lake City in the temple Annex under the hands of Apostles F. M. Lyman and G. F. Richards. Apostle Lyman set Orlando apart and Apostle Richards was mouth when my turn came. We were assured in these blessings that the Lord had called us thru the inspiration of his servant and that if we were faithful the Lord would bless us & make us equal to the undertaking before us. That we should love and be loved by the people with whom we should be called to labor & be the means of accomplishing much good. I had one earnest desire that I might receive some assurance that I might have health to preform my duties & c. After me were all set apart, about 35 elders & his ladies, several of the apostles spoke and it was time to close. I was feeling very humble wondering if I was unworthy to have my prayer answered. Just as they were ready to close Apostle Richards arose & said, "If any of you have failed to receive all they desired in their blessings, if they will ask the Lord in earnest prayer their request shall be granted.

I recognized at once an answer to my secret prayer, & felt more thankful than words can express. With our little family of five children I realized how much more it required to take care of them but felt sure that if the Lord would give me health I could do something for His cause also. Right here I will bear testimony that more times than I will take time to record, have I been brought face to face with the situation in sickness where this blessing has been fulfilled for whenever I most needed, the answer to the prayer of faith has been rewarded in behalf of each of our family. As I sat there in the temple by the side of my husband waiting our turn to be set apart I felt most thankful indeed that the Lord had favored me with such a grand opportunity. So many wives left at home while the husband and father are away fulfilling missions

When Apostle Lyman set Orlando apart in one part he said, "I set you apart for a mission among the Lamanites with your wife for a companion," I felt most unworthy, but determined to prove my appreciation by doing my best.

Cousin Wm O. Clark was set apart the same day for a mission to Eastern States.

We left the children up to cousin Lizzie S. Wilcox is home with my sister Louise and she and cousin Lizzie told us to rest some that they would be all right so we enjoyed the day first class. Cousin Lizzie made us wholly welcome to her home of luxury and we enjoyed seeing her family of talented children. On the same evening John Sharp called there as a teacher in that ward. Upon learning of our trip the next day, he took 10 dollars from his purse and handed it to Orlando. Dr. Wilcox also gave us 5.00. Quite a surprise but Orlando told them both that the Lord would bless them for their liberality. Dec. 9 1908

About noon the D & R. G. Rail Road station was thronged with the friends of the company of 35 elders who were to leave at 2 o'clock.

We breathed a sigh of relief as we were at last seated comfortably & speeding away from our loved Utah home and relatives & friends, not knowing how long we would be gone or just what our future might be. Would the Lord spare out lives to all meet again?

We now had time to think and my mind went back to a patriarchial blessing which Patriarch Syrus Tolman gave both of us in about the year 1899. He said to Orlando, "You will be called to go on another mission in due (line inserted between lines: "Sister Browns vision of our family on Page 67") time, & to me he said in my blessing, "If you desire it with all your heart you will have the privilege of going with him."

I had about come to the conclusion that the chances would be very slim for me to go with him now that I had 5 little children but all the same I desired to go with him if the Lord wanted us all & with a whole heart too.

We were at Sunday School in June of 1907 when Orlando read a letter from the first Presidency asking him if he could go on a mission & when. He answered that he would have his land proved upon in 1 ½ years from then but he would go now if they said go.

He read a reply saying be ready by Dec 1" 1908. From that time we planned in every way we could to bring about conditions favorable for getting as much ahead as possible and it was remarkable how things did come our way.

As nothing had been said in his call about me I had concluded that he might have another mission later in life when our children (line inserted between lines: "when my promise could be fulfilled") were grown perhaps.

In august 1908 at a conference of Star Valley Stake Pres. Joseph F. Smith and Apostle Geo. F. Richards visited us. On Saturday morning of Conference we got over there about 15 minutes before 10 o'clock and as I was walking toward the gate with my little children dressed in white, I shook hands with Pres. Osmond and Apostle Richards with whom I was well acquainted having taught school when he was trustee in Tooele.

We were speaking of some returned (line inserted between lines: "his son Legrand had been in") missionaries and I remarked that Bro Barrus expected to leave for a mission this fall. He turned to me and said, "How would your husband and take the whole family?" I answered, Why Bro. Richards what could I do with all my babies little ones" You could do a great deal" he added. Well said I if there is anything the Lord wants me to do my hand and head are ready to do all in my power. Albert Barrus our

bishop had not heard our conversation but was looking at us. He stepped up and said as he shook hands, "I told her she would go with him." It was less than a week before that I had asked him if he thought it would be all right for me to ask something about the mission as to where it would be for I could not keep the thought out of my mind unless I had been found unworthy, I would have the privilege of going with him and the 8 months remaining was none too much to get a family ready for a trip, I was anxious to know something definite. Albert had told me he felt sure I would know about it at this conference. Apostle Richards talked to us nearly all noon hour on Sunday saying he had been given the duty by the apostles corum to find a family to go on a mission a live for a time among the Catawba Indians in the southern States and that he felt impressed that he had found that very family in us. He said he had spoken entirely by inspiration when the matter was first mentioned to us. He said the matter would be fully looked into, and if all was advisable we would be called later.

"If I desired it with all my heart" as was in my blessing, was yet to have its test. Those having the matter under advisement thought it would be a big undertaking some said almost too big, to take such a large family across the continent and into the southern climate.

They were slow in answering and so Orlando wrote and expressed his willingness to make financial sacrifice such as was necessary and trust the Lord for the outcome. We recd our call in November about the first. While in suspense I found that I did desire it with every bit of my heart if the Lord found me worthy and had something for me to do.

The next three weeks were very busy ones. Our grain had yielded abundantly, while our friends had theirs freeze. We had the threshers several days and arranged for the sale of most all of our furniture cattle and horses & grain & c.

My what a lot of sewing to be done!

Lettie Campbell our Relief Society president volunteered the services of the society to help me one or two days till my sewing was done.

They did so & I fully appreciated the help. The Primary Stake Board & two of the Stake

Presidency surprised me one evening with a big oyster supper. We had a grand time.

We had a farewell dance in the church in Fairview wherein they raised 40 dollars & gave it to us. The Primary officers of all the stake bought me a beautiful gold watch and chain, also a leather bound Primary song book to remember the work by. We had a grand time at a farewell party they arranged for me at Afton and all had our pictures taken in a group. Orlando & Sister Maria J. Allred & I went to visit the Lower Valley to reorganize a primary there & while there the officers of the lower Valley surprised me so we had a grand farewell with all the sister workers in both valleys. I could not help but

feel that I had their love and confidence as they had mine.

I did feel more keenly the parting with aunt Maria than anyone else. We had labored for 12 years together first counselor to her in the Y.L.M.I A. for about 4 yrs. – then when she was chosen Stake Pres of the Primary, I was still with her part of the time secretary & later as her first counsellor. We just naturally love one another & have been blessed in our unity and good fellowship. We have enjoyed so many many delightful rides to the different primaries especially to the lower valley both Summer & Winter the scenery thru the narrows is most beautiful. The river and trees evergreens and cliffs are all an inspiring sight. Our duties among the children also inspired us to pleasant conversation and during all the years we sisters travelled together to visit primaries not one of us were ever injured by accident or took sick as a result of a trip. I always had a baby or two with me and never had one even take cold from exposure but I have had them get well after I took them out, nor have I ever had one come by harm at home as a result of my leaving them. This is one testimony that

the Lord approved of my course & answered my prayers.

It was a peculiar experience for me to be putting one thing and another in the large trunks day after day, wondering under what circumstances I would take them out, wondering also if I ever would return to this lovely little home.

Sometimes a sort of a pain would dart from my heart & almost choke me as I would see them load the furniture onto some ones wagon who had purchased it from us, for I had waited a long long time for a new house and good furniture, but we must furnish a house in the South and Orlando thought we must sell this in order to buy there. Surely it was not easy to part with these things but a feeling satisfaction accompanied it after all for we were called on a mission and could trust the Lord for more furniture. We believed what He has said" "Seek first the Kingdom of God & its richeousness and all else shall be added & "Sacrifice brings forth the blessings of heaven" & c. I am most willing to invest liberally in such blessings for they are more valuable than gold and earthly treasures.

When we were married Feb 3" 1899 Orlando had just returned about a month before from a 3 ½ year mission to the Southern Pacific Islands and of course was not prepared to buy or build a mansion for me – not even a log cabin till we earned the money to buy it with. Therefore we were so fortunate as to be obliged to economise and save and earn to make a start in life together with our hands empty that we might appreciate our possessions more when we did get them. At this time Nov. 1908 after eleven years of labor and sacrifice we have 185 acres of land fenced and under cultivation with

horses, machinery, cattle and a good new five roomed house furnished comfortably – also a buggy harnesses & c all paid for and here we are selling such of it as we could – I mean the movable part, that we might raise money to go on a mission and stay we don't know how long.

My Mason & Hamlin organ I did hate to part with as I had bought it while teaching school in Bountiful in 1896 and I expected it would last me a lifetime. It had been a great blessing to us in this lonely part of the world and I have given music lessons enough to earn a great many little extras to help fix up our home.

A few days before leaving the sisters of the stake board and the Stake Presidency & their wives surprised us with oyster supper and a pleasant evening was spent there at home long to be remembered.

Our Stake Conference held Nov. 22 & 23 1908 we were favored with the presence of Apostles Geo. F. Richards and Geo. Albert Smith. While speaking in conference they each one made mention of us and made us some beautiful promises. We bade good bye to all the folks and recd many good kid wishes expressed by all our friends. When Pres Osmond bade me good bye he said "Sister B. you have been a good girl here and you will be a good girl there.

Apostle Richards said, "They have been called of God as was Aaron"

I attended the evening session at Fairview and was called to speak a few minutes. Orlando stayed home with the children as we could not both leave Sterling who was sick, and he was to stay a nick longer than I and could say good bye later. Orlando administered to him several times and his fever was so high he grunted every breath. It looked more like a siege of pneumonia ahead than starting on a cold trip thru the canyon next day. We however kept on making preparations and felt confident that the Lord would restore our little son to health. I finished packing the trunks after meeting and retired to sleep the last time in our "home sweet home."

Early in the morning I could not help but shed a few silent tears. Orlando asked "Dont you want to go on a mission" I answered "of course I do, but this is certainly not an easy thing to take five little ones out in this cold wind & one of them sick. It took will as well as faith to start but we were soon on our way. We made a bed in the wagon on the hay for Sterling.

By noon he seemed better and by night still more improved. We had plenty of maps but after while the weather moderated & it began to snow.

If we had been going on a pleasure trip people might have thought us crazy taking children out like that. As we jolted along we had time to think and think and I hummed these verses I had written while packing up to leave. Tune „Farewell dear southern home."

Farewell Farewell
Our dear loved mountain home
Farewell Farewell
We leave you now to roam
Southern climes
Where fall no winter snow
The call has come
And cheerfully we go.

To thee we came
In early wedded bliss
To thee we came
To build our little nest
In mountain vales
To build "sweet home's" retreat
Near crystal streams
Mid mild flowers perfume sweet

Each straw & twig
Unitedly we've placed
Our handiwork
Our Father dear has blessed.
Love's labors have
With holy joy been crowned
And clouds we've oft
With silvery linings found

Our home-nest now
Is finished and complete
Where trees and lawns
And flowers bloom so sweet
Our birdlings five
With gratitude we see
All that we have
Was given Lord by thee.

There's one we miss
One we must leave behind
Upon the hill
She sleeps neath grassy mound

A vacant place
Is left which none can fill
In this we bow
To Heavenly Fathe's will

Farewell! Farewell!
Our home & friends most dear
Remember us
When you are bowed in prayer
That we may to
Our Fathe's trust prove true
And in His own
Dear time return to you.

At Garland

The snow fell in the afternoon on our way up to the halfway house where we spent the night with Mrs. Ritson. She would take no pay but gave us a dollar to help us on our way. We arrived at uncle W. W. Clarks the afternoon of the second day and had a short visit with them and bought a few things ready for the start on the train next day.

Orlando saw us off on the train next day & he went back home to settle up his affairs a little better for a week & then he came. We arrived at Garland the same night to with Ma and the family. Thanksgiving dinner next day.

Old friends party

We had a fine time. Clare felt so full of fun she kept us laughing all the time at the dinner. Eva''s children & mine all there together was Ma's special satisfaction. Lera did everything she could to make us have a good time as did George Ellen & Louise & all.

Georgie took me to two good Theatres in Garland while there. Orlando joined us Dec 2nd. On that evening Ma invited about 30 of my old associates who used to live in Farmington when I did and we spent a delightful evening together visiting, feasting, and in pleasant recreation. Ellen & Orlando entertained the folks with humerous reciting and missionary experiences were related by several. Each one bade us God speed and next morning found us at the Depot bidding Ma & Georgie Goodbye. Clares husband was there too. He is a fine young man. Ed Norr.

We spend a few days in our old Farmington home. We had to do some planning to make all ends meet – keep this family looked after in cold weather & all. It makes my head swim to think of it now, but the Lord did certainly fit my back for the burden and everything went off like music.

We left the children with the twins while we went to Salt Lake to get us each a new suit and things for the children we had to have for the trip.

Dr. Wilcox

While coming down the stairs at uncle Almasa's that morning with babe Lera 17 mo. old in my arms I fell and sprained my ankle. It seemed like I would be laid up for a few weeks as a sprain is slower to heal than a break generally. We bathed it in hot water and bound it tightly before I put on my shoe. I felt sure the Lord would not fail at this time of all time to still give me power to do what was required of me. I surely had no time to humer a sprained ankle with only five days between us and the start from SL City on Dec 9. Uncle Almasa and Aunt Susie went with us and we did shopping successfully.

We met cousin Lizzie Wilcox in the Z.C.M.I. and she invited us to spend the night at her home when we came back from Tooele. When we came back from Salt Lake Uncle Almasa took us to the Old Folks Ball in the Opera House. It was a great joy to meet old friends and renew old acquaintences among those with whom I used to associate when I was young.

At Tooele

I could not think of dancing much but did enjoy the visit lunch & program.

I wondered how my ankle would be when I took my shoe off. It is a fact that the Lord was so mindful of me that he blessed me that I did not loose on step which I needed to take, and in a few days it was not even sore.

The Lord heard the prayer of faith and did not turn a deaf ear & I do think him.

Next day we went to Salt Lake & Tooele next day to say goodbye to relatives there & in Grantsville.

Set apart for our mission by <u>Geo F Richards</u> Dec 8 1908

We spent one night at Angelias. Orlando drove down to see his parents and the children & I did not go to Grantsville at all on account of contagious diseases there. They came up however and we all ate several meals together there and enjoyed a real good visit. Monday night we went in to Salt Lake City and accepted cousin Lizzies invitation to her magnificent home. Her sons & daughters were the essence of culture and refinement. Raymond played the piano beautifully. They treated us first class and when we left gave us a 5.00 bill and many good wishes.

On Dec 8 we went to the Temple to be set apart and arrange for transportation & c. Louise came down and kept all the little ones there at Cousin Lizzies so we had a whole day off.

They were just as happy as could be there and we had the day of days for us.

Such a grand gathering of young missionaries, such a beautiful spirit there & c. When Pres Lyman said to O, "I set you apart for a mission to the Lamanites with your wife for a companion" I thot Oh how favored above the many who are left at home without husband. I realized that it would be no easy task ahead but I felt most thankful for the privilege and desire to prove worthy the same.

Ella Pack was going the same day also cousin Wm. O. Clark of Montpelier Idaho. Dec 9"1910 (written over 1908)

Thru Grand Canyon

All aboard at the D&RG station saying farewells & c. 35 elders had a special car until we got to Colorado Springs. We had a pleasant time singing hymns, reading visiting & c. some of the elders had left children at home and a little romp with ours just suited both them and our little ones for they often became fatigued sitting so much when they were used to an active life. It was quite a new and strange experience – Every one of us enjoyed the scenery.

We got well along in the Grand canyon at sunrise.

Dec 10th. The highest point we passed over was Tennessee Pass 13,000 feet above sea level. For a few hours we felt the effects of such high altitude and I was obliged to lie down so I could not see some of the very highest cliffs. It was a source of great satisfaction to feel the assurance that the Lord would protect us from disaster. Oh just to look up for hundreds of feet & see cliffs & down hundreds of feet over cliffs & see the mild soaring grand-river foaming in the bottom of the canyon.

To realize what might result if something should give way and throw our train off this narrow dug way as we climbed higher & higher.

Spring oozing from the cliffs this freezing weather was a grand sight when it formed icicles hundreds of feet down cliffs. We saw miners towns way up the mountains where it did not look to us from the train as tho a bird could find a safe resting place scarcely. At Colorado Springs cousin Wm. O. Clark took another route for his mission in New York. After we had crossed over the Rocky Mountains the first night I was looking out the window & saw the full moon coming up on a level with us I thought it was the head light of another engine nearly upon us.

It did look strange not to see mts. at all.

Jackson Co Misouri

While passing over the plains. I thought of the contrast in our mode of travel & that of the Utah Pioneers in 1846 & 7. We were oh so tired of the train on the comfortable seats – while they walked by their loaded wagons only able to walk a few miles a day – as far as we could ride perhaps in 15 or 20 minutes with our iron horse. If the hundreds of elders who are sent to do missionary work were dependent upon teams instead of trains – how much less would be accomplished each year. Truly the world must be ward and the time is short. God is the author of all this invention. When we arrive at Kansas City we had 7 hrs. wait, so the elders and Miss Pack & we went on the street car to Independence Jackson co. Missouri.

Kansas City

We took the elevated railway. We went up a flight of stairs as high as the tall buildings and bought tickets at the at the elevated rail way station for a ride out to Independence Mo. In about a half hour we had realized the peculiar experience of riding over tall buildings on a street care and were walking the very streets of this historic old place. Indeed we believe that to the location of the garden of Eden as well as the future center stake of Zion where the Temple is to be build. Pres. Bennion ask some of the elders to go from the mission home there with us and we, children & all were favored with the unusual privilege of standing upon the very ground where that great temple is to be erected someday. It was a great satisfaction to take all the little children there. They will never forget it. To walk the very streets in which my grandparents and the early church leaders had walked saw the court house where the prophet had been tried for imaginary crimes & acquitted & c. we ate supper at the mission home and took the train again at about nine O'clock to proceed on our way to S. Carolina. Kansas city is like other of the large cities I have seen out here – built up without much design as to the laying out of the city, with streets running every way. At all these big stations we had to watch the children very close to keep track of them as the crowd was so large it would have been an easy matter to loose them & make trouble finding them again.

At St Louis, we were so worn out from rest that we got a room at a hotel and rested one day and all of one night. Miss Pack & the children & I got on a car and took in the sights for a few hours in the afternoon. The elders went out in the forenoon to look around. St Louis is a big city & like Kansas city without the beauty & charm of wide streets of our western cities. We saw the flatiron building which was at the meeting of five streets & whose front was the point of the triangle (here the author drew the shape of a triangle). It had never occured to me before that any one would think of building a house except with square corners. I have noticed in all these large cities out here that there are fewer large department stores and many little one horse shops filled with trashy trash apparently.

There is so much smoke over the city that the air seemed almost thick. So many people narrow streets – more like alleys. The items of most interest to me there were first the great Mississippi river with its great suspension bridge nearly a mile wide – the large steam boats – tugboats, launches – The long underground ride under the main business part of town through the tunnel. Oh what a wonderful feat to build a Rail Road under a city – under thousands of tons of buildings and to what might happen – It makes one shudder! It felt a degree of satisfaction in the assurance that the Lord has called us thru his servants and will protect us – this did I often thot as we flew over river bridges & trestles, thru tunnels and around steep dugways on the high cliffs.

Union Station

I never had such a horror of a large city as I did of St. Louis. I would rather live on the farm near a city and breathe the air purified by natures elements.

The Union station is an emense affair. Trains coming and going every few minutes and every convenience for those waiting for trains.

At Chattanooga Dec 14 1908

Our next stop was at Chatanooga Tenn. We stayed at the hotel from morning till 8 oclock at night.

The elders came to meet Miss Pack and she went to the mission headquarters to see her sister who is the wife of Pres. C A. Callis of the S.S. Mission. We enjoyed a good rest that day. The children & I slept & rested & bathed. Orlando went up to headquarters on mission business.

That was Dec 14"1908.

We and the missionaries from the office had a few hours of pleasant pastime singing, conversing when they called on us in the evening.

We took the train at 9 o'clock for Columbia.

At Columbia S.C.

We arrived at Columbia after noon & were met by Pres. Paskett of S.C. Conference. He took us to a hotel & we all thot a good warm meal would just suit us – such as hotels we knew set out to eat – after eating cold lunch so long on the train. We were glad to lie down on a bed and sleep once more as we appreciated it more than ever before. We stayed there two days and nights and waited till Pres. Paskett wrote to the nation for them to come and meet us at Rock Hill.

We found the food at the hotel different to western food. Dinner was rice cooked dry & no milk or cream or butter, bacon & sweet potatoes no desert at all.

The children ate very little so the second day we bought our own food and ate in our room.

Columbia is a large city. It has many beautiful mansions. The state buildings were old & interesting. The corner of the state house showed the mark where a cannon ball had struck it during the civil war. It looked strange to see this large building right in the middle of the main street going up to town from the depot.

It seemed odd to see nearly as many [negroes] as white people passing along the street.

At the station are two waiting rooms and no darkey ever goes into the "white" waiting room. In fact it seems to me that the darkies are so well satisfied that they almost pity white people for being white.

Being so near my destination I wondered & wondered.

A dream of the south

The situation was not at all clear to us. We knew we were going among the Indians to live – whether we would be able to get a house to live in or furniture we did not know. We were sure we would need both for the home we must fix up to care for our little family and how we could do this was a real puzzle. While on our way down here among our relatives & friends the question was so often ask (sic_ us where will you live & c & c. We could only answer I don't know. We only know the Lord has called us and He will not forget us when we are nearly 3000 mile from the home we left in the west. I had faith in His watchcare but one night just before we left home I was lying there it seemed to me wide awake and wondering about the place we were going to – If I only knew we would have a comfortable house. A scene passed before my eyes. I saw a house built upon the side like of a kind of a hill. All around it and every way I looked I saw evergreen trees of quite a uniform height making it look like a green covering ever where. After the scene had passed I tried to close my eyes and see it again to get a better view of it but was not able to recall it. I was impressed that it was our home in the forest that I saw and described it to Orlando.

A dream of seeing the Indians

Another night I dreamed we were at our journeys end a house full of the Indians were out to meet us. I heard them singing a song where two voices led and in duett and the rest joined in chorus. I also saw very plainly four indian women.

Jesus Lover of my soule

I also told Orlando this dream & that I was sure I could recognize them if I ever saw them. Both these dreams or manifestations were proven to my satisfaction to have been given me by the spirit of the Lord for sure enough after we arrived at the Indian Nation the first night there were the people I had seen assembled. Only three of the women were there but I saw the fourth one a few days after. Their features were familiar when I met them. They were sisters Watts, Blue, Gordon & Brown. They sang many songs that night but they did not sing "Jesus Lover of my soule" with duett and chorus till I taught it to them & I recognized it just as soon as they sang it as the one I had heard in my dream. This was a very strong testimony to me and I thanked my heavenly Father for the same. These dreams were a source of comfort to me since I of course dreaded the thoughts of taking our family among the Indians. My idea of an Indian was of course the ones I had seen who wore their long unkept hair – male & female – and with blankets & moccasins.

I was thoroughly surprised tho to find a people speaking the English language & natural songsters – dressing as the white people dress and living much the same as the poorer white people of the south live in small houses – poorly furnished having only a homemade table boxes for cupboards – boxes and stumps of wood for chairs – the chairs themselves are an exception. They all have a bed stead or two but very few have the luxury of a good stove. They cook over the fireplace just as their grandparents did 100 years ago. They wash in the proverbial wash-pot over a bonfire at the spring. They have no wells and their houses are built on the hills and the water must be carried up from the hollow below.

Most families have one pressing or flat iron & set it up on end to heat in front of the fire place & wait while it heats.

Their food is mostly corn bread and bacon. Very few raise their own food and tho they could buy a variety of food for the same price that this costs they seem to prefer the bread of corn & bacon. Some raise apples & peaches and there is lots of wild berries that they could put up for winter but very little is used only in the season of it. Their milk is kept in a jar and churned daily. They seldom use sweet milk – buttermilk is preferred by nearly all. A cow is a luxury and few have more than one. I never knew what a real blessing milk was till I came here, and see families without a cow.

I doubt very much if there is more than one or two families have enough dishes to set the table comfortably for all their numbers. Our children will always appreciate the common necessaries of life better having seen how these honest hearted but poor people live.

Like all indians they love to fish and hunt. the catawba river contains fish and the woods on every side are their hunting ground.

They dress as well as possible with their means. they like to wear pretty things and try to imitate batter ways of doing and seem quite willing and anxious to adopt better ways of managing. When we came here they seemed to take much less pride in braiding up their hair and keeping themselves cleaned up. Many times a new dress would be put on Sunday & worn for weeks. Many of them have followed our example of keeping one apron for best & c.

They dress for summer weather and when the few cold spells of winter come they must keep fire on the grate night and day to keep warm.

In case of sickness I have often wondered how they ever get well – houses so very open and no chance to keep a sick person out of draughts. The Lord has been most mindful of them and nearly every case where they send for the elders the administration is a benefit and many have been remarkably healed. Truly I feel sure the Lord intends this tribe to build up and become stronger as they seem as a body to love the Gospel & even those who are not members bear testimony of its divinity. Most of those out of the church are those who have been cut off for immorality – but they still attend church and because the spirit does not cease to strive with them it is an evidence that they are not judged by the same standard, as we who have had greater light for years & years.

Nearly all can read and write and some possess more than average intelligence. Since the gospel has been introduced among them about 25 years ago their morals and habits are greatly improved

At that time very few if any of them were moral. After the custom of Indians – their laws were their customs & their customs their laws. Consent to live together was sufficient marriage then. After the elders came those living together were married and taught to be true to their vows. All seem to be striving now to keep the same with few exceptions.

They have an account of their forefathers for several hundred years back and they have always been a peaceably enclined people. They say one of their number has never been convicted of a murder.

When the colonists were fighting with England these Catawba Indians fought with the white people. In the civil war they also enlisted and some lost their lives. They have not had the educational advantages they deserve. The state leased their land 100 years ago and have not exactly kept their contract. there is a prospect now for them to be paid a part of the money due them.

I have attended funerals weddings and socialables here a few only.

At midnight one indian a carpenter working at Rock Hill fell in love with a white woman a widow and they came down here to the nation to get Bro Barrus to marry them. She seemed quite a nice lady but true to the custom of the southern woman tobacco was necessary for her happiness. She ask me for a chaw of tobaccker. I told her we mormon people believed it to be detrimental to health and were never raised to use it. I explained to her that I had never seen a woman use it till I came south and it seemed strange to hear women of 50 years say they had used it since they were mere babes. I am thankful such habits do not cling to us.

The rising generation here do not use it and the parents are many of them leaving it off and trying to teach the word of wisdom & keep it.

Stealing a bride

It seems quite the thing here to steal the bride and surprise the parents by announcing their marriage rather than asking for their consent. Most of the older men laugh and say "I stole my wife."

There are a number of large families here – the best men have largest families. Nearly every father has lost his first wife and when I think of the way they are cared for in confinement I wonder any of them survive.

The promise made by Apostle Smith that this people would from this time build up it seems to me must be in a measure thru them learning more about their bodies and how to care for them.

One young woman was a bride – mother and a corpse in less than a year. She was only 16 years old and was no more prepared for maried life than a 10 year old child.

After a funeral

I took her food several times. I was not surprised when she died of pneumonia as did her babe one week old. She lay there with only one ragged quilt and blanket over her when we had a warm house & three times that ammount of bedding. They had neither window or shutter in their one room tho plenty of cracks for the warm air to escape before it benefited the sick woman in the opposite corner of the room. She wore only an old waist and skirt in bed and no one seemed to think of a flannel on her chest till I suggested it when she had pneumonia. It is not customary to have more than a few days provisions ahead. it is a puzzle to some to see us plan provisions ahead. We have tried to get them to do the same.

It is customary here for all the indians to quit work while one lay dead & until the funeral is over. then they all meet at the home of the bereaved and sing & sing the night after. As a people they do not seem to be as slow to make up after a falling out as I had expected.

Wheellocks ear

A few days after we arrived a church member Jno. Brown and Mr Whiellock – had a drunken quarrel in which Bro Brown pulled Whiellocks ear clear off. Bro Barrus got them together and reconsiled them and they have been friends ever since. Wheellock said, You should have pulled both ears off, Mr. Brown.

Like all indians they are about crazy when drunk. We have used every bit of influence we could in trying to get them to leave off drinking. The first Xmas here there was the usual cutting up and shooting – the second Xmas there was not any at all.

Old people said it was the first Xmas ever spent here peacefully.

Some who were the worst to drink & c had been cut off the church.

Most of these have since rejoined the church and are trying to help build up this people and their good name.

There have been a few drunken carousals while we have been here but not many and the leaders have reformed now.

Their social pastimes are limited to what they call "plays." All are invited to meet at the certain home and a fiddler plays while they carry on something like they used to call a dance in Utah 50 years ago. They also play games & sing and enjoy themselves in genuine fashion. A sister Brown presented me with a box of raisins thinking it the greatest favor from her at a party. They can't do too much for us, and we loved them as we were promised we would in our blessings.

Arrival at Rock Hill S.C.

When we arrived at Rock Hill Dec 18, 1908. Elder S. T. Blue a Lamanite met us and brought us down here. It was quite a relief to get out of the train and ride out in the mild evening fresh air, after 9 days most of the time on the train or in hotels. The ride was novel – in the evening and it was my first experience going thru the woods and deeper & deeper into the woods. Tall pines – close to each other.

Everything seemed so new and strange. After about 2 hrs. ride we arrived at the Catawba Indian Nation. A reservation of 652 acres. There are are about 130 all told children and all. Many of them are half cast. Very few resemble Indians at all.

I was very much surprised to meet the crowd who were met at Bro. Jno. Browns to welcome us. Not a trace of Indian accent or manner of dress or habits like they are in the west. They speak and sing & dress much as we do. Some have been away to school for 5 & 7 years and are well behaved & in every way intelligent. All seem bright and learn readily and anxiously.

During the first month while we stayed at Bro Brown"s they came in often to talk & sing spenc evening. Bro Brown had an organ and they did enjoy hearing me play it.

Our home builded

Where were we to live was the perplexing question. Bro. Brown had eleven in family and we 8 in family so a house of his rooms besides a cook room was pretty well filled. the first week we cooked over the fire place – a very novel experience, and something I couldent learn very readily. People here prefer the fireplace in general. I don't. After about a week our furniture came from Columbia and we were quite comfortable in the one room, which they vacated for us to use. they way did not seem clear before us to find a place to live. Every house had from one to three families in it and I would hate

to think of living in one of them were they empty. No windows in most of them and not the least comfort or convenience. It was very plain that the Indians were not in circumstances to build a house for missionary purposes since they could not build one for themselves. At a meeting of the council of the chiefs they decided to give a building spot across the street from the church where it would be handy. Orlando proffered to furnish the cho cash to buy the seasoned lumber nails doors, window, paint & c and the Indians agreed to get logs to the saw mill near by sufficient for making the frame work also they would all turn out and build it. Some were good carpenters by trade. John Sanders was a good over seer and gave his time & talent freely. In about three weeks two nice rooms with closet and pantry were ready for us to move in. Orlando worked every day with them and tho we had to line it and paper & paint it after we moved in we were very thankful when we had our family private for I was very anxious to have my children as much to themselves as possible since I could plainly see it would never do to let them mix up too much with the children here and it was our intention to have them play with each other and be friendly but not intimate with the children here. We all soon had "buggie tops" and it took considerable care and trouble to get rid of them which we did in short order – the bugs. When our house was finished I stood on the hill to the east. I recognized exactly the same looking house surrounded by trees in the midst of the forest which had been shown to me in vision before we left home as related heretofore.

Sister Browns vision of us, Buying furniture in Columbia S.C.

Old sister Brown told us soon after we came of a dream she had three years before we came. In this she saw this same house and our family going over to it. she had related this to her son Bro Blue & he verified it to us. This all led us to feel that the Lord overruled the coming of our family here and that he would bless us in our labors if we only did our part – he would do His. While we were in Columbia waiting while Pres. Pasket sent word to the Indians to meet us at Rock Hill – just before leaving the city I felt impressed to ask Orlando if I should not go and see what I could do for second hand furniture. He consented to keep the children & away I went with a prayer in my head – for divine guidance. I was going down the street and something said to me - go over there. I turned at once and walked across the street right into a furniture store. They had some furniture which they had taken from someone moving away I suppose and wanted it out of their way badly. Well they had just exactly what we needed. It only took me about half an hour to arrange for the desired articles to be shipped to Rock Hill.

The prices I will always think were to suit our particular case. The idea of getting an almost new washer & wringer for a dollar – sewing machine for five dollars –a good one too. organ 20.00 two good bedsteads and springs for 7.50 – a table extention – for 3.00 and 7 chairs for 3.50 - & other things accordingly. It seemed remarkable because if we had waited till we got in Rock Hill we would have been obliged to pay at least 3 times as much for the outfit. In this I bear testimony that the Lord knew the conditions and also knew our very great expense bringing our big family so far and blessed us

temporally and spiritually. Oh I wish I could overcome all the weaknesses of the flesh and live so He would always be my guide thru lifes breakers.

The school

Bro Ben Harris a full-blooded Catawba – with brains enough for a senator or lawyer – was teaching the school when we came. He had never been to school, but self educated. He is a great reader & thinker and was doing his best to get the children to read & write and spell correctly.

I let Leone visit one day & she said they sat around a big table and do their best. Each one might recite when he or she had learned a lesson and no system prevailed. Bro Harris gave the school over to Orlando about the middle of January.

Orlando – teacher of the school

The situation was not very encouraging. The first thing he did was put up some lumber shelves to write upon & get some blackboard. The house itself was comfortable but had a no furniture. Bro Harris had been getting a salary and some proposed giving O. remuneration out of the school fund. This he refused to take preferring to see they buy a room full of new desks and books & c. this was done and we now see a room prepared for school better than any for miles around. A bitter opponent to our faith wrote to the Legislature the next setting and objected to the mormon preacher getting away with the Indian money. It happened that the chief and Mr Bordon both non-mormon were there in the interest of the tribe and both openly & strongly refuted the statement. But it was a good thing we did not take any pay. It had a good effect on our cause tho people could not comprehend how a man could work for nothing & board himself and family It was a good lesson on Mormonism. there was only one family who were too hostile to send their children to school.

Sunday School

All the Indians love to go to meetings it seems.

The first Sunday School we attended proved to us that much room there was for improvement. they had the taking turns at reading. And as a result not much accomplished, in either of the classes.

Ben Harris

Orlando & I were put in charge of the two classes and it was not long till we had the plan running according to the S.S. outlines. The lesson given then questions answered by (illegible). It was not long till they could assist in this and soon took up & appreciated the better way. Elder S. T. Blue a half white & half Indian was Supt. He did well indeed and is anxious for better ways. Secy. Ben Harris is a very intelligent man and is studious in his habits in every way. He is very witty and clever. Like Bro Blue he has a good understanding of the gospel but Bro Ben had the advantage since Bro. blue could not read much tho he had a wonderful power of remember and was a very good listener when the elders were preaching. He has an opportunity of defending the principles of often as enquiry is often made of him when at Rock Hill with a load of wood or cotton about the mormons down here. He is an elder and has great faith in the Lord in administering the sick and wonderful inspiration in his speaking. He and Bro Barrus labor here as missionary companions and are very much attached to each other and
have been from the first.

Bro. Blue & John Brown

Bro. John Brown is assistant to Bro Blue. He is a firm believer in the church and has reformed greatly since the elders have brought the gospel message here. He loves the gospel well enough to leave off tobacco and liquor and is trying to overcome what he calls his bad temper. Bro Robert Harris is firm in the faith and is quite talented in music, is a brother of Bro Ben and is also a great reader. the people old and young patronized the SS and meeting and the few who were not members attended quite regular ally. this was especially true of those who had a testimony of the truth and had been cut off the church on account of immorality.

Morals

Until the last 25 years no attempt was made at marrying. After the custom of Indians keeping house together was just as good as a marriage. The elders first came here about 25 yrs. ago and taught them to marry & live lawful according to the morals of the church teachings. Some were disfellowshipped for such things but still the spirit of the Lord never ceased to strive with them, and they would defend the church & bear strong testimony. Five of the eight who were in that condition have now joined the church again having fixed things up and are trying to live right.

It used to be no uncommon thing for a family of six to have three or four different fathers – and indians way of living which they thought all right until taught better.

Night school

Our new house with large double window in the south-west end was quite a novelty to these people as most of their houses have no windows and on a rainy day the shutters must be closed and the fireplace answer for the suns rays. We were very thankful for our comfortable temporary home when we could see so many around us without many of the common necessaries, we would think. During the winter of 1908 and 1909 Bro Barrus taught the school and at night I assisted him in the work at the night school, which we had here at the house. Quite a number of the older people came in and we did what we could to get them to learn reading and writing.

Singing practice

Sunday nights we had a singing practice here at the house because the organ was here & none yet at the church. It was well patronized and they learned a great many hymns and songs for S.S. and meetings. They are unusually apt at music – learning to sing several new songs some times in one practice.

Prohibition

It was nothing unusual when we first came to hear some certain ones in a drunken brawl – often using guns. One night I was very frightened when one chased his wife and children out with a gun and followed here to find her. Bro Barrus & Bro Blue labored often with this class and before the winter was over such things were very rare. There are no saloons here but whiskey is shipped in by any one who wants to send to another state & have it expressed to them.

The weather

The weather was quite a change from that up home where snow covered every thing for about five months. We had not snow at all during the winter months and it did not seem like winter to see the children play out side with wraps on nearly every day, often bare headed yet comfortable.

It looks odd to see icicles freeze straight up out of the ground during a cold spell also to freeze on the leaves as fast as the rain falls until large pine trees become top heavyand fall broken to the ground.

The winds are very piercing the air being o so heavy and damp. It is only about 500 feet above sea level here and it is about 5,500 up home.

Farming

In early March of 1909 they began plowing and getting ready for farm work and the school continued until they had to keep the children out to help plow plant & hoe. In this country all hands must work early and late to bring any successful crop out of this red clay rocks and stumps. Surely they earn their bread by the sweat of their brow. They plow with a little plow more like scratching with a stick around the rocks & stumps. The must buy tons of fertilizer and work it with the soil then turn it over after every rain storm for it rains so swift & hard that the soil is packed like a brick as soon as the sun shines again, and then the seeds cant get up thru the crust or send out roots until it is loosened again. One man said the soil there was too poor to raise the dead.

They farm the top and sides of the hills in patches where they have cleared the timber away.

They must continually keep sprouting or the farm would soon go back to forest.

Five acres is a big patch and requires more hard labor than 50 acres at home, to get a crop of cotton as compared with our dry farm land or even the alfalfa irrigated land crops.

Horse flesh here is hard to get & keep as so few of these folks can raise their feed and corn is so high to buy. The extent of their farming is rated by as, a one hoss farm or a two hoss farm.

Cotton

It is very interesting to see their ancient ways of doing things – To see the cotton planted – growing and harvested. The cotton looks like a bean plant at first – then it grows up to a bush like plant from 1 ½ feet to 3 feet high according to the fertilizing. Each plant has from 15 to 150 blossoms and later cotton bowles as they call them. When mature they burst and the cotton hangs out as if to invite you to pick it up before it falls to the ground. Corn and Cotton are the main products there. It was interesting to see a cotton patch in the harvest season. Negroes from a distance looked like a black

flower among the white cotton boles. It is a common thing to see a basket or box under the bushes with a nursing baby waiting for its meal & its nurse.

Negroes sing as they work and keep time with their hoes or as they gather cotton. Many white families work in cotton also.

When time for dinner comes they all rest while mother gets the dinner, then all out in the field again "Everybody rests but mother." Very few white families own land. In the fall it is a common thing to see a light wagon drawn by one horse sometimes two, with iron beds a small table, boxes & bedding – all their earthly possessions – share croppers. It often happens that these croppers have all the next years wages spent before the crop is planted. The man who hires them owns a store and gives credit on

next years crop. The land owner has in this way has them obligated.

Bro Blue's cotton

Bro Samuel T. Blue was the main man in the Catawba tribe. He owned three mules & a cow. He pd. his tithing strictly – kept the commandments in every way. At one time after he had taken his bales cf cotton to mar. he discovered that they had pd. him 10.00 too much. they next day he called on the buyer at Rock Hill and handed the money back. The mistake had not been discovered. In answer to the question of surprise about his honesty he explained the stand of the mormon people.

Everybody trusted Bro Blue. He was healed by the administration of the elders when his leg had been broken and crushed. It became infected – turned black & Drs said it must be cut off. His family had great faith. They were fine characters

Bro Blues Testimony - The last money found

Pine trees grew very tall & straight. The indians sawed them into blocks & hauled them to Rock Hill for fire wood. Tho Bro blue could neither read or write he was very good in mental arithmetic – had a very good memory. Once he was requested by a number of the indians to bring a small amounts of little articles from the stores at Rock Hill where he sold his wood. Trusting to his memory. 10 & 15 cts worth of this or that. as they came out as he passed he put the change in his pocket. When nearly to Rock Hill he decided to count the money. It was all jolted out of his pocket. He know the indians had confidence in him & walked down the road looking for it. He kneeled down and ask the Lord to show him where to find it. After going a few steps he saw it in a pile by the road. He said the surprising thing about it was that the half dollars were on the bottom of the pile then the quarter, nickels & the dimes on top. He felt sure unseen hands had put the money there in the pile. Bro Blue was a presiding elders one of the Catawba Chiefs.

He and Orlando worked together in many ways – administering to the sick & c. Many were healed. I used to visit the sick a lot, & learned that the greatest favor I could do for them was to take them some of my home made bread & fresh buttermilk. They used biscuits mostly. Pres Callis ask me to teach them make yeast bread. I did & Some of them made good bread.

Nancy Harris

Pres Callis advised me to use my influence to get them to make yeast bread as so many of them had stomach trouble due he said partly to so much bad bread & not enough vegetables in the diet. I believe I succeeded somewhat. Nancy Harris a white woman used to bring a slice of her bread over as proud as can be. She made good bread.

Nancy md an indian – had a firm testimony and had faith to be healed many times while we were there.

One day she came over and ask me if I would pour some oil – she called it aile on her sore finger. After I saw it had proud flesh in I advised her to wash it with a good disinfectant instead of oil.

her faith

The next day she came over again and said "Sister Barrus wont you please let me have just a little aile." I could see that I had made a mistake so I said of course I will. As I poured it on I saw her lips move and I knew she was praying. in abt three days she held her finger up and said I knew the Lords holy consecrated oil would heal it. Ordinarily it would have taken at least 10 days or more. it was an awful looking finger.

Those saints were most interesting and sincere. We used to buy oil quarts of it and never charge them for it. They had faith to use it for every kind of illness. We were glad to fill their bottles.

When I was sick she brot me a bowl of mulligan stew. In it was – a squirrels upper jaw – part of a possum – bacon & c & c. I thanked her and didn"t eat it. They liked it, and are anxious to help make us feel at home.

I heard her tell of having an awful toothache and after being administered to they never did ache again and they were rotted 7 worn to the roots.

I found that she lived up to the light she had quite perfectly.

Ben Harris

Ben Harris was quite a leader – one of the 5 chiefs.

He had a family of about 10 children. His wife did the best she knew. Some of them were bright – some only medium. He was a good speaker and conversationalist.

He had a brow like Webster and a rare ability to remember what he read. Tho self-educated he taught the school after we went home. when Thayer was born he proved his wit & humor. It was on Sunday. At Sunday school and someone told him there was another indian on the reservation born this morning. He answered Jesus was born in a stable but that"s no sign he was a donkey.

Ben like most of the indians was a good singer and never wearied of singing the songs of Zion.

He was quite choice of speech and like the other indians he used no slang or profanity. Speaking of a farmer near the reservation Ben said he was so lazy he hired a [negro] to bat his eyes for him.

How firm a foundation

One incident I must relate as it was impressive & faith promoting.

A few days after arriving at the reservation, I became somewhat discouraged and I lay on the bed & shed a few tears.

Not being able to get good milk for my 17 month old baby (Lera) she became ill. Not having a cow and unable to get a house to live by ourselves & c & c. I was exhausted too from the trip & all. As I lay there a voice seemed to sing in my ear a part of the song.

Fear not I am with you, Oh be not afraid

For I am thy God and will still give thee aid,

I'll strengthen thee help thee

And cause thee to stand

Upheld by my richeous

Omnipotent hand.

If thru the deep water Ive called thee to go – The river of sorrow

Shall not thee overflow

For I will be with thee

They troubles to bless

And sanctify to thee

Thy deepest distress.

I

The soule that on Jesus

Has leaned for repose

Ill never no never desert to his foes

That soule tho all hell

Would endeavor to shake

Ill never no never no never forsake.

My spirit was immediately calmed and courage renewed. I will always love that hymn.

Our cow

One of the first things we did was to try to buy us a cow. They were hard to find. Very few families had more than one cow or one donkey.

Their property was sized up as having "a one hoss farm or a two hoss farm," and one asks another – How many patches do you farm. A patch is an acre or two where trees and underbrush has been cleared for cotton planting.

Orlando and Clark our 8 yr old boy took tracts and day after day went outside the reservation to look for a cow. They found one across the river with a young calf. I think they pd 25.00 for them.

They got the cow in the water & she followed the ferry boat where they had the calf.

We were then at Browns place.

They found it slow work trying to get them to their destination following a narrow trail thru the woods.

Clarks faith

They were overtaken by a very heavy rainstorm and it did pour down. The low part of the river bed was swampy and they could not tell which way they were going.

Clark was just eight years old and he said "Lets pray Pa" They kneeled down in the swamp together and took turns asking the Lord to show them the way to go home. The rain was still coming down in torrents & of course they were wet through.

John Brown

At Bro Browns where I and the other four children were we were sitting around the open fireplace wondering how ever they could find their way with our cow & calf. all at once Bro Brown said "Im going to meet elder Barrus, and went out in the woods calling at the top of his voice, Elder Barrus!"!

Pa said it must have been two or more miles but he heard & shouted back Hello. He said when the call first came they were headed for the big river & didn"t know it.

For an hour or more they drove thru the woods in directions of the calling until they reached home base.

I know the Lord heard that humble prayer and he used Bro Brown to answer the need.

John Brown, son of sister Brown had curley fine black hair. His mother had a child by several different white men – before she joined the church and learned better.

Sister Brown's vision of us

Bro Sam T. Blue was her son & a better man would be hard to find. It was this sister Brown who had what she called a vision abt us being there with our family.

Bro Blue told Pres Callis who in turn told it to the Church Presidency in the apostles meeting with mission presidents.

At that time Pres Jos. F. Smith turned to apostle Richards and said, "I appoint you to find the family to go to the Catawba reservation. Bro Geo F Richards & Pres Smith were up to Star Valley to Stake conference in 1908 in the summer of that year.

Bro Richards used to live in Tooele and was school trustee when I was teaching there. He was born in Farmington where I was also born.

When I went thru the gate at the tabernacle in Afton to go to the conference, he shook my hand and said, "How would you like to go with your husband on a mission." As he said those words I seemed change to the extent that I did not feel the weight of that child in my arms [Lera 17 months old]. The other little ones around my skirts. Clark 7 yrs Leone 11 Zina 5 Sterling & baby 17 mo. Pa was on an errand seeing abt something or other just then. We had a meeting at noon with Pres. Smith and Bro

Richards & the matter was taken under consideration. The result was we made ready to go and were on our way

Dec 1 1908

Our children in 1908

Leone was 11 yrs – a real pal to me always ready to do anything she could to help in the care of the home or the younger part of the family. I always think of the mission as a goodly part hers for she was so trustworthy and dependable beyond her years.

All the while we were there she stood by me and made it possible for my activities in the church and out among the Lamanites I case of visiting them with Bro. Barrus & c.

The Lord surely will find a way for all things to be accomplished that he wants done if we put faith & works together

She has always been a good girl – always thinking of mother in terms of helpfulness – in every way.

Clark was 7 yrs when we went somewhat large for his age and of a kind disposition. We had no trouble controlling him. When he was 8 yrs old his father baptised him and a group of the catawba indians in the big river of that name.

The reservation was in the bend of said river among the pines. He played with the Indian boys. One time they defended him by saying "He cant help it cause hes white," when one of them said Clark was white trash. That was a common expression among the negroes who really felt superior to white people.

The indians had no association with the negroes. Reservation had many plantations near enough that we could hear them singing at night. They often called at our well to drink as they passed thru the reservation.

We bought the powder and the indians & Orlando dug & blasted our well thru solid rock most of the way – very good water. We often went for a bucket of water & gave tracts to those travelers who called there for a drink. We had to carry water abt a quarter of a mile before we dug the well..

Clark & Leone loved to go to church when Elders came thru there to hold meetings. I think they got a great deal more than we knew they were getting. They always seemed to understand the gospel.

Of course we organized all of the auxiliary organizations and they loved to attend & take part.

I had indians for counselors in Relief society and Primary. Indians presided in Sunday School,

Orland appointed Pres. of Conference

Orlando was Presiding Elder with Bro. S. T. Blue, but the second year he was put in Pres of South Carolina conference and spent a greater part of his time away from home & Bro Blue carried on there. He & Geo. Huskinson – Elder. Bro Huskinson and his wife were with us there about 6 months. They were from Sugar City, Idaho and Pres Callis called them there with us. He was conference secy. and she helped me with the organizations. Catawba was the headquarters while we were there much of the time.

Sterling and Zina were sweet little children – easy to manage and all the while a comfort as was Lera 17 mo old but very little trouble. Our home life was a comfort as it always was. W enjoyed each other & the family

Sterlings illness

I will never forget how happy our meetings would be after he had been to some distant part of the state and when he returned to us again.

Sometimes he came home wet through in rain.

I remember one time we were all sitting around the table in the evening. I remarked several times I was afraid Pa would get sick out in that storm. When he came in later Sterling said "There Mama I told you Papa wouldent go dead."

Sterling was not as alert and strong as the other children. He had leakage of theheart. At one time he had what seemed to be pneumonia

Bro Barrus had an appointment in a distant part of the state and it looked like the trip would be impossible. His fever was so high – lungs so congested & c Bro Blue, Bro Huskinson and all of us fasted & prayed for his recovery.

It really looked as if he was slipping away in spite of all we could do for him. After several days of fasting they administered to him & he was instantly healed. All at once he was made well.

While he was so sick I prayed to the Lord so earnestly & promised the Lord if he would spare the little boy to us until we got home I would be willing to give him up if he could not live to grow up, but not to let him die there – we wanted to remain there till our mission was finished.

After we had been back a few yrs – The Lord called him home.

A new baby – Thayer

He seemed to have a stroke and pains around his heart. he suffered so much. He lived until he was 11 ½ yrs old. A dear little fellow with red hair. I felt sure he was not going to get well and often thot cf the promise I made while in the south conserning him & was reconsiled.

Thayer's birth

On Sept 1st 1909 – Sunday Morning Thayer was born at Catawba S. C. Dr Hill the Indian doctor for the reservation attended me also an old Indian woman we all called Aunt Jane Watts.

Sister Huskinson took care of me while in bed, also the baby. For about a month before he was born I had a gathered breast suffered terribly. When he was 2 weeks old Dr Hill lanced it. Oh my, oh my.

Boils & more boils

While I suffered I prayed that my breast might not be spoiled, for I wanted more babies & nourishment for them as well as him. After 6 weeks milk came into the afflicted one and it served for the 3 youngest of the family. I felt that my prayers were answered eve if it was not until later than I had hoped. I always realized temporary relief when I was administered to – often the pain eased and I dropped off into a sleep.

For abt 3 weeks we poultice my breast and finally it healed but my system to be cleansed by boils.

I wonder about the number Job had. I counted till 40 then did not keep track. Some were large carbuncles others just ordinary – but every one – oh my – just boils.

I was Poisened & healed

The indians said they saved me a sickspell.

We used to buy 25 lb boxes of dried prunes – nectarines as we could not get fresh fruit enough for the family.

I had the habit of eating them first thing in the morning. One day I put my hand in the box for a nectarine and I heard a whisper in my ear – "wash the fruit before eating it" I did not heed the prompting, as I was in a hurry to get breakfast over.

After a few hrs I began to get very sleepy & dumpish in a most unnatural way.

The indians had told us that was the way "Rough on rats" affected a rat or a person, then after a long sleep – great pain and death followed, for it is a rank poisen.

We remembered putting "rough on rats on some baits on another shelf to get the pesky rats.

While we kept a lid on the box of fruit there was a knot hole large enough for a rat to get & apparantly they had pulled the paper out that I had pushed into this hole and crawled into the box carrying the poisen on their feet

Well I was apparently poisened by some of it.

There we were abt 2000 miles from home with 5 little children – on a mission.

healed thru faith

Orlando gave me a swallow of consecrated oil and at my request humbly sought the Lord for help – he rebuked the poisen from my system and I bear testimony that the effects of it cleared away almost immediately.

The Lord forgave me for not heeding the prompting, and I thank Him for restoring me. I hope Ill listen & obey next time.

Blackberries & chiggers grew in great abundance. It seemed there were abt 10 of the chiggers to every blackberry

The first few berries we had were so good that we decided to bottle them for winter use. We did so and taught the indians how to bottle them. We gave them our bottles when we left for home – later. The chiggers were pests. Just tiny little insects almost invisible. they fastened themselves on the skin and worked under it - & irritated terribly – itch – oh yes. We learned how to head them off – by tying a cord dip in coal oil around our ankles and wrists they dident bother us.

The elders who came to eat with us enjoyed with us the berries with plenty of sugar and rich jersey cream.

We raised sweet potatoes but there irish potatoes did not flourish We planted a bushel once & only harvested a peck.

The people use sweet potatoes for making pie as well as for a vegetable.

We raised lovely beans and peas. We planted peanuts, by covering the blossoms with sod as they blossom close the ground.

Sterling ask why didnt plant candy too. Peanuts are not good to eat till they are roasted.

We used to gather larger nuts and store them for winter.

The children loved to go gathering them in the fall. they grow on large trees. the frost loosens the outer shells & they fall in large numbers.

The Woods

The **Forest Fires** are a great sight. The underbrush grows so rapidly that it became necessary to cut and burn it away around the lot in case a forest fire came our way. One day Robert Harris, an indian, ask if he might do this for us just as a preventative.

He did do it. A few days later a forest fire came just a short distance from our house & if the underbrush had not been burned away no doubt we would have lost everything as there are no fire-fighting helps there to check it. I saw one forest fire that looked like a whole mountain on fire. Pine trees grow very tall and numerous – long leafed pine mile & miles of "woods"

A plantation is a clearing where they raise cotton. If it were not farms in a few years the trees

& underbrush would cause it to go back to a forest condition.

We used to put our baby in the little buggy and stroll thru the woods for a diversion sometime in the summer evenings. The children loved it especially when we took lunch and called it a party. We gathered nuts. At first I was afraid of snakes but we only a few bad ones.

Visit to Columbia & Charleston

When Thayer was a babe in arms we went to Columbia to attend a conference of the elders. It was not a new experience to take a baby with me on a trip. I had a parcel of a complete outfit for him fresh for every day & got along fine. A very fine conference. Pres Callis treated us with great consideration. One of the Indian women stayed with Leone at the home with the other children.

We also took a trip to the coast when he was abt. a yr. old & visited the saints there.

Pres Callis advised it. It was my first view of the ocean. It was so wonderful.

The Isle of palms

We bought a wicker lunch basket & filled it pretty full of good things to eat and took a trip on a big ship out to the Isle of Palms

It was June and Ill never forget how good the strawberries & cream – a ripe pineapple and cakes & c did taste out there on that Island.

Palm trees were all around and flowers usually found in the windows at home were growing in the gardens so large & more beautiful. We spent all afternoon there. We passed Morro Castle where the first gun of the Civil war was fired.

Sister Dupont

We stayed at the home of a sister Dupont.

She told us of an accident. Her little girl fell into some glass cutting her face and her eyes. They feared for her eyes being blinded.

Sister Dupont wrapped the childs face & sat in a rocker holding the child for days and nights she said. Praying for the Lord to send the elders to administer to it. She had not called the doctor because she thot it entirely too bad a case for any but the great physician. She knew they would come.

Two elders travelling in another part of the state were impressed by the spirit to go to Charleston at once they told Sister Dupont when they arrived at her home.

She testified to us that when they took the bandages off the little girls face the cuts were well and both eyes were open normally. Sister Dupont She was one of the temporal blessing – a missionary"s mother to many many elders who had made her home their head quarters while in Charleston.

The city itself is an old old one. the main street a is about the shape of a letter S. some one said they used to build the first houses on a cow trail and other streets just an off-shoot from it – with not much consideration for the points of the compass.

While in Charleston we saw old cannons which had been used in the civil war also Fort Sumpter where the first gun in the Civil war was fired. Joseph Smith prophesied that this war would start in S.C. many years before it happened.

Whipped but not conquered

I think it was in South Car. that we saw the first movie in 1909. in Charleston as in other parts of the south the Negro population is increasing faster than the white.

At one time I talked with an old negro who came to our door to sell fish.

He said he was a slave and did not want to be free. He loved his master and he would have been happier in serving than otherwise on his own. His master was kind to him.

Our mailman told us that his grandfather was ruined when the slaves were freed as they had been paid for and when they were freed his field went back to undergrowth trees with no on e to hoe the field. One old man said of the war – "We were whipped but not conquered" by the north.

The occasion when I talked with the southern ex civil war veteran was when I went to Rock Hill with Orlando to buy the material for building our house. I was waiting for him in the office at the lumber yard. The soldier noticed our western accent & ask where we were from & c.

I enjoyed answering his questions abt the west – and our mission to the reservation.

I found out from him that the people of the south still had a feeling of dislike almost hate for the north.

This condition prevails I think mainly among the uneducated class, among the older ones, who experienced the war itself.

As we would go to rock hill every week or two – to buy provissions we had many experiences. If Bro Blue even heard a hint that we needed to go to the store his horse & buggy would be at our door as soon as he could get it there – a true friend indeed. We often took all the children with us. They thot it a real treat to go to the city with us.

Sometimes we would leave at noon on a clear day and in an hour a small cloud would be seen & before we could drive the 10 miles the sun would be hidden entirely and the thunder & lightning would warn us to find shelter till the down pour was over.

I dident just rain in came down like a sheet of water.

The white plantations

The hospitality of the southerner is proverbial. Their houses are often surrounded by a wide porch, two story porches. I was told that they sleep on the upper porches in hot weather. When Orlando would enquire if we might sit on the porch thru the shower they made us ever so welcome.

I think it was a rare opportunity for us to answer their questions abt the Mormon question. We usually carried tracts and no doubt sowed seed which might bear fruit some day.

Deep gullies would be washed in the road – few good high ways at that time.

share croppers

It was interesting to see the share croppers jogging along with all their belongings in a smal wagon.

Their few household belongings & 6 or eight children peeping thru the cover going from one cabin to another.

The plantation owners often have a number of such cabins for their hired help. They have sort of a supply house on the plantation and tho not slaves they are nearly always using up next years crop pay to live on this year, so that they are not free to leave because the debt holds them where they are.

Our Well

Negroes seem to be more numerous than white people. We often passed negro churches where grave yards were just out side the church. We could hear the negroes singing as they hoed or picked cotton. They are lovely singers, they would call at our well for a drink of good water as they passed thru the reservation but they showed us every respect.

The Indians understood how to blast 7 dry a well tho there was none there untill ours. We bought the powder and they dug the well of good water.

Only a few inches of good soil covered the lava rock formation. The hilly surface there was pretty well washed by the heavy rainfall, so the hollows were the best places for a garden. We had one in a near by hollow.

When passers by called at our well Pa would empty the bucket of water in the reservoir & pickup a handful of tracts & offer them to the caller

Our baby buggy

The last year we were there Pa was called to preside over the conference. This took him away from home a good part of the time.

Bro & Sister Huskinson were called by Pres Callis to come to the reservation & help with the office work. He was secretary & she helped me in the organizations which we carried on for abt 6 months during which time Thayer was born.

When we bought the furniture a baby buggy was included. So when Pa would go off to visit a conference & we were expecting him back I would put Lera & Thayer in the little buggy and we would go from ½ to a mile in the direction he came from – to meet him.

Hunting hazel nuts

I like to think of those time when we would see him in the distance how Clark & Leone & Zina would shout. There is Papa. He often brot a treat for them.

Those are happy memories.

The Catawba Junction was abt 5 miles away & he would walk that distance home.

He had to flag the train there. in the fall of the year we used to hunt hazel nuts in the woods

They are grown in a shell something like walnuts grow. The frost cracks this outer shell & they fall out of it.

We could get any ammount & store for future use.

A baby buggy for Lera & a sack of nuts to bring back. We would take a picnic basket and enjoyed everything and each other

The catawba river was a slow moving stream abt a quarter of a mile wide. After several days of rain, it would be a mile wide & more. Pa & Bro blue took us across it in a boat one time. We saw an old mill where Civil war people used to grind meal for the soldiers.

The soil on river-bottom land is very rich and the indians raise fine crops of corn there for years at a time then an unusual ammount of rain fall will cause the water to cover the corn & those good people can be seen in little boats gathering as many stalks as they can pull into their canoes to dry & use for food.

They cut hay on river bed for their horse & cow with a scythe. One or two small loads a day is considered a good days work. They just take these things for granted & seldom complain.

Very few of them have more than one horse or mule and only part of them own a cow. One of their main items of food is their turnip patch planted to they gather turnip greens winter & summer.

Bro Blue told us of having his leg broken & blood poisen setting in. It turned purple & the Dr said it much be cut off above the knee. He refused to have it done but prayed for the elders to come. Without any appointment two elders were impressed to come to his home & administered to him. He was healed & went to church the next sunday walking all the way. Truly a miracle.

Bro Blue used to haul wood to Rock Hill abt once a week. He was sort of a father to the whole tribe the main chief. The indians used to send for little & big items by him to the stores & he felt that he owed it to them to do this for them. One time they had given Bro blue several dollars & since he could not read or write he used his wonderful memory to buy & bring to the indians the needed items. As he jolted along the money dropped out of his pocket. He prayed Lord show me where to find that money. After his prayer he took a few steps & found every cent of it in a pile – dollars at the bottom then

halves, quarters & nickels & dimes just as neatly as tho they had been done by human hands.

I heard him bear this testimony & I know he told the truth. Bro Blue is a man God loves. An indian but a good upright one. when our mission was over he took us to the train & cried like a child to see us leave.

He said I love the very ground they walk on.

We had raised chickens or they raised themselves – stole their nests & brot all we could take care of to our coop & we had plenty to eat & enjoyed the eggs too for we had lots of visitors to cook for.

Elders came often on an excuse to get Orlando''s advice & to see the English speaking indians.

Orlando's birthday. 29 May 1909

I remarked to sister Huskinson abt the date & she said it is my husband''s birthday,too. We had a real celebration. Two other pair of elders happened along and the 8 of us partook of every thing we could cook from chicken to lemon pie. That extention table came in just fine for 8 missionaries and our 6 children 14 in all.

Forest Fires

We saw a number of forest fires Pines grew so close together and it was a marvelous sight when a whole mountain side was afire. An Indian suggested to us that we burn the underbrush around the house. We did & if we had not it would have been burned as a forest fire was in line a few days after.

Elders meetings

The elders used to come thru the reservation often and hold meetings several days at a turn.

The indians would leave their work & fill the meeting house Our children would go too and pay good attention.

We helped them to buy a church organ & I played for their services & I did for all the gatherings. They would help me sometimes at noon with a quick dinner. How they did enjoy the rich milk & cream gravies we had. Only a few people there had a cow never more than one.

When I ask to buy irish potatoes – the price of a bushel the clerk at Rock Hill said I have never sold a bushel to one buyer They think them a luxury Sweet Potatoes are their hobby. Potatoes from Maine were ours.

Celebrations in Catawba

The 4th of July does not mean much to the people in Southern States.

The elders who came to our home told us that in the largest cities the 4th was just another day.

We had a special program on July 4th and gave talks abt Declaration of Independence. The Indians helped us to prepare a barbacue and they all joined in a picnic around a long table under the shade trees. Xmas time fire crackers are their great delight.

They have what they call a "play" sometimes. Some one plays a fiddle or mouthorgan & they all join in a reel & enjoy it. Lunch & C. They love to sing & are good singers.

Before we were there it was customary for them to get on a drunk at Xmas day fun. We arrived there just a short time before Xmas and were shocked t hear a big racket over to the neighbors home. The Sanders boys had a quarrel and used knives & guns.
We were very frightened.

John Brown, was sober & tried to get Mr. Whellock to his home. Wheellock chocked Brown & in the scramble Bro Brown bit off Wheellocks ear.

When Bro Brown came in with his hands covered with blood, we were surely filled with horror.

The next day Orlando took Bro B. over to Wheellocks to see if he could make peace between them, not knowing what the outcome might be for him. Bro B. was willing to be peacable but Wheellock was not a Mormon

A peace maker

I was pretty anxious but Orlando came back in less than an hour.

The first thing Bro Brown said to his foe was – "I"m sorry I bit off your ear Arch. Wheellock said, "I deserved it & if I get drunk again, I wish you would bit the other one off." When they got acquainted with our ideals – they refrained entirely from that drinking habit while we were there.

We were shown every consideration in their power to bestow upon us all the time.

Members & non members came to church & joined in singing. We helped them buy an organ for their church and I helped some of the girls to learn to play hymns.

school at night

Orlando invited all who had a desire to come to night school to meet at our home. Only a few of the older ones could read We had night school thru the winter months. They learned rapidly.

All they need is opportunity. They are anxious to learn in every way.

When the time came for us to leave the Indians fairly wept – some of them. they like us had learned to love each other . When I was set apart for the mission it was said, "You will learn to love them. We sold our organ for 10.00 to a negro and most of the articles for housekeeping for abt what we had paid for them 2nd hand. We gave dishes & such things to them. They prized everything

Leaving for home

Nancy Harris came over and helped me make up half a dozen lunch boxes with chicken sandwiches & c. We fried fleshy parts to all the chicken we could use and gave the rest to them dead & alive. The elders who were to take over to preside were there and besides getting six children & the two of us all ready to leave I had to get dinner over for visitors & us & be off to the meet the train in Rock Hill soon after noon.

I was exhausted indeed. Im sure I was at the near end of my endurance.

Several of the Indians went with us to Rock Hill depot. When the train pulled out we could not find dear Bro Sam Blue. They said he was behind the house crying & couldent say goodbye. We will look for him in Heaven.

The two extra large trunks that we took with us and the roll of bedding were all tied up O.K. & I found the only thing left out was my 12 silver knives & forks & spoons. I must not leave them.

Orlando opened up a trunk & dumped them all in the till on top of the girls summer hats I had packed so carefully.

When we arrived home we had a good laugh, the forks & the straw hats had apparently enjoyed themselves. It look like a pile of straw in a flower garden.

It was quite an experience on the way home. We came an entirely different route.

We went north to Chicago then west.

Blue Ridge Mts

Going thru the blue ridge mts was awful. So many tunnels

the smoke would fill the car & abt the time it cleared & could breathe easy, we would run into another tunnel. but we saw things – even some oxen pulling loads of wood in Virginia. I could imagine elders visiting country districts to those home up on those side hills. Very little level space for homes in the Blue Ridge country. Their RR stations seemed 100 years behind ours in contrast.

When we left home Lera was 1 ½ yrs old & when we were on our way home every now & then when the trains changed she would say, "Is this home."

In Chicago

In the south Negroes had a separate car from the Whites. As we neared the Chicago, both classes rode in the same cars.

Those negros were real cocky. They are not the least bit like Indians who are invariably humble, and can ride or sit in a theatre where they choose.

We made quite a line up in Chicago. Six children in an enormous station. Pa went out to find a hotel where we could spend a few days & rest up. He dident find one. The children were good to mind & behaved well.

In a hotel

I gave him the baby, Thayer, after I had nursed him & c & told him I would try my luck. I was impressed to ask the guide in the station for the address of a hotel with a mormon proprietor. I found one abt 2 blocks from the depot.

She said they could not have children there. I said are you a mother she answered oh yes. Then I said put your self in my place with six little tired children would you want a place to put the to bed? Oh yes yes come bring them in." I told her they were too tired to make a noise. I gave them a bath & supper & they were soon asleep.

Pa had to go & see abt. the transfer of luggage 7 did not get back till 9-30. I dident sleep. I prayed for him to find his way back safely – The sweetest music every heard was his footsteps coming down the hall that night.

The room we got was an extra & with extra bedding all slept on the floor but we knew the Lord was watching over us & protected us

He never will forsake those who trust him. I know.

We took the children out to Jackson Park to see all kinds of animals & tropical plants growing in hot houses. Tea Coffee bannanas oranges & c. We had quite a time getting on & off street cars as they only stopped still long enough for a grown person to hop on & off.

Strangers would say – Are they all yours, and gasp.

We crossed a swinging bridge over Chicago river.

While preparing for the trip home I had made black sateen dresses and bloomers for the girls and trimmed with red ribbon – the boys with blouses to match. We stepped in a completely fresh outfit & left our old clothes there at Catawba.

At home again

The Church paid us 200.00 for our house & with that cash we were enabled to buy furniture to replace the things we sold to begin housekeeping again in the home in Fairview.

Uncle Emery met us at the depot in Montpelier with a big white top carriage. It was cold but we had plenty of wraps. When we passed a pasture in Fairview where a band of horses were feeding one young horse came running whinning to the fence & tried to jump over. It was one we had raised from a colt & sold. It actually seemed to know us after 2 years.

Readjustments – Oh yes – plenty of them. While we were gone someone had tried to jump our dry farm. We had spent the 2,000 we had raised to with & used the last 25.00 we had left of it to fight a law suit to hold our claim on the hill.

Ruth born June 1911

We won, but had to refile and live seven out of 12 mo. for the next few yrs.

We would like to have settled in our comfortable home but had to have a new kind experience.

We could only guess who it was who made this new trouble for us.

There was a cabin on the dry farm and we built a room on front of it for a living room with a bedroom over head and a lean to on the front for a cookroom. The log room also for a bed room.

Ruth was born 6 mo after we came home so now there were 9 of us. in those close quarters was a lot of fun_ Sometimes 17 meals during breakdowns & rain & c.

Cooking for the threshers
giving music lessons

We rented in Fairview for the 5 mo between dry farm seasons and left the home vacant again –

the new house

We prepared the old house in Fairview as well as the one on the dry farm.

Weve always tried to make the place we lived in look as cosy as was in our power. While we were living across the street from the church there I had as many music pupils as I could find time to teach. I earned two dandy pair of all woollen blankets, a baby buggy & a dresser giving piano lessons. It was a common thing for me to wrap a baby up & go out in the wind & snow & give a lesson or two in the evening. Quite an experience two moves a year on the dry farm & off again with the family. How I have always appreciated my darling husband in all the changing vicitudes we met – so true so helpful – dependable so faithful.

Orlando – High council In 1910 & Bp of the Ward 1912

In 1910 he was called into the High Counsil.

In 1912 he was set apart as a Bishop of Fairview. The call came in Conference.

By this time I was building up hopes of our going to Logan to work in the temple and

when this call came to him I went out to our white top buggy & cried a real cry of disappointment. I knew it was the last thing in the world Orlando would desire.

Uncle Emery said, "Dont cry Mamie, It isn"t life imprisonment."

Stake Boards

I became reconsiled and tryed in every way to help him as he tried to help me in the things I was called upon to do. He made a good bishop, and served abt 12 years

He was loved by every one even by one or two old cats – she cats – good to his face & snarlers at his back – always a few like that.

We wore out 4 buggies and two white top carriages during the time we lived in Star Valley, before we had a car, also several bible & other church books for we both taught Sunday School class and held stake positions as well. During the 20 years I served on the stake board of Primary before our mission & the mutual after returning, I drove many hundreds of miles with a baby on my lap – sometimes two or 3 others tucked in besides.

I never had a child get sick from taking such trips but often brought them home feeling better than they were when I started. I lived on the end of the line & very often took other members of the board on trips to visit organizations or to help hold conferences.

I was counsellor in the Mutual to Maria Allred in the ward & she chose one counsellor when she was Stake Pres of Primary.

Sometimes in cold weather I have come home after bed time too cold to take off my shoes & Orlando would put me in bed & after I warmed up take my shoes off. Eight of our 9 children were born in Star Valley – Thayer while we were in Southern States.

Looking backward 1950
I love flowers

I have always loved flowers. I remember when we first bought the Sprague place in Star Valley, how we planted trees all around it – planted lawn & a border of perennials – pansies – sweet Williams & c. A yellow rose bush by the south kitchen window. I had windows filled with geraniums – begonias – lilies & c. One night the dog pushed the door open in March & the plants all froze. I felt so dissapointed. Some time afterward I had a dream I saw a large house & said to Orlando who planned this 7 he said, I did. There were nice flowers in front of it & a voice said, "Now you may have

all the flowers you want."

Surely that has been fulfilled when we lived 17 years with all the beautiful flowers on temple hill right in front of our door. That big appartment house was Orlando"s planning not mine but it was a blessing to us. While we lived there we were able to make it almost pay for itself & furnish us 3 rooms to live in besides. Four 2 room apts to rent to students & c

We made many lasting friends. After living in it 17 years we sold it for about what we paid for it. Of course we made improvements many of them.

Keeping up the apts – papering painting and renewing fixtures & all got to strenuous. During those years it was a common thing for us to be papering a room at 10 or 11 oclock at night. We sold it to Bro Woodbury. Laurence bought our dry farm in 19__ and we finished paying for the apt house and we had a chance to buy this nice bungaloo on 275 blvd.

It is certainly a dream of a lifetime come true. It is furnace heated & we can wash & dry our clothes down in basement. I always thot basements & c were for others, not for me, but now it has come for us & we do appreciate it.

I often tell Orlando that I am enjoying the reward he earned when he slept 3 ½ years under the palm trees with his bible for a pillow while he was on a mission in Samoa. Ill try and deserve the place we have. We are in Logan 11th ward. Wm Horlacher is Bp here.

Leone, Ruth & Merle all live in Logan.

Leones husband died

Jan 7"1949 Laurence Webber passed to the other side simply closed his eyes and went to sleep. They had gone to a home social the night before and enjoyed everything & everyone. They said their prayers before going to bed as usual & laughed as they discussed the party they had enjoyed together. They also discussed the fact that at the beginning of this year he felt good abt having settled his tithing up to date.

It was a fearful shock when Leone spoke to him after he had gone to sleep as she thot & found him lifeless.

They phoned to us that day & we went up on the bus. Arlene was here with us going to the college We arrived there in Freedom abt. nine o'clock at night

It was 50 below and the snow was nearly 3 feet on the level. We found a heartbroken family. It was a terrible shock.

The day after when Sterling & Lanece & Nola & Arlene went up to Afton to arrange some things, I dreaded to see them come back, but they rec"d a testimony while there of the death & came back thoroughly calmed. When Lanece went into the room where he lay she said, „Oh Daddy" & he spoke to her spirit & said "That is not me." He had lived a full life and was ready for a promotion. Bp Robinson spoke at his funeral and said if Laurence ever did a wrong deed I never knew of it & we have associated together all our lives.

April Conference 1950

Samuel Tayler Blue came to Salt Lake to attend Conference. Elders who had filled a mission to the south who knew Bro Blue sent a little contribution for his expenses and he and sister Blue had the privilege of going to the Temple, also.

We went down on Saturday and met him by appointment. Tho it had been 40 years since we were there at the reservation we knew each other & it was a happy reunion. Tears kept coming in his eyes. He is one of God"s noblemen. A man He loves for his unabiding faith and living a life above reproach. I told him if he would take family group sheets and get as many of the dead people as could & send them to us we would have their work done. He spoke in Conference Sunday morning

8th of June Today is the

Elder Orlando Clark Barrus   --   SSM 1920-1922

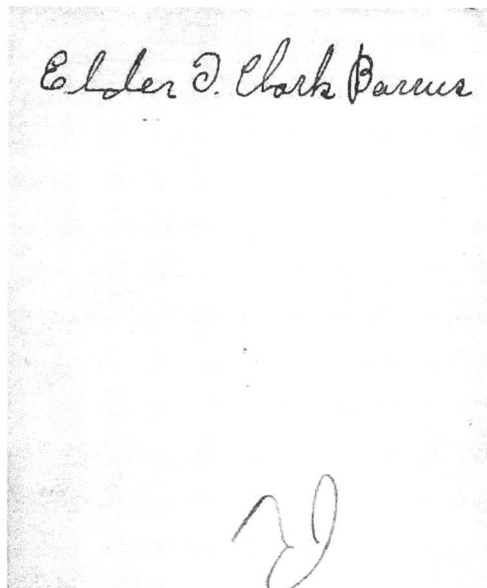

PHOTO 75   ELDER ORLANDO CLARK BARRUS

Birth date, place - 18 August 1902, Fairview, Uinta, Wyoming, United States
Death date - 8 August 1922 -- Died In The Field
Baptism date - 18 August 1909   --   Baptism by - Orrin Orlando Barrus
Father's name - Orrin Orlando Barrus -- Mother's name - Mary Elizabeth Mamie Clark

Southern States -- November 1920–August 1922 - Age Called: 18
Southern States
Set Apart: 16 November 1920 -- Departed From Home: 17 November 1920
End Date: 8 August 1922 -- Died In The Field: 8 August 1922
Mission type: Proselytizing
Marital Status: Single
Priesthood office: Elder
Called From: Fairview, Lincoln, Wyoming, United States
Set apart by: Charles Henry Hart

Ermaline Harris
Lula Blue
Elder Clark Barrus
Vera Blue
May 1922

LIAHONA THE ELDERS' JOURNAL

ELDER ORLANDO CLARK BARRUS MEETS DEATH BY DROWNING.

By Chas. A. Callis, President Southern States Mission.

The hearts of the missionaries are filled with sorrow because of the death of one of our faithful elders. A telegram came to Mission headquarters, Tuesday, August 8, bringing the sad news that Elder Orlando Clark Barrus had been drowned that day in the Chauga river, near Westminster, South Carolina.

The particulars of this distressing accident are as follows: Some members of the Church had arranged a picnic. Elder Barrus and Elder Ben

Elder Orlando Clark Barrus.

S. Riggs, his companion, were invited to take part in it. A few of the party and the elders went bathing in shallow water. Suddenly and unexpectedly, while walking in the stream, Elder Barrus stepped into deep water. Two others of the bathers went with him. With that inbred spirit of service which works against self-interest to benefit one's fellows, he assisted in helping one of them out of the dangerous place.

This effort evidently exhausted him, for while the other one was being rescued he sank and was drowned. In the excitement that prevailed he was overlooked. He was considered a good swimmer. The body was recovered after a search that lasted thirty-five minutes. It was embalmed and brought to Atlanta, where it was prepared for burial to be sent home. President Noel H. Dastrup of the Georgia Conference and Elder M. L. Olsen of the South Carolina Conference

accompanied the remains home. Memorial services were held in the Atlanta chapel Thursday evening, August 10. Appropriate remarks were made by President M. E. Moody and Elder M. L. Olsen of the South Carolina Conference; Elder Noel H. Dastrup, Sister Grace E. Callis and President Chas. A. Callis.

Elder Barrus had labored for twenty-one months in South Carolina. Had he lived ten days longer he would have been twenty-one years of age. His home was in Fairview, Wyoming. Twelve years ago, his father, Orlando Barrus, now bishop of the Fairview ward, and his mother, Mary Clark Barrus, filled a mission in South Carolina. They were stationed in the Catawba Indian Nation. The names and good works of these faithful missionaries are held in affectionate and honorable remembrance by the Lamanite saints. While they were on this mission one of their children was born.

Elder Barrus preached the word in the power of the Holy Ghost and his words went to the hearts of the people, carrying conviction of the truth of the everlasting Gospel. He sounded the Gospel trumpet with no uncertain sound. What he was his clean, upright life, his humility combined with courage in proclaiming the Gospel message, spoke louder than words, and stamped him a faithful minister of Jesus Christ. His missionary labors were blessed of the Lord and his death lamented and mourned by all the missionaries and the people whose hearts and souls he gladdened and blessed with his presence and teachings.

To his Master's service he gave the precious years of his young manhood, and the Father, who keeps and fulfills His promises, will bless him with immortality and eternal life. He stood nobly for the Lord and he will share with all the faithful sons of God in the glories of the resurrection of the just.

Sublime faith—the faith that death cannot extinguish and which survives the sorrow that comes from the death of loved ones, the faith that is a gift from God as well as a holy, trusting spirit of submission to His will—is shown in letters received from Bishop and Sister Barrus since the death of their son. The sacrifice they have made is sacred in the sight of the Lord. We mourn with them in this great sorrow. God doeth all things well. "What I do thou knowest not now," He said, "but thou shalt know hereafter." We pray God to fill the hearts of the bereaved with the peace and comfort which passeth understanding.

To give happiness and to do good, there is our only law, our anchor of salvation, our beacon light, our reason for existing. All religions may crumble away; so long as these survive we have still an ideal, and life is worth living.—*Amiel.*

months old and needed work. She wanted to go back home. Her parents were dead and her older brother and his wife had reared her. Her brother owned a large furniture store in Winston Salem, N.C. and was quite well off. His social position was important to him and he wouldn't let her come home with her baby. Flora (her name) worked for Mae and decided if she could find a good home for her baby she would give him up.

I was ten years old at that time. My folks decided to take the baby. Flora brought the baby boy up to our house and gave him to Papa and Mama after having a sincere talk with them. She was willing to let them adopt him but Papa said no, they wouldn't adopt him but would raise him as they had raised their own, and if she ever married and she and her husband wanted him back, he and Mama would give him back. She said she would not treat them like that. Well, we took the baby and the whole family loved him and gave him our name. We changed his given name which was James Edward. There was already an Edward in the family and they changed it to Julian (Mama's name was Julia) Crews (that was Flora's sir name). Now we had a baby boy to add to our big family—Julian Crews Haney. When Julian come to us he had a digestive problem and couldn't tolerate any of the formulas we tried. Finally, the doctor told us to get a goat and feed him goat milk. Paul and Jason got a nanny goat. She soon had twins. The milk agreed with our baby, and he was soon a healthy, happy little boy.

Those goats were a nuisance but lots of fun. One day someone left the front door open and they went into the house. We had our school books on the stairs. When we heard the goats on the tin roof of the porch running around, we ran up the stairs. They had jumped through the window at the head of the stairs. I don't remember how we got them off but we managed. When we saw what a mess they had made of our books we were flabbergasted! We knew Papa didn't have money to replace all those books for all four of us. (At that time, at our school, we had to furnish all our own books.) The goats had eaten our dictionary too. Somehow we managed. The goats had served their purpose and we got rid of them.

My Bathing Suit. Mamie Edrie Haney, 1924.

It was summertime and the season for our annual family get together. We had a houseful with all our family and Mae's sister and the Mormon elders. We decided to have a picnic at Chauga Creek (it was more the size of a river than a creek). There was a place

page 39

Mamie: Through the Years with Laughter and Tears

where people went swimming with a make shift dressing room by it. Those who wished to do so swam. We "young 'uns" waded around in the shallow water at the edge of the swimming hole.

Preparations were made and early in the morning the wagon was ready—boards were fixed across the wagon box so they wouldn't slip off. The food was stored in the wagon for our picnic. It was cloudy when we started out. Jonah and his family weren't with us; neither was Ed and his family—they were to meet us at the picnic site.

Soon after we started out the rain started. We made it to the cotton gin across town from our home. Papa drove the mules under a wagon shed by the cotton gin where we waited for the rain to stop. Everyone was in a gala mood, having a great time talking and laughing, joking and singing some. One person was not joining in the festivities wholeheartedly—one of the elders was very quiet. He had gotten out of the wagon and was standing by himself—he had an expression on his face as if he were in a deep study about something. Even I, who was only ten years old, noticed it. Papa was very concerned for fear Elder Barrus was ill but when he asked, Elder Barrus only smiled a little and said no, he was fine.

The rain ceased, the clouds broke away and the sun shone through again. Everyone got back in the wagon and off we went. Soon we arrived at the picnic grounds and everyone started having fun. We had lunch and some of the grown ups went swimming. The girls swimsuits consisted of an old dress and underpants. The men wore improvised swim pants. At least everyone was more modest than today's fashions! The elders, Barrus and Riggs, went swimming also.

Effie and Mae's sister, Margie, were playing around in the deep water. Neither of them could swim but they were holding onto one end of a plank while Elder Barrus was pulling the other end walking backwards. Suddenly he stepped into a deep hole. The girls floundered, Margie grabbed Elder Barrus around the neck and wouldn't let loose. He was still trying to hold onto the plank that Effie still clung to. He held onto it for as long as he could. Suddenly he went limp and started under. The last we saw of him was his right hand as it gave a little wave and he was gone. The girls were rescued by some of the older men. Elder Barrus never surfaced again.

Different ones tried to dive down but none could find him. Finally Papa took a rope he had in the wagon with a hook on one end an dived down. It took a little while to find him. Papa fastened the hook in Elder Barrus' swimming suit and started up with him, having the men on shore pulling the end of the rope. By the time they had got him out a doctor was there and also the district president of the

S.C. Mission. Elder Riggs had called them, and had also called President Callis, President of the Southern States Mission.

The doctor worked over him for a long while but wasn't able to a get a drop of water out of his lungs. The doctor thought he had ruptured a major blood vessel just as he stepped down in the hole.

That surely was a sad experience for all. When we arrived home Papa went into the Elders room and saw Elder Barrus' diary on the table lying open to the last entry of the morning. The following is what he had written: "—Today we are going on a picnic with the Haney family for their annual reunion. We have been looking forward to this event; but today I have doubts on whether we should go or not. I had a dream last night of being in the water struggling with a woman. It makes me sad. I don't want to ruin the reunion for the Haneys." There was more in the entry but that is all I can remember Papa reading to us.

Flora Flowers and Paul Haney,
1923.

He gathered all of Elder Barrus' personal things together and put the diary with them. President Spencer took all his things and sent them to his family in Star Valley in Wyoming.

The companion, Elder Riggs, told Papa that Elder Barrus had related the dream to him that morning but after discussing it they decided to go because he didn't want to ruin the party for the family. Papa was very disturbed because he was a firm believer in dreams and had he known about it, he would never have permitted the Elders to go. But it was too late then and so many people were affected by the tragedy. Our hearts went out in sympathy to his family and his sweetheart who was waiting for him.

There is an ending to this tragic happening that I would like to relate at this time.

Several years after this took place we were grown up, married and lived in Idaho. My sister, Lyda, and her husband, Walter Harris were living here also. One day their stake went to the Logan temple and they went. While in the temple they met the parents of Elder Barrus. They had retired and moved to Logan from Star Valley where they were officiators in the temple. They were so happy to see Walter because they knew him when he was a young boy. Mr. Barrus was a school teacher then and was sent to the Catawba Indian Reservation in South Carolina where Walter lived. Their son, Clark, was two years older than Walter but they became good friends for several years while his father taught school there. When they knew who Lyda was they remembered the sad death of their son, Clark. Mrs. Barrus told them this true story: For several years after Clark's death she was so bitter she would not accept it and was very despondent. She couldn't understand why the Lord would permit such a thing to happen to her son when he was doing the Lord's work. No one could console her and her testimony was getting weaker—in fact she was pulling away from the church. One night, when she had reached the depth of despair, she went to bed feeling that life wasn't worth living. Finally she went to sleep and had this dream: Clark came to her and his countenance was extremely sad. He spoke to her. He told her she was sinning by grieving like that. He said, "Mother, it was my time to go, also to go in that manner. I had a mission here and have been laboring here. I know you were saddened by the tragedy but Heavenly Father is not pleased with your actions and I am saddened grievously. Please renew your faith in the Lord and continue serving Him". She said it was so real that she knew he really was there. When she awoke she realized how far she had drifted from the faith. From that time on she changed her attitude about the whole thing and accepted it as her son had pled with her to do.

After the tragedy of Elder Barrus, life went on. Some non-members tried to start a scandal about the Mormons. They told others that the "Mormon preachers" had the two girls out swimming in the nude and were having a drunken orgy when it happened. So many good people knew us too well and didn't believe their vicious lies.

Two new missionaries were assigned to our area and we had cottage meetings with our neighbors attending. even though we often remembered Elder Barrus with love and sadness in our hearts, we enjoyed the visits of the new missionaries and the cottage meetings.

Here's an interesting story that happened about that time. A family lived just off the highway on our way to and from town. The man made moonshine and he really had a thing going! The deputy sheriff was in cahoots with him. There was a cut along the road with high banks on each side just east of the man's house. The deputy would hide out on the high bank where he couldn't be seen but he could still watch the house. When the customers would leave the house he would jump in his car and chase them until he caught them. Then he would take the whiskey from them and charge them a fine then "so they wouldn't have to stand trial and maybe go to jail", he told them. They would pay him, he'd take the whiskey and when they

Elder Edward James Gibbons -- SSM 1911-1914

PHOTO 76   EDWARD JAMES GIBBONS

Birth date, place - 24 September 1876, Laketown, Rich, Utah Territory, United States
Death date - 12 July 1961
Baptism date - 28 September 1884 -- Baptism by - Joseph Weston
Father's name - Joseph Gibbons -- Mother's name - Mercy Weston

Southern States -- November 1911–January 1914 -- Age Called: 35

Southern States
Set Apart: 7 November 1911 -- Arrived At Home: 27 January 1914
Mission type: Proselytizing -- Priesthood office: Elder
Called From: Logan, Cache, Utah, United States
Set apart by: Joseph W McMurrin

Missionary Department missionary registers, 1860-1959, Vol. 4, p. 118, line 688.
First Presidency missionary calls and recommendations 1877-1918: CR 1 168, Church History Library.

RECEIVED
JUN 17 '11
PRESIDENT'S OFFICE

Logan 6/13/11

President Joseph F. Smith,
Salt Lake City Utah;

Dear Brother;—

I am willing to take a mission to the Southern States as you have selected.

Your Brother in the Gospel

Edward J. Gibbons
Oscar F. Rice.

P.S. Preferably not until Nov 15/11

Elder William George Ogilvie -- SSM 1907-1910

PHOTO 77   WILLIAM GEORGE OGILVIE

Birth date, place - 28 February 1885, St John, Apache, Arizona
Baptism date - 3 May 1893   --   Baptism by - Morten Jensen
Father's name - George William Ogilvie   --   Mother's name - Cosmelia Ellen Farnsworth

Southern States   -   November 1907–May 1910 - Age Called: 22

Southern States
Set Apart: 5 November 1907   -   End Date: 23 May 1910
Priesthood office: Elder
Called From: Richfield, Sevier, Utah, United States
Set apart by: Geo F Richards

Missionary Department missionary registers, 1860-1959, Vol. 4, p. 23, line 712.

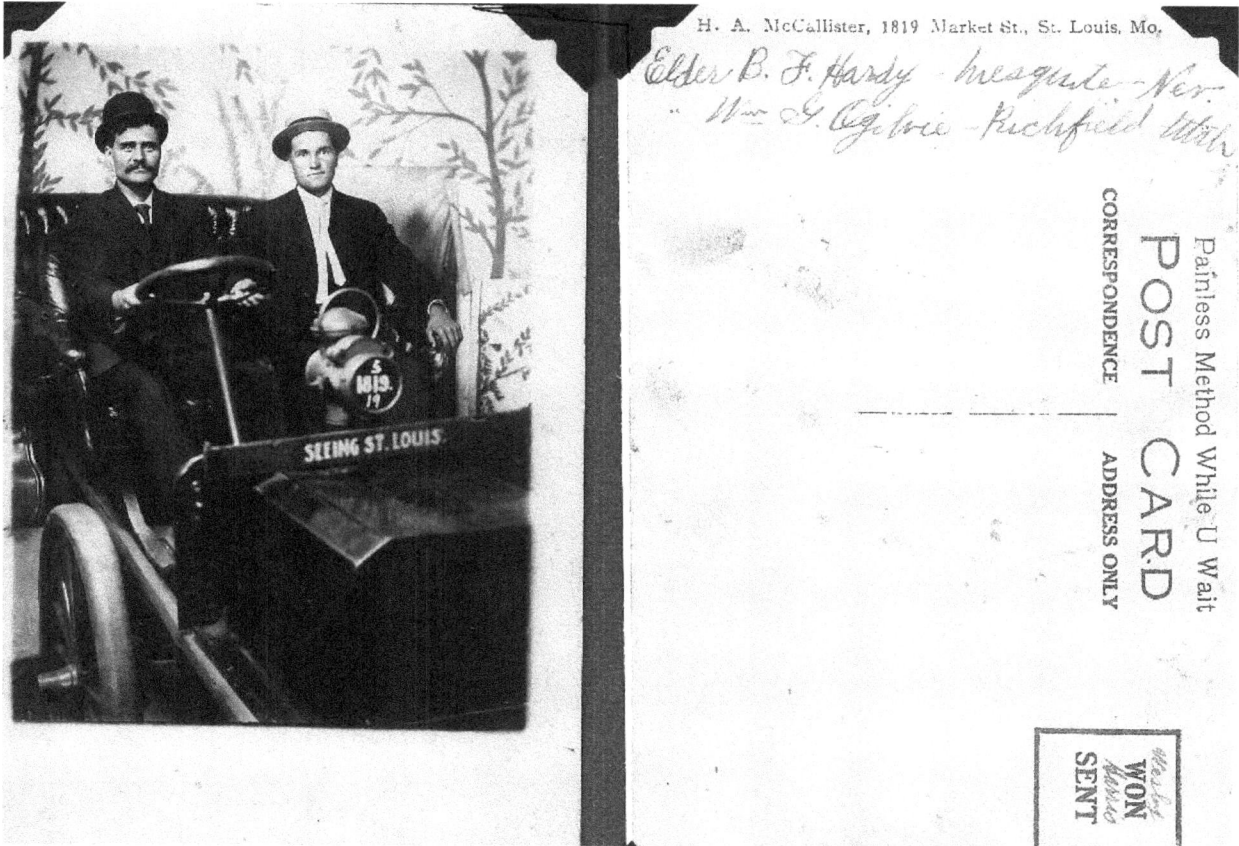

PHOTO 78   BRIGHAM FRANKLIN HARDY AND WILLIAM GEORGE OGILVIE

Elder Brigham Franklin Hardy   --   SSM 1909-1910

PHOTO 79   BRIGHAM FRANKLIN HARDY   ON THE LEFT

Birth date, place - 8 September 1881, St George, Washington, Utah
Death date - 23 September 1945 - Nampa, Canyon, Idaho, USA
Father's name - Warren Hardy -- Mother's name - Caroline Blake

Southern States - May 1909–May 1910 - Age Called: 27

Southern States -- Virginia Conference
Set Apart: 25 May 1909 -- Arrived In Field: 30 May 1909
Released: 19 May 1910 -- Arrived At Home: 24 May 1910
Mission type: Proselytizing -- Marital Status: Married
Priesthood office: Elder
Called From: Mesquite, Lincoln, Nevada, United States -- Set apart by: John Henry Smith
Notes: Released due to illness

PHOTO 80 BRIGHAM FRANKLIN HARDY AND WIFE ON LEFT – HEADSTONE OF B F HARDY AND WIFE ON RIGHT

Elder James William Hurren - SSM 1911-

PHOTO 81 ELDER JAMES WILLIAM HURREN

Birth date -- place 2 December 1889,   Hyde Park, Cache, Utah
Death date -- 9 July 1960
Baptism date -- 7 December 1897 -- Baptism by -- Geo H Tibbitt
Father's name - J W D Hurren -- Mother's name - Margaret A Ashcroft

Southern States -- October 1911–Unknown -- Age Called: 21

Southern States
Set Apart: 10 October 1911
Priesthood office: Elder
Called From: Hyde Park, Cache, Utah, United States
Set apart by: Jos W Mc Murrin

Missionary Department missionary registers, 1860-1959, Vol. 4, p. 113, line 491.

When grandpa would talk in church he never had notes [because during his mission he never used purse or script. Everything was memorized.] Regarding his mission in the Southern States he said that he was once tarred and feathered and driven out of town. He was married when he went on his mission. (1911 through 1913). From history on family search

Sister Rosa Emmeline Durrant   --   SSM 1912-

PHOTO 82   ROSA EMMELINE DURRANT

Birth date, place - 19 November 1893, Franklin, Oneida, Idaho
Death date - 17 September 1981
Baptism date - August 1902 -- Baptism by - Bishop Wm Bromley
Father's name - John Durrant - Mother's name - Elizth J G Miller

Southern States - September 1912–Unknown - Age Called: 19

Southern States
Set Apart: 17 September 1912
Marital Status: Single
Called From: American Fork, Utah, Utah, United States
Set apart by: George F Richards

Missionary Department missionary registers, 1860-1959, Vol. 4, p. 134, line 443.

Elder Streeter Wallace   --   SSM 1914-1916

PHOTO 83   STREETER WALLACE

Birth date, place: 21 May 1889, Beechville, Metcall, Kentucky
Death date: 8 October 1956
Baptism date: 12 August 1901   --   Baptism by - Joseph Later
Father's name - Benjamin Bruce Wallace   --   Mother's name - Nancy Perry

Southern States - June 1914–September 1916   --   Age Called: 25

Southern States
Set Apart: 23 June 1914   --   End Date: 5 September 1916
Departed From Home: 24 June 1914
Priesthood office: Elder
Called From: Ammon, Boniville, Idaho, United States
Set apart by: Rulon S Wells

Missionary Department missionary registers, 1860-1959, Vol. 4, p. 173, line 374.
First Presidency missionary calls and recommendations 1877-1918: CR 1 168, Church History Library

PHOTO 84 -- SOUTHERN STATES MISSIONARIES -- GROUP PHOTO
FRONT ROW L TO R: STREETER WALLACE; ALBERT JARVIS
SECOND ROW L TO R: WILLIAM P MERRILL; ARTHUR T SHURTLEFF

RECEIVED
JUN-9'14
PRESIDENT'S OFFICE

Ozone Bonneville Co Idaho
June 7 1914

Mr Joseph F Smith
Dear Bro I will ans your
Letter as regarding going
on a Mission I Will Be at
Salt Lake on the 24 of June
for my departure

Your Brother in the Gospel

Streeter Wallace

Leonard Ball
Bishop Ammon Ward.

Elder Samuel Carloss Hall -- SSM 1910-1913

PHOTO 85   SAMUEL CARLOSS HALL

Birth date, place - 10 April 1890, Bennington, Bear Lake, Idaho
Death date - 12 May 1959
Baptism date - 12 May 1898 -- Baptism by - Austin M Brown
Father's name - Saml R Hall --- Mother's name - Mary E Perkins

Southern States -- October 1910–March 1913 - Age Called: 20

Southern States -- South Carolina Conference

Set Apart: 11 October 1910 -- Arrived In Field: 16 October 1910
Released: 23 February 1913 -- Arrived At Home: 2 March 1913
Mission type: Proselytizing -- Marital Status: Single -- Priesthood office: Elder
Called From: Pennington, Bear Lake, Idaho, United States
Set apart by: Joseph W McMurrin

Missionary Department missionary registers, 1860-1959, Vol. 4, p. 93, line 640.
First Presidency missionary calls and recommendations 1877-1918: CR 1 168, Church History Library.
         October 2, 1908 recommendation for service
First Presidency missionary calls and recommendations 1877-1918: CR 1 168, Church History Library.
         April 24, 1910 letter accepting mission call
Southern States Mission history, 18332-1964: LR 8557 2, Church History Library. -- Mission index
Southern States Mission history, 18332-1964: LR 8557 2, Church History Library.
March 2, 1913 return home

Missionaries who served in the Southern States Mission

PHOTO 86 -- SOUTHERN STATES MISSIONARIES ABOUT 1911
FRONT ROW L TO R: GEORGE WILLIAM GRAFF; JOSEPH EUGENE COBBLEY;
BACK ROW L TO R: SAMUEL CARLOSS HALL; CHARLES FREDRICK BARNES.

PHOTO 87 -- SOUTHERN STATES MISSIONARIES - GROUP PHOTO, SOUTH CAROLINA CONFERENCE -- CA 1911
FRONT ROW L TO R: THOMAS R JONES; ROBERT L ISON; EUGENE COBBLEY; UNIDENTIFIED; LEROY BLACK
SECOND ROW L TO R: UNIDENTIFIED; UNIDENTIFIED; CLARENCE HART; UNIDENTIFIED; UNIDENTIFIED; UNIDENTIFIED
THIRD ROW L TO R: SAMUEL C HALL; UNIDENTIFIED; CHARLES F BARNES; UNIDENTIFIED; UNIDENTIFIED
FOURTH ROW L TO R: UNIDENTIFIED; WILLIAM P ROWLEY; GEORGE W GRAFF; HENRY WHITTAKER

Elder Hurbert Record   SSM 1913-1915

Elder Hubert Record taken at end of his mission to Southern States May 17th 1915.

Birth date, place 2 July 1894, Kingsville, Lincoln, Kentucky, United States
Death date 5 November 1979
Baptism date 4 July 1903 - Baptism by Thomas Yates
Father's name Benajah Julius Record Mother's name Lena Quimby

Southern States - November 1913–September 1915 - Age Called: 19

Southern States
Set Apart: 11 November 1913 -- End Date: 10 September 1915
Departed From Home: 12 November 1913
Priesthood office: Elder -- Priesthood: Elder
Called From: Deweyville, Box Elder, Utah, United States
Set apart by: J Golden Kimball

Missionary Department missionary registers, 1860-1959, Vol. 4, p. 161, line 717.
First Presidency missionary calls and recommendations 1877-1918: CR 1 168, Church History Library.

Deweyville, Utah. Oct. 13, 1913.

Pres. Joseph F. Smith:-
Salt Lake City, Utah.

I have received a call as a missionary to the Southern States, I accept the call and will be ready to leave at the date set, Nov. 12th 1913.

Your Brother in the Gospel,
Hubert Record.

Elder Arland L A Davidson   --   SSM 1914-1915

PHOTO 88   ARLAND L A DAVIDSON

Birth date, place - 8 July 1890, Fairview, Sanpete, Utah
Death date - 4 September 1979
Baptism date - 9 August 1898 -- Baptism by - Daniel B Hill
Father's name - Lorenzo Davidson -- Mother's name - Anna Louise Petterson

Southern States - October 1914–December 1915 - Age Called: 24

Southern States -- South Carolina Conference
Arrived In Field: 28 October 1914 - Released: 17 December 1915
Arrived At Home: 3 January 1916
Mission type: Proselytizing
Priesthood office: Elder
Called From: Swedish Mission
Set apart by: Joseph W McMurrin

Missionary Department missionary registers, 1860-1959, Vol. 4, p. 160, line 698.
First Presidency missionary calls and recommendations 1877-1918: CR 1 168, Church History Library.
Sweden Stockholm Mission manuscript history and historical reports 1850-1971: LR 8865 2, Church History Library
Southern States Mission history 1832-1964:LR 8557 2, Church History Library

PHOTO 89 -- L TO R: WILLIAM A SHULDBERG; ARLAND LORENZO DAVIDSON; JOHN ALMA JANSON

Parker Idaho
Oct. 19th 1913

President Joseph F Smith
Dear brother.
In answer to your letter of Oct. 13th stating that my name has been accepted as a missionary to Sweeden. I feel willing to act and labor in such a calling. believing it a soloma duty, I expect to present myself at your office on the time indicated, desiring an interest in faith and prayers of the members of this faith, along with the other laborers of this cause.
I wish to remain true to the Cause with respect

Arland L. Davidson

Elder Miles Greener -- SSM 1909-1910

Birth date, place - 10 June 1873, Kanosh, Millard, Utah Territory, United States
Death date - 7 January 1943
Baptism date - 13 February 1899 -- Baptism by - George A Black
Father's name - Thomas Richardson Greener -- Mother's name -

PHOTO 90 ELDER MILES GREENER

Southern States -- June 1909–December 1910 - *Age Called: 36*

Southern States
Set Apart: 22 June 1909 -- Arrived At Home: 13 December 1910
Mission type: Proselytizing -- Priesthood office: Elder
Called From: Hinckley, Millard, Utah, United States
Called From: Hinckley, Millard, Utah, United States
Set apart by: J Golden Kimball

Missionary Department missionary registers, 1860-1959, Vol. 4, p. 64, line 489.

Elder David Lorin Turner -- SSM 1912-1914

PHOTO 91   DAVID LORIN TURNER

 Birth date, place - 11 June 1891, Giles, Wayne, Utah
Death date - 1 November 1974
Baptism by - F Archie Young
Father's name - Lorenzo Turner --   Mother's name - Lydia Hall

Southern States --   September 1912 – December 1914 --   Age Called: 21

Southern States
Set Apart: 17 September 1912 - End Date: 31 December 1914
Priesthood office: Elder
Called From: Wayne, Utah, United States
Set apart by: Joseph F Smith Jr

Missionary Department missionary registers, 1860-1959, Vol. 4, p. 134, line 442.

Elder George William Graff   --   SSM 1909-1911

RGE WILLIAM GRAFF - MISSIONARY

PHOTO 92   GEORGE W GRAFF

Birth date, place - 9 August 1887, Cannonville, Garfield, Utah Territory, United States
Death date - 9 May 1952
Baptism date - 1 January 1896   --   Baptism by - W W Willis
Father's name - Johan Jacob Graff   --   Mother's name - Lucy May Bramall

Southern States   --   May 1909–December 1911 - Age Called: 21

Southern States
Set Apart: 25 May 1909   --   Arrived At Home: 1 December 1911
Mission type: Proselytizing
Priesthood office: Elder
Called From: Cannonville, Garfield, Utah, United States
Set apart by: John Henry Smith

Missionary Department missionary registers, 1860-1959, Vol. 4, p. 60, line 346.

Elder P. Eugene Johansen -- SSM 1914-1915

PHOTO 93   P. EUGENE JOHANSEN

Birth date, place - 16 January 1893, Huntington, Emery, Utah Territory, United States
Death date - 19 December 1953
Baptism date - 31 August 1901 -- Baptism by - Albert Guyman
Father's name - Peter Johansen -- Mother's name - Zora Cook

Southern States - October 1914–December 1915 - Age Called: 21

South Carolina Conference
Arrived In Field: 28 October 1914
Released: 9 December 1915
Mission type: Proselytizing
Marital Status: Single
Priesthood office: Priest
Called From: Scandinavian Mission
Set apart by: Charles H Hart

Notes: Transferred. Completed his mission in the United States along with other missionaries who were released from European missions due to the war.

Missionary Department missionary registers, 1860-1959, Vol. 4, p. 157, line 567.
Index to the British Mission manuscript history and historical reports 1841-1971: LR 1140 32, Church History Library
Scandinavian Mission Manuscript history and historical reports 1855-1920: LR 9332 2, Church History Library
Southern States Mission history 1832-1964: LR 8557 2, Church History Library

P. EUGENE JOHANSEN--ACTIVITY RECORD

Born January 16, 1893, Huntington, Utah

Ordained Deacon 1905; Ordained Teacher 1908; Ordained Priest 1911

Secretary Ward MIA 1912

Called on mission August, 1913 to Scandinavian Mission; Transferred to Southern States Mission, USA, October 1914. Released December 1915.

Worked in Stake MIA, Ward MIA, Ward Sunday School 1916 to 1925

Moved to Carbon Stake 1925--Alma Fullmer chosen Presiding Elder there, and I and Russell Williams were chosen as Councilors with Guy Ware as Clerk

Moved home to Castle Dale 1930.

Chosen 2nd Counselor to Bishop Elmer Nielson 1932; later Ward Clerk

Chosen Castle Dale Ward Bishop in April, 1944. Released in 1951.

Chosen 2nd Counselor in Stake High Priest Quorum with William L. Guymon

From 1921 to 1953 have never been out of a Church office. A subscriber of Improvement Era from 1912 to 1954 inclusive.

MISSION TO NORWAY AND TO SOUTHERN STATES

About October 12, 1914, the Mormon Missionaries were ready to leave Norway. World War I had been declared, and the majority of missionaries were being called to the United States from Europe. There were about 50 of us, and i certainly did hate to leave a few Elders (Nephi Williams, my best pal) and the saints behind. We were about 10 days on the water to New York. The lights had to be turned off at dark. We were very happy to get to the United States. Ernest Jensen landed there two days before me and we had a very good 2 days together.

I was sent to the Southern headquarters at Chattanooga, Tennessee. I visited Washington DC and many interesting places. I was appointed to labor in South Carolina, arriving there the latter part of October. At this time a Branch Conference was being held in Greenville, South Carolina with Arther T. Shurtleff as President and Charles A. Callis as Mission President. All Elders and Lady Missionaries spoke in Conference. At the close of Conference, I was appointed to labor with Elder George W. James from Enoch (near Cedar City, Utah). Elder Jones and I had gone through the Salt Lake Temple together October 8, 1913. We were appointed to labor in the country for about four months. The homes were very scattered and backwoodsy. One peculiar thing about so many of the houses was that they didn't have much foundation--a pile of rock at each corner and a few along the side. They had a very large fireplace at one end of the house from the ground up. In the cold weather of winter, the pigs roosted at the bottom of the chimney.

Each pair of Elders would have a new mailing place 50 to 100 miles apart where they would clean their clothes, receive and answer mail, make out reports, and hold meetings from Friday until Monday. During the week they would do tracting, hold cottage meetings when and where the people would take us in and give us food, bed, and lodging. Some parts of the country where we were laboring were and had been very bitter against the Mormons. I recall one good old faithful Brother, Richard Smothers (known as Dick), sitting on his porch with his shotgun on his lap while the Mormon Elders slept.

After our spring conference other elders were assigned as companions. At the close of the meeting Elder Winfield Hurst, a big redheaded man came up to me and said, "Can you sing." Our first mailing place was just over the line to North Carolina at the home of Brother Groves. We went out into the woods, selected about four songs to be used to hold Sacrament meeting on Sunday. We learned them well enough for that.

Occasionally the Elders were called in to labor in the cities for a change. As new Elders came out from home and old ones returned, we would be given changes quite often. At the close of the Fall Conference I was appointed a young Elder about three months from home. We just got located in our field of labor for a few months when word was sent for us to appear at a special conference. We decided to spend the week tracting through the country to conference. The first day out didn't have very good luck getting entertainment for the night. It made no difference what kind of talks we gave, we received no results. I had been out over two years and had never been refused before. We asked our Father in heaven for help. When time was getting close to midnight, we could see a light some distance from the road in the woods. We knocked at the door and a young woman answered. I asked if her husband was home. Just then I could see him at the far end of the room reaching for his gun. Then he came over to the door and we stated our message but were refused. On leaving here we could see a light some distance away on a hill--the only light to be seen. They invited us in but said not to mention religion. Soon after he made a fire, we arose and got ready to leave. The room and bed were very clean and neat, with white sheets, etc., a large white pitcher, and a bowl of fresh water. We had such a good restful night. He asked us to stay and have breakfast, asked us to offer grace, and before the meal was over he brought up the subject of polygamy. This gave us the privilege of explaining our gospel.

After the special meeting, we were sent back to our field of labor. Soon after this, we received a letter from a member of the church asking if we could hold a meeting or service for a child who had been dead and buried a couple or three months. We accepted. During the stay there we held several meetings and baptized six persons. We felt well paid. We then went through the district keeping up the regular work.

In the early part of December, 1915, I received my release to go home. Two other Elders and I were to leave the same time; we visited a lot of interesting places on the way and reported at headquarters in Salt Lake. We stayed there with our old Conference President, Arthur L. Shurtleff. We bade farewell in Salt lake and I took the train east to Price, then the stage to Castle Dale over dirt roads on December 21 or 22. Father and the children met me with the big white top buggy; Ernest Jensen met me next. I then went into the Co-op Store to say hello to my girlfriend, Oral, and visited with her that night. I was so happy to be home with family and friends, but very sorry my dear Mother was missing. Christmas holidays, visiting and so many other things coming on kept everybody so busy.

HEBER WRIGHT DEAD

NEVER RALLIES FROM EFFECTS OF OPERATION AND IN- JURIES.

Passes From Sleep Into Death—Fun- eral Will be Announced Later.

Heber Wright, who sustained such serious injuries beneath the wheels of a gravel train at Promontory Tuesday morning, died this morning at 1:25 o'clock at the Ogden General hospital.

Immediately after the accident Mr. Wright was brought into Ogden by special train and taken to the hospital. His condition was such for several hours after arrival here that he could not be operated upon, due to the weakness resultant from the shock at the time of the accident. Between 4 and 5 o'clock Tuesday afternoon the crushed arm was amputated at the shoulder. After the operation he conversed with his wife and others who were there. "Well, Janey, our cut-off days are over," said he and with these words he went to sleep. He never awoke again, but passed into the sleep that knows no awakening.

Mr. Wright was a well-known resident of this city. He was sheriff of Weber county for one term about ten years ago, but since that time up to the time of his death has been working on the railroad.

A wife and five daughters mourn the loss of husband and father. The family residence is at 554 Twenty-eighth street. The remains of the deceased were taken in charge by Undertaker Lindquist, who will announce the date of funeral.

FUNERAL SERVICES OVER HEBER WRIGHT

IMPRESSIVE SERVICE HELD AT THE FAMILY RESIDENCE.

Remains Sent to Willard Where Inter- ment Will Take Place.

Short but impressive funeral services were held at the family residence, 554 Twenty-eighth street, this morning over the remains of Heber Wright, who died Wednesday morning from injuries sustained while at work the previous day, on a gravel train at Promontory Point.

George Shorten, counselor to the Bishop of the Second Ward conducted the services. Music for the sad occasion was furnished by the ward choir. John A. Boyle, H. H. Goddard and George Shorten gave a few brief eulogistic remarks about the deceased. They testified to his worth as a man and spoke with much feeling concerning the manner of his death. The rainbow of hope was held out before the eyes of sorrowing wife and children and they were assured of a grand re-union with husband and father on the other shore.

At the conclusion of the services at the home a funeral cortege formed and the remains were taken to the Union depot and were shipped to Willard, where interment will take place.

The deceased was formerly sheriff of Weber county and had a great number of friends in and around Ogden. Surviving him are wife and five daughters, most of whom are grown up.

Elder Ephraim Larson -- SSM 1916-1918

PHOTO 94   ELDER EPHRAIM LARSON AND WIFE SISTER LARSON

Birth date, place - 13 January 1882, Snow Flake, Apache, Arizona
Death date - 1 January 1981
Baptism by - Lehi Larson
Father's name - Mons Larson -- Mother's name - Olivia L Eklund

Southern States - January 1916–March 1918 - Age Called: 34

Southern States
Set Apart: 25 January 1916 - End Date: 11 March 1918
Departed From Home: 26 January 1916
Served with children
Priesthood office: Elder
Called From: Graham, Arizona, United States
Set apart by: Heber J Grant
Notes: Served with wife Lilly Celestia Larson

Missionary Department missionary registers, 1860-1959, Vol. 4, p. 200, line 107.
First Presidency missionary calls and recommendations 1877-1918, CR 1 168, Church History Library.
First Presidency missionary calls and recommendations 1877-1918: CR 1 168, Church History Library.
First Presidency missionary calls and recommendations 1877-1918: CR 1 168, Church History Library.
First Presidency missionary calls and recommendations 1877-1918: CR 1 168, Church History Library.

Lilly Celestia Barney-Larson -- SSM 1916-1918

PHOTO 95   LILLY CELESTIA BARNEY-LARSON

Birth date, place - 27 September 1883, Kanosh, Millard, Utah
Death date - 25 January 1931
Baptism date - 6 October 1892 - Baptism by - Austin Evans
Father's name - Walter Turner Barney -- Mother's name - Sarah Matilda Farr

Southern States - January 1916–March 1918 - Age Called: 32

Southern States
Set Apart: 25 January 1916 - End Date: 11 March 1918
Departed From Home: 26 January 1916
Served with children
Called From: Graham, Arizona, United States
Notes: Served with husband Ephraim Larson

Missionary Department missionary registers, 1860-1959, Vol. 4, p. 200, line 108.
First Presidency missionary calls and recommendations 1877-1918, CR 1 168, Church History Library.
First Presidency missionary calls and recommendations 1877-1918, CR 1 168, Church History Library.
First Presidency missionary calls and recommendations 1877-1918, CR 1 168, Church History Library.
First Presidency missionary calls and recommendations 1877-1918: CR 1 168, Church History Library.

Notes
Name also spelled "Lillie"

Elder Winfield Hurst -- SSM 1914-1916

PHOTO 96   WINFIELD HURST

Birth date, place - 12 January 1892, Logan, Cache, Utah Territory, United States
Death date - 3 May 1879
Baptism date - 28 January 1901   --   Baptism by - Alsoup
Father's name - Samuel H Hurst   --   Mother's name - Elizabeth Bateman

Southern States - March 1914–June 1916 - Age Called: 22

Southern States
Set Apart: 17 March 1914   --   Arrived At Home: 8 June 1916
Departed From Home: 18 March 1914
Mission type: Proselytizing
Marital Status: Single
Priesthood office: Elder
Called From: Woodville, Bingham, Idaho, United States
Set apart by: Joseph F Smith Jr

Missionary Department missionary registers, 1860-1959, Vol. 4, p. 167, line 135.
First Presidency missionary calls and recommendations 1877-1918: CR 1 168, Church History Library.
Southern States Mission History
See page 191 of the Index for his entries

Elder Joseph Eugene Cobbley   --   SSM 1909-1912

PHOTO 97   JOSEPH EUGENE COBBLEY

Birth date, place - 5 December 1889, Pleasant Grove, Utah, Utah
Death date - 13 February 1957
Baptism date - 5 February 1898   --   Baptism by - Benj Walker
Father's name - James Cobbley   --   Mother's name - Emma Thorne

Southern States   --   November 1909–April 1912   --   Age Called: 19

Southern States
Set Apart: 2 November 1909   --   End Date: 2 April 1912
Priesthood office: Elder
Called From: Blackfoot, Bingham, Idaho, United States
Set apart by: J Golden Kimball

Missionaries who served in the Southern States Mission

PHOTO 98 -- SOUTHERN STATES MISSIONARIES ABOUT 1911 -- FRONT ROW L TO R: GEORGE WILLIAM GRAFF; JOSEPH EUGENE COBBLEY; -- BACK ROW L TO R: SAMUEL CARLOSS HALL; CHARLES FREDRICK BARNES.

PHOTO 99 -- SOUTHERN STATES MISSIONARIES -- GROUP PHOTO, SOUTH CAROLINA CONFERENCE -- CA 1911
FRONT ROW L TO R: THOMAS R JONES; ROBERT L ISON; **EUGENE COBBLEY**; UNIDENTIFIED; LEROY BLACK
SECOND ROW L TO R: UNIDENTIFIED; UNIDENTIFIED; CLARENCE HART; UNIDENTIFIED; UNIDENTIFIED; UNIDENTIFIED
THIRD ROW L TO R: SAMUEL C HALL; UNIDENTIFIED; CHARLES F BARNES; UNIDENTIFIED; UNIDENTIFIED
FOURTH ROW L TO R: UNIDENTIFIED; WILLIAM P ROWLEY; GEORGE W GRAFF; HENRY WHITTAKER

Sister Mamie Cornelia Nelson -- SSM 1918-1920

PHOTO 100   MAMIE CORNELIA NELSON

Birth date, place - 28 October 1893, Logan, Cache, Utah
Death date - 24 July 1956
Baptism date - 4 August 1907 -- Baptism by - Joseph S Campbell
Father's name - Olof Nelson -- Mother's name - Hilda Olson

Southern States - June 1918–February 1920 - Age Called: 24

Southern States
Set Apart: 11 June 1918 - End Date: 19 February 1920
Departed From Home: 12 June 1918
Priesthood: Sis
Called From: Logan, Cache, Utah, United States
Set apart by: Rudger Clawson

Missionary Department missionary registers, 1860-1959, Vol. 4, p. 233, line 147.
First Presidency missionary calls and recommendations 1877-1918: CR 1 168, Church History Library.

PHOTO 101   SISTER M C NELSON AND SISTER BETTY LEE TUCK

Sister Betty Lee Tuck -- SSM 1918-1919

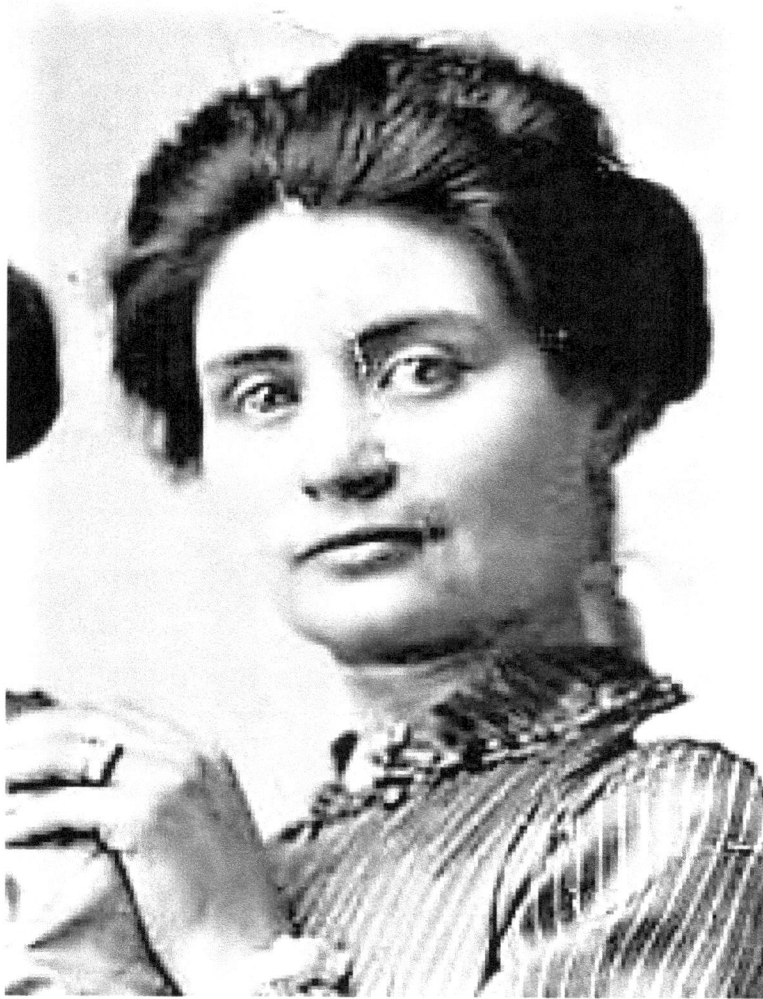

PHOTO 102   BETTY LEE TUCK

Birth date, place -- 19 September 1883, Franklin Junction, Pittsylvania, Virginia
Died -- 5 September 1940 -- Ogden, Weber, Utah, United States
Baptism date - 13 September 1898
Baptism by - Saml E Taylor
Father's name - John W Tuck -- Mother's name - Nannie F Hogan

Southern States - April 1918–October 1919 - Age Called: 34

Southern States
Set Apart: 9 April 1918 - End Date: 20 October 1919
Departed From Home: 10 April 1918
Called From: Fremont, Idaho, United States
Set apart by: Jos F Smith Jr

Missionary Department missionary registers, 1860-1959, Vol. 4, p. 231, line 80.
First Presidency missionary calls and recommendations 1877-1918: CR 1 168, Church History Library.

Southern States Missionaries
Who Served between 1921-1935

Elder William Peter McCormack   --   SSM 1921-1923

PHOTO 103   WILLIAM PETER MCCORMACK WITH DOG AND A PICTURE YOUNGER AND OLDER

Birth date, place - 22 October 1898, Flagstaff, Cocinino, Arizona
Death date - 9 December 1959
Baptism date - 5 August 1911   --   Baptism by - Gregersen Jensen

Father's name - Larry Hewitt   --   Mother's name - Eliza Carter

Southern States   --   May 1921–July 1923 - Age Called: 22

Southern States
Set Apart: 17 May 1921   --   End Date: 31 July 1923
Departed From Home: 18 May 1921
Priesthood office: Elder
Called From: Pocatello, Bannock, Idaho, United States
Set apart by: Joseph Fielding Smith
Missionary Department missionary registers, 1860-1959, Vol. 5, p. 50, line 340.

PERSONAL RECORD

		IMPORTANT EVENTS
Name in full	William Peter McCormack.	List below and on the reverse side items such as schools attended, vocation and business activities.
Father's name	William Adamson McCormack.	Church positions, places of residence, special talents and interests, unusual and faith promoting
Mother's maiden name	Eliza Roxana Drake.	experiences, travel, genealogical and temple work. Church leaders and other outstanding characters
When born (day, month, year)	22 October-1898	you have met, etc. I left school after leaving the eighth grade
Where born (town, county, state)	Flagstaff, Coconino County, Arizona.	Then I started working on the railroad in various
When blessed (day, month, year)		departments. I taught the church history class in the
By whom		second ward, after I returned from my mission. I taught
When baptized (day, month, year)	5-August-1911.	the church history class for three years. My chief
Where baptized	Pocatello, First Ward.	interest is collecting historically church events.
Baptized by	Georgeson Jensen.	I have traveled in the states of Nevada, California,
When confirmed	6 august-1911. By whom	And many of the southern states. I am now devoting
Priesthood ordinations:	All at Pocatello, Ida.	My time to Temple work and genealogy. I have met and
Office Deacon	By Whom Pat Cannon. Date 27-Jan-1017	talked with President Heber J. Grant. Elder, Melvin J.
Office Teacher	By Whom A.Y.Satterfield Date 11-Feb-1918	Ballard, President George Albert Smith. I have met
Office Priest	By Whom A.Y.Satterfield Date 3-Nov-1919	President William Howard Taft, and Theodore Roosevelt.
Office Elder	By Whom W.A.Hyde Date 9 May-1921	I was a boxer, and was in the ring for three years.
Office Seventy	By Whom Rudger Clawson Date 25 Feb-1928	I was classed as a middle weight, fighting at 155 Lbs.
Office High Priest	By Whom A.Y.Satterfield Date 15-Aug-1954	All my fights were here in Pocatello. This was before
Married to	Effie Mae Beatrice Haney. Date 26-June-1928	I left for my mission, prior to 1921. I have been a
Where married	Salt Lake Temple by George F. Richards.	member of the wards here in Pocatello, since 1905.
Where endowed	Salt Lake Temple Date 18 May-1921	I was in my first Sunday school in the first ward.
Where sealed	Salt Lake Temple Date 26-June 1928	Then the second ward, then the fifth, and last the eighth.
To whom (husband or wife)	Wife	I was given stake appointments by President Wm.A.
Patriarchal blessing by	Hyrum G. Smith Date 3-Dec-1923	Hyde, until the time of his release. I have delivered
Departed for mission to	Southern States Date 18 May 1921	gospel sermons in the first, third, four, firth,
When returned	I Agust-1923.	sixth, fifteenth wards. Also American Falls, Rockland,
Special appointments	2 Years in North Pocatello stake Mission.	Inkom, Fort Hall, and Lava wards. I have performed
	2 Years in Indien Mission.	baptisims in the Idaho Falls temple. And have done
When died	Date	work in the Salt Lake temple.
Where buried	Date	

Printed in the U.S.A. Distributed by Deseret Book Company—Salt Lake City, Utah—Copyright 1936.

Symbols: Bap-Baptised. Conf-Confirmed.Chr.Christened. F-Father.M-Mother.	IMPORTANT EVENTS
14th-1921-Chr.John Hiram Wilson-F-John Wilson-M-Emma A.Wright.	Feb-14-1923-Baptised-Leon Jackson Cutter at Santee Swamp.
Oct-22-1921-Chr.Elsie Nelson-F.Freddie Nelson-M-Mary Wilson.	Mar.28-1923-Baptised Alvin McCleod at Bay Branch.
June-17-1921-Con.Willie Leslie Welch,F.David Welch-M.Carrie Jones.	Mar.28-1923-Baptised Richard McCleod at Bay Branch.
8-Oct-1921.Conf.John Allen-F.Marion Allen-M-Lizzie Cooper.	Mar.28-1923-Baptised-Rody Adkinson at Bay Branch.
21-Oct-1921-Bap.Horace Thos.Dees-F.Butler Dees.M.Tressy Threat.	May-25-1923- " Wade Franklin Chambers at Williamston Creek
26-Nov-1921-Conf.Lesco Chambers-F.Frank Chambers.M.Donnie Webb.	
20Feb1922-Chr.Ulee Rowena Patrick.F.Bishop Patrick.M.Mary Moberly.	
9-Mar-1922Chr.Maggie Lee Cutler.F.Thos.Cutler.M.Lela Fair.	
6-Mar-1922.Chr.Rbt.Lee Tobias.F.Luther Tobias.M.Mary Broud.	
9-Jan-1922.Chr.Henry Harris.F.Tom Harris.M.Mary Player.	
3-June-1922.Chr.Ruth Mary Cook.F.Jake Cook.M.Mary Cook.	
24-Aug-1922.Conf.Leatha May Harrell.F.R.Howell.M.Lilly Allen.	
24-Aug-1922-Bap.Nancy Jane Thompson.F.David Thompson.M.Flora Braboy.	
24-aug-1922.Conf.Nancy Jane Thompson.	
15-Feb-1923.Conf.Maud Lee Cutter.F.L.W.Cutter.M.Lula Shepherd.	
1-Apr-1923.Chr.Mae Lula Welch.F.Henry Welch.M.Annabell Harris.	
29-Apr-1923-Chr.Eugen McKinley Medlock.F.Otis.M.Lillian Cleveland.	
20-June-1923.Conf.Chas.Barness Ebernickle.F.John.M.Lila Cleveland.	
20-June-1923.Conf.Mozelle Ebernickle. " " " " "	
July-1-1923.Conf.Mary Venetta Tucker.F.Major.M.Verda Cobia.	
June-17-1921-Baptised Florence Atkinson at Society Hill.	
June-26-1921 " Lamar Hunter at Gren Plains.	
Aug-11-1921 " Gary Edwin Benton at Greenville.	
Oct-21-1921 " Horace Thomas Dees at Centerville.	
June-3-1922 " Lillian Idoria Hair at Hairs Mill.	
July-23-1922 " Boggy Archie Powers at Sutters Mill.	
Aug-24-1922 " Nancy Jane Thompson at Gum Swamp.	
" " " " Cain " " " "	
Feb-14-1923 " Charles Hampton Cutter at Santee Swamp.	

The Beganning or my own history.

Birth.

I was born in Arizona in the year 1898, the 22nd of October. In the city of Flagstaff, Coconino County, Arizona. My father died when I was six weeks old, in the city of Phoenix. Leaving me with my mother and oldest brother. We came to Pocatello that year, I898. Where we lived for four years and left for Portland,Oreon. After living there a year, we moved on the San Fransisco.We lived there untill I904. Then left in the month of April for Pocatello. The next year, l905, Was the year of the great earthquake. I have all my ordinations to the priesthood on file teacher to High Priest.Also Patriarchal blessings, Mission calls and releases.I have pictures of missionary companions, the mission president etc. am in possession or all the names I have worked for in the Idaho Fails Temple.

Elder Benjamin "Ben" Smith Riggs -- SSM 1921-1923

PHOTO 104 — LEFT — ELDER BEN S RIGGS AND RIGHT — ELDER J L VANCE

PHOTO 105 -- ELDER BENJAMIN SMITH RIGGS

Benjamin Smith Riggs
Birth – 19 October 1899, Dos Cabezas, Cochise, Arizona
Death – 20 March 1937, Tucson, Pima, Arizona
Burial- Riggs Family Cemetery, Cochise, Arizona

Baptism date - 1907
Baptism by - Elder Ammon M Tenney

Father's name - Brannick Benjamin Riggs   -   Mother's name - Martha Smith

Southern States Mission - November 1921–December 1923 - Age Called: 22

Southern States
Set Apart: 8 November 1921 -- End Date: 5 December 1923
Departed From Home: 9 November 1921
Mission type: Proselytizing
Priesthood office: Elder
Called From: St David, Cochise, Arizona, United States
Set apart by: Joseph Fielding Smith

Missionary Department missionary registers, 1860-1959, Vol. 5, p. 59, line 695.
Missionary Department missionary registers, 1860-1959, Vol. 6, p. 29, line 1123.

Elder John Lewis Vance -- SSM 1921-1923

PHOTO 106 -- LEFT :ELDER BEN S RIGGS — RIGHT; JOHN LEWIS (J L) VANCE

PHOTO 107 -- JOHN LEWIS VANCE

Birth date -- 11 July 1892, Alpine, Utah, Utah
Death date -- 14 May 1974, Alpine, Utah, Utah
Baptism date -- 1 September 1900 -- Baptism by -- T F Carlisle
Father's name - Lewis Jefferson Vance -- Mother's name - Mary Frances Ferrell

Southern States - May 1921–July 1923 - Age Called: 28

Southern States
Set Apart: 3 May 1921
End Date: 7 July 1923
Departed From Home: 4 May 1921
Priesthood: Seventy
Called From: Alpine, Utah, Utah, United States
Set apart by: Seymour B Young

> Missionary Department missionary registers, 1860-1959, Vol. 5, p. 49, line 307.

John Lewis Vance
Utah, Missionary Department Missionary Registers
Name   John Lewis Vance
Event Type   Mission
Event Date   1921
Event Place   Southern States
Residence Place   Alpine, Utah, Utah, United States
Birth Date   11 Jul 1892 - Birthplace   Alpine, Utah, Utah
Baptism Date   01 Sep 1900
Date Returned   07 Jul 1923
Departure Date   04 May 1921
Father's Name Lewis Jefferson Vance   --   Mother's Name   Mary Frances Farrell

Page   49 - Volume   Missionary Register v. 5
By Whom Baptized   T F Carlisle
By Whom Set Apart   Seymour B Young   --   Date Set Apart   03 May 1921

Citing this Record
"Utah, Missionary Department Missionary Registers, 1860-1937," database, FamilySearch
(https://familysearch.org/ark:/61903/1:1:QKDW-1DS7 : 26 February 2016), John Lewis Vance,
Southern States; records extracted by FamilySearch and images digitized by Church History library,
The Church of Jesus Christ of Latter-day Saints; citing Missionary Register v. 5, Missionary
department missionary registers 1860-1959, CR 301 22, Church History Library, Salt lake City, Utah.

Elder Blaine Haycock Liston - SSM 1922-1925

PHOTO 108 BLAINE HAYCOCK LISTON

Birth date, place --   18 April 1904, Escalante, Garfield, Utah
Death date -- 8 September 1961
Baptism date -- 18 August 1912   Baptism by -- Jed Eyre
Father's name -- Oscar Liston   Mother's name -- Elizabeth Haycock

Southern States - October 1922–January 1925 -- Age Called: 18
Southern States
Set Apart: 10 October 1922 -- End Date: 26 January 1925
Departed From Home: 11 October 1922
Served with companion: William Peter McCormack
Priesthood office: Elder
Called From: Escalante, Garfield, Utah, United States
Set apart by: Jos Fielding Smith
Missionary Department missionary registers, 1860-1959, Vol. 5, p. 79, line 635.

PHOTO 109 -- BLAINE H LISTON AND WILLIAM PETER MCCORMACK

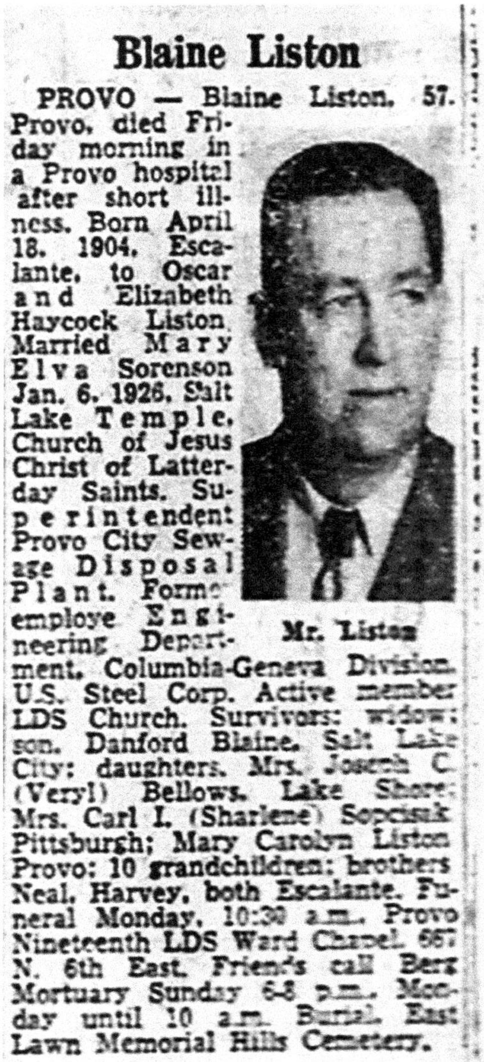

Blaine Liston

PROVO — Blaine Liston, 57, Provo, died Friday morning in a Provo hospital after short illness. Born April 18, 1904, Escalante, to Oscar and Elizabeth Haycock Liston. Married Mary Elva Sorenson Jan. 6, 1926, Salt Lake Temple, Church of Jesus Christ of Latter-day Saints. Superintendent Provo City Sewage Disposal Plant. Former employe Engineering Department, Columbia-Geneva Division, U.S. Steel Corp. Active member LDS Church. Survivors: widow; son, Danford Blaine, Salt Lake City; daughters, Mrs. Joseph C. (Veryl) Bellows, Lake Shore; Mrs. Carl I. (Sharlene) Sopcisak, Pittsburgh; Mary Carolyn Liston, Provo; 10 grandchildren; brothers Neal, Harvey, both Escalante. Funeral Monday, 10:30 a.m., Provo Nineteenth LDS Ward Chapel, 667 N. 6th East. Friends call Berg Mortuary Sunday 6-8 p.m., Monday until 10 a.m. Burial, East Lawn Memorial Hills Cemetery.

Mr. Liston

PHOTO 110 – DEATH OF BLAINE HAYCOCK LISTON

Elder August Wilhelm Ossmen   --   SSM 1925-1926

PHOTO 111   AUGUST WILHELM OSSMEN

Birth date, place - 14 August 1860, Elbrona, Tjärstad, Östergötland, Sweden
Death date - 10 August 1936 -- Rexburg, Madison County, Idaho, United States
Baptism date - 18 February 1884 - Baptism by - George Ossmen
Father's name - Johannes Ossmen - Mother's name - Anna Lena Persson
August Wilhelm Ossmin

Scandinavian -- July 1898–Unknown -- Age Called: 37
Scandinavia
Set Apart: 22 July 1898
Mission type: Proselytizing
Marital Status: Married
Priesthood office: Seventy -- Quorum: 106th
Called From: Rigby, Fremont, Idaho, United States
Set apart by: J G Kimball

Western States   Colorado -- December 1907–December 1909 -- Age Called: 47
Western States
Set Apart: 10 December 1907 -- Arrived At Home: 25 December 1909
Mission type: Proselytizing
Marital Status: Married
Priesthood office: Seventy - Quorum: 130th
Called From: Rigby, Fremont, Idaho, United States
Set apart by: Heber J Grant

Southern States -- December 1925–March 1926 -- Age Called: 65
Southern States
Set Apart: 1 December 1925 -- Arrived At Home: 25 March 1926
Mission type: Proselytizing
Marital Status: Married
Priesthood office: High Priest
Called From: Rigby, Fremont, Idaho, United States
Set apart by: David O McKay

Missionary Department Missionary Registers, 1860-1959, Vol. 3, p. 77, line 568.
Missionary Department missionary registers, 1860-1959, Vol. 4, p. 27, line 901.
Missionary Department missionary registers, 1860-1959, Vol. 5, p. 157, line 1083.
First Presidency missionary calls and recommendations 1877-1918: CR 1 168, Church History Library
First Presidency missionary calls and recommendations 1877-1918: CR 1 168, Church History Library
First Presidency missionary calls and recommendations 1877-1918: CR 1 168, Church History Library
First Presidency missionary calls and recommendations 1877-1918: CR 1 168, Church History Library
Alternative names: August Wilhelm Osmin, Ossmin

Rigby. March. 18/ 98.
Geo. Rynolds
    Dear Brother
yours of March 11 received.
I saw Apostle Teasdale and had a talk
with him Monday 14 at Lewisvill
He told me to report to you when I
am ready to go on a mission. I cannot tell if
I am ready or not till I find out
what the cost will be. Pleas write
and let me know all potielars. if
the expspencies are not to high I wiee
be ready at any time
        Your Brother in the gospel
        Augest Wm Osspneered
Pleas address to
LaBelle
    Fremont co Idaho

Rigby   April 10/ 98
Geo. Reynalds
        Dear Brother
    I have received a letter from
W. C. Spencer stating the raite
to Copenhagen I am ready or
will be in about three weaks
I should have retten sooner
but was delayed on account of sickness
I buried my only son a weak ago
My wife has also been sick. but
with the help of god I ham ready
when ever you see fit to send me.
    your Brother in the gosple

        A. W. Osmen.
address to   Labelle Fremont Co.
        Idaho.

Rigby April 25/98

Geo. Reynolds

Dear Brother

Your letter of April 20 was received

I will say in answer to your request. I was call by the Bishoprick of Rigby ward Feb 27/98 to go on a foren mission. Received a letter from you dated March. 11/98 requesting me to see Apostle Geo Teasdale at our Quarterly Conference at Lewisville and have a talk with him regarding my mission, which I did. he instructed me to to write to you, when I was ready. But as to the time and place, I have not been notified. I received a letter from W. C. Spencer & I will inclose his letter, It may help you find where the mistake lies. I am ready to go on my Mission eny time. you see fit to send me.

Your Brother in the Gospel

A. W. Ossmen

Rigby April 30/98

Pres. Wilford Woodruff

Dear Brother. Your letter of April 26 received

I willingly accept of the call to go on a mission. With the help of God I desire to do all the good, I can preaching the gospel. I desire to be obedient to the call of the priesthood at all times.

Your Brother in the gospel

A. W. Ossmen.

Geo. A. Gordon Bp.

Rigby April 10/98

Geo. Reynolds

Dear Brother

I have received a letter from W. C. Spencer stating the raits to Copenhagen. I am ready or will be in about three weaks I should have ritten sooner but was delayed on account of sickness I buried my only son a weak ago My wife has also been sick. but with the help of god I ham ready when ever you see fit to send me.

Your Brother in the gospel

A. W. Ossmen.

address to Labelle Fremount Co.
Idaho.

A. W. Ossmen

Nov. 18, 1907.

Rigby, Ida. Nov. 18 - 1907

Pres. Joseph. F. Smith

Salt Lake City

Dear Brother

Your favor of Nov. 9 is received
With the help of the Lord I
will in Salt Lake City at the
appointed time to be set apart
for a mission.

I am your Brother in the Gosple

A. W. Ossmen.

Bros. A. Cordon Bp

Elder Delbert Odell Boice   --   SSM 1926-

PHOTO 112 DELBERT ODELL BOICE

Birth date, place - 3 November 1905, Bountiful, Conejos, Colorado
Death date - 22 October 2000
Baptism date - 1 March 1914   --   Baptism by - G W Rogers
Father's name - John E Boice   --   Mother's name - Alta A Ball

Southern States   November 1926–Unknown   -   Age Called: 21
Southern States
Set Apart: 16 November 1926   -   Departed From Home: 19 November 1926
Priesthood office: Elder
Called From: Manassa, Colorado, United States
Set apart by: John A Widtsoe

Missionary Department missionary registers, 1860-1959, Vol. 5, p. 192, line 1064.

PHOTO 113   HEADSTONE FOR DELBERT ODELL BOICE

Elder Orlan Cox   --   SSM 1927-

PHOTO 114   ORLAN COX HIGH SCHOOL PIC. AND ON THE LEFT SHORTER ONE AND MISSION CONFERANCE

1952

PHOTO 115   ORLAN COX IN 1952

Birth date, place - 26 October 1907, Lovell, Big Horn, Wyoming
Death date - 13 June 1992
Baptism date - 2 July 1916   --   Baptism by - Elias Johnson
Father's name - Orlan L Cox   --   Mother's name - Ada E Asay
Family Search logo

Southern States - November 1927–Unknown - Age Called: 20
Southern States
Set Apart: 8 November 1927
Departed From Home: 15 November 1927
Priesthood office: Elder   --   Priesthood: Elder
Called From: Lovell, Wyoming, United States
Set apart by: Rudger Clawson
Stories and Documents

Missionary Department missionary registers, 1860-1959, Vol. 5, p. 218, line 824.

PHOTO 116 -- GROUP PHOTO, SOUTHERN STATES MISSIONARIES IN SOUTH CAROLINA

L TO R: WESLEY SCOTT; ORLAN COX; WILLIAM H FOSTER; ERNEST ROBINSON

Elder Walter Clyde Shelley -- SSM 1928-1930

PHOTO 117   WALTER CLYDE SHELLEY

Birth date, place   14 February 1895, Heber, Navajo, Arizona
Death date   9 January 1967

383

Baptism date   30 August 1903 -   Baptism by   James E Shelley
Father's name   James E Shelley   --   Mother's name   Margaret Hunter

Southern States   February 1928–March 1930   Age Called: 33
Florida District; Columbia, South Carolina
Set Apart: 21 February 1928
Departed From Home: 24 February 1928   Arrived In Field: 28 February 1928
Released: 2 March 1930   Arrived At Home: 15 March 1930
Mission type: Proselytizing   Marital Status: Married
Priesthood office: Elder
Called From: Joseph City, Arizona, United States
Set apart by: David O McKay

Missionary Department missionary registers, 1860-1959, Vol. 5, p. 229, line 226.
Southern States Mission history, 1832-1964: LR 8557 2, Church History Library.
Mission index

Page 345   SOUTHERN STATES MISSION INDEX
Shelley, Walter Clyde - 1928   Feb 28 - Arr in Miss:to Fla Dist Nov 30 tr to office
                        1929   Sep 1 At conf, Columbia, South Car olina
                        1930   Mar 2 At conf, released

Missionary Department missionary registers, 1860-1959, Vol. 5, p. 229, line 226.
Southern States Mission history, 1832-1964: LR 8557 2, Church History Library.

PHOTO 113 -- ELDER WALTER CLYDE SHELLEY, THIRD FROM LEFT, WITH CATAWBA INDIANS -- ELSIE BLUE, SECOND FROM THE LEFT

PHOTO 119   ELDERS WALTER CLYDE SHELLEY AND JOSEPH MARK WINDER

PHOTO 120   WALTER C SHELLEY'S MILITARY HEADSTONE

Elder Joseph Mark Winder - SSM 1928

Joseph Mark Winder
Birth date, place   15 December 1906, Salt Lake City, Utah
Death date   11 February 2006
Baptism date   1915   Baptism by   Frank Cutler
Father's name William C Winder   Mother's name Rosalie Taylor

Southern States   June 1928–Unknown   Age Called: 21
Southern States
Set Apart: 19 June 1928
Departed From Home: 22 June 1928
Priesthood office: Seventy
Called From: Salt Lake City, Salt Lake, Utah, United States
Set apart by: Rudger Clawson

Missionary Department missionary registers, 1860-1959, Vol. 5, p. 237, line 530.

PHOTO 121   WINDER AND SHELLEY ON BANKS OF CATAWBA RIVER 1928

PHOTO 122   WALTER C SHELLEY AND JOSEPH MARK WINDER

PHOTO 123   ELDER JOSEPH MARK WINDER, BROTHER H LINDE AND ELDER WESLEY SCOTT

Elder Richard Clarence Carter   SSM 1914 -1916

PHOTO 124 - ELDER RICHARD CLARENCE CARTER

Richard Clarence Carter
Birth date, place: 4 April 1891, Provo, Utah, Utah
Death date: 12 January 1927
Baptism date: 18 May 1901
Father's name: Richard Carter   --   Mother's name: Ada Clark

Southern States   -   February 1914–June 1916 -- Age Called: 22
Set Apart: 3 February 1914 -- End Date: 3 June 1916
Departed From Home: 4 February 1914
Priesthood office: Elder   --   Called From: Provo, Utah, Utah, United States
Set apart by: Anthony W Ivins

Missionary Department missionary registers, 1860-1959, Vol. 4, p. 166, line 76.
First Presidency missionary calls and recommendations 1877-1918: CR 1 168, Church History Library

BISHOP'S OFFICE
_____Ward

_____Provo___ Utah, _Jan. 13,_ 19_14_

Mr. Joseph F. Smith
Dear Brother, I accept the call to fill
a mission to the Southern States, and will
be there at Feb. 9, to be set apart.
Your brother
Richard Clarence Carter,

James H Jenkins P.E.

PHOTO 125   RICHARD CLARENCE CARTER'S SOUTHERN STATES MISSION LETTER OF ACCEPTANCE

Elder James Lael Simmons -- SSM 1920-1922

PHOTO 126   JAMES LAEL SIMMONS

Birth date, place -- 12 December 1900, Tabiona, Fremont, Idaho
Death date -- 5 March 1989
Baptism date - 5 November 1909   --   Baptism by - D H Hopkins
Father's name - John S Simmons   --   Mother's name - Mary Jane

Southern States -- October 1920–December 1922   --   Age Called: 19
Southern States
Set Apart: 19 October 1920 -- End Date: 24 December 1922
Departed From Home: 20 October 1920
Priesthood office: Elder
Called From: Cassia, Idaho, United States
Set apart by: Joseph Fielding Smith.

Missionary Department missionary registers, 1860-1959, Vol. 5, p. 35, line 653.

Elder Dewey Wallice Sabin -- SSM – 1920-1922

Birth, 21 December 1898, St David, Cochise, Arizona
Death date 7 October 1979
Baptism date 2 May 1908 -- Baptism by Crozier
Father's name Parley P Sabin - Mother's name Sarah Cecelia Smith

Southern States October 1920–1922 - Age Called: 21

Southern States Set Apart: 12 October 1920 -- End Date: 1922
Departed From Home: 13 October 1920
Priesthood office: Elder
Called From: Cochise, Arizona, United States
Set apart by: Orson F Whitney

PHOTO 127 -- ALABAMA CONFERENCE, BIRMINGHAM, ALABAMA MISSION PHOTOGRAPH -- CA 1921

1ST ROW, L TO R: ELDER WATT; EDWIN T. VEST; ELDER FOUNDS; CLARENCE SILVER; ELDER STAUFFER; PAUL ROSS.

2ND ROW, L TO R: CARL EDVALSEN; ELDER WILLOWBY; ELDER PERKINS; PRES. WM. C. OLSON; PRES. CHAS. A. CALLIS; TED LEWIS; A. C. ELLIOTT; ELDER HUNT.

3RD ROW, L TO R: ELDER LEE; IVON R. HOWELL; J. GILBERT FULLER; ELDER CHRISTENSEN; GRANT SMITH.

4TH ROW, L TO R: J. CLAYTON WATTS; W. W. HARDY; ELDER WELKER; CLOYD BROWN; FLOYD O. CRANDALL; ELDER TOONE; **DEWEY SABIN**; UNKNOWN

Elder John Andrew Hunt   SSM 1923-1925

PHOTO 128   ELDER JOHN ANDREW HUNT

Birth date, place - 16 January 1901, Tuba City, Arizona
Death date - 15 July 1999
Baptism date - 1909 -- Baptism by - Harman Brinhall
Father's name - William Hunt   -- Mother's name -- Elese S Hunt

Southern States - October 1923–December 1925 - Age Called: 22
Southern States
Set Apart: 9 October 1923 - Arrived In Field: 15 October 1923
Released: 11 December 1925 - Departed From Home: 10 October 1923
Priesthood office: Seventy - Quorum: 77th
Priesthood: Seventy 77th Quo
Called From: San Juan, New Mexico, United States
Set apart by: Geo Albert Smith

Missionary Department missionary registers, 1860-1959, Vol. 5, p. 99, line 556.

He was a missionary companion to Elder Willard J Andersen

Elder William Whiting   --   SSM 1920-1922

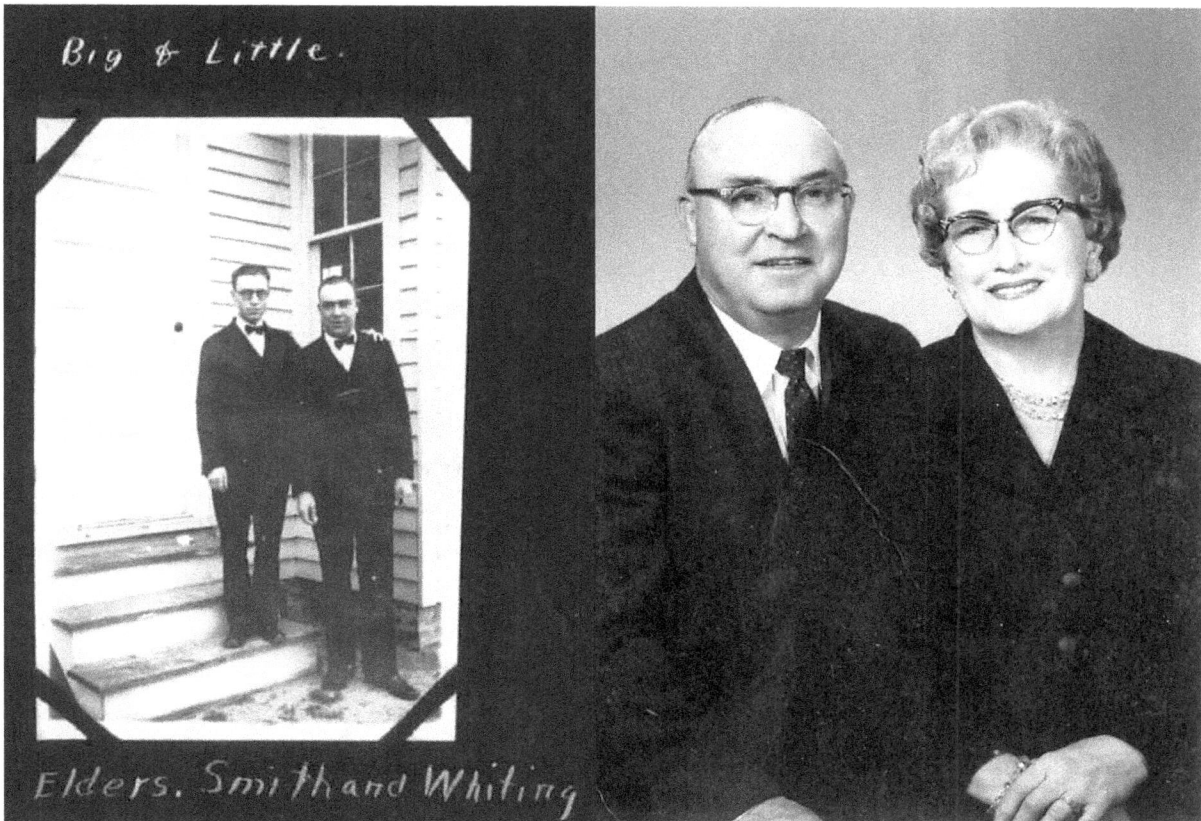

PHOTO 129   1ST ELDER WILLIAM WHITING AND ELDER J M SMITH AND 2ND WILLIAM WHITING AND WIFE

Birth date, place - 7 December 1901, Robin, Bannock, Idaho
Death date - 11 August 1987
Baptism date - 10 September 1910   --   Baptism by - Orson Christensen
Father's name - Lorenzo S Whiting   --   Mother's name - Flora Natterman

Southern States - November 1920–December 1922 - Age Called: 18
Southern States
Set Apart: 23 November 1920   -   End Date: 25 December 1922
Departed From Home: 24 November 1920
Priesthood office: Elder   --   Priesthood: Elder
Called From: Power, Idaho, United States
Set apart by: Stephen L Richards

Missionary Department missionary registers, 1860-1959, Vol. 5, p. 39, line 802.

Elder James Frederick Farr -- SSM 1920-1923

PHOTO 130   JAMES FREDERICK FARR

Birth date, place - 14 August 1899, Ogden, Weber, Utah, United States
Death date - 13 July 1961
Baptism date - 14 August 1907   --   Baptism by - Carl E Peterson
Father's name - David Farr   --   Mother's name - Margaret Williams

Southern States - November 1920–March 1923 - Age Called: 21
Southern States
Set Apart: 23 November 1920 - Arrived At Home: 27 March 1923
Departed From Home: 24 November 1920
Mission type: Proselytizing
Marital Status: Single
Priesthood office: Elder
Called From: Ogden, Weber, Utah, United States
Set apart by: George F Richards

Missionary Department missionary registers, 1860-1959, Vol. 5, p. 39, line 800.

SOUTHERN STATE MISSION INDEX
Page 128

Farr, James Frederick	1920	Nov 28	Arr in miss: E Ky conf.
	1921	Apr 13	app pres: E Ky miss
	1922	May 1	July 31, Sep 10, Nov 5 at conf
	1923	Mar 5	Released Mar 7

Elder Walter Glen Phillip Perkins   SSM   1923-1926

PHOTO 131   ELDER WALTER GLEN PHILLIP PERKINS

Walter Glen Phillip Perkins -   Gender - Male
Birth date, place --   29 November 1900, Wellsville, Cache, Utah
Death date --   2 June 1976
Baptism date -   5 December 1908
Baptism by --   Richd Brenchley
Father's name -   Samuel John Perkins   Mother's name -   Margaret Glenn

Mission   - July 1923–February 1926 -   Age Called: 22
Netherlands
Set Apart: 13 July 1923
End Date: 21 February 1926
Departed From Home: 14 July 1923
Priesthood office: Elder   Priesthood: Elder 6th Quo
Called From: Wellsville, Cache, Utah, United States
Set apart by: Melvin J Ballard

Elder Morris Willis Teeples -- SSM 1925-1926

PHOTO 132 MORRIS WILLIS TEEPLES ON RIGHT AND BY HIMSELF ON RIGHT

Birth date, place - 20 July 1901, Shelley, Bingham, Idaho
Death date - 29 March 1978
Baptism date - 1 August 1909 -- Baptism by - Ransford H Teeples
Father's name - Ransford H Teeples -- Mother's name - Lodisa E Killian

Southern States - November 1920–March 1923 - Age Called: 19
Southern States
Set Apart: 9 November 1920 - End Date: 15 March 1923
Departed From Home: 10 November 1920
Priesthood office: Elder
Called From: Goshen, Bingham, Idaho, United States
Set apart by: Richd R Lyman

Southern States - December 1925–June 1926 -- Age Called: 24
Southern States
Set Apart: 8 December 1925 -- End Date: 30 June 1926
Priesthood office: Elder
Called From: Shelley, Bingham, Idaho, United States
Set apart by: R R Lyman

Missionary Department missionary registers, 1860-1959, Vol. 5, p. 159, line 1190.
Missionary Department missionary registers, 1860-1959, Vol. 5, p. 37, line 720.

Elder Willard J Andersen   --   SSM 1925-1929

PHOTO 133   WILLARD J ANDERSEN

Birth date, place - 16 July 1907, Mendon, Cache, Utah, United States
Death date - 1 August 1996
Baptism date - 30 June 1917   --   Baptism by – Lorenzo B Evans
Father's name – John C Andersen   --   Mother's name – Sena Sorensen

Southern States -- January 1925–May 1927
Age Called: 17
Southern States
Set Apart: 20 January 1925   --   Arrived At Home: 1 May 1927
Departed From Home: 21 January 1925
Mission type: Proselytizing
Marital Status: Single
Priesthood office: Elder
Called From: Arbon, Power, Idaho, United States -- Set apart by: George Albert Smith

Southern States -- November 1928–April 1929   Age Called: 21
Southern States
Set Apart: 27 November 1928   --   Arrived At Home: 28 April 1929
Departed From Home: 29 November 1928
Mission type: Proselytizing   --   Marital Status: Single
Priesthood office: High Priest
Called From: Arbon, Power, Idaho, United States   --   Set apart by: Melvin J Ballard

Left Elder Willard J Andersen

Elder Willard J Andersen - front middle
(Left) second from right

PHOTO 134 - ELDER WILLARD J ANDERSEN

PHOTO 135 LUCILE BLUE, ELDER WILLARD J ANDERSON AND ELSIE BLUE

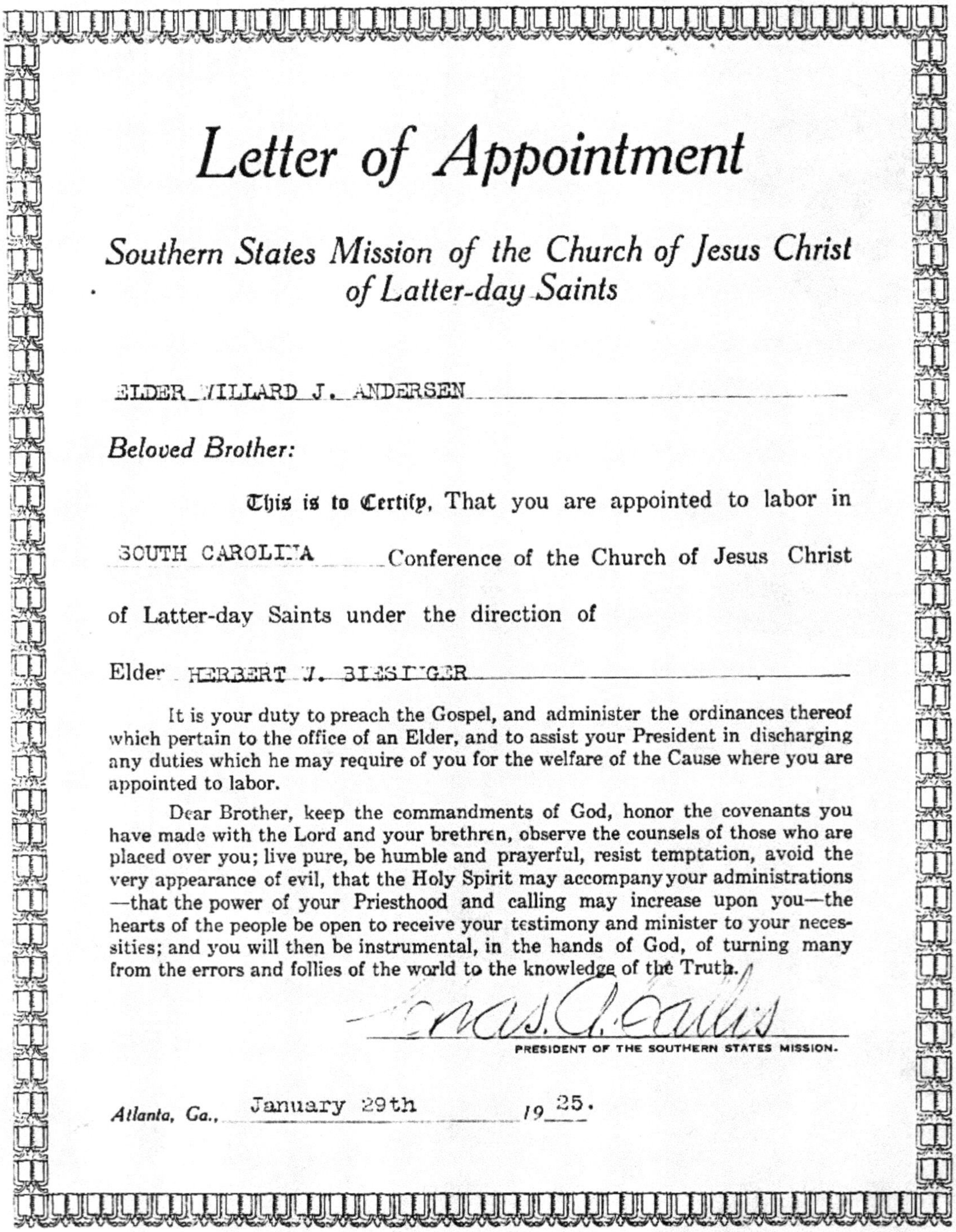

Letter of Appointment

Southern States Mission of the Church of Jesus Christ of Latter-day Saints

ELDER WILLARD J. ANDERSEN

Beloved Brother:

This is to Certify, That you are appointed to labor in

SOUTH CAROLINA _____ Conference of the Church of Jesus Christ

of Latter-day Saints under the direction of

Elder HERBERT J. BLESINGER

It is your duty to preach the Gospel, and administer the ordinances thereof which pertain to the office of an Elder, and to assist your President in discharging any duties which he may require of you for the welfare of the Cause where you are appointed to labor.

Dear Brother, keep the commandments of God, honor the covenants you have made with the Lord and your brethren, observe the counsels of those who are placed over you; live pure, be humble and prayerful, resist temptation, avoid the very appearance of evil, that the Holy Spirit may accompany your administrations —that the power of your Priesthood and calling may increase upon you—the hearts of the people be open to receive your testimony and minister to your necessities; and you will then be instrumental, in the hands of God, of turning many from the errors and follies of the world to the knowledge of the Truth.

PRESIDENT OF THE SOUTHERN STATES MISSION.

Atlanta, Ga., January 29th 19 25.

PHOTO 136   W J ANDERSEN- SOUTHERN STATES MISSION LETTER OF APPOINTMENT

Pages from the Missionary Journal of elder Willard J Andersen

46

July ∴∴ August.

At night we went to Tagons for supper after supper we went to a baptist prayer meeting and spent the night with Tagn

Thu. 30 traced the rest of the mill village and studyed some Held a fine meeting that night good crowd out and spent the night with Bro. Savoy

Fri. 31. went over to Bro. threats where we had dinner and at 2.30 P.m. we left for Chester on the Bus, again 4.00 went to Bro. Winters where we spent the night

Sat. 1. arose bright and early at 3.00 o'clock and walked to the depot about one mile and left before the Chickens were up for Edgemoor to get our mail And to wait till 7.00 o'clock. to get our mail and after we got our mail we wrote some letters at the depot. and studyed some. at 7.00 P. m. we took the train for Catawba went to the ball game and then we went home with some of the Indians went to Bro. Blue where we got aquainted with the Blue family had a fine supper after supper they had a box supper in the Hall and I bought a box cost 80 cents. Stayed with Bro. Blue that night.

Sun. 2. went to Sunday School in the morning and held two fine meeting one at 2.00 P.m. and the other at 7.20 o'clock and still spent the night with Bro. Blue again

Mon. 3. Practiced playing ball with Indians most of the day when we were not studying held another fine meeting that night and stayed with Bro. Nelson Blue.

Tue. 4. rained all day like old sixty so we studyed and wrote some letters Stayed with Bro. Sam Blue again.

Wed. 5. In the after noon we went to the junction where the Indians were going to play ball that day I played with them. Then we went to Bro Browns for the night. Had all the water mellon we could eat, and spent the night

Thur. 6. Walked to the Inn, and caught the train for Kershaw went to Bro. Crollys and spent the night

Fri 7 Studyed some and I walked around town wrote some letters that night we went through the first catton mill for me spent the night with Bro Crollys

48

Sat. 8. Sept. Kershaw at 9.13 train for westville where we got our mail and walked to Bro. Dixon wrote a letter home and went and saw a negro ball game. not much ~~think~~ Walter Dixon and I went to a baptist preaching services. sure not much like ours.

Sun. 9. Had all the watermellon we could eat. and spent the day in talking and after dinner we went to Camden with Bro. Dixon and on the way back we went to see the monument that is put up in memory of De Kalb. where he was fatally wounded went back to the house after supper we went to two different places to hear ~~some music~~

Mon. 10. After eating a big breakfast. we went to the watermellon patch and got a mellon all we could carry. sure had all we could eat. then we went to westville and took the train for Camden went to Bro. Selligner had dinner and then went up town and got a good bath. went to Bro owitches and had supper after supper we went to Bro. Hancock.

on the Wateree mill village and
spent the night.

Tue. 11. Walked back to Bro Pettigrew
and wrote some letters studyed
some and spent the night there.

Wed. 12. Packed up for Conference studyed
on our sirmons we had to
preach Held a meeting on the
Wateree Village had a good
crowd walked back to Bro.
Pettigrew and spent the night.

Thur 13. Got up early left Camden at
4.00 Oclock on the sea board
A. R. after walking 2 miles and
toteing our big grips. when
we got on Elder Tempest & Brockbank was there also. went to
Macbee there we had to
wait two hours for the
train. Elder Tempest & Brockbank
got of at Hartsville and we went on
to Darlington there we meet Elders
Hardy & Cole went to the picture
show and spent the night with
Bro. & Sis Cadell.

Feb 14. Left Darlington for the Hills
the four of us about half way
Elder Tempest & Brockbank
got on that made six of us
Elders Elders Hardy & Tempest,
Brockbank, & Cole and my self and
Elder Hunt got to the Hill about

50

11.30 o'clock went to the Post
office and got our mail and
then we went to Bro. Lithis
where Sis. Lithe fixed dinner
for eight of us. had a real
fine dinner after dinner we
hit the trail for Bro. Freemans 4 miles from town.
Some of the Elders went over
to the church and helped
the other Elders with the brush
arbor I stayed and helped Elder
Scott wash. then we went
to the branch and had a good
dip then we went to priest
Hood meeting and arranged
things for the Conference. and
went to our different places to
stay that night. 4 of us went
to Bro. Earl Wilcks. I was with them

Sat. 15, after breakfast we went to
Bro. Pete Freemans and cleaned
up for the big day. walked
over to the brush arbor to wait
the arival of Pres. Callis He came
at 9.30 also Elder Holt. the mission
Secretary and Sis Ellen Jenkins
Jenkin mission recorder. He greeted
all of us. and then we proceeded
with the meeting, and as it happened
I was the Second speaker and

52

up the road aways. and Elder
Moon & Far Joined in with us
Elder Toon & I rode in the buggy
over half way and then we
walked and let Elder Frost & Scott
ride. got to Bro. Crolley and
he took us to Bro. Halls
in his car. there we held
a little cottage meeting and
spent the night.

Tue. 18. One of Bro Halls Boys took
us to Mauber where we caught
the train for columbia I got
off at Camden and got a horse
to take me to Sis Pettigrew
and got my stuff cast me
70¢ then I took the next
train to Columbia got there
at noon walked to Chrystle
Lake and had a good bath
and swim then came back
and got ready for the party
that night. a farewell for
Elder Hardy & Pres. Spencer. Had
a real fine party at 12000 that
Elder Hardy and Elds Hunt, Holt, Gibbe
and Elder Cole left afor their field
of labor Elder Hardy for Atlanta
Elder Scott & I spent the night
with Sis Smith that night.

Wed. 19. got up early and got ready
to leave for Spartanburg but

missed the noon train but
caught the 4.00 o'clock train got
in Spartanburg at 7.00 o'clock.
went out to Sister's __ eaton's and
spent the night.

Thu. 20. Adw Scott put his pictures
in his new album and b
walked up town mailed some
letters and studyed some. spent
another night there.

Fri 21. Walked up town and got our
mail heard good news from
home and wrote some more
letters and studyed some.

Sat. 22. Caught the train for Gaffney
went up to Bro. Hills to spend
the night Had corn bread and
butter milk to eat. sure some eats

Sun 23. Same kind of eats for breakfast
held Sunday School at Bro.
Hills, that night we held a
fine Cottage meeting at Bro. Black
and spent the night there.

Mon 24. went back to Bro. Hills and done
a little studing and writing straiten
up things some. and spent the night there.

Tue 25; Studyed some more walked
down town and mailed some
letters and went to Bro. Black for the
night.

Wed. 26. Studyed some more and that
evening we rode out in the

54

country with Bro. Sanders there
we had a change from corn
bread and butter milk some supper
spent the night there.

Thur. 27. After breakfast we hit the road
at 9.00 o'clock for Bro. Harrises
about 1½ miles in to N.C. 14 miles
from Gaffney there we had another
fine dinner after dinner we picked
Horseshoe some with the boys
and then we went back to
Gaffney with them save walking
"don't blame us, do you." spent
the night with the hounds (&
bed bugs.) and had some more corn
bread and butter milk.

5 Fri 28. Bro. Hill got us up before
daylight and got us fooled
again at the table by the 8.00
o'clock we went to town to
get our mail good new from
Home again answered it and
studyed some then we walked
out to Sister warrens. Spent the
night there and had good eats.

Sat. 29. Walked back to town and
spent the night with Bro.
Black.

Sun. 30. Went up to Bro. Hill where we had
the lesson over and held Sunday
School pretty good crowed Mr. B.
to charge had dinner with

August + September

Bro. Hill then we went down to
Bro. Burdetts for supper played
Bro Burdetts a few games of Chicks
he beat me all to pieces went to
Bro. Dave whites where we held
preaching we stayed there that
night and fought the skeeters
all night some Job. I'll say.

Mon 31 Went up to Bro. Hills and
washed our clothes went out in
the park took a picture as two
then we went to Bro. Sprouses
and tried to baptise his little
girls but the old lady wouldn't
listen to it went to Bro. millwoods to spend the night well
we sure had a time the bugs
tried to takes us but we gave
them the bed and moved as far
as we could on the floor tryed
to get away from them but a few
found us but they wasnt so bad.

Tue 1 Went to Bro. Hills packed up
our grips and took the High
way for blacksburg walked to
Bro moss there we had supper
and a fine bed to sleep in

Wed. 2. Walked 2 miles to blacksburg
there we tracted a mill village
and caught the train for Gastonia
got there at 12:00 P.m. stayed there
till 4:00 P.M. left on the train

56

for Clover got there at 4.30 P.m.
and at 5.00 P.m. we left for
Rock Hill about 23 miles on foot.
the members had moved that
lived at Clover so we couldent
catch a ride, and had to walk
well we walked till 10.00 o'clock
and couldent get a place to
stay so we had to sleep
with uncle Sam that night
and got a lot of furters
bits and made a bed mid
velvet bean vines and corn
stocks did sleep much that
night

Thu. 3. Balled out at 6.00 o'clock in
the morning never had to dress
but cleared up a little and
but the road to Rock Hill got
a ride all the way sure did
take fine cause we sure was
tired got there at 7.30 o'clock
went to the cafe and got our
breakfast then started to
find Bros. Blue failed to find
him but found Bro. Stovens
had dinner with them then
we found Bro. blue after a
little map and supper we went
to the Indian nation to preach
Preaching there Elders Scott & Co.
Stud the preaching then we

went back to Rockhill and
spent the night with Bro. Blue

Feb 4. Had breakfast and Eld. Hunt
went after the mail got
letter from home and report
Eld. J.C.H. and receipt of check
for $100.00 went to the movie
cost 10¢ then we wrote a letter
or two and spent the night with
Bro. Walter Harris at Rockhill.

5. Got up feeling fine and
brushed up some and studyed
some at 1.30 oclock Bro. Brown
came along and we went with
him to the Indian Nation
after we arrived there helped
eat a nice little watermellon
weighing 65 lbs. left our grips
with Bro Blue and went on
to the Junction where Eld. Scott
& I joined in with the Indians
in a base ball game had a
fine game beat the other team
12 to 5. went back with Bro.
Nelson Blue and ate a snack
with Bro. Sam Blue and held a
fine meeting spent the night
with Bro. Sam. Blue.

Feb 6. Got up feeling like a Hundred and fasted till noon held
a fine sunday school and
then a meeting then we went

58

to Bro. Sanders for dinner.
where we sure did fill up on
sweet potatoes and chickens & fruit.
went back to the Church there
we studyed some and at 2.30
P. m, we held a fine meeting
and another at 7.30 P. m. spent
the night. after a fine bite to eat.
with Bro. Sam Blue.

Mon 7. after another fine breakfast
we went to the Church there
we studyed till 9.30 A. m. then
we went to the River where
we had a glorious Swim then
we came back and after dinner
we studyed some more and
held another fine meeting and
again we spent the night at.
Bro. Sam. Blues.

Tue. 8. After a fine breakfast we
walked around to see some of.
the members and the gave us
some of the pottery then Bro.
Brown's boy came up there and
we got him to take us to Rock
Hill there we stayed with Bro.
Walter Harris.

Wed. 9. Left Rock Hill at 9.00 o'clock for
Charlotte m. c. there we went to
a show. called "The Sea Hawk." and
saw some of the town then we
left about noon for Gastonia

no. 2, went to the Victory Cotton mills and found Bro. millsap had a fine supper and spent the night there. with a few bed hounds.

Fri 10 Tracted some in the fore noon we had fine luck. put out 211 tract apiece and sold 15 little books Elder Scott 17. at 4.00 oclock Bro. millsap took us to Bessemer city there we caught the train for Jacksburg there we got part of our mail and walked out to Bro. moses and spent the night.

Fri 11. After breakfast we walked back to Jacksburg where we got some more of our mail and left for Gaffney on the train took our Grips to Bro. Hills then we went to Bro. west-morlands and spent the night

Sat 12. about noon we went to the swamps with Bro. westmorland and helped him build his dam worked till dark and it was eight oclock when we got back to the house there we made a big freezer of Ice cream and after supper we had all the cream we could eat. then Elder Scott & I went up town got a hair cut and came back about 12. 30 P.m.

62

September & November.

Sun. 20. Held a fine Sacrement meeting with the family And spent the day in talking and studying and again we spent the night there.

Mon. 21. of September thru 5 of nov. Missed Diary From Sept 21 to November 5. 1926. Left Gaffney for Blacksburg on the train got part of our mail and then we walked to Bro. Masson and there we had a fine supper and also a fine Cottage meeting and spent the night there also

Fri. 4. Got up pretty early and after breakfast we both took the road to Blacksburg again there we got the rest of our mail and I got a real fruit Cake from Home. at 9.00 o'clock Elder Scott left to go back to Gaffney and I left for Rock Hill arriving there about noon. went to see Bro. Harris and Bro Harris & I went to a Vadaville then & spent the night at bro. Harris.

Sat. 7. Left Bro Harris at 4.00 a. m. and walked to the depot there I caught the train for winnsbaro got there at 9.00 a. m. Elder C. C. toon being at the station to meet me then we walked to bro nelsons after dinner we walked back to town mailed a cupple letter then went back

to bro Nelsons had a fine supper
and also a good cottage meeting +
spent the night with Bro Nelsons.

Sun. 8. Got up feeling fine after breakfast
we went to Sunday School, and
also had dinner where we held
S. C. then about 3.00 P. m. we walked
back to Bro Collins then we held
another meeting after that we went
back to bro Nelsons and spent the
night again.

Mon. 9. Studyed in the fore noon. and
went to bro Wilsons for dinner
spent most of the after noon at
bro Wilsons and went back to bro
Nelsons for the night.

Tue 10 after breakfast Elder toon decided
to go to the races at Charolette
He left at 11.00 a. m. so I spent the
rest of the day at bro Nelsons studying
and also the night again.

Wed. 11. Studyed most of the day had
dinner with bro Collins, and spent
the night again at bro Nelsons.

thu. 12. I left bro Nelsons to go to centerville got to the depot to early.
so I went to the post office and
there wasnt any mail so I went
back to the station found my Grip
was gone. waited and looked
around for it about two hours
missed the train. and then a

went to Bro Sam. Beanhams Jr. and
got the names of the Family then
we got a ride to Sis _____ there
we stayed a little while Had dinner
and about 4.30 P.m. Bro Linder Br,
Came along in his Car road as far
as Bro Joines there we spent the
night. also seen the 5 live oppossens
he had in a box.

Wed. 18. Got up feeling fine Walked to
Bro Linders that morning there &
spent the day in reading the book
named "added upon." sure was fine
Elder tempest & Bunnell came in
on us from Blainy So we had a
real good visit and spent the
night all by our selves in a lone
house sure did have a fine nights
rest.

thur 19. Elder tempest got one of the
members Car and took Elder
toon & I to Bro toms Beanhams. then
he went back to Elder Bunnell. sure
had a fine supper and also a good
nights rest.

Fri 20. Got up pretty early went to
Blythewood where we had
mailed got there and couldent
get our mail so I took the train
to Columbia. Elder toon waited
for the mail. Igot in Col. there I
met Elders Clement, Bush, Plumb,

and west. then I went right up
town got my shoes half soled then
went back to the room Elder toon
had came in while I was out.
I waited a little while and he came
in I read my mail over then I
went down and got me a pair of
pants. then we all went to the
Y. M. C. A. got a good bath then
Elder Plumb I'd went down to sis
Smiths and spent the night.

Sat. 21. we all met at the room all of
the Elders but Elder Plumb & I decided
to go to Atlanta for the dedication
Elder Plumb & I went up, and seen the
dentist seen when he could work
on my teeth then we left for
Smallwood had to walk nearly
all the way to Centerville spent
the night at Bro Sam. Branhams.

Sun 22. went to meeting at 10.00 a.m. officers
& teachers meeting then at 1.00 Sunday
School. then at 3.00 P. m. we held
another preaching service I spoke
on the God Head. at 4.00 P. m. another
preaching & I spoke on the Kingdom
of God. spent the night at S. R.

Mon 23. Studyed some wrote a litter or two
then we went to Sis Freemans for
dinner sure had a fine dinner
then we went back to Bro Sams &
studyed some more went to bro Frank Br.
and spent the night.

Nov 24 Got up feeling fine after breakfast
we walked over to to see how Sis Wilson
was and found she was improving then
we walked back to Bro Sams B. a
little while and then we went to Bro
Sam Jr. and had dinner after dinner
we visited a little while then we
went to Bro Christesens God old
pal of Elder Plumbs there we had a
fine supper and also a fine visit
had a good nights rest also.

Nov 25 Elder Plumb & I went to Sis Sams
and carried Sis Christesens meat
over to her. had a fine dinner
after dinner we went to Bro Sams
and got our Grips and hit the road
for Bro Toms. Got a ride to smallwood
walked the rest of the way 8 miles
there we had a fine supper and
also a good nights rest.

Nov 26 Thanksgiving day at bro toms Branham
my first thanksgiving day in the
mission field Sure had a fine
dinner rained most of the day
but we enjoyed our selves anyway
Spent the day in visiting with the
family also spent that night there.

Nov 27 after a very fine breakfast Elder
Plumb drove the ford to Blythewood
took the girls to school and waited
for our mail got our mail about 9:30
a. m. went back to bro Branhams

read our mail over then we took
our Strips and hit the Highway for
Columbia walked about 2 miles then
we got a ride the rest of the way.
I went and seen the Dentist made a
date with him and we spent the
night at sis Smithdales.

Sat 28. Got up feeling bine and after breakfast
we studyed some I wrote a letter and
went to the Dentist and get my tooth
fixed again at sis Smithdale.

Sun 29. Got up feeling fine fast day
fasted went to Sunday School &
then preaching afterwards. then
we went to dinner with sis Smith
after dinner we all went to the
opening exercises of the new school
that the jounion order gave they
presented the Flag & Bell to the
School, after that we went back
to the hall there we had a fine
meeting but I took up all the time
Elder Plumb didnt get to speak
we went and spent the night at sis
Smith.

Mon 30. walked up town and after a little
studing I went back to the Dentist
and he finished the work on my
tuth. studyed some more then
we went to a meeting at ~~Brio~~
Feldus had a fine meeting and we
went and spent the night at sis

December 1, 1926

Tue. 1.
After breakfast at sis. Smiths we went to the room there we played for a while then we walked down to the ferferine Hotel where we studyed some or till 4.30 P. M., then we went back to the room there we meet Elder Brockbank & Farr they had come in from the dedication after talking some Elder Plumb & I went to Bro. Davis for supper then we went to sis Bullards also we meet the two [?] in that [?] his [?] for Book of morming Glass then we [?] & sis Beck Elder Brockbank & I went and get their [?] went back to the room and spent the M.

Wed. 2.
Romed around town most of the day and studyed some then at night we all went to mutual there they had a debat and I was put on judge for one side but I lost for them sure was fine after which we went to our room for the M.

Thur. 3.
Got up feeling fine Elder Plumb & I hit the Highway for Centerville got a ride to winnsboro so we took it went to Bro Nelsons had dinner appointed a meeting then we studyed some had a fine meeting and I gave a B of m. to Mr. Tanner. spent the night with Bro Nelson.

Fri. 4.
Mail day and 12 miles from our mail so we jes got out and took the Highway as usually got a ride to Ridgeway didn't get our mail and so we started for Bro Sam Branham got to sis meddlins had dinner then went on to Bro Sams after reading our mail we write some letters and went to Bro

70

Morgan nelsons for supper after supper
we went to the Church there we held a
fine preaching services went to Bro
Sam Beanhams Jr. for the night.

Sat 5: after breakfast we went back to Bro
Sam. Beanhams and we pop and
finished the Candy I got from Melvin &
Julia then we studyd some more and
went to Bro margons nelsons for the night.

Sun 6. Fast day so we fasted went to
Priest Hood meeting then officers & teachers
meeting and Sunday School and a testimony
meeting. then we went to Bro Sams B.
for dinner after dinner we had to
study some held another meeting at
200 o'Clock. and again at 7.30 P. M. again
at Bro Sam. B. for the night.

Mon 7. Got up before daylight had breakfast
then road to Smallwood with him
and started for Col. On the highway
walked about 7 miles past Blythewood
and got a ride all the way to Col. went
to the room saw the other two Elders and
then we went to dinner, after dinner
Elder Brockbank & I went to see some of
the members that hadent seen any Elders
for quite a while and when
we came back to the room we went
tracting for a while put out tracts
a piece and I gave out one B. of m. then
we went to a Cottage meeting on the mill
village the two Ladys m & Fars spoke
then after meeting the Ladys home we spent the
evening.

Tue 8. after a hasty breakfast Elder Plum & I started for Greenville for Confrence walked about 2½ miles and got a ride to Lexington then we walked about 15 miles and got a ride to newberry there we took the Bus on to Greenville arriving just in time to go to meeting 7.30 P.m. after meeting we all went to our rooms for the N.

Wed. 9. after breakfast we all went to the Church Held a fine meeting at 10.00 a.m. at 12.00 o'clock Pres Richard Pres Callis & Sis Richard Came lunch was served at 2.00 P.m. another meeting was held. and right after that a fine Priest Hood meeting then Preaching again at 7.30

Thur 10. after the eats we all meet at the Church & got my black eye at the room that morning before leaving fooling doing something I hadent aught to. meeting at 10.00 A. m. lunch at 12.30 meeting at 20.0 o'clock. P.m. then Priest Hood right after that and meeting again at 7.30 P.m. we sure recieved some very fine instructions went back to the room for the night.

Fri 11 Mail day at Greenville got our mail good news from Home went and had our pictures taken then we bid all the Elders good=by that was leaving and we stayed at the same place as we'd been staying.

Sat. 12. after settling up for our rooms we

72

moved over next door 12 academy St. and some more of the Elders left out for their Counties. and Elder Ward (Short termer) & I spent the night to-gether.

Sun. 13. First Sunday for me in Greenville went to Sunday School & meeting Elder Ward & I. Sis Berg & Thorpe went to Bro aikens for dinner, sure had a fine time Elder Ward & I went and spent the night with Bro. Settles.

Mon. 14. Rained all day so we didn't do much only stay in and study wrote some letters ect. still at the Boarding

Tue 15. Still kind stormy but we went out tracting had pretty good luck nothing extra. Elder tempest & Plume left for their Counties so Elder Ward & I moved to 19 academy st where we were to stay while in Greenville. still storming.

Wed. 16. went to the cafeteria for breakfast held our meeting at 9 a. m. then we went out tracting. when we came back we cooked our own supper and say we sure did have a real supper.

Thu 17. Breakfast, our usually meeting in the morning and tracting then we had another of them real suppers Elder Ward being the Chief Cook & Bottle washer.

Fri 18. Got up early and went to Spartan where my other belongings were Had dinner with sis Heaton then I took

my stuff and went back to Greenville
where the other Elders were. there I heard
about the Sad news of the death of
Elder wards little boy sure was to
bad. got may mail and read that.

Sat 19. Rained nearly all day so we didnt
do very much only hold our little meeting
and studyed & wrote letters.

Sun. 20. Got up feeling fine after breakfast
we went to Church had Sunday
School & Preaching then we got
aquainted with some of the saints
I went back to the room and studyed
some then back to preaching that
night still at the room.

Mon. 21. after breakfast and our moral meeting
we went tracting had pretty good
luck and then we had another good
home Cooked Supper.

Tue 22. about the same thing happed today
as yesterday. nothing very exiting.

Wed 23. wrote a few letters and studyed some
then Elder ward & I went to the Brunette
Hotel and wrote some more when we
came out we met Elder & Bros. Stead and
two more new Elder Elder merrell from
Blackfoot Idaho & Elder Revell T. Smith
from Draper Utah Came back to the
room and talked matter over a bit
and visited with the new Elders.

Thur 24. didnt go out tracting that day but
stayed in and studyed & wrote some

74

letters then in the evening Elder
Merrell & I went to Bro Haney's for
supper sure had a real supper too. then
we went out to the Hall to the Program
sure had a fine time. but that day
I got some fine packages from Home,
Xmas Cakes & Candies. sure did have
a real fine time.

Dec.
Fri 25
(Christmas)

First Christmas in the mission
Field and at Greenville well we all
met at the room where we had our
class then we all went out to Bro & Sis
Crosbys for dinner. there the two
Lady mis was also there so that made
9 of us there Bros Steif Elfers ward,
Low, ossmen, merrell, Smith and
myself. Sis olive Berg & Sis Thacker [make]
we sure had a real time, a real
dinner one day spent long to
be remembered "yours but not to be
forgotten." it almost seemed like
we was back home. Candy & nuts
and the wonderful treatment the
people showed to us. sure did
hate to see the day come to a end
but it came. we went back to our
rooms well satisfied with the day.

Sat. 26.

Received some more Cakes & Candys
from home say sure sure distressed
our old stomach. it sure is a good
thing Christmas comes once a year.
Elder merrell & I went out tracting for a

little while didn't have much success
Came back and went up the street
to hold a meeting had pretty good
crowd but it was awful cold. after
the meeting Pres Steed & Elder ward went
to Gaffney.

Sun. 27. Went to Sunday and had a pretty
good meeting, after meeting Elders
ward, Smith & my self. the two
Lady mis went to sis Crosbys mothers
for dinner sure did have a real
feast, again. after the dinner we went
back to the Church to get ready for
the funeral of Bro. Ginns. one of the
old members. Elder Low & organen
preached the funeral then we went
back to the Church for the lys meeting
then we all retired back to our rooms.

Mon. 28. wrote some letters studyed some
then at 2.00 P, m. Elder merrill left
Elder Smith & I for Columbia to met
Elder Sheffield then Elder Smith & I
straightened up things for the night
so we could be ready for work

Tue 29. Got up feeling fine after breakfast
& our class we went tracting had
pretty good luck then at night we
went to mutual had a fine Class.

Wed. 30. Breakfast then our class and then
we tracted some more no more luck
they usually spent the night at
the room. study my ect.

76

December 1925 & January 1926.

Thur 31 about the same thing as usually.
after tracting we went out to the
Church. there we had a fine time
associating with each other. then at
12.06 P. m. that night we watched
the old year out and the new one
come in. the Celebrated with fire
works and by ringing the bells &
blowing the whistles. Bro. crosby &
the Lady. m'o took Elder Smith & I
home. went to bed at 1.30 a.m.
1926 of the new year.

Fri 1. Elder Smith & I spent most of the
day at the room studying and wrote
some letters. in the after noon we
went over to visit Bro. Low & examine
then we came back the room for the night

Sat. 2. Studyed some more & wrote a letter
Had our usual class at the room. at
3.00 o'clock we went up on the
street to hold a street meeting
had a pretty good meeting. the Lady.
m'o helped us sing. when we had
finished Elder ward came up so
we slept three in a bed that night
we glad to see Elder ward back.

Sun. 3. Got up at 6.00 a. m., and Elder Low & I
went to seneca there we wandered around
trying to find the Church but couldent
find it so we went on to town and
found Bro. moar after a fine dinner
we held a little meeting at 3.45. P. m.

1- Reana George
Born May 17, 1917
Baptzed June 6, 1936
Confirmed " "Cata___

2- Cecil Randoff
Baptzed June 6, 1936
Confirmed "
Rock Hill -

3 Fannie Minervia ____
B- May 13, 1918
Baptzid 6/6/36 -   By   H. J. a
Confirmed " "   "   J. a.
address R#3 Catawba ___

May and June. 1926,

then we went with him to a cematary
where a bablist preacher was preaching
well there was about 300 people there
and after the minister got through
he ask if any one else wanted to
speak well I jumped at the appertunity
and spoke a few min. then after
the services some of the people
wanted to hear us speake some
more so we went down to Bro.
Sanders and held a fine openair
meeting we had about 30 there. then
we went back to town had preaching
again at Bro M. Burditt.

Mon 31. Well we sure didnt do much today
we attended the Corner's inquest at
the Court House. for the killing of
a "Bohim" fellow. Elmond Warren
is mixed up in the affair the
first inquest & we attended spent
the night at Stacys.

Tue 1. Rather cool for the first of June.
well we worked with Stacy again
hoeing Potatoes, then I wrote a letter
and Elder Smith went and set out
some sweet potatoes spent the night
again at Stacys.

Wed. 2 after a good nights rest and
a fine breakfast we put in a full
day tracting in the Limestone
met with pretty good success.
had a few real turndowns.

110

Thur #.3 worked with Stacy again this a.m. nearly feel like a real Southern Farmer now. after dinner we put our missionary clothes on again and tracted on the alma mill. well we had pretty good luck. always get a few hard heads. met Bro. & Sis. Brown. Came on back to Stacys for the night.

Fri. #.4 tracted on the Irene mill. had some real cold turn downs there about the same as I found them last summer. didn't have much success. mail day also at Goffney good news from Home.

Sat. #.5 Got up pretty early this morning after breakfast we caught the train for Rock-Hill then we went to Bro. Robert Blues where we spent the night.

Sun. #.6 Got up feeling fine after breakfast Bro Blue took us to the Nation there we met many more of the Lamanite Brethren. also Elder Clement & Pearce from Chester had a fine visit Sunday School at 10.30 a.m. testimony right after then we went to Bro Blues for dinner. at 2.30 P.m. meeting again had a fine crowd. Preaching again at 7.30 Elder Pearce & I spoke at the evening meeting. Elder Clement & I went to Bro. S.T. Blues for the night Elder Pearce & Smith went to Bro Robert Harris for the night. Oh! boy. have a good nights rest.

Mon. 7 after breakfast Bro. Elder went
to the Catawba River for a swim and
had a fine time to I'll say during
the afternoon we had a baptismal
services which 5 more were added to
the fold. Elder Smith performing the
ordinances, held another fine meeting
that night the house being full. Elder
Clement & I were at Bro. S. F. Blue to-
night. Elders Pearce & Smith at Bro. Harris.

Tue. 8 Studied some played Horseshoe till
noon then Elder Smith and I were
going to leave but we changed our
mind. So we appointed another meeting
and the house was full again. We
went again to Catawba river for a
swim oh! boy what a time we had
there were two girls from Columbia
up there may white & Bessie Rowe.
this night Elder Clement & I went
to Bro. Roberts Harris for the nite

Wed. 9 we got up early after breakfast
we bid the Saints & Elders adieu
and rode to Rock Hill with Bro.
Brown. Spent the night with Bro.
Herbert Blue that night.

Thur. 10 tracted some in Rock Hill to-day
had pretty good success we went
over and visited Bro. & Sis Harris a
little while and spent the night
again at Bro. Herberts Blues after
eating supper with Sis Harris

112

Fri 11. Mail day and here we are in Rock
Hill. about 12.30, we caught the train
for Gaffney. there we met Pres Tempest.
at Stacys after a good little chat.
I spent the night at Hells and Pres.
& Elder Smith spent the night with
Stacys.

Sat. 12 Visited and studyed some this
morning. this after noon we held
a street meeting but we never
had much of a crowed.

Sun. 13 We went to Bro Mawin Buditts
and held a Priest Hood meeting
all three of we Elders went to Stacys
for dinner after dinner we went to
Bro Joe Blacks at 2.30 we held a
fine open air meeting Pres. & I spoke,
at 4.45. another Preaching service
at Bro, David Whites Pres & Elder Smith
preached. we administered to sis Frye.
& Bro Hill we all three spent the nite
at Bro Hill.

Mon. 14 Didnt do much to-day visited
with Pres. wrote a letter or studyed
some,

Tue 15. After a good nights rest. and a fine
breakfast & dinner Elder Smith & I
went to Spartanburg on the Pres cost
50¢ rented a room & Pres came in
on the 6.30 train Elder Smith went
to meet Him that night from my
window I say with my own eyes the

first lady smoker in my life. in the Franklin Hotel.

Wed. 16. Studyed some this morning about 1:00 P.m. we went tracting had pretty good success.

Thur. 17. after our breakfast and studying a little we all three went out tracting Bro. was going to show us how to sell books. when we came in that night Bro. had sold one, Elder Smith 3 & me 1. sure struck a hard bunch to deal with Bro. & Elder Smith went out to visit Sis Deaton Bro. also left for

Fri. 18. Columbia. so Elder Smith & me alone again to-night.

Mail Day in Spartanburg got our mail and went down town and blowed in $16.50. for a new summer suit I sold a B. of m. to the Clerk. came back to the room nearly Broke. good news from Home again

Sat. 19. Left this morning about eleven o'clock for Greenville only walked about ½ mile and Bro. Wm Hollis came along and picked us up stoped at Greer and got 10¢ worth of Ice cream for 5¢. went on to Greenville then we met Elder Lance & Plumb. had a fine visit. Elder Lance & Plumb had moved from the Mr. David apt. to 9 whitsin Street. we went out and spent the night with Bro & Sis Crosby

To spend the fourth of July, caught the train for Rock Hill changed trains at Blacksburg & Elder Smith lost his ticket. got in Rock Hill about 11.30 and met Bro Blue & Bro. Walter Harris and they were just going to leave for the nation. So we took the train back way and Herbert Blue was there to meet us. just got to the nation to ask the Blessing on the food and help eat it which we sure did enjoy very much. then we played Horseshoes a while and then went to the Junction and played Ball with the Indians but got beat but oh! boy it was fun. Came back and had a meeting to night we stayed with Bro. Blue.

Sun. 4. Held fine meeting to day with the house full at all meetings Elder Clement & Pearce Came in about noon from Greatfalls. with some of the members. we sure did enjoy our selves very much. Elder Clement & I spent the night at Bro. S. A. Blues.

Mon. 5. Still at the nation well we played horseshoe nearly all day, in the afternoon we went to the River picked a gallon of blackberries and had a fine swim in the River then we Came back and held a fine meeting. Elder Clement & I went up to Bro. Robert Harris for the night.

118

Tue. 6. after a good breakfast we played Horseshoe's again and had a fine Visit with each other after dinner we went down to the river again we four picked four gallons of blackberries to day. Elder Smith & ~~Clement~~ went in the river again went back up to the house after supper we held another fine meeting Clement & I stayed with Bro. S. F. Blue for night

Wed. 7. Eldr Clement & I visited some this morning ~~played~~ horeshoe again Sure had lots of fun well after coming from the river we had another meeting to night had a good crowd out it was a Priest Hood meeting Elder Smith & I bid them all adue then we went home with Bro. Robert Harris.

Thur. 8. Sure got up early today after breakfast we went to Rockhill with Bro. Whullock then went to Bro. Herbert Blue spent most of the day there and Bro. Walter Harris & I went to the Show, after we came back we spent the night with Bro. Walter Harris.

Fri. 9. we stayed at Rockhill till about noon then took the Bus to Cloven there we found the members and had a good visit with them also spent the night with them (their names were Brookouts)

Sat. 10. after a fine breakfast we

went tracting for about a hour
we met with fairly good success
after dinner we was going to stage
a Street but was unsuccessful
no one on the Streets so we took
the Highway to Gastonia 12 miles
well we good a ride nearly all the
way. Stayed in Gastonia for about
an hour then we dicided to go to
Bro. Bethunes about 17 miles — So we
hit the Highway again and arrived
there about 6.30 P.m, only annie may
Home but the others came in later.
Sure had a fine Visit Spent the nite
with them to-night.

Sun. 11.   after breakfast we walked
around with Bro. Bethune and
saw the Peacock's sure are pretty.
Came back to the house after
dinner, we spent most of the
time talking to a Russellight
on the Gospel. again we stayed there
sure had a fine Visit Ice Cream
& all the good things to eat.

Mon 12.   well we should leave but dicided
to wash. — So I got a pair of over-
alls and helped Sis. Bethune wash
Eldy Smith went with the boys to
the river for a boat ride made
somemore Ice Cream. in the evening
we sang a few Songs then had
Prayer then Elder Smith took

120

Crow one of the boys to work.
Annie may & Sis Bethune went with
him. Sue had a good nights rest.

Thur 13.   after another good breakfast &
dinner we had to leave Bro. Bethune
carried us 4 miles then we hit the
Highway for Gaffney. 47 miles well
it was. 2.00 P.m. then got 8 different
rides walked about 12 miles and was
in Gaffney by 7.00 P.m. Just to
late to get our mail went to
Stacys for the night.

Fed 14.   Went to the post office &
got our lost Fridays mail
good news from Home if it was
late. Studyed most of the day
went to Bro. Mc. Daniels and
held a fine meetings during the
day we saw the Cotton parade.
Spent the nights at Stacy's.

Sat. 15.   Went to the swamps with
Stacy but there was a sick
baby so didnt do much only lay
around. after dinner we came
back to the house and all I
did was play around. Spent the
night at Stacy's again.

Fri 16.   my birth day also 20 years old.
Stacy carried us to Blacks-
burg there we got our mail &
got a box from Home but sent
it back with Stacy. we went
on down to Bro. Will masses the

439

a visit & dinner we went out tracting
had pretty good success appointed
a meeting had a fine crowed out
to our open air meeting spent the
night at Bro. moss

Sat 17.   Still feeling bad but had to
go to Gaffney so we took the
Highway to Gaffney got a ride
nearly all the way went to Stacys
left our Grips and went out to
Bro. Browns for the night sure had
a good nights rest.

Sun. 18.   Got up feeling a little better
Sis Brown fixed me a bowl of
soup. oh! boy it was good Bro.
Brown carried us to Stacys there
we got ready for the meeting went
to Bro. Blacks held a fine open air
meeting then we went to Bro. David
White and held a sacrement meeting
had good attendence went back to
Stacys for the night.

Mon. 19.   Studyed some to day then
went to the swamp and helped
Stacy pick beans again at Stacys

Tue 20.   didnt do much to-day tried
to study & write but it was to
hot so we just hunted the coolest
place we could find and some
Ice Cream that sure tasted fine
went to Bro. millwoods for supper
then he carried us to Wilkinsville
(12 miles)

a visit & dinner we went out tracting had pretty good success appointed a meeting had a fine crowd out to my open air meeting spent the night at Bro. moss,

Sat. 17. Still feeling bad but had to go to Gaffney so we took the Highway to Gaffney got a ride nearly all the way went to Stacys left our Grips and went out to Bro. Browns for the night sure had a good nights rest.

Sun. 18. Got up feeling a little better Sis Brown fixed me a bowl of soup. Oh! boy it was good Bro. Brown carried us to Stacys there we got ready for the meeting went to Bro. Blacks held a fine open air meeting then we went to Bro. David Whits, and held a sacrement meeting had good attendance. went back to Stacys for the night

Mon. 19. Studyed some to day then went to the swamp and helped Stacy pick beans, again at Stacys

Tue. 20. didnt do much to-day tried to study & write but it was to Hot so we just hunted the coolest place we could find and some Ice cream that sure tasted fine went to Bro. millwoods for Supper then he carried us to wilkinsville 12 miles

122

where we held a fine open air meeting
with some nonmembers. had a fine
ride back to Gaffney in the call
of the evening. went back to
Stacys for the night on account
of the bed (hounds).

Wed 21. went to the swamps again
with Stacys pulled fuild a day
& say bay it was hot work. Smith
was on the sick list to day. at Stacys.

Thur 22. After breakfast Stacy had a
good heart and took me to
Cherokee Falls. stoped at Bro.
McDaniels and ate a watermellon
then went on down to the Falls.
went to Bro. Luther Martins. jot
there at 12.30 P. m. after a little nap
we went out tracting on the pasture
Village Had pretty good Success.
appointed a meeting Sue had a
good meeting, under a street meeting
all but one family on that Hill was
out. about 65 or 70. Spent the night
at Bro. Luther martins.

Fri 23. After breakfast we went out tracting
had pretty good Success. at noon
we left on the Highway for Cowpens.
Sue was a hot old day got a ride
to Gaffney stayed there about 2
hours and left for Cowpens 12 mile
& Had to walk all the way. arving
at 10. P. m. went to Bro. Tom Henderson &

woke him up and he fixed the bed sure was glad to roll in I'll say.

Sat. 24. Mail day at Cowpens. got my mail answered a letter or two studyed some about 3.30 P.m. we went up town and staged a street meeting with good success then took the Highway to Gaffney getting a ride most all the way. when we got there we were called to preach a funeral of a little baby that had died 6 month old. at 7.30 P.m. we held the meeting the body was buried that morning spent the night with Bro. & Sis. Mace father & mother of the child.

Sun. 25. Bro. Maces Father requested we call there and talk to his wife on the resurrection. so we did so, Had a fine visit then we went to Stacys and got ready for meeting Bro. Stacy was sick so. Elder Smith drove the car down to Bro. Blacks there we held another fine meeting went to the creek & baptised Bro Black little girl I performing the ordinance. got back just in time to escape the rain storm. held another Sacrement meeting at. Bro. David whits with pretty good attendance.

Mon. 26. I went to the Swamps with Stacys and helped pick beans.

124

and other garden, Stuff, he took
up town. After dinner with Stacys
He carried us. about 12 miles.
within a mile of Bro andy Greens.
Left Stacy and walked on to Bro.
Greens. where we spent the night.

Thrus 27, Got up kinda late raining
So we didnt do much only Visit
and sleep,

Wed. 28. Still at. Andys Greens. more
rain Sure did rain a lot. I put a
Supper on a hive of bees for Bro Gray
and only got one sting Spent the
night again at. Andys.

thu 29. More rain Got up feeling fine
after breakfast and after it cleared
up a little, we took the Highway to
Cowpens got a ride all the way went
to Bro. Hendersons for the night.

Fri 30. Mail day again at Cowpens good
News from Home answered a letter
Home. then we took the Highway
for Spartan. got a ride nearly all
the way. went back to the Caroline
for the night.

Sat. 31 Well here we are again in Spartan
wrote some diary & letters. Studied
quite a bit, went over to Bro. Deaton
and had a pretty good Visits
went back to the Room for the
night. more picture Show fans
our room in the Hotel Franklin.

August for 1926,

Sun. 1.   Got up early went over to Bro
Deatons and then we went to
Greenville with Him to visit got
there in time to attend the S.S.
Class. after Sunday School we
Had a testimony meeting. then
Elder V.G. Lines, LeBaron, Smith &
I went to Bro. Josew Honnup for
dinner Sure had a fine dinner.
Priesthood meeting at. 6 P.m Preach
ing at. 7.30 P. m. Elder Smith & I had
the preaching I spoke on pre-existence
Spent the night at. Bro. Crosbys.

Mon. 2.   after breakfast at Bro. & Sis. Crosbys
and a Short visit we took our grips
and went over to 214 Green ave.
where the other Elders were at and
there we had a fine visit with
them stayed there most all day
went to a show at night. "Chasing
Trouble." Spent the night at Sis
Goggins the same place where the
other Elders were staying.

Tue 3.   Stayed in all day visiting
with each other. about 7.30 Elder
LeBarron & I went one way Elder
Smith & Lines went another to
Hold a Street meeting we met
with good Success had a good
crowd came back and helped
make some Ice cream. then we
retired still at Sis Goggins.

126

Wed. 4. Got up feeling pretty good. After a bite to eat. Elder Lewis & LeBaron went to the depot with us. We bed them adieu and went to the Limon where we spent the day in tracting. Had fine success. took the Highway to Spartan went back to the Carolina for the nite.

Thu. 5. Got up late feeling pretty good. though rested all day Sundays & wrote a letter or two us. then we went out to Bro Deatons & Played rook for a while. back to the room.

Fri. 6. Mail day in Spartan. again good News from Home. answered the Home letter as usual. then we went out by the Saxon mill and tracted some. had pretty good success. back to the room for the night.

Sat. 7. After a little bite to eat we took the Highway to Goffney. got a ride nearly all the way. Appointed a meeting at Bro David whits. told all we could about the meeting. and went Home with Stacys again.

Sun. 8. After our arrival. Daily dozen we visited mostly with Stacy & family that night we went to Bro whits and had a fine crowed out to our meeting. Appointed a meeting for Tues & went Home again with Bro. Stacy Westmoreland.

Mon. 9. Still at Stacys, visited some more and advertised the meeting a little more, then about 6.40 we were at the Depot to meet Pres. H. S. Tempest & Elder Sheffield. They came all O K. we talked a while then we walked on out to Bro. Brown for the night.

Tue. 10. Got up, feeling fine after breakfast we walked to Sis Warrens there we had dinner then went on up to Bro. Hills where Bros. Tempest & Sheffield was had a fine visit with them went to Bro. Whites for the meeting had a fine crowd out. Elder Smith & I stayed at Bro. H. S. Hills. Bros & Sheff at Stacys.

Wed. 11. we all meet at Bro. Hills where we held a fine Priest Hood meeting, all ate dinner with Bro. Hills that night we had another fine meeting, Bros. & Sheff. Spoke. Elder Sheff. & I went to Stacys for the night.

Thur 12. after breakfast we all took the train for Spartan & stopped at Cowpens Pres. Tempest went on to Columbia to marrie a couple, I went to Bro. Parkers left my Grip & went out tracting came in for dinner and went out again spent most of the day at it had pretty good Success spent the night with Bro. Parker & Family after a short visit with Sis Henderson & Bro. Burdett.

128

Fri 13. Mail day at Cowpens & got both my
mail & Elder Smith aged at 10.00 a.m.
I took the train for Spartan. went to
the room and found all everything o.k.
gave Elder Smith His mail at 12.00 a.m.
we went to the arkright and held
a fine meeting with about 65 present.
went back to the room. I stayed in
Elder Smith and Sheff. went teaching
at the room again to-night.

Sat. 14 Studyed most of the day Elder Smith &
Sheffield went around and visited
the members & apointed to meeting
for the Sunday at Bro. Deatons. read
mostly all day. Stayed in at the
room for the night.

Sun. 15: after a little bite to eat. we
went over to Bro. Deatons where we
held a Sacrement meeting with the
members. Elder Sheffield being the
main speaker apointed a meeting
at Sis. Mosleys for that night went
back to the room studyed some
more. went and held another meeting
not many out only women folks
apointed a meeting for tue and
retired to the room for the night

Mon. 16. after a little more studying Elder
Sheffield & I went teaching for a
while had pretty good success
went to the station to meet Bros.
then we went to the room where we

Thu. 17. Layed around in the room most of the day reading & studying etc. Visiting with each other. also spent the night at the room. after holding a meeting at Sis Moffleas but only Lady folks were there. Bro. Tempest & Elder Smith spoke

Wed. 18. Still at Spartanburg. well we went out tracting some. went to the Saxon & held a meeting then we came back to the room Bro. Tempest and Elder Smith went out and Visited Sis Deaton & Family. Elder Shuffield went to a Show seen the three musketeers. at the room again to night

Thurs, 19. went down to the depot to see Bro. & Sheff. off for Greenville we went back to the room and studyed most the rest of the day. alone again to night Elder Smith & I.

Fri 20. Mail day in Spartan. Sure heard good news again to-day. rested some more today & wrote a few letters & studyed quite a bit. still at the room & we signed up for another week. thats some more.

Sat. 21. after making out our reports & studying a little we went tracting a little sold 6 little books & I. B. for went to Bro Deatons where we visited some more. and stayed quite late typewriting etc. then we went back to the room.

130

Sun. 22. Another Sunday in Spartanburg, we slept till late had breakfast & dinner together then we went out to Rev. Deaton where we held a fine meeting and then we also had a fine visit with the folks.

Mon. 23. Got up felt pretty good after a bite, over went out to the big mill and held a meeting with the men. Came back to the room after tracting some. had pretty good success.

Tue. 24. As usual again this morning went out to the arkwright but was unable to hold a meeting so we tracted some again came back to the room.

Wed. 25. went out to the Saxon to hold a street meeting but failed, so we hit the road to the arkadia mills. where we visited 30 homes. came back with a gas man. Just got a ride in time or we would of got wet we went down town after it quite raining and got a box of candy for Sis. Deaton for her Birthday. but it rained. So we couldn't get back from Deatons so we spent the night with them.

Thu. 26. Got up pretty early after breakfast we went up town packed up our grips and took the train to Union where we got a room and went out tracting quite a bit but had fine success spent the nite at the room.

Fri.27. Mail day at Union. A good letter from and news of conference. Home again to day. after reading over the mail we went out tracting again. here had good success again came back pretty tired was going to hold a meeting but the boss wouldn't let us.

Sat. 28. Still in union went out tracting again this morning for a while sold 2 little books and had many good conversations. was going to hold a street meeting but the Salvation army beat us to it so we took the Highway for Gaffney. got a ride with a preacher to Cowpens. then got another ride to Gaffney. took the train there made 46 miles in 3½ hours. apointed some meeting for sunday & stayed with Stacy to-night.

Sun. 29. Got up feeling fine again this morning. after dinner we went to Bro. Blacks where we held a good open air meeting. then we went on back up Town with Stacy. where we studyed some & then at 7.30 P.M. we went to Bro. Hill where we held another fine meeting. Spent the night again at Stacys.

Mon. 30. after breakfast we went with stacy after giving us his bees) out to the Alma mills went to sis merrins Had dinner & tasted fresh sis worrings little boy 8 years old that we went to Bro. Browns good visit with them. for the night

132

August and September 1926

Tue, 31. after breakfast we walked to Stacys then on to Bro. McDaniels to see about baptising the boys. went back to Stacys for dinner and then we went down and bathed the boys. came back got our Grips & left on the Highway for Cowpens. got a ride after walking 5 miles. went to Bro. Parkers for the night after a short visit to Bro. & Sis. Henderson. heard that the North Carolina Elders were coming down also to Greenville to meet with us.

Wed. I after a good nights rest and a breakfast we hit the Highway for Spartanburg got a ride all the way went to the Carolina for the night got our other suits and put our light suits in the wash. then we spent the night at the room to night.

Thu 2. Got up early to day after a little bite to eat we went and got our suits and went to the arkright mill to hold a meeting but we were again unsuccessful. So we caught a jitney back to town and then went out to Daytons and left some of our things then we hit the Highway for Greenville we got a ride all the way. went to 214 Green ave. reported to Pres and then went and had supper then Elder Smith & I went out to Sis Croshys for the night they wasn't Home but we went in any way & made our selves to Home.

Fri. 3. Mail day in Greenville after a good
nights rest, we went up town got our
trips and reported at the Virginia Hotel
read our mail then I went down town
& got me a pair of $6.00 Shoes for 5.00 then
we walked back to 214 Green ave again
and visited a little while met many
of the Elders. Both M.C. & S.C. most
of us had registered at the Hotel by
now. So we went there for the night.
after a good Priest Hood meeting at the
Church where we all reported.

Sat. 4. up early went for breakfast then to the
Church for Conference. meeting at 10,30
a.m. I was called on first to break the
ice. Sure had a fine meeting at 12.50.
Bro. Chas. A. Callis & wife came with
two Ladys m's & one of His Daughters.
meeting again at 2.30 & 7.30, P.m. which
many of the Elders Preached & bore their
testimonys. back to the room for the nite
Elder Staffer & I rode over to town with Sis
Carrie Connoly Dessie mcclenen & Louise Bethune
also we went to see part of the Show free.

Sun. 5. after breakfast we went to the Church
where men were ready for the second
day of conference. Elders Cole & I had to
take care of the water 3 more Public
meeting again today two more Lady
m's & one of Bro. Callis Daughters came
in also today and the Lady m's &
Grace & Josephine Callis Sang at the meeting

134

Bro Callis being the the last speaker
Sun. Elder Staffer & I road again to town
in the Buick Roadster.

Mon 6. At 9.00 o'Clock we all meet at the
Church again for Priest Hood meeting which
was held four hour many questions being
ask and discussed then at 4 P.m we
met again for our asignments. Elder
D. R. LeBarron to be my Companion & to
labor in Kershaw & Chester Co. went back
to the Hotel for the night visited quite
a bit with the N.C. Bro. before retiring.

Tue. 7. Biding the Elders good by. 16 of the
N.C. Elders left out this morning
on the Highway for their Counties. some
had over 400 miles to go. many of the
S.C. Elder's left also. Elder Brockbank &
Riding, LeBaron & I went to Spartan.
with Bro Goggins went to the Caroling
and got a room. then I took Elder Brock
bank & Riding around & Showed them
where the Joint lived then Elder
Brockbank & I went to a Show. came
back to the room about 11.00 P.m. ready
for the bed

Wed. 8. After breakfast we went and got a place
seen Sparto Circus Parade. then we
went out to Deatons got our Grips &
took the train to Columbia at 1.5.6. after
biding Elder Brockbank & Riding adiue..
Cost us 2.30 arrived in Columbia at 4.43..
went to another Show spent the night
at 1015 resembly st;

Elder Marcus Charles Ellis   --   SSM 1927-1929

PHOTO 137 MARCUS CHARLES ELLIS 1926 AND THEN LATER

Birth date, place   - 2 August 1908, North Ogden, Weber, Utah
Death date -- 30 April 1971
Baptism date -- 6 August 1916   --   Baptism by -   B E Chatelam
Father's name - Chas Wm Ellis   --   Mother's name -   Louise Brown

Southern States -   April 1927–June 1929   -   Age Called: 18
Southern States
Set Apart: 12 April 1927   -   End Date: 4 June 1929
Departed From Home: 15 April 1927
Priesthood office: Elder
Called From: North Ogden, Weber, Utah, United States
Set apart by: O F Whitney

Missionary Department missionary registers, 1860-1959, Vol. 5, p. 203, line 266.
First Presidency missionary calls and recommendations 1877-1918: CR 1 168, Church History Library
11/28/1906 Recommendations to call for a missionary course along with James Jackson Cude. He served a Southern States

North Ogden
Nov 28, 1896.

Pres George Reynolds.

Dear Bro:

If compatable we would like the
presidency to call, Elders Charles Ellis,
& James Cude to take a short-
missionary course to the Weber
Stake Acodemy prepatory to filling
a mission to the nations of
the earth.

Please notify them as soon as
possible as I have arranged with
Apostle David O., McKay for them
to enter.

Your Bro:
James Ward. Bp

Elder Burton Rasmus Scott -- SSM 1923-1926

Burton Scott
Southern States, 1923–25

PHOTO 139   BURTON RASMUS SCOTT

Born: 27 January 1904 Park City, Summit, Utah –
died 5 December 2001 Layton, Davis, Utah.
Baptism date 1912 -- Baptism by John E Johnson
Father's name - George Albert Scott --   Mother's name - Anna C Anderson

Mission Southern States -- November 1923 – March 1926 --   Age Called: 19

Southern States
 Set Apart: 6 November 1923 -- End Date: 25 March 1926
 Departed From Home: 7 November 1923
Priesthood office: Elder   - Called From: Provo, Utah, Utah, United States
Set apart by: Seymour B Young
Missionary Department missionary registers, 1860-1959, Vol. 5, p. 102, line 652.

Elder Willard Anderson on his mission in South Carolina with Elder Burton R. Scott, one of his companions.

PHOTO 140   ELDER WILLARD ANDERSEN AND ELDER BURTON R SCOTT

Elder Claudius C Toone -- SSM 1924-1926

PHOTO 141 - CLAUDIUS C TOONE

Birth date, place -- 25 January 1902, Croydon, Morgan, Utah
Death date -- 10 March 1980
Baptism date -- 17 June 1911 -- Baptism by -- W H Toone
Father's name -- Wilford Toone -- Mother's name -- Harriet Grover

Southern States - March 1924–May 1926 - Age Called: 22
Southern States
Set Apart: 25 March 1924 - End Date: 13 May 1926
Departed From Home: 26 March 1924
Priesthood office: Elder
Called From: Croydon, Morgan, Utah, United States
Set apart by: Melvin J Ballard

Missionary Department missionary registers, 1860-1959, Vol. 5, p. 112, line 220.

Elder Owen William West -- SSM 1925-1927

PHOTO 142 - ELDER OWEN WILLIAM WEST AND TWO CATAWBA GIRLS

Birth date, place - 26 May 1905, Hoytsville, Summit, Utah
Death date - 9 February 1909
Baptism date - 26 July 1913 -- Baptism by - Chas M Mulin
Father's name - Charles H West -- Mother's name - Hannah M Brown

Southern States - October 1925–December 1927 - Age Called: 20

Southern States -- Catawba Indian Nation, South Carolina Conference
Set Apart: 27 October 1925 -- Departed From Home: 29 October 1925
Arrived In Field: 2 November 1925
Released: 12 December 1927 -- Arrived At Home: 29 December 1927
Mission type: Proselytizing -- Marital Status: Single
Served with companion: Willard John Andersen Vearl Arthur Lines
Priesthood office: Elder
Called From: Hoytsville, Summit, Utah, United States
Set apart by: J Golden Kimball

Missionary Department missionary registers, 1860-1959, Vol. 5, p. 147, line 721.
Southern States Mission history, 1832-1964: LR 8557 2, Church History Library.
Southern States Mission history, 1832-1964: LR 8557 2, Church History Library.
July 3, 1927 branch conference with Catawba Indians

PHOTO 143   ELDER OWEN WILLIAM WEST - SAM AND LOUISA BLUE – ELBER VEARL ARTHUR LINES

Elder Vearl Arthur Lines   --   SSM 1925-

PHOTO 144   VEARL ARTHUR LINES

Birth date, place - 2 September 1906, Pima, Graham, Arizona
Death date - 6 April 1969
Baptism date - 4 September 1914   --   Baptism by - Phil C Merrell
Father's name - William Arthur Lines   --   Mother's name - Sarah Evaline Anderson

Southern States - October 1925–Unknown - Age Called: 19

Southern States -- Catawba Indian Nation, South Carolina Conference, Georgia District
Set Apart: 7 October 1925   --   Departed From Home: 8 October 1925
Arrived In Field: 13 October 1925
Released: 21 November 1927
Mission type: Proselytizing   --   Marital Status: Single
Served with companion: Owen William West
Priesthood office: Elder
Called From: Graham, Arizona, United States
Set apart by: Charles H Hart

Missionary Department missionary registers, 1860-1959, Vol. 5, p. 144, line 597.
Southern States Mission history, 1832-1964: LR 8557 2, Church History Library.
Mission index

PHOTO 145   VEARL ARTHUR LINES AND J M SMITH 1927

PHOTO 146 TR T SMITH, J M SMITH AND V A LINES

PHOTO 147   ELDERS J M SMITH AND V A LINES

Elder Don Raymond LeBaron   --   SSM 1925-1928

PHOTO 148   DON RAYMOND LEBARON

 Birth date, place - 25 December 1900, Santaquin, Utah, Utah
Death date   - 19 March 1978
Baptism date - 18 September 1909 --   Baptism by -- Geo W LeBaron
Father's name - George W LeBaron --   Mother's name - Mary A Openshaw

Southern States - October 1925–April 1928 --   Age Called: 24

Southern States
Set Apart: 20 October 1925 -   End Date: 27 April 1928
Departed From Home: 22 October 1925
Priesthood office: Elder
Called From: Santaquin, Utah, Utah, United States
Set apart by: Rudger Clawson

Missionary Department missionary registers, 1860-1959, Vol. 5, p. 146, line 685.

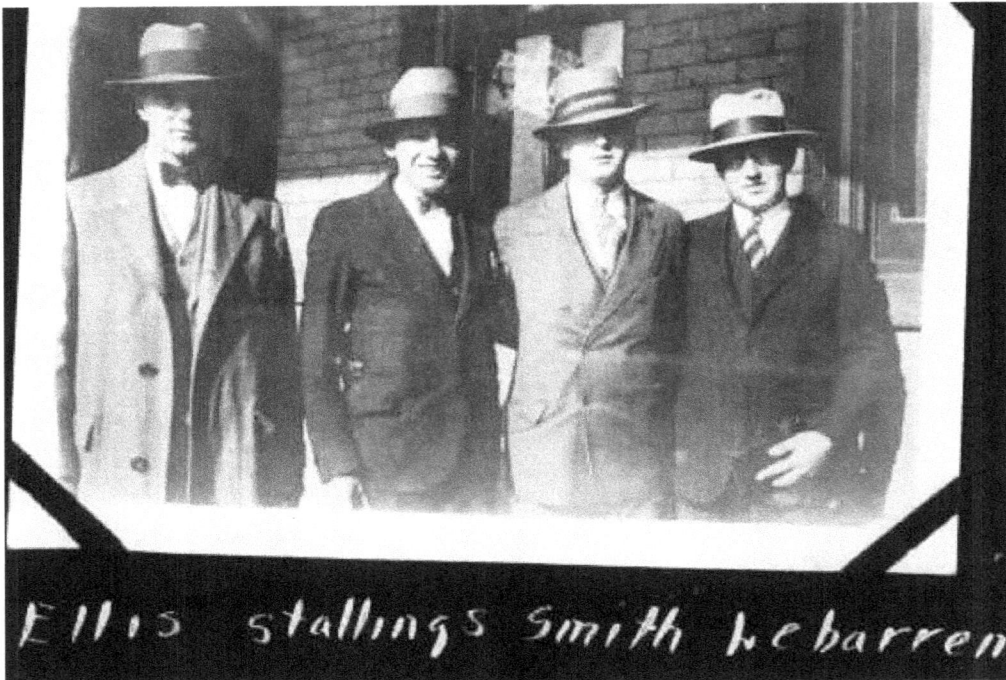

PHOTO 149   ELDERS- ELLIS, STALLINGS, SMITH, LEBARREN

PHOTO 150   ELDERS – AT SOUTH CARLINA CONFERENCE - NAMES LISTED BELOW

Joseph Matt Smith -- (1906-1992) KW8N-DG7
Elder Bosgarter -- Ernest Wilford Bosgieter - (1904-1996) KWZF-S7F
Elder Branham - Estill Green Branham - (1908-1992) KW8F-PWN
Elder Stalling -- LaVon Stallings - (1907-1964) KW88-PCG
Elder Chadwick - Ellwood Chadwick - (1906-1965) KWCD-5NZ
Elder Merrill - Eugene Hyde Merrill - (1908-1973) KWZX-C8Q
Newel Bernard Cox - (1894-1978) KWCW-BLJ

Elder Scott - Wesley Scott - (1902-1992) KWZK-K44
Elder Roos - Samuel Andrus Roos - (1902-1988) KWZ6-6C2
Elder West - Owen William West - (1905-1989) KWZ2-LBL
Elder Page - Lawrence P Page - (1905-1984) KWZD-TND
Elder Riding - James Regnald Riding - (1907-1955) KWJZ-1C1
Elder Plumb - Alma John Plumb - (1901-1988) KWZ4-9MD
Elder Pearce - William Edward Pearce Jr. - (1899-1979) KWC6-54N
Elder LeBaron - Don Raymond LeBaron - (1900-1978) KWCV-MX9
Bror Henry Linde - (1902-1976) KWZ3-871
Elder Smith - Revell Terry Smith - (1904-1969) KWCG-M

Sister Alice Elenora Ohlson -- SSM 1926-1928

PHOTO 151 ALICE ELENORA OHLSON

Birth date, place - 27 January 1907, Sandy, Utah
Death date - 5 December 1973
Baptism date - 7 March 1915 -- Baptism by - Abel Johnson
Father's name - Gustave L Ohlson -- Mother's name - Esther E Sodergren

Southern States - October 1926–April 1928 - Age Called: 19

Southern States
Set Apart: 19 October 1926 - End Date: 27 April 1928
Departed From Home: 22 October 1926
Called From: Sandy, Salt Lake, Utah, United States
Set apart by: R R Lyman

Missionary Department missionary registers, 1860-1959, Vol. 5, p. 187, line 877a

Elder Joseph Matt Smith   --   SSM 1927-1929

PHOTO 152   JOSEPH MATT SMITH

Birth date, place - 4 May 1906, West Jordan, Salt Lake, Utah Territory
Death date   -   15 March 1992
Baptism date - 5 September 1914   --   Baptism by - R W Palmer
Father's name - August O Schmidt - Mother's name - Ettie H Palmer

Southern States   -   June 1927–June 1929   -   Age Called: 21

South Carolina Conference
Set Apart: 7 June 1927 -   End Date: 17 June 1929
Departed From Home: 10 June 1927
Priesthood office: Elder
Called From: Sandy, Salt Lake, Utah, United States
Set apart by: J Golden Kimball

PHOTO 153   ELDERS- ELLIS, STALLINGS, SMITH AND LEBARREN

PHOTO 154 - JOESPH MAT SMITH

PHOTO 155   ELDERS — ROOS, PIERCE, NUNNELL, SMITH AND LABARREN

467

PHOTO 156   ELDER J M SMITH AND UNKNOWN AND 2ND ELDER VEARL LINES AND JOSEPH MATT SMITH

PHOTO 157   ELDER JOSEPH MATT SMITH AND VERNON HORTIN JENSEN

I was called on my mission to the Southern States Mission by President Heber J. Grant on April 29,

1927 to enter the Mission Home in Salt Lake Monday, May 30. I was ordained a Seventy and set apart for my mission by J. golden Kimball in June 1927 and left Salt Lake on June 10th for Mission Headquarters in Atlanta Georgia. President Charles A. Callis was the Mission president. I spent my entire mission in South Carolina. After I had been in the mission field for about five months, I developed appendicitis and was sent home for surgery. I was operated on in the LDS Hospital by Dr. Middleton, assisted by Dr. J. O. Jones. After being home about a month I went back and finished my mission. It wasn't a very fruitful mission, but I enjoyed it. While I was there, I don't know why, but every time there was a funeral in our district, it seemed as though I was called on to be one of the missionaries to help conduct the service. I helped conduct eleven funerals while I was there.

One time we went up to Rock Hill to the Indian Reservation. These people were all members of the Church and it was a delight to go there. A man by the name of Brother Blue was the president of the branch and they treated the missionaries royally whenever we went there.

One day four of us Elders were studying our talks for conference in the chapel when the door opened about half-dozen young people came in. The boy walked up to us and said, "We want to get married. Will you perform the marriage for us?" We weren't supposed to perform a marriage unless there wasn't anyone else there to do it. The girl was 15 and the boy was 17. I was the senior Elder and so I thought the best way to handle the situation so we wouldn't get into trouble, was to give Elder Jensen the authority to perform the ceremony. I thought I never would get an opportunity to perform a wedding ceremony.

About two months later we went to the northwest corner of the State of South Carolina, Walla Walla was the name of the little area. We went there by assignment from our district president to hold a conference. When we were there a couple came and said they would like to get married, but the girl said that her parents wouldn't allow her to join the Church until after they were married. There were no phones so I couldn't get in touch with anyone, so I went ahead and performed the ceremony.

I was released from my mission June 8, 1929. The mission had cost $605. For 24 months. That is quite different from the cost of a mission now. When I first came home from my mission I worked for the John J. F. Schmidt family doing farm work.

"One time we went up to Rock Hill to the Indian Reservation. These people were all members of the Church and it was a delight to go there. A man by the name of Brother Blue was the president of the branch and they treated the missionaries royally whenever we went there." from the history of Joseph Mat Smith

Elder Morris Theodore Bunnell - SSM 1925-1927

PHOTO 158   MORRIS THEODORE BUNNELL AND 2ND BUNNELL AND JOSEPH M SMITH   1927

Birth date, place - 5 November 1905, Spring City, Sanpete, Utah, United States
Death date - 7 June 1988
Baptism date - 10 November 1913   --   Baptism by - John Baxter Jr
Father's name - Stephen L Bunnell - Mother's name - Helena Reese

Southern States   -   October 1925–October 1927   --   Age Called: 19

Southern States
Set Apart: 7 October 1925 - End Date: 21 October 1927
Departed From Home: 8 October 1925
Priesthood office: Elder
Called From: Spring City, Sanpete, Utah, United States
Set apart by: Charles H Hart

Missionary Department missionary registers, 1860-1959, Vol. 5, p. 144, line 598.

Elder Wesley Scott   -   SSM   1927-1930

Wesley Scott   Gender - Male
Birth date and place   --   21 June 1902, Colonia, Oaxaca, Mexico
Death date -- 28 February 1992
Baptism date -- 21 June 1910   Baptism by -- Geo W Scott
Father's name -- Franklin Scott   --   Mother's name -- Sophronia R Morton

Southern States   -   October 1927–March 1930 -   Age Called: 25

Southern States
Set Apart: 11 October 1927
End Date: 15 March 1930
Departed From Home: 12 October 1927
Priesthood office: Elder   Priesthood: Elder
Called From: Prescott, Arizona, United States
Set apart by: J Golden Kimball

Missionary Department missionary registers, 1860-1959, Vol. 5, p. 213, line 642.
Vol. 5, p. 213, line 626 thru 662, Column for Departed date in book has incorrect year of "10/12/1928". Further research shows Correct date "10/12/1927" .

Elder Vernon Hortin Jensen -- SSM 1927-1930

PHOTO 159   VERNON HORTIN JENSEN

Early Mormon Missionaries
Vernon Hortin Jensen
 Birth date, place -- 10 July 1907, Salt Lake City, Utah
Death date - 27 September 1998
Baptism date - 24 June 1916   --   Baptism by - Denton Thomson
Father's name - Joseph E Jensen   --   Mother's name - Grace Hortin

Southern States - December 1927–March 1930 -- Age Called: 20

Southern States
Set Apart: 6 December 1927 - End Date: 23 March 1930
Departed From Home: 7 December 1927
Priesthood office: Elder
Called From: Salt Lake City, Salt Lake, Utah, United States
Set apart by: J Golden Kimball
Stories and Documents

Missionary Department missionary registers, 1860-1959, Vol. 5, p. 222, line 997.

Elder William E Pearce -- SSM 1926-1928

PHOTO 160   WILLIAM E PEARCE

Birth date, place - 20 December 1899, Vernal, Uintah, Utah
Death date - 31 October 1979
Baptism date - 3 July 1909 -- Baptism by - Thos Bingham
Father's name - William E Pearce -- Mother's name - Minnie C Lewis

Southern States - January 1926–January 1928 - Age Called: 26

Southern States
Set Apart: 12 January 1926 - End Date: 18 January 1928
Departed From Home: 13 January 1926
Priesthood office: Elder
Called From: Vernal, Uintah, Utah, United States
Set apart by: Geo Albert Smith
Missionary Department missionary registers, 1860-1959

PHOTO 161   BACK L-R SMITH AND LeBARREN – FRONT L-R ROOS, PEARCE AND BUNNELL

Elder Newell Bernard Cox -- SSM 1928-1930

PHOTO 162   NEWELL BERNARD COX AND IN GROUP PHOTO HE IS THIRD FROM RIGHT IN BACK

Birth date, place - 12 March 1894, Fairview, Sanpete, Utah Territory, United States
Death date - February 1978
Baptism date - 13 April 1902 --   Baptism by - Peter Nielson
Father's name - Amasa Bernard Cox   -   Mother's name - Anna Caroline Hansen

Southern States - January 1928–March 1930   --   Age Called: 33

Southern States
Set Apart: 17 January 1928 --   Arrived At Home: 5 March 1930
Departed From Home: 20 January 1928
Mission type: Proselytizing
Marital Status: Married
Priesthood office: Seventy
Called From: Fairview, Utah, United States
Set apart by: Richard R Lyman

Missionary Department missionary registers, 1860-1959, Vol. 5, p. 224, line 59.

Elder Bror Henry Linde   --   SSM 1927-1929

PHOTO 163   BROR HENRY LINDE

Birth date, place - 19 January 1902, Lidensboda, Sweden
Death date - 25 September 1976
Baptism date - 10 June 1910   --   Baptism by - Elder Johnson
Father's name - Joseph F Theodore Linde   --   Mother's name - Alida Kristina Alsin

Southern States   --   June 1927–October 1929   --   Age Called: 25

Southern States
Set Apart: 21 June 1927   -   End Date: 4 October 1929
Departed From Home: 10 June 1927
Priesthood office: Elder
Called From: Bellingham, Washington, United States
Set apart by: Stephen L Richards

Missionary Department missionary registers, 1860-1959, Vol. 5, p. 206, line 402.

Elder Revell Terry Smith -- SSM 1925-1928

PHOTO 164   REVELL TERRY SMITH

Birth date, place -- 22 October 1904, Draper, Salt Lake, Utah
Death date -- 6 October 1969
Baptism date -- 20 July 1913 -- Baptism by - A W Walbeck
Father's name - Jos Edw Smith -- Mother's name - Clarissa A Terry

Southern States - December 1925–May 1928 -- Age Called: 21

Southern States
Set Apart: 15 December 1925 - End Date: 8 May 1928
Departed From Home: 16 December 1925
Priesthood office: Elder
Called From: Ioka, Duchesne, Utah, United States
Set apart by: Stephen L Richards

Missionary Department missionary registers, 1860-1959, Vol. 5, p. 161, line 1270.

PHOTO 165   REVELL TERRY SMITH AND HIS BROTHER JOSEPH MATT SMITH

PHOTO 166   REVELL TERRY SMITH AND ELDER WHITING

Elder Samuel Andrus Roos   --   SSM 1926-1928

PHOTO 167   SAMUEL ANDRUS ROOS

Birth date, place - 16 April 1902, Bedford, Lincoln, Wyoming
Death date - 30 October 1988
Baptism date - 30 June 1910 -- Baptism by - John U Moser
Father's name - Carl W Roos -- Mother's name - Emma J Merritt

Southern States - August 1926–December 1928 - Age Called: 24

Southern States
Set Apart: 24 August 1926 - End Date: 4 December 1928
Departed From Home: 27 August 1926

Priesthood: Elder
Called From: Montpelier, Idaho, United States
Set apart by: Geo F Richards
Missionary Department missionary registers, 1860-1959, Vol. 5, p. 181, line 656.

Elder William James Beus -- SSM 1924-1926

PHOTO 168   WILLIAM JAMES BEUS

Birth date, place - 20 April 1905, Clinton, Davis, Utah, United States
Death date - 5 March 1989
Baptism date - 4 September 1913   --   Baptism by - Orlando D Haddock
Father's name - Michael Ezra Beus   --   Mother's name - Olive R Baker

Southern States -- February 1924 – March 1926 -- Age Called: 18

Southern States
Set Apart: 19 February 1924   --   Arrived At Home: 19 March 1926
Departed From Home: 20 February 1924
Mission type: Proselytizing
Marital Status: Single
Priesthood office: Elder
Called From: Hooper, Weber, Utah, United States
Set apart by: Melvin J Ballard

Southern States -- December 1927-April 1928 -- Age Called: 22

Southern States
Set Apart: 6 December 1927   --   Arrived At Home: 1 April 1928
Departed From Home: 7 December 1927
Mission type: Proselytizing
Marital Status: Married
Priesthood office: Elder

Called From: Hooper, Weber, Utah, United States
Set apart by: Melvin J Ballard

Missionary Department missionary registers, 1860-1959, Vol. 5, p. 110, line 173.
Missionary Department missionary registers, 1860-1959, Vol. 5, p. 222, line 994.

Elder William Oscar Clouse -- SSM 1925-1927

PHOTO 169   WILLIAM OSCAR CLOUSE

Birth date, place -- 15 August 1903, Graham, Graham, Arizona
Death date - 2 September 1981
Baptism date - 6 April 1912 -- Baptism by - George Skinner
Father's name - Oscar Clouse --   Mother's name - Mary Francis Ann Stuart

Southern States - August 1925–September 1927 - Age Called: 22

Southern States
Set Apart: 25 August 1925 --   End Date: 24 September 1927
Departed From Home: 27 August 1925
Priesthood office: Elder
Called From: Virden, Greenlee, Arizona, United States
Set apart by: Joseph Fielding Smith

Missionary Department missionary registers, 1860-1959, Vol. 5, p. 142, line 509.

"Bill and Edith decided to get married before he left for his mission if it seemed right with their parents and others concerned. Things worked out in that direction. A farewell party was held and funds raised to assist Bill in his preparation for the mission field.

Bill and Edith caught a train in Lordsburg on 1 August 1925. They planned on getting married at the Salt Lake Temple but it was closed so they had to go to Logan where they were married on 5

August 1925. Edith stayed at a hotel while Bill was in the mission home. Edith boarded a train on the 26th of August to return home and Bill left by train for Atlanta, Georgia the following day.

Bill was assigned to work in the Alabama District with his first companion, Sterling W. Sill, a future General Authority. Bill was a dedicated missionary and was quite successful in his efforts. "During my mission, I baptized twelve people, was the first District President from Virden. My brother, Charles was the second, and my pal, Ivan Payne, was the third. I do not say this boastfully, but humbly, knowing that the Lord was with me, and that circumstances made such things possible."

"From familysearch"

PHOTO 170   WILLIAM OSCAR CLOUSE AND CHARLES IRA CLOUSE SERVING AS MISSIONARIES IN THE SOUTHERN STATES.

Elder Earl Leaver Page -- SSM 1920-1921

PHOTO 171   EARL LEAVER PAGE

Birth date, place -- 8 April 1899, Payson, Utah, Utah, United States
Death date -- 7 July 1980
Baptism date -- 5 May 1907   --   Baptism by - Francis M Elmer
Father's name - Jonathan Socwell Page   --   Mother's name - Lilyus Curtis

Southern States - November 1920–April 1921   -   Age Called: 21

Southern States
Set Apart: 2 November 1920 - Arrived At Home: 22 April 1921
Departed From Home: 3 November 1920
Mission type: Proselytizing
Marital Status: Married
Priesthood office: Elder
Called From: Payson, Utah, Utah, United States
Set apart by: George F Richards

Missionary Department missionary registers, 1860-1959, Vol. 5, p. 36, line 687.

Elder Henry Golden Tempest -- SSM 1924-1926

PHOTO 172 HENRY GOLDEN TEMPEST

Birth date, place - 10 February 1902, Herriman, Salt Lake, Utah
Death date - 2 January 1981
Baptism date - 7 July 1910 -- Baptism by - Valentine Smith
Father's name - Henry J Tempest -- Mother's name - Sarah E Freeman

Southern States - June 1924–December 1926 -- Age Called: 22

Southern States
Set Apart: 17 June 1924 - End Date: 10 December 1926
Departed From Home: 18 June 1924
Priesthood office: Elder
Called From: Salt Lake, Utah, United States
Set apart by: James E Talmage

Missionary Department missionary registers, 1860-1959, Vol. 5, p. 118, line 445.

Elder James Reginald Riding -- SSM 1926-1928

Birth date, place - 15 January 1907, Panguitch, Garfield, Utah
Death date -- 11 November 1955
Baptism date - 1 August 1915 -- Baptism by - John A Bishop
Father's name - Job Hall Riding -- Mother's name - Catherine Steele

Southern States - June 1926–July 1928 - Age Called: 19

Southern States
Set Apart: 22 June 1926 - End Date: 16 July 1928
Departed From Home: 25 June 1926
Priesthood office: Elder
Called From: Delta, Millard, Utah, United States
Set apart by: David O McKay

Missionary Department missionary registers, 1860-1959, Vol. 5, p. 178, line 549.

Page 325

SOUTHERN STATES MISSION INDEX

Ridgeway Branch, South Car	1897 Jul 3	Br conf, church burned Jul 4	
	1921 Apr 13	Samuel Branham is pres of	
	1928 Nov 28	Chapel dedic by S L Richards	
	1941 Dec 7	Chapel dedic, G A Smith	
	1947 Oct 19	Became part of So Carolina Stake	
Riding, Christopher L.	1900 Jul 18	Set apart Jul 23 arr:to Va Conf	
	1901 Mar 23	At conf Sep 21 at conf	
	1902 Jun 15	at Conf Jul 3 tran to Middle States Mission	
Riding, Franklin Dee	1926 Aug 30	Arr in Miss:to S Car Conf Sep 5	
	1927 May 22	At conf	
	1928 May 27	Sep 12 released	
Riding, James Regnald	1926 Jun 29	Arr in Miss:to N Car Conf Sep 5 Dec 5	
	1927 May 29	Aug 31 Sep 23	
	1928 Jul 8	Released	
Riding, John Anaelious Jr	1951 Feb 3	Arr in Miss:to S Fla Dist Dec 15 tr to S Car Dist	

Elder Ephraim E Twitchell   --   SSM 1926-1929

Eph Twitchell just a few days
before leaving on mission to
Southern States. 1926.

PHOTO 173   EPHRAIM E TWITCHELL

Ephraim E Twitchell
 Birth date, place --   14 February 1906, Manila, Uintah, Utah
Death date -- 2 May 1993
Baptism date -- October 1917   --   Baptism by - Pace Odekirk

Southern States - October 1926–January 1929 --   Age Called: 20

Southern States
Set Apart: 19 October 1926 - Released
: 18 January 1929
Departed From Home: 22 October 1926
Priesthood office: Elder
Called From: Abraham, Utah, United States
Set apart by: Geo Albert Smith

Missionary Department missionary registers, 1860-1959, Vol. 5, p. 187, line 881.

PHOTO 174 TYRRELL SQUIRES TOONE ON RIGHT AND EPHRAIM E TWITCHELL ON LEFT

Elder Lawrence P Page   --   SSM 1927-

PHOTO 175   LAWRENCE P PAGE

Birth date, place - 28 January 1905, Syracuse, Davis, Utah, United States
Death date - 2 May 1984
Baptism date - 3 August 1913 --   Baptism by - Francis Bone
Father's name - Orson M Page - Mother's name - Annie Parker

Southern States - June 1927–Unknown   --   Age Called: 22

Southern States
Set Apart: 7 June 1927 -   Departed From Home: 10 June 1927
Mission type: Proselytizing
Marital Status: Single
Priesthood office: Elder
Called From: Layton, Davis, Utah, United States
Set apart by: Melvin J Ballard

Missionary Department missionary registers, 1860-1959, Vol. 5, p. 205, line 358.

PHOTO 176 LAWRENCE P PAGE WITH THE MISSIONARIES AT SALT LAKE MISSION HOME - JUNE 1927

Salt Lake Mission Home   --   Group Photo ca June 1927 -   Missionaries identified from L-R

On steps: Le Roi Clarence Snow, Burma Celia Snow, Ilene Martha Schick, Norma Stewart,
       Helen Eliza Rich, Ada Stephens
1st Row (on Grass): Myrtle Orton, William Isom Palmer Lawrence Page, Leo Beavan Hill,
       Kenneth Shipley Summers, Wayne E Chadwick, Joseph Matt Smith, Theodore McAllister
       Silver
2nd Row: Marius Oman Evans, Earl Hillstead Wirthlin, Lavelle Singleton, unidentified, Leroy
       Larson, John Ethridge Litster
3rd Row: Willard Goodwin Nobel, Richard Welling Roskelley, Eric Bennett Pearson, Sieman
        Bouwman, Joseph Charles Rich
The Date on the picture is May 2, 1927 but most of the Missionaries in the picture were set apart
       on June 7, 1927

PHOTO 177 LAWRENCE P PAGE WITH THE MISSIONARIES AT SALT LAKE MISSION HOME - JUNE 1927

Salt Lake Mission Home Missionaries.   ---   ca. June 1927
Row 1, L to R: Lawrence P Page; Burma Celia Snow; Le Roi C Snow.
Row 2, L to R: Earl H Wirthlin; Wayne E Chadwick; unidentified; Joseph Matt Smith.
Row 3, L to R: Marius Oman Evans; Joseph Charles Rich; Willard G Noble; Richard W Roskelley; Theodore
M. Silver
Row 4, L to R: Lavelle Singleton; William Isom Palmer.

Sister Grace Mickelsen -- SSM 1927-1929

PHOTO 178   GRACE MICKELSEN

Birth date, place - 19 September 1908, Draper, Salt Lake, Utah
Death date - 12 November 1993
Baptism date - 15 July 1917   --   Baptism by - H Alva Fitzgerald
Father's name - S J Mickelsen   --   Mother's name - Mina Garff

Southern States -- August 1927–June 1929 -- Age Called: 18

Southern States
Set Apart: 3 August 1927 -- End Date: 7 June 1929
Departed From Home: 2 September 1927
Called From: Draper, Salt Lake, Utah, United States
Set apart by: Richard R Lyman

Missionary Department missionary registers, 1860-1959, Vol. 5, p. 209, line 514.

PHOTO 179   LEFT- GRACE MICKELSEN AND 2ND GRACE THE ONLY SISTER MISSIONARH - WITH OTHER MISSIONAR

PHOTO 180   SOUTHERN STATES MISSIONARIES -- GRACE MICKELSEN, THIRD FROM THE LEFT: ALBERT GRANT STREET, FAR RIGHT

Elder Ernest Wilford Bosgieter   --   SSM 1927-1929

PHOTO 181   ERNEST WILFORD BOSGIERTER

Birth date, place - 15 April 1904, Salt Lake City, Utah
Death date - 20 November 1996
Father's name - John Bosgieter   --   Mother's name - Jemima C Wheat

Southern States - November 1927–December 1929 --   Age Called: 23

Southern States
Set Apart: 8 November 1927 - End Date: 18 December 1929
Departed From Home: 15 November 1927
Priesthood office: Elder
Priesthood: Elder
Called From: Los Angeles, Los Angeles, California, United States
Set apart by: Rulon S Wheat

Missionary Department missionary registers, 1860-1959, Vol. 5, p. 218, line 822.

PHOTO 182   LEO NEPHI HUISH IN SOUTHERN STATES MISSION FIELD AND ERNEST WILFORD BOSGIETER 2ND FROM RIGHT

PHOTO 183 CONFERENCE AT GREENVILLE SOUTH CAROLINA - OCTOBER 1927 -- ERNEST WILFORD BOSGIETER IS 2ND FROM LEFT IN BACK ROW

Elder Estill G Branham -- SSM 1927-1928

PHOTO 184   ESTILL G BRANHAM TOP LEFT

Birth date, place - 21 May 1908, Tripplet, Rowan, Kentucky
Death date - 25 November 1992
Baptism date - 3 September 1922   --   Baptism by - H O Eitner
Father's name - Samuel T Branham   -   Mother's name - Bertha Lee Pitts

Southern States - October 1927–April 1928   --   Age Called: 19

Southern States
Set Apart: 11 October 1927 - End Date: 27 April 1928
Departed From Home: 12 October 1927
Priesthood office: Elder
Priesthood: Elder
Called From: Salt Lake City, Salt Lake, Utah, United States
Set apart by: J Golden Kimball

Missionary Department missionary registers, 1860-1959, Vol. 5, p. 213, line 638.
Vol. 5, p. 213, line 626 thru 662, Column for Departed date in book has incorrect year of "10/12/1928". Further research shows Correct date "10/12/1927" .

Elder Tyrrell Squires Toone -- SSM 1926-1928

PHOTO 185 TYRRELL SQUIRES TOONE

Birth date, place - 16 October 1903, Salt Lake City, Salt Lake, Utah, United States
Death date - 17 January 1997
Baptism date - 1 September 1912 -- Baptism by - David M Whitaker
Father's name - George H Toone -- Mother's name - Mary A Smith

Southern States -- November 1926–December 1928 -- Age Called: 23

Southern States
Set Apart: 30 November 1926 - Arrived At Home: 15 December 1928
Departed From Home: 3 December 1926
Mission type: Proselytizing
Marital Status: Single
Priesthood office: Elder
Called From: Salt Lake City, Salt Lake, Utah, United States
Set apart by: Melvin J Ballard

Missionary Department missionary registers, 1860-1959, Vol. 5, p. 194, line 1163.

PHOTO 186 TYRRELL SQUIRES TOONE ON RIGHT AND EPHRAIM E TWITCHELL ON LEFT

Elder William Melvin Turpin -- SSM 1926-1929

PHOTO 187   WILLIAM MELVIN TURPIN

Birth date, place - 20 April 1903, Salt Lake City, Salt Lake, Utah, United States
Death date - 6 May 1970
Baptism date - 7 July 1912 -- Baptism by - W W Covington
Father's name - Edward James Turpin -- Mother's name - Florence L Goodwin

Southern States - December 1926–March 1929 -- Age Called: 23

Southern States
Set Apart: 14 December 1926 -- Departed From Home: 17 December 1926
Arrived At Home: 7 March 1929
Mission type: Proselytizing
Marital Status: Married
Priesthood office: Elder
Called From: Blackfoot, Bingham, Idaho, United States
Set apart by: Orson F Whitney

Missionary Department missionary registers, 1860-1959, Vol. 5, p. 196, line 1223.

PHOTO 188   WILLIAM MELVIN TURPIN WITH OTHER MISSIONARIES

Elder Alma John Plumb -- SSM 1925-

PHOTO 189   ALMA JOHN PLUMB

Birth date, place - 9 April 1901, St David, Cochise, Arizona
Death date - 19 March 1988
Baptism date - 25 June 1910 -- Baptism by - Ed T Lofgrean
Father's name - Charles R Plumb - Mother's name - Mary W Smith

Southern States - October 1925–Unknown - Age Called: 24

Southern States
Set Apart: 20 October 1925 - Departed From Home: 22 October 1925
Priesthood office: Elder
Called From: St David, Cochise, Arizona, United States
Set apart by: Rudger Clawson
Stories and Documents

Missionary Department missionary registers, 1860-1959, Vol. 5, p. 146, line 684.

Elder Lavon Stallings -- SSM 1927-1930

Lavon Stallings at Ricks College

Lavon Stallings as a school teacher

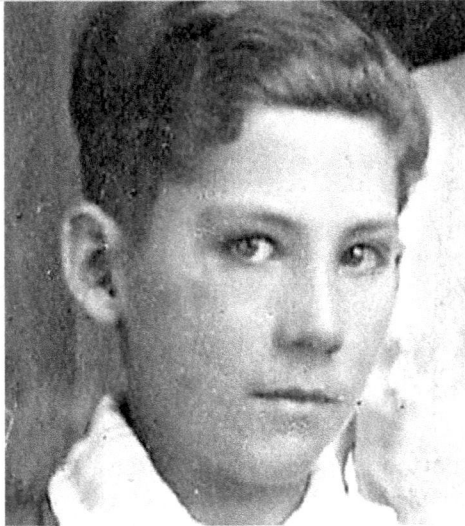

PHOTO 190   LAVON STALLINGS

Birth date, place -- 23 August 1907, Lewisville, Jefferson, Idaho
Death date -- 13 August 1907
Baptism date -- 3 August 1918   --   Baptism by -- William Jardine
Father's name - Don Carlos Stallings - Mother's name - Mary Ann Gibbs

Southern States - August 1927–March 1930 - Age Called: 20

Southern States
Set Apart: 30 August 1927 - End Date: 29 March 1930
Departed From Home: 2 September 1927
Priesthood office: Elder
Called From: Lewisville, Idaho, United States
Set apart by: Richard R Lyman
Missionary Department missionary registers, 1860-1959, Vol. 5, p. 210, line 518.

Elder Elwood Poinsett Chadwick -- SSM 1927-1930

PHOTO 191   ELWOOD POINSETT CHADWICK

Birth date, place -- 28 October 1903, Hyrum, Cache, Utah
Death date -   21 January 1989
Baptism date   - 14 May 1912   --   Baptism by - Jacob Miller
Father's name -p William Chadwick   --   Mother's name - Mary Hansen

Southern States   -   October 1927–January 1930   -   Age Called: 23

Southern States
Set Apart: 18 October 1927   -   End Date: 8 January 1930
Departed From Home: 28 October 1927
Priesthood office: Elder
Called From: Morgan, Utah, United States
Set apart by: Melvin J Ballard

Missionary Department missionary registers, 1860-1959, Vol. 5, p. 215, line 710.

Sister Mildred Molen - SSM - 1928-1930

Lady missionaries
Sister Bonham - molen

892

Birth   -   11 June 1909, St Anthony, Idaho
Death date - 27 December 1990
Baptism date - 17 August 1917 --   Photo 192 -- Mildred Molen on the right   Baptism by -
John A Johnson
Father's name - Kenneth L Molen   --   Mother's name -- Minerva Richards

Southern States - September 1928–April 1930 - Age Called: 19
Southern States
Set Apart: 4 September 1928
End Date: 1 April 1930
Departed From Home: 7 September 1928
Called From: Vaughn, Montana, United States
Set apart by: Rudger Clawson
Missionary Department missionary registers, 1860-1959, Vol. 5, p. 239, line 626.

500

Sister Thelma Oneta Bonham -- SSM -- 1928-

PHOTO 193 -- THELMA ONETA BONHAM

Sister Thelma Oneta Bonham on the left

Birth date -- 3 July 1906, Ogden, Weber, Utah
Death date -- 4 July 1995
Baptism date -- 3 July 1914 --- Baptism by - Bowen Hadlock
Father's name - F E Bonham -- Mother's name - Mary Patterson

Southern States -- June 1928–Unknown -- Age Called: 21

Southern States
Set Apart: 5 June 1928
Departed From Home: 9 June 1928
Priesthood office: Elder
Called From: Burley, Idaho, United States
Set apart by: Stephen L Richards

Missionary Department missionary registers, 1860-1959, Vol. 5, p. 235, line 459.

Elder Monrad Fred McBride - SSM 1930-

Birth --11 September 1908, Hyrum, Cache, Utah
Death date - 5 August 1969
Baptism date - 30 September 1916 -- Baptism by - A A Allen Jr
Father's name - Henry N McBride -- Mother's name - Margaret A Anderson

Southern States - May 1930–Unknown - Age Called: 21

Southern States
Set Apart: 13 May 1930
Departed From Home: 15 May 1930
Priesthood office: Priest - Priesthood: Priest
Called From: United States
Set apart by: Melvin J Ballard

Missionary Department missionary registers, 1860-1959, Vol. 6, p. 8, line 306.

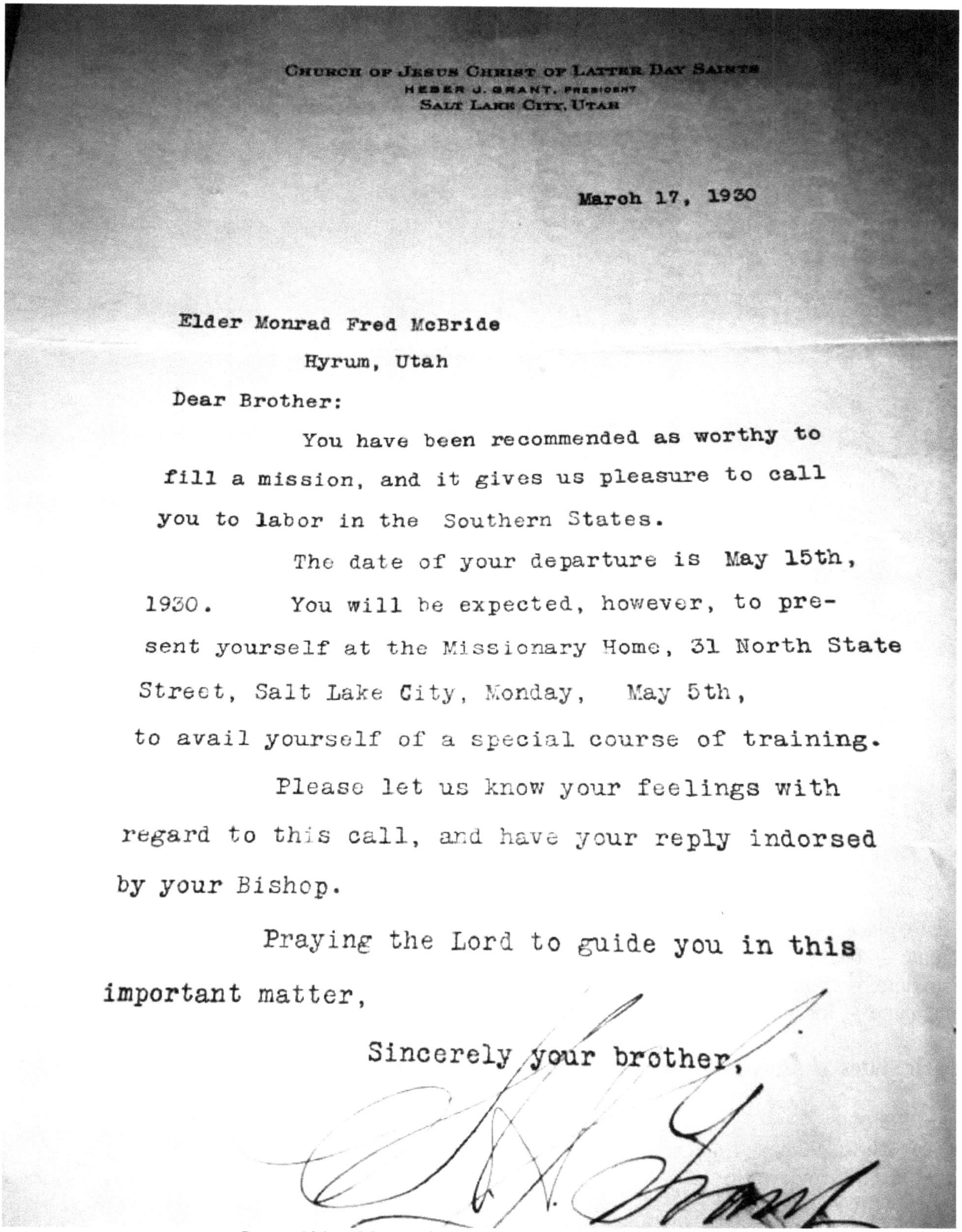

CHURCH OF JESUS CHRIST OF LATTER DAY SAINTS
HEBER J. GRANT, PRESIDENT
SALT LAKE CITY, UTAH

March 17, 1930

Elder Monrad Fred McBride

Hyrum, Utah

Dear Brother:

You have been recommended as worthy to fill a mission, and it gives us pleasure to call you to labor in the Southern States.

The date of your departure is May 15th, 1930. You will be expected, however, to present yourself at the Missionary Home, 31 North State Street, Salt Lake City, Monday, May 5th, to avail yourself of a special course of training.

Please let us know your feelings with regard to this call, and have your reply indorsed by your Bishop.

Praying the Lord to guide you in this important matter,

Sincerely your brother,

PHOTO 194 -- MONRAD'S MISSION CALL SIGNED BY HEBER J GRANT

Elder Eugene Hyde Merrill -- SSM 1928-1930

PHOTO 195 EUGENE HYDE MERRILL

Birth date, place - 25 June 1908, Salt Lake City, Utah
Death date - 4 January 1973
Baptism date - 25 June 1916 -- Baptism by - Jos F Merrill
Father's name - Joseph F Merrill - Mother's name - Annie Laura Hyde

Southern States - July 1928–September 1930 -- Age Called: 20

Southern States
Set Apart: 3 July 1928 - End Date: 17 September 1930
Departed From Home: 6 July 1928
Priesthood office: Elder
Called From: Salt Lake City, Salt Lake, Utah, United States
Set apart by: Jos Fielding Smith

Missionary Department missionary registers, 1860-1959, Vol. 5, p. 238, line 574.

Elder Heber George Bott -- SSM 1928-1931

PHOTO 196 HEBER GEORGE BOTT

Gender   Male
Birth date, place -- 19 December 1907, Brigham, Box Elder, Utah
Death date - 26 July 1931
Baptism date - 5 February 1916 -   Baptism by, Isaac A Jensen
Father's name - George Henry Bott   Mother's name - Nancey Bankhead

Southern States - December 1928–March 1931 Age Called: 20

Southern
Set Apart: 11 December 1928   -   End Date: 13 March 1931
Departed From Home: 14 December 1928
Priesthood: Elder
Called From: Brigham City, Box Elder, Utah, United States
Set apart by: Brigham H Roberts

Missionary Department missionary registers, 1860-1959, Vol. 5, p. 253, line 1161.

BRIGHAM CITY, July 27.—Two boys were killed and three others seriously injured when the car in which they were riding went over the dugway a short distance from the horseshoe bend in Sardine canyon, shortly before 2 o'clock on Sunday morning.

Orland Sorensen, 27, son of Mr. and Mrs. Joseph Sorensen of Bear River City, was instantly killed and Heber Bott, 23, of Brigham City lived only a few minutes after the car rolled several hundred feet down a steep embankment. Melvin Bott, brother of the dead boy, suffered a broken back. His brother, Crosby Bott, suffered a crushed skull, and Eugene Bott, also a brother, was cut and bruised.

The boys were returning from a party at Wellsville and were attempting to pass another car on the grade when they hit a rock, causing a tire to blow out and swerve the car over the embankment. The car turned over several times and was demolished.

Heber Bott is the son of George Bott of East Bear River City and Mrs. Paul Forrester of Brigham City, and is survived by the three brothers, Eugene, Melvin and Crosby Bott, who are in the hospital at Logan. Mrs. Charles Burt of Brigham City is a sister. Funeral services will probably be held for the Bott boy on Tuesday at 1 o'clock, but the place was not designated.

Orlando Sorensen was the son of Mr. and Mrs. John Sorensen of Bear River City, and is survived by his aged parents, three brothers, Elac, Herbert and Silas Sorensen, and three sisters, Hildred and Harriet Sorsensen of Bear River City, and Mrs. Essie Peterson of California. Both boys had recently returned from missions.

The Ogden Standard-Examiner, 27 Jul 1931

Elder John Eldon Ladle -- 1929-1932

PHOTO 197 – JOHN ELDON LADEL

Birth date, place - 11 July 1909, Salt Lake City, Salt Lake, Utah
Death date - 24 July 1991
Baptism by - Elder Fred Schwenderman
Father's name - John J Ladle -- Mother's name - Emma Bull

Southern States - December 1929–February 1932 - Age Called: 20

Southern States
Set Apart: 10 December 1929 - End Date: 8 February 1932
Departed From Home: 12 December 1929
Priesthood office: Elder
Called From: Sugar City, Idaho, United States
Set apart by: Melvin J Ballard

Missionary Department missionary registers, 1860-1959, Vol. 5, p. 281, line 1033.

Elder Arthur Clinton Adair -- SSM 1935

PHOTO 198 - CLINTON ADAIR AND CHESTER HARRIS — 2 MORE PICTURES OF CLINTON ADAIR

Birth - 13 September 1912 - Luna, Catron, New Mexico, United States
Death - 10 December 1996 - Lewis, Montezuma, Colorado, United States
Father - Charles Newton Adair -- Mother - Mary Elva Woolsey

Mission in the Southern States 1935

"Working with Arthur Clinton Adair was just as enjoyable, but for different reasons. His ranching background had given him a quiet strength, a mirthful sense of humor, and an understanding of other two legged creatures. He was somewhat diffident about speaking in public or pushing himself to the front at social affairs, but was very effective as a missionary one to one. We spent the two months from mid-March to mid-May of 1936 tracting and holding meetings in the small town of Kinston and had a week together without purse or scrip in Robeson County. An excerpt from my March 1936 diary brings back fond memories of Clint Adair. "Adair decided to preach on Word of Wisdom (at the Albertson Chapel) which he had never attempted before. He said that some scientists allowed a leech to suck the blood from a person who was an habitual tobacco user. The leech was not long in dying after gorging itself on this contaminated blood. Then this man of science allowed a leech to fill itself on the blood of a person who didn't use tobacco and it thrived. Adair said that he could prove it from his own experience for he had spent the night at a member's home in the hills of North Carolina, and the next morning he was covered with bed- bug bites and he could see stuffed bed- bugs crawling away. He said that the people up there use tobacco and liquor and therefore bed-bugs couldn't live off them, but when they got near these two Elders they knew that the famine was over." Adair and I did our job and enjoyed each other's company. In September 1935 while we were traveling for a few days without purse or scrip, Adair and I went methodically from door to door for two hours in Parkton (population 450), starting with the minister, asking for a night's lodging. We finally found hospitality in the fourth to the last house; but later I recorded, " Got a place to stay at first house we asked which is unusual" It was with a certain amount of relief that I recorded returning to the home of a good Saint Furnie Harper in Deep Run: first square meal I've had for a month. When one elderly woman asked me for baptism I agreed to perform the ceremony but becoming slightly ill asked if Adair could officiate. She refused. If I wouldn't baptize her she wouldn't join the church I acquiesced, though with some personal misgivings about the strength of her convictions. Adair played the guitar and had a good tenor voice, in Kingston we got in the habit of taking his guitar to our cottage meetings then singing for the congregation afterwards. We were soon at attracting such large crowds that our sermons became shorter and our performances stretched out to as much as two hours. Adair's favorite music was cowboy songs, so we soon branched out from hymns, and I developed a real fondness for Western music as well including Adair's signature tune "When It's Night Time in Nevada." We made a lot of friends for our church. Who knows perhaps this pleasant approach was as effective in improving the reputation of the Mormons and leading some to investigate as my public sparring with ministers in Tennessee. Money was always tight in contrast to the present, there was no great emphasis on placing or selling copies of the book of Mormon, but at least once such a sale was a godsend. Harris and I sold one to the barber in the small town of Pembroke: we have had $.20 apiece for about two weeks now-no more, no less so it ($.50) came in handy. On another occasion Adair and I got down to $.13 between us but were saved when he received a money order for $40. My diary records frequent disapproval of the prices charged in 1936. $12 a month for room in Kinston and $.10 for a large hamburger with all the trimmings. When Adair's trousers needed mending in April 1936, he had to stay in our room all day while the tailor worked. Holding open and street meetings was much more difficult in North Carolina than in Tennessee where they had been part of the Bible Belt culture. A carnival was set up just across the street from our meeting place as we started to sing our opening him the carnival Calliope started up at full volume. Our meeting came to an abrupt end and I silently paid my compliments to a very devious official. In Kinston, Adair and I were unable to get permission to hold street meetings, and the city officials just laughed when we asked to hold a preaching service in the courthouse. At Parkton in Roberson County when Adair and I attended a Baptist Sunday school, the minister asked Adair to give the opening prayer and had me teach the adult class. One day Adair and I caught a ride with the man to whom, as we rolled along, we explained Mormonism and that our church did not believe in paid ministry. Only as we were getting out of the car did he politely mention that he was a Methodist minister."

From AGAINST THE GRAIN by Brigham D Madsen

Elder Brigham D Madsen

PHOTO 199V BRIGHAM D MADSEN

PHOTO 200 HEADSTONE OF BRIGHAM MADSEN

Brigham served a mission in the southern states. He seems to have doubts about the gospel even then. He served willingly and vigorously. One of his callings took him to North Carolina where he met Chester Harris, a Catawba Indian from York county, South Carolina. He also met Clint Adair from New Mexico, who had or would serve in Catawba because he told the author that he knew Chief Blue many years later.

Elder Madsen did his share of preaching and singing, singing mostly with elder Adair who was quite the singer and musician. Madsen's observations are found in the Adair and Chester Harris pages.

He was instrumental in building several small chapels around the area and did a lot of administrating the mission.

I don't find any other interaction with the Catawba.

Brigham D Madsen and Chester Harris

Elder Antone C Christensen   SSM 1926-1934

PHOTO 201 ANTONE C CHRISTENSEN

Antone C Christensen   --   Birth date, place 5 November 1859, Riverdale, Weber, Utah
Death date 8 November 1942
Baptism date 1867   Baptism by Warren G Child
Father's name Anders C Christensen -- Mother's name Mary Sopha Ipsen

Missions served
Northwestern States, 1886–1886, Age 26
 Southern States, 1926–1927, Age 66   --   **Southern States, 1926–1926, Age 67**
Southern States, 1929–1931, Age 69   --   **Southern States, 1931–1931, Age 71**
Southern States, 1932–1933, Age 72   --   **Southern States, 1934–1934, Age 74**

So Brother Christensen labored as a missionary to give unto other the knowledge of the truthfulness of the Gospel that they might realize the joy which was his.

Charles A. Callis, who presided over him during several of his missions, wrote the following in a letter to the Elder: "In the Spanish American War General Shafter commanded the American army in Cuba. His reports were few and far between like angels visits. The Secretary of the War Department said, 'General Shafter is fighting, not writing'. We have not been favored with many reports from you; but we know you have been fighting the good fight."

South Carolina People Who Helped the LDS Missionaries that Served in That Area.

Richie Harkness

Richie Harkness
    Gender   Male   Birth date, place
    22 May 1850, Yorkville, York, South Carolina
    Baptism date - 6 January 1885 --   Baptism by - Joseph Willey
    Father's name - Addison Davis Harkness -   Mother's name - Frances Emeline Dover

Southern States
    May 1898–Unknown --   Age Called: 47   Southern States
    Set Apart: 18 May 1898
    Priesthood office: Seventy --   Priesthood: Elder Ord Seventy
    Called From: Salt Lake City, Salt Lake, Utah, United States
    Set apart by: S B Young

This information was obtained from Family Search and written (By Shelly Rushton Jeppson (a Great- Great Granddaughter))

Richie wrote of these experiences in his diary:

"Was driven from home April 20, 1885. Was ordered by Hence Broome at Cherry Chee fall (Cherokee Fall) factory to leave in 10 minutes was followed and shot at 5 times, this was the 9th day of February 1886 after July 1887 a mob of 125 men came to my place [and] fired two shots at my wife, then took me about ½ mile from home, stripped me to the skin, hit me 20 times with a forked hickory stick, opening the skin in 17 places from 1to3 inches long." "On the 1st morning of December 1884 while lying on my bed meditating the gospel, a voice spoke to me and said, 'If you will obey me and keep my commandments you shall have long life and many days with tribulations and persecutions.' On the 6th day of January 1885, I was baptized into the Church of Christ. About the first of April1885, my once special friends gathered together to mob me, so I had to leave my home or be mobbed, so on the 20th day of April I took my family and went about 20 miles South where I lived in peace the rest of the year. I was ordained an Elder on the 2nd day of November 1885…on February 1886 I was sent to visit some of my old friends at the 99 islands on Broad River, while there I went to Cherry Chee Falls (Cherokee Falls) Factory. When I had gone about 1mile I was followed and shot at 5 times, one ball passing so near my head I could feel the air of it. This was late in the afternoon. I had nothing to eat since early morning, nor did I get anything to eat before I got a place to stop. This occurred on the 8th day of February 1886. The following summer we raised up a branch of Saints [in] the upper part of the county. So the next spring all the Elders were driven out of the county. I was the only one left and one priest. We continued to visit the Saints in that part, until July. In May I and Brother Joseph A. Smith, a priest. Was that the spirit says to me you had better go so we started for home, through the woods so we wouldn't be seen. We had not been gone above

a half hour before the house was surrounded by a howling mob. So sure was they that they had us that they searched the house for us, but the Lord had bid us to go and we had done his bidding. Nevertheless we continued to visit the Saints and baptize men converts until July 19th, 1887 a mob of 125 men came to my place about midnight, broke [into] the house. My wife knocked one down with a chair, he shot twice at her. One ball stuck in the window frame a few inches of her head." "They took me about ½ mile from home, stripped me to the skin and hit me 20 licks with a forked hickory stick about 3 ½ feet long, split my skin in 17 places and bruised me fearful. But I did not suffer much for the Lord caused boils to rise which carried off the bruised blood. I was compelled to leave the state in 10 days, so I had to sacrifice all I had to save my life and my family. My wife thought they would kill me but I told her in their presence that they would not kill me for I remembered what the spirit of the Lord had told me." "I stopped in Spartanburg County, South Carolina, for one month. I could not get work so I went to Ashwell, North Carolina. I stopped about four months when we came to Alabama to mother's. Stopped with her one year. When I baptized her in fulfillment of a dream I had about three prior to that time. I was three years in that state when in November 1890 I came to Salt Lake City. I remained there nine months, I went to Lehi. Helped to finish sugar factory. I stopped there one year then went to

On 5 February 1898 Richie received a call to serve a mission for the Church of Jesus Christ of Latter-day Saints. He was called to serve in the Southern States Mission. Part of his mission was served in South Carolina; the very state he had been driven from years earlier. He served in the days when missionaries traveled without purse or script.

Richie's wife, Mary Elizabeth, supported him while he was on his mission by selling milk and butter that she gathered from the four cows that they owned. His children, Dave and Lenora, worked to raise money while he was on his mission as well. His family was able to send him 25 dollars each month while he was on his mission. This was quite an accomplishment for Mary Elizabeth because she was also unable to read and write.

(From Diary of Richie Harkness.)

Our family history is that Richie was originally a preacher in another Church. He was baptized into the LDS Church on 6 January 1885! He was first mobbed in April 1885 by many of his former friends and he moved 20 miles to the south on 20 April 1885. He had been establishing a branch of the Saints in the upper part of the county! On 19 July 1887 a mob of about 125 men attacked Richie at home. They took two shots at my G-G- Grandmother narrowly missing her! They took Richie about 1/2 mile from his home, stripped him to the skin and beat him 20 times with a forked hickory stick that was about 3 1/2 feet long! It split his skin in 17 places! He was ordered to leave the State in 10 days and he first went to North Carolina, then down to Alabama and then he came to Salt Lake City in

November 1890! His son's history states that it was the Klan who attacked my Grandfather!

Richie was later called to serve a Southern States mission. He received his mission call on 5 February 1898. Part of his mission was in South Carolina but he was also in Tenessee and other Southern States! There is an article called "Mormons Among the Catawba" which was published by the South Carolina Historical Society which talks about Richie Harkness and other missionaries teaching the Catawba Indians.

baptism and mob

"This completes my labors as a missionary: signed Joseph Wiley. Items of interest on my mission: August 1883, visited the Cherokee Indians. September 26, 1883 I stood over elder C.E. Robison when he breathed his last breath. September 28 we put his corpse on the train home, got bit by a dog had one meeting broken up by two Baptist ministers. Had one gun pointed at me. Laid out 15 nights. Went 30 hours without food. Walked 3,600 miles. Held 113 meetings. Organized one Sunday school, ordained one priest. (John Alonzo Canty) Baptized 34 and assisted in baptizing 59. Baptize the first Catawba Lamanite that ever give obedience to the gospel in this dispensation. Baptized one preacher (Richie Hartness). "

from the missionary journal of Joseph Willey

Saturday, Oct 25, Heavy frost last night. Started at 10 am, walked 6 miles through the sand. Called to get a drink of water and the Ladie of the house ask us to come in the house and take a seat in the piazza. We told her our business, she got us some dinner and said she wished us to go and see her son John Robin. She said he would be pleased to entertain us over night so we went. When we reached his place we found he was not at home, but there was a Baptist preacher there who was calculating to preach near there the next day when he found out we were ministers he sent a boy off to get help. Soon the man of the house came and brought several with him. After supper Mr. Hartness {Ritchie} and the minister ask where the thief that hung with Jesus went to. I readily answered his questions which seemed to astonish him as it was never answered before to his satisfaction. We divided the time and talked some three hours on the first principles of the Gospel. He became excited and said he would retire for the night. The gentleman of the house tried to get him to stay all night, but he would not. I ask him where he got the authority to preach. He said he took his authority from the Bible, Mark, chapter 8, where Jesus commanded his Disciples to go and preach. I then asked him if he believed the Father, Son and Holy Ghost to be one or three seperate persons. He said the "Bible could not be understood, good night!"

Sunday Oct.26, Weather fine. We was calculating to go and hear Mr. Harten preach but a gentleman came to us and said it would not be safe for us to go to meeting. He said he was a friend to us and knew that the people would not reason with us, but would use violence and mobb us. So we passed on. We met Mr. Harten and a minister of the Methodist church in the road early that morning but they seemed to be very distant. Walked several miles through the sand. Was turned of several times, staid with a gentleman, but could not learn his name.

James Carson Russell

When James Carson Russell was born on July 10, 1804, in Abbeville, South Carolina, his father, Matthew, was 32 and his mother, Mary, was 26. He married Juda Tinsley and they had two children together He also had one son with Susan Russell. He died on December 13, 1874, in Dallas, Alabama, at the age of 70.

." Next with Bro. Taylor George and had quite a lively time and staid in the city till late in the evening and started to J.C. Russells plase which was 12 miles west. The evening was very cold. We reached Bro. Russells plase about 9 o'clock in the night where I met with my aunt and 4 cousins of that family and 4 cousins of another family. I met with Elders Joseph Willey who had been laboring in our part for some time and Elders W. E. Bingham and Cragun. They had a fine time that night singing the songs of Zion. I concluded that I would stay at Bro. Pattersons and write for the company that was going in February and about the same time had found out that they was no company going from SC. I staid in the country and worked until April 1. I heard they was some Saints going to Colorado so I thought I would go then and the 3rd day of April I quit work to fix up to go. I left and walked 10 miles that evening. Come to Martinsville P.O. SC and there I got a letter from home stating that my mother was sick, bad off, no life expected for her. She said that she wanted me to come home and, see her one more time so went on to Bro. Russells got there about sundown. Staid there till 12 o'clock that night getting ready to go home." from Journal of Pinkney Head.

Nov. 29th had a long talk with Mr. Simkins and Mr. Mathews. Mr. Mathews said he was a Bible lover. I had a long talk on apostacy from the primitive church. Mr. Mathews got very angry that evening. I called a meeting a requested all the Saints to come together. I called on Br. George and Harris to make a public confession for getting intoxicated and ask the Saints forgiveness. They made a humble confession and the Saints freely forgave them. I spoke some time on the duty of the Saints. Bro. Russell had come to move the Saints.

November 30, 1884, Sunday, I preached my farwell sermon at the Rock Hill Branch. A good spirit prevailed. Bro. James Russell had now come to move the Saints to his place to tend his farm in Spartenburg Co. The Lamanites that went with him numbered 22. This broke up the Rock Hill Branch of the Church. The Saints wished be to go with them as several of them was sick with the chills and fever. I did so. The distance they had to move was 65 miles over a very rough road. They had two wagons to and took to cows.

December 1, 1884. We started for Spartanburg Co. Traveled 9 miles campes in the woods. Had a large fire, cooked supper, had prayers and all laid down on the ground.

Dec. 2, weather very cold and cloudy. We started on our journey as soon as it was light. It was so cold that most of the children was obliged to walk to keep warm. We reached Bro. Moses Gordons at 6 PM a distance of 20 miles. Camped in an old house that is the Lamanites did. I slept with Elder W. S. Cragun who was laboring thar.

Dec. 3, The weather was fine. We camped in the woods that night. Everything was all right. We ask the Lord night and morning to temper the elements.

Dec. 4, 1 1884, We had a good nights rest. The night of the 3rd, I went with Bro. Russell to see one Mr. Blacks who was a strong believer in the Gospel, to see if he wished to rent his large plantation td some of the Rock Hill Saints. We got enough land for 6 of the Saints and wrote for them to make calculations to move in 2 weeks. On the 4th we reached Bro. Russells at 2pm without an accident and we all gave the Lord the praise for taking us safe through. It never rained or snowed on the road. After we got moved in the houses the rain come down in torrents and continued to rain all night. 5th and 6th visited the Saints and read the papers.

Dec, Sunday, the 7th 1 held a meeting at Bro. James Russells. Thar was quite a number of the neighbors come. After meeting I baptized Edward Harris in the Pacolet River. December 8, Elders W. E. Bingham and R .M. Humphrey who had been trying to open a new field of arrived at Bro. Russells (where) I met them.

Willard Melton Hayes

Willard Melton Hayes – interviewed by Emma Reid Echols, accompanied by Mrs Frances Wade

E: This is Emma Reid Echols, Rock Hill, South Carolina, Route 6, Box 260. This is August 20, 1973. I'm visiting in the home of Mr. and Mrs. Willard Hayes in Gaffney, South Carolina. I have brought with me Mrs. Frances Wade, who will be talking with them a little bit later. Mr. Hayes, give me your full name and your address.

H: I'm Willard M. Hayes. This is 704 Peddy Hill Street in Gaffney, and we've been living here since 1967. I was at the Catawba School from September, 1935, until June, 1942. I moved from there to Spartanburg.

E: I have been visiting among the Catawba Indians. So many of them have told me about what Mr. Willard Hayes meant to them as a teacher. He was not only a teacher, but he was a Boy Scout leader, he was their advisor, their helper and their friend. So this is a special day when I get to talk with him about his work among the Indians. Mr. Hayes, let's get the physical set-up of the school. Do you remember the school building and the equipment that you had to use?

H: Yes. The school building was a two-room school when I went there. Miss Ethel Smith of Columbia came as the assistant teacher and she taught first and second grade, I believe. Possibly third. Do you remember, Frances?

W: No, I sure don't.

H: You were there, wasn't you?

W: Well, I do remember   day.

H: I had the upper grades. There was one that was doing ninth grade work. She was studying. She had the ninth grade books, and I helped her with her ninth grade work. That was Brothers Sanders' oldest girl, married William Watts, and I can't think of her name.

W: Euliss?

H: Yeah.

W: Euliss Sanders.

E: So Euliss Sanders was doing the ninth grade work.

H: When I went there in 1935, none of them were going to high school in Rock Hill. They had no way of getting out, back and forth. No transportation to high school. But before I left, Samuel was running the bus, wasn't he? To the high school?

E: That's be 1942 when you left.

H: Yes. They'd been going to high school after some time, though, and they'd take them out. Samuel would take them on, he had a big old bus or something.

W: I can't quite remember that. I remember the Indian agent appointed Mama to use her car. Maybe Samuel was driving it.

H: No, she probably used her car at first, but he got a big old long car that he could carry a whole hunch in and he would take them. He took the high school students there, part of the time, I know. How about your mother. I can't recall just what arrangements was made for the first ones that went to high school, but we started them going to high school. Who paid her that? That came out of school funds, didn't it?

W: Well, I'm not too clear that came out of some sort of fund. The Indian agent paid it, though, once a month.

H: Yes, the county didn't do anything about the Indian school at all.

E: Mr. Hayes, who was the one who drove the first bus, as you remember?

H: I don't know whether it was the first one or not, but I know that Samuel Beck...he lived up there-- house burned, I believe, didn't it?

W: Yes.

H: He's had two or three burned-up houses.

W: Yes.

H: But, what was that old place up there where he and Helen lived?

W: You mean just above Doris Blue's?

H: Yes, right in there.

E; That would be a difficult thing you did, teaching so many grades. Tell us just about....

H: One year, it seems to me the second year I was there, they didn't have an assistant. Sister Davis didn't want to come back or didn't come back. I didn't have an assistant and I taught all the grades. That was a very primitive-type school.

E: Do you remember how many students you would have?

H: I don't know, the room was jam-packed. What I would do was to give them an assignment, some of them, the ones that were supposed to be studying, and I'd bring the class that I was working with up to the front of the room. We'd have a place at the front for them. We had to do that to get the class you was working with separated from the ones that were not particularly interested in what you were doing. Riding herd on that bunch that was supposed to be studying and getting some work out of the onen that were supposed to have their recitation was quite a problem sometimes.

E: What about the materials you could find to use, such as books, writing paper, pencils, things of that kind, was that provided?

H: Yes, that was provided by the Indian agent. They set aside a certain part of the general appropriation that was provided for the Indians for school. I'm not sure, I think the first year I went there I received $90.00 a month.

E: Do you know how that salary would compare with the salary of other teachers in the district?

H: At that time, no, I don't. I don't know what they were paying the other teachers. The most I ever made while I was there was $135.00 a month.

E: What about the transportation for children who came to school? The roads were very poor.

H: There were no transportation to the elementary school. But we did get arrangements made to take those to high school that wanted to go to high school. I can't recall just when that was or how soon after I went there, but when I went, there was only one person that was even studying on the high school level. She came there to that school, and I helped her what I could with her lessons. That was all we had in the way of a high school until we got enough of them that wanted to go to high school where we could get them up there. So they started going to high school. I don't know whether any had gone to high school when Brother Davis was there, do you know?

W: I think that Samuel was the first one that went, and he didn't go real long.

E: My. Hayes, what did you do about janitorial services? Did your boys and you make the fires and sweep the building?

H: Yes, I usually made the fire, and the girls liked to have something to do other than lessons, so they'd sweep the floor to get out of their lessons.

E: And then where did you bring your water from?

H: Let's see, we didn't have a well right at the schoolhouse. I don't know what...they went down to....

W: They carried it from the spring, Brother Hayes. You know how we would....

H: I believe it was the spring. They had to go and take a bucket and get the water. I remember teaching how to make paper cups and we wasted an awful lot of paper making paper cups to drink from.

E: I suppose there'd be a shelf on the little porch to hold the bucket of water?

H: No, they had a bucket in the back corner of the room, as I remember. They had a dipper, and to get them to use the individual cups, I showed them how to make--do you know how to make a paper cup?

W: Yes, sir, I sure did.

H: The agent furnished them everything, the textbooks, their writing paper and pencils, and that thing. We'd just get a supply of pencil tablets and pencils, and as they needed a pencil, we'd just issue them a pencil. So everything was furnished for the school. In the spring we'd let them go home for lunch because we didn't have a lunch program, you see, nothing for them there at first, but we got one eventually. But there was no lunch program, so in the spring, they'd go hone for lunch and a lot of the boys wouldn't come back lots of times. The next day that they'd gone fishing. When the fish started biting, I started having bad attendance at school.

E: The children were talented in art. Were there any art supplies pro¬vided: crayons, papers, clay, anything of that kind provided by the school?

H: No, I started having them do beadwork. We got some beads. I don't know where the money came from or how we got it, but I bought some of these little bend looms and needles and thread and different colored beads. We learned to do rings. They put rings and beads on wire and they'd make rings and bracelets and watchfobs and necklaces. Were you there when we made one for Mrs. Eleanor Roosevelt?

W: No, I don't remember it.

H: We made a special one and wove it into the thing, the Indian reservation as it was originally set aside, 140,000 acres, and then we put one little black bead in among the red beads, I believe, to show the amount of land that they had now. She came to Rock Hill to go to college for something, and Chief Blue presented that to her and we got a note of thanks. I wonder what ever became of that--but we got a note of thanks from Mrs. Roosevelt after she got back for that necklace.

E: That is most interesting. That's the only time anyone has ever told me this story. If you ever find that note of thanks, I hope you'll let me have a copy of it.

H: I haven't any idea what became of it, where it is. It should be pre¬served somewhere, but I don't know what became of it. But Chief Blue was dressed and he had his uniform on and headdress, and he presented Mrs. Roosevelt the necklace that we'd made there in the school. I think we arranged to have every pupil to put on a few beads on the necklace.

E: The girls and boys both participated in that beadwork?

H: Oh, yes. Then Just about every week there'd come a busload of school children from somewhere over the state to visit the reservation. They'd come by the school and we'd sell them our rings, bracelets, and so on, and from doing that we could buy more supplies. Was you in-volved in that beadwork?

W: I remember making some. We did rings, especially.

H: Yes, a lot of them. That would keep alot of busy little fingers occu-pied when they should behave themselves, when they probably wouldn't be if they didn't have something to do. The boys could take that wire and make the rings with the piece of wire and the different colored beads. They'd decide on the design they wanted to put in there. We, one time, had a whole bunch of that on hand and when the children would come from other schools we'd have some souvenirs that they could buy. Helped get our craft program going.

E: That's interesting. What about sports for your children? What did you do in the line of sports?

H: You'd give them a baseball and a bat and that's all they wanted. They were great ballplayers. They liked to play. Girls played and boys played and everybody played ball. They still like to play ball.

E: Were you provided with playground equipment?

H: So far as I know. I don't remember how we got them. But somebody would find a bat and sometimes I think they used a piece of board, take an axe and hack out of it, or a paddle or a saw and saw it out.

You could take a big, a big piece of board and saw a bat out of it and made the bat out of that. Sometimes they'd take their stockings and unravel them and wind the string around the--I don't know whether they put a rock in the middle of it or what. They started winding around something and they'd wind that thread on there. Then you'd take a needle and thread and sew back and forth around it to keep that from unraveling. It'd get real fuzzy sometimes, though, beginning to break and all, and when it got wet it was always soggy. But they made their own balls sometimes like that.

E: Your salary and your supplies came from the Indian agent.

H: That's right.

E: Do you remember any of the Indian agents who worked with you?

H: Tome Flowers was the agent when I went there. He'was the fire chief at Rock Hill. He's the one that I wrote to make application. I was teaching in the C.C.C. camp down at Walterboro when Brother Davis decided to move to Salt Lake City. The school position was open, and they had nobody to teach. So I wrote to Mr. Flowers, Tom Flowers, T. 0. Flowers, and then I believe he died. They got a man named Wingate, and he lived up above town somewhere. I can't recall even if he lived out in the country. He was the one that reduced my salary to $90.00 a month. I think Mr. Flowers give me a $120.00. He was going to use that money to build up a fund of some kind, I don't know what it was he had in mind. Then Mr....

W: Crier Lesslie?

H: I don't know whether he was next or not. Was there anybody else after Wingate? I can't recall.

W: I can't remember either.

H: It seems to me too that Mr. Grier Lesslic was the next one. He stayed there and he was the agent when I left.

E: Do you remember Mr. Tom Boyd? He was interested in the school and I think tried to help the school at some point.

H: Boyd.

E: He lived in Neely's Creek church.

H: I don't recall. I don't remember him.

E: What about the economic standards of these boys and girls. Their health, I'm concerned about. Did they have enough food and clothing? What about their health conditions?

h: So far as I could see, they were about like the kids in the white community where I grew up here at the Cowpen Junction. We were all poor as church mice, but we got by. They seemed to me to be as well-clothed as the average country child, and I don't know of any of them that were undernourished. There might have been. But we got a lunch program. They ate at a little lunchroom on the left-hand side and Sister Sanders--I can never think of her name....

W: Arzada?

H: Arzada, yeah, Arzada Sanders, she'd prepare the lunch and they got the food from the government like the other schools did, you know. I don't think we charged anybody for food, did we? There was no charge for the lunch, every kid got something to eat, and so on. We had the lunch program there for I don't know how many years. I was there for seven years, but as soon as we could get one started after I got there, we got a lunch program.

E: Mr. Hayes, what do you remember about the relationship of the white people of the community to the Indians? Was there cooperation and friendship?

H: So far as I knew, there was no ill feelings between them. I don't know of any white people that were concerned or that came about the reservation except the church officials, and the missionaries would come in, but I don't recall anybody coming or having any....

E: Was there any relationship between your school and Winthrop College? H: No, not that I know of.

E: Mr. Hayes, who followed you when you left in June of '42? Who was the next teacher? Do you know?

H: Well, gracious me, I certainly don't. I can't recall.

E: Let's go back to some of the students that you taught. I'm sure you've followed and you know what some of them are doing today. Who were some of the students that you taught and what are they doing in life today?

H: The people that I became acquainted with there were not...Samuel Beck wasn't in the school, he was in the C.C.C. camp; and Helen Canty, she wasn't in school. But I used to go up to the C.C.C. camp and get Samuel. Helen was working, I believe, in a restaurant in Rock Hill, and I'd bring them down to help with the M.I.A. program in the church there. I'd go once a week, get them and bring them down. I probably had a part of play as Cupid, because they wound up by getting married, Helen and Samuel. Florence Harris and Gladys Gordon and Euliss Sanders, those were the oldest girls, I believe, when I first went there. Florence and Gladys and Euliss, and I don't recall any of the other larger girls then, but those were the largest girls when I first went there. Of course, Gladys is dead now, and Euliss is living in Salt Lake City. She married William Watts. How many children did Euliss and William have?

W: Five.

H: Some of them went on missions.

W: I knew two of them did.

H: How many boys did he have?

W: Three.

H: Three boys?

W: Three boys and two girls.

H: Then you're sure that two of those boys went on missions for the church, and they seem to be doing quite well. I tried to contact them when I was out there last summer but nobody was home. I got their phone number to call. Euliss was the one that was in the ninth grade when I went there. She married William Watts. William was in the seventh grade, I believe. He was an outstanding person. He was real intelligent and just a fine person. He and Euliss got married and decided to move to Salt Lake where they'd have more advantaged in the church and more economic advantages, I guess. Heywood Canty, her [Frances Wade's] brother, was one of the sharpest students that I ever taught. Heywood would come to me if the problem was something he couldn't understand and I'd explain it to him.

That's be all I'd ever have to do for Heywood. He'd go back there and he could get any problem done using that princi¬ple. I taught several thousand students and Heywood was one of the outstanding students. I think with the mind that he had, he could have done anything that he wanted, just about. He was real smart. And then, of course, there was Frances. I can't remember ever having any trouble with her. But the Canty children were real smart and they were always clean and neat. I'll never forget Heywood. They'd play marbles and he had a board, a little piece of board, that he'd put down and he'd kneel on that board when he was shooting marbles. I said, "Heywood, why you doing that?" He said, "It's hard work to wash these clothes:"

E: He was thinking of his mother, wasn't he? That was very thoughtful.

H: His mother had impressed upon them the importance of keeping those clothes clean. But they were always neat.

E What about Alberta? Did you teach Alberta, too?

H: Yes, I taught Alberta. She wasn't as friendly and outgoing as Helen and Frances. I never was as close to her as I was to Helen and Frances. They were all talented and good students.

E: What about the Blue family? Did you teach any of the Blues?

H: Oh, yes. That Mildred was the most surprising thing I ever saw. For the first six weeks I was there, the only answer I ever got her to give me in class was, "I don't know." I'd ask her a question, "I don't know." But when I gave a written test, she'd get every answer correct. She was just so shy she wouldn't say a thing. But Betty was just the opposite. Man, she was a ball of fire. Mildred, she surprised me. I said, "Well, the poor girl, there must be something the matter with her. She can't learn," because I could never get her to answer a ques¬tion. But when I gave a written test, she came through with flying colors. She knew them all. She just wasn't going to say anything out loud in class. That, I learned, was one of their characteristics. The Indian people don't like to show their hand, as the saying is, until they get pretty well acquainted with you. I remember there was a missionary that came down there. They asked him to teach a class one night at M.I.A. and he kept asking them questions. It was the first time he'd been there and since he was a missionary, they put him in charge of the class. So he'd ask questions, nobody would answer. Finally he said, "You folks just act like a bunch of wooden Indian. You won't say a thing." He couldn't get a discussion going. They just say there and never cracked a smile or said a word. But for years after that, you'd mention him and they'd laugh about him calling them wooden Indians. They just wouldn't talk out. But once they get acquainted, it's quite different.

When I went there, one of the first things that I did was to get a Scout troop going among the boys.

The girls got a little jealous, said there ought to be something for the girls. So Hesse over there took them out camping. Say, did you go on camping trips with her?

E: Now, Odessa who?

H: My wife. Not Odessa, just Dessa, D-e-s-s-a.

E: Your wife? That's fine.

H: She went on a lot of camping trips with them. They had some exciting adventures, and various things going on.

E: You were telling me about those students. Any other students you remem¬ber? You started with the Blues, Mildred and Betty, any of the other ones you remember?

H: Yes. Floyd Harris, that's Sister Georgia Harris's boy, and Thomas, Fred and William Sanders, and the Beck boys, Samuel, Major Beck, and Fletcher. Eugene Beck was in school when I first went there. He was one of the older boys. He was close to Samuel's age, and he was getting on in years.

E: What about the chiefs? Who was chief when you were there, and what do you remember about the chiefs?

H: Chief Blue was the chief when I went there, and sometime during the time that I was there Brother Harris.. what was his name? The old man? I can't recall his name now.

W: Wasn't it Robert?

H: Robert. Yeah, old man Robert Harris.

E: Robert.

H: Robert Harris was chief. It seems to me that Douglas Harris was chief there for a year or so.

E: What impressed you about the relationship of the chief to the tribe or the people?

H: Chief Blue, when he was chief, he was also the branch president of the church there so everybody looked to him for leadership. Any problem they had, they'd usually take it up with him. If they got sick, they'd want him to come and see them. I've gone all hours of the day and night with him to see the sick.

E: What did you think about the medicines that he made himself? Did you think they were effective and good?

H: I don't know. I went with him into the woods many times. One time we had a booth at the fair in which we displayed Indian medicines. That was up at Rock Hill. The Indian medicines was one of the most attractive things at the fair that year. We went and we got samples of the roots and herbs and barks and berries and things he used and put down what it was and what the Indians used it for as medicine. I don't recall anybody using those as medicines while I was there because if anybody got a headache, all they had to do was go to Dr. Blackburn. I'd frequently take people to the doctor up there when I felt, I'm sure, worse than they did. But I had to pay and they didn't, so if they got sick or they felt bad, they'd go to the doctor. So they got away from the old Indian medicines pretty fast when they received the state appropriations paid the doctor so much, I don't know how much they paid him. But anybody that was sick, why, they'd go to the doctor and he'd treat them. So they didn't have to use herbs when I was there. But Chief Blue knew the different things that they had used in the past and that display that we got up for the fair was quite attractive and quite interesting to the public. Sister Blue or Sister Gordon or some of them might have used some of the things there to make a tea or something good for anything, but I couldn't say. I think that one of the experiences I had was the fact that I was about the last white man alive that ever heard the Catawba language used in conversation. Chief Blue could speak the Catawba language and Sister Cordon--what was her first name?

W: Sally.

H: Sally Gordon?

W: Sally Gordon.

H: She lived out back of the church and Chief Blue lived right across in front of the church. They have a well there, and she'd come out to the well. I lived right across the road the first year I was there, at LeRoy Blue's place. I had a room with them. She'd come to the well in the morning to draw water and they'd talk to each other in the Catawba language. I'd listen to then, but I didn't understand what they were saying. They'd carry on a conversation in their language. Then Dr. Frank Speck--have you heard about him?

E: Yes, I have.

H: He came and he could speak the language. He has it recorded at the University of Pennsylvania, I believe that's where he worked. He was an old man when I went there in '35, and he would come just about every year and spend some time, several days there, talking with Chief Blue and getting everything from him that he could concerning their stories, their traditions, their language, and everything. He has that recorded somewhere among his material. He's probably dead by now, but among his material at the University of Pennsylvania he has the lan¬guage and he devised a phonetic alphabet so that he could write that Catawba language so it could be read. He recorded everything that he possibly could get from Chief Blue in the way of their stories and their history and every word that he could get out of Chief Blue. I know he came there one time. I saw Chief Blue that day and he says, "I don't feel good today." And I said, "Why?" He said, "Well, I've been doing something that I haven't done since I was a little boy." I said, "What's that?" He said, "Dr. Speck was asking me to give him all the dirty words in the Catawba language that I could remember." So he'd made a list of all the dirty words that Chief Blue hadn't even used for years, he said hadn't been in his mind. He'd been trying to recall all of those words. So if you could get hold of Dr. Speck's material, you'd find quite a bit of information there, I'm sure.

E: Did you never learn to speak any of the language although you heard it sometimes?

H: Oh, yes. I can say sookahooglonee. That's all I know.

E: There're very few people on the reservation now that know the meaning of the words. I have found that they disagree among themselves. They'll have a certain word and they will disagree as to the meaning of that word. Have you heard Gilbert Blue do the chants his grand-father used to do?

H: Yes, I have. He's performed at church functions where we'd have dance festivals and things like that. I don't know how much of his grand father's stories that Gilbert learned, because Gilbert was just a small child when I lived there. He's grown up since I left. But Chief Blue told me that it was quite difficult to get anyone interested in the language because they aren't using it, you see, and it's hard to get them to learn anything.

E: Are you amazed that a man who didn't have any formal education as Chief Blue hadn't, became the outstanding leader, religiously and in every way, of his tribe? Are you amazed at that?

H: He was quite a guy, there's no doubt about it. He would have been an outstanding person, I think, anywhere he would've been. He had leadership qualities. A lot of the leadership that he had was because he was forced into leadership of the church there. When he received the priest-hood and became an elder in the church, they put him to work in the church as a leader, so his church work developed his leadership qualities. But he was just a natural-born leader, I think.

E: You think he was a natural-born actor, too?

H: Oh, yes. He could get up and stand in the pulpit and quote a passage of Scripture and preach a sermon on it. You would think that he had read it out of the Bible. He could quote more Scripture than any person just about that I ever knew, and how he learned it, I don't know. He told me how he learned when he received the priesthood and was made an elder in the church. When you administer the sacrament in the church, you have to...she's written in here that I taught him to write his name. When I was going to Salt Lake City to get married in the temple at Salt Lake, you have to have a recommendation from your branch president or bishop before you can get in the temple. He was the branch president so I taught him how to write his name so he could sign my temple recommendation.

E: He had never written his name before?

H: That's right.

E: That's amazing.

H: But I got his name on my temple recommendation to go to the temple.

E: Do you remember when Chief Blue went to Salt Lake City?

H: Oh, yes. That was after I left there, but I remember it quite well. He was quite thrilled with the opportunity he had to go. But when he had to learn the prayers on the sacrament so he could administer the sacrament, he said he would have his daughter read them over to him because they have to be given letter-perfect.. If you mispro-nounce a word, you have to start over. So he wanted to learn them perfectly. He said he would get out and walk around over the reser-vation at night, going over those prayers to see if he had them right. If he couldn't get one, he'd go back and have his daughter read it to him again, read it on, read it over, and he kept on with that until he got them perfect. He must have had a very retentive memory because he'd get up in the pulpit and quote the Scripture and preach a sermon from it. He was a very effective speaker. I have a story that he told when he was speaking in the Tabernacle when he got out to Salt Lake City. This professor at Brigham Young University heard that and he copied down to use it as a very effective means of expression. He was astounded and thrilled that Chief Blue was devoted to express himself in the English language.

E: You have that in a booklet form, I believe.

H: It's just a short story that he got from Chief Blue's talk while he was in the Tabernacle.

E: This is wonderful. I'll read it in just a moment. We can continue our conversation.

H: Yes.

E: Which one of the daughters helped him in memorizing his prayers? Do you remember?

H: That was the daughter that died. I've forgotten her name.

W: Lily?

H: Who?

W; Lily?

H: It might have been. She was dead when I went there, but she could read, evidently, and she taught him. She would read these prayers over and he'd memorize them.

E: That was an outstanding family. It still is. You've known all these groups of Indians by families. Do you find that their intelligence and their talents are handed down through a family line, usually, or are there some outstanding students even in a very poor, underprivileged family?

H: There were some outstanding families, like the Canty family, I don't remember any stupid ones in the family. Of course, Betty and Mildred Blue were outstanding. Most of them were average or better, but there were some that didn't have much ability at all or at least they wasn't interested in learning.

E: I've followed, and I know you have too, the occupations that some of these Indians are doing now. Will you mention some of the occupations that you know they're engaged in?

H: When I was there about the only occupation that any of them were engaged in was textiles. They worked in the textile mills in Rock Hill. A few of them farmed a little bit. There was very little farming as an occupation on the reservation when I was there. Most of the work was in Rock Hill there at the textile mills and the finishing plant. What were some of those mills up there?

W: Industrial Cannery.

H: Industrial mills.

E: Rock Hill Printing and Finishing Company.

H: Yes.

F.: But now, the Indian, to my way of thinking, never liked mill work. They wanted to be doing something with their hands more constructive or ingenious.

H: Samuel Beck was an electrician.

W: He's an electrician.

H: What does Gary do?

W: He builds cabinets.

E: Builds cabinets?

H: The opportunities for work was pretty limited. Textiles was about all an unskilled person could hope to find.

E: What about the homes? I know as you ride through the reservation, you see a great improvement in the type of homes they live in.

H: Yes.

E: And the roads.

H: When I went there, there were no paved roads at all anywhere close to the reservation and it looked like they would never get any roads out there. But they finally got some decent roads. I think that the state said that this little place here is not even South Carolina. They did nothing. That appropriation that they made for the Indians took care of everything so far as the state was concerned.

They discharged their obligation by just giving them an appropri¬ation and appointing an agent to disperse the funds. Nobody seemed to care what happened to them. There was a lady there that got interested in the Catawba Indians. She began to approach the people in Washington and get them interested, and eventually the federal government came down and began to do something there. That expanded the reservation, they bought more land, and it finally ended up by them dividing up the property and making the Catawba group a part of the nation, because the federal government ignored them completely. The federal government just put them off on 640 acres, I believe it was, and just made the general appropriation every year and the agent divided it up between the schools and the doctor. What was left after the schools was taken care of and the doctor, every summer. What was it they called the day that they got their checks? They divided up what was left of the appro¬priation equally.

W: Drawing money.

H: The what?

W: The drawing money.

H: Drawing money, and a lot of them would be drunk before dark came on drawing day.

E: Would they have a big feast or something?

H: No, they'd just go to town. I never did attend it, I just knew that

they'd go to town and they'd get a check--did they give them cash or a check?

W: I tell you, I just really don't know.

H: You never did get one?

W: Well, the heads of families....

H: Would get the check for the whole family.

W: Yes.

E: The type home has completely changed. There were log cabins on the reservation when you were there. They're all gone today.

H: There were a few log cabins, but most of the houses were board.

E: Board.

H: lilt huh.

E: When the people are owning their own homes, building them, and some of them have deeds to them, they have a pride in their ownership.

H: Well, of course.

E: Many of them away from the reservation have bought homes in other sections of Rock Hill.

H: Oh, yes.

E: What do you think about the pride of the Indian and his heritage? Do you think that they are proud that they are Indians?

H: I didn't notice any difference in them. In the church there's no difference between them and anybody else in the church. So far as the members of the church arc concerned, they're members of the church and that's all there is to it. They have a contribution to make, their heritage and their arts and crafts and their background, their story, is something Chat they should be proud of. The approach that we have toward the Indian is quite different from anyone else in the world because we think that they're choice people, that they're descendants from the children of Israel and that they have a heritage, and that the Lord has promised them tremendous blessings. I think right now that the Indians are beginning to receive the blessings that the Lord has promised them as members of the house of Israel. What our church is doing now in the Indian program is...I think that if the nation would use the same approach, we'd have an entirely different attitude among the Indian people. You wouldn't have Wounded Knee, for instance, like they had here and all this at the beginning of the year for weeks and weeks and weeks, because the church's offering to the Indian people is so vastly different from what the government's offering that there's no comparison to it. I think that in the next generation we'll see, certainly in Mexico and Central and South America, thousands and thousands of them coming into the church. It's always been predicted that in the Mormon church by the end of this century, Spanish will be spoken more than English because many of the Spanish-speaking people among the Indian people are coming into the church. We're sending doctors and nurses and teachers and dieticians and everything, agricultural experts, over to help them. We aren't just handing them food, we're teaching them how to produce their own food.

E: Of all the Indians you love, your particular love is for the Catawba group?

H: That's the only ones that I know very well.

E: That's right.

H: I know some of the Cherokees and they're fine. But the Catawbas have a special place in my heart because I know them.

E: How true. One more question. When you taught these children, did they ever tell any of their stories or their myths or their legends of the past? Did they seem to know anything of their past?

H: Not that I recall. Chief Blue was the only one that I talked with that could tell me very much about their past history, and the old man Robert Harris was pretty well-versed.

E: Won't you tell me about Robert Harris? What do you remember about him?

H: He was a very fine old man, very faithful and had the interests of the Catawbas at heart.

Mrs. H: He was so courteous.

H: Oh, yes, he was very, very courteous and very polite.

E: Very courteous. What did he look like?

H: He was a very dignified old man.

Xr. H: He was full-blooded, wasn't he? Almost?

H: I believe he was.

E: Robert and Ben Harris were the last two full-blooded Indians, so the history records.

H: But you'll never find a person that was more polite and more courteous and gentle than Robert Harris.

E: Who did Robert Harris marry?

H: I don't know.

E: Now Ben married Mary.

H: Just before he died, he married some woman. Not too long before he died, didn't he, Frances?

W: Yes, she wasn't an Indian.

H: No, she wasn't an Indian, but he married somebody just a few years before he died.

E: I think that's recorded somewhere.

H: But he was a very nice person and he knew quite a bit about the Indian story and the Indian traditions. But he lived in Rock Hill and I didn't get as close a contact with him as I did with Chief Blue, because I was with Chief Blue just about every day I was down there.

E: What about Ben Harris, do you remember him? That's the one they called Toad.

W: No. No, Ben is not Toad.

E: Oh, Ben Harris that married Mary, do you remember him?

H: No, I don't. I might have met him, but I don't recall.

E: You don't remember this, I'm sure, but did you ever hear the story of the Thomas Stevens, the man who froze to death and is buried in the old cemetery? Did anyone ever tell you that story?

H: Not that I recall.

E: I just wondered. Now before we finish the tape, maybe I haven't asked the questions I should. Is there anything else that you-want to tell me that you remember about the Catawba Indians that I haven't asked?

Mrs. H: Did you tell her about the leasing of the city of Rock Hill?

H: The leasing of the land, that happened ages ago. It was a colonial government that set aside 140,000 acres for them, and when the king decided to divide the colony--you've hear that story, how the line run around the Indian reservation, and in Rock Hill. In the library, there's a copy of the petition that the Indians gave to the king asking to leave them in South Carolina, because the old cemetery of the Catawbas is across the river on the Lancaster side of the river. The new cemetery was the one on this side, and then they have one up at the church now which is the new cemetery. As I say, most of the stories that ihave are mostly stories that Chief Blue told me, are very closely connected with the church and the activities of the church and the coming of the missionaries there to the reservation and their story. I have a tape recording that I nade of a man who was there in 1887 as a missionary, and I taped his story when he was 102 years old. He told about going to the reservation and the conditions that were there when he went. But Chief Blue, I don't think I've ever known anyone who had any greater faith in God than he did. He had a tremendous amount of faith, and the events and things that took place there at the reservation in connection with the church are some of the most inspiring stories imaginable. I could write a book-¬but I'm too lazy, I reckon--of the stories that Chief Blue told me about his experiences there.

E: We'll record some more about the things that you remember along that line.

Frances Wade interviewing Willard Hayes

W: This is Frances Wade. I'm a Catawba Indian. I live at Route 3, Box 304, Rock Hill. Actually, I live on what's known as the old reservation. Today I'm visiting in the home of Mr. and Mrs. Willard M. Hayes. I'm so used to calling them "Brother and Sister Hayes" that it's hard for me to say "Mr." Hayes. Brother Hayes, would you tell us a little about yourself?

H: I became acquainted with the Catawba people when I went there to teach school. I had known ever since I had been in the church that they were members of the church, and I had met Brother Herbert Blue. I don't remember meeting Chief Blue until I was applying for the position to teach the school. I went there in September of 1935 and became quite well acquainted with Chief Blue because I relied upon him to give me guidance on how to go about getting the school set up and operating it, and who to contact to get supplies, and various things. As soon as I got there, I became active in the church activities. When I went they were having, so far as I know, Sunday school and sacrament meeting, and Mutual Improvement Asso¬ciation, Partial Relief Society. I don't know whether they had a primary or not. But the men were not very active in the church. There was two men there that held the priesthood, Brother Blue and Brother Wade Gordon. Chief Blue was the branch president and Brother Gordon was the Sunday school superintendent. Then Brother Maroni George was working in the Sunday school, but I don't believe he held an auxilliary priesthood. He might have been a priest but I don't believe he was an elder. But they did have a Sunday school, and so I became a Sunday school teacher. Pretty soon we had a Scout troop. I was the Scoutmaster and I had the group of the kids in Sunday school, so they really got a dose of me, in church and in school too. I was there all the time. But the experiences that I had with Brother Blue and the stories that he told were some of the choice experiences of my life because I learned something about the early history of the church.

The first missionaries of the church that went in there went in around 1880. Brother Harris, I believe it was Robert, had a baptismal certificate that was dated in 1882. The first missionaries went there in May of 1882, and they held a service at the home of Nancy Harris. The first Latter Day Saint hymn that was sung on the reservation was "We Thank Thee, 0 God, for Our Prophet." The In¬dians became interested in this new religion because it was something pertaining to them and to their story and their

history. According to Chief Blue, there was very little religious activity on the reser¬vation.
Occasionally some traveling preacher would come by, hold a service and preach and move on. Then
sometime later someone else would come through. There had been some attempts to bring
Christ¬ianity to the Catawbas, but they were rather half-hearted and not very successful. The
Presbyterians at one time had a building. We have a picture of that building in there, but I don't know
whether that was before or after the missionaries came. Apparently there was very little religious
activity among the Indians, and the white people on the outside of the reservation took no interest in
them. So when the missionaries came and began to visit the reservation and to teach them, they began
to join the church. Pretty soon the vast majority of them were baptized into the Mormon church.
That was during the time of revolution in the South. We had just had the Civil War, and we had just
had the Reconstruction period, which aroused tremendous animosity and bitterness in the hearts of the
Southern people toward anything that was strange, foreign or from the outside. So when these
missionaries came in it wasn't long before the mob spirit became pretty evident. They went to the
reser¬vation, and seven men--and I don't know their identities--brought a paper signed by almost 100
people warning them to get out, to leave the reservation and stay away from the Indians. They didn't
heed the warning. So one night a mob of white men gathered at the home of one of the Indians. It was
at the home where George Harris and Douglas lived when they were raising their children back over
there. Chief Blue was only about eight or ten years old, and he was in the house the night that the mob
came. They began to fire their guns, yell and carry on out in the yard, and the person who lived in the
house--I don't know who he was, Chief Blue might have told me, but I don't remember told the others
to run. One of them went to the kitchen door, went out into the yard and crossed into the woods. As he
crossed the yard, the mob saw him and began to fire. Chief Blue said that they heard this elder scream
and they knew he had been hit, but they didn't know how seriously. They broke into the house and
took the other elder up there to where Peggy and Alfred Harris lived, right there just in that area there
where they live now. They stripped him down to the waist and tied him to a tree, and a man weighing
250 pounds took a hickory switch in both hands and beat him forty lashes on the neck and back. Then
they tried to force him to drink some whiskey. They'd hold him and pour the whiskey in his mouth. He
told them that they could put it in his mouth but they couldn't make him swallow. They told him if he
didn't leave the reservation that they'd probably kill him the next time. So they turned him loose and
he went back to the house, and of course the Indian people were there.

The other elder was still out in the woods, hiding out. They didn't know where he was. So Elder
Froughten, the one that got beat, signaled, whistled or shouted or gave some signal to the Elder Lylie
G. Kraygen, the one that got allot. When he learned that it was safe to come back, he came out of the

woods. He'd been shot in the face and his jaw had been broken. Chief Blue said that they walked back and forth in the house. Elder Kraygen was the senior companion and he told him what to do. So he finally asked Elder Froughten, "Did you promise the mob anything?" He said, "Yes, I promised them we'd leave the reservation." He says, "Did you pro¬mise them we wouldn't come back?" He said, "No, I didn't promise them that." He says, "Well, we'll keep your promise. We'll leave tomorrow, but we'll come back again." They walked from Catawba ten miles to Old Rock Hill, to my grandmother's place up at Cowpens Battlegrounds.

They stayed at her home until they recovered from this mobbing. My mother was just a tiny little girl then. She said that they were both crying when they got to the house. They asked them why, and what was the matter? Grandmother had two dogs that had been taught to shake hands with people who took their paw. When they saw these two missionaries coming up the road, the dogs ran down the road and shook hands with them. They said that that touched them so much that that's why they were crying because that was the first friendly thing that had happened to them since they left Catawba.

W: Brother Hayes, as much as I can remember, when you first came to Catawba, you wasn't married.

H: No.

W: I'd like for you to tell us a little bit about Sister Hayes and the big part she played in our religious life in Catawba.

H: I went there in '35 and during that winter, the district held a Going Green Ball at Gaffney. I came up. I was supposed to be master of ceremonies for the banquet and then the ball that followed. They were going to crown the queen for the Going Green Ball. When I went into the hotel up here, the Carroll Hotel, a bunch of girls from Greenville were there decorating the place. She came crawling out from under a table where she'd been pinning some paper to the table and that's the first time I remember seeing her. She had a mouthful of pins where she'd been pinning that paper under the table. They said, "This is Dessa Chapman." That's the first I remember. Then I was put in as first counsellor to the district president. The first district for the local people were given leadership of the church in South Carolina. I was the first counsellor to President William 0. Harris. We needed a leader for the young men's M.I.A., and so President Harris assigned me the job of being district president of the young men's Mutual Improvement Association. We needed a young woman, so I suggested that they put her in as the young women's presi¬dent. So she and I worked together in the M.I.A. Finally asked her to marry me and she took off to Salt Lake City. I followed here on out there. When I got there, she'd gone forty miles further west to Tulsa. But we finally got together and got married.

W: You know how we in Catawba feel about you. We got to have that same feeling for Sister Hayes because she played a big part in our religious life also. So what were some of the things that you can remember that she helped the Catawbas with?

H: She worked in relief society there, and she worked. I don't know whether she did anything in Sunday school or not. Did you do anything in the Sunday school?

Mrs. H: No, the M.I.A.

H: M.I.A. and you did work in the relief society. I don't know how much, but you was a relief society worker. She worked with the young girls, taking them out and interesting them in camping activities together as a group. I never could have done anything in the church if it hadn't been for her. She always supported me in every effort and every activity. She was responsible for bringing up kids while I was away from home. There was hardly a Sunday that I wasn't gone somewhere.

W: When we was in school every morning, the first thing before we had any lessons, we always had a devotional. Will you tell us something about that?

H: The purpose of the devotional was to get our minds set for the day and to remember that the Lord had a part in our lives. We'd usually sing a song and maybe read a Scripture and have a prayer or tell a story or something that would be inspirational, some type of inspira¬tional activity for the school. What do you remember about it?

W: I remember that it was always the good part. It was there I learned the Articles of Faith.

H: Is that right?

W: I remember that we all enjoyed it.

H: I enjoyed it. When I taught out here at White Plains, I did the same thing. I went there in 1950, and just a few weeks ago I met her at a funeral. Out there at the cemetery, after the benediction was given at the graveside, she came down and she was talking about those devotionals, said that some of the most inspiring moments of her teaching career was those devotionals we used to have out at White Plains. So I think that we ought to take tine to turn our thoughts to the Lord when we start our day's activities.

W: When you came to Catawba and started teaching us, which were the most interesting to teach as far as trying to learn, the boys or the girls?

I couldn't tell much difference. Some of the girls were real out¬standing in their efforts to learn, and so were the boys. Gladys and Florence would always knock their seat down when they wanted to raise a row in the classroom. We had the old scats and they should have been thrown away years before. They sat right in the back of the room, and they had a seat that if you moved it just right, it'd collapse. So right in the middle of the class when everything was going just fine, bang: Down would go that seat and little girls would be sitting flat on the floor. But all in all, we had a very enjoyable time. I couldn't say which was the smartest or who did the best. Moving from the front of the room, you could look back and it'd look like nobody's learning anything, but they do.

W: I remember your sister, Brother Hayes, Janie.

H: She came there for a couple of years. She lived with me dawn there.

W: Would you tell us something about your family?

H: My sister was the only member of my family that joined the church other than myself. My aunt joined the church when the missionaries first came to this part of the world. But I joined in 1928, and my sister joined in 1935. Then she stayed with my aunt. My aunt was helpless for many years. She was in bed, couldn't get out of bed and my sister stayed there and looked after her. When my aunt died, she had no place to stay, and I suggested that she come down there and stay with me and she could cook for me. I had been living with the Blues the first year, Leroy and his wife. So the next year we rented a house from Mr. Weiss. She needed a place to stay and I needed a cook, so we just got together. Until I got married, she stayed with me. When my mother died, she had requested that we leave the property to her and give her a deed to it. The boys , because we could look after ourselves, she wanted us to give the property to my sister. So all the boys did and my dad signed the deed, and we gave my mother's property to her. It was supposed to be hers, so we built her a house up there on the place and she moved back up there to live. That's when I got married. That's where she wanted me all the time, back at home.

W: I was young when you came to Catawba, but you taught me in school and I'll have to say I learned lots and I really appreciate it, things I'll never forget. But in your own mind, do you think we have pro-gressed much in that length of time? Where most do you think we've made the progress that we've ma de?

H: I think when you started going to high school, that was the secret of your success. As soon as you get an education. there's no hope for people...well, I'll take Chief Blue. With all his native intelligence and personality and leadership ability, he was handicapped because he didn't have an education. So I think that the secret of success was an education. As soon as we could get you to high school, even a high school education would widen the horizon, your opportunities would be ouch greater. You've got a bunch of people that have been to college or arc in college now, haven't you?

W: We sure have.

H: So without that, there's not much hope. I think that getting that car and going to Rock Hill with some high school students was about the finest thing that ever happened. Then, getting the men active in the church, getting the priesthood there and getting the church program going....You probably can't remember, but when I went there, most of the men just sat outside under the trees.

W: I do remember that.

H: You do?

W: Yes.

H: Chief Blue and Brother Cordon would fight trying to carry on the church, but the men just didn't come in. They didn't hold the priesthood, and I think alcohol and tobacco was the problem.

W: I'm new at this taping, and I'm not following my chain of thought to the end, but maybe you ought to tell us about your children, Brother Hayes.

H: Willard Harley's the only one that was born while we were down there. He was born up there at the Catholic hospital. What was the name of that hospital, Saint...?

W: Saint Philip's.

H: Saint Philip's Hospital. It's been torn down now, they built when he was born. He was born while we were there. When we moved to Spartanburg, the others were all born. He's the only Indian in the family.

W: Just a few minutes ago, you talked about the moral standards, especially of the smoking and drinking while church was going on, all the men sitting on the outside. Can you make a comparison with today?

H: Oh, there's no comparison. It's so vastly different now. You have a great many men and the young boys and girls are active in the church. They participate in the state activities. I don't know whether you're doing much in the Charlotte or not, but here the Catawbas were outstanding, especially in mathematics. In fact, when we had to go against Catawba, we knew we was going to have a fight on our hands, a contest. Of course, they took part in the music program and the dance program. It was quite pleasing to me to see the progress and development. I couldn't get anybody to do an Indian war dance. Even there at school, we had a real hard time getting anybody to do anything. We'd go down to the church and put on Christmas plays and Christmas programs. Did we have graduation programs? Oh, yeah, we had school closing programs then, every year. We'd put on plays, recite poems and sing songs and get them on their feet before the public. I think that helped to get them out, to bring out their talents and their abilities, to get them doing some¬thing. That fact has happened now, and your participation in the church program is certainly much greater than it was then, locally, and even in the state activity. Of course, we didn't have a state activity or district activities then, so you've had tremendous growth and development.

Dr. Frank G. Speck said when he first came there, that the only way he could get from Rock Hill out to the Indian reservation was to get some white man who was coming out to see an Indian woman to take him down there. The moral standards were very low. He stood up there in a meeting one night and said that the change that he had seen since he had been coming there...he started as a young man

541

and when I got there he was an old man, so he was there about the time of the turn of the century, certainly. He'd been coming for many years. He started when he was a graduate student in college and he'd been all over North and South America when I saw him. So he said that the moral standards on the reservation were so far superior to what they were when he started going there that he gave the church credit for it, for helping to get the Indians straightened out and getting them to living a better life. So, yes, there's been a tremendous change. Some of those kids you have down there, Kelly Harris, I don't see how he can fail to be a tremendous leader because he has, I think, the qualities of leadership and the spirituality of Chief Blue, but he'll have a college education.

The story of Roy Brown is such an inspiring one to people in the church. It shows the tremendous faith that Chief Blue had and the confidence that the people on the reservation had in Chief Blue. When the people were dying all over, particularly a great many of them died there at the Indian reservation. In fact, in the Brown family, I believe there'd been at least two or three other deaths before Roy died. Chief Blue was up on the upper end of the reservation cutting wood, and he brought a load of wood down. As he came into the highway down below the house where they lived, they hollered down to him and told him that Roy was dead. They wanted him to come over, so he went home, put up his mule and probably changed clothes to go over to arrange for the funeral. When he got there, the boy had been dead for some time. I don't know how long he'd died before Chief Blue came down out of the woods. But anyhow, Roy's father insisted that Chief Blue administer to him. Administration in the Mormon church is you anoint them with olive oil and then you seal that anointing on them, give them a blessing, that is for the sick. Roy's father insisted that Chief Blue administer to Roy. The chief told him there was no need to do that, he's been dead for some time now. But he insisted that he do it. so Chief Blue anointed him with the oil and then put his hands on his head and sealed that anointing. According to Chief Blue, when he took his hands off the boy's head, he opened his eyes, and he's still living.

Brother Hayes, I think, too, they said that the children that had died, all of them had died within a week's time. At the time, there was two more children in bed sick beside Roy.

H: Yes. But Chief Blue's leg there, that is a tremendous story. Because when he got it broken, and the doctors had told him that there was no way they could save his life except to cut that leg off, he said no. He wouldn't stand for that. So they went out in the yard, consulted together and decided that since there was no way to save him, he was going to die. They would just put some chloroform on a handkerchief, go into the room and put it over his face right quick. He'd pass out and they'd take his leg off and save his life. His wife heard the plans, Sister Blue, and so she told him, "They're going to put chloroform on you and take your leg off." Up over the front door they had some forked sticks there like that, nailed to the wall, and he'd put his gun up there. So he told her to bring him the gun. When the doctors came to the door, there he lay on the bed with a gun laid across his chest and he told them not to come any closer. They said, "We're leaving, then, because there's nothing further we can do for you." He had already told his wife and his children to find the elders. At that time they'd come by and visitawhile and then they'd go on to another town and visit there, and another. They just moved around from place to place, the Mormon missionaries did. So he evidently knew what town they were in or somehow he'd contacted them and sent for them. They came and he had them administer to him. He said when they anointed him with the oil and sealed that anointing, that he felt the bones going back into place in his leg. That was on a Thursday, and he went to church the next Sunday.

E: Mr. Hayes, what doctors were these that...?

H: I don't know. I don't even remember that he told me the names of the doctors.

E: Will you tell us how this leg was injured?

H: This tree fell when he was cutting wood. The tree fell and broke it. That isn't the end of the story, because he walked out in the woods one day after he got to where he could walk on the leg, and a stump- a tree had been cut and the stump had rotted out and there was a hole there--he stepped in that hole with that leg and broke it all over again. This time the doctors again told him that there was no hope for saving the leg, that it would have to be taken off. He was administered to again and the leg was healed.

W: We know that Indians like to chew tobacco. Will you tell us how Uncle Sam broke that habit?

H: To administer the ordinances, preach, baptize and carry on the acti-vities of the church, you have to hold the priesthood, at least be an elder in the church. So when he decided that he wanted to be an elder, he had been chewing tobacco ever since he could remember. He said he couldn't remember when he started chewing tobacco. All of his life that he could remember, he'd been chewing tobacco. But he decided that he was going to get rid of the habit. Well, he couldn't do it. He tried and he failed, he tried and he failed. So he started fasting one day, it was in the summer, and he was plowing in the river bottoms. Now fasting means that you don't cat food and you don't drink water. But he went all day, fasting. and when he'd feel like he had to have a chewing tobacco, he'd stop his mule and go out in the woods and pray for strength to keep on going. The next day he went back and plowed sone more, prayed some more and fasted some more. It was the third or fourth day of fasting, and he still had that craving for tobacco. So he said he went in the woods and he knelt down and he said, "Lord, I've done all I can do. Now, if I get up from this prayer and I still want to chew tobacco, I'm going to chew it!" He said that when he said that to the Lord, that every desire for tobacco left him. Many, many years later he said. "I've never wanted to chew in my mouth since that day." To go for three days in the summertime without food or water takes quite a bit of courage, and working all the time too, but he was determined to get rid of that habit and he did.

W: I know the stories that he's told, there's many of them, but even at my age, I can remember the time when the Mormon church would have come to a complete standstill, I guess...

H: Without him.

W: ...without him. Do you remember anything about that?

H: They had no leadership. About the only thing the church could have done was to send missionaries back in there to carry on the activities if he hadn't been there to keep it going. Yes, he was a mighty force in the church there, and the people on the outside of the reservation recognized his leadership from the fact that he was keeping it going. I don't know the man's name, I can't recall his name now, but he told me his name when he told me the story. He was a very wealthy landowner that had land close to the reservation, and Chief Blue had twenty-three children. One December just before Christmas he was hauling wood to Rock Hill. He'd cut a load of wood, haul it to Rock Hill, and sell it for fifty cents. He was trying to get some money so he could buy something for Christmas for his children. He was coming home on the evening, cold, wet, and rainy. Then he met this man who was riding in a buggy and had a nice lap robe over him, was nice and comfortable, and Chief Blue had his wagon going home. They stopped to pass the time of day. This man asked him, "Sam, how're you doing?" He said, "Well, I'm not doing so well. I'm just trying to get some money together here so I can get some things for the chil¬dren for Christmas." This man used a bad word and says, "Well, Sam, I'll give you $1000.00 if you'll get out of that 'blank' Mormon church!" Chief Blue says, "$1000.00!" Says, "That was more money than I'd even seen all put together in my life. There I sat, with a big family at home and it Christmas and me with no money, and here was $1000.00." A tremendous amount of money. But he said, "I thought a moment and I just told him that I couldn't accept his offer." And he says, "Why?" And he said, "Well. I'm not Judas, and I'm not Esau, so I can't afford to take it!" One of the most interesting ones was when the missionaries had gotten mobbed on the reservation. They didn't dare come in there together. They'd go one at a time. It was a signal. If they saw two strange men going toward the Indian reserva¬tion, they knew they were Mormon elders. So one at a time would go in. They knew there was an elder coming from toward Gaffney down that road and he didn't know the way to the reservation. So they sent Chief Blue and another boy up the road to above Rock Hill there to meet him. There's a church there at the little town of Percyville, and they went walking up the road. Chief Blue was real dark when he was a boy. So as they went up the road they kept looking for somebody they thought might be the elder. They passed this church and they saw a man sit¬ting on the steps of the church reading a letter. They went on up and Chief Blue says,

"You know, I believe that was the elder sitting back there at that church." The other boy said, "Well, you want to go back?" They decided to go back and they went walking back down the road. This elder looked at them and he couldn't decide whether they were Indian or Negro boys. He was afraid to ask them, but fin-ally he decided on a question he could ask them that he'd find out whether they were friends or enemies or not. He said as they came down the road, "Boys, are you boys Laymanites?" They said, "Yeah!" They knew he was the elder then because no other white man in the country would have known, they would have thought they were Indians. In the Book of Mormon, the Indian people are referred to as Laymanites. So when be asked them whether they were Laymanites, they knew he was the elder. If they'd been colored boys, they wouldn't have known what he meant, so they couldn't have given him away.

W: Brother Hayes, you mentioned something a few minutes ago that I didn't know. The Uncle Sam that I remember, he was not a dark-skinned person.

H: I know that.

W: A lot of people might have mistaken him even for white. So I wonder what happened in between there. You mentioned that he was dark.

H: The Book of Mormon promises the Indian people that they'll become white in the eyes of people if they'll accept the Gospel and live it. I don't know why he changed, but he showed me a picture of one of his sons, I believe the one that was shot, that was real dark, and he says, "I was darker than he was when I was a little boy." But he wasn't dark when he died. If he wasn't sunburnt, he'd be as white as anyone. In fact, when he'd get a haircut sometimes, it'd show.

W: There was such a crowd at Uncle Sam's funeral. To people who won't recognize the name, Chief Blue is who we're talking about. There were so many people there. Were you there? At his funeral?

H: Oh, yes.

W: What do you remember about his funeral?

H: I think it was a wonderful experience. It was a very spiritual ex¬perience to me because shortly before he died, I visited. I asked him, "Brother Blue, how are you?" He says, "I'm not doing any good. I'm just riding my stick-grip." Of course nobody would know what that meant if they didn't know the story of the church. Because, the Book of Mormon, we call it the Stick of Joseph, and the Bible is the Stick of Judah. So when the missionaries would come out, they'd have a little satchel, a little grip, and they'd carry these books in it, and they'd call it their stick-grip. Somewhere in there they'd usually have a clean pair of underwear and a clean shirt or something. So when they get ready to go home, when they get released from the mis¬sion--they stay in the mission field until they get a release from their mission president. So when they're expecting their mission to be up, they start watching for that letter to come. They'll get their stick-grip and everything all packed and ready to go. When a missionary begins to think about going home, the others just tell him he's "riding his stick-grip," getting ready to go home. So Brother Blue says, "I'm just riding my stick-grip." He was prepared to go and had suffered intensely from cancer. What he meant was that he had everything packed up and ready to go, just waiting for his call.

W: I remember at his funeral there was a great many of what I consider important men from Rock Hill.

H: That's right.

W: Ministers.

A great many people who knew him, respected him and honored him as a fine person.

Mrs. H: The bishop from the Episcopalian Church was there. He spoke.

W: Yes, he did. Reverend Lumpkin spoke, yes.

E: Do you have a tape of the service?

H: No, I don't. I'm sorry, but I don't. I never have taped a sermon, and I've preached a great many sermons in my life. Most of them were very close and dear friends. I had trouble getting emotionally involved when I'd try to preach a sermon. But Chief Blue was a very dear friend and a very wonderful person.

W: To the people in Catawba and especially me, his influence was felt by all of us. We all really learned to love him. He taught us a lot, because we all knew he didn't have an education and we all knew he couldn't even write, but he taught us lessons that we couldn't have gotten from any source other than him.

H: A great many of you received your blessing from him.

W: Yes.

H: He baptized and confirmed you, and when you were sick he came and administered to you.

W: Well, he gave advice, too. He gave sound advice.

H: That's right, he gave advice. He preached--I don't know how many sermons that man preached in his life. They were all interesting and all inspiring to me. His testimony of the Gospel was so strong and so sure that, as I said, when he saw that his life was coming to a close, he was prepared to go on. He was anxious to get it over with and get on into the next pahse of his existence.

E: Do you remember the music that you had at that service, the funeral service for Chief Blue?

H: No I don't. I'm almost sure that they sang "0 My Father".

E: Is that a special Mormon song?

H: Yes, it is.

E: Could you sing it?

Mrs. H: You could let Frances sing it.

W: Oh, no! I haven't got a good voice.

H: She can sing it.

Mrs. H: I'd rather Frances sang it.

W: I can't.   I just....

H, W, Mrs H: singing 0 my Father,

E: That was "0 My Father" recorded by Mr. and Mrs. Hayes and Frances Wade. It's taken from the hymns of the Church of Jesus Christ of the Latter Day Saints. "0 My Father" was sung at the funeral service of Chief Samuel Blue.

PHOTO 202 -- WILLARD M HAYES IN THE MIDDLE BACK ROW

Louisa Hayes

PHOTO 203 -- LOUISA HAYES

LOUISA FACING DOWN THE MOB

Contributed By **reginalouisahayes1** · 22 June 2014 ·

LOUISA FACING DOWN THE MOB There was once a woman who lived with her husband, daughter and 4 sons. They lived on the land that her father had deeded to her before he died. It was on part of the land that is now used as a State Park, called Cowpens Battle Ground. An important Revolutionary battle was fought there. There was soon to be another battle on this land and Grandmother Louisa would be the victor. Louisa was a mid-wife and was very knowledgeable of herbal medicine. Because they lived far from town the country folk would go to her for any sickness and leave the more serious ailments for the city doctor. Now this area was infested with gun toting, tar and feather carrying Mormon haters. Grandmother Louisa was a God-fearing Baptist and followed the 'good books' teachings. Matter of fact she went to the New Pleasant Baptist Church. Her teenage son, Willard taught one of the Sunday school classes. The church resided on land that was given to them by one of her relatives. Toward nightfall two Mormon Elders came to my grandmother's door looking for refuge, rest and possibly a little food to sustain them. Grandmother took them in, gave them food and sleeping quarters. Later that same evening a mob came carrying their guns, tar and feathers and their torches, so they could see if they were doing a good job of tar and feathering those two-low life Mormon scum. They shouted, "give us those two no account Mormon boys we know you have 'um. We're going to teach them how we take care of varmints like them. Grandmother Louisa came out on the porch with fire in her eyes and welding a shotgun with this statement. "You'll have to go thru me if you plan on harming these Mormon fellers. Meanwhile inside were the two Mormon elders, both scared out of their wits, and wondering if one strong willed woman they had just met, would be able to hold off that mob who were after their skin. One of the elders chose, to his later regret, to take his chances and run for it out the back ways toward the woods. A sharp-eyed mobster caught movement out of the corner of his eye, and hollered, "There goes one of 'um headed for the woods, let's get him". As the shots whizzed by his head, one shot made it's mark and took off his left ear. The mob figured that was punishment enough and took their tar, feathers and torches and went on their way. Meanwhile back at grandmother's house, the other elder, who chose to stay under the protection of my grandmother Louisa, thanked grandmother, Heavenly Father and his good sense to lay low in the back-bed room like he was told.

Regina Louisa Hayes

John Shaw Black

PHOTO 204 -- JOHN SHAW BLACK

From the journal of Mononi Ferrin 1887

John S Black furnished two teams and went with me to Cowpens Station after Pres. John Morgan and Brother John Wilson the former president of the southern states mission and the latter a local priest from Oconee County South Carolina.

19th- I borrowed a team from JS Black and Elder Bingham, Brother Sidney Berry and I went and got Sister. Davis her family and baggage and brought them to Brother A Canty's. We packed up part of Sister Davises things and also Sister Pattersons. Elders Humphreys, Peck, and I took supper with JS Black. Elders Bingham, Redd, Humphreys and I stayed overnight with him. Our enemies were here prowling around the house. Mr. Black got his gun and scared them away but no shooting was done as they stayed out of Mr. Blacks sight. 20th Sunday we finished packing up the baggage for the Saints, held meeting and had a good time. The emegration Saints were taken to Cowpen Station with the team of JS Black and Alexander Bridges. Accompanied by a number of the Saints, friends and Elders. We hired a room in a hotel for the people to stay in overnight. Elders Bingham, Stookey, Redd, Humphreys, Johnson and I stayed with them. We had scarcely got settled we stayed up all night and sit by the fire in our room when the scoundrel(George Bishop a merchant at Cowpen Station) disturbed our peace by his demonic presents.

On learning that he had come therefore licentious purpose and had been insulting our Sisters we saw it was necessary to invite him from the room which we did, but he soon returned and continued. Returning making himself bolder and bolder until it became necessary to keep him out by force. But he made so much disturbance that we called upon the Constable of that place to take him and keep the peace.

The Constable replied by coming in and insulting one of our Sisters. The task of getting rid of them both was now before us, by the aid of our faithful friend JS Black, we finally succeeded in doing so without resorting to any great violence, although Mr. Blacks knife was waived through the air somewhat. Walked 8 miles"

From Alexander Redd's Journal

"1887 - Feb. 27th- Sunday held two meetings - considerable interest - went down to Cowpens at night to see Bros. Wright and Fraughten off for home - got back to J. Black's at daylight - slept till noon and heard John Black bear testimony of the blessings of the Lord manifested to him by feeding the servants of the Lord - in a public gathering when Elders Wright and Fraughten were leaving Nov. 18th - Sunday - go to Bro. Sarratts - hold S.S. and meeting - not many present - a good spirit manifest - D, S and stay all night with Bro. Evan Watts. I don't have any more of his mission journal. I remember him saying that when he was released he didn't have the money to come home. Then the church didn't pay their way home as they do now. He went to Mr. Black who has been mentioned many times. Mr. Black was not a member, but a very good friend. He was a Justice of the Peace or some such thing and stood out on the courthouse steps and gave quite a speech. He said he was going to lend this man $50.00. He had been out here paying his own way for them and their welfare. He wouldn't lend anything to a sectarian minister, but he was going to lend it to this man, Mr. William A. Redd from Utah, because he would pay it back. He was an honest man and could be trusted."

LAST SURVIVOR OF FAMOUS COMPANY HAS PASSED AWAY

John S. Black, Civil War Soldier of Highest Quality, Dies After Short Illness.

John S. Black, believed to be the last surviving member of Company "H," Palmetto Sharpshooters, who served gallantly throughout the Civil War, died at a local hospital late Wednesday following an illness of only three days. Mr. Black was well known to many Gaffney and Cherokee county people. He was about 80 years of age.

Mr. Black's wife has been ill in a hospital here for some time. He had been visiting her regularly, and on Sunday he went to see her. While at the hospital he had a chill. The next morning he was found practically unconscious at his home on West Meadow street. He was taken to the hospital where he lived until Wednesday evening.

The funeral arrangements have not been made yet, it having been decided to postpone the burial until Mrs. Black is able to attend.

Besides his wife, Mr. Black is survived by an adopted son, Joe Black.

The deceased was a gallant Confederate soldier, having served throughout the war in Company "H," Palmetto Sharpshooters, General Jenkins' brigade. He was wounded at the battle of Sharpsburg. He was a brave and courageous soldier, according to his comrades. Once, it is said, his captain remarked that with half a million men like Mr. Black he could capture the entire federal army and go on and take Canada.

A number of the older men formerly prominent in this section were members of Company "H," Palmetto Sharpshooters. A few days before his death Mr. Black told friends that so far as he knew he was the last surviving member of that famous old company, although there are a few of the members widows still living.

Mr. Black was a native of this county. He married Miss Mary E. Williams, of the Battleground section, about 30 years ago. He had been living in Gaffney nearly 20 years, having moved here after saving a competence from hard and industrious labor on his farms in the Thickety Mountain section of the county.

Delivered 9 April 1950 General Conference By George Albert Smith

This is the last address delivered to the Saints by President George Albert Smith prior to his death. The occasion was the 120th Annual General Conference of the Church.

George Albert Smith, Conference Report, April 1950, p.145 - p.146 I pray the Lord to bless us that we may be worthy because of our lives to keep this testimony, that not only we, but all we can reach may receive that witness and carry it to our brothers and sisters of all races and creeds, and particularly to the descendants of Lehi, until we have done our duty by them. I am sure that when the time comes for the resurrection, that all who are in their tombs and worthy shall be raised from their graves, and this earth shall become the celestial kingdom, and Jesus Christ, our Lord, will be our King and our Lawgiver -- that we will rejoice that we have availed ourselves of the truth and applied it in our lives. That is what the gospel teaches us. That is what the gospel offers to us if we will accept it, and I pray that we may be worthy of it in the name of Jesus Christ. Amen.

When I was twenty-one years of age, I was sent on a mission to the southern states. I became secretary of the mission, and while there was called to Columbia, South Carolina, because some of our elders had become seriously ill. It was difficult to get word back and forth, so I got on a train and went down there. I found that they were improved and getting along all right.

MISSIONARY EXPERIENCE

When I bade them good-bye, I boarded the train and started home, and we passed a little Indian settlement at the side of the track. I saw evidence that there were quite a number of Indians there, so I reached over and touched the man who was sitting in the seat in front of me, and I said, "Do you know what Indians these are?"

He said, "They are the Catawbas." That is the tribe that Chief Blue represents, who has just spoken to us.

I asked, "Do you know where they come from?"

He said, "Do you mean the Catawbas?"

I replied, "Any Indians."

He said, "Nobody knows where the Indians came from."

"Oh," I said, "yes they do." I was talking then to a man about forty-five or fifty years old, and I was twenty-one.

He questioned, "Well, where did they come from?"

I answered, "They came from Jerusalem six hundred years before the birth of Christ."

"Where did you get that information?" he asked.

I told him, "From the history of the Indians."

"Why," he said, "I didn't know there was any history of the Indians."

I said, "Yes, there is a history of the Indians. It tells all about them." Then he looked at me as much as to say: My, you are trying to put one over on me.

But he said, "Where is this history?"

"Would you like to see one?" I asked. And he said that he certainly would. I reached down under the seat in my little log cabin grip and took out a Book of Mormon and handed it to him.

He exclaimed, "My goodness, what is this?"

I replied, "That is the history of the ancestry of the American Indian."

He said, "I never heard of it before. May I see it?"

I said, "Yes" and after he had looked at it a few minutes, he turned around to me and asked, "Won't you sell me this book? I don't want to lose the privilege of reading it through."

"Well," I said, "I will be on the train for three hours. You can read it for that long, and it won't cost you anything." I had found that he was getting off farther on, but I had to get off in three hours.

In a little while he turned around again and said, "I don't want to give up this book. I've never seen anything like this before."

I could see that he apparently was a refined and well-educated man. I didn't tell him I really wanted him to read the book, but I said, "Well, I can't sell it to you. It is the only one I have." (I didn't tell him I could get as many more as I wanted.)

He said, "I think you ought to sell it to me."

I replied, "No, I'll tell you what I'll do. You keep it for three weeks, and at the end of that time you send it to me at Chattanooga," and I gave him my card with my address on, secretary of the mission.

So we bade one another good-bye, and in about two weeks he wrote me a letter saying, "I don't want to give this book up. I am sure you can get another, and I will pay you any price you want for it."

Then I had my opportunity. I wrote back, "If you really enjoy the book and have an idea it is truly worthwhile, accept it with my compliments." I received a letter of thanks back from him.

I speak of that because that was the first time I had ever heard of the Catawba Indians, and there were only a few of them. I understand now from Chief Blue that ninety-seven percent of them are members of the Church of Jesus Christ of Latter-day Saints.

MEETING 15 YEARS LATER

Coming back to this book again--Brother B. H. Roberts and I were sent some fifteen years later down into the southern states to visit the mission. When we arrived at the hotel at Columbia, we registered and went into our room, and soon after a knock came at the door and a colored man said, "There's a man downstairs that wants to see George A. Smith." That was the way I used to write my name, and I wrote it that way before I was married.

I said to Brother Roberts, "What will we do?" and he replied, "Send him up," so the man went back, and pretty soon up came a man and knocked on the door, and we opened it.

He reached out his hand and said, "My, I am glad to see you."

I said, "I am glad if you're glad to see me; I am happy to see you, but who are you?" and he gave me his name.

I asked, "What can I do for you?"

He said, "Don't you remember me?"

I told him, "Remember you? I don't believe I ever saw you before."

He said, "Isn't your name George A. Smith?" and I said, "Yes."

"Well, he replied, "I am sure you're the man. I met George A. Smith years ago as he was doing missionary work here."

I answered, "Oh, that is easily explained, there was another George A. Smith here doing missionary work, too."

"Oh," he said, "it wasn't any other George A. Smith. It was you. Nobody that ever saw that face would forget it."

"Well," I said, "I guess I must be the man."

Then he related this story. He said, "You were on a train, and we passed the Catawba Indian Reservation."

I interrupted, "I remember all about it now." It all came back in an instant.

He said, "I want to tell you something. I read that book, and I was so impressed with it that I made up my mind I would like to take a trip down into Central America and South America and I took that book with me in my bag when I went down there. As a result of reading it I knew more about those people than they knew about themselves.

"I lost your address; I didn't know how to find you, and all these years I wanted to see you, and today after you registered downstairs I happened to be looking at the hotel register and I saw your name. That is how I found you."

"I am a representative of the Associated Press for this part of the United States. I understand you are here in the interest of your people."

And I answered, "Yes, Mr. Roberts and I both are here for that purpose.

"And he said, "If there is anything I can do for you while you are here, if you want anything put in the press, give it to me and it won't cost you a cent. But," he continued, "I want to tell you one other thing, I have kept your missionaries out of jail; I have got them free from mobs; I have helped them every way I could; but I have never been able to get your address until now."

CHIEF BLUE AND CATAWBA INDIANS

So you may be interested, brethren and sisters, in knowing that I am delighted in seeing Chief Blue here today, representing that tribe of fine Indians. I have seen some of them since. I have met one very fine young woman who is a schoolteacher, and others I have met of that race; in fact, I have some trinkets in my office that were sent to me by members of that tribe.

I am happy to have this good man here who represents one of the tribes that descended from Father Lehi as well as some of the others that are in our audience today. One good man that I am looking at here came to the temple during the week and was sealed to his wife. They are coming into the Church all around, and I am so grateful this morning to be here and hear this man who for sixty years has been a faithful leader among his people and now comes to this general conference and bears testimony to us.

It is a great work that We are identified with. Not the least of our responsibilities is to see that this message is carried to the descendants of Lehi, wherever they are, and give them an opportunity to accept the gospel of Jesus Christ.

George Albert Smith

PHOTO 205 - GEORGE ALBERT SMITH

ADDITIONAL KNOWLEDGE

How glorious it is to know that we have that information, and we have the knowledge that there were others resurrected, as recorded in the New Testament. And then we have the information in the Book of Mormon of the coming of the Savior to this western hemisphere, and we have the appearance of John the Baptist, and Peter, James, and John, and the Father and the Son to Joseph Smith on these latter days. No other people have what we have. I don't know of any people who ought to be so anxious and willing and grateful to be able to celebrate this day that is recognized in the world as the anniversary of the resurrection of the Redeemer of mankind, and that meant the opening of the grave for all humanity.

Group Pictures of Southern States Missionaries

PHOTO 206 -- EARLY SOUTHERN STATES MISSION MISSIONARIES

PHOTO 207 -- SSM 1911 - SOUTH CAROLINA CONFERENCE OF THE SOUTHERN STATES MISSION

Group Pictures of Southern States Missionaries

PHOTO 208 -- SSM 14 JANUARY 1883 - KOSSUTH DYAL – BR – 6TH FROM LEFT.

PHOTO 209 -- SSM 1921 – ALABALMA COPNFERENCE OF SOUTHERN STATES MISSION

Group Pictures of Southern States Missionaries

Top row. Smith, Bosgiter, Brunham, Stalling, Chadwick, Merrill, Cox, Scott, Ellis, Bottom row West Page, Riding, Plumb, Pearce, Lebaron, Linde, Smith

PHOTO 210 -- SSM 1927 - SOUTH CAROLINA CONFERENCE OF THE SOUTHERN STATES MISSION

PHOTO 211 - SSM 1929 -- SOUTH CAROLINA - SOUTHERN STATES MISSION

Group Pictures of Southern States Missionaries

L-R -- Elders, Hune, Tempest, Goble, Cole, Scheffield, Scott, Farr, Pres Calis, Toone, Buse, Hardy, Brockbank, Anderson, Pres. Arrington, , Clement.

PHOTO 212 -- SSM 1922 – SOUTH CAROLINA, SOUTHERN STATES MISSION

PHOTO 213 -- SSM 1926 - SOUTH CAROLINA, SOUTHERN STATES MISSION (WELder ANDERSEN- FRONT SECOND FROM RIGHT)

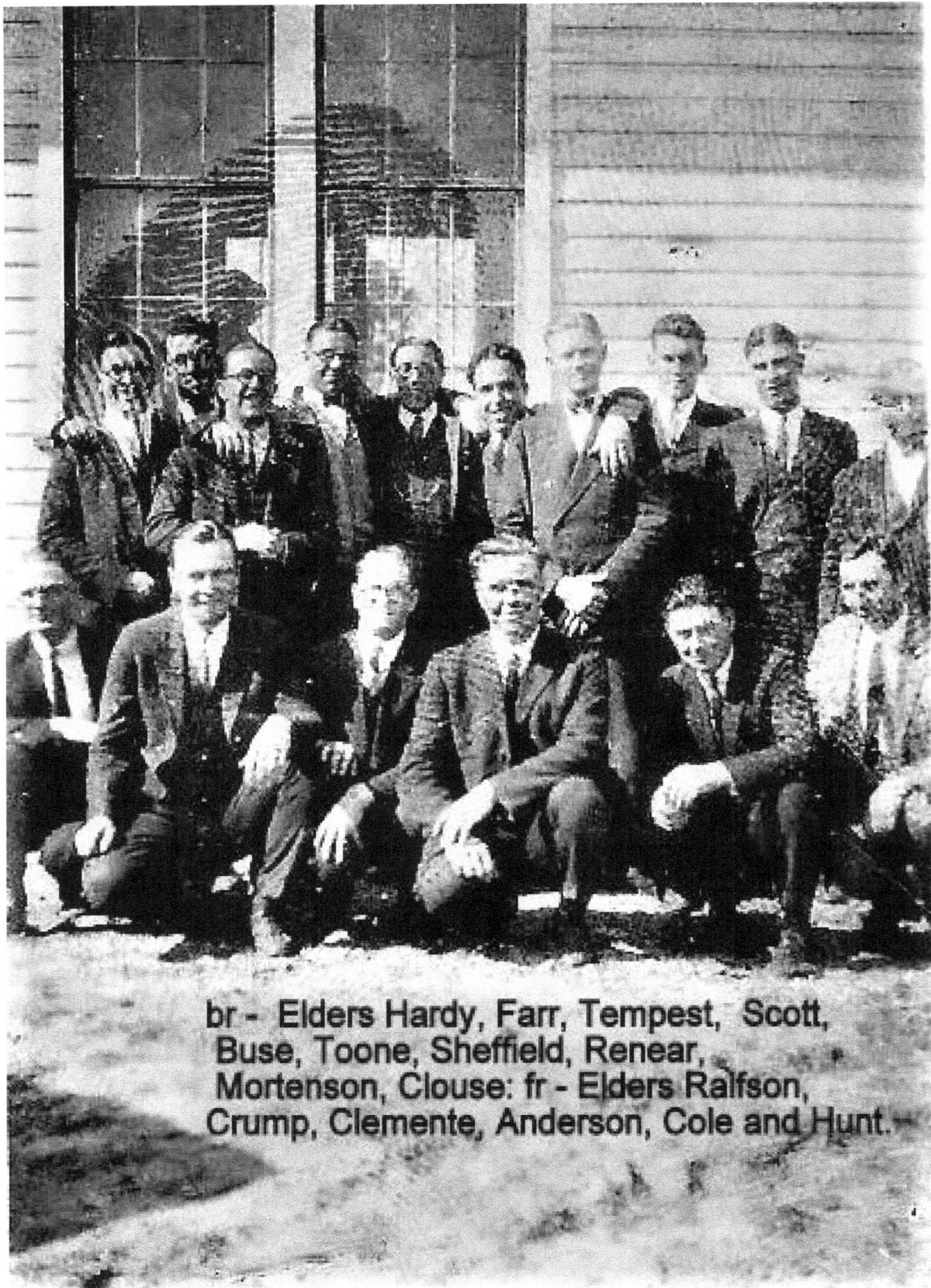

br - Elders Hardy, Farr, Tempest, Scott, Buse, Toone, Sheffield, Renear, Mortenson, Clouse: fr - Elders Ralfson, Crump, Clemente, Anderson, Cole and Hunt.

PHOTO 214 -- SSM 1927 -- SOUTH CAROLINA - SOUTHERN STATES MISSION

Group Pictures of Southern States Missionaries

PHOTO 215 -- SSM 1922 - PRESIDENT CALIS- CENTER FRONT, AND ELDER MCCORMACK – 3RD FROM RIGHT BACK.

PHOTO 216 -- SSM 1927 - SALT LAKE MISSION HOME

PHOTO 217 - SSM 1930 -- SALT LAKE MISSIONARIES AT MISSION HOME – DECEMBER 1930

Unknown - South Carolina – Southern States Mission Missionaries

Elder Sarber

Elder F. Dee Fidling

INDEX

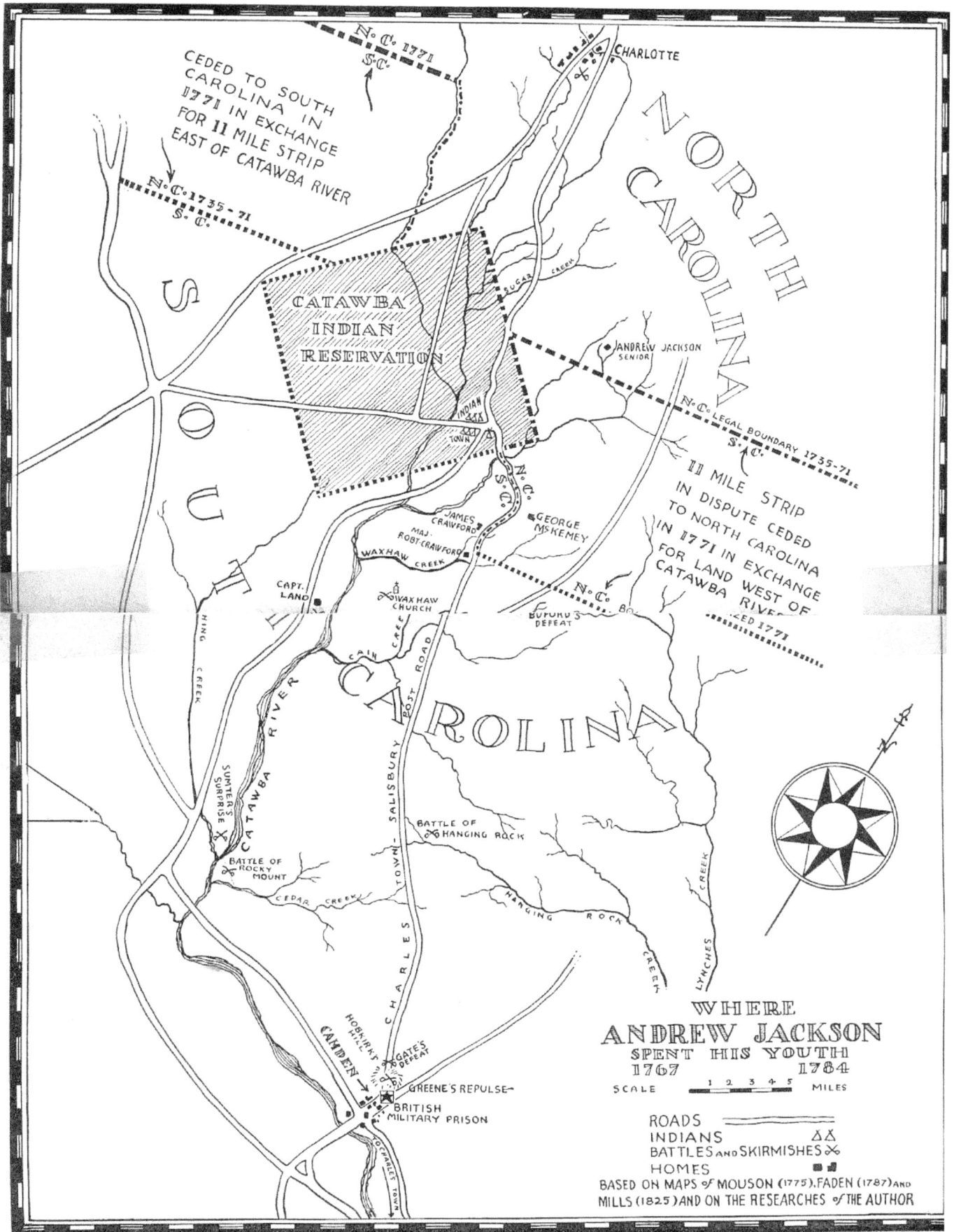

CEDED TO SOUTH CAROLINA IN 1771 IN EXCHANGE FOR 11 MILE STRIP EAST OF CATAWBA RIVER

N.C. 1771 S.C.

N.C. 1735-71 S.C.

CHARLOTTE

NORTH CAROLINA

SOUTH

CATAWBA INDIAN RESERVATION

SUGAR CREEK

ANDREW JACKSON SENIOR

N.C. LEGAL BOUNDARY 1735-71 S.C.

11 MILE STRIP IN DISPUTE CEDED TO NORTH CAROLINA IN 1771 IN EXCHANGE FOR LAND WEST OF CATAWBA RIVER CEDED 1771

INDIAN CREEK

TOWN

N.C. S.C.

JAMES CRAWFORD

MAJ. ROBT. CRAWFORD

GEORGE McKEMEY

WAXHAW CREEK

N.C. 80

CAPT. LAND

WAXHAW CHURCH

BUFORD'S DEFEAT

CAIN CREEK

CAROLINA

KING CREEK

CATAWBA RIVER

POST ROAD

SALISBURY

CHARLES TOWN

SUMTER'S SURPRISE

BATTLE OF ROCKY MOUNT

BATTLE OF HANGING ROCK

CEDAR CREEK

HANGING ROCK

LYNCHES CREEK

CREEK

HOBKIRK'S HILL

GATE'S DEFEAT

CAMDEN

GREENE'S REPULSE

BRITISH MILITARY PRISON

TO CHARLES TOWN

WHERE ANDREW JACKSON SPENT HIS YOUTH 1767 1784

SCALE 1 2 3 4 5 MILES

ROADS
INDIANS △△
BATTLES AND SKIRMISHES ✕
HOMES ▪ ◼

BASED ON MAPS OF MOUSON (1775), FADEN (1787) AND MILLS (1825) AND ON THE RESEARCHES OF THE AUTHOR